OPEN BRITAIN 2010

The definitive travel guide to accessible Britain

tourismforall RADAR the disability network NATIONAL FEDERATION OF Shopmobility AA

OPENBRITAIN.NET

OPEN BRITAIN

OpenBritain | Contents

Contents

Foreword by Tessa Jowell MP	5
Welcome	7
Foreword by Chris Holmes MBE	9
Tourism for All	10
RADAR	13

How to use this guide

How to use this Guide	17
Ratings and Awards	19
Schemes Explained	20
Accommodation Entries Explained	22
OpenBritain Symbols	24
Location Maps	420

Features

The Alnwick Garden	31
The Caravan Club	34
RYA Sailability	37
Chatsworth	40
Ken Hames	47
Rail Travel (ATOC)	50
South West Coastal Path	53
The Wheelyboat Trust	57
Shopmobility	61
Historic House Association	63
Scotland Outdoors	67
Mobilise	73
Park House	76

Around Britain

Information region by region on attractions, tourist information centres and accommodation.

• England	86
• South West	88
• South East	136
• London	168
• East of England	184
• East Midlands	210
• Heart of England	230
• Yorkshire and Humber	246
• Northwest	268
• North East	294
• Scotland	312
• Wales	344

Getting there... and back

Advice on Air, Rail, Road and Sea Travel, with all the contacts you will need for a hassle free journey.

Travel Planning	366
Air Travel	370
Road Travel	390
Rail Travel	404
Sea Travel	412

Useful Indexes

Accessible Scheme Index	435
Display Advertisers	441
Index by Place Name	444
Index by Property Name	449

Tourism for All UK is a national charity dedicated to standards of world class tourism which are welcoming to all. Tourism for All UK contains the knowledge gained over the past 30 years in providing information to the public, especially to disabled or older people, on where their access needs can be met so that they can fully participate in travel and leisure. Registered Charity 279169

RADAR is a national network of disability organisations and disabled people. RADAR represent their members by fast-tracking their opinions and concerns to policy-makers and legislators in Westminster and Whitehall, and launching campaigns to promote equality for all disabled people. Registered Charity 273150

VisitBritain is Britain's national tourism agency, responsible for marketing Britain worldwide and for developing England's visitor economy. VisitBritain work in partnership with thousands of organisations from across the UK.

www.openbritain.net

OpenBritain | Contents

Region	Counties	Page
England		86
South West	Cornwall, Isles of Scilly, Jersey, Devon, Dorset, Gloucestershire, Somerset, Wiltshire	88
South East	Berkshire, Buckinghamshire, Hampshire, Isle of Wight, Kent, Oxfordshire, Surrey, East Sussex, Werst Sussex	136
London		168
East of England	Bedfordshire, Cambridgeshire, Essex, Hertfordshire, Norfolk, Suffolk	184
East Midlands	Derbyshire, Leicestershire, Lincolnshire, Northamptonshire, Nottinghamshire	210
Heart of England	Herefordshire, Shropshire, Staffordshire, Warwickshire, West Midlands, Worcestershire	230
Yorkshire and Humber		246
North West	Cheshire, Cumbria, Lancashire, Greater Manchester, Merseyside	268
North East	Co. Durham, Northumberland, Tyne & Wear	294
Scotland		312
Wales		344

www.openbritain.net

Get 1/3 off rail fares for you...

Disabled Persons Railcard

and a companion...

£18 For a one-year Railcard

Only £48 For a three-year Railcard

You qualify if you meet any one of the criteria below:

- ✓ You receive Attendance Allowance
- ✓ You receive Disability Living Allowance (at either the higher or lower rate for getting around or the higher or middle rate for personal care)
- ✓ You are registered as having a visual impairment
- ✓ You have epilepsy and have repeated attacks or are currently prohibited from driving because of epilepsy
- ✓ You are registered as deaf or use a hearing aid
- ✓ You receive severe disablement allowance
- ✓ You receive War Pensioner's Mobility Supplement for 80% or more disability
- ✓ You are buying or leasing a vehicle through the Motability scheme

To find out how to apply see the leaflet 'Rail Travel Made Easy' (available at stations) or contact us:

Web
www.disabledpersons-railcard.co.uk

Email
disability@atoc.org

Telephone
0845 605 0525

Textphone
0845 601 0132

Foreword

**by the Rt Hon. Tessa Jowell MP,
Minister for the Olympics, Cabinet Office and London**

When London bid for the Olympic and Paralympic Games, we promised that we would welcome the world to Britain in 2012.

Building a fully accessible Games, with the best ever facilities for disabled people, is a fundamental part of that commitment, but it only scratches the surface of London 2012's potential in helping to drive progress towards achieving disability equality in this country.

The Olympic and Paralympic Games are a truly global event, and their unique inspirational power means that hosting them in Britain offers us a once in a lifetime opportunity to change perceptions of disabled people, break down barriers, and create a nationwide legacy of accessibility.

This guide is a necessary and timely contribution to that process. Not only is it an invaluable and long-awaited resource for travellers with disabilities and access requirements, it also serves as a powerful incentive for those businesses that are not listed here to raise their game.

It will encourage them to look again at their facilities, to re-appraise their ability to meet accessibility needs, and to act to ensure that staff and managers are well equipped to provide high-quality services to disabled people.

How businesses respond to this challenge will determine how fully they can benefit from the two billion pound nationwide boom for tourism that will accompany the 2012 Games.

It is the businesses listed in this guide that are setting the gold standard for accessible tourism, and it is these businesses that will, as the global spotlight falls on this country in 2012, help us to make the Olympics and Paralympics a showcase for a Britain without barriers.

Tessa Jowell.

From relaxing to exploring
From business to leisure

Access for all...
Our hotels offer a range of facilities for guests with a perspective on disability including accessible bars, restaurants, washrooms and guest rooms, interconnecting carer's rooms, designated Blue Badge parking, induction loops and menus in large print.

Ceiling track hoist facilities now provided in the following locations: Crowne Plaza London – Heathrow, Holiday Inn London – Bloomsbury, Holiday Inn London – Kensington Forum, Holiday Inn Birmingham M6, Jct. 7 and Holiday Inn Cardiff City Centre.

Winners of the **Enhanced Accessibility Award** (2005) and **Employment Award** (2007) in the RADAR People of the Year Awards.

Gold Winners of the **Accessible Tourism Award** in the Visit London Awards 2007.

Discover the accessible world of IHG
call **0800 40 50 60**
or visit **www.ihg.com**

IHG
InterContinental Hotels Group

INTERCONTINENTAL HOTELS & RESORTS | CROWNE PLAZA HOTELS & RESORTS | hotel INDIGO | Holiday Inn | Holiday Inn Express | STAYBRIDGE SUITES | CANDLEWOOD SUITES

Welcome

Jenifer Littman MBE, Chief Executive of Tourism for All UK, welcomes readers to the first edition of the OpenBritain guide to accessible places to stay and visit.

This exciting new guide has been produced in an historic collaboration between two major UK disability charities – Tourism for All UK (TFA) and RADAR – who previously published their own guides – 'Easy Access Britain' by TFA and VisitBritain, and RADAR's "Where to Stay" and 'How to Get There". As a result, this guide includes all the accommodation inspected under the National Accessible Scheme (NAS) operated by VisitEngland, along with those known to the Scottish and Welsh tourism agencies. In addition, all the providers listed in the former RADAR guides have been invited to join OpenBritain and be subject to randomized checks of their facilities. This system is being applied to other new providers such as attractions.

Readers should therefore be aware that there is a distinction between those properties who have been officially inspected, and those who are self-assessed but subject to a random check. OpenBritain cannot take responsibility for information which has been wrongly supplied to us. We are keen to include a wide range of choice for you, the traveller looking for accessible facilities, and as all the schemes in the UK are voluntary rather than statutory, there is no one comprehensive, reliable source. It is also evident that what will suit one person may not suit another. However, with the new OpenBritain website, www.openbritain.net, we hope that you can help us build the level of information available by giving feedback that will help other travellers. This will provide a further source to help you in your decisions.

You will shortly start to see the OpenBritain logo appearing in the windows of those establishments that have chosen to support us. It is your indicator that specific information has been supplied by that establishment pertaining to access availability and will be readily available within the Guide itself or via www.openbritain.net.

This will soon be expanded to cover restaurants and visitor attractions etc – in short, a visually recognisable sign of access awareness.

We also look forward to receiving your recommendations for new places to include in the future – please send these either via the website or to info@openbritain.net We are always seeking new examples of good practice.

The charities Tourism for All UK and RADAR share a raison d'etre in seeking to influence the public sector and industry to attain the highest standards of accessibility – to take the 'disability' out of people's lives.

We are delighted to have been joined by so many partners in this endeavour – from Government Ministers who helped us launch this initiative – our thanks to Barbara Follett MP, Tessa Jowell MP and Jonathan Shaw MP – to the tourist boards, VisitEngland, Visit Wales and VisitScotland, the regional development agencies, and a whole range of industry associations including the British Hospitality Association, the AA, the Association of Train Operating Companies, the Historic Houses Association, the National Trust, and individual companies of all sizes, as well as charities including the National Federation of ShopMobility.

In the context of Britain hosting the Olympic and Paralympic Games in 2012, where we are as a country pledged to provide 'the most accessible Games ever', we need all the help we can get to make this happen. Please play a part – join our campaigns, and give us your feedback and your nominations of good providers. In this way, we can create a true legacy from 2012 for disabled citizens and visitors alike.

Thank you for your support.

Jenifer Littman

British Airways is continually looking at ways to ensure that all our disabled customers have full access to all of our facilities, whether they are onboard, in our terminals or visiting our website. Here are a number of ways in which we support our disabled customers during their journey with us.

proud airline partner of the Paralympic Games

- London Heathrow Terminal 5 offers greater accessibility throughout for disabled customers, more people than ever are able to take their wheelchairs to the aircraft side and have them returned at the gate

- Individual onboard safety briefings for sight-impaired customers make sure they understand and are confident about our safety procedures

- Certified Assistance Dogs for blind, deaf or disabled passengers travel free of charge in the aircraft cabin on all British Airways services within the UK

- Assistance Dogs that are compliant with the Pet Travel System may be carried in the cabin of the aircraft on certain international routes

- Visually impaired customers who wish to listen to the content of ba.com can use Browsealoud, a free tool that converts written text into verbal data

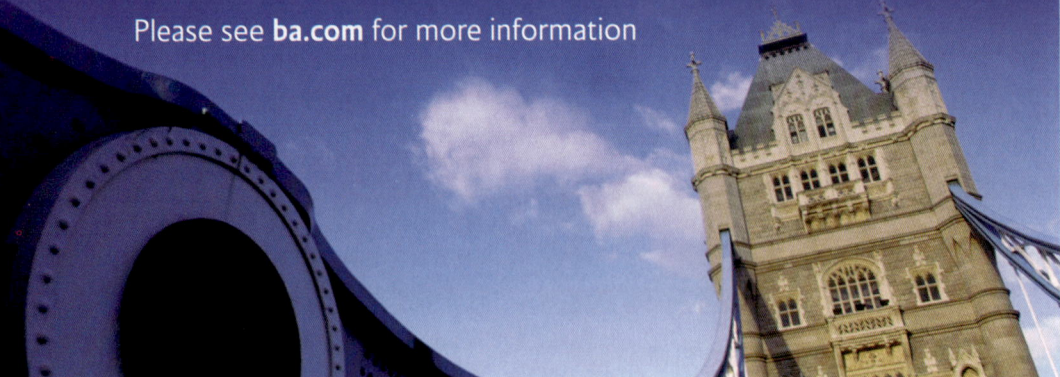

Please see **ba.com** for more information

BRITISH AIRWAYS

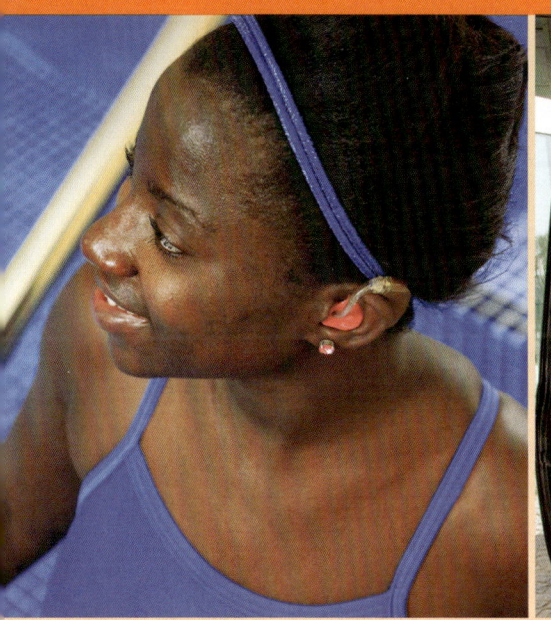

Foreword

by Chris Holmes, Tourism for All UK Patron, Britain's most successful Paralympic swimmer

As we are all living longer, more and more of us are experiencing the need for facilities in order to take advantage of opportunities to travel and enjoy leisure facilities and activities.

There are over 10 million people in the UK with a disability, and over 87 million in Europe who are wanting to take part in travel and holidays.

This is a huge and growing market, and needs to be catered for not as a 'special group' but as a normal part of customer service.

Going the extra mile is what good customer service is all about. It's important for all those serving customers to have the right attitude, knowledge and training, and appropriate facilities. Communicating to the public is last and most vital part of the equation.

Disabled people often find it hard to know if, when and where they are going to be able to use a service. That is what OpenBritain is all about.

For providers of services, those included here have recognised the need to take those steps. And with an OpenBritain sticker to display, you can readily be identified. This guide will be the principal means for the traveller with access needs to find what he or she needs, backed up by the comprehensive new website, www.openbritain.net

I am delighted that this fresh new initiative has been launched at a time when we need to be joining forces to offer a welcome to all in the biggest visitor event Britain has ever hosted, the Olympics and Paralympics in 2012. The hosting of the Paralympics in the UK in 2012 represents the best opportunity to change attitudes to disability, once and for all, that we are ever likely to have.

I urge every reader to use the facilities offered, get involved, and give us feedback.

Chris Holmes

OpenBritain | Tourism for All

Worried about finding the right place to stay?
Frustrated by not being able to identify what you need?

Help is at hand....

Tourism for All UK is the UK's central source of holiday and travel information for people with access requirements.

Our new guide and website **OpenBritain** is a vital resource in this objective. But you may find a human voice on the phone or someone who can answer your detailed enquiries by email is the only way to gain the level of assurance you need. Tourism for All UK operates the only free helpline and independent information service that provides this. With 30 years of expertise as an organisation, we hope to answer all your questions.

Photo: Paralympian Gold winner Chris Holmes (TFA Patron) with Carrie-Ann Fleming who runs the TFA Information service (its Carrie-Ann on the front cover of this guide!) helping launch OpenBritain at the Best of Britain exhibition.

The free TFA helpline is funded by charitable support, along with fees from those who choose to join us as Friends. We invite all readers of this guide to consider joining TFA as a Friend. This not only helps us to secure the future of this vital service, but also provides you with a range of benefits.

Benefits of making friends

- A newsletter packed with items about accessible tourism, from new developments, places to stay and visit, changes in the law, and much more

- An exclusive rate at both the Copthorne Tara Hotel in Kensington, which has a number of fully adapted rooms, including two with hoists

- A special rate from InterContinental hotels worldwide - which include Holiday Inn, Holiday Express, and Crowne Plaza hotels. The Kensington Forum Holiday Inn also has rooms with hoists

- Many other time-limited offers which are published in the newsletter and on the TFA website
  www.tourismforall.org.uk

- Free publications on specific topics, such as financial help for holidays, overseas travel, extra services such as care support (worth £3.00 - £6.00 each)

- Access to special members' only areas of the website including a members' forum

All this for **only £25.00** - which you can save in a single hotel booking.

www.tourismforall.org.uk

OpenBritain | **Tourism for All**

Tourism for All Services

Tourism for All Services is a wholly owned subsidiary of the charity that offers access audits, destination audits, and consultancy to business and public sector organisations seeking to improve their accessibility or comply with the Disability Discrimination Act.

Businesses advised by TFA Services have gone on to win Access Awards.

"I cannot thank Brian Seaman and Tourism for All enough for all their help and advice – the whole accessible issue was made easy with their guidance and support. Put simply, we could never have done it, or done it so well, without you".
Mortons House Hotel, Dorset

For TFA Services contact:
Brian Seaman
t 01293 776225 or
e brian@tourismforall.org.uk

Access for All training

We can also offer assistance with staff training and access to our online training programme in welcoming guests with disabilities. The Access for All training has been developed with the help of people with impairments and industry professionals, and is endorsed by the Institute of Hospitality.

For Access for All training contact:
Tim Gardiner
e timgardiner@tourismforall.org.uk

Tourism for All Services Limited donates 100% of all profits to the charity Tourism for All UK Registered Charity 279169. A company limited by guarantee Registered in England No 02567422 VAT No: GB 602 6087 66. Registered Office: 16 Swordfish Drive, Christchurch, Dorset BH23 4TP

tourismforall

Join today!

To join, or for information call **t 0845 124 9971**

To make a reservation, call **t 0845 124 9973**

e info@tourismforall.org.uk

Join online on
www.tourismforall.org.uk/Membership.html

Or write to us at: **Tourism for All UK, c/o Vitalise, Shap Road Ind. Est, Shap Road, Kendal LA9 6NZ**

Tourism for All UK is a registered charity No 279169 and a company limited by guarantee No 01466822 VAT registration 884 5432 93

www.openbritain.net

11

There's more to life than shopping

There's the beach ▪ park ▪ woods ▪ hills ▪ walks ▪ jogging ▪ canoeing ▪ fishing ▪ sailing

Get out there in style and rise to new challenges in comfort in our lightweight, fun and stylish range of Delta All-Terrain Buggies, or the Hippocampe Amphibious Wheelchair.

To experience new environments, enjoy previously inaccessible places or just hit the beach, call Delichon on **01725 519405**, or visit **www.delichon.co.uk** There **is** more to life than shopping.

Delichon Ltd.
Performance Seating Systems

Kings Yard, Martin, Fordingbridge, Hants SP6 3LB
T: 01725 519405   **E**: info@delichon.co.uk

OpenBritain | RADAR

RADAR is a national network of disability organisations and disabled people. RADAR represent their members by fast-tracking their opinions and concerns to policy-makers and legislators in Westminster and Whitehall, and launching campaigns to promote equality for all disabled people. Registered Charity 273150

Books which open doors to independent living

To help people living with ill-health, injury or disability lead as independent a life as possible. RADAR has published two valuable guides.

If Only I'd Known That A Year Ago

A guide for newly disabled people, their families and friends

A self-help guide signposting to valuable support and specialist information on social and health care, welfare rights and benefits

National Key Scheme Guide (NKS) 2009: accessible toilets for disabled people

A guide to the 7000 accessible disabled toilets around the UK fitted with the National Key Scheme lock.

An important part of freedom is having the confidence to go out, knowing that public toilets will be available that are accessible and meet your requirements.

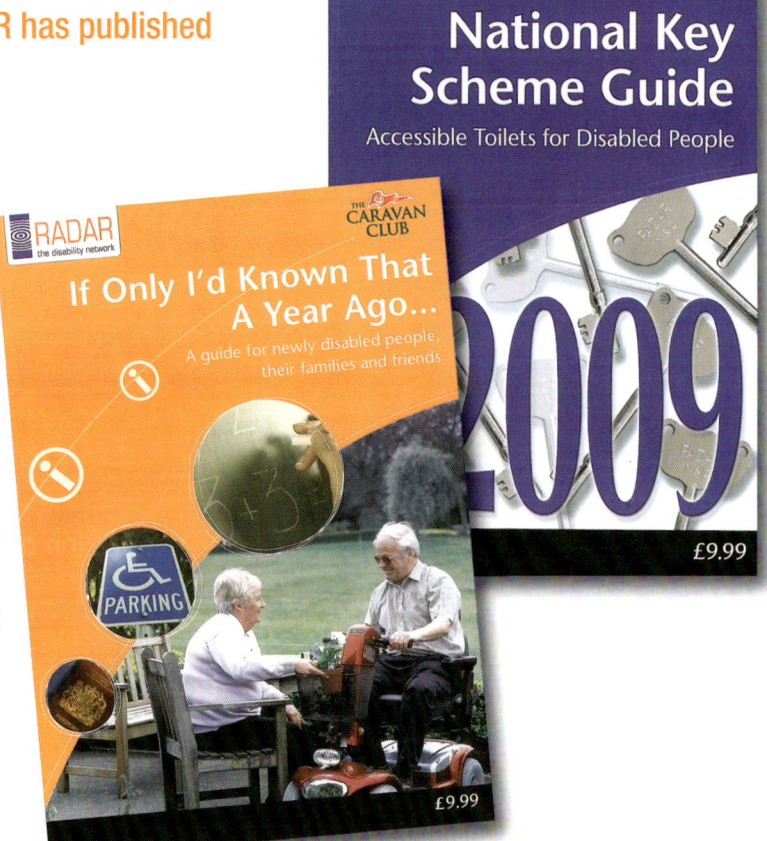

Copies are available from RADAR t 020 7250 3222
e radar@radar.org.uk   minicom 020 7250 4119   web www.radar-shop.org.uk

Over 2000 stations with accessible information

The improved Blue Badge map is just the ticket . . .

The new Blue Badge rail map contains information on accessible facilities for more than 2000 train stations.

We've searched the UK and also found information for you on accessible football stadiums, tube stations, airports, public toilets, beaches, petrol stations and much more.

www.direct.gov.uk/bluebadgemap

Directgov
Public services all in one place
www.direct.gov.uk

Blue Badge — **be sure you know before you go**

www.direct.gov.uk/disability

Directgov is the website to visit for the latest information and services from government. It's clearly written, useful and the information is all in one place.

There's a large section for disabled people covering:

- home and housing
- financial support
- disability rights
- employment
- health and support

Find out about equipment, adapting your home or vehicle, direct payments (arranging your own care and services), social care assessments, the Blue Badge parking scheme – including an interactive UK-wide map, travel and transport, accessible technology – and much more.

There's also information for carers and links to charities and helpful organisations supporting disabled people.

Motability
The leading car scheme for disabled people

it changed our lives!

"The use of a reliable car is vital for our day-to-day routine. As the servicing, breakdown cover, tax and insurance are all included it saves me money as well as time. The car is comfortable and the peace of mind I have now is invaluable."

Emma, Charley's mum

where will yours take you?

use your mobility allowance to get mobile...

Simply exchange it for an all-inclusive worry-free mobility package, including:

- New car, powered wheelchair or scooter
- Insurance
- Servicing and repairs
- Tyres
- Breakdown cover

freephone 0800 093 1000

or visit www.motability.co.uk for further details and quote 'AbilityNI'

How to use this guide

19	Ratings & Awards
19	Accommodation Types
20	National Accessible Scheme
22	Accommodation Entries Explained
24	OpenBritain Symbols

OpenBritain is the new definitive guide for visitors to the UK with access needs. Packed with easy to use information - where to stay, how to get there, and what to see and do when you arrive. Working with organisations and companies throughout the UK, all offering products and services dedicated to making Britain more accessible.

OpenBritain offers you a wide choice of accommodation, from hotels to B&B's, self catering properties to caravan parks. All the accommodation within this guide must either be accessed under the National Accessible Scheme (NAS) or a member of VisitScotland, Visit Wales, Visit London schemes or self-assessed though **OpenBritain.** Those with NAS inspection are flagged to offer you the highest level of reassurance.

Looking for great places to visit whilst you are there? At the end of each accommodation section you will find attractions for that region. **OpenBritain** members offer you more detailed information on what facilities they provide and look out for the 'AS' symbol, which is your at-a-glance guide to those with an Access Statement.

OpenBritain helps you with 'getting there...and back'. The travel section will give you up-to-date, useful information, hints & tips on travelling in and around the UK. All the information you need on planes, trains and automobiles.

Don't forget, home or away, the UK is accessible. **OpenBritain** members are offering you a whole range of facilities, equipment, services and experiences you might never have considered before. Look inside to find out much more about what is available.

OPENBRITAIN.NET
The one-stop-shop for all your travel needs.

www.openbritain.net

Up to
60% off every day. 100% shopper satisfaction.

HUGO BOSS   L.K.BENNETT   JAEGER   TED BAKER   & MANY MORE

With so much to see and do, McArthurGlen is the fashionable day out. And with free 10% discount cards for group bookings, free meal vouchers for drivers, fully accessible centres and dedicated parking, they're guaranteed to be days out that pack more in.

Ashford ▪ Bridgend ▪ Cheshire Oaks
East Midlands ▪ Livingston ▪ Swindon ▪ York

McArthur Glen Designer Outlets

McArthurGlen.com

OpenBritain | **How to use this guide**

Ratings

Star ratings are internationally recognisable and give you a guide to the standard of quality for accommodation. Whether rated by VisitEngland, VisitScotland, VisitWales or the AA, these ratings give you information at a glance.

Star ratings made simple

★	No frills, basic facilities
★★	Well maintained with a good level of service
★★★	Friendly, very good quality and well presented
★★★★	Excellent standards, high quality facilities and attentive service
★★★★★	Exceptional service and surroundings. An extra bit of luxury

More detail can be found on

www.theaa.com/travel

www.enjoyengland.com/stay

www.visitscotland.com/guide/where-to-stay

www.visitwales.co.uk/holiday-accommodation-in-wales

Awards

★★★★★ **Gold and Silver Awards -** Highlighted by ★★★★★ gold or silver coloured stars, these colours denote properties offering the highest levels of quality within their star rating (part of the EnjoyEngland scheme).

Accommodation types

The following types of accommodation can be found in this guide:

Hotels: Hotel, Small Hotel, Country House Hotel, Town House Hotel, Metro Hotel, Budget Hotel, Restaurant with Rooms, Serviced Apartments

Guest Accommodation: Guest Accommodation, Bed & Breakfast, Guest House, Farmhouse, Inn

Hostel Accommodation: Hostel, Group Hostel, Activity Accommodation, Backpacker, Bunkhouse, Camping Barn

Self Catering: Self Catering, Approved Caravan Holiday Homes, Chalets, Campus Accommodation

Camping & Caravan Parks: Camping Park, Touring Park, Holiday Park, Holiday Village, Forest Holiday Village

Detailed descriptions of these accommodation types can be found at **openbritain.net**

www.openbritain.net

19

National Accessible Scheme

England

Accommodation is assessed under VisitBritain's National Accessible Scheme, which includes standards useful for hearing and visually impaired guests in addition to standards useful for guests with mobility impairment.

Accommodation taking part in this scheme will display one or more of the mobility, visual or hearing symbols shown on this page.

When you see one of the symbols, you can be sure that the accommodation and core facilities have been thoroughly assessed against demanding criteria. If you have additional needs or special requirements, we strongly recommend that you make sure these can be met by your chosen establishment before you confirm your booking.

Visual Impairment Symbols

Typically provides key additional services and facilities to meet the needs of visually impaired guests.

Typically provides a higher level of additional services and facilities to meet the needs of visually impaired guests.

Hearing Impairment Symbols

Typically provides key additional services and facilities to meet the needs of guests with hearing impairment.

Typically provides a higher level of additional services and facilities to meet the needs of guests with hearing impairment.

Mobility Impairment Symbols

Typically suitable for a person with sufficient mobility to climb a flight of steps but who would benefit from fixtures and fittings to aid balance.

Typically suitable for a person with restricted walking ability and for those who may need to use a wheelchair some of the time and can negotiate a maximum of three steps.

Typically suitable for a person who depends on the use of a wheelchair and transfers unaided to and from the wheelchair in a seated position. This person may be an independent traveller.

Typically suitable for a person who depends on the use of a wheelchair and needs assistance when transferring to and from the wheelchair in a seated position.

Access Exceptional is awarded to establishments that meet the requirements of independent wheelchair users or assisted wheelchair users shown above and also fulfil more demanding requirements with reference to the British Standards 858300:2001.

London

This Guide lists hotels in London that have not been assessed under VisitBritain's National Accessible Scheme. These establishments do, however, have bedrooms suitable for wheelchair users and have been audited on behalf of the London Development Agency by Direct Enquiries. For more information go to directenquiries.com/LDAhotels.

Scotland

All kinds of accommodation are assessed by VisitScotland Quality Advisors, based on criteria drawn up with the co-operation of organisations which deal with wheelchair users. This is part of the VisitScotland grading schemes. Criteria can be found on **visitscotland.com/accommodation/accessiblescotland** Accommodation accessibility is checked every three years. Entries show one of three symbols.

- **Category 1 -** Accessible to a wheelchair user travelling independently.
- **Category 2 -** Accessible to a wheelchair user travelling with assistance.
- **Category 3 -** Accessible to a wheelchair user able to walk a few paces and up a maximum of three steps.

Wales

Owners of all types of accommodation in Wales should have a full Access Statement available to visitors.

The criteria VisitBritain and national regional tourism organisations have adopted do not necessarily conform to British Standards or to Building Regulations. They reflect what the organisations understand to be acceptable to meet the practical needs of guests with special mobility or sensory needs and encourage the industry to increase access to all.

Accommodation entries explained

All the establishments featured in this guide must be either inspected under the National Accessible Scheme (NAS), operated by VisitEngland, or under those operated by VisitScotland, VisitLondon or other regional schemes, OR accommodations, attractions, or services who have joined OpenBritain on a self-assessed basis, and are subject to random checks. The former offer a higher level of assurance and are clearly flagged.

1. Locations

Entries are listed alphabetically by town name, by county, within each region. Some properties, where located in a small village may be listed under a nearby town (within 7 miles).

Complete addresses are not given for Self Catering properties for security reasons and the town(s) listed may be a distance from the establishment. Please check the location at time of booking.

2. Map References

Maps can be found starting on page 420 of the guide.

3. Contact Information

Establishment name and booking details including telephone number.

Note: Prices and ratings shown were supplied to us by the proprietors in Summer 2009. These may have been changed after this guide has gone to press and we advise that you check at time of booking.

Prices are shown in pounds sterling and include VAT where applicable.

Properties and attactions which have OpenBritain symbols in their entries have paid to be featured.

4. Prices

Bed & Breakfast: Per room for B&B and per person for evening meal (d=Double s=Single)

Hotels: Per room for B&B and per person for half board (d=Double s=Single).

Evening Meal: Prices shown are per person per night.

Self Catering: Prices shown are per unit per week for low and high season (inc. VAT)

Camping and Caravan Parks: Per pitch per night for touring pitches; per unit per week for caravan holiday homes.

5. Opening

Indicates when the establishment is open.

6. Symbols

An at-a-glance view of services and facilities available. The key to these symbols can be found on page 20

7. Access Statements

'AS' denotes that an Access Statement is available. These can be viewed on openbritain.net

8. Ratings

Quality Rating awarded to the establishment. For more information see pg 19

9. Travel Directions

OpenBritain | How to use this guide | **Accommodation Entries Explained**

Sandringham | **Park House Hotel**

AS

3B1

Enjoy England ★★

Open: All year

Rooms per night:
s: £110.00–£158.00
d: £186.00–£288.00
p/p half board:
d: £108.00–£173.00
Meals: £15.00–£17.50

Shop: 1.5 miles
Pub: 1.5 miles

Access:

General:

Room:

Sandringham PE35 6EH
t 01485 543000 e parkinfo@lcdisability.org
parkhousehotel.org.uk

Located on the Royal Sandringham Estate, the hotel has 8 single and 8 twin rooms and is adapted for people with mobility difficulties/disabilities with or without carers/companions. The hotel is fully accessible and care is available if required.

Location: From King's Lynn follow A149 towards Hunstanton, follow brown tourists signs. Park House is on right before Sandringham Visitor Centre.

www.openbritain.net

23

Key to symbols

Information about many of the accommodation and attractions services and facilties is given in the form of symbols.

Access: Accommodation & Attractions

- Access trained staff
- Staff available to assist by arrangement
- Large print information
- Braille information
- Induction loop system at reception
- Facilities for service dogs
- Hoist available
- Designated wheelchair accessible public toilet
- Wheelchair accessible bedroom
- Wheelchair accessible leisure facilities
- Wheelchair accessible restaurant
- Wheelchair accessible ground floor
- Wheelchair accessible gardens
- Fully wheelchair accessible
- Tactile routes
- Visual alarm system
- Audible alarm system

Hotels and Guest Accommodation

Rooms

- Bedroom(s) on ground floor
- Text phone/inductive coupler
- Typetalk available
- TV listening device
- TV with subtitles
- Tea/coffee facilities in all bedrooms
- Level-entry shower
- Seating in shower
- Toilet seat raiser

General

- Children welcome
- Designated parking
- Ramped or level entrance
- Licensed bar
- Evening meal by arrangement
- Special diets by arrangement
- Lift
- Garden/patio

National Accessible Scheme

For information on the National Accessible Scheme symbols, see page 20

OpenBritain | How to use this guide | **Key to symbols**

Self Catering Accommodation

Unit

	Ramped or level entrance
	Bedroom(s) on ground floor
	TV listening device
	TV with subtitles
	Text phone/ inductive coupler
	Wheelchair accessible bedroom
	Adapted kitchen
	Embossed kitchen equipment
	Level-entry shower
	Seating in shower
	Toilet Seat Raiser
	Daily servicing of unit
	Garden/patio
	Wheelchair accessible leisure facilities

General

	Children welcome
P	Parking next to unit
	Laundry facilities
	Weekend/midweek bookings

Camping, Caravan and Holiday Parks

General

	Overnight holding area
	Motor home pitches reserved for day trips off-site
	Electrical hook-up points for caravans and tents
	Calor Gas/Camping Gaz purchase/exchange service
	Chemical toilet disposal point
	Motor home waste disposal point
	Showers
	Laundry facilities
	Food shop on site
	Restaurant on site

Pitches

	Caravans
	Motor caravans
	Tents
	Caravan holiday homes
	Log cabins/lodges
	Chalets/villas

Attractions

General

	Designated disabled parking
	Ramped or level entrance
	Virtual tour
	Licensed bar
	Garden
	Restaurant

www.openbritain.net

PLAN A GREAT DAY OUT

DISCOVER GARDEN PERFECTION

For an altogether more relaxing and inspiring day out, visit an RHS Garden near you. Enjoy glorious vistas, year-round beauty and ever-changing colour across a wide variety of heavenly garden landscapes.

Each RHS Garden is a scented experience and offers limited pre-booked wheelchair availability, wheelchair routes and free admission for assistance dogs and a carer. Each garden also features a Plant Centre, Gift Shop, Coffee Shop(s) and free parking with disabled bays.

RHS GARDEN WISLEY, SURREY
- Limited pre-booked electric scooters
- Free mobility buggy
- Guided walks available on request
- Hearing loop in Shop and Plant Centre
- Call **0845 260 9000** to arrange your requirements before your visit

RHS GARDEN HARLOW CARR, NORTH YORKSHIRE
- Limited pre-booked electric scooters & wheelchairs
- Guided walks available on request
- Large print guides available on request
- Tel: **01423 565418**

RHS GARDEN ROSEMOOR, DEVON
- Guided walks available on request
- Tel: **01805 626810**

RHS GARDEN HYDE HALL, ESSEX
- Free mobility buggy
- Braille and large print guides
- Tel: **01245 400256**

www.rhs.org.uk

WITH THE RHS

Royal Horticultural Society

DISCOVER SUMMER FLOWER SHOWS

A firm favourite of the calendar, each RHS Show is a must-see Summer attraction. With their own unique style and personalities, the RHS shows are a perfect blend of gardening inspiration, retail therapy and expert advice, providing the perfect day out.

RHS FLOWER SHOW DATES 2010

RHS Show Cardiff
16 – 18 April

RHS Chelsea Flower Show
25 – 29 May

RHS Hampton Court Palace Flower Show
6 – 11 July

RHS Show Tatton Park
21 – 25 July

RHS FLOWER SHOWS

- Limited disabled parking spaces available (except at RHS Chelsea Flower Show). Spaces may be a short distance from showground entrances

- Parking spaces for those who have pre-booked wheelchairs are 150m from gate entrances

- Event Mobility Charity Trust provide a limited number of manual wheelchairs and electric scooters* at all shows (*excluding RHS Chelsea Flower Show). A small donation is requested. Advance booking is recommended for all shows except RHS Show Cardiff. Please call **0845 260 7000** from 11 January 2010 to reserve

- One companion is admitted free of charge and assistance dogs are welcome

- Hearing loops are set up in the talks area

- For more information visit **www.rhs.org.uk/flowershows**

RHS Registered Charity No: 222879/SC038262

The RHS, the UK's leading gardening charity

Welcome to Accor hotels

Where friendly staff are on hand in over 130 accessible hotels across Britain – whatever your needs, whatever your budget.

SOFITEL LUXURY HOTELS
Three elegant 5 star French Art de Vivre hotels situated in St James, London, Gatwick and Heathrow T5.

NOVOTEL
31 contemporary 4 star hotels across the UK.

Mercure
31 individual 3 and 4 star mid-market, UK hotels.

ibis HOTEL
52 economy hotels situated in all major city locations throughout the UK.

Etap HOTEL
16 low-cost UK hotels offering the smart traveller a no frills experience at very competitive rates.

For more information and bookings visit or call 0870 609 0961 / **accor**hotels.com

OpenBritain | Features

"Too long have people been put off packing their bags and heading for an adventure by a lack of access and information; its time to get out there with the help of OpenBritain."

Ken Hames

Features

From the painted halls of Chatsworth House to the snow-topped mountains of Scotland, OpenBritain has discovered the best Britain has to offer in accessible travel.

However, like any seasoned traveller, we know there's always more to see. Why not share your experiences with us on www.openbritain.net?

The Alnwick Garden	31
The Caravan Club	34
RYA Sailability	37
Chatsworth	40
Ken Hames	47
Rail Travel (ATOC)	50
South West Coastal Path	53
The Wheelyboat Trust	57
Shopmobility	61
Historic House Association	63
Scotland Outdoors	67
Mobilise	73
Park House	76

www.openbritain.net

OpenBritain | Advertorial | **MS Society**

"Have you still got MS?"

"Yes, I've got it for life. There's no cure."

Ian Williams *living with MS*

MS
Multiple Sclerosis Society

No one knows what causes MS and they've yet to find a cure. But with the MS Society's support, I have a rich and fulfilling life. They've got a freephone helpline **0808 800 8000** and you can visit **www.mssociety.org.uk** to find out more or make a donation.

MS Society. Putting the pieces together.

The Multiple Sclerosis Society of Great Britain and Northern Ireland is a charity registered in England and Wales (207495) and Scotland (SC016433)

Ian had been experiencing a variety of unexplained symptoms for around two years.

The symptoms Included a loss of sensation in his legs, difficulties with his balance and an inability to co-ordinate his movements, but when he started experiencing blurred vision in his left eye he decided a trip to the doctors was necessary.

He didn't know what the symptoms meant, and had certainly never heard of multiple sclerosis (MS).

Ian went for tests and an MRI showed lesions on his brain; doctors confirmed he had MS - a condition of the central nervous system which causes the body's immune system to attack myelin, a substance surrounding nerve fibres, causing confusion and delay in messages from the brain and spine.

MS can cause a variety of symptoms including loss of balance and mobility, extreme fatigue, depression and mood swings. There is currently no cure and few effective treatments, but with the right support and information people can continue their lives.

That's where the MS Society comes in. Every year the charity funds millions of pounds worth of MS research, runs respite care centres, funds MS nurses, physiotherapists and grants and financial assistance and provides information on everything to do with MS – from managing relapses to claiming the right benefits.

The charity's **freephone helpline (0808 800 8000)** is a great benefit to thousands of people, as is the website **www.mssociety.org.uk.**

Ten years after his diagnosis Ian lives a full and happy life. Encouraged by his local branch of the MS Society he began to play disabled sport and, after completing a course at a local college, has qualified as a holistic therapist specialising in reflexology.

"I hope my story shows that MS can be a catalyst for new opportunities. With the right help life doesn't have to stop when MS starts," explains Ian

www.openbritain.net

The Alnwick Garden

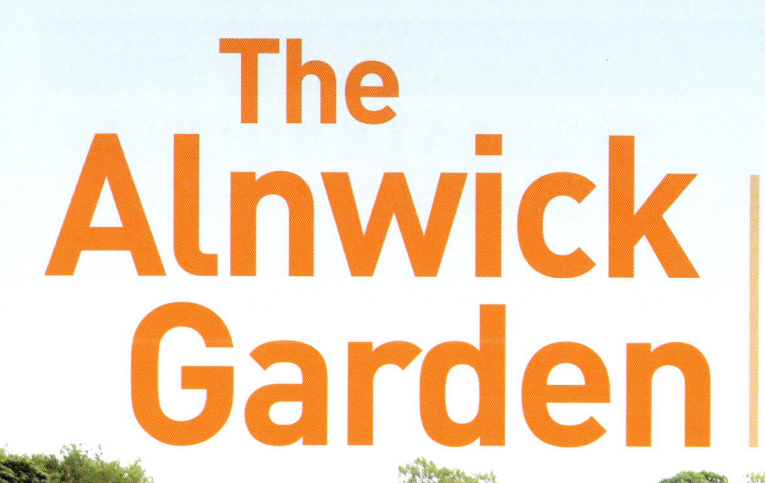

One Of The Most Exciting Contemporary Gardens In The World

Something extraordinary has been happening in Northumberland; the creation of The Alnwick Garden; one of the most exciting contemporary gardens to be developed anywhere in the world in the last one hundred years.

The inspiration of the Duchess of Northumberland and designed by the world-renowned Wirtz International, The Garden's design mixes eclectic gardens, planting, structures and features, and brings them to life with water. The fascinating landscape is a sequence of quiet and busy spaces, and full of surprises.

The Grand Cascade is The Garden's centrepiece; a magnificent tumbling mass of water and the largest water feature of its kind in the country. The Cascade's spectacular water displays appear regularly, with shooting water jets splashing onto the middle terrace. At the lower basin, children play on mini tractors with buckets to collect the water cascading down the walls. A change of clothes for children is essential in this garden as it's tempting to get wet. You can watch the Cascade's displays from the sheltered terraces of The Pavilion and Visitor Centre, over coffee, lunch or afternoon tea. ▶

www.openbritain.net

ACCESSIBLE HOLIDAYS

3 GREAT CHOICES!

Specialist holidays for People with Disabilities

EASY ACCESS FOR WHEELCHAIRS EN-SUITE ROOMS ADJOINING ROOMS
ELECTRIC HOISTS OVERHEAD TRACKING HOIST ELECTRIC BEDS COT SIDES
MODERN SPACIOUS BAR & RESTAURANT SPECIAL DIETS CATERED FOR
HYDROTHERAPY POOL CONFERENCE FACILITIES CAR PARK
LIVE CABARET SHOW EVERY NIGHT
PICK-UP AND RETURN SERVICE

BOND HOTEL Blackpool
120, Bond Street, Blackpool, FY4 1HG

BOND HOTEL St. Annes
The Beach, 69-71 South Promenade, St Annes on Sea, FY8 1LZ

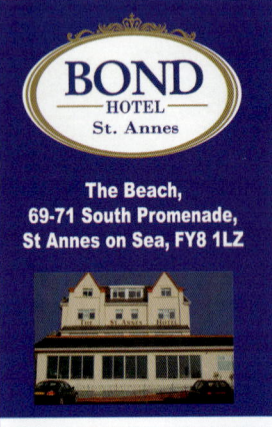

BOND HOLIDAY HOMES
Marton Mere Holiday Village

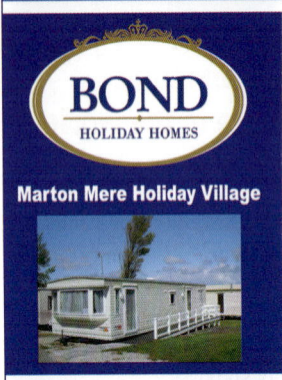

BOND ACCESSIBLE COACHES LIMITED

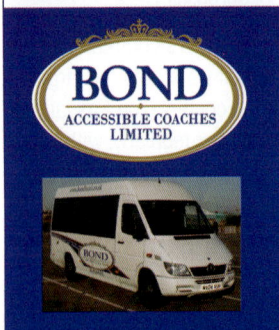

PARTY at the Bond Hotel Blackpool, where the great fun atmosphere is a very popular choice for many of our guests. The hotel has 65 bedrooms, most of which are wheelchair-accessible, and all the extra facilities that you might require during your stay. With great food, and nightly entertainment, this hotel offers the perfect Blackpool holiday!

RELAX in our sophisticated new hotel in St Annes. Recently refurbished to the highest possible standard, this stylish 26-room hotel overlooks the sea, and offers a choice of luxurious wheelchair-accessible accommodation - from single rooms up to 3-room suites. The new Bond Hotel, St Annes is the ideal venue for those looking for the chance to unwind in style.

ENJOY our de-luxe holiday homes at scenic Marton Mere. If you would prefer a self-catering break, these superbly appointed holiday homes could be just the thing. They sleep up to six, have central heating and all mod cons, are fully accessible, and overlook the beautiful lake and wildlife area at this popular resort.

LUXURY travel wherever you choose to stay, you will have access to Bond Accessible Coaches Ltd who will pick you up and take you home at very reasonable prices.

So come and explore a whole world of special holidays for very special guests. Whether it's a week with the stars of "Coronation Street or Emmerdale", a break on a nature reserve, or a luxury room with a great sea view, we can provide it - and at a great price too!

To find out about our Special Offers please contact Karen on 01253 341218

sales@bondhotel.co.uk • Booking hotline 01253 341218
www.bondhotel.co.uk

OpenBritain | The Alnwick Garden

The Garden has an eclectic programme of events and activities throughout the year, with music, performances, storytelling, workshops, exhibitions, classes, tours, and much more. Much of the programme is free to Garden visitors. Visitors can meet the gardening team to take a look behind the scenes, or join a course in garden design. Children can learn how to plant their own vegetable plot or even pot a pumpkin ready for carving next Halloween. As well as all that, there's fabulous **locally-inspired food** and great shops stocked with plants, local produce and gifts from Northumberland. There really is something to enjoy on every one of the 364 days a year that The Garden's open.

▶ The walled **Ornamental Garden** is a peaceful, restful garden with inviting pathways bordered by lavender and fruit trees and secret places to catch the sun. At its centre lies a bubbling pool, spilling into shallow rills that are perfect for splashing and paddling. Taking the path from the Ornamental Garden through the trees and past Barbara Hepworth's sculpture, 'Ascending Form', visitors arrive in the **Rose Garden**, with pergola-lined pathways and walkways covered in climbing and shrub roses mixed with clematis and honeysuckle. There are more than 3000 roses, and in summer the colours and scents are wonderful.

The **Cherry Orchard** is a new feature, and the only place to see more than three hundred Great White Cherry trees all planted together. The Taihaku tree is known as the Great White thanks to its large, double-petalled white flowers, which fall like snow to create drifts on the ground.

The Alnwick Garden is also home to one of the **world's largest wooden tree houses**, high in the trees outside The Garden's walls and featuring walkways in the sky and wobbly rope bridges. The restaurant at the heart of The Treehouse is open for lunch every day and for dinner on Thursday, Friday and Saturday evenings, and is known for delicious menus of seasonal, local produce. **The Woodland Walk** begins below The Treehouse, along a path lined with mature trees and offering panoramic views.

Accessibility

The paths that lead around The Garden, the sloping aerial path that leads onto The Treehouse, the bridges and the walkways have all been designed to be suitable for scooters, wheelchairs and pushchairs, to make sure that everyone can have a wonderful day. You can hire a scooter or wheelchair for your visit at no charge, by calling 01665 511350. Pick up a special map to plan a suitable route, and talk to the helpful staff to make sure you don't miss anything. Before visiting, download an audio tour from www.alnwickgarden.com to be guided around the landscape and hear more about this exciting project from its visionary, the Duchess of Northumberland. Accompanying carers enter The Garden free of charge, and of course accessibility dogs are welcome.

It's a wonderful garden, but an even better day out ■

w www.alnwickgarden.com
e info@alnwickgarden.com   t 01665 511350

Why Motorhomes and Caravans?

Avid Caravan Club members, Gerry and Christine Bullock give their advice and opinions on why caravanning is a great way to holiday for people with disabilities.

If suddenly, for whatever reason, you find yourself having to use a wheelchair, you and your family will have to look at your lifestyle, including your holidays, in a different way.

Altering your home can be difficult, but most things are possible. Then you start to think about your holidays and really, with a bit of thought, all things are possible. You may even want to take your pet on holiday with you and you like the outdoor style of life. So what are your options?

We have owned motorhomes for nearly 30 years, so let us explain as simply as possible, the benefits of caravans and motorhomes. Christine has, for all this time, had a deteriorating spinal problem, which has left her relying on her wheelchair for getting around outside. I myself, have a leg full of metal and various bits in my wrist (a cheaper version of the bionic man!).

If your finances allow you to run two vehicles, then a **motorhome** is a possibility. This type of vehicle can be built to meet **your specific needs**. Wide doors, lifts and ramps can be put in when the vehicle is new, but there are things that can be added to make current motorhomes, either large or small, more user friendly for wheelchair users. Alterations can also be made to smaller campers and then you only need the one vehicle. This can become your everyday transport as well, with the added bonus of having bathroom facilities with you at all times. For example, handrails and grab rails can easily be fitted, taps and fittings can have levers. Cupboards can have handles or knobs which you are able to use and other less visible requirements can be sorted.

This also applies to caravans. New caravans can be built to your requirements - lifts, wide doors, ramps and lots more. Again smaller, less major adjustments can be done to standard caravans to make them user friendly.

Once your transport and sleeping has been sorted, you then need places to go and stay with your holiday home. One of the most reliable clubs that offer sites where wheelchair users can spend time in their caravan/motorhome is The Caravan Club. ▶

OpenBritain | Why Motorhomes and Caravans?

▶ The facilities offered by The Club for disabled people are second to none and are always built to a very high standard and kept to a high quality of cleanliness at all times. They offer good handrails both in their specialist disabled rooms and also their able-bodied facilities. The disabled rooms have been designed as wet rooms, where the shower and toilet are all in one unit, with the vanity sink at the correct height and all light switches are pull cords. An emergency alarm is also fitted.

The **disabled rooms** are normally kept locked and can mostly be opened with a RADAR key. These keys can be borrowed from the site office or you can obtain your own.

The locations of Caravan Club sites, where you will find these facilities, are across the UK. The sites usually offer pitches which are also wheelchair friendly, many on hard standing, with rollout mats available to use on gravel. Also the kerbs have been lowered at access points around the sites.

The buildings, such as the reception, the washing-up area and other such amenities, are accessible. Most of the roads are level and tarmac, although where it is a hilly site, you could need assistance!

Every Club site has an access statement, which gives in detail every door width and available space in all rooms and access all around the site.

All Caravan Club site staff are most helpful - they will pitch you at the most convenient spot for your needs, so pre-booking and passing on your information is very important. They can then offer assistance on what to see and do in their particular area.

We have owned many motorhomes throughout our camping career and have been lucky enough to assist The Caravan Club with access issues. We have found that they have the attitude that all their members or visitors are important, and they take special care of those less able and do whatever they can to make a stay on one of their sites as pleasant and relaxing as possible, for all the family, including your pets!

Gerry and Chris Bullock, 2009 ▶

www.openbritain.net

35

SPINAL HOME CARE

Your Life - Your Way

Spinal Home Care is an established specialist nationwide provider of quality live-in care and assistance

- We build our packages to cater for your individual needs, which we can meet on a short term respite basis or on a permanent basis

- We can also provide assistance on a live-out basis in and around Lancaster/Lune Valley area

- Our highly attentive staff are appropriately trained and supported by our very experienced management team

- Care Quality Commission and ISO accredited

For further information call us on
01539 730777
email
enquiries@spinalhomecare.co.uk
or visit
www.spinalhomecare.co.uk

You can go sailing

"When I go out on the boat I leave the wheelchair on the shore to take care of itself - and I enjoy the sailing. The boat and I become one"

Judy Figures has sailed all her life; being diagnosed with Multiple Sclerosis didn't stop her from continuing.

Sailing is one of the few sports that no matter what your disability or age you can get onboard and sail a boat – yourself. You don't need to have previous experience of sailing - just a desire to face new challenges offering you excitement and freedom.

Through RYA Sailability 20,000 people with a disability of all ages have been able to experience sailing and/or are sailing regularly. ▶

Open Road
ACCESSIBLE RENTALS

Freedom to Explore

If you or someone you're travelling with uses a wheelchair, the new rental service from Allied Mobility means you can now have the freedom to explore where you want, when you want, anywhere in the UK.

- ✓ **Wide range of wheelchair accessible vehicles**
- ✓ **Choice of short, regular or extended hire**
- ✓ **Easy collection or delivered direct to you**
- ✓ **Full comprehensive insurance available**

*All of our vehicles are also available to buy or through the Motability Scheme

0800 916 0042
www.alliedmobility.com

Allied Mobility
Driving for Perfection

▶ Whether its leisure sailing on the coast or inland, or racing in national championships or the Paralympics. We can do this for you too. It's easy; visit **www.rya.org.uk/sailability** and find out how you can get on the water!

Clubs and centres across the country

There are clubs and centres across the country where you can try sailing with a wide range of special facilities including hoists, launching ramps and specially adapted changing rooms. As well as a choice of boats to suit your needs. Go to RYA Sailability; find your nearest club or centre; see the boats and watch the fun of sailing on **www.ryasailability.tv**

Many centres offer training and formal courses. The courses and all safety issues are regulated by the RYA and such centres are RYA recognised training centres; these centres are inspected and approved annually. Look for the RYA tick mark.

Freedom and independence

Lucy Hodges is visually impaired and sails a Skud 18. She has competed in the National and European Blind Championships and won a silver medal at the World Blind Championships. *"I think it's a nice sport to do. Being visually impaired you can't just jump in a car and drive yourself somewhere. But I find that sailing's my little way of getting out and having a bit of freedom, rather than someone having to take me somewhere all the time."*

In 2007 **Geoff Holt** was the first disabled sailor to circumnavigate the UK. Watch his inspirational journey on **www.ryasailability.tv**.

A great family activity

Sailing allows all the family to participate, learn and have fun together and on equal terms.

Jackie Griffith *"As a family it's really important that we have meaningful days out together and sailing can provide that unique opportunity. There is nothing else that I have found that we can all participate, all enjoy, and all improve together."*

Jackie's daughter, Tilly, has a neuromuscular disease called Spinal Muscular Atrophy which means that she has profound muscle weakness throughout her body. She can't roll, walk or crawl – but she can sail.

Come sailing with RYA Sailability

Whether you or someone you know is in a wheelchair, has restricted mobility, is visually or hearing impaired or indeed deaf and or blind, or experiences learning difficulties sailing has something to offer.

RYA Sailability is the charity of the Royal Yachting Association and promotes sailing and boating for disabled adults and children in Britain. It provides:

- Support and advice for people wishing to start sailing and ongoing support
- Links and opportunities to become involved with competitive sailing
- Grants to develop sailing opportunities ■

RYA Sailability, RYA House, Ensign Way, Hamble, Southampton SO31 9FD
t 0844 55 69 550   e sailability@rya.org.uk
web www.rya.org.uk/sailability

OpenBritain | Chatsworth

Chatsworth

500 years of innovation

Chatsworth has been a place of innovation and change over five centuries, and it has welcomed visitors for most of that time. ▶

www.openbritain.net

OpenBritain | Chatsworth

▶ The current five year Masterplan, a £14 million investment in the building, renewing its services and improving visitor facilities, is the latest phase of change. Central to this project was the desire of the entire Chatsworth team, led by the Duke and Duchess of Devonshire, to make the house, a complex structure with important rooms on three different floors, more easily accessible to all visitors.

The Chatsworth House Trust, the independent charity established by the Devonshire family in 1981 to manage and improve Chatsworth for the long term benefit of visitors, is funding the bulk of the Masterplan. This is only possible thanks to the revenue it receives from visitor admissions and events, which goes entirely towards the running costs and conservation of the house, landscape and collections.

The current programme of refurbishment includes a significant investment, of more than £½million, to ensure less mobile visitors have a totally inclusive experience in the house. March 2010 sees the introduction of a new lift which will allow people with restricted mobility to travel between all floors of the house, and to stay with their family and friends throughout their visit.

Construction of the new lift

The lift will make a huge difference to everyone in terms of access, and at the same time we have to ensure the safety of every visitor in the event of an emergency during which we might have to evacuate the building.

With this in mind, we are allowed to accommodate two visitors who use wheelchairs on the top floor at any one time. To minimise any delay, we always recommend that people contact us before they come, so that we can discuss the entire visit in advance. Planning the day can make a real difference.

We are also improving the route for all visitors by removing more than a third, the number of stairs (something like 160) visitors formerly had to negotiate if they wanted to see the 2nd floor rooms (which are open until the end of October, but do not feature in our winter opening) ▶

www.openbritain.net

41

MOBILITY SMART

WHERE SERVICE AND CARE MATTERS

Sales Service Repairs

- Over 5000 Healthcare Aids
- FREE Home Demonstrations *
- FREE Delivery *
- Walking Aids
- Toileting & Incontinence Equipment
- Access Ramps
- Adjustable Beds

www.mobilitysmart.cc

Stair Lifts Bath Lifts Riser Recliners Wheelchairs

We also supply the NHS, Nursing Homes and County Councils. Call for more information.

Freephone 0800 567 7222

BHTA British Healthcare Trades Association

FSB Member of the Federation of Small Businesses

Mobility Smart Limited | Unit 10 | Creamery Industrial Estate | Kenlis Road | Barnacre | Preston | Lancashire | PR3 1GD
Registered in England 5251905 · VAT Registration Number 852 0340 59 · * Terms & Conditions apply

OpenBritain | Chatsworth

The Painted Hall

▶ The installation of new ramps means that the main visitor entrance, the North Front Hall, will be accessible to all for the first time. And when they reach the top floor, all our visitors will now be able to see the 1st Duke's State Rooms, new galleries created by the Masterplan, our temporary exhibitions, treasures like the magnificent 'trompe l'oeil' painting of a violin by Van der Vaardt on the inner door in the **State Music Room**, and the magnificent views of the Cascade (designed for the 1st Duke by Grillet in 1696) and the **Emperor Fountain** (built for the 6th Duke by Joseph Paxton c. 1850) from the windows.

> "All in all a wonderful day out. Going on such visits with someone who is wheelchair bound is always a bit daunting. So it gave me great peace of mind to know in advance what to expect, and enhanced our visit greatly to be looked after in such a friendly way by all of the staff we came across." **M Manton**

Pre-dating the Masterplan work, the garden and the farmyard have been made increasingly accessible for visitors who use manual wheelchairs and electric scooters; we provide a plan of the garden which shows details of paths of varying length and ease so it should be possible to find a route to most of the features that interest you. The paths which are unsuitable for wheelchairs and scooters - either because the camber on the path would make it unsafe, or there are steps or other obstacles - are clearly marked. The map can be downloaded from the 'Accessibility' page on our website prior to your visit. We also offer four electric scooters which can be borrowed for use in the garden, and eight manual wheelchairs with wide profile front castors for use in the house and the garden. ▶

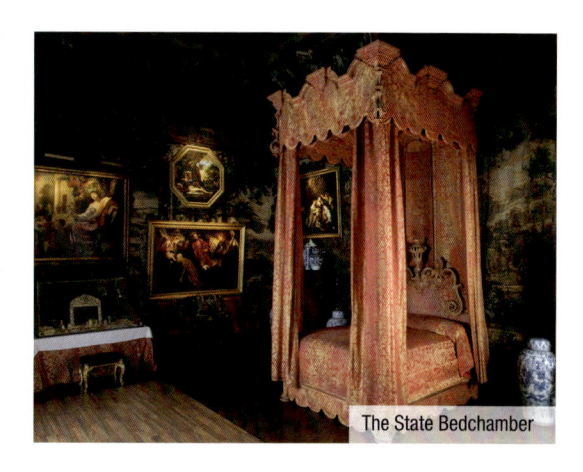

The State Bedchamber

www.openbritain.net

43

Over 100 award-winning camp sites

The Camping and Caravanning Club
The Friendly Club

Cannock Club Site

If you love camping as much as we do, you'll love staying on one of The Camping and Caravanning Club's 109 UK Club Sites. Each of our sites are in great locations and are an ideal base for exploring the UK.

There's just one thing: once you've discovered the friendly welcome, the excellent facilities and clean, safe surroundings, you'll probably want to join anyway!

To book your adventure or to join The Club call **0845 130 7633** quoting code **2741** or visit **www.thefriendlyclub.co.uk**

- More choice of highly maintained, regularly inspected sites
- Friendly sites that are clean and safe, so great for families
- Preferential rates – recoup your membership fee in just 6 nights' stay
- Reduced site fees for 55's and over and special deals for families
- Exclusive Member Services including specialist insurance and advice.

OpenBritain | Chatsworth

Van der Vaardt trompe l'oeil

View of the cascade

▶ To improve access around the car park, and between the house and stables, where shops and restaurants are housed, we provide a free six seater golf buggy, driven by a member of staff, from the main visitor entrance up to the stables. Another golf buggy is available to take visitors on a half hour tour of some of the 5 miles of footpaths in the 105 acre garden. A 28 seat access trailer offering rides, with a commentary, to the woods and lakes behind the house is fully wheelchair accessible. There are small additional charges for both these rides. To ensure availability, we recommend that visitors using wheelchairs pre-book the trailer ride.

Chatsworth House Trust continues to be committed to making access for visitors with disabilities as fully inclusive as possible, responding where possible to peoples' needs. It is always wonderful to get feedback from visitors, and to know when they have had the experience they hoped for, and visitors who have required assistance are usually the ones who take the most trouble to write:

"I just wanted to say how smooth our visit to Chatsworth went on Saturday - thank you for arranging the wheelchairs for my parents and please pass on our thanks to all the staff who could not have been more helpful and pleasant with us. It made for a very happy day and we all enjoyed our visit very much." **J Dismore**

Get in touch

For queries about access or other related issues, please contact Chatsworth via their 24 hour switchboard t 01246 565300. More details at w www.chatsworth.org

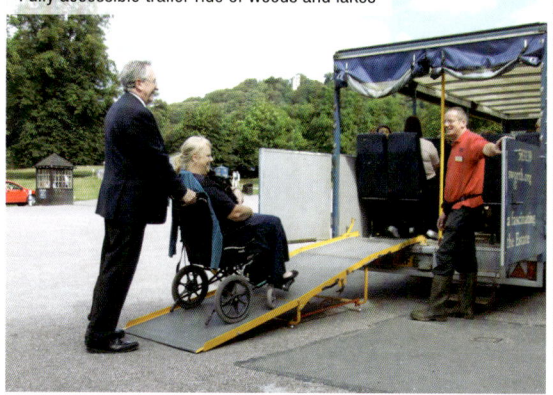

Fully accessible trailer ride of woods and lakes

The free buggy service

www.openbritain.net

45

Hotel breaks for all

Whether you prefer a weekend break by the sea, or a longer stay in the countryside, Vision Hotels offer AA Three Star ✱✱✱ accommodation at a price that won't break the bank.

We work hard to ensure that we're accessible to all. We particularly welcome visually impaired guests and have excellent facilities for Guide Dogs.

Our hotels provide a warm and friendly atmosphere, the highest level of service, home cooked cuisine and a range of leisure activities, excursions and entertainment.

To make a booking, just call our friendly staff at your chosen hotel. Please mention OpenBritain when making an enquiry.

For more details, visit www.actionforblindpeople.org.uk

In Association with RNIB
Registered Charity no: 205913
(England and Wales) Sc040050 (Scotland)

Cliffden Hotel
Teignmouth, South Devon
Tel: 01626 770052

Lauriston Hotel
Weston-super-Mare, Somerset
Tel: 01934 620758

Russell Hotel
Bognor Regis, West Sussex
Tel: 01243 871300

Windermere Manor Hotel
Lake District
Tel: 01539 445801

Action for blind people

Beyond Boundaries

Ken Hames, motivational speaker and presenter of BBC2's 'Beyond Boundaries', explains the importance of seeing the person first and not the disability, and how he believes OpenBritain will inspire disabled travellers to discover their own sense of adventure! ▶

Volkswagen Caravelle
wheelchair accessible

Invatravel's Caravelle conversion, fitted with an underfloor lift, has been the ultimate family transport for the past 25 years.

INVATRAVEL CONVERSIONS
Tel: 01704 506608

HOME DEMONSTRATION, NEW, EX-DEMONSTRATOR & SECOND HAND VEHICLES, SHORT AND LONG TERM HIRE

Visit our website www.invatravel.com

97 Lytham Road, Southport, Merseyside PR9 9UG, Fax: 01704 506607, Email: sales@invatravel.com

Northern Agent for Brotherwood conversions of VW Sharan, VW Caddy Life, VW Caddy Maxi, Peugeot Partner Tepee, Fiat Multipla (travel beside the driver) and Brotherwood's 'Red Label' conversion of the Kia Sedona.

▶ Getting the right information to people with disability about suitable accommodation and leisure activities has always been a challenge. Indeed, in the UK there seems to have been a lack of awareness and empathy to the needs of our disabled community of 11 million people. When I left the Army I knew nothing about people with disability until I went climbing with someone who was blind who opened my eyes so to speak to the possibilities for disabled adventurers. It started me thinking that given the right support and challenge there was absolutely no reason why people with disability shouldn't be introduced, indeed challenged, to do what the able bodied do.

OpenBritain 2010 seeks to change the lives of disabled travellers by collating masses of useful data into a single digestible publication and website. This unique contribution to both the disabled community and the UK tourist industry has many interesting features. Not only does it make important links and introductions into communities all over our islands but it inspires people to provide a service and gateway to exciting opportunities. I believe this is crucial to the disabled community of all ages and functions. Too long have people been put off packing their bags and heading for an adventure by a lack of access and information; its time to get out there with the help of OpenBritain. Last year we took 8 wheelchair users to the top of Ben Nevis in Scotland and it proved that there were no boundaries. A lot of the support for the challenge came from local resources and it also proved that when local communities are aware of people's aspirations they will do a lot to help and support. Most tourist areas have numerous organisations that provide adventure or leisure activities and there is usually a lot more there then meets the eye.

One of my most important learning points when trying to give exciting opportunities to people with disability was to see the person first and not the disability. If I had, for a minute, looked at the disability before the person then I reckon none of my expeditions would have got off the ground! The notion of people first, I champion but it only takes us so far. We also need to recognise the needs of varied function. Wheelchair access, stair lifts and disabled toilets are not rocket science but it always surprises how people with disability are denied access to some really fantastic locations and venues for the sake of a ramp! The Beyond Boundaries series of programmes on BBC2 proved beyond all doubt that people with disability are exceptionally determined and only need the minimum amount of help to get them going. They remained undeterred by volcanoes and swamps, deserts and mountains and have since the expeditions changed the face of disability and persuaded large charities to adapt their charters to encompass, greater understanding and opportunities for adventurous activities.

> "Too long have people been put off packing their bags and heading for an adventure by a lack of access and information."

Additionally they do provide huge inspiration to all of us overcoming difficulties and challenges that would make most of us fill with trepidation. This is why we need to think big and not be deterred by bureaucracy and petty health and safety criteria. OpenBritain seeks to promote awareness and get better access for all into the future.

OpenBritain will inspire everybody in the tourist industry to think carefully about their facilities and indeed the activities and attractions available nearby. We are in the middle of planning a very large challenge for people with disability using parts of the West Highland Way and taking on three sections of it for 3 days ending in Fort William. It will take place in July 2010 and will see teams from all the disabled communities battle it out in the Scottish Highlands. It will be unique in that the A stream will be racers, the B stream walkers and runners and the C stream motorised wheelchairs and it will probably be the biggest gathering of people with disability that UK has ever witnessed. We have already had promises of support from all parts of Scotland and in particular access for motorised wheelchair users will be a key factor.

OpenBritain 2010 is more than just a hotel guide. I recommend you take advantage of it. It represents a way of life that should be accessible to all and seeks to offer exciting opportunities to disabled travellers. I fully endorse it and its ethos and hope it will be a source of inspiration for all.

Ken Hames ■

OpenBritain | Rail travel

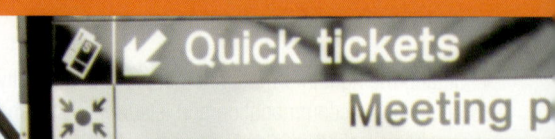

Better than ever

Britain's rail network is now more accessible than it has ever been.

Most trains now have facilities for customers with disabilities. Information screens and audible announcements have removed the uncertainty once felt by many customers with sensory impairments. Many stations have been refurbished so that there are step free routes to train services and the Department for Transport is now four years into its 10-year Access for All scheme which will revolutionise access at a further 200 stations. Discount schemes for disabled people, such as the Disabled Persons Railcard, have also helped keep train travel as an affordable alternative to other modes of transport.

Planning your Journey

If you want to make sure that every leg of your journey is accessible there are a number of services available to help you. If you have a computer you can go to the National Rail enquiries website at **www.nationalrail.co.uk** and use its Journey Planner to plan your route. Once you've done this you can state your access needs on the Stations Made Easy page and find the route through each station that best suits your preferences.

For those of you who prefer human contact you can call **National Rail enquiries on 08457 48 49 50** or call your train company directly. If you're no fan of the phone, you can always visit the nearest staffed station. Travel advice is also available on **www.disabledpersons-railcard.co.uk**.

www.openbritain.net

Assistance

Train companies can also provide you with help using their services. If you need assistance, you should book it at least 24 hours before you travel. This lets the train companies check the accessibility of the stations you will be using and if necessary, arrange alternative transport to or from the nearest accessible station. If you're planning to travel at a time when a station is usually unstaffed, the 24 hour notice period also allows time for staff to be relocated.

Rail staff will help you get on and off of trains but they cannot escort customers throughout the whole of their journey, nor can they provide personal care (for example, help with eating and drinking, taking medication or using the toilet) or carry heavy luggage.

Wheelchairs

There are a limited number of spaces for wheelchair users on each train so, where reservations apply, it is recommended you book your space in advance. Most trains accommodate wheelchairs that are within the dimensions 700mm wide by 1200mm long. The maximum combined weight of a person and their wheelchair that can be conveyed is limited by two things: the capabilities of the member of staff assisting the passenger and the stated maximum safe working load of the ramp (between 230kg and 300kg).

Powered scooters

Because scooters come in a wide variety of shapes and sizes, many have problems on trains, including: tipping backwards on ramps; being heavier than the ramp's safe working load; or being the wrong shape to manoeuvre safely inside a carriage. These problems mean that some companies have trains that cannot carry scooters. If you are a scooter user you should contact the train company you want to travel with or check its scooter policy on **www.nationalrail.co.uk**.

The Disabled Persons Railcard

If you have a disability that makes travelling by train difficult you might qualify for the Disabled Persons Railcard. The Railcard allows you (and a friend if you're not travelling alone) to get 1/3 off most rail fares throughout Great Britain.

A one-year card is £18 and a three-year Railcard is £48. You must provide proof that you are eligible. If you have: a visual impairment, a hearing impairment, epilepsy, or are in receipt of a disability-related benefit you are likely to qualify. Application forms detailing the evidence you must send in can be downloaded from **www.disabledpersons-railcard.co.uk**, requested by phone from **0845 605 0525** or found in the leaflet Rail Travel Made Easy (available from stations and disability information providers).

For contact details of Britain's rail operators see 'Getting there and back' page 404

www.discountmobilityshop.co.uk

The lowest Prices in the UK

	Mobility Scooters from Only £349 Delivered to your Home		**Pride - Shoprider** **Mercury - Freerider** **OVER 75 MODELS**
Lightweight - Travel Chairs - Sports & ELECTRIC		**Wheelchairs** from Just £79 Over 100 Models	
	Rise Recline Chairs from Only £439 **FREE DELIVERY**		**Bath Lifts** from Just £249 Safe Relaxation
Electric Beds Less Than £397 **Plus Memory Foam Mattress**		**Walking Frames** from Just £34 30 Models	

DMS

Buy Securely Online Or call us Free on
08000 430357

Visit our site to see why So many people get More Mobility For Less Cost

Apartments • Cottages • Villas
Hotels • Castles

England • Scotland • Wales
Ireland • Spain • Italy • France
Turkey • Portugal • Florida

Sign Up For Our Free Newsletter

accessible accommodation.com

HOLIDAY MOBILITY HIRE

Do you need to hire Mobility Scooters and More when you go on Holiday?

Spain • Costa del Sol • Costa Blanca
Mallorca • Ibiza • Tenerife • Lanzarote
Gran Canaria • Algarve • Portugal
Cyprus • Ireland • Florida

MobilityAbroad

Book Online at
www.mobilityabroad.com
Or call on 0871 277 0888

OpenBritain | South West Coast Path National Trail

Stair Hole cove, near Lulworth Cove, Dorset

Easy Going Walks
on the South West Coast Path National Trail

The South West Coast Path is renowned as one of the world's best walks.

Its 630 mile long journey around the edge of the Westcountry is like no other as it passes through five Areas of Outstanding Natural Beauty, seventeen Heritage Coasts, a National Park, two World Heritage Sites, a UNESCO Geopark and Britain's first UNESCO Biosphere reserve.

The contrasting landscapes of wild, rugged beauty, bustling seaside resorts, idyllic fishing villages, woodland, pastures and sandy beaches along the coast from Minehead to the shores of Poole Harbour, are truly inspirational and every day walking the path brings stunning new experiences.

Whilst the nature of the coastline means that the Coast Path crosses many steep coastal valleys, there are also plenty of gentle sections. The most attractive of these gentle sections have been audited by the South West Coast Path Team, and displayed on their website www.southwestcoastpath.com as 'Easy Going' walks.

All of these easy-going walks are along fairly flat paths that are at least 2'6" (850mm) wide, and have a minimal cross camber. However in recognition of the varying abilities of people with mobility problems, and the capability of some mobility scooters to tackle uneven ground and slopes, some of the walks do not meet 'urban' accessibility standards.

To enable you to decide whether a particular walk is suitable for you before you make a trip, a detailed map and description of each one with photographs illustrating the nature of the walk can be viewed and printed from the website. Variations in gradients, cross-slopes and path surface, as well as the width and type of any gates are also all noted. ▶

www.openbritain.net   53

Electrically Adjustable Beds

MOTION TECHNOLOGY

With over a decade of experience in the manufacture of bespoke adjustable beds, we can offer high quality sleeping solutions that have your specific needs in mind. We offer a range of sizes from 2ft 3" to 6ft 0" and a number of different upholstered and wooden base options. However our pride and joy is our selection of mattresses, which offer both fantastic comfort and very high longevity.

We also offer a range of accessories, including full divan bases, storage draws, wireless handsets, and our special "Carer-Assist" bed lifter, which can be fitted to beds from 3ft to 4ft 6".

Contact us for more information on our products!
Website: www.motiontech.co.uk
Telephone: 01636 816455

OpenBritain | South West Coast Path National Trail

▶ Examples of some of the stunning locations with an easy-going walk are Lynton and Baggy Point in North Devon, North Cliffs and Godrevy in North Cornwall, Bolberry Down, Berry Head and Budleigh Salterton in South and East Devon and Durlston and Studland in Dorset. Currently over 20 are listed, and there are plans to add more in the future.

These easy-going walks can be found by clicking on the 'Search for a short walk' link on the home page of the South West Coast Path website. On this next page, type in the place name of where you are staying, and the nearest easy going walks are then shown on the map. Click on them, and it will bring up a brief description of the walk, with a link to display more details.

Cornborough Cliff, near Westward Ho!, Devon

Two of the country parks on the coast (Berry Head, Brixham & Durlston, near Swanage) have 'off-road' mobility scooters that can be borrowed on a similar basis to the Shopmobility scheme. A project is planned that will expand this scheme to include around 15 countryside sites around the south west region by August 2010, with a similar number being added in the following year. News of the progress of this project will be added to the website.

Coast Path near Padstow, Cornwall

If you don't have access to the internet, please give the South West Coast Path Team a ring t **01392 383560** and they will send you copies of walks in any area you're interested in visiting.

If you try any of these walks they would really appreciate any feedback (good or bad) about the walks, along with any ideas for improving them, or suggestions for other walks they could add. They can be contacted through the website (each walk has a 'Review this Walk' button), or give them a ring.

The South West Coast Path is one of 15 National Trails in England and Wales that offer some of the best walking, riding and cycling experiences and pass through our finest landscapes. They are managed by highway authorities and the National Trust, and largely funded by Natural England and the Countryside Council for Wales. To find out more about these, visit the website **www.nationaltrail.co.uk**

South West Coast Path
NATIONAL TRAIL

Botallack, West Cornwall

www.openbritain.net

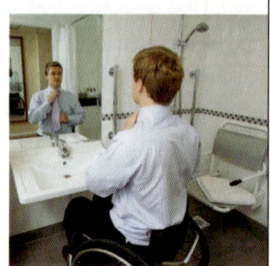

Award-winning hotels, medal-winning performers

Clare Strange, Paralympian

Holiday Inn & Holiday Inn Express are proud to have been confirmed as the Official Hotel Services Provider to the London 2012 Olympic and Paralympic Games.

To find out more about our award winning accessible hotels or to book call **0800 40 50 60** or visit **www.holidayinn.co.uk**

OpenBritain | Wheelyboat Trust

Wheels on water

The Coulam 15 Wheelyboat on the River Tweed

Andy Beadsley, Director of the Wheelyboat Trust, explains how getting out and about on Britain's waterways is getting easier.

The Wheelyboat Trust is a small national charity dedicated to providing disabled people with hassle-free access to waterborne activities such as angling, pleasure boating and nature watching. Formed in 1985 as The Handicapped Anglers Trust, the Trust has supplied more than 120 specially designed wheelchair accessible Wheelyboats to fisheries, water parks and other venues open to the public all over the UK.

I have been Director of the Trust since 2002 but my relationship with Wheelyboats goes back much further. I first used one in the mid-1980s, probably no more than a year or two after the Trust had been formed. I was a fairly recent paraplegic following a motorcycle accident and had not long fallen for the charms of fly-fishing. Wheelchairs and the aquatic environment do not go together at all well so I had to choose my fishing carefully. Unfortunately and unsurprisingly I was not spoilt for choice. Then I came across the Wheelyboat – a marvellous machine that resembled a small landing craft. As the fleet began to spread throughout the UK the horizons of wheelchair users like me and other disabled anglers broadened considerably.

It soon became apparent, however, that Wheelyboats have a much wider appeal than just as angling boats. The features that make them ideal for angling also make them ideal for pleasure boating and nature watching and, consequently, the Trust has always been very keen to broaden their use beyond the fishing lake. Currently, 50% of the Wheelyboats we supply are used for activities other than fishing and as a consequence the impact we are making is bigger and we are helping larger numbers of disabled people get out and about on water.

The Trust's principal role is to promote and provide Wheelyboats to fisheries and other public venues enabling them to accommodate the needs of their disabled visitors. We can help these venues acquire their own Wheelyboat by fundraising to discount its cost. ▶

www.openbritain.net 57

collinscare
the mobility specialists

OFFICE OF FAIR TRADING

Making Mobility Affordable

- Stair Lift
- Walking Sticks
- Rise & Recline Chair
- Tri Walker
- Wheelchair
- Scooter

FREE Demonstrations   FREE Delivery   FREE Catalogue

2 Sprowston Road, Norwich, Norfolk NR3 4QN
Tel: 01603 483 883
Open Monday to Friday 9am to 5pm & Saturday 10am to 4pm
www.collinscare.co.uk

BHTA
British Healthcare Trades Association

---

constables mobility

SETTING YOU FREE...

Keeping our eye on affordability...

- Air conditioning in all our vehicles is optional – to keep running costs lower, and
- There's no need to add a winch - in our conversions they're simply not necessary

...while you keep your eye on the road!

At Constables, our customers' freedom comes first and so our lowered floors offer:

- Extra headroom for that feeling of space
- Great eye-lines and better views!

Tell us what freedom means to you - call us today for a free demonstration

01323 76 75 74

VCA CERTIFIED PRODUCT   VCA REGISTERED FIRM   Motability CONVERTER PARTNER   PEUGEOT   RENAULT

▶ The Trust's most versatile Wheelyboat to date is the Mk III. Its design is very straightforward and has many of the features found in its two predecessors, the most notable being the hinged bow which lowers to form a ramp. Its shallow draught means it can be driven ashore for boarding and disembarking directly from the bank or a slipway. The flat deck ensures its disabled users can reach all corners of the boat enabling them to helm the boat independently without having to rely on help from others. In standard boats, wheelchair users need lifting in and out and once on board are completely reliant on a boat partner. In a Wheelyboat, disabled people can do everything for themselves and are thus provided with a measure of dignity and independence not available from other craft. The latest innovation for the Mk III is its drive-from-wheelchair console.

The Trust supplies three models at present with more on the drawing board. Ever since I became Director I have been keen for the Trust to develop a portfolio of craft suited to different activities, rather than a one-size-fits-all solution. To this end, we have developed two specialist angling boats in conjunction with JM Coulam Boatbuilders. The Coulam 15 Wheelyboat is a purpose-built river fishing boat and was designed for large rivers (two are currently in use on the River Tweed). The Coulam 16 Wheelyboat is a larger version of the 15 and is ideal for fishing on large stillwaters where the handling, looks and performance of the standard fishing boat it is based on are important to its disabled users. This model won the 2008 CLA Game Fair's Most Innovative Product Award.

Below: The Mk III Wheelyboat on Siblyback Lake, Cornwall

Mk III Wheelyboat with drive-from-wheelchair console

We are small charity that makes a big impact. I've been a beneficiary of its work for more than twenty years and it is a real privilege to be at its helm providing others with the opportunity, freedom and access to participate in waterborne activities alongside and on equal terms with their able-bodied counterparts. Long may we continue! ■

For more information about the work of the Trust and the Wheelyboat, please contact: **Andy Beadsley, Director, The Wheelyboat Trust, North Lodge, Burton Park, Petworth, West Sussex, GU28 0JT**
t **01798 342222** e **wheelyboattrust@btconnect.com**, web **www.wheelyboats.org**.

emp
evacuation : mobility : products

SWALLOW EVACUATION AND MOBILITY PRODUCTS

- We are an experienced and committed company who want to improve the experiences for people, in as many situations as possible. We believe we can provide a solution for your specific situation as we believe that one product can't cover all situations. Our range covers basic downward evacuation to a powered mobile lift (SuperTrac) that will take motorised wheelchair and also for moving bariatric people.

- We have a fantastic range of products for customers with disabilities and also for evacuation purposes. The huge advantage of our range is that they do not rely on the physical strength of the operator and therefore, helpers / buddies are happy and confident when using them.

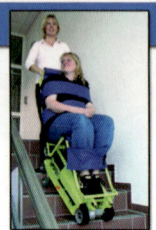

Power-trac
provides easy ride up and down stairs for people who are unable to climb stairs.

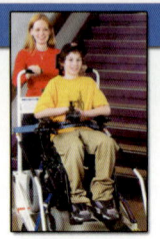

Super-trac
carries all types of wheelchairs. It is the world's only portable inclined platform lift.

Stair-mate
is an easy to use, portable wheelchair lift designed to attached under most manual wheelchairs

Beach-buggy
A comfortable wheelchair, which can be used on uneven ground and also soft and sandy beaches, with a brake/lock, safety bar and umbrella

C-max
The only chair that can travel up & down spiral and curved staircases.

Also ... Evac-track
is an evacuation device used to move people with a disability or injury down stairways quickly and safely during an emergency.

Swallow Evacuation & Mobility Products. 197 Vicarage Road, Kings Heath, Birmingham B14 7QQ.
0121 444 3690 - 07789 766652 - www.swallowemp.com - info@swallowemp.com

---

The world's best mobility and seating solutions

Alber e-fix E25 and **E26** electrical add-on drives combine the benefits of power and manual chairs. With a range of over 18 miles and now, with **E26**, up to 25 stone user weight limit, **e-fix** can be operated even without full hand functionality. Most current manual wheelchairs can be retrofitted with **e-fix**, so you can continue to use a chair that has been adjusted to suit you.
e-fix can easily handle ramps and gradients up to 20% and, because of its low weight, **e-fix** is easy to load into the boot of a car.

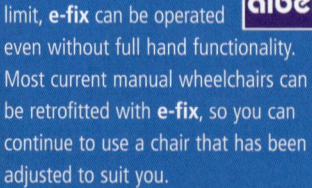

alber **e-fix**®

- LIGHTWEIGHT WHEELCHAIRS
- POWERCHAIRS
- STAND UP WHEELCHAIRS
- COMFORT WHEELCHAIRS
- POWERDRIVES
- WHEELCHAIR SEATING
- PRESSURE AREA CARE
- WALKING AIDS

Get out more.

GERALD SIMONDS

9 March Place, Gatehouse Way, Aylesbury, Bucks HP19 8UA
Freephone: 0800 220975   Fax: 01296 380279
email: info@gerald-simonds.co.uk

Visit **www.gs-direct.co.uk** your new, on-line source for aids to daily living. Quality products, designed to make life easier.

Shopmobility
...the freedom to get around

What Is Shopmobility?

Shopmobility is a Scheme which lends manual wheelchairs, powered wheelchairs and powered scooters to members of the public with limited mobility, to shop and to visit leisure and commercial facilities within the town, city or shopping centre. It aims to:

- Enable people with temporarily or permanently impaired mobility to engage or re-engage with their community and travel with confidence, thus enhancing their quality of life, and providing them and their carers with independence

- Set uniform and trustworthy standards of safety and service for Shopmobility users, and encourage good practice and consistency of approach

- Act as a national network helping disabled and older people to travel with ease and enjoy shopping, leisure and other facilities

- Encourage equality of access for disabled and older people to all main towns and city centres

How Much Does It Cost?

All Schemes operate slightly differently; some provide **Shopmobility** as a free service while others make a charge. Most Schemes welcome any donations you wish to make.

Who Can Use Shopmobility?

Shopmobility is for anyone, young or old, whether their disability is temporary or permanent. It is available for those with injuries, long or short-term disabilities – anyone who needs help with mobility.

Shopmobility is about the freedom to get around. You do not need to be registered disabled to use it.

How Do I Use Shopmobility?

Each Scheme varies so it is important to contact the Scheme you wish to visit prior to using the service. A member of staff or volunteer will give you all the information you need.

Most Schemes ask that you bring identification containing your name and address on your first visit; this is so that Schemes can complete a registration form and keep a record of your details. Many Schemes will issue you with a membership card, and on your next visit you can simply show this card.

NATIONAL FEDERATION OF Shopmobility

w www.shopmobilityuk.org
e info@shopmobilityuk.org   t 08456 442446

GM Coachwork were awarded 'The National 2009 Award' for their 'Wheelchair Accessible Vehicle Conversions' by Motability - the biggest Government vehicle leasing company in Europe.

gm coachwork

Motability Operations
WAV PARTNER OF THE YEAR
WINNER 2009

wheelchair accessible vehicles

Motability Enquiry Line   0800 3169 327

Home Demonstration Nationwide

www.gmcoachwork.co.uk

VCA   WAVCA   Motability

BE INSPIRED

EXPERIENCE

JOIN IN

The Mobility Roadshow

1st, 2nd, 3rd July 2010

East of England Showground, Peterborough

Open 10am daily • Free Admission & Parking

Showcasing the widest choice of products and services to aid an independent lifestyle

- **Be inspired** see the latest mobility innovations
- **Feel the experience** test drive vehicles, wheelchairs, powerchairs and scooters plus travel, leisure and home products
- **Join in** demonstrations and activities for all the family

For more information go to www.mobilityroadshow.co.uk or call 0845 241 0390

The Mobility Roadshow®
the future of mobility

the UK's premier mobility event for over 25 years

the UK's premier mobility & lifestyle event

HISTORIC HOUSES ASSOCIATION

The access challenge

Valerie Wenham, who provides access advice to members of the Historic Houses Association, champions best practice in some of the least accessible places.

Since becoming an Access Adviser to members of the Historic Houses Association seven years ago, I have visited more than 150 privately-owned houses, gardens and estates that are opened to the public. Providing detailed access reports and guidance for Disability Discrimination Act requirements has been part of this wonderful role - but the opportunity to see so many of the places that hitherto had been just names to me was an added bonus.

I was delighted to find at the outset that many of these houses had already provided a great deal of access for every visitor - including those with more severe disabilities, such as wheelchair users - not an insignificant feat, as the many castles we saw had been built to 'keep people out'. I first heard this phrase when I visited the Tower of London many years ago, and it is constantly repeated - a cliche now, it is nevertheless true.

A case in point is the romantic **Duart Castle** on the Isle of Mull, which is not easy for people who find stairs difficult. If visitors are able to manage two flights of steps with handrails, they will gain access to the main floor of the Castle where, in the Banqueting Hall, there is a video of the remainder of the tour. ▶

< Mark Ellis, Lincolnshire Association for People with Disabilities, exploring the temple of the winds at Doddington Hall in Lincolnshire during development of the sensory tours, supported by the HLF.

BOMA OFF ROAD WHEELCHAIR

Where could a Boma take you?

Contact:
01908 585648
07773 278768

FREEDOM, INDEPENDENCE, ENJOYING THE OUTDOORS

www.moltenrock.co.uk

Whatever your needs we have the mobility solution for you.

Sirus Automotive are the UK's leading provider of compact 'Drive From Wheelchair' and 'Passenger up Front' vehicles

We also convert rear entry WAV's and provide an adaptations service offering seating solutions, boot hoists, and many driving modifications.

For further information or a no obligation home demonstration, please contact us on 0121 505 7777 email info@sirusautomotive.co.uk or visit www.drivefrom.com

Motability

SIRUS
Live your Life

OpenBritain | Historic Houses Association

The award winning Brewhouse Education Centre at Burghley House, supported by the HLF

▶ A most important point, reiterated by HHA members and managers in literature and on the web, is to encourage all visitors, disabled or otherwise, to contact the property in advance of a visit should they need advice. There is nothing more discouraging for all concerned than to have to leave an elderly or disabled person sitting alone in the garden or house, unable to complete a tour, when this could have been avoided by making one telephone call.

So many adjustments can be made to provide an enjoyable visit for people unable to climb stairs. Although many historic house owners have found ways to provide passenger lifts and hoists, this is a difficult issue, as the integrity of the building must not be compromised, and such provisions are very costly. When all else fails, technology such as CCTV, a video, or a touch-screen presentation may provide more information than a tour of the building! And booklets of pictures of inaccessible rooms are appreciated, such as those provided at **Hartland Abbey** in Devon, and **Markenfield Hall** in Yorkshire, where there is limited wheelchair access. These supplement the guide book while companions are completing their tour of the property.

Many HHA members' houses stand out for the innovative way they have approached this challenge. For instance **Wilton House** in Wiltshire which, with its garden, is fully accessible for wheelchair users, has provided so much more for people with disabilities, including a large print guide, an induction loop in the theatre for hearing-aid users, and scented plants, fountains and a 'whispering seat' in the gardens, all attractive to people with impaired vision.

Burghley House in Lincolnshire has a visitor reception area in the Brewhouse, with a display projected on the walls of events in the history of the house, so readily accessible to all visitors.

At **Sutton Park** near York there is a lift inside the house, and an electric buggy is provided for people to tour the grounds.

Other houses, like **Holkham Hall** in Norfolk, have provided stairclimbers - independent devices which take a wheelchair user on their own (or a borrowed) manual wheelchair up and down flights of stairs. They are conducted by a trained member of staff, and are a safe and economical method of providing a full visit for wheelchair users.

Gardens and parkland can present access problems, but HHA members are equal to this, and have provided a large degree of access. Wheelchairs are normally available for people who may not be accustomed to this method of progress, but find long distances daunting. At an increasing number of places, there are electric buggies, self-drive or staff-driven.

At **Newby Hall** in North Yorkshire, there are three buggies and three wheelchairs for loan to explore the extensive gardens, and a miniature railway offers a fascinating tour of the grounds. Most of the major rooms in the house are on the ground floor which is fully accessible. **Great Dixter** in East Sussex provides a plan showing wheelchair accessible routes through this magnificent garden.

Most Members' websites now give full details of access, allowing visitors to decide whether a visit will be suitable for them. This is extremely important, as the majority of people with disabilities rely on the web for information.

As technology continues to improve, I am sure HHA members will continually find different and magical ways to enhance their houses, gardens and estates for the majority of visitors, in the years to come.

Valerie Wenham ■

Joanna Boyson assisting Valerie at an advisory visit to Holkham Hall

www.openbritain.net

65

What public transport services are there for me?

just ask nexus.org.uk

If you have a question about public transport, nexus.org.uk has the answer. Use it to plan great days out, renew your travel pass or find the right ticket for your journey. And of course, it's the place to go for all Tyne and Wear bus, Metro and ferry timetables.

Discover today's YHA...

YHA has over 200 properties across England and Wales with 45 suitable for people with accessibility requirements. We are constantly updating and improving accessibility - check out the website for further information.

A selection of our most accessible YHA's are:

YHA Blaxhall	YHA London Central
YHA Borrowdale	YHA London St. Pancras
YHA Helmsley	YHA Manchester
YHA Lee Valley	YHA National Forest
YHA Lockton	YHA Whitby

Visit www.yha.org.uk or phone 0800 0191 700

Scotland Outdoors

High on the wish-list for visitors to Scotland are the landscape, the great outdoors and the wildlife. The mountains, the moorlands, the glens and the coastline are spectacular and varied and the thrill of watching an eagle soaring above the glens will stay with you forever. Your first thought may be, "Great, but what happens if I can't get around so easily and negotiating rocky paths is definitely out". The news is that access to Scotland's countryside is improving and there are many places which can be visited. ▶

ScotRail's Fort William - Mallaig service crossing the Loch nan Uamh Viaduct © Norman McNab

www.bath-knight.co.uk
STRESS FREE BATHING

The easiest way to get in and out of the bath

BK8009

FREE BROCHURE
FREE TRIAL   FREE FITTING

CALL TODAY
0800 1 690 690

Bath-Knight

STOP PRESS
our **NEW**
SCOOTER WEBSITE
is NOW OPEN

www.road-knight.co.uk

with wheelchair boarding **RAMPS**, a **SPACIOUS** dedicated area for two wheelchairs, a tip-up **COMPANION SEAT** adjacent to each wheelchair space, wheelchair boarding door **CLEARLY INDICATED**, laptop **SOCKETS** and **FOLD-AWAY** tables, **IMPROVED** access to 20% of seats, **CLEARER,** visible and audible announcements, **EASIER** access to toilet facilities...

...our Pennine Class 185 trains make life **EASIER FOR EVERYONE**.

Book now at **www.tpexpress.co.uk** or for assisted travel bookings call **0800 107 2149**

First transforming travel

transpennine express

OpenBritain | Scotland Outdoors

▶ A magnet for visitors is the **Cairngorms National Park** in the Highlands, where you need not be a mountaineer to reach the high plateau; the funicular railway takes visitors to a viewing terrace just below the summit of Cairn Gorm, the UK's sixth-highest mountain. From here there are spectacular views – and it's the ideal place for weather-watching, with four seasons in under an hour! The funicular travels from 635m to 1,097m above sea level and is fully accessible, as is the terrace and the restaurant.

There is also a network of way-marked paths through the **Cairngorm forests** and special electric buggies are available from **Badenoch and Strathspey Community Transport** so you can explore the trails, starting off from the **Glenmore Visitor Centre**, near Aviemore. It is best to book twenty-four hours in advance and longer in the main season; there is no charge, but donations are welcome. You can also borrow a scooter if you are on holiday in the area.

For wildlife-watching you can spend time in **Speyside Wildlife's** specially adapted hide on the **Rothiemurchus Estate** in the Cairngorms. This company specialises in bird and wildlife-watching and being with an expert means that you are more likely to see a tawny owl, a great spotted woodpecker, a pine marten or a badger and learn more about them and their way of life.

The Forestry Commission in Scotland has been particularly active in upgrading their paths in several areas so that wheelchair-users can find it easier to enjoy their forests. Their leaflets highlight paths which are accessible, such as the **Dunmore Walk** at Faskally north of Pitlochry where visitors may be surprised to see ducks nesting in trees, a peculiarity of the goldeneye duck! The forest is a mixture of deciduous and conifer trees so the spring and autumn colours are particularly spectacular and there are birds and animals aplenty to be seen, including the elusive red squirrel. At **Craigvinean** near Dunkeld, the Pine Cone Point Walk leads to a viewpoint from which there are spectacular views over Perthshire.

Bird-watching is especially fascinating in spring and autumn when migrating birds flock to Scotland in their thousands. The Royal Society For The Protection of Birds (RSPB) has several sites where accessible paths have been laid out and there are adapted hides. Perhaps the most famous is **Loch of Garten** which ospreys have made their home for many years and their arrival each spring results in a flurry of interest to find out whether the same birds have returned. It is easy to get to the osprey centre where there are viewing slots, telescopes and binoculars at different levels. Also to be seen are Scottish crossbills, crested tits and red squirrels. ▶

Ben Lomond

A guided walk in the Galloway Forest Park

View from Corpach, Ben Nevis

www.openbritain.net

69

STAIRLIFTS FROM HELP THE AGED WE WILL®

Low Price Guarantee* From A Name You Can Trust

Call for a quotation or information
0800 019 8625

*Please ask an advisor for details.

Age Concern England and Help the Aged merged on the 1st April 2009. Together they have formed Age UK (charity No. 1128267), a single charity dedicated to improving the lives of older people. 50% of all stairlift profits go directly to the charity. Help the Aged working in partnership with Minivator Group.

ADAPTED CAR HIRE
Car hire for disabled drivers and passengers

- Broad range of cars and adaptations
- Cars with push pull hand controls
- Wheelchair Accessible Vehicles (WAV)
- Cars with flip down left foot accelerators
- Automatic vehicles
- Online and telephone booking
- Door-to-door delivery and collection service
- Insurance included
- Reasonable rates
- Unlimited mileage
- Brand new vehicles

Adapted Car Hire provides a broad range of specially adapted vehicles to cater for the needs of disabled drivers and passengers.

Vehicles can be hired on a daily, weekly and monthly basis and we provide a door-to-door delivery and collection service.

We run a variety of rental schemes tailored to the needs of the individual customer, as well as regular promotional and special offers.

All vehicles supplied and adapted by Motability accredited suppliers.

Please visit our website **www.adaptedcarhire.co.uk**, email us at info@adaptedcarhire.co.uk or call us on **0845 68 62 007** for further information.

www.adaptedcarhire.co.uk

Help on hand 24 hours a day

TRY IT! No obligation demonstration

AGE Concern — Personal Alarm Service
Call for a demonstration or buy online and install with **Easy-Connect**. Quote: AID0471

Freephone 0800 77 22 66
www.aidcall.co.uk/openbritain

The four national Age Concerns in the UK have joined together with Help the Aged to form new national charities dedicated to improving the lives of older people. **Demonstration does not apply if you buy online and Easy-Connect.**

OpenBritain | Scotland Outdoors

The Steamship Sir Walter Scott, Loch Katrine

▶ In the south west is the RSPB's **Mersehead Nature Reserve**, near Dumfries, between the Solway Firth and the hills. This is home to a variety of wildlife, including lapwings, snipe, geese (up to 15,000 at a time), skylarks, dragonflies, butterflies, natterjack toads – and starlings, whose aerial acrobatics at dusk are sensational. The hides are accessible, as are the paths. Near Glasgow is the **RSPB Lochwinnoch Reserve**, one of the largest wetlands in Scotland and best known for its water birds – whooper swans, teals, goosanders, goldeneyes, and great crested grebes. There are trails and hides and a visitor centre, all of them accessible.

If you want to join a group for an extended walk, then there are **Disabled Ramblers' Associations** in some areas, one of these being the Forth and Tay Disabled Ramblers, which organises a dozen excursions between April and October and welcomes visitors. If you prefer to explore trails on your own, then get a copy of the guide book, **"Walking on Wheels"**, by Eva McCracken, with descriptions of fifty wheel-friendly trails, all barrier-free and graded according to wheel size. There is also a detailed map, photographs and a fact-file.

For a thoroughly enjoyable family day out, try **Cream o' Galloway** near Gatehouse of Fleet – and enjoy their delicious ice-cream. This organic farm has a range of activities, including a farm tour, two miles of nature trails, pond-dipping and a wildlife hide, all of which are accessible, as is the Ready Steady Freeze where you can try your hand at making ice-cream.

If you prefer to watch the scenery glide by while you sit and relax, then opt for a trip on the steamship *Sir Walter Scott* on **Loch Katrine** in the Trossachs, a hilly and wooded area. This most beautiful of lochs is in the heart of Rob Roy MacGregor territory and you can enjoy a cruise whilst admiring the scenery.

Another relaxing way to enjoy the Scotland's mountainous landscape is to catch a **ScotRail** train on one of the most scenic routes in the world. There are four in Scotland: **Glasgow to Oban** or to **Fort William via Loch Lomond** and the remote **Rannoch Moor** and on to **Mallaig**; **Inverness to the Kyle of Lochalsh** through the heart of the Highlands; and **Inverness to Thurso and Wick** in the far north. The stunning scenery guarantees that a book is definitely surplus to requirements!

Choose Scotland for your next holiday and enjoy the great outdoors! ◾

Factfile

CairnGorm Mountain
t 01479 861261 web www.cairngormmountain.co.uk

Badenoch and Strathspey Community Transport
t 01479 810004
e maggie@bsctc.wanadoo.co.uk

Speyside Wildlife
t 01479 812498 web www.speysidewildlife.co.uk

Forestry Commission
t 0845 3673787 web www.forestry.gov.uk/scotland

RSPB
t 0131 311 6500 web www.rspb.org.uk/reserves/guide

Forth and Tay Ramblers Association
web www.ftdr.com

Cream o' Galloway:
t 01557 814040 web www.creamogalloway.co.uk

Loch Katrine/Sir Walter Scott
t 01877 332000 web www.lochkatrine.com

ScotRail
t 0800 912 2 901 web www.scotrail.co.uk

Walking on Wheels
t 01383 733724 web www.cualann.com

www.openbritain.net

Welcome to mobilise
Promoting mobility for disabled people

JOIN NOW!!!

Membership

As well as help, advice and campaigning from our fully trained Information Officers, members of Mobilise also receive a monthly magazine, can request up-to-date information leaflets and enjoy concessions and benefits from a range of different companies including ferries and Eurotunnel.

For further information visit our website

www.mobilise.info

the UK charity that promotes mobility for disabled people

...looking after your Mobility

Mobilise is a national charity fighting to improve mobility and access for all disabled people including drivers, passengers, Blue Badge holders, scooter and wheelchair users.

The charity campaigns at national and local government level and works closely with other organisations such as Motability and the Department for Transport. Mobilise is run by people with disabilities and a number of staff are also disabled.

One of Mobilise's most notable and long-running campaigns is to seek improvements to the Blue Badge parking scheme. We were heavily involved in the government's recent Blue Badge consultation. Another ongoing campaign is to secure a national relief scheme from congestion charging. It is because of the hard work of Mobilise that all Blue Badge holders are exempt from the London congestion charge. Mobilise is also concerned by the growing number of local authorities removing the disabled parking concession from their car parks.

Mobilise Director of Policy and Campaigns, Helen Smith told OpenBritain "As a disabled person I know just how important mobility is and I believe the work of Mobilise is vital in ensuring disabled people have the same access rights as everyone else. We want to ensure that disabled people are exempt from high parking charges at hospitals, can get fuel at petrol stations and are exempt from road pricing"

Membership of Mobilise is open to everyone with a disability. Those without a disability are also welcome to join as an associate member. Benefits of being a member include access to a helpline run by experienced information officers, plenty of concessions including ferries, Eurotunnel and car hire and a monthly magazine.

The membership magazine is always packed with interesting reports. Recent features have included a trip to Venice by a wheelchair user, a mobility scooter formation team and a round Britain sailing trip. We also keep members up to date with our current campaigns and new legislation. Our information officers also investigate new inventions to make life easier for disabled people and in recent years one of the best inventions has been the beach wheelchair.

Accessible Beaches

Sand and rocks are two of the hardest surfaces to either walk on or push a wheelchair over but Britain's beaches have now become much more accessible with the growing number of beach wheelchairs available for hire.

Mobilise receives quite a few calls in the summer months from members wanting to know how and where they can hire beach wheelchairs so to find out more Mobilise Information Officers Jim Rawlings and Marta Bartosiewicz took a trip to some beaches in East Anglia.

Need to hire a Wheelchair Accessible Vehicle?

We provide Wheelchair Accessible Vehicles (WAVS), people carriers and minibuses to private customers, local authorities, schools and NHS Trusts throughout the UK for rental. Our extensive knowledge and experience means we provide the best possible individual services

- WAV, minibus and people carrier rental specialists
- Competitive daily, weekly and weekend hire rates: 1 day - 3 years
- Hire before you buy - make sure you choose the right vehicle for your needs
- Fully comprehensive or customers' own insurance available
- Individual specifications available
- Extensive WAV fleet, from single person vehicles to minibuses
- Countrywide delivery
- Used WAV sales

Please contact us with your requirements, we will be able to help...
Nationwide Lo-Call: **0845 603 9464**
e-mail: sgamvale@btconnect.com
or visit: www.amvalemobility.co.uk

Amvale mobility

BRIDGESTONE
PASSION for EXCELLENCE

General Enquiries
Bridgestone UK
Athena Drive
Tachbrook Park
Warwick (Leamington Spa)
CV34 6UX

www.bridgestone.co.uk

25 000 LIVES TO SAVE
European Road Safety Charter

Bridgestone is a signatory of the European Road Safety Charter

---

Break
All about Caring

Registered Charity No. 286650

Everyone deserves a Break

Break provides a range of specialist holidays and respite care for people with disabilities

• **Supported holidays** - for children and adults with learning disabilities, including those with high level care needs

• **Self-catering chalets** - for families with special needs

To book please call **01263 822161**
or email bookings@break-charity.org

www.break-charity.org

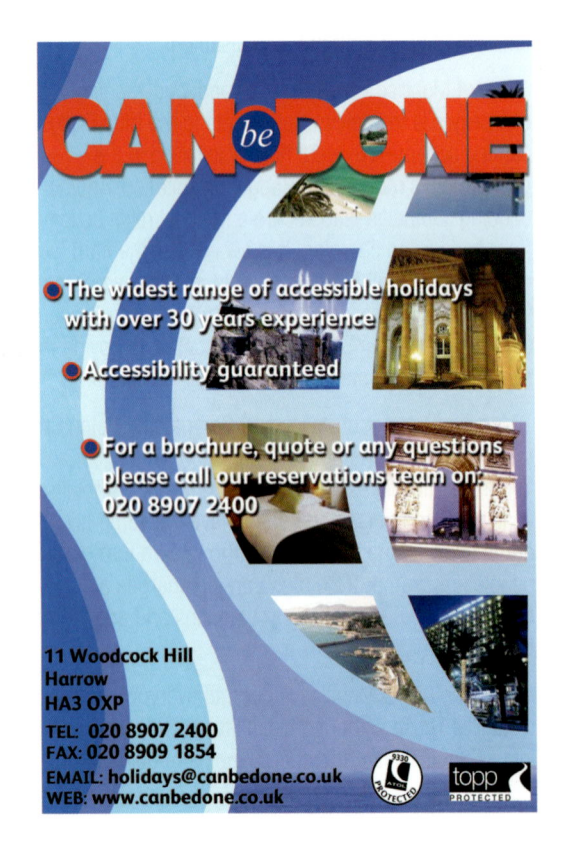

CAN be DONE

- The widest range of accessible holidays with over 30 years experience
- Accessibility guaranteed
- For a brochure, quote or any questions please call our reservations team on: **020 8907 2400**

11 Woodcock Hill
Harrow
HA3 0XP
TEL: 020 8907 2400
FAX: 020 8909 1854
EMAIL: holidays@canbedone.co.uk
WEB: www.canbedone.co.uk

9330 PROTECTED | topp PROTECTED

74

Our Top Tips:

1. Always phone in advance to check there is a beach wheelchair available
2. Check what documentation you will be required to have to hire the wheelchair
3. Find out how much money you will need for the deposit
4. Find out how long you can hire the chair for
5. Always ask for a demonstration and read the instructions

Aldeburgh

Aldeburgh is a picturesque village steeped in maritime history and famous for its fish and chips. On Aldeburgh's beach, a short distance north of the town centre, stands a sculpture, The Scallop, dedicated to Benjamin Britten. Visitors to the sculpture are encouraged to sit on it and watch the sea. We wanted to do just that, but to do so Jim needed an all terrain wheelchair. Fortunately there is such a wheelchair in Aldeburgh, which can be hired for up to two hours.

Excited at the prospect, we went to Aldeburgh Tourist information Centre. All we needed to do was to leave a driving licence for security, collect a key to the shed where the chair is stored and head for the beach. We found the shed located next to the disabled parking spaces by the beach. But, unfortunately things did not go according to plan!

The padlock locking the shed simply would not budge – it was just too rusty. Back at the Information centre we highlighted the problem. Because they were not aware of it, we wondered when the wheelchair was last hired. "A long time ago" sprung to mind. Waste of fantastic equipment, we thought. The lady at the centre apologised and reassured us that the padlock will be changed shortly. We were very disappointed and Jim could only look at the sculpture from a distance.

Great Yarmouth

Not to be defeated, we decided to head for Great Yarmouth hoping Jim would eventually be able to test the elusive, so far, beach wheelchair.

After arranging our appointment, we turned up at Great Yarmouth Tourist Information centre. We were told they have 5 of the wheelchairs in question and we were very welcome to take one of them to the beach. It was as easy as that. After leaving £20 fully refundable deposit and a proof of identity, we headed for the beach.

Jim had a slight problem getting in and out of the chair, but once in it he enjoyed the ride. The chair was easy to push on the sandy beach ■

Join mobilise

Mobilise membership costs just £16 a year. For more information about Mobilise, its ongoing campaigns, and how to become a member, please call 01508 489449, email enquiries@mobilise.info or visit our website www.mobilise.info

mobilise

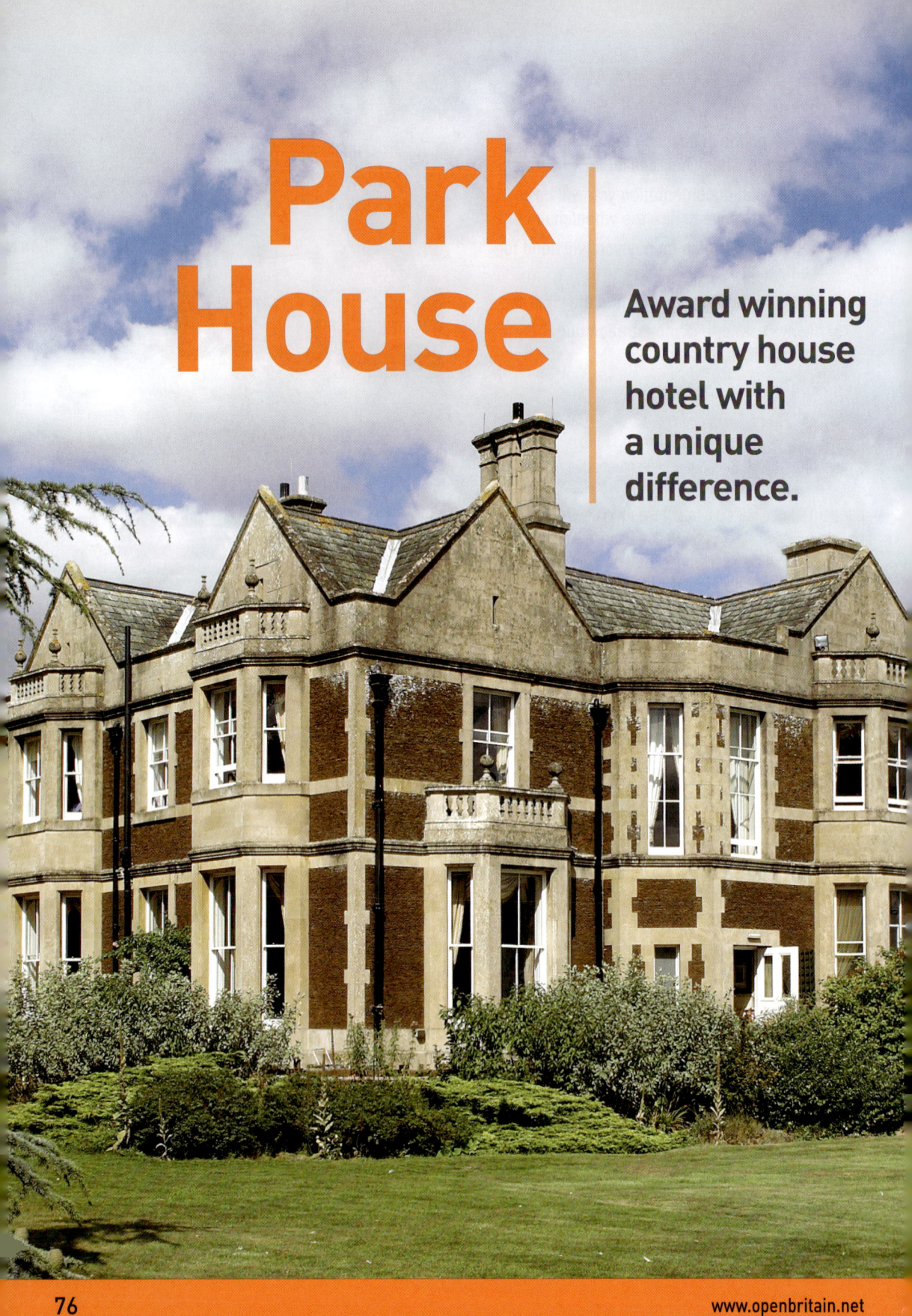

Park House

Award winning country house hotel with a unique difference.

Located on the Royal Sandringham estate near King's Lynn in West Norfolk and operated by the charity Leonard Cheshire Disability, the hotel offers a holiday experience for people with mobility difficulties or disabilities, with or without their carer or companion. The hotel's in-house care team, headed by a registered nurse, ensures that everyone has a break.

Park House is an impressive Victorian country house set in its own grounds amidst the soaring trees and rolling parklands of the Estate. The main house itself was the birthplace of Princess Diana and was made available to the charity by Her Majesty the Queen in 1987. After a national fundraising campaign, the hotel was completely renovated and specially designed to meet the needs of disabled guests.

Experienced nurses and care staff are employed by the hotel to ensure every guest has the opportunity to enjoy a completely relaxing and revitalizing holiday all year round. Discreet and unobtrusive personal assistance is on hand if required 24 hours a day. Whether it is a helping hand getting in and out of bed, 'peace of mind' or full nursing care, the hotel is able to accommodate most requirements.

Park House has been equipped to the very highest of standards. All 16 bedrooms (8 single and 8 twins) are en-suite and most are provided with a digital TV, radio, a direct dial telephone and tea & coffee making facilities. The main reception rooms and all of the bedrooms have been refurbished to a very high standard and the spacious conservatory provides a social meeting place at the very heart of the building.

Lifts, ramps and automatic doors provide easy wheelchair access and all bedrooms and bathrooms have been specially equipped, some with overhead hoists and electronic controls to doors. The bedrooms now incorporate leading edge technology beds - designed to accommodate specialist needs. Arjo jacuzzi baths are available, with assistance if required.

Facilities within the hotel include a shop, a well-stocked library with talking/large print books, complimentary broadband enabled computer system, a spacious, relaxing lounge which includes; a 42" television and movie/games room, a piano and art equipment. Most evenings at the hotel there is some form of optional entertainment, ranging from talented local musicians to quiz nights and demonstrations.

The picturesque grounds at Park House are fully accessible and include a terraced patio, raised flower beds and wheelchair paths leading through woodland areas. Several accessible terraces are available for relaxing during summer months, particularly popular is the area over looking Sandringham cricket pitch. A heated outdoor swimming pool with Arjo hoist is also available between May and September. ▶

National Trust

For a copy of our **Access Guide**, or to request an **Admit One Card** for an essential companion of a disabled visitor, or **Links Pass** for disability group visits, contact our Membership Department:
National Trust, PO Box 39, Warrington WA5 7WD. Tel 01793 817634, or e-mail enquiries@thenationaltrust.org.uk

For general enquiries tel 0844 800 1895.

For other access enquiries email accessforall@nationaltrust.org.uk

---

PB Conversions — giving you freedom

"Specialists in vehicle adaptations for people with disabilities"

- Hand Controls
- Drive from the Wheelchair
- Auto Adapt Platinum Dealer
- On site service available
- 20 years experience
- Left foot Accelerators
- Infra Red systems
- Annual service reminders
- 3 Year warranty on PBC products

Motability — The leading car scheme for disabled people

Call for friendly service and Free advice on
01525 850588
www.pbconversions.co.uk

PB Conversions, Unit 6 Acacia Close, Cherrycourt Way, Leighton Buzzard, Beds, LU7 4QE
Tel: 01525 850588   Fax: 01525 850588   E-mail: pbconversions@aol.com

---

24 stunning UK family holiday parks

In Cornwall, Devon, Dorset, Hampshire, Norfolk, South Wales & Scotland

Choose from 24 fantastic holiday parks by some of the UK's most stunning beaches, beautiful rolling countryside or peaceful woodlands.

- Top quality wheelchair friendly caravan holiday homes
- Central heating & double glazing available
- Easy access into venues for wheelchair users
- Heated indoor & outdoor pools
- FREE kids' clubs, from tots to teens
- FREE live family entertainment
- Cafés, bars & restaurants
- Superb touring & camping facilities at 11 parks

Parkdean
parkdean.com   0844 335 3746

REHAB PROSTHETICS

Are you an amputee who is:-
   Satisfied with the service from your Limb Centre?
   Walking as well as you'd like?
   Receiving the best possible assessment for your needs?
   Wearing the most appropriate prothesis?

Then you probably don't need to contact us!

Our service is tailored to suit your requirements. We have experienced physiotherapists to help you walk better. Your assessment will be undertaken by prosthetist and physiotherapist working together. We have access to the whole prosthetic range, worldwide.

Maybe you do need to contact us.

15, The Courtyard, Whitwick Business Park, Coalville, Leicestershire LE67 4JP
T: 01530 813555   W: www.rehabprosthetics.com   E: info@rehabprosthetics.com

▶ Throughout the year a fully optional program of escorted excursions are organised to the un-spoilt local countryside, coastline, nature reserves and stately homes that surround Park House. The hotel's fleet of adapted minibuses ensures that all guests have the chance to take in their choice of local attractions.

The Royal residence at Sandringham House is adjacent to the hotel and is also a popular destination, along with the myriad other stately homes within the local area such as Oxborough and Blickling.

All in all, Park House is the ideal country house destination for people with mobility difficulties or disabilities, providing peace of mind and a holiday for everyone.

For further details regarding personalised booking service or any further queries, please contact the hotel or visit the comprehensive website. A booking form is available online, however after initial contact the hotel prefers to communicate with guests individually by telephone to ensure special requirements are met ■

Park House Hotel, Sandringham,
King's Lynn, Norfolk PE35 6EH
t 01485 543000 e parkinfo@LCDisability.org
w www.parkhousehotel.org.uk

I am **disabled** on land... but everything changes on the **water!**

Find out how you can get afloat - visit
www.rya.org.uk/sailability

RYA Sailability

---

holiday homes

The Trust has 12 caravans and 1 chalet and provides low cost self-catering holidays on 11 fully commercial holiday parks (eg Haven, Hoburne) for any family or group with special needs or low income and one parent families – in fact any family or group in which the quality of life is diminished by disability, infirmity or misfortune.

No Scouting or Guiding connection is required.

More information from
www.scouts.org.uk/holidayhomes

or
Scout Holiday Homes Trust,
Gilwell Park,
Chingford,
London E4 7QW

Scope **Inclusion** Team

"Scope's inclusion team offers much-needed support to help disabled people achieve inclusion in the wider community."

- care
- therapy
- nursing
- education support

For more information please contact Scope's inclusion team on:
01752 840059, by fax on: 01752 846162
or email: andrew.mullen@scope.org.uk

scope
About cerebral palsy
For disabled people achieving equality.

Time to get equal
Scope is a Registered Charity no208231/SC039409

unwin
Safety Systems

Unwin wheelchair restraints are the strongest in the world. Tested to secure a 120kg (300lbs) wheelchair as standard, this range along with Unwin's seat fixings and flooring systems provide unrivalled passenger safety.

tel: +44 (0)1935 827740

email: sales@unwin-safety.co.uk
www.unwin-safety.com

SHOP EASY THROUGH SHOPMOBILITY

Registered Charity Number 1079758 n   Company Limited by Guarantee Number 3689727

NATIONAL FEDERATION OF Shopmobility

The National Federation of Shopmobility UK
PO Box 6641 Christchurch BH23 9DQ

info@shopmobilityuk.org   www.shopmobilityuk.org

T: 08456 442446

(24hr answerphone service)

"The sign of a quality service"

The Shopmobility word and symbol is a UK Registered Trademark No. 2185606

AYLESBURY
Aylesbury Shopmobility Civic Centre Car Park, Exchange Street, Aylesbury, Bucks HP20 1DG

Office: 01296 336725 **Fax:** 01296 398688
Open: Monday to Friday: 9.00am to 4.00pm
Saturday 9.00am to 1.00pm
Notes: Staff can meet you at the bus or train station if notice is given. Blankets and wet weather coveralls given. Childrens wheelchairs and 3 travel scooters also provided for hire purposes.

BOGNOR REGIS AND WORTHING
Bognor Regis Shopmobility
Old Fire Station, Town Hall, Belmont Street Car Park, Bognor Regis, West Sussex PO21 1LD

Office: 01243 830077 **Fax:** 01243 830077
Email: bognorshopmobility@jrmaiol.co.uk
Open: Monday to Friday: 10.00am to 4.00pm
Saturday 10.00am to 2.00pm
Notes: Butlins, Bognor Regis. The scheme can arrange for delivery of scooters to Butlins as may be required.

BRIXHAM
Brixham Shopmobility c/o Barclays Bank, Central Car Park, Brixham TQ5 4BW

Office: 01803 858304
Email: andy.young@torbay.gov.uk
Open: Summer: 10.00am to 4.00pm
Winter: 10.00am to 2.00pm

CAMBRIDGE
Cambridge Shopmobility Grand Arcade car park first right at entrance

Office: 01223 457452 and
Grafton Centre east car park level 4
Office: 01223 461858

COATBRIDGE
North Lanarkshire Shopmobility Exchange Place, Coatbridge, North Lanarkshire, Scotland ML5 3RB

Day: 01236 605795 **Fax:** 01236 605795
Open: Monday to Friday: 10.00am to 4.30pm
Saturday 10.00am to 4.00pm
Notes: Registration charge for all users is £1. Long term loan of manual wheelchairs only.

Direct Mobility HIRE

Specialising in short term rental of all mobility equipment including:-

- Wheelchairs (all types)
- Commodes (all types)
- High Seat Armchairs
- Electric Scooters
- Hoists

All equipment Delivered Installed & Collected
All Major Credit & Debit Cards Accepted

+44 (0)20 8370 7888

Hire & Sales Showroom: Warren House 201a Bury Street, Edmonton, London N9 9JE

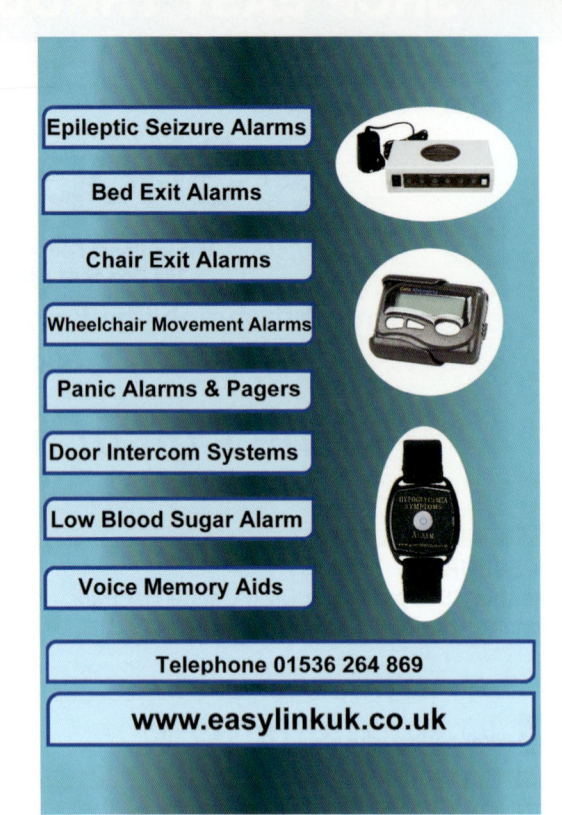

- Epileptic Seizure Alarms
- Bed Exit Alarms
- Chair Exit Alarms
- Wheelchair Movement Alarms
- Panic Alarms & Pagers
- Door Intercom Systems
- Low Blood Sugar Alarm
- Voice Memory Aids

Telephone 01536 264 869

www.easylinkuk.co.uk

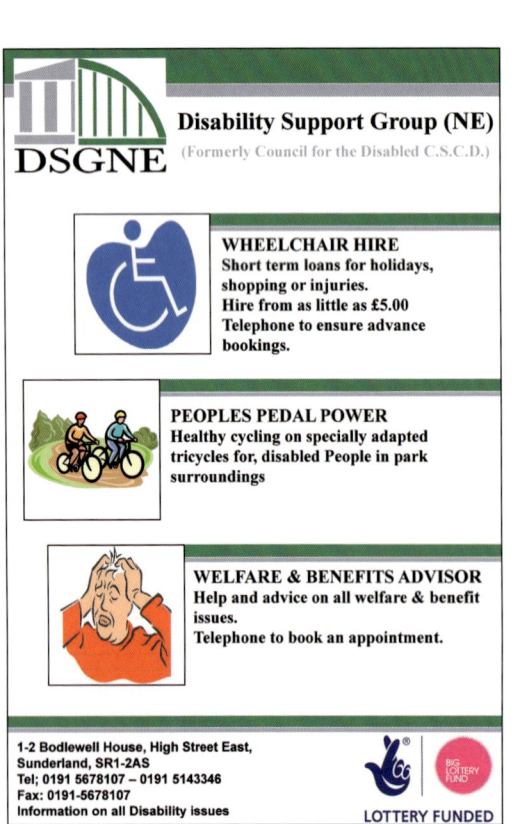

Disability Support Group (NE)
(Formerly Council for the Disabled C.S.C.D.)

WHEELCHAIR HIRE
Short term loans for holidays, shopping or injuries.
Hire from as little as £5.00
Telephone to ensure advance bookings.

PEOPLES PEDAL POWER
Healthy cycling on specially adapted tricycles for, disabled People in park surroundings

WELFARE & BENEFITS ADVISOR
Help and advice on all welfare & benefit issues.
Telephone to book an appointment.

1-2 Bodlewell House, High Street East,
Sunderland, SR1-2AS
Tel; 0191 5678107 – 0191 5143346
Fax: 0191-5678107
Information on all Disability issues

LOTTERY FUNDED

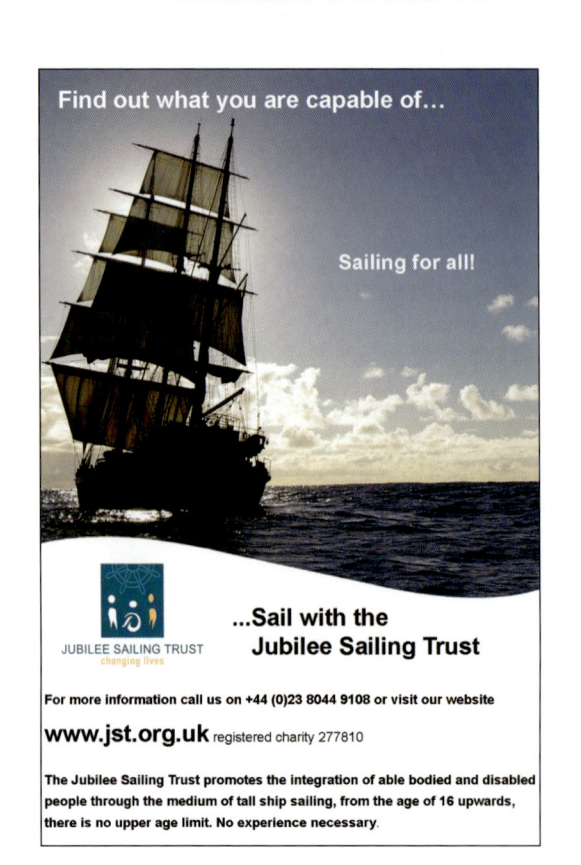

Find out what you are capable of...

Sailing for all!

...Sail with the **Jubilee Sailing Trust**

JUBILEE SAILING TRUST
changing lives

For more information call us on +44 (0)23 8044 9108 or visit our website
www.jst.org.uk registered charity 277810

The Jubilee Sailing Trust promotes the integration of able bodied and disabled people through the medium of tall ship sailing, from the age of 16 upwards, there is no upper age limit. No experience necessary.

SHOP EASY THROUGH SHOPMOBILITY

GOSPORT
Gosport Shopmobility
Bus Station, South Street, Gosport, Hampshire
PO12 1ET

Day: 02392 502692
Email: shopmobility@gvaprojects.org.uk
Open: Tuesday, Friday and Saturday: 10.00am to 3.00pm

HARROW
Harrow and Wealdstone Shopmobility
37 St. George's Centre, St. Ann's Road, Harrow, Middlesex HA1 1HS

Office: 02084 271200   **Fax:** 02084 271200
Email: harrowshopmo@tiscali.co.uk
Open: Monday to Friday and FIRST Saturday of every month: 10.00am to 4.00pm
Notes: Booking is advisable but not essential. Other equipment available, details on request.

HIGH WYCOMBE
High Wycombe Shopmobility
Newlands Meadow, Eden, High Wycombe, Bucks
HP11 2BZ

Office: 01494 472277   **Fax:** 01494 472277
Email: hw.shopmob@btconnect.com
Open: Monday to Saturday: 9.30am to 5.00pm
Sunday: 12.00pm to 4.00pm
Notes: Long term loans available on manual wheelchairs only.

HUNTINGDON
Hunt's Shopmobility
Princes Street Car Park, Malthouse Close, Huntingdon, Cambridgeshire, PE29 3AN

Day: 01480 432793
Email: Shopmobility@huntsforum.org.uk
Open: Tuesday to Saturday: 9.30am to 3.30pm
Notes: Charges are either £20 per year or £3.50 per visit.

IPSWICH
Ipswich (Buttermarket)
Ipswich Shopmobility Buttermarket Shopping Centre, Lower Ground (Car Park Level), St Stephens Lane Ipswich, Suffolk IP1 1DT

Office: 01473 222225
Email: Heather.richards@ipswich.gov.uk
Open: Monday to Saturday: 9.30am to 4.30pm

LEEDS (MERRION CENTRE)
Leeds Shopmobility
Unit 92, Merrion Centre, Leeds, West Yorks LS2 8LY

Office: 01132 460125   **Minicom:** 01132 460125
Open: Monday to Saturday: 9.30am to 4.30pm
Notes: Child scooter available.
Parking Facilities: For Blue Badge Holders free spaces are available in the nearby Brunswick Terrace, and staff will bring the Wheelchair/ Scooter to your car.

LONDON, KENSINGTON, CHESHIRE AND WESTMINSTER
Kensington and Chelsea Shopmobility
" Out and About", Westway Community Transport, 240 Acklam Road, Kensington and Chelsea, London W10 5YG

Helpline: 020 89608774   **Fax:** 020 89695733
Office: 0208 8964 4928   **Email:** scooter@westwayct.org.uk
Open: Please contact the helpline between 10.00am and 1.00pm for times and location of operation of this mobility scheme.

THE WHEELYBOAT TRUST

Wheelyboats provide disabled people with hassle-free and independent access to waterborne activities such as nature watching, pleasure boating and angling. 120 have now been supplied by the Trust to venues open to the public all over the UK. To discover your nearest Wheelyboat and the activities it provides access to, contact the Director or visit the website.

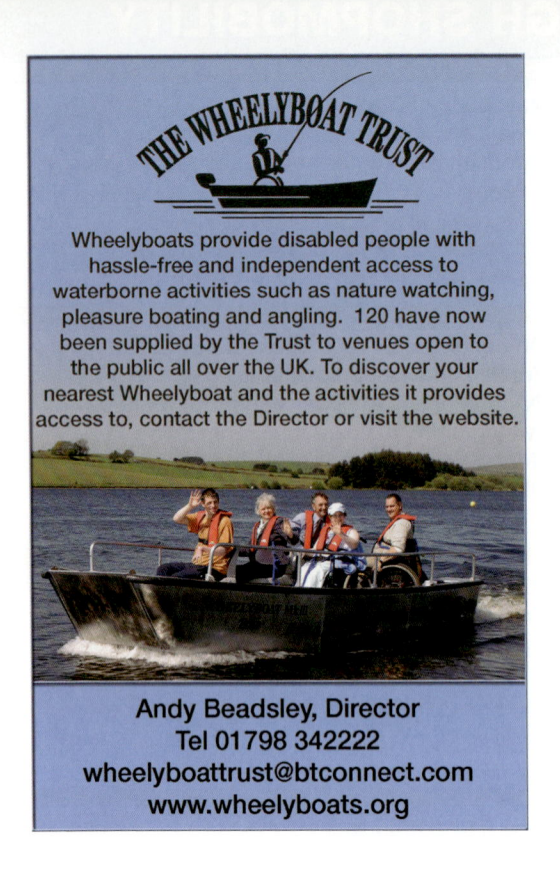

Andy Beadsley, Director
Tel 01798 342222
wheelyboattrust@btconnect.com
www.wheelyboats.org

Best wishes from

Forest Laboratories (UK) Ltd

Forest Laboratories UK Ltd
Riverbridge House
Anchor Boulevard
Crossways Business Park
Dartford, Kent
DA2 6SL

Tel: (0) 1322 421 800   Fax: (0) 1322 291 306

RSC ROYAL SHAKESPEARE COMPANY

THE RSC WELCOMES PEOPLE WITH DISABILITIES TO ITS THEATRES. WE OFFER THE FOLLOWING SERVICES:

- Discounted tickets
- Assisted performances - Audio described and captioned
- Free membership of our access mailing list including our newsletter
- Loop and radio systems to give assisted hearing facilities

For more information and a schedule of plays please call Pat Collcutt on
01789 272227 or
07896 417721 or email
access@rsc.org.uk

Dedicated booking line
01789 430435

www.rsc.org.uk

Speciality Brandy Snaps

SHARP & NICKLESS
The Biscuit Makers
Est. since 1888

SHARP & NICKLESS LTD

77 College Street
Long Eaton
Nottingham
NG10 4NN

Telephone / Fax:
0115 973 2169

---

fairhaven
WOODLAND & WATER GARDEN
Registered Charity No. 261059

Wheelchair accessible
Dogs on leads welcome
Children's nature trail

Tearoom, Gift shop
and Plant sales

South Walsham, Norwich,
NR13 6DZ   01603 270449
www.fairhavengarden.co.uk

FOCKE & CO (UK) LTD.
Packing Machines

Focke & Co (UK) Ltd
Courtenay Works, Monument Way East,
Woking, Surrey GU21 5LY

Tel: 01483 756094
Fax: 01483 756099

OFFICIAL TOURIST BOARD GUIDE

Enjoy Every Minute
Enjoy England
Enjoy The Books

B&B 2010

Now available in good bookshops and online at...

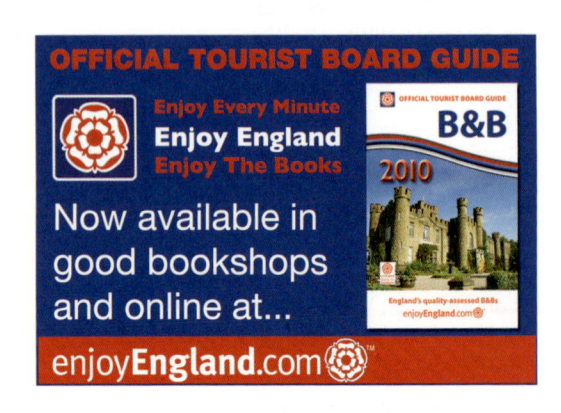

enjoyEngland.com

SHOP EASY THROUGH SHOPMOBILITY

NEWBURY
Newbury Shopmobility
1 Bolton Place, Northbrook Street, Newbury, Berkshire RG14 1AJ

Office: 01635 523854
Email: info@vcwb.org.uk
Open: Monday to Saturday: 9.30am to 4.00pm
Notes: Charge made for long term loan.

Norwich
Norwich Shopmobility
Car Park Level 1, Chaplefield, Norwich, NR2 1RS
Office: 01603 7533350 **Fax:** 01603 623899
Email: shopmobility@btconnect.com

Open: Monday to Saturday: 9.am to 6.00pm
Thursday extended opening from 9.00 to 8.00pm
Sunday: 11.00am to 5.00pm
Note: Also at: 2 Castle Mall, Norwich, NR1 3DD. Monday to Saturday 10.00am to 4.30pm. t:01603 283148 f:01603 764109 Further facility for members only at the Bus Station of one scooter and one manual chair.

NUNEATON
Nuneaton & Beadworth Shopmobility
Unit 1, Rope Walk Car Park, Cotton Road, Nuneaton, Warwickshire CV11 5TQ

Office: 02476 325908
Email: mbeaumont@nbdial.com
Open: Monday to Saturday: 9.30am to 4.30pm
Notes: Satellite: Bedworth Shopmobility, Open Tuesday and Friday: 10.00am to 2.00pm
Call 02476 325908 for further information.

PLYMOUTH
Plymouth Shopmobility and Community Transport Mayflower East Car Park, Mayflower Street, Plymouth, Devon PL1 1QJ

Office: 01752 600633 **Fax:** 01752 229826
Minicom: 01752 229826
Email: plymshopmobilityct@googlemail.com
Open: Monday to Friday: 9.15am to 4.30pm
Saturday: 9.15am to 4.00pm
Satellite at Plymouth Drake Circus t: 01752 221530

REDDITCH
Redditch Shopmobility
Car Park 3, Kingfisher Centre, Redditch, Worcs. B97 4HL

Office: 01527 63271 **Fax:** 01527 63271
Email: shopmobility@redditchbc.gov.uk
Open: Monday to Saturday: 9.00am to 5.00pm
Bank Holidays and Sunday running up to Christmas: 10.30am to 4.00pm, please ring for more information.

SOUTH SHIELDS
South Shields Shopmobility
35 Mile End Road, South Shields, Tyne and Wear NE33 1TA.
Office: 0191 4546286 **Fax:** 0191 4552068

Email: info@ssshopmobility.wannadoo.co.uk
Open: Monday to Saturday: 10.00am to 4.00pm
Closed Tuesdays
Notes: Private car park for members to left of the building with 10 spaces and service call available. Long term hire available on powered scooters and manual wheelchairs.

NATIONAL FEDERATION OF Shopmobility

www.shopmobilityuk.org

OpenBritain | England

Stonehenge

Imperial War Museum Duxford

Enjoy England!

England is a country of impressive diversity and variety, divided into nine distinct regions – each with its own unique personality. From the rolling hills of the Cotswolds and bustling city life of Manchester, to the charms of sleepy Cornish villages and the dramatic coastal splendour of the North East.

Home to 21 of Britain's UNESCO World Heritage Sites, including **Hadrian's Wall** in the North East, **Stonehenge** in the South West, **Canterbury Cathedral** in the South East and the **Tower of London** and **Maritime Greenwich** in London, you can also find all seven of Britain's Heritage Cities in England.

In every region of England there are hundreds of fantastic attractions to enjoy. As well as London's world-famous attractions, you'll find historical sites like **Stonehenge**, ecological attractions such as the **Eden Project** and great family attractions ranging from zoos and safari parks to picnic spots and beaches.

So whether you're visiting a quaint market town or charming cathedral city, shopping in a vibrant city centre or exploring its rugged coastline, England has an impressive range of things to do and places to see.

Accessible England

Tourism businesses are working hard to make their facilities and services more accessible to everyone.

So whether **The Great North Museum** (Newcastle-upon-Tyne) takes your fancy, **The National Theatre** (London), **Imperial War Museum** (Duxford), **Windsor Castle** (Berkshire) or **Bosworth Battlefield** (Leicestershire), you are sure of a warm welcome.

Accommodation providers may have introduced a large print menu, which will be of great use to those who forget their reading glasses, and attractions may have added low level interpretation boards for children to read. All of these little improvements will help you and your family to have a better holiday in England.

National Accessible Scheme

VisitEngland runs a scheme to highlight those accommodation businesses which have improved their accessibility. The National Accessible Scheme (NAS) is great if you have a visual, hearing or mobility impairment giving you the confidence to book somewhere which suits your specific needs. A trained assessor has checked it out before you have checked in. So remember - next time you book your accommodation in England look out for the NAS logos. You can also search for NAS accredited accommodation at **www.enjoyengland.com/access**. See page 20 for more information.

OpenBritain | England

The National Theatre

Windsor Castle

England

88	South West	230	Heart of England
136	South East	246	Yorkshire & Humber
168	London	268	Northwest
184	East of England	294	North East
210	East Midlands		

Information is key

All VisitEngland star rated accommodation and quality assured attractions are now required to provide information on their facilities and services to help you 'know before you go'. This information is presented as an Access Statement, which is simply a document that tells you lots of useful details about the premises and its surroundings. Typical information may include, for example, the frequency of buses, useful telephone numbers, the number of steps to the front door and the availability of subtitles on televisions. So, when you are next researching which accommodation to stay at and attractions to visit, ask to see their access statements.

EnjoyEngland.com now has a dedicated information section for people with physical or sensory needs. Whether you're travelling on foot, by car, bus, taxi or train, in fact whatever type of transport you're using, there's a section containing all you need to know about travelling around England. To make your travels around England easier and more enjoyable for you, we've put together some practical information we hope you'll find useful. So if you need to use accessible toilets, information on the RADAR National Key Scheme and Changing Places is available. Find out more at www.enjoyengland.com/access.

enjoyEngland

Further information

Travel and tourism information for people with physical and sensory needs:

www.enjoyengland.com/access

www.openbritain.net

Eden Project

Sensational South West

You might be surprised at the scale of experiences that await you in the South West. Bristol and Bath, Cornwall and the Isles of Scilly, Devon, Dorset, Gloucestershire and the Cotswolds, Somerset and Wiltshire - each part of the region has its own special character. Fascinating history, stunning scenery, exciting cities, adrenaline fuelled outdoor pursuits, world heritage sites, music, food and drink, and arts festivals all woven together by our warm and welcoming locals.

The natural environment is one of the biggest draws of people here; rolling hills, rugged coast, quaint villages, beautiful gardens, dramatic wind swept moor-land and sandy beaches are all waiting to be discovered. The impressive **South West Coast Path** covers 630 miles of coast line offering inspiring views and every stretch of the path is graded online in terms of its difficulty of terrain, with many sections wheelchair accessible (**southwestcoastpath.com**).

A trip to the South West is not complete without trying some of our famous local produce. Visit one of many Michelin starred restaurants, country pubs or local farmers markets and try a range of mouth watering food and drink, from ruby red beef and sweet Somerset cider to our famous clotted cream.

There's plenty on offer for those who enjoy the great outdoors too; surf a few waves, kayak down a river, climb a Tor, or ride a horse across moor land. There are countless other fun filled activities, all readily available throughout the region, with many centres offering hands on experiences to visitors with a wide range of abilities and accessibility needs.

Why not indulge in some boutique shopping at the recently redeveloped **Cabot Circus** in **Bristol**, visit **Roman Bath Spa** or maybe catch a show at the award winning cliff-side **Minack theatre** at Porthcurno near Lands End? The stunning gardens at the world-famous 18th-Century National Trust estate of **Stourhead**, Wiltshire, make an ideal place for an afternoon stroll and the Palladian mansion filled with Georgian treasures is a must-see too.

The famous **Eden project** in Cornwall offers the opportunity to experience the sights, sounds and humidity of a South American jungle. **Explore-At-Bristol** features innovative science collections, many of which are designed to challenge all of your senses, or why not take in an art exhibition featuring the cream of local, national and international talent at the **Tate St Ives**?

Myth and legend abounds in the South West, you'll marvel at mysterious **Stonehenge** in Wiltshire, and if you're heading that way then beautiful **Salisbury Cathedral** boasts the tallest spire in the country! (There is wheelchair access to the Cathedral and ▶

OpenBritain | South West

Durdle Door

Salisbury Cathedral

South West

Cornwall	Dorset
Isles of Scilly	Gloucestershire
Jersey	Somerset
Devon	Wiltshire

▶ touch models and written guides are available). Imagine fighting off invaders and pirates from the battlements of the 450 year old **Pendennis Castle** in Falmouth, discover the mysteries of King Arthur at **Tintagel** or step back in time to the industrial revolution at Brunel's **SS Great Britain**, Bristol, the world's first steam powered ocean liner perfectly preserved.

Gawp at the nettle eating competition in Dorset, watch the annual Cheese Rolling in Gloucestershire or enjoy the Ottery St Mary flaming tar barrel festival on bonfire night in Devon. If you fancy something a little gentler then watch hundreds of balloons float off at the annual Bristol hot air balloon festival, or gaze skywards in awe at the firework championships on Plymouth's Hoe. A vibrant calendar of traditions and festivals thrives throughout the year.

Whether you are looking for long walks, fantastic restaurants, great beaches, historic landscapes and monuments or adventure, South West England is a great destination for all.

Find out more

web www.visitsouthwest.co.uk ■

Newquay ©Visit Cornwall

www.openbritain.net 89

Tourist Information Centres

Tourist Information Centres are a mine of information about local and regional accommodation, attractions and events. Visit them when you arrive at your destination or contact them before you go:

Avebury	Avebury Chapel Centre	01672 539425	all.tic's@kennet.gov.uk
Bath	Abbey Chambers	0906 711 2000	tourism@bathtourism.co.uk
Bodmin	Shire Hall	01208 76616	bodmintic@visit.org.uk
Bourton-On-The-Water	Victoria Street	01451 820211	bourtonvic@btconnect.com
Bridport	47 South Street	01308 424901	bridport.tic@westdorset-dc.gov.uk
Bristol: Harbourside	Wildwalk @Bristol	0906 711 2191	ticharbourside@destinationbristol.co.uk
Brixham	The Old Market House	01803 211 211	holiday@torbay.gov.uk
Bude	Bude Visitor Centre	01288 354240	budetic@visitbude.info
Burnham-On-Sea	South Esplanade	01278 787852	burnham.tic@sedgemoor.gov.uk
Camelford	North Cornwall Museum	01840 212954	manager@camelfordtic.eclipse.co.uk
Cartgate	South Somerset TIC	01935 829333	cartgate.tic@southsomerset.gov.uk
Cheddar	The Gorge	01934 744071	cheddar.tic@sedgemoor.gov.uk
Cheltenham	Municipal Offices	01242 522878	info@cheltenham.gov.uk
Chippenham	Yelde Hall	01249 665970	tourism@chippenham.gov.uk
Chipping Campden	The Old Police Station	01386 841206	information@visitchippingcampden.com
Christchurch	49 High Street	01202 471780	enquiries@christchurchtourism.info
Cirencester	Corn Hall	01285 654180	cirencestervic@cotswold.gov.uk
Coleford	High Street	01594 812388	tourism@fdean.gov.uk
Corsham	Arnold House	01249 714660	enquiries@corshamheritage.org.uk
Devizes	Cromwell House	01380 729408	all.tic's@kennet.gov.uk
Dorchester	11 Antelope Walk	01305 267992	dorchester.tic@westdorset-dc.gov.uk
Falmouth	11 Market Strand	01326 312300	info@falmouthtic.co.uk
Fowey	5 South Street	01726 833616	info@fowey.co.uk
Frome	The Round Tower	01373 467271	frome.tic@ukonline.co.uk
Glastonbury	The Tribunal	01458 832954	glastonbury.tic@ukonline.co.uk
Gloucester	28 Southgate Street	01452 396572	tourism@gloucester.gov.uk
Looe	The Guildhall	01503 262072	looetic@btconnect.com

OpenBritain | South West

Lyme Regis	Guildhall Cottage	01297 442138	lymeregis.tic@westdorset-dc.gov.uk
Malmesbury	Town Hall	01666 823748	tic@malmesbury.gov.uk
Moreton-In-Marsh	High Street	01608 650881	moreton@cotswold.gov.uk
Padstow & Wadebridge	Red Brick Building	01841 533449	padstowtic@btconnect.com
Paignton	The Esplanade	01803 211 211	holiday@torbay.gov.uk
Penzance	Station Road	01736 362207	pztic@penwith.gov.uk
Plymouth	Plymouth Mayflower Centre	01752 306330	barbicantic@plymouth.gov.uk
Salisbury	Fish Row	01722 334956	visitorinfo@salisbury.gov.uk
Shepton Mallet	70 High Street	01749 345258	sheptonmallet.tic@ukonline.co.uk
Sherborne	3 Tilton Court	01935 815341	sherborne.tic@westdorset-dc.gov.uk
Somerset Visitor Centre	Sedgemoor Services	01934 750833	somersetvisitorcentre@somerset.gov.uk
St Austell	Southbourne Road	01726 879 500	tic@cornish-riviera.co.uk
St Ives	The Guildhall	01736 796297	ivtic@penwith.gov.uk
Stow-On-The-Wold	Hollis House	01451 831082	stowvic@cotswold.gov.uk
Street	Clarks Village	01458 447384	street.tic@ukonline.co.uk
Stroud	Subscription Rooms	01453 760960	tic@stroud.gov.uk
Swanage	The White House	01929 422885	mail@swanage.gov.uk
Swindon	37 Regent Street	01793 530328	infocentre@swindon.gov.uk
Taunton	The Library	01823 336344	tauntontic@tauntondeane.gov.uk
Tetbury	33 Church Street	01666 503552	tourism@tetbury.org
Tewkesbury	100 Church Street	01684 855043	tewkesburytic@tewkesburybc.gov.uk
Torquay	Vaughan Parade	01803 211 211	holiday@torbay.gov.uk
Truro	Municipal Building	01872 274555	tic@truro.gov.uk
Wareham	Holy Trinity Church	01929 552740	tic@purbeck-dc.gov.uk
Warminster	Central Car Park	01985 218548	visitwarminster@btconnect.com
Wells	Town Hall	01749 672552	touristinfo@wells.gov.uk
Weston-Super-Mare	Beach Lawns	01934 888800	westontouristinfo@n-somerset.gov.uk
Weymouth	The King's Statue	01305 785747	tic@weymouth.gov.uk
Winchcombe	Town Hall	01242 602925	winchcombetic@tewkesbury.gov.uk
Yeovil	Hendford	01935 845946/7	yeoviltic@southsomerset.gov.uk

www.openbritain.net

South West | Cornwall

Albaston | Todsworthy Farm Holidays

Enjoy England ★★★★ Mr Pellow, Todsworthy Farm Holidays, Albaston, Gunnislake PL18 9AW
t 01822 834744 e jon@todsworthyfarmholidays.co.uk
todsworthyfarmholidays.co.uk

Access: General: Unit:

Alverton | Penzance Youth Hostel

Enjoy England ★★ Castle Horneck, Alverton, Penzance TR18 4LP
t 01736 362666 e penzance@yha.co.uk

Bodmin | Churchtown Lodges

The Bookings Team Vitalise, Churchtown, Lanlivery, Bodmin, Cornwall PL30 5BT   t 0845 345 1970 e churchtown@vitalise.org.uk
vitalise.org.uk

Access: General: Unit:

Bodmin | Vitalise Churchtown

Lanlivery, Bodmin, Cornwall PL30 5BT
t 01208 872148 e churchtown@vitalise.org.uk
vitalise.org.uk

Access: General: Room:

Boscastle | The Old Coach House

Enjoy England ★★★★ Tintagel Road, Boscastle PL35 0AS
t 01840 250398 e stay@old-coach.co.uk
old-coach.co.uk

Access: General: Room:

Chapel Amble | The Olde House

Enjoy England ★★★-★★★★ Mrs Coralie Goodfellow, The Olde House, Chapel Amble, Wadebridge PL27 6EN
t 01208 813219 e info@theoldehouse.co.uk
theoldehouse.co.uk

Davidstow | Pendragon Country House

Enjoy England ★★★★★ Davidstow, Camelford PL32 9XR

Fowey | South Torfrey Farm

Enjoy England ★★★★★ Mr & Mrs Andrews, South Torfrey Farm, Golant, Fowey PL23 1LA
t 01726 833126 e debbie.andrews@southtorfreyfarm.com
southtorfreyfarm.com

Access: General: P Unit:

92 www.openbritain.net

South West | Cornwall

Golant | Penquite Farm Holidays

Enjoy England
★★★★-★★★★★

Mrs Ruth Varco, Penquite Farm Holidays, Penquite Farm, Golant, Fowey PL23 1LB   t 01726 833319   e ruth@penquitefarm.co.uk

penquitefarm.co.uk

Golberdon | Berrio Mill Holiday Cottages

Enjoy England   ★★★★

Mr & Mrs Ivan Callanan, Berrio Mill Holiday Cottages, Berrio Mill, Golberdon, Callington PL17 7NL   t 01579 363252   e enquiries@berriomill.co.uk

berriomill.co.uk

Harlyn Bay | Yellow Sands Cottages

Enjoy England ★★★-★★★★★

Mrs Sharon Keast, Yellow Sands Cottages, Treliver Farm, Ruthvoes, St Columb TR9 6HU   t 01637 881548   e keast3@btinternet.com

yellowsands.co.uk

Helston | The Stables

National Trust, The Stables, Penrose, Helston, Cornwall
t 0844 8002070

nationaltrustcottages.co.uk/south_west/

Higher Laity | Higher Laity Farm

Enjoy England   ★★★★★

Mrs Lynne Drew, Higher Laity Farm, Portreath Road, Redruth TR16 4HY
t 01209 842317   e info@higherlaityfarm.co.uk

higherlaityfarm.co.uk

Illogan | Trengove Farm Cottages

Enjoy England
★★★★-★★★★★

Mrs Lindsey Richards, Trengove Farm Cottages, Trengove Farm, Cot Road, Illogan TR16 4PU   t 01209 843008   e richards@farming.co.uk

trengovefarm.co.uk

Kerrier | Gwel an Mor Lodges

Owner, Gwel an Mor Lodges, Portreath TR16 4PE

OPEN BRITAIN

GETTING THERE IS NOT A PROBLEM!
See Getting there.....
and back section (p364)
Everything you need for a
hassle-free journey

For symbols see pg 24

South West | **Cornwall**

Kilkhampton | Forda Lodges & Cottages

Enjoy England ★★★★-★★★★★

Units: 12 Sleeps: 2-6
Open: All year

Low season p/w: £525.00
High season p/w: £1200.00

Mr & Mrs Jim Chibbett, Kilkhampton, Bude EX23 9RZ
t 01288 321413 e info@forda.co.uk

forda.co.uk 1C2

In a beautiful valley, only minutes from coastal beaches. Fishing, indoor pool, sauna, spa treatments.

Access: abc **General:** **Unit:**

Lanhydrock | Lanhydrock Hotel & Golf Club

Enjoy England ★★★

Lostwithiel Road, Bodmin PL30 5AQ
t 01208 262570 e info@lanhydrockhotel.com
lanhydrockhotel.com

Lanreath | Bocaddon Holiday Cottages

Enjoy England ★★★★

Mrs Alison Maiklem, Bocaddon Holiday Cottages, Bocaddon Farm, Lanreath, Looe PL13 2PG   t 01503 220192 e holidays@bocaddon.com
bocaddon.com

Access: **General:** **Unit:**

Looe | Tudor Lodges

Enjoy England ★★★★

Units: 6 Sleeps: 2-6
Open: All year

Low season p/w: £195.00
High season p/w: £755.00

Shop: 2 miles

Mr & Mrs M Tudor, Tudor Lodges, Morval, Looe, Cornwall PL13 1PR t 01579 320344 e mollytudor@aol.com

tudorlodges.co.uk 1C2

Six 2007/08 individual award winning accessible countryside lodges. Sleeps 2 to 6 persons. (Two person discount). Three double bedrooms. Balconies front/rear. Profiling beds. Electric hoists, rise/recline chairs. Large level entry wheelchair accessible shower. Ideal touring base. Eden Project.

Location: Looe 3 miles, sandy beaches/fishing port. Polperro 8 miles. Fowey via ferry 11 miles. Eden Project 22 miles.

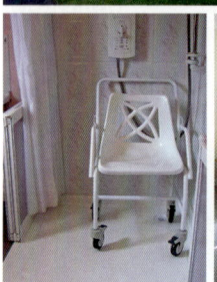

Access:
General:
Unit:

94 www.openbritain.net

South West | Cornwall

Lostwithiel | Brean Park

Enjoy England ★★★★★
Units: 1   Sleeps: 1-8
Open: All year

Low season p/w: £850.00
High season p/w: £2195.00

Shop: 5 miles
Pub: 5 miles

General:
Unit:

Mrs Janet Hoskin, Brean Park Farm, Lostwithiel PL22 0LP
t 01208 872184   e breanpark@btconnect.com

breanpark.co.uk   1B2

Spectacular views of Lanhydrock House and parkland, this single storey luxury barn offers accommodation of the highest standard in Cornwall. Spacious and easily accessible throughout. All bedrooms are En Suite. Relax and enjoy the countryside and nature at its best.

Location: Accessible from A30 and A38. A few minutes drive from Eden Project. Convenient for North and South coast beaches.

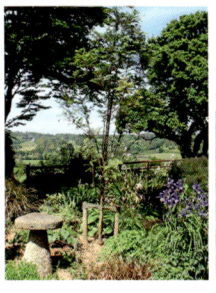

Lostwithiel Fowey | Hartswheal Stables

Enjoy England ★★★★
Units: 1   Sleeps: 1-4
Open: All year

Low season p/w: £380.00
High season p/w: £700.00

Shop: 1 mile
Pub: 1 mile

Access:
General:
Unit:

Mrs Wendy Jordan, Hartswell Farm, Saint Winnow, Lostwithiel Fowey PL22 0RB
t 01208 873419   e hartswheal@connexions.co.uk

connexions.co.uk/hartswell   1B3

A Cornish smoke-free working farm. The Stables is the lower floor of an old granary, specially converted for wheelchair access, with garden and friendly livestock. The twin bedroom has profiling electric bed and ceiling hoist, tracking to bathroom.

Location: Centrally located off the A390, 1 mile east of Lostwithiel, and 5 miles from Fowey, the Eden Project and Bodmin.

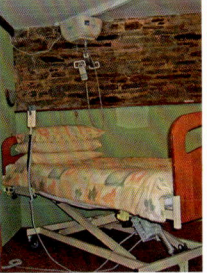

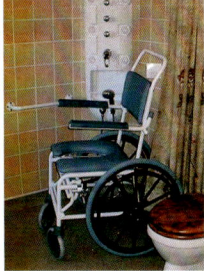

For symbols see pg 24

South West | Cornwall

Marazion | Ocean Studios

Enjoy England ★★★★

Mrs Heather Wenn, Mounts Bay House, Turnpike Hill, Marazion TR17 0AY
t 01736 711040   e enquiries@mountsbayhouse.co.uk

mountsbayhouse.co.uk

General: | Unit:

Mount Hawke | Ropers Walk Barns

Enjoy England ★★★★
Units: 1   Sleeps: 4
Low season p/w: £350.00
High season p/w: £885.00

Mr & Mrs Pollard, Ropers Walk Farm, Rope Walk, St. Agnes TR4 8DW   t 01209 891632   e peterandliz@roperswalkbarns.co.uk

roperswalkbarns.co.uk   1B3

Spacious single storey barn conversion. Level site, peaceful setting. Convenient north coast, Truro and A30.

General: | Unit:

Padstow | Arum House Bed and Breakfast

Enjoy England ★★★★

Arum House, 3 Grenville Road, Padstow PL28 8EX
t 01841 532364   e emmathompson@talktalk.net

padstow-bed-and-breakfast.com

Pillaton | Kernock Cottages

Enjoy England ★★★★-★★★★★
Units: 4   Sleeps: 2-6
Open: All year
Low season p/w: £350.00
High season p/w: £1650.00
Shop: 4 miles
Pub: 0.5 miles

Mrs Beth Bailey, Owner, Pillaton, Saltash, Cornwall PL12 6RY
t 01579 350435   e hughbeth@kernockcottages.com

kernockcottages.com   1C3

Heather Barn is a beautifully converted 5* NAS M3a single level barn conversion set in a private orchard garden in our 25 acre estate. 2 Double (or twin) bedrooms, one with level-entry shower, large parking area, private terrace & BBQ.

Location: Just outside the village of Pillaton, only 10 miles from Plymouth; ideally placed for exploring SE Cornwall and South Devon.

General:
Unit:

South West | Cornwall

Penzance | Hotel Penzance

Enjoy England ★★★

Britons Hill, Penzance TR18 3AE
t 01736 363117 e reception@hotelpenzance.com
hotelpenzance.com

Polzeath | Manna Place

Enjoy England ★★★★

Mrs Ann Jones, 14 Trenant Close, Polzeath PL27 6SW
t 01208 863258 e anniepolzeath@hotmail.com
mannaplace.co.uk

General: **Unit:**

Porthtowan | Rosehill Lodges

Enjoy England ★★★★★

Units: 10 **Sleeps:** 1-6
Open: All year
Low season p/w: £482.00
High season p/w: £1580.00
Shop: 0.5 miles
Pub: 0.5 miles

Mr John Barrow, Rosehill Lodges, Porthtowan, Cornwall TR4 8AR
t 01209 891920 e reception@rosehilllodges.com
rosehilllodges.com   1B3

Eco Elegance on the Cornish coast. Pamper yourself. King size beds, log burners, your own personal hot tub spa. Level access throughout. Glass covered decking for dining alfresco and those stargazing nights. Easy level access from car to lodge.

Location: Rosehill is located within the coastal village of Porthtowan on the North coast of Cornwall, just 100yds past beach road.

Access:
General:
Unit:

Portscatho | Pollaughan Farm

Enjoy England ★★★★-★★★★★

Mrs Valerie Penny, Pollaughan Farm, Portscatho, Truro TR2 5EH
t 01872 580150 e holidays@pollaughan.co.uk
pollaughan.co.uk

Redmoor | Chark Country Holidays

Enjoy England ★★★★

Mrs Jenny Littleton, Chark Country Holidays, Redmoor, Bodmin PL30 5AR
t 01208 871118 e charkholidays@tiscali.co.uk
charkcountryholidays.co.uk

For symbols see pg 24

South West | Cornwall

Roche | Owls Reach
Enjoy England ★★★★
Mrs Diana Pride, Owls Reach, Colbiggan Farm, Roche, St Austell PL26 8LJ
t 01208 831597 e info@owlsreach.co.uk
owlsreach.co.uk

Ruan High Lanes | Trelagossick Farm
Enjoy England ★★★-★★★★★
Mrs Rachel Carbis, Trelagossick Farm, Ruan High Lanes, Truro TR2 5JU
t 01872 501338 e enquiries@trelagossickfarm.co.uk
trelagossickfarm.co.uk

Ruan High Lanes | Trenona Farm Holidays
Enjoy England ★★★★
Units: 2   Sleeps: 2-6
Open: All year
Low season p/w: £275.00
High season p/w: £975.00

Mrs Pamela Carbis, Trenona Farm Holidays, Trenona Farm, Ruan High Lanes, Truro TR2 5JS
t 01872 501339 e pam@trenonafarmholidays.co.uk
trenonafarmholidays.co.uk

1B3

Single storey cottage with 3 En Suite bedrooms. Own garden/patio. Level 2 mobility.

General: P S   Unit:

Sithney | Tregoose Farmhouse
Enjoy England ★★★★
Mrs Hazel Bergin, Tregoose Farmhouse, Trelo, Southern Cross, Boundervean Lane, Camborne TR14 0QB   t 01209 714314   e hazel.bergin@dsl.pipex.com
tregooselet.co.uk

St. Endellion | Tolraggott Farm Cottages
Enjoy England ★★★★
Mrs Harris, Tolraggott Farm Cottages, Tolraggott Farm, St Endellion, Port Isaac PL29 3TP   t 01208 880927
rock-wadebridge.co.uk

St. Just | Swallow's End
Enjoy England ★★★★
Mr David Beer, Swallow's End, Kelynack Moor Farmhouse, Bosworlas, Penzance TR19 7RQ   t 01736 787011   e enquiries@westcornwalllets.co.uk
westcornwalllets.co.uk

St. Martin | Bucklawren Farm
Enjoy England ★★★★-★★★★★★
Mrs Jean Henly, Bucklawren Farm, St. Martin, Looe PL13 1NZ
t 01503 240738   e bucklawren@btopenworld.com
bucklawren.com

www.openbritain.net

South West | Cornwall

St. Mary's | Atlantic Hotel
Enjoy England ★★★ Hugh Street, St. Mary's TR21 0PL
t 01726 744444

St. Veep | A Little Bit Of Heaven
Enjoy England ★★★ Mrs Daphne Rolling, A Little Bit Of Heaven, Manelly Fleming Farm, St Veep, Lostwithiel PL22 0NS   t 01208 872564   e daphne@alittlebitofheaven.co.uk
alittlebitofheaven.co.uk

St Agnes | Trenerry Farm
Mingoose, Mount Hawke, Truro, Cornwall TR4 8BX
t 01872 553755
babatrenerry.co.uk

Access: General: Unit:

The Lizard | Lizard Point Youth Hostel
Enjoy England ★★★★ Lizard TR12 7NT
t 0870 770 6120
yha.org.uk

Tintagel | Trewethett Farm Caravan Club Site
Enjoy England ★★★★★ Trethevy, Tintagel, Cornwall PL34 0BQ
t 01840 770222

(142)   £13.70–£19.55
(142)   £13.70–£19.55
(20)

caravanclub.co.uk   1B2

142 touring pitches
Open: 27 March - 9 November

Shop: 2.5 miles
Pub: 2.5 miles

The site boasts a cliff top setting, with breathtaking views over Bossiney Cove with its safe and sandy beach. The coastal path borders the site and there are spectacular walks. Tintagel is a popular resort with shops and restaurants aplenty.

Location: A30, A395 (Camelford), A39 (Bude), left before transmitter, B3266 (Boscastle), B3263. Site on right in 2 miles.

Access:
General:
Pitch:

For symbols see pg 24   99

South West | Cornwall

Treator | Woodlands Country House

Enjoy England ★★★★★

Open: All year except Xmas and New Year

Rooms per night:
s: £59.00-£71.00
d: £88.00-£112.00

Treator, Padstow, Cornwall PL28 8RU
t 01841 532426 e enquiries@woodlands-padstow.co.uk

woodlands-padstow.co.uk   1B2

Accommodation, our famous breakfast, with a touch of splendour, and views of the Cornish coastline.

Access:
General: Room:

AS

Tresmeer | An-Skyber

Enjoy England ★★★

Mr & Mrs Walters, An-Skyber, Tresmeer, Launceston PL15 8QT
t 01566 781339 e juliewalters@uwclub.net

Trevalga | Reddivallen Farm

Enjoy England ★★★★★

Boscastle PL35 0EE
t 01840 250854 e liz@redboscastle.com

redboscastle.com

Truro | The Captain's Quarter

National Trust, The Captain's Quarter, St Anthony-in-Roseland, Truro, Cornwall
t 0844 8002070

nationaltrustcottages.co.uk/south_west/south_cornwall/

Truro | Engine House

National Trust, Engine House, Trelissick, Feock, Truro
t 0844 8002070

nationaltrustcottages.co.uk/south_west/south_cornwall/

Truro | The Major's Quarter

National Trust, The Major's Quarter, St Anthony-in-Roseland, Truro, Cornwall
t 0844 8002070

nationaltrustcottages.co.uk/south_west/south_cornwall/

HUDSONs

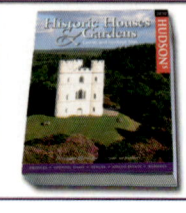

Hudson's is the definitive guide to historic houses & gardens.

Up to date information on over 2000 properties with clear information symbols for accessibility and facilities.

Historic Houses & Gardens
Castles and Heritage Sites

Order online at:
www.hhgroup.co.uk/hudsons

South West | Cornwall/Isles of Scilly/Jersey

Truro (7 miles) | Treworgans Farm Holidays   AS

Units: 2 **Sleeps:** 1-6
Open: All year

Low season p/w:
£375.00
High season p/w:
£1085.00

Shop: 1 mile
Pub: 1 mile

Access:
General:
Unit:

Treworgans Farm, Ladock, Truro, Cornwall TR2 4QD
t 01726 883240   e info@treworgansfarm.co.uk

treworgans.co.uk   1B3

Recently converted detached barns on family farm. Sleeps 4-6 people. Fully wheelchair accessible. Electric beds, hoists, riser recline chair and other equipment available. All rooms En Suite with wetrooms or bathrooms. Care available locally. Farm produce and meals available.

Location: Located in central Cornwall 5 miles from the A30, Truro is only 15 minutes away. Near to Eden Project.

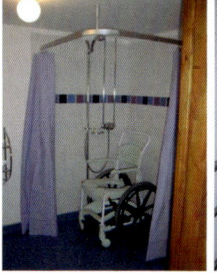

St. Mary's | Isles of Scilly Country Guest House

Enjoy England   ★★★

Sage House, High Lanes, St Mary's TR21 0NW
t 01720 422440   e scillyguesthouse@hotmail.co.uk

scillyguesthouse.co.uk

Jersey | Hotel L'Horizon

AA   ★★★★

St. Brelade, Jersey, Channel Islands JE3 8EF
t 01534 743101   e lhorizon@handpicked.co.uk

handpicked.co.uk/lhorizon

Access: **General:**   **Room:**

Jersey | La Rocco Self-catering Apartments   AS

Units: 2 **Sleeps:** 1-5
Open: All year

Low season p/w:
£456.00
High season p/w:
£1635.00

La Pulente, St Brelade, Jersey JE3 8HG
t 01534 743378   e mail@laroccoapartments.com

laroccoapartments.com   1D3

La Rocco self catering apartments have one/two bedrooms with coastal views from the balconies.

General: **Unit:**

For symbols see pg 24   101

South West | Jersey/Devon

Jersey | Maison Des Landes Hotel

p/p half board:
d: £59.50-£69.50

Shop: 2 miles
Pub: 2 miles

St Ouen, Jersey Channel Islands JE3 2AA
t 01534 481683 e contact@maisondeslandes.co.uk

maisondeslandes.co.uk

Established for over 40 years, the hotel provides carefree holidays for the disabled and their families. Nine miles from St. Helier, on gorse and heather covered headlands, with panoramic views of St. Ouen's Bay and the Atlantic.

Location: Flights to Jersey from most UK Airports and Ferries from Weymouth, Poole and Portsmouth.

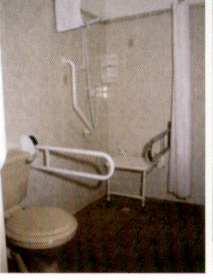

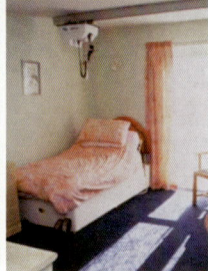

Access:
General:
Room:

Beesands | Beeson Farm Holiday Cottages

Enjoy England ★★★★

Mr & Mrs Robin Cross, Beeson Farm, Beeson, Kingsbridge TQ7 2HW
t 01548 581270 e info@beesonhols.co.uk

beesonhols.co.uk

Access: General: Unit:

OPEN BRITAIN

Join today!

Become a member of OpenBritain today.

Share your own travel and accommodation experiences and help Britain become more open!

visit **www.openbritain.net**

102 www.openbritain.net

South West | **Devon**

Brixham | **Hillhead Caravan Club Site**

Enjoy England ★★★★★

🚐 (239) £14.60–£27.40
🚙 (239) £14.60–£27.40
⛺ (12)

239 touring pitches
Open: 27 March – 4 January

Access:
General:
Pitch:

Hillhead, Brixham, Devon TQ5 0HH
t 01803 853204

caravanclub.co.uk   1D2

Set in 22 acres of Devon countryside near Brixham, with many pitches affording stunning views. There's plenty of entertainment on site - an outdoor heated swimming pool, skateboard ramp and entertainment complex housing a games room, shop, restaurant and bar.

Location: A380 (Newton Abbot) onto A3022 (Brixham). Right onto A379. Two miles keep left onto B3025. Site entrance on left.

Broadclyst | **Hue's Piece**   AS

Enjoy England ★★★★
Units: 1   **Sleeps:** 4
Open: All year
Low season p/w: £270.00
High season p/w: £780.00

Mrs Anna Hamlyn, Hue's Piece, Paynes Farm, Broadclyst, Exeter EX5 3BJ   t 01392 466720   e annahamlyn@paynes-farm.co.uk

paynes-farm.co.uk   1D2

3-bedroomed converted barn on National Trust farm. 2008 Tourism Excellence Gold Award for accessibility.

Access: **General:**   **Unit:**

OPEN BRITAIN PLANNING A DAY OUT? WHY NOT MAKE IT A SHORT-BREAK?
Fabulous 'Places to Stay' in every region

For symbols see pg 24   103

South West | Devon

Buckland Brewer | West Hele

AS

Enjoy England ★★★★
Units: 2   Sleeps: 4-6
Open: All year

Low season p/w: £300.00
High season p/w: £880.00

Shop: 1.5 miles
Pub: 1.5 miles

Mrs Lorna Hicks, West Hele, Buckland Brewer, Bideford EX39 5LZ
t 01237 451044   e lorna.hicks@virgin.net

westhele.co.uk   1C1

Beautiful rural area. Come and see the stars. Listen to the birds. Beef farm. Extensive attractive gardens. Spacious and comfortable rooms. Ground floor bedrooms with wet rooms. 6 miles to RHS Garden Rosemoor. 10 miles to dramatic North Devon Coastline.

Location: West Hele is 6 miles from Bideford and Torrington and 1½ miles south of the village of Buckland Brewer. SS425188.

Access:
General:
Unit:

Budleigh Salterton | Badgers Den

AS

Enjoy England ★★★★
Units: 1   Sleeps: 2-6
Open: All year

Low season p/w: £300.00
High season p/w: £760.00

Leo & Mandy Dickinson, Badgers Den, Dalditch Lane, Knowle, Budleigh Salterton EX9 7AH
t 01395 443282   e mandydickinson3@btinternet.com

holidaycottagedevon.com   1D2

Traditional thatched cottage. Ideal for restful holidays. Well equipped. Beach 1.5 miles, pub 200 yards.

Access:
General: Unit:

High Bickington | Country Ways

Enjoy England ★★★-★★★★★

Mrs Kate Price, Country Ways, Little Knowle Farm, High Bickington, Umberleigh EX37 9BJ   t 01769 560503   e kate@country-ways.net

country-ways.net

Holcombe Rogus | Old Lime Kiln Cottages

Enjoy England ★★★★

Mrs Sue Gallagher, Old Lime Kiln Cottages, Holcombe Rogus, Wellington TA21 0NA   t 01823 672339   e bookings@oldlimekiln.freeserve.co.uk

oldlimekilncottages.co.uk/

www.openbritain.net

South West | **Devon**

Honiton | **Combe House**　　　　　　　　　　　　　　　　　　　　　AS

| AA | ★★★ | Gittisham, Honiton, Devon EX14 3AD |
| Enjoy England | ★★★ | t 01404 540400　e stay@thishotel.com |

thishotel.com

Access:　**General:**

Long Barn | **Creedy Manor**

| Enjoy England | ★★★★ | Mrs Sandra Turner, Creedy Manor, Long Barn Farm, Crediton EX17 4AB |
| | | t 01363 772684　e sandra@creedymanor.com |

creedymanor.com

Modbury | **Broad Park Caravan Club Site** THE CARAVAN CLUB

Enjoy England ★★★★　Higher East Leigh, Modbury, Ivybridge, Devon PL21 0SH
t 01548 830714

(112) £12.00–£17.95

(112) £12.00–£17.95

caravanclub.co.uk　　　　　　　　　　　　　　　　　　1C3

112 touring pitches
Open: 27 March – 9 November

Shop: 1 mile
Pub: 1 mile

Situated between moor and sea, this makes a splendid base from which to explore South Devon. Head for Dartmoor, or seek out the small villages of the South Hams.

Location: From B3027 (signposted Modbury), site on left after 1 mile.

Access:

General:

Pitch:

Moretonhampstead | **Budleigh Farm**

| Enjoy England | ★★★ | Mr Arthur Harvey, Budleigh Farm, Moretonhampstead, Newton Abbot |
| | | TQ13 8SB　t 01647 440835　e harvey@budleighfarm.co.uk |

budleighfarm.co.uk

Northleigh | **Smallicombe Farm**　　　　　　　　　　　　　　　　AS

| Enjoy England | ★★★★ | Northleigh, Colyton EX24 6BU |
| | | t 01404 831310　e maggie_todd@yahoo.com |

smallicombe.com

Access:　**General:**　**Room:**

For symbols see pg 24　　　　　　　　　　　　　　　　　　　　　　　**105**

South West | Devon

Northleigh | Smallicombe Farm Self Catering

Enjoy England ★★★★ Mrs Maggie Todd, Smallicombe Farm Self Catering, Northleigh, Colyton EX24 6BU t 01404 831310 e maggie_todd@yahoo.com
smallicombe.com

Access: General: Unit:

Okehampton | Beer Farm

Enjoy England ★★★★ Mr & Mrs Annear, Beer Farm, Okehampton EX20 1SG
t 01837 840265 e info@beerfarm.co.uk
beerfarm.co.uk

Plymouth | Haddington House Apartments

Enjoy England ★★★ Mr & Mrs Luxmoore, 42 Haddington Road, Stoke Damerel, Plymouth PL2 1RR t 07966 256984 e luxmoore@btinternet.com
Units: 1 Sleeps: 4
Open: All year
plymouth-self-catering.co.uk   1C2

Low season p/w: £300.00
High season p/w: £350.00

Haddington House makes the ideal choice for self catering holidays in Plymouth.

General: Unit:

Plymouth | Holiday Inn Plymouth

AA ★★★★ Armada Way, Plymouth, Devon PL1 2HJ
t 01752 639988 e hiplymouth@qmh-hotels.com
holidayinn.co.uk

Access: abc General: Room:

Sandford | Ashridge Farm

Enjoy England ★★★★ Ashridge Farm, Sandford, Crediton EX17 4EN
t 01363 774292 e info@ashdridgefarm.co.uk
ashridgefarm.co.uk/

Looking for something else?

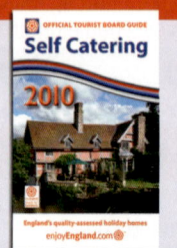

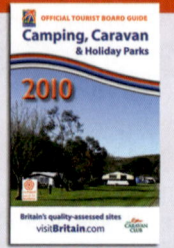

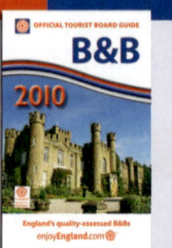

OFFICIAL TOURIST BOARD GUIDE — Pets Come Too! 2010 — Pet-friendly accommodation — enjoyEngland.com

OFFICIAL TOURIST BOARD GUIDE — Self Catering 2010 — England's quality-assessed holiday homes — enjoyEngland.com

OFFICIAL TOURIST BOARD GUIDE — Camping, Caravan & Holiday Parks 2010 — Britain's quality-assessed sites — visitBritain.com

OFFICIAL TOURIST BOARD GUIDE — B&B 2010 — England's quality-assessed B&Bs — enjoyEngland.com

OFFICIAL TOURIST BOARD GUIDE — Hotels 2010 — England's quality-assessed hotels — enjoyEngland.com

If you haven't found what you are looking for in OpenBritain, VisitBritain's Official Tourist Board Guides offer a wide choice of assessed accommodation which may meet your needs.

South West | **Devon**

Sidbury | Putts Corner Caravan Club Site

Enjoy England ★★★★

(117) £12.00–£17.95
(117) £12.00–£17.95
117 touring pitches
Open: 27 March - 9 November

Shop: 2.5 miles
Pub: 1 mile

Putts Corner, Sidbury, Sidmouth, Devon EX10 0QQ
t 01404 42875

caravanclub.co.uk　　　1D2

A quiet site in pretty surroundings, with a private path to the local pub. Bluebells create a sea of blue in spring, followed by foxgloves.

Location: M5 jct 25 onto A375 (Sidmouth). Turn right onto B3174. In about 0.25 miles turn right into site entrance.

Access:
General:
Pitch:

South Molton | Stable Cottage

AA ★★★★★
Enjoy England ★★★★★
Units: 1　Sleeps: 6
Open: All year

Low season p/w: £390.00
High season p/w: £835.00

Mrs V Huxtable, Stable Cottage, Stitchpool Fm, Sth Molton EX36 3EZ　t 01598 740130　e stitchpoolcottage@hotmail.co.uk

stitchpoolfarm.co.uk　　　2C1

Peaceful countryside setting on farm, 5 star M3A barn conversion, 3 bedroom, Jacuzzi bath, Gardens.

Access:
General:　Unit:

Torquay | Atlantis Holiday Apartments

Enjoy England ★★★-★★★★★
Units: 6　Sleeps: 2-5
Open: All year

Low season p/w: £220.00
High season p/w: £660.00

Mrs Pauline Roberts, Solsbro Road, Chelston, Torquay TQ2 6PF
t 01803 607929　e enquiry@atlantistorquay.co.uk

atlantistorquay.co.uk　　　1D3

Award winning, accessible apartments, near seafront, shops, railway station and attractions. No meters. Wi-fi access.

Access:　General:　Unit:

For symbols see pg 24　　　107

South West | **Devon**

Torquay | **The Crowndale**
Enjoy England ★★★★ 18 Bridge Road, Torquay TQ2 5BA

Torquay | **Crown Lodge**
Enjoy England ★★★★ 83 Avenue Road, Torquay TQ2 5LH
t 01803 298772 e stay@crownlodgehotel.co.uk
crownlodgehotel.co.uk

Access: | General: | Room:

Torquay | **South Sands Apartments**
Enjoy England ★★★ Mr & Mrs Paul & Deborah Moorhouse, South Sands Apartments, Torbay Road, Livermead, Torquay TQ2 6RG t 01803 293521 e info@southsands.co.uk
southsands.co.uk

Ugborough | **Venn Farm**
Enjoy England ★★★★ Mrs Stephens, Venn Farm, Ugborough, Ivybridge PL21 0PE
t 01364 73240

Whitnage | **West Pitt Farm**
Enjoy England ★★★–★★★★★ Owner, West Pitt Farm, Whitnage, Tiverton EX16 7DU

Yealmpton | **Kitley House Hotel and Restaurant**
Enjoy England ★★★
Open: All year

Rooms per night:
s: £79.50–£99.50
d: £99.50–£149.50
Meals: £22.50–£29.95

Kitley Estate, Yealmpton, Plymouth PL8 2NW
t 01752 881555 e sales@kitleyhousehotel.com
kitleyhousehotel.com 1C2

Built of silver-grey Devonshire marble. Originally Tudor Revival house. Remodelled in c1820s by George Repton. Grade I Listed building.

Access: | General: | Room:

OPEN BRITAIN
DECIDED WHERE TO GO?
SEE ATTRACTIONS FOR WHAT TO DO
Ideas and information at the end of each regional section

©Britainonview / Martin Brent

South West | Devon/Dorset

Yelverton | Overcombe House

AS

Enjoy England ★★★★
Open: All year
Rooms per night:
s: £45.00-£60.00
d: £70.00-£75.00

Old Station Road, Horrabridge, Yelverton PL20 7RA
t 01822 853501   e enquiries@overcombehotel.co.uk

overcombehotel.co.uk   1C2

Comfortable, fully En Suite, guest accommodation, situated in Dartmoor National Park between Tavistock and Plymouth.

Access: General: Room:

Abbotsbury | Character Farm Cottages

AS

Enjoy England ★★★★
Units: 7   **Sleeps:** 2-9
Open: All year
Low season p/w: £235.00
High season p/w: £1050.00

Mrs Ann Mayo, Higher Farm, Rodden, Weymouth DT3 4JE
t 01305 871347   e jane@mayo.fsbusiness.co.uk

characterfarmcottages.co.uk   2A3

Beautifully converted barn, high quality facilities. Heritage coast. Smaller properties with downstairs bedrooms and showers.

Access: General: Unit:

Abbotsbury | Gorwell Farm Cottages

Enjoy England ★★★★

Mrs Mary Pengelly, Gorwell Farm Cottages, Gorwell, Abbotsbury, Weymouth DT3 4JX   t 01305 871401   e mary@gorwellfarm.co.uk

gorwellfarm.co.uk

Alton Pancras | Bookham Court

AS

Enjoy England ★★★★★
Units: 4   **Sleeps:** 4-8
Open: All year
Low season p/w: £235.00
High season p/w: £1160.00

Mr & Mrs Andrew Foot, Whiteways, Bookham, Dorchester DT2 7RP   t 01300 345511   e andy.foot1@btinternet.com

bookhamcourt.co.uk   2B3

Luxury barn conversions with panoramic views, games room, wildlife hide, fishing walks. 30 minutes to sea.

Access: General: Unit:

Beaminster | Stable Cottage

Enjoy England ★★★★

Mrs Diana Clarke, Stable Cottage, Meerhay Manor, Beaminster, Dorset DT8 3SB   t 01308 862305   e meerhay@aol.com

meerhay.co.uk

Access: General: Unit:

For symbols see pg 24

South West | Dorset

Bridport | Tamarisk Farm Holiday Cottages
Enjoy England ★★★★ Mrs Josephine Pearse, Tamarisk Farm, West Bexington, Dorchester, Dorset DT2 9DF t 01308 897784 e holidays@tamariskfarm.com
tamariskfarm.com/holidays

Access: **General:** **Unit:**

Charmouth | The Poplars
Enjoy England ★★★ Mrs Jane Bremner, Wood Farm Caravan and Camping Park, Axminster Road, Charmouth, Bridport DT6 6BT t 01297 560697 e holidays@woodfarm.co.uk
woodfarm.co.uk

Corfe Castle | Isolation Hospital 2
National Trust, Isolation Hospital 2, Corfe Castle, Dorset
t 0844 8002070
nationaltrustcottages.co.uk/south_west/dorset/

Corfe Castle | Mortons House Hotel
AA ★★★ 45 East Street, Corfe Castle, Dorset BH20 5EE
Enjoy England ★★★ t 01929 480988 e stay@mortonshouse.co.uk
Open: All year
mortonshouse.co.uk

Rooms per night:
s: £75.00-£100.00
d: £130.00-£155.00
p/p half board:
d: £160.00-£195.00
Meals: £25.00-£30.00

16th century Elizabethan Manor House with four award winning 'accessible' rooms. A very special place!

Access: General: Room:

Fifehead Magdalen | Top Stall
Enjoy England ★★★ Mrs Kathleen Jeanes, Top Stall, Factory Farm, Fifehead Magdalen, Gillingham SP8 5RS t 01258 820022 e kath@topstallcottage.co.uk
topstallcottage.co.uk

Isle of Purbeck | The Farmhouse
National Trust, The Farmhouse, Middlebere Farm, Isle of Purbeck, Dorset
t 0844 8002070
nationaltrustcottages.co.uk/south_west/dorset/

Long Bredy | Whatcombe Stables
Enjoy England ★★★★ Ms Margarette Stuart-Brown, Long Bredy, Dorchester DT2 9HN
t 01305 789000 e admin@dream-cottages.co.uk

South West | Dorset

Poole | 5 Dolphin Quays

AS

Enjoy England ★★★★★ Mrs Helen Challis, Quay Holidays, 1 Grand Parade, High Street, Poole, Dorset BH15 1AD t 01202 683333 f 01202 684444 e stay@quayholidays.co.uk

quayholidays.co.uk

Access: | General: | Unit:

Poole | Holton Lee - Gateway & Woodland Cottages

AS

Enjoy England ★★★ East Holton, Holton Heath, Poole, Dorset BH16 6JN

Units: 3 **Sleeps:** 8-12
Open: All year

holtonlee.co.uk   2B3

Low season p/w: £378.00
High season p/w: £1512.00

Twin rooms in each accommodation. Fully accessible, in 350 acres, views of heath & woodland.

Access: | General: P | Unit:

Poole | Holton Lee - The Barn

Open: All year except Xmas and New Year

East Holton, Holton Heath, Poole, Dorset BH16 6JN
t 01202 631063 e director@holtonlee.co.uk

holtonlee.co.uk   2B3

Rooms per night:
s: £65.00-£82.00
d: £100.00-£134.00
Meals: £10.00

Friendly, family style accommodation. 10 twin En Suite, fully accessible bedrooms with personal assistance.

Access:
General: | Room:

Stoke Abbott | Lewesdon Farm Holidays

Enjoy England ★★★★ Mr & Mrs Micheal & Linda Smith, Lewesdon Farm Holidays, Lewesdon Farm, Stoke Abbott, Beaminster DT8 3JZ
t 01308 868270 e lewesdonfarmholiday@tinyonline.co.uk

lewesdonfarmholidays.co.uk

Swanage | 9 Quayside Court

Enjoy England ★★★ Mr Graham Hogg, 9 Quayside Court, Lilliput Avenue, Chipping Sodbury, Bristol BS37 6HX t 01454 311178 e graham.hogg@blueyonder.co.uk

bythequayholidays.co.uk

Become a member of OpenBritain today.
Share your own travel and accommodation experiences and help Britain become more open!

visit www.openbritain.net

OPEN BRITAIN

For symbols see pg 24

111

South West | **Dorset**

Swanage | Haycraft Caravan Club Site

Enjoy England ★★★★★

Haycrafts Lane, Swanage, Dorset BH19 3EB
t 01929 480572

(53) £13.70–£19.55
(53) £13.70–£19.55
53 touring pitches
Open: 27 March – 9 November
Shop: 0.5 miles
Pub: 1.5 miles

caravanclub.co.uk   2B3

Peaceful site located five miles from Swanage, with its safe, sandy beach. Spectacular cliff-top walks, Corfe Castle, Lulworth Cove and Durdle Door are within easy reach. The Swanage Railway is a favourite with young and old alike.

Location: Take A351 from Wareham to Swanage, at Harmans Cross turn right into Haycrafts Lane, site 0.5 miles on the left.

Access:
General:
Pitch:

Tincleton | Tincleton Lodge and Clyffe Dairy Cottage

Enjoy England ★★★★★

Mrs Jane Coleman, Tincleton Lodge and Clyffe Dairy Cottage, Eweleaze Farm, Tincleton, Dorchester DT2 8QR
t 01305 848391   e enquiries@dorsetholidaycottages.net
dorsetholidaycottages.net

Weymouth | Jubilee View Apartment

Enjoy England ★★★

Mrs Jennifer Deagle, Jubilee View Apartment, 41 Melrose Road, Southampton SO15 7PG   t 023 078 0301   e jubileeview@googlemail.com
jubileeview.com

Weymouth | Wimborne & Ferndown Lions Club Caravans

Frank Fortey, 23 Egdon Drive, Wimborne, Dorset BH21 1TY
t 01202 886022
lions.org.uk/wimborne-ferndown/

General: P **Unit:**

Winterborne Houghton | Houghton Lodge

Enjoy England ★★★★★

Mrs Clarice Fiander-Norman, Houghton Lodge, Winterborne Houghton, Blandford Forum DT11 0PE
t 01258 882170   e enquiries@houghtonlodge.com
houghtonlodge.com

South West | Dorset/Gloucestershire

Woolland | Ellwood Cottages

Enjoy England ★★★★ Mr & Mrs John & Ann Heath, Ellwood Cottages, Woolland, Blandford Forum DT11 0ES t 01258 818196 e admin@ellwoodcottages.co.uk
ellwoodcottages.co.uk

Awre | The Priory Cottages

Enjoy England ★★★★ Ian Cowan, The Priory Cottages, Awre, Newnham GL14 1EQ
t 07919 407128 e rigc@onetel.com

Bristol | Holiday Inn Bristol Filton

Filton Road, Hambrook, Bristol BS16 1QX
t 0870 400 9014 e Bristol@ihg.com
holidayinn.co.uk

Access: **General:** **Room:**

Bristol | Winford Manor

Enjoy England ★★★
Open: All year

Rooms per night:
s: £75.00–£85.00
d: £85.00–£165.00
p/p half board:
d: £50.00–£100.00
Meals: £9.95–£35.00

Shop: 1 mile
Pub: 1 mile

Old Hill, Bristol BS40 8DW
t 01275 472292 e reservations@winfordmanor.co.uk
winfordmanor.co.uk

2A2

Set in the Chew Valley not far from Bristol Airport, Winford Manor offers accommodation to suit every budget. Fabulous, accessible services, complimented by friendly professional service. The hotel's Labyrinth restaurant caters for all dietary requirements with delicious simplicity.

Location: Just off A38, near Bristol Airport, see website for full directions.

Access:
General:
Room:

Chipping Campden | Cotswold Charm

Enjoy England ★★★★ Mr & Miss Michael & Margaret Haines, Cotswold Charm, Blind Lane, Chipping Campden GL55 6ED t 01386 840164 e info@cotswoldcharm.co.uk
cotswoldcharm.co.uk

South West | **Gloucestershire**

Cirencester | Bibury Court Hotel

AA ★★★
Open: All year

Rooms per night:
s: £140.00-£220.00
d: £170.00-£250.00
Meals: £15.00-£45.00

Bibury, Cirencester, Gloucestershire GL7 5NT
t 01285 740 337   e info@biburycourt.com

biburycourt.com   2B2

A Jacobean mansion in the heart of the Cotswolds, in 6 acres of glorious countryside.

Access: General: Room:

Forest of Dean | Dryslade Farm

AA ★★★★

English Bicknor, Coleford, Gloucestershire GL16 7PA
t 01594 860259

drysladefarm.co.uk

Access: General: Room:

Gloucester | Express by Holiday Inn Gloucester South

Telford Way, Nr. Quedgeley, Gloucester, Gloucestershire GL2 2AB
t 0870 720 0953   e gloucester@morethanhotels.com

ichotelsgroup.com/h/d/ex/1/en/hotel/glcuk

Access: General: Room:

Gloucester | Holiday Inn Gloucester-Cheltenham

AS

Crest Way, Barnwood, Gloucester, Gloucestershire GL4 7RX
t 0870 400 9034   e reservations-gloucester@ihg.com

holidayinn.co.uk

Access: General: Room:

Gloucester | The Lodge

Enjoy England   ★★★★

Mr Brian C Morgan, Little Allaston farm, Driffield Road, Lydney, Gloucester GL1 4EU   t 01594 843745

GETTING THERE IS NOT A PROBLEM!
OPEN BRITAIN   See Getting there..... and back section (p364)
Everything you need for a hassle-free journey

South West | Gloucestershire

Moreton-in-Marsh | Moreton-in-Marsh Caravan Club Site

Bourton Road, Moreton-in-Marsh, Gloucestershire GL56 0BT
t 01608 650519

caravanclub.co.uk 2B1

Enjoy England ★★★★★
🚐 (183) £14.60–£20.85
🚙 (183) £14.60–£20.85
183 touring pitches
Open: All year
Shop: <0.5 miles
Pub: <0.5 miles

An attractive, well-wooded site within easy walking distance of the market town of Moreton-in-Marsh. On-site facilities include crazy golf, volleyball and boules. Large dog-walking area.

Location: From Moreton-in-Marsh on A44 the site entrance is on right 250yds past end of the speed limit sign.

Access:
General:
Pitch:

Parkend | The Fountain Inn

Enjoy England ★★★
Parkend, Lydney GL15 4JD
t 01594 562189 e thefountaininn@aol.com
thefountaininnandlodge.co.uk

Prestbury | Prestbury House

Enjoy England ★★★★
The Burgage, Prestbury, Cheltenham GL52 3DN
t 01242 529533 e enquiries@prestburyhouse.co.uk
prestburyhouse.co.uk

Woodchester | 1 Woodchester Lodge AS

AA ★★★★
Enjoy England ★★★★
Southfield Road, Woodchester, Stroud GL5 5PA
t 01453 872586 e anne@woodchesterlodge.co.uk
woodchesterlodge.co.uk

Access: General: Room:

HUDSONs

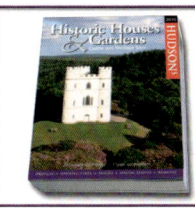

Hudson's is the definitive guide to historic houses & gardens.

Up to date information on over 2000 properties with clear information symbols for accessibility and facilities.

Historic Houses & Gardens
Castles and Heritage Sites

Order online at:
www.hhgroup.co.uk/hudsons

South West | Gloucestershire/Somerset

Yorkley | 2 Danby Cottages

Enjoy England ★★★
Units: 1 Sleeps: 1-6
Open: All year

Low season p/w: £300.00
High season p/w: £850.00

Gareth Lawes, 23 Cotham Road South, Bristol BS6 5TZ
t 0117 942 2301 e glawes@tiscali.co.uk

2danbycottages.co.uk 2B1

Comprehensively equipped six person, two bathroom cottage: heart of forest, pets, children welcome, walks, views.

Access: General: Unit:

Bath | Carfax Hotel

Enjoy England ★★★
Open: All year except Xmas

Rooms per night:
s: £80.00-£161.00
d: £110.00-£165.00
p/p half board:
d: £119.95-£177.95
Meals: £9.95-£12.95

13-15 Great Pulteney Street, Bath BA2 4BS
t 01225 462089 e reservations@carfaxhotel.co.uk

carfaxhotel.co.uk 2B2

A trio of Georgian town houses in the centre of Bath. Lifts, lounge and carpark.

Access: General: Room:

Bishops Lydeard | Redlands

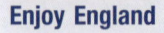

Enjoy England

Trebles Holford, Taunton TA4 3HA
t 01823 433159 e redlandshouse@hotmail.com

escapetothecountry.co.uk

OPEN BRITAIN DECIDED WHERE TO GO? SEE ATTRACTIONS FOR WHAT TO DO
Ideas and information at the end of each regional section

116 www.openbritain.net

South West | Somerset

Blue Anchor | Primrose Hill Holidays AS

Enjoy England ★★★★
Units: 4   Sleeps: 1-6
Open: March to November,
Low season p/w: £340.00
High season p/w: £560.00
Shop: <0.5 miles
Pub: <0.5 miles

Access: abc 🐾 ☺
General: 🪃 📺 P S
Unit: [symbols]

Mrs Jo Halliday, Owner, Wood Lane, Blue Anchor, West Somerset TA24 6LA   t 01643 821200   e info@primrosehillholidays.co.uk

primrosehillholidays.co.uk   1D1

Three 2 bedroomed and one 3 bedroomed bungalow. Wheel in wet rooms. Accessible private enclosed gardens. Level access. Panoramic views over Blue Anchor Bay and the West Somerset Railway, Dunster Castle and Exmoor. Quiet location. Adjacent parking. Winner Accessible Somerset 2008.

Location: Situated at Blue Anchor Bay near Minehead within easy reach of all that West Somerset and Exmoor has to offer.

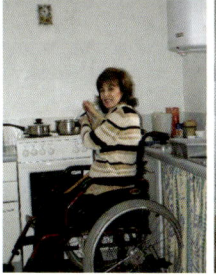

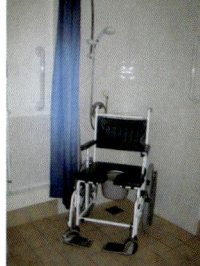

Bridgewater | Buzzard Heights

Enjoy England ★★★
Aethandune, Tower Road, Stawell, Bridgewater, Somerset TA7 9AJ
t 01278 722743   e Teresa@buzzardheights.co.uk

buzzardheights.co.uk

Access: abc [symbols]   General: [symbols]   Room: [symbols]

Burnham on Sea | Wall Eden Farm

Enjoy England ★★★
Mr Andrew Wall, Manager, Wall Eden Farm, New Road, East Huntspill, Highbridge, Somerset TA9 3PU   t 01278 786488   e walleden@btinternet.com

walledenfarm.co.uk

Access: abc [symbols]   General: 🪃 📺 P S   Unit: [symbols]

Cannington | Blackmore Farm

Enjoy England ★★★★
Blackmore Lane, Nr Bridgwater TA5 2NE
t 01278 653442   e dyerfarm@aol.com

dyerfarm.co.uk

OPEN BRITAIN

PLANNING A DAY OUT? WHY NOT MAKE IT A SHORT-BREAK?
Fabulous 'Places to Stay' in every region

For symbols see pg 24   117

South West | **Somerset**

Chard | Tamarack Lodge

AS

Enjoy England ★★★★
Units: 1 Sleeps: 12
Open: All year

Low season p/w: £320.00
High season p/w: £950.00

Matthew Sparks, Fyfett Farm, Otterford, nr. Chard, Somerset TA20 3QP
t 01823 601270 e matthew.sparks@tamaracklodge.co.uk

tamaracklodge.co.uk 1D2

Hand crafted log cabin, suitable for wheelchairs, beautiful views on family livestock farm, Blackdown, Somerset.

Access:
General: Unit:

Cheddar | Cheddar YHA

Enjoy England ★★★

Hillfield, Cheddar BS27 3HN
t 01934 742494 e cheddar@yha.org.uk

yha.org.uk

Chewton Mendip | The Garden House

Enjoy England ★★★★★
Units: 1 Sleeps: 8
Open: All year

Low season p/w: £945.00
High season p/w: £1695.00

Ms Jane Clayton, Owner, The Garden House, Lilycombe Farm, Chewton Mendip, Somerset BA3 4NZ
t 01761 241080 e jclayton@janeclayton.co.uk

lilycombe.co.uk

Sleeps 8 in 3 king size doubles and 1 twin. 3 bathrooms.

General: Unit:

Clanville | Clanville Manor Tallet and Lone Oak Cottage

Enjoy England ★★★★

Mrs Snook, Clanville Manor Tallet and Lone Oak Cottage, Clanville Manor, Clanville, Nr Castle Cary BA7 7PJ
t 01963 350124 e info@clanvillemanor.co.uk

clanvillemanor.co.uk

Croscombe | St Marys Lodge

Enjoy England ★★★★

Mrs Jane Hughes, St Marys Lodge, Coombe Cottages, Croscombe, Wells BA5 3QU t 01749 342611 e hirtemp@hotmail.co.uk

st-marys-lodge.co.uk

Exford | Westermill Farm

Enjoy England ★★★

Mr Oliver Edwards, Westermill Farm, Exford, Exmoor, Minehead TA24 7NJ
t 01643 831238 e swt@westermill.com

westermill.com

South West | Somerset

Fitzhead | Linnets

Enjoy England ★★★★

Mrs Patricia Grabham, Linnets, Church Road, Nr Wivliscombe TA4 3JX
t 01823 400658 e patricia.grabham@onetel.net
linnetsfitzhead.co.uk

Godney | Swallow Barn

Enjoy England ★★★★
Units: 1 **Sleeps:** 2-8
Open: All year
Low season p/w: £350.00
High season p/w: £800.00

Mrs Hilary Millard, Swallow Barn, Double Gate Farm, Nr Wells BA5 1RX t 01458 832217 e doublegatefarm@aol.com
doublegatefarm.com and doublegatefarm.co.uk

National Award winning accommodation. Breakfast available. Fishing from the garden. Central for all attractions.

Access: **General:** **Unit:**

High Littleton | Greyfield Farm Cottages

Enjoy England ★★★★–★★★★★

Mrs June Merry, Greyfield Road, High Littleton BS39 6YQ
t 01761 471132 e june@greyfieldfarm.com
greyfieldfarm.com

Access: **General:** **Unit:**

Lower Godney | Double-Gate Farm

AA ★★★★
Enjoy England ★★★★
Open: All year except Xmas and New Year

Rooms per night:
s: £60.00-£75.00
d: £70.00-£100.00

Shop: 3 miles

Double-Gate Farm, Godney, Nr Wells BA5 1RX
t 01458 832217 e doublegatefarm@aol.com
doublegatefarm.com

2A2

Lovely Georgian farmhouse on working farm. Farmhouse bedrooms: first floor En Suite. Four riverside suites: ground floor, double wheelchair turning space, wet rooms, patio doors to riverside terrace. Three x double/single bed. One x double/2 single beds; all movable.

Location: From Wells A39 south to Polham. Turn right, continue 3 miles. Farm on left after Inn.

Access:
General:
Room:

For symbols see pg 24

South West | **Somerset**

Lympsham, Weston-Super-Mare | Hope Farm Cottages

Enjoy England ★★★★
Units: 4 Sleeps: 1
Open: All year

Low season p/w:
£200.00
High season p/w:
£650.00

Malcolm & Aline Bennett, Brean Road, Lympsham, Weston-super-Mare, Somerset BS24 0HA
t 01934 750506 e hopefarmcottages@gmail.com

hopefarmcottages.co.uk 1D1

4 x 4* cottages beautifully converted from former farm buildings set in a peaceful location.

Access:
General: Unit:

Minehead | The Promenade

Enjoy England ★★★
Open: All year

Rooms per night:
s: £40.00-£50.00
d: £80.00-£100.00
p/p half board:
d: £55.00-£70.00
Meals: £14.99

Shop: 0.5 miles
Pub: <0.5 miles

The Esplanade, Minehead, Somerset TA24 5QS
t 01643 702572 e promenade@livability.org.uk

livability.org.uk 1D1

The Promenade, Minehead is accessible by wheelchair users travelling independently and has TFA NAS category 1 status. We offer a range of amenities including 8 accessible rooms with colour TV and tea/coffee making facilities, a bright conservatory and beautiful garden.

Location: Minehead is on the edge of Exmoor National Park. With good road links to the county of Somerset and beyond.

Access:
General:
Room:

Minehead | Woodcombe Lodges

Enjoy England ★★★★
Units: 8 Sleeps: 2-10
Open: All year

Low season p/w:
£195.00
High season p/w:
£1375.00

Mrs Nicola Hanson, Woodcombe Lodges, Bratton Lane, Minehead, Somerset TA24 8SQ
t 01643 702789 e nicola@woodcombelodge.co.uk

woodcombelodge.co.uk

4 star lodges sleeping 4-10 persons. Peaceful rural setting but near to sea & shops.

General: Unit:

www.openbritain.net

South West | Somerset

Stathe | Walkers Farm Cottages

Enjoy England ★★★★
Units: 4   Sleeps: 2-6
Open: All year

Low season p/w:
£200.00
High season p/w:
£600.00

Mr & Mrs William Tilley, Walkers Farm Cottages, Walkers Farm, Stathe, Burrowbridge, Bridgwater TA7 0JL
t 01823 698229   e info@walkersfarmcottages.co.uk

walkersfarmcottages.co.uk

Superb quality cottages offering real peace and tranquility with wonderful views over open countryside.

General: Unit:

Stogumber | Wick House

AS

Enjoy England ★★★★
Open: All year

Rooms per night:
s: £35.00-£50.00
d: £70.00-£80.00
p/p half board:
d: £53.00-£72.00
Meals: £18.00-£22.00

Brook Street, Stogumber, Taunton, Somerset TA4 3SZ
t 01984656422   e sheila@wickhouse.co.uk

wickhouse.co.uk

1D1

Relax in our 4star friendly family B&B. Lovely village setting. Quantock Hills and Exmoor NP.

Access: General: Room:

Stoke St. Gregory | Holly Farm Cottages

Enjoy England ★★★★

Mr & Mrs Robert & Liz Hembrow, Holly Farm Cottages, Holly Farm House, Meare Green, Stoke St Gregory, Nr Taunton TA3 6HS
t 01823 490828   e robhembrow@btinternet.com

holly-farm.com

Taunton | Holiday Inn Taunton M5 J25

AA ★★★

Deane Gate Avenue, Taunton, Somerset TA1 2UA
t 0870 4009080

holidayinn.com/tauntonm5

Access: General: Room:

Tytherington | Lighthouse Guest House

Enjoy England ★★★★

The Grange, Tytherington, Frome BA11 5BW
t 01373 453585   e contact@lighthouse-uk.com

Wells | Manor Farm

Dulcote, Wells, Somerset BA5 3PZ
t 01749 672125

wells-accommodation.co.uk

Access: General: Room:

For symbols see pg 24

121

South West | **Somerset**

Wembdon | Ash-Wembdon Farm Cottages

Enjoy England ★★★★ Mr Clarence Rowe, Ash-Wembdon Farm Cottages, Ash-Wembdon Farm, Hollow Lane, Bridgwater TA5 2BD t 01278 453097 e c.a.rowe@btinternet.com
ukcottageholiday.com

Weston-Super-Mare | Beverley Guest House

11 Whitecross Road, Weston-super-Mare BS23 1EP

Weston-Super-Mare | Milton Lodge Guest House

Enjoy England ★★★★ 15 Milton Road, Weston-super-Mare BS23 2SH
t 01934 623161 e info@milton-lodge.co.uk
milton-lodge.co.uk

Weston-Super-Mare | The Royal Hotel

Enjoy England ★★★
Open: All year
Rooms per night:
s: £69.00
d: £99.00-£140.00
p/p half board:
d: £89.00-£180.00
Meals: £15.00-£25.00

1 South Parade, Weston-super-Mare, North Somerset BS23 1JP
t 01934 423100 e reservations@royalhotelweston.com
royalhotelweston.com   1D1

Sea Front Location. Restaurant & Bars. Lift, Carpark. Shopping Centre 200 Yards. Entertainment. Disabled Friendly.

Access: abc ... **General:** ... **Room:** ...

Weston-Super-Mare | Spreyton Guest House

Enjoy England ★★★ 72 Locking Road, Weston-super-Mare BS23 3EN
t 01934 416887 e info@spreytonguesthouse.com
spreytonguesthouse.com

Worle | Villa Ryall

Units: 1 Sleeps: 8
Open: All year
Low season p/w: £280.00
High season p/w: £530.00

Livability Self catering holidays, PO Box 36, Cowbridge, Vale of Glamorgan CF71 7TN
t 08456 584478 f 01446 775060 e selfcatering@livability.org.uk
livability.org.uk   1D1

Beautiful four-bedroom bungalow with 2 ground floor accessible bedrooms. Weston-Super-Mare 3 miles.

Access: ... **General:** P S **Unit:** ...

South West | **Wiltshire**

Britford | The Old Stables

Enjoy England ★★★★　Mr Giles Gould, The Old Stables, Bridge Farm, Lower Road, Salisbury SP5 4DY
t 01722 349002　e mail@old-stables.co.uk
old-stables.co.uk

Malmesbury | Best Western The Mayfield House Hotel　AS

AA ★★★　The Street, Crudwell, Malmesbury, Wiltshire SN16 9EW
Open: All year
t 01666 577409　e reception@mayfieldhousehotel.co.uk
mayfieldhousehotel.co.uk　2B2

Rooms per night:
s:　£74.00-£124.00
d:　£84.00-£139.00
p/p half board:
d:　£60.00-£87.50
Meals:　£12.00-£26.00

Traditional country hotel offering visitors a warm Cotswold welcome and the best of local fare.

Access:　General: 　Room:

Swindon | Best Western Premier Blunsdon House Hotel

AA ★★★★　Blunsdon, Swindon, Wiltshire SN26 7AS
t 01793 721701　e reservations@blunsdonhouse.co.uk
blunsdonhouse.co.uk

Access:　abc　General:　Room:

Warminster | Longleat Caravan Club Site

Enjoy England ★★★★★　Warminster, Wiltshire BA12 7NL
t 01985 844663

(165)　£14.60-£21.45
(165)　£14.60-£21.45
caravanclub.co.uk　2B2

165 touring pitches
Open: 27 March - 9 November

Shop: 3 miles
Pub: 1 mile

Close to Longleat House, this is the only site where you can hear lions roar at night! Cafés, pubs and restaurants within walking distance.

Location: A362 (Frome), at roundabout 1st exit into Longleat Estate. Through toll booths, follow caravan and camping signs for 1 mile.

Access:
General:
Pitch:

For symbols see pg 24　123

South West | Wiltshire/Attractions

Winsley | Church Farm Country Cottages

Enjoy England ★★★★

Mrs Trish Bowles, Church Farm Country Cottages, Church Farm, Winsley, Bradford-on-Avon BA15 2JH
t 01225 722246 e stay@churchfarmcottages.com

churchfarmcottages.com

Falmouth | Pendennis Castle

Open: For opening hours and prices, please call 0870 333 1181 or visit www.english-heritage.org.uk/properties

Pendennis Headland, Falmouth, Cornwall TR11 4LP
t 0870 333 1181 e customers@english-heritage.org.uk

english-heritage.org.uk/pendennis

The perfect day out for families as there is so much to see and do!

Access: abc **General:**

Newquay | Newquay Zoo

Trenance Park, Newquay, Cornwall TR7 2LZ
t 01637 873342 e info@newquayzoo.org.uk

newquayzoo.org.uk

St Mawes | St Mawes Castle

Open: For opening hours and prices, please call 0870 333 1181 or visit www.english-heritage.org.uk/properties

St.Mawes, Nr Truro, Cornwall TR2 5DE
t 0870 333 1181 e customers@english-heritage.org.uk

english-heritage.org.uk/stmawes

Sat overlooking the Sea, the elaborately decorated Castle offers families a great day out.

Access: abc **General:**

Summercourt | Dairyland Farm World

Nr. Newquay, Cornwall TR8 5AA
t 01872 510349 / 01872 510246 e info@dairylandfarmworld.co.uk

dairylandfarmworld.com

Great Torrington | RHS Garden Rosemoor

Great Torrington, Devon EX38 8PH
t 01805 624067 e rosemooradmin@rhs.org.uk

rhs.org.uk/rosemoor

Access: **General:**

124 www.openbritain.net

South West | **Attractions**

Okehampton | Okehampton Castle

Open: For opening hours and prices, please call 0870 333 1181 or visit www.english-heritage.org.uk/properties

Castle Lodge, Okehampton, Devon EX20 1JA
t 0870 333 1181   e customers@english-heritage.org.uk

english-heritage.org.uk/okehampton

Let our free audio tour bring this romantic ruin to life. There's plenty to explore!

Access: General:

Plymouth | Plymouth Gin

Blackfriars Distillery, 60 Southside Street, Plymouth PL1 2LQ
t 01752 828951   e richard.smith@plymouthgin.com

plymouthgin.com

Totnes | Woodlands Leisure Park

Blackawton, Totnes, Devon TQ9 7DQ
t 01803 712598   e pat@woodlandspark.com

woodlands-leisure-park.co.uk

Blandford Forum | Royal Signals Museum

Blandford Camp, Blandford Forum, Dorset DT11 8RH
t 01258 482248   e adam@royalsignalsmuseum.com

royalsignalsmuseum.com

Poole | Tower Park

Poole, Dorset BH12 4HY
t 01202 723 671

towerparkcentre.co.uk

Portland | Portland Castle

Open: For opening hours and prices, please call 0870 333 1181 or visit www.english-heritage.org.uk/properties

Liberty Road, Castletown, Portland, Dorset DT5 1AZ
t 0870 333 1181   e customers@english-heritage.org.uk

english-heritage.org.uk/portland

Discover one of Henry VIII's finest coastal forts and enjoy a great family day out.

Access: General:

For symbols see pg 24

South West | Attractions

Bristol | Bristol Hippodrome

Saint Augustines Parade, Bristol BS1 4UZ
t 1173023310 e steve.jones@livenation.co.uk
Bristolhippodrome.org.uk

Access: abc **General:**

Gloucester | Gloucester Cathedral

12 College Green, Gloucester, Gloucestershire GL1 2LX
t 01452 528095
www.gloucestercathedral.org.uk

Winchcombe | Hailes Abbey

Open: For opening hours and prices, please call 0870 333 1181 or visit www.english-heritage.org.uk/properties

Nr Winchcombe, Cheltenham, Gloucestershire GL54 5PB
t 0870 333 1181 e customers@english-heritage.org.uk
english-heritage.org.uk/hailesabbey

Enjoy a fascinating day out, take the audio tour and discover the history.

Access: abc **General:**

Winchcombe | Sudeley Castle

Winchcombe, Gloucestershire GL54 5JD
t 01242 602308 e enquiries@sudeley.org.uk
sudeleycastle.co.uk

Bath | St Michaels Without

Broad Street, Bath BA1 5LJ
t 01225 447103 e office@stmichaelsbath.org.uk
stmichaelsbath.org.uk

nr Amesbury | Stonehenge

Open: For opening hours and prices, please call 0870 333 1181 or visit www.english-heritage.org.uk/properties

Nr Amesbury, Wiltshire SP4 7DE
t 0870 333 1181 e customers@english-heritage.org.uk
english-heritage.org.uk/stonehenge

Britain's most intriguing prehistoric monument. Uncover the mysteries guided by a complimentary audio tour.

Access: abc **General:**

South West | Attractions

Salisbury | Old Sarum

Open: For opening hours and prices, please call 0870 333 1181 or visit www.english-heritage.org.uk/properties

Castle Road, Salisbury, Wiltshire SP1 3SD
t 0870 333 1181   e customers@english-heritage.org.uk
english-heritage.org.uk/oldsarum

With 5,000 years of history, the iron age hill fort is an impressive site.

Access: abc 🐕 ☺ ♿wc ♿ ☼ 🚻 ♿   **General:** P♿ 🚭 ♿

Swindon | STEAM - Museum of the Great Western Railway

Kemble Drive, Swindon, Wiltshire SN2 2TA
t 01793 466602   e hbarnes@swindon.gov.uk
steam-museum.org.uk

Warminster | Longleat

Longleat, Warminster, Wiltshire BA12 7NW
t 01985 844400   e enquiries@longleat.co.uk
longleat.co.uk

Access: 🐕 ♿wc ♿ ☼ ♿ ♿G   **General:** P♿ 🚭 ♣ ♿

Hall for Cornwall

For symbols see pg 24

OpenBritain | South West

MONKEY WORLD
APE RESCUE CENTRE

To make the park more enjoyable for our less-abled visitors, Monkey World is pleased to offer the following:

Mobility scooters & wheelchairs **Disabled swings** **Sensory statues & guided tours**

where families matter

Over 230 rescued and endangered apes and monkeys in a 65-acre park!

Near Wool, Dorset BH20 6HH
Tel: 01929 462537   Email: apes@monkeyworld.org

FREE INFO LINE 0800 456600   www.monkeyworld.org

OpenBritain | South West

Quay HOLIDAYS

Poole's Premium Letting Specialists

We only offer the highest quality self-catering holiday accommodation, comprehensively and comfortably furnished

Short breaks or longer stays welcome - call 01202 683333 for rates

Quay Holidays, 1 Grand Parade, High Street, Poole Dorset, BH15 1AD
www.quayholidays.co.uk

enjoyEngland.com
4★-5★ SELF CATERING

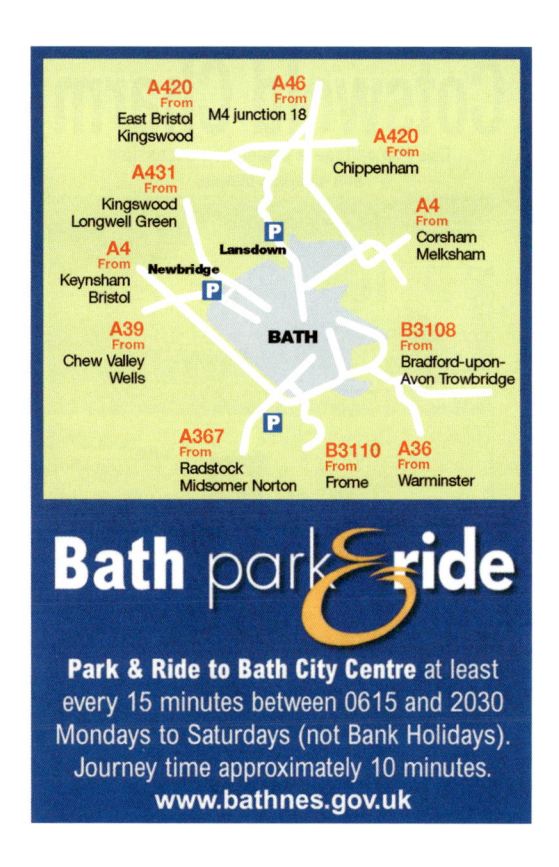

Bath park & ride

A420 From East Bristol Kingswood
A46 From M4 junction 18
A420 From Chippenham
A431 From Kingswood Longwell Green
A4 From Corsham Melksham
A4 From Keynsham Bristol
Lansdown
Newbridge
BATH
A39 From Chew Valley Wells
B3108 From Bradford-upon-Avon Trowbridge
A367 From Radstock Midsomer Norton
B3110 From Frome
A36 From Warminster

Park & Ride to Bath City Centre at least every 15 minutes between 0615 and 2030 Mondays to Saturdays (not Bank Holidays). Journey time approximately 10 minutes.
www.bathnes.gov.uk

THE BRISTOL HIPPODROME

A LIVE NATION VENUE

Musicals · Ballet · Opera · Family · Comedy · Concerts

Welcoming all visitors with Access requirements

Telephone: 0117 302 3222
Mon - Fri 10am - 6pm · Voice or minicom

email: trish.hodson@livenation.co.uk

www.bristolhippodrome.org.uk
for show and venue info

OpenBritain | South West

VisitCornwall

For information on accessible accommodation, attractions and events tel: 01872 322900 or www.visitcornwall.com

BROADwindsor
CRAFT AND DESIGN CENTRE

Shopping for all the family - the main shop & individual craft studios are the ideal place to shop or browse.

Meals and refreshments are served in the relaxed atmosphere of the restaurant and conservatory. For lunch, homemade soups, hot dishes and salads are created daily using local produce. Fine coffee, teas, homemade cakes and Dorset cream teas are served throughout the day.

The attractive setting is well complemented by the warm and friendly services.

The main shop, restaurant and conservatory are now fully air-conditioned.

Open daily all year
10am - 5pm
Large free car park
Coaches welcome

Broadwindsor DT8 3PX
Tel: 01308 868362
www.broadwindsorcrafts.co.uk

Cotswold Charm
Ewe Pen cottage is wheelchair accessible and sleeps 5 people.

info@cotswoldcharm.co.uk
01386 - 840164

OpenBritain | South West

Use public transport confidently...

The Devon Access Wallet scheme is designed to help make journeys by bus or train in Devon easier and give people the support to travel independently.

For more information call 01392 383509
Email: accesswallet@devon.gov.uk
www.devon.gov.uk/devonaccesswallet

Devon County Council

HALL FOR CORNWALL

Do you love theatre?

Situated in the heart of Truro, HfC is an access-friendly venue hosting a wide range of shows.

Our helpful staff will be happy to discuss your needs and offer you a very warm welcome.

For more information:
call **01872 262 466**
or log onto
www.hallforcornwall.co.uk

Also visit our restaurant and coffee shop!

Theatre narration for people with sight problems

Discover Falmouth

Falmouth Tourist Information Centre has a comprehensive list of accessible accommodation and offers a booking service.

The centre is fully accessible, stocks a good range of maps, guides and books, and helpful staff can provide detailed information for visitors with specific needs on what to do, where to go and how to get around the area.

Shopmobility scooters are available 10am - 4.30pm Mon-Fri. Book through Falmouth Town Management in the One Stop Shop 24 hrs in advance. Tel: 01326 313553 email: ruth@falmouth.co.uk

All-terrain wheelchair for easy access onto Gyllyngvase Beach and into the sea available through Gylly Beach Café.
Tel: 01326 312884 or e-mail: café@gyllybeach.com

Falmouth Tourist
Information Centre
11 Market Strand,
Prince of Wales Pier,
Falmouth, Cornwall.
TR11 3DF
Tel: 01326 312200
info@falmouthtic.co.uk

www.discoverfalmouth.co.uk
www.visitfalmouth.com
(Falmouth and District Hotels Association)

Tourist Information

Falmouth Town Council

PLYMOUTH - The Smooth ENGLISH GIN

DISTILLERY & TOUR · BRASSERIE COCKTAIL LOUNGE · SHOP

Discover gin's colourful history and over 200 years of distilling at Black Friars Distillery - the working home of Plymouth Gin since 1793.

Take a guided tour and learn about the art of making the world famous Plymouth Gin and discover more secrets behind the taste of this unique and original gin.

Plymouth Gin Black Friars Distillery
60 Southside Street,
Plymouth. PL1 2LQ
T: 01752 665292
E: rose@plymouthgin.com
W: www.plymouthgin.com

The distillery is open from 10 am - 5.30pm Monday to Saturday and 11am - 5.00pm Sunday, except for Christmas.

PLYMOUTH
DRINKAWARE.CO.UK

131

RHS GARDEN ROSEMOOR

A JEWEL NESTLING WITHIN A WOODED DEVON VALLEY

www.rhs.org.uk/rosemoor
01805 624067
GREAT TORRINGTON, DEVON EX38 8PH

Registered Charity no. 222879/SC038262

The RHS, the UK's leading gardening charity

SOUTH SOMERSET
A GUIDE FOR VISITORS WITH DISABILITIES

Picturesque villages, country walks, historic houses and gardens—South Somerset has so much to offer for all abilities.

Please contact Yeovil Tourist Information on 01935 845 946 for our updated guide.

www.visitsouthsomerset.com

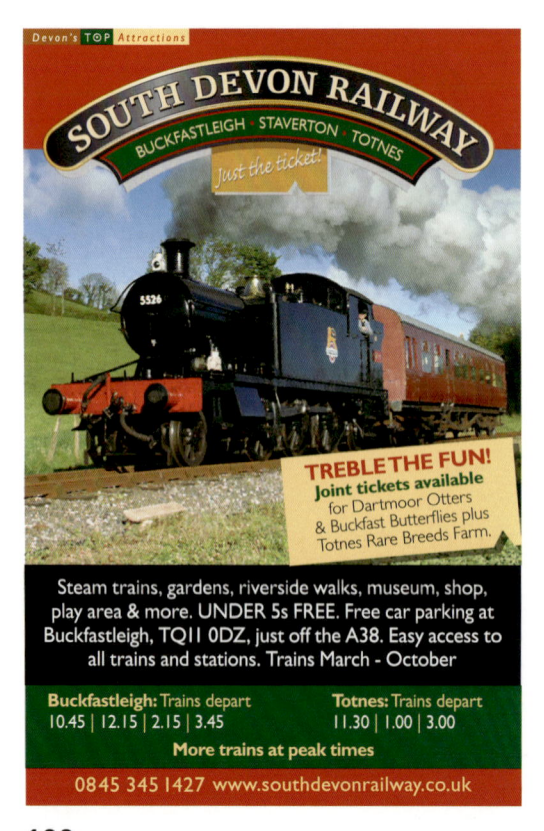

Beacon Authority

SOUTH DEVON RAILWAY
BUCKFASTLEIGH · STAVERTON · TOTNES
Just the ticket!

Devon's TOP Attractions

TREBLE THE FUN!
Joint tickets available for Dartmoor Otters & Buckfast Butterflies plus Totnes Rare Breeds Farm.

Steam trains, gardens, riverside walks, museum, shop, play area & more. UNDER 5s FREE. Free car parking at Buckfastleigh, TQ11 0DZ, just off the A38. Easy access to all trains and stations. Trains March - October

Buckfastleigh: Trains depart
10.45 | 12.15 | 2.15 | 3.45

Totnes: Trains depart
11.30 | 1.00 | 3.00

More trains at peak times

0845 345 1427   www.southdevonrailway.co.uk

STEAM GWR
Museum of the Great Western Railway

A first class day out

Open daily - Kemble Drive, Swindon.
Tel: 01793 466646
www.swindon.gov.uk/steam

Supported by the National Lottery through the Heritage Lottery Fund

Swindon BOROUGH COUNCIL

OpenBritain | South West

Taunton's Shopmobility Centre

Adding to Life — pluss

Taunton Deane Borough Council

Shopmobility is a **free** loan service of manual and powered wheelchairs and electric scooters to **anyone** with temporary or permanent limited disability.

Shopmobility is at **Paul Street** Old Market Shoppers Car Park

To book your vehicle
Tel: Taunton
(01823) 327900

Makes Shopping Easier!

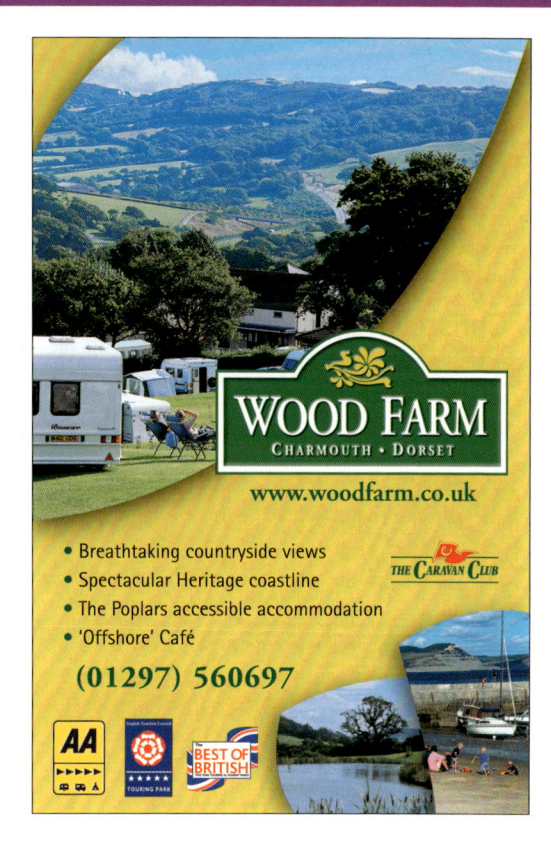

Wood Farm

Charmouth • Dorset

www.woodfarm.co.uk

- Breathtaking countryside views
- Spectacular Heritage coastline
- The Poplars accessible accommodation
- 'Offshore' Café

(01297) 560697

THE CARAVAN CLUB
AA *****
TOURING PARK
BEST OF BRITISH

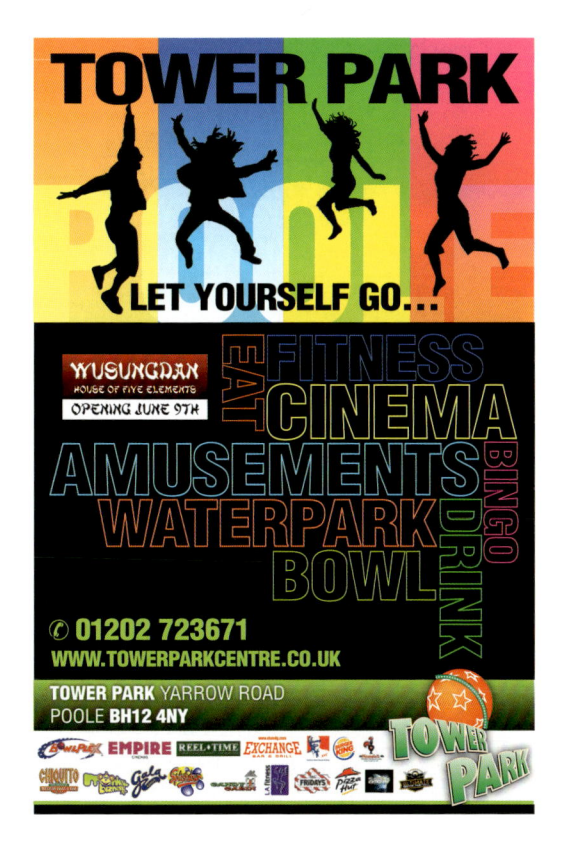

TOWER PARK

LET YOURSELF GO…

WUSUNGDAN - HOUSE OF FIVE ELEMENTS - OPENING JUNE 9TH

EAT • FITNESS • CINEMA • AMUSEMENTS • WATERPARK • BOWL • BINGO • DRINK

01202 723671
WWW.TOWERPARKCENTRE.CO.UK

TOWER PARK YARROW ROAD
POOLE BH12 4NY

Bath CitySightseeing

If you are local or visiting the area, you will be amazed what you learn on our two Bath CitySightseeing tours.

Tel: 01225 330444

The Bull Pen at DairyLand Farm World

Non-stop all weather action in The Bull Pen
Over 12,000 sq.ft. Indoors

NOVEMBER to EASTER
Open every Thur, Fri, Sat, Sun plus school holidays

EASTER to NOVEMBER
The Bull Pen and DairyLand are open 7 days a week

On the A3058, 4 miles from Newquay. TR8 5AA
www.dairylandfarmworld.com   Infoline: 01872 510349

133

OpenBritain | South West

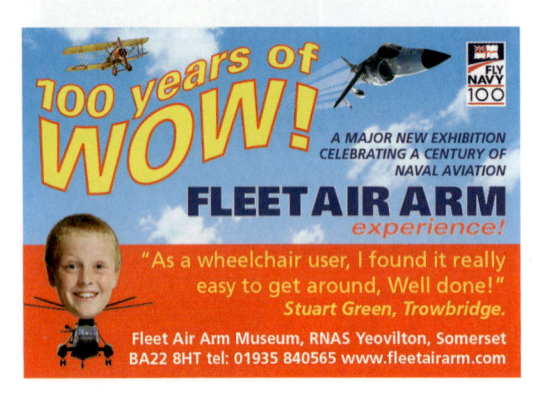

Discover Centuries of character when you visit Christchurch

Whatever the time of year, historic Christchurch is the perfect choice for a well-deserved short break, a longer stay or for just a few hours.

Christchurch
Mudeford • Highcliffe • Hurn
For FREE brochure Tel: 01202 471780
www.visitchristchurch.info

Christchurch ...where time is pleasure

NEWQUAY ZOO — Meet our meerkats!

For all the latest news please visit our website
EXPERIENCE THE WORLD'S WILDLIFE
01637 873342 www.newquayzoo.org.uk

100 years of WOW!

FLY NAVY 100
A MAJOR NEW EXHIBITION CELEBRATING A CENTURY OF NAVAL AVIATION

FLEET AIR ARM experience!

"As a wheelchair user, I found it really easy to get around, Well done!"
Stuart Green, Trowbridge.

Fleet Air Arm Museum, RNAS Yeovilton, Somerset
BA22 8HT tel: 01935 840565 www.fleetairarm.com

St Michael's Without

Welcome to St. Michael's Without

Come and visit us in our beautiful church. All are welcome; find a peaceful spot away from the bustle of the city, enjoy our café, explore our building or find out about forthcoming concerts and events.

St. Michael's Without, Broad Street, Bath, BA1 5LJ (Next to the main post office and Podium shopping centre)

Open 10.00am – 5.00pm Monday to Saturday, Sunday services at 9.00am and 10.30am

www.stmichaelsbath.org.uk tel:01225 447103

A warm welcome awaits you at Gloucester Cathedral

- one of the finest medieval buildings in the country

- Magnificent stained glass
- Royal tombs
- Medieval cloisters
- Rich musical heritage

Phone 01452 528095
email reception@gloucestercathedral.org.uk
www.gloucestercathedral.org.uk

SUDELEY CASTLE

Access our award-winning gardens

t. 01242 602308 | w. sudeleycastle.co.uk

Les Rocquettes Hotel

St Peter Port, Guernsey
3 ★★★

Good location with parking
Attractive garden and terraces
Indoor pool, gym and Jacuzzi
Excellent restaurant and popular bar
51 ensuite bedrooms and lift

www.rocquettes@sarniahotels.com
Tel : 01481 722146

Woodlands FAMILY THEME PARK DARTMOUTH

SPECIAL DISCOUNTS

WE CARE YOUR DAY IS SPECIAL

Blackawton, Totnes, Devon TQ9 7DQ • Tel: 01803 712598 • www.woodlandspark.com
Wheelchairs may require strong pusher for hills

OpenBritain | South West

Live your life

with the Etac Balder F280 powerchair

Experience the liberating feeling of enjoying the outdoors with peace of mind in the Etac Balder F280. Renowned worldwide for unparalleled reliability, functionality and comfort, this Scandinavian designed powerchair lets you live life to the full. Be yourself in a powerchair you can trust – the Etac Balder F280.

T: 01256 767181 E: info@etacuk.com
www.etacuk.com

Etac UK Limited, 29 Murrell Green Business Park
London Road, Hook, Hampshire RG27 9GR

etac®
Creating possibilities

135

Winchester Cathedral

Great days out in the South East

The South East is your quintessential slice of England. Meander around an English country garden, explore outstanding castles, enjoy colourful festivals and savour English wine. From 400 miles of glorious coastline, to the dreaming spires of Oxford, there's so much to discover.

Making history

Relive the 1066 Battle of Hastings and take the interactive audio tour at the **Abbey and Battlefield**. Board the world-famous **HMS Victory** at **Portsmouth Historic Dockyard**. Explore one of the many breathtaking castles, including **Windsor**, **Arundel** and **Leeds** (Kent). Admire elegant cathedrals and hear gentle sounds of evensong at **Oxford**, **Canterbury** or **Chichester**. Behold 'the finest view in England' according to Winston Churchill's mother, at World Heritage Site **Blenheim Palace**, Oxfordshire.

Full-on fun

Ride the Jungle Coaster at **Legoland**, Windsor, meet colourful characters at **Dickens World**, Kent, delight in the fantabulous award-winning **Roald Dahl Museum and Story Centre**, Buckinghamshire, or discover over 250 exotic and endangered species at **Marwell Wildlife**, Hampshire.

Shore pleasures

Unwind on our own unspoilt island; the **Isle of Wight**, home to Queen Victoria's **Osborne House**. Visit the charming beaches of **Brighton**, **Eastbourne** and **Margate**, all popular Victorian playgrounds. Save your small change for the slot machines on the pier or tasty fish and chips. Wander the sand dunes at **West Wittering**, watch kite surfers at **Pevensey Bay**, see the spectacular **White Cliffs of Dover**, or sample an unrivalled number of water-sports at **Calshot Activities Centre**, Hampshire.

OpenBritain | South East

The Nurse's Cottage

Blenheim

South East

Berkshire
Buckinghamshire
Hampshire
Isle of Wight
Kent
Oxfordshire
Surrey
East Sussex
West Sussex

At one with nature

Savour a picnic in Kent, the 'Garden of England', home to the iconic **Sissinghurst Castle Garden**. Explore the **RHS's flagship garden at Wisley**, Surrey, or international gardens at **Paradise Park**, East Sussex. Devour a tasty pub lunch then traverse the tracks of the **South Downs Way**, or Ridgeway and Thames Path then explore the vibrant **River Thames**. If it's escapism you crave, retreat to the **New Forest National Park** for ancient woodland and picturesque villages, wild deer, ponies and cattle.

Festival fever

Be inspired by a true celebration of the arts, at the hip **Brighton Festival** every May. Dress up for **Glyndebourne's opera** for the epitome of elegance. Revel with jolly folks in Victorian costumes during the **Broadstairs Dickens Festival**. Enjoy rock, pop and hip hop mixed with a liberal dose of mud at August's **Reading Festival**. Don't forget the **Henley Royal Regatta**, where rowers demonstrate their sporting prowess, or fill your lungs with invigorating sea air at the internationally acclaimed **Cowes Week**.

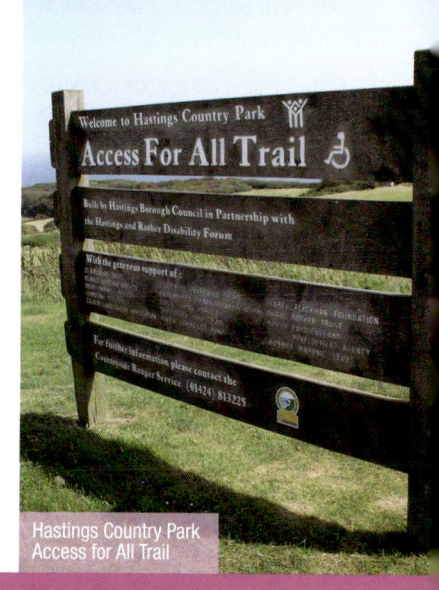

Hastings Country Park
Access for All Trail

www.openbritain.net

OpenBritain | **South East**

Windsor Castle

Welcoming all to South East England

South East England offers an increasing range of accessible accommodation to meet the needs of all visitors. Sample the culinary delights of the 'Nurse's Cottage Restaurant with Rooms' in the New Forest, or stay on a working farm at Heath Farm Self Catering Cottages, Sussex. Indulge in luxury leisure facilities at the Holiday Inn Windsor/Maidenhead, enjoy the great outdoors at Burford Caravan Site, or explore Oxford from the local YHA.

Many historic attractions across the region have been modernised to offer excellent accessibility, including **Waddesdon Manor** in Buckinghamshire, **Blenheim Palace** in Oxfordshire, the **Abbey** and **Battlefield** at Hastings in Sussex and **Pallant House Gallery** in Chichester, winner of numerous accessibility awards.

Enjoy accessible outdoor attractions including **Marwell Wildlife** in Hampshire and **Legoland** in Windsor. Savour hot doughnuts at **Brighton Pie**r, marvel at over 1000 years of history at **Winchester Cathedral**, or shop 'til you drop at **West Quay, Southampton**.

Wheelchair users can access the flying areas, bird hides and picnic areas at the **Hawk Conservancy Trust** in Andover, which also boasts interactive sessions and large print.

For something completely different, visit **Dickens World**, Kent, **Denbies Wine Estate**, Surrey, **Paradise Park**, East Sussex or the **Roald Dahl Museum and Story Centre**, Buckinghamshire.

Historic properties, gardens, eateries, shops, family attractions and entire towns and cities are going the extra mile to welcome all visitors. Investment in staff disability awareness training, facilities, adaptations and building work is increasing in an effort to become the most accessible region in the UK. **Brighton**, **Winchester** and **Windsor** have undertaken full city centre access audits. Buckinghamshire boasts the unique position of being the birthplace of the Paralympics at Stoke Mandeville in 1948 and hosts the Olympic rowing at **Dorney Lake** in 2012.

Find out more

web www.visitsoutheastengland.com

Tourist Information Centres

Tourist Information Centres are a mine of information about local and regional accommodation, attractions and events. Visit them when you arrive at your destination or contact them before you go:

Aylesbury	The Kings Head	01296 330559	tic@aylesburyvaledc.gov.uk
Banbury	Spiceball Park Road	01295 259855	banbury.tic@cherwell-dc.gov.uk
Bicester	Bicester Village	01869 369055	bicester.vc@cherwell-dc.gov.uk
Brighton	Royal Pavilion Shop	0906 711 2255	brighton-tourism@brighton-hove.gov.uk
Burford	The Brewery	01993 823558	burford.vic@westoxon.gov.uk
Canterbury	12/13 Sun Street	01227 378100	canterburyinformation@canterbury.gov.uk
Chichester	29a South Street	01243 775888	chitic@chichester.gov.uk
Cowes	9 The Arcade	01983 813818	info@islandbreaks.co.uk
Croydon	Croydon Clocktower	020 8253 1009	tic@croydon.gov.uk
Dover	The Old Town Gaol	01304 205108	tic@doveruk.com
Gravesend	Towncentric	01474 337600	info@towncentric.co.uk
Hastings	Queens Square	01424 781111	hic@hastings.gov.uk
Lewes	187 High Street	01273 483448	lewes.tic@lewes.gov.uk
Maidstone	Town Hall, Middle Row	01622 602169	tourism@maidstone.gov.uk
Margate	12-13 The Parade	0870 2646111	margate.tic@visitor-centre.net
Marlow	31 High Street	01628 483597	tourism_enquiries@wycombe.gov.uk
Newbury	The Wharf	01635 30267	tourism@westberks.gov.uk
Newport	The Guildhall	01983 813818	info@islandbreaks.co.uk
Oxford	15/16 Broad Street	01865 726871	tic@oxford.gov.uk
Portsmouth	Clarence Esplanade	023 9282 6722	vis@portsmouthcc.gov.uk
Portsmouth	The Hard	023 9282 6722	vis@portsmouthcc.gov.uk
Ramsgate	17 Albert Court	0870 2646111	ramsgate.tic@visitor-centre.net
Rochester	95 High Street	01634 843666	visitor.centre@medway.gov.uk
Romsey	Heritage & Visitor Centre	01794 512987	romseytic@testvalley.gov.uk
Royal Tunbridge Wells	The Old Fish Market	01892 515675	touristinformationcentre@tunbridgewells.gov.uk
Ryde	81-83 Union Street	01983 813818	info@islandbreaks.co.uk
Rye	The Heritage Centre	01797 226696	ryetic@rother.gov.uk
Sandown	8 High Street	01983 813818	info@islandbreaks.co.uk
Shanklin	67 High Street	01983 813818	info@islandbreaks.co.uk
Southampton	9 Civic Centre Road	023 8083 3333	tourist.information@southampton.gov.uk
Winchester	Guildhall	01962 840500	tourism@winchester.gov.uk
Windsor	Royal Windsor Shopping Centre	01753 743900	windsor.tic@rbwm.gov.uk
Witney	26A Market Square	01993 775802	witney.vic@westoxon.gov.uk
Woodstock	Oxfordshire Museum	01993 813276	woodstock.vic@westoxon.gov.uk
Worthing	Marine Parade	01903 221066	tic@worthing.gov.uk
Yarmouth	The Quay	01983 813818	info@islandbreaks.co.uk

www.openbritain.net

South East | Berkshire/Buckinghamshire

Maidenhead | Holiday Inn Maidenhead   AS

AA ★★★★ Manor Lane, Maidenhead, Berkshire SL6 2RA
t 0870 4009053 e joanna.murphy@ichotelsgroup.com
holiday-inn.co.uk

Access: · abc · · · · · · · General: · · · P · · · Room: · · · · · · ·

Slough | Holiday Inn Slough Windsor   AS

Church Street, Chalvey, Slough, Berkshire SL1 2NH
t 01753 551 551 e reservations@slough.kewgreen.co.uk
holiday-inn.co.uk

Access: abc · · · · · General: · · · P · · · Room: · · · ·

Wokingham | Cantley House Hotel

Open: All year except Xmas and New Year

Rooms per night:
s: £90.00–£155.00
d: £100.00–£160.00
Meals: £24.00

Milton Road, Wokingham, Berkshire RG40 5QG
t 0118 978 9912 e reception@cantleyhotel.co.uk
cantleyhotel.co.uk

Beautiful country house hotel set within 50 acres of parkland with splendid gardens.

Access: · · · · General: · × P · · Room: · · · ·

Aylesbury | Holiday Inn Aylesbury

AA ★★★ Aston Clinton Road, Aylesbury, England HP22 5AA
t +44 0 871 9429002
holiday-inn.co.uk

Access: abc · · · · · · General: · · × P · · Room: · · · ·

High Wycombe | Holiday Inn - High Wycombe

AA ★★★ Handy Cross, High Wycombe, England HP11 1TL
t +44 0 870 4009042
holidayinn.co.uk

Access: abc · · · · · General: · · × P · Room: · ·

Leckhampstead | Weatherhead Farm

Enjoy England ★★★★ Leckhampstead, Buckingham MK18 5NP
t 01280 860502 e weatherheadfarm@aol.com

Milton Keynes | Holiday Inn Milton Keynes

AA ★★★ 500 Saxon Gate West, Milton Keynes MK9 2HQ
t 01908 698508
holiday-inn.co.uk

Access: abc · · · · · · General: · · × P · · · Room: · · ·

www.openbritain.net

South East | **Hampshire**

Fareham | Holiday Inn Fareham

Cartwright Drive, Titchfield, Fareham PO15 5RJ
t 0871 9429028   e reservations-fareham@ihg.com
holiday-inn.co.uk

Access: ⋯ abc 🚗 ☺ ♿ ♿ General: 🪑 🍽 🍷 P♿ ✿ ♿   Room: ☕

Lymington | Bench Cottage and Little Bench   AS

Units: 2   **Sleeps:** 2-4
Open: All year

Low season p/w: £250.00
High season p/w: £785.00

Shop: 0.5 miles
Pub: 0.5 miles

Mrs Mary Lewis, Owner, Lodge Road, Pennington, Lymington, Hampshire SO41 8HH
t 01590 673141   e enquiries@ourbench.co.uk
ourbench.co.uk   2C3

Cottages are fully accessible. The master bedroom can be made up as a double or twin beds, with electric foot and head raiser beds, and Bench Cottage has the benefit of a second bedroom which is a twin room.

Location: From the A337 to Lymington turn off at Pennington Village and through village centre. Turn off opposite Pennington Common.

Access:
🏨 abc
General:
🪑 P S
Unit:
♿ ♨ ♿ ♿ 🛏 S ♿ ✿

Southampton | Holiday Inn Southampton

AA   ★★★   Herbert Walker Avenue, Southampton SO15 1HJ
t 08719429073
holiday-inn.co.uk

Access: ⋯ 🚗 🐾 ♿ ♿ ♿   General: 🪑 🍽 🍷 P♿ 🛗 ♿   Room: S ☕

Southampton | Vitalise Netley Waterside House   AS

Abbey Hill, Netley Abbey, Southampton SO31 5FA
t 02380 453686   e netley@vitalise.org.uk
vitalise.org.uk

Access: 🏨 🐾 ☺ ♿ ♿ ♿   General: 🍽 ✕ 🍷 P♿ ✿ 🛗 ♿   Room: ♿ ♨ ♿ S ☕

Southampton, Eastleigh | Holiday Inn Southampton - Eastleigh   AS

Leigh Road, Eastleigh SO50 9PG
t +44 0 871 9429075
holiday-inn.co.uk

Access: ⋯ abc 🐾 ☺ ♿ 🐾   General: 🪑 🍽 ✕ 🍷 P♿ 🛗 ♿   Room: ♿ ☕

For symbols see pg 24

South East | Hampshire/Isle of Wight

Sway | The Nurse's Cottage
Enjoy England ★★★★ Station Road, Sway, Lymington SO41 6BA
t 01590 683402 e nurses.cottage@lineone.net
nursescottage.co.uk

Borthwood | Borthwood Cottages
Enjoy England ★★★ Mrs Anne Finch, Borthwood Cottages, Sandlin, Borthwood Lane, Sandown PO36 0HH t 01983 403967 e anne@borthwoodcottages.co.uk
borthwoodcottages.co.uk

Newchurch | Southland Camping Park
Enjoy England ★★★★★ Winford Road, Newchurch PO36 0LZ
t 01983 865385 e info@southland.co.uk
southland.co.uk

Shanklin | Laramie
Enjoy England ★★★★ Mrs Sally Ranson, Laramie, Howard Road, Shanklin PO37 6HD
t 01983 862905 e sally.ranson@tiscali.co.uk
laramieholidayhome.co.uk

Shanklin | Sunny Bay Apartments
Enjoy England ★★★★ Mrs Julia Nash, Sunny Bay Apartments, Alexandra Road, Shanklin PO37 6AF
t 01983 866379 e info@sunnybayapartments.com
sunnybayapartments.com

St Helen's | The Old Club House
National Trust, The Old Club House, St Helen's, Isle of Wight
t 0844 8002070
nationaltrustcottages.co.uk/south_east/isle_of_wight/

Looking for something else?

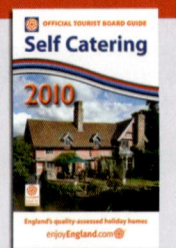

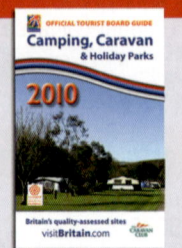

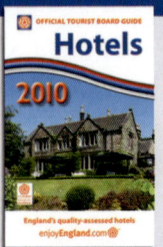

Official Tourist Board Guides: Pets Come Too! 2010 · Self Catering 2010 · Camping, Caravan & Holiday Parks 2010 · B&B 2010 · Hotels 2010

If you haven't found what you are looking for in OpenBritain, VisitBritain's Official Tourist Board Guides offer a wide choice of assessed accommodation which may meet your needs.

South East | Isle of Wight/Kent

Yarmouth | West Bay Club

Enjoy England ★★★★
Units: 2 Sleeps: 1-4
Open: All year

Low season p/w: £280.00
High season p/w: £1110.00

West Bay Club (formerly The Savoy), Halletts Shute, Yarmouth, Isle of Wight PO41 0RJ
t 01983 760355 f 01983 761277 e info@westbayclub.co.uk

westbayclub.co.uk   2C3

West Bay Club is a four star self-catering village in acres of landscaped grounds. Featuring two specially designed accessible cottages each with two twin bedrooms, wet room, adapted kitchen, lounge, parking and hoist to heated indoor pool.

Location: Located approximately 1 mile from the ferry terminal at picturesque Yarmouth in the popular West Wight area of the Island.

Access:
General:
Unit:

Ashford | Holiday Inn Ashford Central

AA ★★★
Canterbury Road, Ashford, Kent TN24 8QQ
t 08719429001 e reservations-ashford@ihg.com
ihg.com/ashfordcentral

Access: General: Room:

Betteshanger | Updown Park Farm

Enjoy England ★★★★
Mrs J R Mongomery, Updown Park Farm, Little Brooksend Farm, Birchington CT7 0JW   t 01843 841656 e info@montgomery-cottages.co.uk
montgomery-cottages.co.uk

Biddenden | Heron Cottage

Enjoy England ★★★★
Biddenden, Ashford TN27 8HH
t 01580 291358 e susantwort@hotmail.com
heroncottage.info

Bromley | Best Western Bromley Court Hotel

Bromley Hill, Bromley BR1 4JD
t 020 84618600 e enquiries@bromleycourthotel.co.uk
bw-bromleycourthotel.co.uk

For symbols see pg 24

South East | **Kent**

Cliftonville | Smiths Court Hotel

Enjoy England ★★★
Open: All year

Rooms per night:
s: £50.00–£60.00
d: £75.00–£85.00
p/p half board:
d: £64.75–£76.75
Meals: £14.75–£16.75

Access:
General:
Room:

21-27 Eastern Esplanade, Cliftonville, Kent CT9 2HL
t 01843 222310 e info@smithscourt.co.uk

smithscourt.co.uk 3C3

The Smiths Court has all the modern conveniences expected by the discerning traveller, but retains a quintessentially English charm. Set on the clifftops with 43 individually decorated rooms and suites, some enjoying superb sea views and spectacular 'Turner' sunsets.

Location: A299 roundabout, 2nd exit onto A28 Canterbury road, A28 roundabout 2nd exit to Marine Terrace, left at lights, 1.1 miles

Densole | Garden Lodge Guest House & Restaurant

Enjoy England ★★★★

324 Canterbury Road, Densole, Folkestone CT18 7BB
t 01303 893147 e stay@garden-lodge.com

garden-lodge.com

Edenbridge | Hay Barn & Straw Barn

Enjoy England ★★★★
Units: 2   Sleeps: 2-4
Open: All year

Low season p/w:
£345.00
High season p/w:
£535.00

Mr J Piers Quirk, Watstock Farm, Wellers Town Road, Chiddingstone, Edenbridge TN8 7BH
t 07770 762076 e info@watstockbarns.co.uk

watstockbarns.co.uk 2D2

Two units for 2 to 6 persons. Converted 2007 on family farm, all ground-floor.

Access:
General: Unit:

OPEN BRITAIN
DECIDED WHERE TO GO?
SEE ATTRACTIONS FOR WHAT TO DO
Ideas and information at the end of each regional section

©BritainonView / Martin Brent

South East | Kent

Folkestone | Black Horse Farm Caravan Club Site

Enjoy England ★★★★★

385 Canterbury Road, Densole, Folkestone, Kent CT18 7BG
t 01303 892665

caravanclub.co.uk   3B4

(140) £12.00–£17.95
(140) £12.00–£17.95
(20)

140 touring pitches
Open: All year

Shop: <0.5 miles
Pub: <0.5 miles

Set in the heart of farming country in the Kentish village of Densole on the Downs. This is a quiet, relaxed country site, ideally for families wishing to visit the many interesting local attractions including the historic city of Canterbury.

Location: M20 jct 13 onto A260 to Canterbury, 2 miles from junction with A20, site on left 200yds past Black Horse.

Access:
General:
Pitch:

Rochester-Chatham | Holiday Inn Rochester Chatham

AA ★★★

Maidstone Road, Chatham, Kent ME5 8NS
t 0870 400 9069   e reservations-rochester@ihg.com
holidayinn.com/rochesterchath

Access: General: Room:

St. Michaels | Little Silver Country Hotel

Enjoy England ★★★

Ashford Road, Tenterden TN30 6SP
t 01233 850321   e enquiries@little-silver.co.uk
little-silver.co.uk

Tunbridge Wells | The Brew House Hotel

Enjoy England ★★★★

1 Warwick Park, Royal Tunbridge Wells TN2 5TA
t 01892 520587   e reception@brewhousehotel.com
thebrewhousehotel.net

Become a member of OpenBritain today.
Share your own travel and accommodation experiences and help Britain become more open!

visit www.openbritain.net

OPEN BRITAIN

For symbols see pg 24

South East | **Oxfordshire**

Burford | Burford Caravan Club Site

Enjoy England ★★★★

Bradwell Grove, Burford, Oxfordshire OX18 4JJ
t 01993 823080

caravanclub.co.uk 2B1

(119) £12.00–£17.75
(119) £12.00–£17.75

119 touring pitches
Open: 3 April – 9 November
Shop: 3 miles
Pub: 1.8 miles

Attractive, spacious site opposite Cotswold Wildlife Park. Burford has superb Tudor houses, a museum and historic inns. A great base from which to explore the Cotswolds.

Location: From roundabout at A40/A361 junction in Burford, take A361 signposted Lechlade. Site on right after 2.5 miles.

Access:
General:
Pitch:

Headington | YHA Oxford

Enjoy England ★★★★

2A Botley Road, Oxford OX2 0AB
t 01865 727275 e oxford@yha.org.uk

yha.org.uk

High Cogges | Springhill Farm Bed & Breakfast

Enjoy England ★★★

Cogges, Witney OX29 6UL
t 01993 704919 e jan@strainge.fsnet.co.uk

High Cogges | Swallows Nest

Enjoy England ★★★★
Units: 1 **Sleeps:** 4
Open: All year

Low season p/w: £260.00
High season p/w: £450.00

Mrs Jan Strainge, Swallows Nest, Cogges, Witney OX29 6UL
t 01993 704919 e jan@strainge.fsnet.co.uk

swallowsnest.co.uk 2C1

Cosy country barn conversion, one mile from Witney. Oxford, Blenheim and Cotswolds within easy reach.

Access: **General:** **Unit:**

146 www.openbritain.net

South East | Oxfordshire/Surrey

Oxford | Abbey Guest House

Enjoy England ★★★★
Open: All year

Rooms per night:
s: £45.00–£50.00
d: £70.00–£78.00
Meals: £6.50–£9.50

Shop: <0.5 miles
Pub: <0.5 miles

136 Oxford Road, Abingdon, Oxford OX14 2AG
t +44 0 1235 537020 or +44 0 7976 627252
e info@abbeyguest.com

abbeyguest.com

Friendly, homely, non-smoking 5 bedroom guesthouse close to Oxford and Abingdon. 'Easy access' room, with En Suite wet-room on ground floor. More information on website, or telephone and we will be pleased to discuss how we can accommodate your requirements.

Location: By car: via A34 (North Abingdon exit) or the A415. By bus: from Oxford/Didcot, stop outside the door.

Access:
General:
Room:

Oxford | Holiday Inn Oxford

Peartree Roundabout, Oxford OX2 8JD
t 0871 423 4931
holidayinn.co.uk

Access: **General:** **Room:**

Croydon | Jurys Inn Croydon

AA ★★★

26 Wellesley Road, Croydon, Surrey CR0 9XY
t 020 84486000   e jurysinncroydon@jurysinns.com
jurysinns.com/croydonhotels

Access: **General:** **Room:**

Farnham | High Wray

Enjoy England ★★★

Mrs Alexine Crawford, High Wray, 73 Lodge Hill Road, Lower Bourne, Farnham GU10 3RB   t 01252 715589   e alexine@highwray73.co.uk
highwray73.co.uk

General: **Unit:**

Guildford | Holiday Inn Guildford

Egerton Road, Guildford, Surrey GU2 7XZ
t 0870 4009036   e gary.lewendon@ihg.com
holiday-inn.co.uk

Access: **General:** **Room:**

For symbols see pg 24

South East | **Surrey**

Holmbury St. Mary | **Bulmer Farm Self-catering**

Enjoy England ★★★★ Mrs Sue Walker, Bulmer Farm Self-catering, Holmbury St. Mary, Dorking RH5 6LG t 01306 731871 e enquiries@bulmerfarm.co.uk
bulmerfarm.co.uk

Horley | **Holiday Inn Gatwick Airport**

Provey Cross Road, Horley, Surrey RH6 0BA
t 0871 9429030 e reservations-gatwick@ihg.com
holiday-inn.co.uk

Access: **General:** **Room:**

Redhill | **Alderstead Heath Caravan Club Site**

Enjoy England ★★★★ Dean Lane, Merstham, Redhill, Surrey RH1 3AH
t 01737 644629

(150) £12.00–£17.75
(150) £12.00–£17.75
(10)

caravanclub.co.uk   2D2

150 touring pitches
Open: All year
Shop: 2.5 miles
Pub: 2.5 miles

A quiet site with views over the North Downs. Denbies Wine Estate is nearby. For day trips try Chessington and Thorpe Park and the lively city of Brighton. Non-members welcome.

Location: M25 jct 8, A217 Reigate, left to Merstham, left - A23, right - Shepherds Hill (B2031), left - Dean Lane.

Access:
General:
Pitch:

Sutton | **Holiday Inn Sutton**

Gibson Road, Sutton, Surrey SM1 2RF
t 020 8770 1311
holiday-inn.co.uk

Access: **General:** **Room:**

Woking | **Holiday Inn Woking**

Victoria Way, Woking, Surrey GU21 8EW
t 01483221000 e info @hiwoking.co.uk
hiwoking.co.uk

Access: **General:** **Room:**

148   www.openbritain.net

South East | **East Sussex**

Battle | Normanhurst Court Caravan Club Site

Enjoy England ★★★★★

🚗 (149) £12.00–£17.75
🚙 (149) £12.00–£17.75

149 touring pitches
Open: 27 March – 9 November

Shop: 1.5 miles
Pub: 1.5 miles

Access:
General:
Pitch:

Stevens Crouch, Battle, East Sussex TN33 9LR
t 01424 773808

caravanclub.co.uk　　3B4

Situated in former gardens with magnificent specimen trees, and colourful rhododendrons in spring. Located close to the 1066 Trail, great for walkers, nature lovers and families. The seaside towns of Eastbourne and Hastings are just a short drive away.

Location: From Battle, turn left onto A271. Site is 3 miles on left.

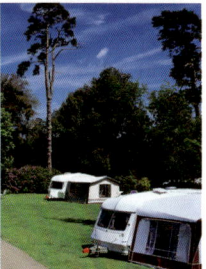

Brighton & Hove | Sheepcote Valley Caravan Club Site

Enjoy England ★★★★★

🚗 (169) £14.60–£21.55
🚙 (169) £14.60–£21.55
⛺ (80)

169 touring pitches
Open: All year

Shop: 0.5 miles
Pub: 0.5 miles

Access:
General:
Pitch:

East Brighton Park, Brighton, East Sussex BN2 5TS
t 01273 626546

caravanclub.co.uk　　2D3

Located on the South Downs, just two miles from Brighton. Visit the Marina, with its shops, pubs and restaurants, and tour the exotic Royal Pavilion. Brighton is a lively town with all the attractions of a seaside holiday resort.

Location: M23/A23, join A27 (Lewes). B2123 (Falmer/Rottingdean). Right B2123 (Woodingdean). Right at traffic lights (Warren Road). Left (Wilson Avenue).

For symbols see pg 24

South East | East Sussex

Eastbourne | Hydro Hotel

Enjoy England ★★★ Mount Road, Eastbourne BN20 7HZ
t 01323 720643 e sales@hydrohotel.com
hydrohotel.com

East Dean | Beachy Head Holiday Cottages

Enjoy England ★★★★ Ms Michelle Hilton, Estate Office, The Green, East Dean BN20 0BY
t 01323 423878 e michelle@beachyhead.org.uk
beachyhead.org.uk

Access: **General:** **Unit:**

Glynde | Caburn Cottages

Enjoy England ★★★★
Units: 9   Sleeps: 2-6
Open: All year

Low season p/w: £240.00
High season p/w: £600.00

Rosemary Norris, Ranscombe Farm, Glynde, nr Lewes, East Sussex BN8 6AA
t 01273 858538 e enquiries@caburncottages.co.uk
caburncottages.co.uk   2D3

A group of flint and brick cottages, very comfortable, well equipped. Bed linen, towels provided.

Access: **General:** **Unit:**

Hastings | Grand Hotel

Enjoy England ★★★★★
Open: All year

Rooms per night:
s: £35.00-£80.00
d: £48.00-£120.00
p/p half board:
d: £55.00-£120.00
Meals: £20.00-£40.00

1 Grand Parade, St. Leonards, Hastings, East Sussex TN37 6AQ
t 01424 428510 e info@grandhotelhastings.co.uk
grandhotelhastings.co.uk

Seafront traditonal boutique hotel. Provides comfort and welcome for all.

Access: **General:** **Room:**

©Britainonview / Adrian Houston

OPEN BRITAIN — DECIDED WHERE TO GO? SEE ATTRACTIONS FOR WHAT TO DO
Ideas and information at the end of each regional section

South East | **East Sussex/West Sussex**

Lewes | **Heath Farm**

Enjoy England ★★★★
Units: 2　　Sleeps: 4-6
Open: All year

Low season p/w:
£425.00
High season p/w:
£667.00

Shop: 1 mile
Pub: <0.5 miles

Mrs Marilyn Hanbury, South Road, Plumpton Green, Lewes, East Sussex BN8 4EA　t 01273 890712　e hanbury@heath-farm.com

heath-farm.com　　　　　　　　　　　　　　　　　　2D3

Two luxury self-catering cottages on small family working farm in beautiful countryside, close to South Downs, coast and easy access to London. Parlour cottage sleeps 4, Stable cottage 5/6.

Location: A272 through Haywards Heath, follow B2112, left into Wivelsfield Green, right into South Road, left at roundabout, mile on left.

General:
Unit:

Bognor Regis | **Farrell House**

Units: 1　　Sleeps: 8
Open: All year

Low season p/w:
£280.00
High season p/w:
£550.00

Livability Self catering holidays, PO Box 36, Cowbridge, Vale of Glamorgan CF71 7TN
t 08456 584478　f 01446 775060　e selfcatering@livability.org.uk

livability.org.uk　　　　　　　　　　　　　　　　　2C3

This property sleeps up to 8 people with an accessible twin and single bedrooms downstairs.

Access:
General:　　**Unit:**

Historic Houses & Gardens
Castles and Heritage Sites

Hudson's is the definitive guide to historic houses & gardens - open to visitors.

Up to date information on over 2000 properties with clear information symbols for accessibility and facilities.
Order online at: www.hhgroup.co.uk/hudsons

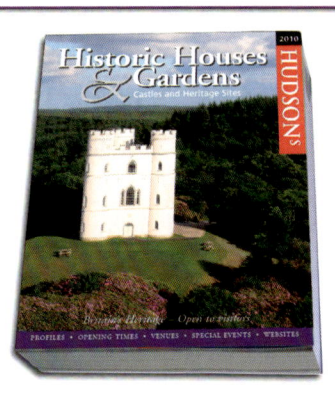

HUDSONS

For symbols see pg 24　　　　　　　　　　　　　　　　151

South East | West Sussex

Bognor Regis | Rowan Park Caravan Club Site — THE CARAVAN CLUB

Enjoy England ★★★★★

🚐 (94) £12.00–£17.75
🚍 (94) £12.00–£17.75
⛺ (6)

94 touring pitches
Open: 3 April – 9 November

Shop: <0.5 miles
Pub: 0.5 miles

Rowan Way, Bognor Regis, West Sussex PO22 9RP
t 01243 828515
caravanclub.co.uk

Conveniently situated about 2 miles from the beach, and close to the traditional seaside resort of Bognor Regis. For the theatre goer you are not far from the Chichester Festival Theatre, or from Arundel Castle.

Location: Turn left into Rowan Way at roundabout on A29 (1 mile north of Bognor). Site 100yds on right, opposite Halfords.

Access:
General:
Pitch:

Bracklesham Bay | Tamarisk

Units: 1 Sleeps: 6
Open: All year

Low season p/w: £280.00
High season p/w: £540.00

Livability Self catering holidays, PO Box 36, Cowbridge, Vale of Glamorgan CF71 7TN
t 08456 584478 f 01446 775060 e selfcatering@livability.org.uk
livability.org.uk

2C3

Fully accessible 3 bedroom bungalow only a few minutes walk from the sea.

Access:
General: **Unit:**

Chichester | George Bell House

Enjoy England ★★★★★

4 Canon Lane, Chichester PO19 1PX
t 01243 813581 e bookings@chichestercathedral.org.uk
chichestercathedral.org.uk

Coldwaltham | The Labouring Man

Enjoy England ★★★★

Old London Road, Coldwaltham, Pulborough RH20 1LF
t 01798 872215 e philip.beckett@btconnect.com
thelabouringman.co.uk

152   www.openbritain.net

South East | **West Sussex**

Compton | **The Barn**

Enjoy England ★★★★
Units: 2 Sleeps: 2-6
Open: All year

Low season p/w:
£250.00
High season p/w:
£750.00

Shop: <0.5 miles
Pub: <0.5 miles

General:
Unit:

Robin Bray, Compton Farmhouse, Compton, Chichester, Sussex PO18 9HB t 02392 631597/631022 f 02392 631022 e robin.bray4@btopenworld.com

bookcottages.com 2C3

This listed barn has been especially adapted for disabled access on the ground floor. Sleeps up to 6. Compton is a quiet downland village with a pub and shop/tearoom. Twin bedroom downstairs has En Suite level entry shower with showerchair.

Location: M25 to A3 to Petersfield, B2146 to Compton, turn left into village square, 120metres, behind farmhouse.

Compton | **The Bull Pen**

Enjoy England ★★★★
Units: 2 Sleeps: 2-4
Open: All year

Low season p/w:
£250.00
High season p/w:
£650.00

Shop: <0.5 miles
Pub: <0.5 miles

General:
Unit:

Mr Robin Bray, Compton Farmhouse, Compton, Chichester, Sussex PO18 9HB t 02392 631597/631022 f 02392 631022 e robin.bray1@btopenworld.com

bookcottages.com 2C3

Former farm buildings especially adapted for easy disabled access in quiet downland village with pub and shop/tearoom within 130 metres. Double room En Suite, twin room En Suite level entry shower, shower chair and support rails.

Location: M25 to A3 to Petersfield, B2146 to Compton, turn left into village square, 120 metres, opposite farmhouse, next to church.

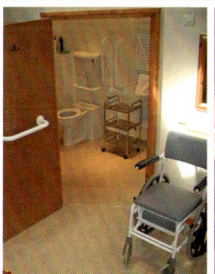

South East | **West Sussex**

East Grinstead | Felbridge Hotel and Spa

AA ★★★★
London Road, East Grinstead, West Sussex RH19 2BH
t 01342 337700 e sales@felbridgehotel.co.uk
felbridgehotel.co.uk

Access: 　　　　　 General: 　　　　　 Room: 　　　　

Felpham | Beach Lodge

Units: 1   Sleeps: 9
Open: All year
Low season p/w: £330.00
High season p/w: £550.00

Livability Self catering holidays, PO Box 36, Cowbridge, Vale of Glamorgan CF71 7TN
t 08456 584478 f 01446 775060 e selfcatering@livability.org.uk
livability.org.uk   2D3

Beach Lodge is a large property adapted for wheelchair users, suitable for groups or families.
Access: 　　　
General: 　　 Unit: 　　　　　

Haywards Heath | Birch Hotel   AS

AA ★★★
7 Lewes Road, Haywards Heath, West Sussex RH17 7SF
t 01444 451565 e info@birch-hotel.co.uk
bw-birchhotel.co.uk

Access: 　　　　　 General: 　　　　　 Room: 　　

Hill Brow | The Jolly Drover

Enjoy England ★★★★
London Road, Hill Brow, Liss GU33 7QL
t 01730 893137 e thejollydrover@googlemail.com
thejollydrover.co.uk

Horsham | The Springfields Hotel

Enjoy England ★★★★
Springfield Road, Horsham RH12 2PG
t 01403 246770 e bookings@springfieldshotel.co.uk
springfieldshotel.co.uk

Runcton | Cornerstones

Enjoy England ★★★★
Viv & Roland Higgins, Corner Cottages, Greenacre, Goodwood Gardens, Runcton PO20 1SP   t 01243 839096 e v.r.higgins@dsl.pipex.com
cornercottages.com

OPENBRITAIN.NET
The one-stop-shop for all your travel needs. Go online and see how we can help you get in, out ...and about.

South East | **West Sussex/Attractions**

Selsey Bill | **Seagulls**

Units: 1 **Sleeps:** 6
Open: All year
Low season p/w: £280.00
High season p/w: £540.00

Livability Self catering holidays, PO Box 36, Cowbridge, Vale of Glamorgan CF71 7TN
t 08456 584478 f 01446 775060 e selfcatering@livability.org.uk

livability.org.uk   2C3

Fully accessible bungalow is right on the Coastal Walk. It sleeps six in 3 bedrooms.

Access:
General: **Unit:**

Westhampnett | **Chichester Park Hotel**

Enjoy England ★★★

Madgwick Lane, Westhampnett, Chichester PO19 7QL
t 01243 786351 e info@chichesterparkhotel.com

chichesterparkhotel.com

West Marden | **Grandwood House**

AA ★★★
Open: All year
Rooms per night:
s: £45.00–£60.00
d: £50.00–£85.00

Watergate, West Marden, Chichester, West sussex PO18 9EG
t 02392 631436 e info@grandwoodhouse.co.uk

grandwoodhouse.co.uk   2C3

Lovely quiet location in the Southdowns within easy reach of Christchurch and Portsmouth historic dock.

Access: abc   **General:**   **Room:**

Bracknell | **Look Out Discovery Centre**

Nine Mile Ride, Bracknell, Berkshire RG12 7QW
t 01344 354400 e Liz.blunt@bracknell-forest.gov.uk

bracknell-forest.gov.uk/lookout

Great Missenden | **Roald Dahl Museum and Story Centre**

81-83 High Street, Great Missenden, Buckinghamshire HP16 0AL
t 01494 892192 e admin@roalddahlmuseum.org

roalddahlmuseum.org

Access: abc   **General:**

OPEN BRITAIN

PLANNING A DAY OUT? WHY NOT MAKE IT A SHORT-BREAK?
Fabulous 'Places to Stay' in every region

For symbols see pg 24   155

South East | Attractions

Tilbury | Tilbury Fort

Open: For opening hours and prices, please call 0870 333 1181 or visit www.english-heritage.org.uk/properties

No 2 Office Block, The Fort, Tilbury, Essex RM18 7NR
t 0870 333 1181   e customers@english-heritage.org.uk
english-heritage.org.uk/tilburyfort

Fascinating for war enthusiasts. View WWI & II gun emplacements and explore the extensive site.

Access: General:

Alton | Jane Austen's House and Museum

Chawton, Alton, Hants GU34 1SD
t 01420 83262   e enquiries@jahmusm.org.uk
jane-austen-house-museum.org.uk

Beaulieu | Beaulieu

John Montagu Building, Beaulieu, Brockenhurst, Hampshire SO42 7ZN
t 01590 612345   e info@beaulieu.co.uk
beaulieu.co.uk

Chichester | Royal Military Police Museum

Defence College of Policing & Guarding, Southwick Park, Chichester, Hampshire PO17 6EJ   t 023 9228 4372   e museum_rhqrmp@btconnect.com
armymuseums.org.uk

New Alresford | Mid Hants Railway Plc

Railway Station, New Alresford SO24 9JG
t 01962 733810   e marketing@watercressline.co.uk
watercressline.co.uk

Nr Andover | Hawk Conservancy Trust

Sarson Lane, Weyhill, Nr Andover, Hampshire SP11 8DY
t 01264 773850 Ex 223   e gale@hawkconservancy.org
hawk-conservancy.org

Southampton | Nuffield Theatre

University Road, Southampton SO17 1TR
t 02380 371771   e info@nuffieldtheatre.co.uk
nuffieldtheatre.co.uk

South East | **Attractions**

Cowes | Osborne House

Open: For opening hours and prices, please call 0870 333 1181 or visit www.english-heritage.org.uk/properties

East Cowes, Isle of Wight PO32 6JX
t 0870 333 1181   e customers@english-heritage.org.uk

english-heritage.org.uk/osbornehouse

Osborne House is one of the Isle of Wight's top attractions, a great day out.

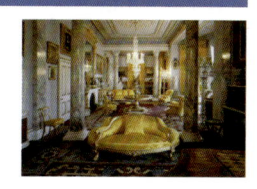

Access: **General:**

Isle of Wight | Carisbrooke Castle

Open: For opening hours and prices, please call 0870 333 1181 or visit www.english-heritage.org.uk/properties

Newport, Isle of Wight PO30 1XY
t 0870 333 1181   e customers@english-heritage.org.uk

english-heritage.org.uk/carisbrookecastle

March the battlements and meet the famous donkeys on a day out to remember.

Access: **General:**

Cranbrook | Sissinghurst Castle Garden

The Biddenden Road, Cranbrook, Kent TN17 2AB
t 01580 710700   e jenny.rogers@nationaltrust.org.uk

nationaltrust.org.uk

Access: abc **General:**

Deal | Walmer Castle & Gardens

Open: For opening hours and prices, please call 0870 333 1181 or visit www.english-heritage.org.uk/properties

Deal, Kent CT14 7LJ
t 0870 333 1181   e customers@english-heritage.org.uk

english-heritage.org.uk/walmercastle

Surrounded by beautiful gardens, with a rich history and a charm all of it own.

Access: abc **General:**

Looking for something else?

If you haven't found what you are looking for in OpenBritain, VisitBritain's Official Tourist Board Guides offer a wide choice of assessed accommodation which may meet your needs.

For symbols see pg 24

South East | **Attractions**

Dover | **Dover Castle**

Open: For opening hours and prices, please call 0870 333 1181 or visit www.english-heritage.org.uk/properties

Dover, Kent CT16 1HU
t 0870 333 1181   e customers@english-heritage.org.uk

english-heritage.org.uk/dovercastle

Explore the medieval world of Henry II's royal court and discover the secret WWII tunnels.

Access: .: ♿ ♿ ⊡ ♿ **General:** P♿ ⊡ ✿ 🖥

Downe | **The Home of Charles Darwin, Down House**

Open: For opening hours and prices, please call 0870 333 1181 or visit www.english-heritage.org.uk/properties

Downe, Kent BR6 7JT
t 0870 333 1181   e customers@english-heritage.org.uk

english-heritage.org.uk/darwin

A fascinating day out, discover the home of Darwin, with new exhibits and audiovisual tours.

Access: .: ♿ ♿ ☀ ♿ ♿ **General:** P♿ ⊡ ✿ ♿ 🖥

Eynsford | **Lullingstone Roman Villa**

Open: For opening hours and prices, please call 0870 333 1181 or visit www.english-heritage.org.uk/properties

Eynsford, Kent DA4 0JA
t 0870 333 1181   e customers@english-heritage.org.uk

english-heritage.org.uk/lullingstoneromanvilla

Become Tony Robinson for a few hours at one of England's most exciting archaeological finds.

Access: ♿ ⊡ **General:** ✿ ♿

Burford | **Cotswold Wild Life Park**

Bradwell Grove, Burford, Oxfordshire OX18 4JP
t 01993 823006   e feedback@cotswoldwildlifepark.co.uk

cotswoldwildlifepark.co.uk

Guildford | **Guildford Cathedral**

Stag Hill, Guildford, Surrey GU2 7UP
t 01483 547860   e reception@guildford-cathedral.org

guildford-cathedral.org

South East | **Attractions**

Wisley | **RHS Garden Wisley**

Wisley, Woking, Surrey GU23 6QB
t 01483 211113 e info@rhs.org.uk

rhs.org.uk

Access: **General:**

Battle | **1066 Battle of Hastings, Abbey & Battlefield**

Open: For opening hours and prices, please call 0870 333 1181 or visit www.english-heritage.org.uk/properties

Battle, East Sussex TN33 0AD
t 0870 333 1181 e customers@english-heritage.org.uk

english-heritage.org.uk/battleabbeyandbattlefield

From interactive exhibits to a themed play area it's perfect for all ages!

Access:

Pevensey | **Pevensey Castle**

Open: For opening hours and prices, please call 0870 333 1181 or visit www.english-heritage.org.uk/properties

Pevensey, East Sussex BN24 5LE
t 0870 333 1181 e customers@english-heritage.org.uk

english-heritage.org.uk/pevenseycastle

Towering ruins, dark dungeons and fascinating exhibition, a fun day out for the whole family.

Access: **General:**

OPEN BRITAIN DECIDED WHERE TO GO? SEE ATTRACTIONS FOR WHAT TO DO
Ideas and information at the end of each regional section

For symbols see pg 24

OpenBritain | South East

harpers
health & fitness

Good value and facilities for all

Stoke Mandeville – the birthplace of the Paralympics and the home of British Wheelchair Sport

- Olympic Lodge hotel
- Olympic & Paralympic training camp venue
- Swimming pool
- Corporate & conference facilities
- Fully accessible

Enquire now quoting 'Paralympic12' to receive 10% discount on accommodation or corporate bookings at Stoke Mandeville Stadium

Visit Buckinghamshire
So much to see. So much to do.
Events – Eating Out – Entertainment
www.visitbuckinghamshire.org

For London 2012 opportunities in Buckinghamshire visit
www.buckssport.org/2012

Stoke Mandeville Stadium & Olympic Lodge Hotel
01296 484848

Guttmann Road, Stoke Mandeville, Aylesbury, Buckinghamshire HP21 9PP

WheelPower
British Wheelchair Sport

Bucks 2012

Stoke Mandeville Stadium is managed by Leisure Connection Limited on behalf of WheelPower.

stoke.mandeville@harpersfitness.co.uk
www.stokemandevillestadium.co.uk
www.harpersfitness.co.uk

OpenBritain | South East

CANTERBURY
SIMPLY INSPIRATIONAL

Make your visit truly inspirational

The cathedral city of Canterbury, with museums, galleries, heritage sites and great shopping. Seaside towns of Herne Bay with its attractive promenade and Whitstable with its excellent seafood restaurants and harbour. Twenty-five villages in beautiful countryside.

Canterbury Visitor Centre on 01227 378 100 or go to www.canterbury.co.uk

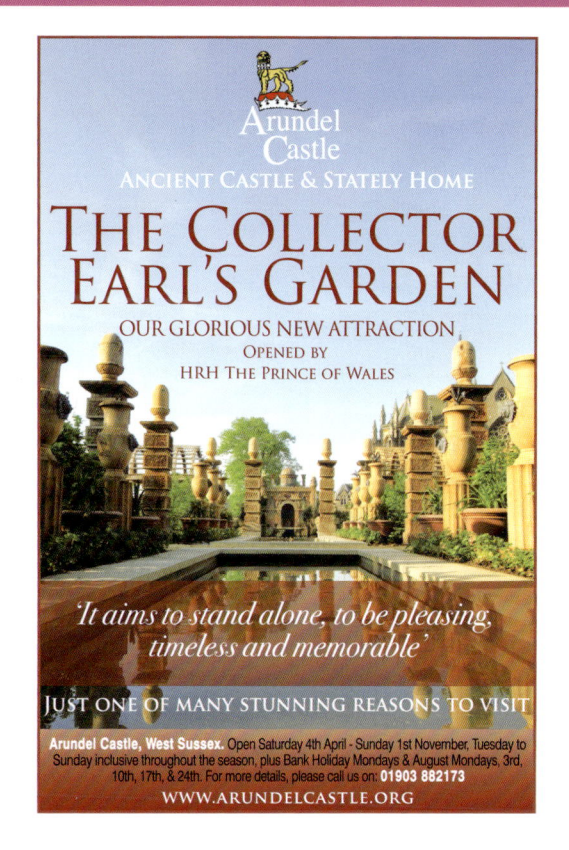

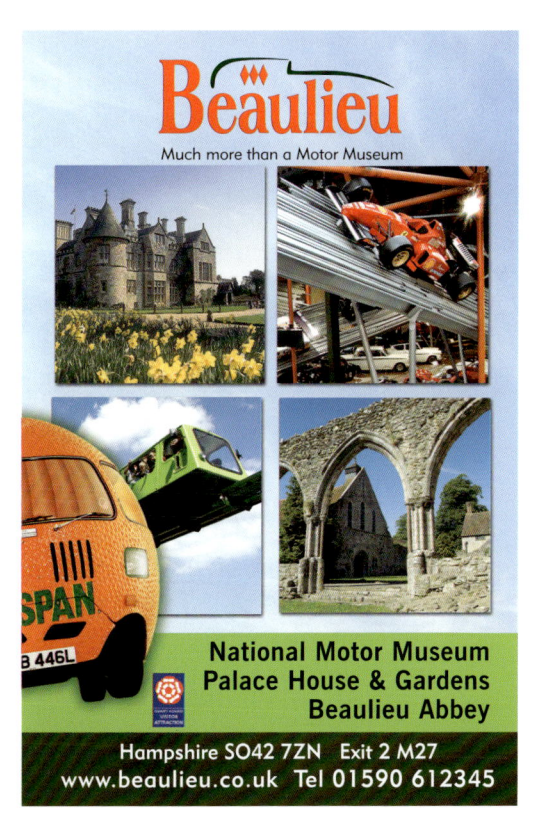

Arundel Castle
ANCIENT CASTLE & STATELY HOME

THE COLLECTOR EARL'S GARDEN

OUR GLORIOUS NEW ATTRACTION
OPENED BY
HRH The Prince of Wales

'It aims to stand alone, to be pleasing, timeless and memorable'

JUST ONE OF MANY STUNNING REASONS TO VISIT

Arundel Castle, West Sussex. Open Saturday 4th April - Sunday 1st November. Tuesday to Sunday inclusive throughout the season, plus Bank Holiday Mondays & August Mondays, 3rd, 10th, 17th, & 24th. For more details, please call us on: 01903 882173
WWW.ARUNDELCASTLE.ORG

Beaulieu
Much more than a Motor Museum

**National Motor Museum
Palace House & Gardens
Beaulieu Abbey**

Hampshire SO42 7ZN   Exit 2 M27
www.beaulieu.co.uk   Tel 01590 612345

161

OpenBritain | South East

Fun filled family holidays

Choose from 3 Holiday Parks
FREE Family Leisure Pools
FREE Children's Fun Clubs
FREE Big Named Entertainment
Spacious Family Accommodation
Bars, Restaurants and Cafés
Outdoor Play Areas
Fantastic South Coast location
in Selsey, West Sussex
1 mile of Beach... and more

Call today 01243 606080

bunnleisure.co.uk   Let the fun shine

BUNN Leisure

---

breeze up

to the Downs at Devil's Dyke, Ditchling Beacon and Stanmer Park by bus from Brighton.

Phone Brighton & Hove City Council on 01273 292480 or visit www.brighton-hove.gov.uk/breezebuses for times and leaflets.

*see 'Breeze' leaflets for details

Train travellers' discount*

COTSWOLD Wildlife Park and Gardens

OPEN DAILY From 10am

from **ANTS** to **WHITE RHINOS** and **BATS** to **BIG CATS** in 160 acres of Landscaped Parkland

- ADVENTURE PLAYGROUND
- CHILDREN'S FARMYARD
- CAFETERIA · PICNIC AREAS
- NARROW GAUGE RAILWAY
  (Runs from April to October)

TEL: 01993 825728

BURFORD • OXON OX18 4JP
(Mid way between Oxford and Cheltenham)

www.cotswoldwildlifepark.co.uk

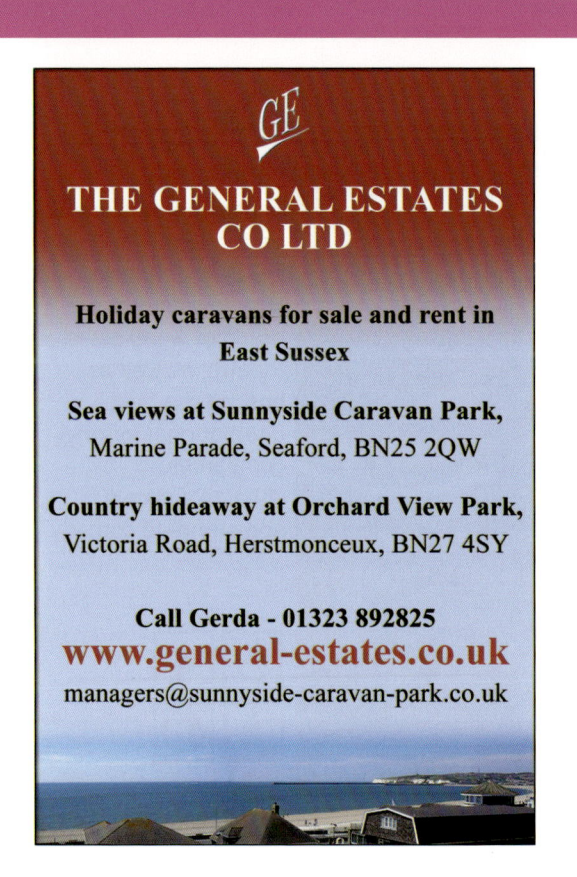

OpenBritain | South East

THE GENERAL ESTATES CO LTD

Holiday caravans for sale and rent in East Sussex

Sea views at Sunnyside Caravan Park,
Marine Parade, Seaford, BN25 2QW

Country hideaway at Orchard View Park,
Victoria Road, Herstmonceux, BN27 4SY

Call Gerda - 01323 892825
www.general-estates.co.uk
managers@sunnyside-caravan-park.co.uk

HAVANT & HAYLING ISLAND

If you are mobility impaired then Havant & Hayling Island is a wonderful place to visit, especially if you want to be beside the sea.

- Beach boardwalks for mobility impaired
- Specially designed picnic tables
- Radar key toilets
- Special parking areas
- Specially adapted beach huts for hire
- Variety of accommodation with range of access
- Topography suitable for wheelchairs

For a full colour brochure contact:
Hayling Island Visitor Centre,
Sea Front, Hayling Island PO11 0AG
Tel/Fax: 023 9246 7111
Email: tourism@havant.gov.uk
www.visithavant.co.uk

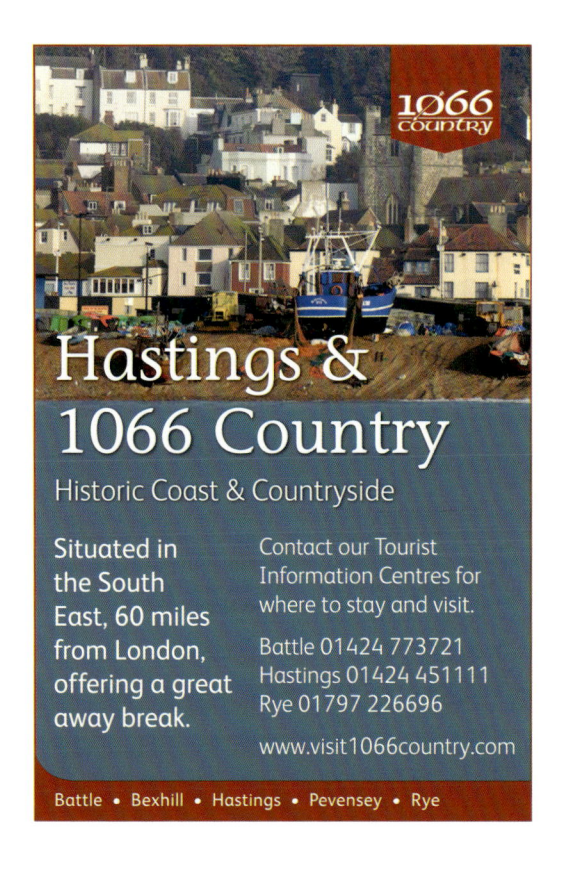

Hastings & 1066 Country

1066 country

Historic Coast & Countryside

Situated in the South East, 60 miles from London, offering a great away break.

Contact our Tourist Information Centres for where to stay and visit.
Battle 01424 773721
Hastings 01424 451111
Rye 01797 226696

www.visit1066country.com

Battle • Bexhill • Hastings • Pevensey • Rye

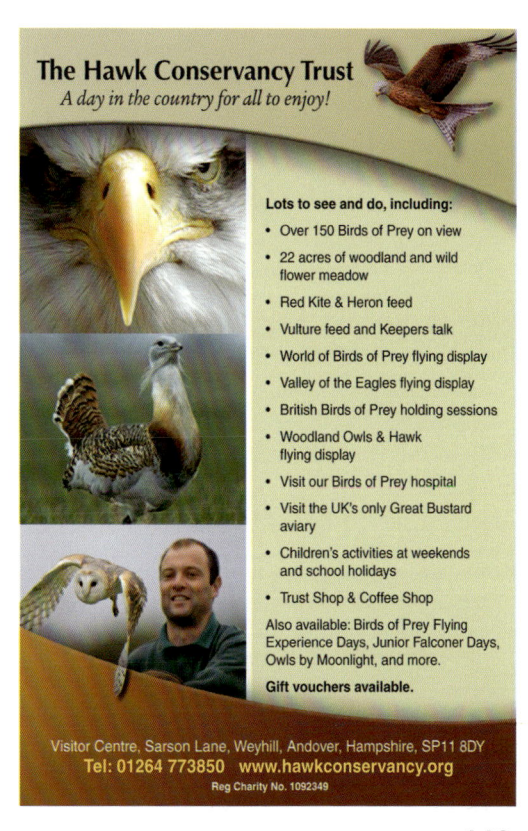

The Hawk Conservancy Trust
A day in the country for all to enjoy!

Lots to see and do, including:
- Over 150 Birds of Prey on view
- 22 acres of woodland and wild flower meadow
- Red Kite & Heron feed
- Vulture feed and Keepers talk
- World of Birds of Prey flying display
- Valley of the Eagles flying display
- British Birds of Prey holding sessions
- Woodland Owls & Hawk flying display
- Visit our Birds of Prey hospital
- Visit the UK's only Great Bustard aviary
- Children's activities at weekends and school holidays
- Trust Shop & Coffee Shop

Also available: Birds of Prey Flying Experience Days, Junior Falconer Days, Owls by Moonlight, and more.

Gift vouchers available.

Visitor Centre, Sarson Lane, Weyhill, Andover, Hampshire, SP11 8DY
Tel: 01264 773850   www.hawkconservancy.org
Reg Charity No. 1092460

OpenBritain | South East

Be Amazed...
The Look Out Discovery Centre

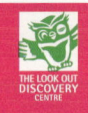

A Great Family Day Out, Whatever the Weather!

Hands on Science and Nature Exhibition - Over 80 Exhibits

Open Daily 10am - 5pm

- Children's Adventure Playground
- Coffee Shop
- 1,000 hectares of Crown Estate Woodland
- Gift Shop
- Mountain Bike Hire - Seasonal
- Free Car Parking

Hands-On Science Fun

HOW TO FIND US
Follow the brown tourist signs:-
Junction 10 off the M4 or Junction 3 off the M3
The Look Out Discovery Centre
Nine Mile Ride, Bracknell,
Berkshire, RG12 7QW
Tel: 01344 354400

www.bracknell-forest.gov.uk/be

---

the Nuffield southampton

Southampton's only professional producing theatre, creating it's own brand of world class theatre, as well as hosting the finest international touring companies, children's shows and stand-up comedy

023 8067 1771
www.nuffieldtheatre.co.uk

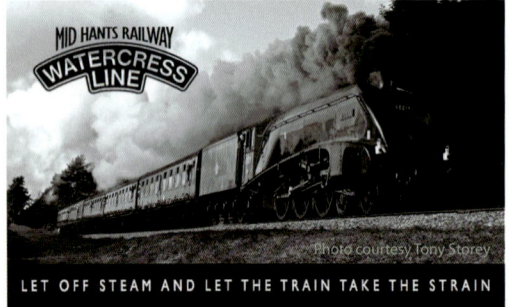

MID HANTS RAILWAY WATERCRESS LINE

Photo courtesy Tony Storey

LET OFF STEAM AND LET THE TRAIN TAKE THE STRAIN

WE ARE A DISABLED FRIENDLY RAILWAY WITH DISABLED FACILITIES AT ALTON, ROPLEY AND ALRESFORD STATIONS. FOR CUSTOMERS CONFINED TO A WHEELCHAIR OR WITH WALKING DIFFICULTIES, WE RECOMMEND YOU JOIN THE TRAIN AT ALRESFORD STATION WHERE THE PLATFORM ACCESS IS ON ONE LEVEL

DISABLED PARKING IS AVAILABLE AT ALRESFORD AND ALTON STATIONS

ONE CARER PER REGISTERED PERSON CAN ENTER FREE OF CHARGE WITH ONE FULL FARE PAYING DISABLED PERSON. FOR GROUPS OF 15+, PLEASE CALL RESERVATIONS FOR DISCOUNTED FARES

OPENING TIMES
WEEKENDS JANUARY TO NOVEMBER PUBLIC HOLIDAYS, HALF TERMS & SELECTED MID-WEEK DAYS FROM MAY TO SEPTEMBER

FINDING US
A31 WINCHESTER TO ALTON ROAD FROM M3 JUNCTION 9/10 OR SAT NAV ALRESFORD STATION, SO24 9JG

CONTACT US
T: 01962 733810
WWW.WATERCRESSLINE.CO.UK

PRESERVING HAMPSHIRE'S RAILWAY HERITAGE

Discover Royal Windsor

To get the most out of your stay visit the Royal Windsor Information Centre. Open 7 days a week, our friendly and knowledgeable staff are waiting to help.

Royal Windsor Information
www.windsor.gov.uk

INFORMATION HOTLINE 01753 743900
OR TO BOOK ACCOMMODATION 01753 743907

OpenBritain | South East

THE NATIONAL TRUST
Time well spent

Relaxing in stunning surroundings is time well spent

Sissinghurst

Biddenden Road
Cranbrook
Kent
TN17 2AB

Discover peace and tranquility within the walls of this exsquisite Garden

www.nationaltrust.org.uk/sissinghurstcastlegarden

Registered charity No: 205846

Winchester City Council

Public toilets are provided in the City Centre and surrounding area. All have facilities for disabled people.

The RADAR key scheme is in use and keys are available for loan or purchase from the Tourist Information Centre or the City Council's Offices, Colebrook Street.

For further information visit the Winchester City Council website **www.winchester.gov.uk**.

©Britainonview / Rod Edwards

OPEN BRITAIN — DECIDED WHERE TO GO? SEE ATTRACTIONS FOR WHAT TO DO
Ideas and information at the end of each regional section

165

OpenBritain | South East

Guildford Cathedral

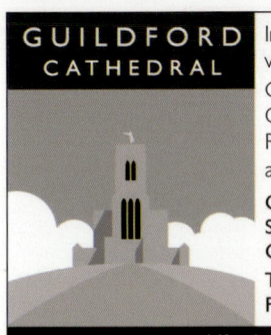

In a peaceful rural setting with spacious parking. Come and visit our lovely Cathedral, also our Restaurant, Gift Shop and Book Shop.

Guildford Cathedral
Stag Hill, Guildford
GU2 7UP
Tel: 01483 547860
Fax: 01483 303350

www.guildford-cathedral.org

Royal Military Police Museum

The Royal Military Police Museum located in the historic Southwick Park, the Museum traces the history of the Redcaps from their medieval origins to their current operations in Iraq and Afghanistan.

Open Mon - Fri 9:30 - 4:30 - visiting is strictly by appointment.

Tel 023 9228 4651 / 4372
FREE Admission

Hurley Riverside Park

- Family-run Park situated alongside the River Thames
- Ideal for visiting Legoland® Henley and Oxford
- Discounted tickets for Legoland, Thorpe Park & Chessington
- We welcome Motorhomes, Tourers & Tents
- Multi-service, hard-standing and electric hook-ups
- Shop, laundry, free showers, slipway, WiFi, fishing
- Fully serviced Caravan Holiday Homes and ReadyTents for hire

Tel: 01628 824493
Email: info@hurleyriversidepark.co.uk
Web: www.hurleyriversidepark.co.uk

OPENBRITAIN.NET

The one-stop-shop for all your travel needs.

Go online and see how we can help you get in, out ...and about.

Join today!

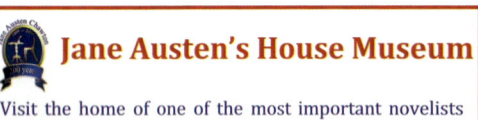

Jane Austen's House Museum

Visit the home of one of the most important novelists England has produced. This 17th century house tells the story of Jane Austen and her family and where she spent the last eight years of her life.

In this house Jane wrote Mansfield Park, Emma and Persuasion

Enquiries regarding Jane Austen's House Museum: Louise West
T: 01420 83262
Jane Austen's House Museum,
Chawton, Alton, Hants, GU34 1SD
www.jane-austens-house-museum.org.uk

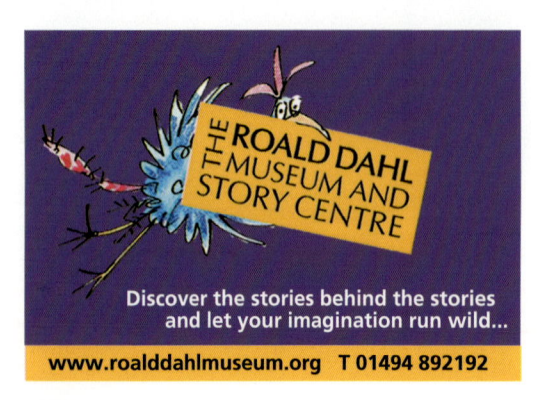

The Roald Dahl Museum and Story Centre

Discover the stories behind the stories and let your imagination run wild...

www.roalddahlmuseum.org   T 01494 892192

OPEN LONDON

Coming soon.... early 2010

The new **OpenLondon** guide is the definitive guide for visitors to London with access needs. The guide contains everything required to enjoy London to the full.

NEW

VISIT LONDON   MAYOR OF LONDON

LONDON DEVELOPMENT AGENCY   VISIT LONDON   MAYOR OF LONDON

www.openbritain.net | openlondon@hhgroup.co.uk | 01603 813740

OpenBritain | South East

BROOK MILLER
MOBILITY LIMITED

Brook Miller Mobility are more than just 'Motability Specialists', we are a company dedicated to providing solutions to a multitude of mobility problems. The company was built on foundations of customer care and professionalism. We believe the service and products we offer are without equal, our customers seem to think so too as they come back time after time.

Talk to Brook Miller Mobility, you'll discover people that listen and a depth of understanding that can only be achieved through years of dedication.

Brook Miller Motability, our reputation means everything to us and a great deal more to you.

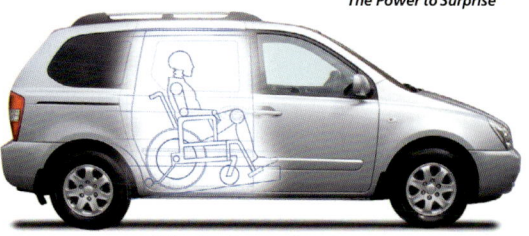

KIA MOTORS
The Power to Surprise

Kia Sedona Centro.
Long Floor Rear Access Wheelchair Vehicle

Kia Sedona Access.
Rear Access Wheelchair Vehicle

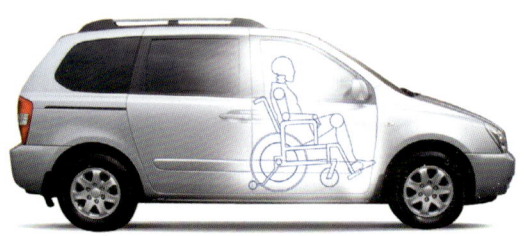

Kia Sedona Up Front Passenger:
Side Access

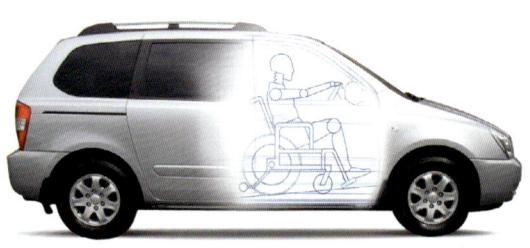

Kia Sedona Pilot: Drive From Wheelchair

FREE HOME DEMONSTRATION ON VEHICLES ANYWHERE IN THE UK MAINLAND

Unit 1A,
Elland Lane,
Elland, Halifax,
West Yorkshire,
HX5 9DZ

Motability

BROOK MILLER
MOBILITY LIMITED

FREEPHONE
0800 0644454
E-MAIL office@brookmiller.com

Opening Times:
Mon - Fri 9:00am - 5:30pm,
Sat 10:00am - 1:30pm

www.brookmiller.com

River Thames and London Eye

London - spoilt for choice!

Whatever your interests, you'll be spoilt for choice in London. From world-class museums, galleries and theatres to top sporting venues, there's plenty to keep you entertained.

See the Sights

London has an extensive travel network allowing you to get around easily. All public buses and Docklands Light Railway trains plus many of London's tours are accessible to wheelchair users. The Merlin Entertainments **London Eye** will take you graciously up into the sky giving dramatic views of the many landmarks on the River Thames and beyond.

Take a cruise down the Thames to get a different perspective. **City Cruises** and **Thames Clippers** are wheelchair accessible and provide a hassle-free way to soak up the atmosphere and navigate between the sites. Join **Original London Sightseeing Tours** open-top buses for an entertaining guide through the city past and present (a third of vehicles are wheelchair accessible).

Soak Up The Culture

London is a true culture capital with 70 large museums and over 30 major art galleries – with a good number providing enhanced access facilities. The **British Museum** offers sound guides and sign language interpreted tours giving you an insight into hundreds of years of world art and artefacts. Audio guides, Touch Tours and BSL interpreted events are all provided at the **Tate Modern**'s extensive modern art collection and **Tate Britain**'s collection of pieces from 1500 to the present. Visit the huge collection at **The Natural History Museum** including the magnificent Darwin Centre where you can see world-leading scientists at work and incredible specimens. The **Science Museum** offers hundreds of interactive exhibits and an IMAX 3D Cinema. Take an adventure through seafaring history at the **National Maritime Museum** in Greenwich. The **National Theatre**, Gold Award Winner for the Visit London Accessible Tourism Award 2008, produces theatre of international acclaim from classics to newly commissioned works.

OpenBritain | London

Wembley Stadium

British Museum

London

170	Tourist Information Centres
171	**Accommodation**

Sporting Triumphs and Musical Legends

How about a tour of the home of your sporting legends? Many clubs provide guided visits. Try the Arsenal **Emirates Stadium** which is fully wheelchair accessible or walk in the footsteps of your sporting heroes on the accessible **Wembley Stadium** tour.

If it's musical entertainment that you're after, **The O2** is a world class entertainment venue in the iconic Greenwich dome and home of the O2 arena which plays host to big name musical acts and sporting events throughout the year.

Retail Therapy and Relaxation

Westfield is the largest in-town shopping centre in Europe with over 265 shops and varied dining facilities. Shopmobility motorised scooters can be booked in advance and wheelchairs are available on site. In the West End, visit **Hamley's** on Regents Street – every child's dream with seven floors of toys and delights accessed by lift or escalator.

Finally, if you need time to relax after your hectic schedule, why not take some time in one of the Royal Parks such as **St James's** or **Regent's Park**. Take in the views and enjoy the cultivated gardens.

VISIT LONDON
VISITLONDON.COM

Get in touch

For general information and advice on accommodation:

Visit London

t 08701 566 366
e visitorinfo@visitlondon.com
web www.visitlondon.com

Accessible accommodation:
www.visitlondon.com/
accommodation/accessible/

www.openbritain.net

169

OpenBritain | London

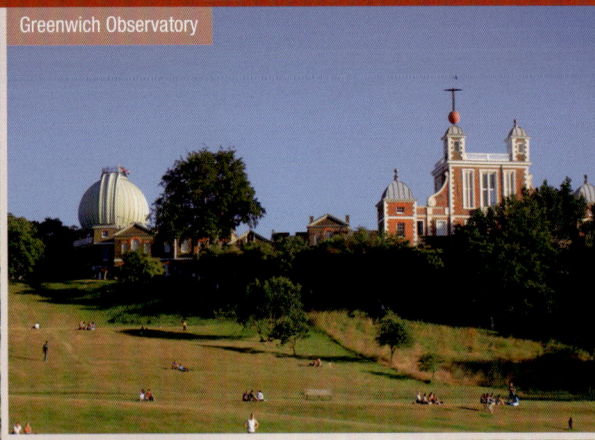

Greenwich Observatory

Regents Park

Natural History Museum

Tourist Information Centres

Tourist Information Centres are a mine of information about local and regional accommodation, attractions and events. Visit them when you arrive at your destination or contact them before you go:

Bexley Hall Place	Bourne Road	01322 558676	touristinfo@bexleyheritagetrust.co.uk
Britain & London Visitor Centre	1 Regent Street	0870 1566366	blvcinfo@visitbritain.org
City of London	St Paul's Churchyard	020 7332 1456	
Greenwich	46 Greenwich Church Street	0870 608 2000	
Harrow	Gayton Library	020 8427 6012	info@harrow.gov.uk
Holborn	Opp. Holborn tube station		
Kingston	Market Place	020 8547 5592	tourist.information@rbk.kingston.gov.uk
Lewisham	Lewisham Library	020 8297 8317	tic@lewisham.gov.uk
Richmond	Old Town Hall	020 8940 9125	info@visitrichmond.co.uk
Swanley	Swanley Library & Information Centre	01322 614660	touristinfo@swanley.org.uk
Twickenham	Civic Centre	020 8891 7272	info@visitrichmond.co.uk

www.openbritain.net

London | Inner London

London E14 | Radisson Edwardian Providence Wharf

Enjoy England ★★★★

Radisson Edwardian Providence Wharf, London E14 9PG
t 020 7987 2050 e resnpw@radisson.com
radissonedwardian.co.uk

London E16 | Crowne Plaza London - Docklands

AS

Royal Victoria Dock, Western Gateway, London E16 1AL
t 0207 055 2111
crowneplazadocklands.co.uk

Access: General: Room:

London SE2 | Abbey Wood Caravan Club Site

Enjoy England ★★★★★

(210) £14.60-£21.55
(210) £14.60-£21.55
(100)

210 touring pitches
Open: All year
Shop: <0.5 miles
Pub: 3 miles

Federation Road, Abbey Wood, London SE2 0LS
t 0208 311 7708
caravanclub.co.uk   2D2

It feels positively rural when you reach this verdant, gently sloping site with its mature trees and spacious grounds. This site is the ideal base for exploring the capital or nearby Greenwich, which offers its own blend of fascinating attractions.

Location: Turn off M2 at A221. Turn right into McLeod Road, right into Knee Hill. Site 2nd turning on right.

Access:
General:
Pitch:

London SE16 | YHA London Thameside

Enjoy England ★★

20 Salter Road, London SE16 5PR
t 0870 770 6010 e thameside@yha.org.uk
yha.org.uk

London SW6 | Jurys Inn Chelsea

Imperial Road, Imperial Wharf, London SW6 2GA
t 0207 411 2200 e jurysinnchelsea@jurysinns.com
jurysinns.com

Access: General: Room:

For symbols see pg 24   171

London | Inner London/Outer London

London SW7 | Holiday Inn London Kensington AS
AA ★★★★
London SW7 4DN
t 0871 9429100
lonhi-reservations@ihg.com

Access: General: Room:

London SW7 | Meininger City Hostel & Hotel London
Enjoy England ★★★★
65-67 Queen's Gate, London SW7 5JS
t 020 3051 8173   e welcome@meininger-hostels.com
meininger-hostels.com

London W1 | Holiday Inn London - Regents Park AS
AA ★★★★
Carburton Street, London W1W 5EE
holidayinn.co.uk

Access: General: Room:

London W1 | Holiday Inn London Mayfair
3 Berkeley Street, London W1J 8NE
t 020 7493 8282
holiday-inn.co.uk

Access: General: Room:

London W1 | YHA London Central
Enjoy England ★★★★
104-108 Bolsover Street, London W1W 6AB
yha.org.uk

London W3 | Express by Holiday Inn London - Park Royal AS
Victoria Road, London W3 6UP
hiexpress.co.uk

Access: General: Room:

London WC1 | Holiday Inn London - Bloomsbury
Coram Street, London WC1N 1HT
t +44 0 871 942 9222   e bloomsbury@ihg.com
holidayinn.com/bloomsbury

Access: General: Room:

Hounslow | Renaissance London Heathrow Hotel
AA ★★★★
Bath Road, Hounslow, Middlesex TW6 2AQ
t 020 8897 6363   e rhi.lhrbr.sales.reservations@renaissancehotels.com
renaissanceLondonheathrow.co.uk

Access: General: Room:

www.openbritain.net

London | Outer London

London | Holiday Inn London - Bexley AS
AA ★★★ Black Prince Interchange, Southwold Rd, Bexley DA5 1ND
t 01322 625579
holiday-inn.co.uk

Access: abc ... General: ... Room: ...

London, Newbury Park | Holiday Inn Express - Newbury Park, London
713 Eastern Avenue, London IG2 7RH
t 0871 423 4876
hiexpress.co.uk

Access: abc ... General: ... Room: ...

London - Kingston South | Holiday Inn London - Kingston South AS
Kingston Tower, Portsmouth Road, Surbiton, England KT6 5QQ
t +44 0 208 7866565
holidayinn.co.uk

Access: abc ... General: ... Room: ...

London NW2 | Holiday Inn Brent Cross AS
AA ★★★ Tilling Road, Brent Cross, London NW2 1LP
t 0870 4009112
holiday-inn.co.uk

Access: abc ... General: ... Room: ...

London SE19 | Crystal Palace Caravan Club Site
Enjoy England ★★★★★

🚐 (126) £14.60–£21.55
🚙 (126) £14.60–£21.55
⛺ (30)

126 touring pitches
Open: All year
Shop: 0.5 miles
Pub: 0.5 miles

Crystal Palace Parade, London SE19 1UF
t 0208 778 7155
caravanclub.co.uk   2D2

A busy but friendly site on the edge of a pleasant park with many attractions for children. In close proximity to all of London's attractions, Tower Bridge, Imperial War Museum, London Eye and Lords Tour to name but a few.

Location: Turn off A205 South Circular at West Dulwich into Croxted Road. The site is adjacent to television mast.

Access: ...
General: ...
Pitch: ...

For symbols see pg 24   173

London | Outer London/Attractions

Shepperton | Holiday Inn London Shepperton
AA ★★★★ Felix Lane, Shepperton, Middlesex TW17 8NP
t 01932 899988
holidayinn.co.uk

Access: General: Room:

West Drayton | Crowne Plaza Heathrow
AA ★★★★ Stockley Road, West Drayton, Middlesex UB7 9NA
t 01895 445555 e LONHA.reservations@ihg.com
crowneplaza.co.uk

Access: General: Room:

West Drayton | Holiday Inn London Heathrow   AS
Sipson Road, West Drayton, Middlesex UB7 0JU
t 0870 400 8595 e andreas.boettger@ichotelsgroup.com
holiday-inn.co.uk

Access: General: Room:

London E2 | Geffrye Museum
132 Kingsland Road, London E2 8EA
t 020 7739 9893 e info@geffrye-museum.org.uk
geffrye-museum.org.uk

London N1 | London Canal Museum
12-13 New Wharf Road, London N1 9RT
t 020 7713 0836 e webmaster@canalmuseum.org.uk
canalmuseum.org.uk

Access: General:

London N5 | Arsenal Football Club
Emirates Stadium, 75 Drayton Park, London N5 1BU
t 0207 619 5000
arsenal.com

London NW3 | Kenwood House
Open: For opening hours and prices, please call 0870 333 1181 or visit www.english-heritage.org.uk/properties

Hampstead, London NW3 7JR
t 0208 348 1286 e customers@english-heritage.org.uk
english-heritage.org.uk/kenwood

Make the most of the weekend and holidays with a free family day out.

Access: General:

174   www.openbritain.net

London | Attractions

London SE9 | Eltham Palace

Open: For opening hours and prices, please call 0870 333 1181 or visit www.english-heritage.org.uk/properties

Court Yard, Eltham, London SE9 5QE
t 0870 333 1181 e customers@english-heritage.org.uk

english-heritage.org.uk/elthampalace

A perfect day out for anyone interested in art, stylish interiors and grand gardens.

Access: 🚹♿ **General:** 🅿️

London SW1 | Houses Of Parliament

House Of Commons, Westminster, London SW1A 0AA
t 0207 2194 272

parliament.co.uk

London SW1 | Westminster Cathedral

42 Francis Street, London SW1P 1QW
t 020 7798 9055

westminstercathedral.org.uk

London W2 | Royal Parks

The Old Police House, Hyde Park, London W2 2UH
t 0207 298 2000 e MIler@royalparks.gsi.gov.uk

London W4 | Chiswick House & Gardens

Open: For opening hours and prices, please call 0870 333 1181 or visit www.english-heritage.org.uk/properties

Burlington Lane, Chiswick, London W4 2RP
t 0870 333 1181 e customers@english-heritage.org.uk

english-heritage.org.uk/chiswickhouse

A family friendly day out in London? A day trip to Chiswick House is perfect.

Access: 🚹♿ **General:** 🅿️

London WC2 | Donmar Warehouse Theatre

41 Earlham Street, Seven Dials, London WC2H 9LX
t 0844 871 7624

donmarwarehouse.com

For symbols see pg 24

175

London | **Attractions**

London | Marble Hill House

Open: For opening hours and prices, please call 0870 333 1181 or visit www.english-heritage.org.uk/ properties

Richmond Road, Twickenham, London TW1 2NL
t 0870 333 1181   e customers@english-heritage.org.uk
english-heritage.org.uk/marblehillhouse

Built as a retreat from the hustle and bustle, the perfect spot for afternoon tea.

Access: abc ♿ ♿   **General:** P♿ 🔲 ✿ ♿

London Canal Museum

176   www.openbritain.net

OpenBritain | London

Explore
Lee Valley Regional Park

The Lee Valley Regional Park is 10,000 acres of award-winning parklands and sports venues just waiting to be discovered.

From ice skating, horse riding, golf and birdwatching in East London to the tranquillity and peaceful surroundings of River Lee Country Park in Essex, where you can walk and cycle for miles on many accessible pathways or relax by the river with a picnic - we really do have something for everyone. Want to stay longer? We have two campsites and there's a Youth Hostel too.

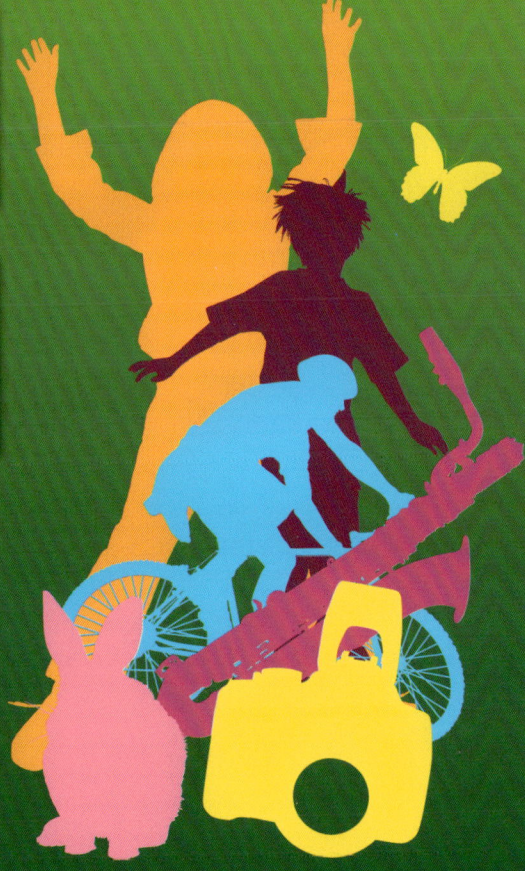

Easy access from the North Circular and M25 or trains from Liverpool Street.

08456 770 600
www.leevalleypark.org.uk

Lee Valley Park
Open spaces and sporting places

Immerse yourself in natural beauty in the heart of London

DisabledGo guides are available at
www.royalparks.org.uk

The Royal Parks are: Bushy Park, The Green Park, Greenwich Park, Hyde Park, Kensington Gardens, The Regent's Park & Primrose Hill, Richmond Park, St James's Park

THE ROYAL PARKS

OpenBritain | London

COPTHORNE TARA HOTEL

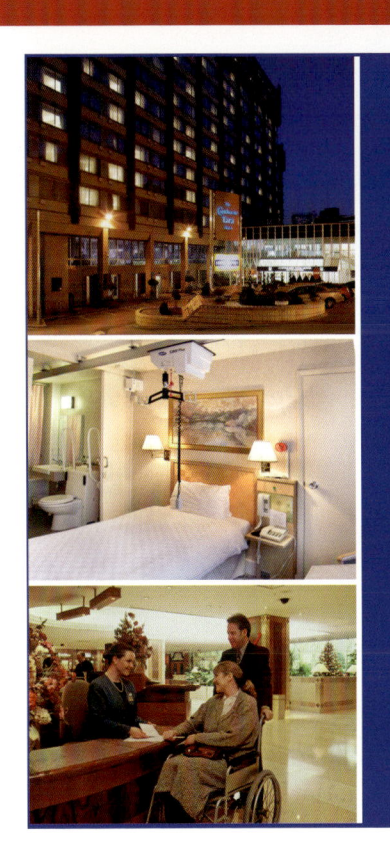

Proud to be one of the UK's award-winning hotels for providing high specification specially accessible bedrooms and hotel facilities

- Hotel fully accessible
- Disabled parking available
- Connecting rooms for carer or family members
- 2 rooms with electric ceiling hoist systems
- Bedside control panel for TV, Radio & Light
- Close-O-Mat automatic toilet

Copthorne Tara Hotel London Kensington
Scarsdale Place, Kensington. London W8 5SR
T: 020 7872 2000 | F: 020 7937 7211
E: reservations.tara@millenniumhotels.co.uk
www.millenniumhotels.co.uk/tara

MILLENNIUM
HOTELS AND RESORTS
MILLENNIUM • COPTHORNE

Guildhall Art Gallery

An historic collection in a modern building, purpose-built for disability access.

Re-opened in 1999, Guildhall Art Gallery displays London subjects and portraits from the 17th century to the present day and a fine collection of Victorian paintings including works by Constable, Landseer, Tissot and the Pre-Raphaelites. In addition there is a programme of temporary exhibitions. The remains of Roman London's amphitheatre are also on view.

Guildhall Art Gallery
Guildhall Yard London EC2V 5AE

Open Monday-Saturday 10am-5pm (last admission 4.30pm)
Sunday noon-4pm (last admission 3.45pm)

Telephone: 020 7332 3700
Textphone: 020 7332 3803
Fax: 020 7332 2242
email: guildhall.artgallery@cityoflondon.gov.uk
website: www.guildhall-art-gallery.org.uk

CITY OF LONDON

Dante Gabriel Rossetti: *La Ghirlandata*, 1873

OpenBritain | London

National Theatre
Accessible and welcoming to all.

- Audio-described and captioned performances
- FREE synopsis and CD programme notes
- Regular touch tours
- NEW initiative for partially hearing people to enjoy backstage tours
- Ticket concessions for disabled people

Tickets £12 plus companion at the same price.

Join our free mailing list for regular updates access@nationaltheatre.org.uk
Box Office 020 7452 3000 • **Information** 020 7452 3400
boxoffice@nationaltheatre.org.uk • **Fax** 020 7452 3030

ARTS COUNCIL ENGLAND

A warm welcome…

At the Renaissance London Heathrow Hotel, we understand it's the small things that make a big difference. With the Lobby, Concierge, restaurant, bar and Reception all on the ground floor, specially designed disabled bedrooms and bathrooms, and friendly staff; your stay is bound to be comfortable and enjoyable with us.

Awaiting your arrival…

For each disabled room booked and stayed in on a Friday, Saturday or Sunday until 31st December 2010 you will receive a complimentary bottle of house wine in your room.

To take advantage of this offer please call 020 8897 6363 and ask for Internal Reservations quoting OBG10. Alternatively you can email the hotel's Internal Reservations department on rhi.lhrbr.sales.reservations@renaissancehotels.com please remember to quote OBG10.

Renaissance London Heathrow Hotel Bath Road, Hounslow, Middlesex TW6 2AQ
Tel: 020 8897 6363   Fax: 020 8897 1113   www.renaissancelondonheathrow.co.uk

London Borough of Barking & Dagenham

Barking & Dagenham Leisure Centre Services

For all your Health and Fitness Needs

Abbey Sports Centre
Axe Street
Barking IG11 7LX
Telephone: 020 8270 6800

Dagenham Swimming Pool
Althorne Way
Dagenham RM10 7AY
Telephone: 020 8270 6600

Wood Lane Sports Centre
Wood Lane
Dagenham RM8 1JX
Telephone: 020 8270 6880

Goresbrook Leisure Centre
Ripple Road
Dagenham RM9 6XW
Telephone: 020 8227 3976

Greenwich
where time begins!

Greenwich is just a short hop by rail or river from the centre of London. • A World Heritage Site and famous for the Royal Observatory, and home of Greenwich Mean Time. • Stay longer to explore nearby attractions at The O_2, Eltham Palace and the Royal Arsenal.

Greenwich Tourist Information Centre
46 Greenwich Church Street,
London SE10 9BL
Tel: 0870 608 2000
Email: tic@greenwich.gov.uk
From early 2010, our location changes to:
Pepys Building, 2 Cutty Sark Gardens,
London SE10 9LW

Host venue to London 2012 Olympic and Paralympic Games

www.greenwichwhs.org.uk

Greenwich Council

Explore 400 years of English Homes and Gardens at London's Geffrye Museum

- Period rooms and gardens from 1600 to the present day
- Accessible displays and toilets
- Free talks, handling sessions and art workshops in BSL or for blind and partially-sighted visitors
- Two parking bays for disabled visitors

Admission Free
136 Kingsland Road, London E2 8EA
Tel: 020 7739 9893
www.geffrye-museum.org.uk

HORNIMAN MUSEUM
London Visitor Attraction Silver Award 2007

Explore Your World

Discover world cultures, music and environments plus an acclaimed new Aquarium, all set in 16 acres of beautiful Gardens. Facilities for people with disabilities include lift access to all spaces and pre-booked on-site parking.

Open daily
10.30am – 5.30pm

100 London Road • Forest Hill • London SE23
Tel 020 8699 1872 • www.horniman.ac.uk

OpenBritain | London

Discover the LONDON CANAL MUSEUM

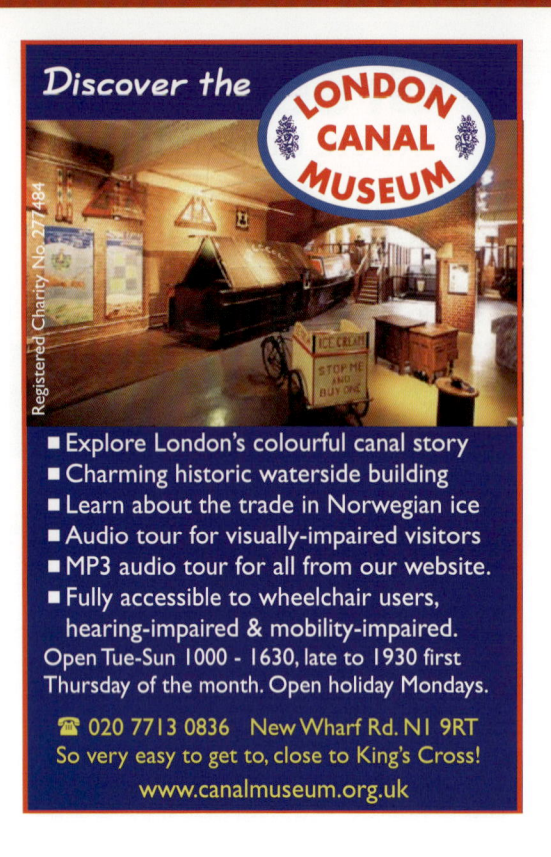

Registered Charity No 277484

- Explore London's colourful canal story
- Charming historic waterside building
- Learn about the trade in Norwegian ice
- Audio tour for visually-impaired visitors
- MP3 audio tour for all from our website.
- Fully accessible to wheelchair users, hearing-impaired & mobility-impaired.

Open Tue-Sun 1000 - 1630, late to 1930 first Thursday of the month. Open holiday Mondays.

☎ 020 7713 0836   New Wharf Rd. N1 9RT
So very easy to get to, close to King's Cross!

www.canalmuseum.org.uk

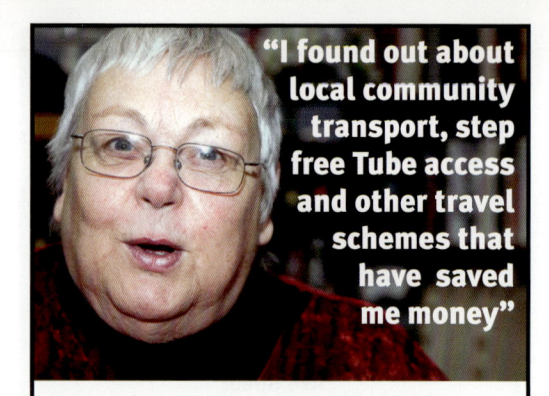

"I found out about local community transport, step free Tube access and other travel schemes that have saved me money"

We provide free expert advice and information on all transport benefits and services.

Call us on 020 7737 2339 or email contactus@transportforall.org.uk
www.transportforall.org.uk

Transportforall
Accessible transport is our right

HOUSES of PARLIAMENT
Summer Opening 2010

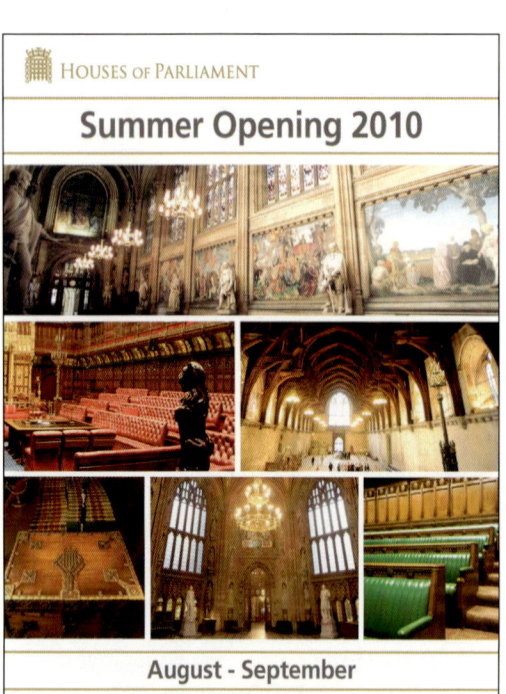

August - September

Tickets on sale February 2010
Please call +44 (0)844 847 1672 for further information
For groups call +44 (0)844 847 2498
or visit: www.ticketmaster.co.uk/housesofparliament

ticketmaster

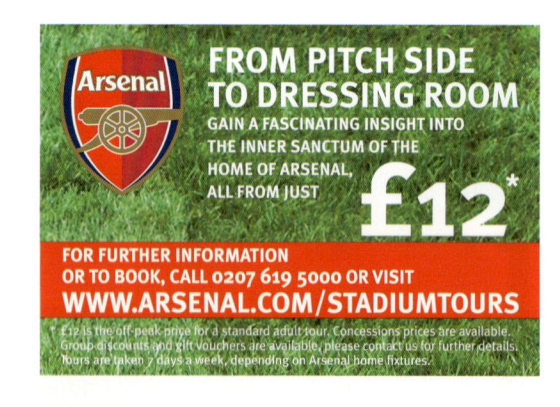

FROM PITCH SIDE TO DRESSING ROOM

GAIN A FASCINATING INSIGHT INTO THE INNER SANCTUM OF THE HOME OF ARSENAL, ALL FROM JUST £12*

FOR FURTHER INFORMATION OR TO BOOK, CALL 0207 619 5000 OR VISIT
WWW.ARSENAL.COM/STADIUMTOURS

*£12 is the off-peak price for a standard adult tour. Concessions prices are available. Group discounts and gift vouchers are available, please contact us for further details. Tours are taken 7 days a week, depending on Arsenal home fixtures.

DONMAR

For every production the Donmar Warehouse provides a signed, audio-described & captioned performance.

donmarwarehouse.com/access
020 7845 5822
Donmar, Covent Garden WC2H 9LX

OpenBritain | London

London Borough of Redbridge

London Borough of Redbridge is pleased to support the "OpenBritain 2010 Guidebook"

For information and where to find about our public conveniences, please go to

www.redbridge.gov.uk

OPEN BRITAIN — Join today!

The one-stop-shop for all your travel needs.

Go online and see how we can help you get in, out ...and about.

- Fully searchable database of accommodation, days out and where to eat and drink
- MyOpenBritain trip planner
- User reviews, blog and forums

OPENBRITAIN.NET

WESTMINSTER CATHEDRAL

one of London's greatest secrets...

Westminster Cathedral is the mother-church of the Roman Catholic Archdiocese of Westminster

Open from 7:00am to 7:00pm Monday-Saturday

The Cathedral closes after 7:00pm Mass on Sunday and after 5:30pm Mass on Public Holidays.

We do not charge for admission.

For Mass times and more information please visit our website:

www.westminstercathedral.org.uk

NATIONAL FEDERATION OF Shopmobility 2009/2010

The directory of Shopmobility Schemes in the UK, Channel Islands & ROI

Get trained - Get out - Get independent

The Shopmobility experience is not just about shopping!

www.shopmobilityuk.org

OpenBritain | East of England

King's College, Cambridge

Discover the unexpected pleasures and treasures of the East of England

Watch swan-white sails and cotton wool clouds racing over the rippling waters of The Broads. Drift along 'The Backs' in a punt past the manicured lawns and medieval colleges of historic Cambridge. Stroll from castle to ancient churches in the cobbled streets of Norwich. Freewheel down country lanes bordered with scarlet poppies, stopping off for a well-earned pint of real ale at a half-timbered inn.

Get a fascinating glimpse of Her Majesty the Queen's life 'off-duty' at **Royal Sandringham**, and of the treasures of a mystery Saxon king in the burial ship at **Sutton Hoo**.

Step into an 18th C. landscape painting in Constable Country. The water meadows, river and mill are all there still, just as the Great Master painted them. Or follow in the footsteps of those magnificent men in their flying machines with a visit to the **Imperial War Museum Duxford**. Whatever your interest, you'll find something to fascinate you in this unspoilt and very special corner of England.

Beautiful coastline, unspoilt countryside, historic cities and fascinating heritage, the East of England has it all, plus a unique and charmingly quirky character which is all its own. It's a short train ride from the bright lights and frenetic twenty first century life of London into another more serene and peaceful world, a world where time takes a breather. In fact, it slows down so much that snail racing is a popular sport in the village of Grimston (nr. King's Lynn) in Norfolk. And you may well come across a steam train or a traction engine puffing gently along through the untroubled countryside.

The East coast offers something for everyone from the excitement of **Southend-on-Sea** to the lonely curlew's cry on the salt marshes of North Norfolk and Suffolk. Childhood memories spring into life in old-fashioned seaside havens like **Sheringham** and **Southwold**, while sleek yachts and sturdy fishing smacks jostle for position in picturesque ports. Hire a boat and sail off into the sunset on a reed-fringed **Broad** or explore the peaceful waterways of **The Fens** on a traditional narrow boat. ▶

www.openbritain.net

OpenBritain | East of England

Marshes at Brancaster Staithe

Luton Carnival

East of England

Bedfordshire
Cambridgeshire
Essex
Hertfordshire
Norfolk
Suffolk

▶ Get on your bike and pedal off on almost car-free roads, stopping off to explore little towns and villages. Rest in the cool stillness of medieval churches and revel in the kaleidoscopic colours of country gardens. Follow in the footsteps of Kings and Queens to sumptuous stately homes and palaces like **Woburn Abbey**, **Hatfield House** and **Knebworth House**.

Or why not take a few days' city break just shopping and sightseeing? You'll find even the cities in the East are more laid back than others in the rest of England. **Norwich** is a treat with its Norman castle, cathedral and its medieval market place - plus it is in the top ten shopping destinations in the UK. **Cambridge** - a treasure house with its unique academic ambience and medieval architecture, and little **Ely** a delight, sitting demurely beneath its triumphant cathedral. Wherever you go, keep an eye out for the East of England's magic ingredient - a quirky individuality that's been around for centuries. It pops up unexpectedly in an extravagant folly, an eccentric tradition, a weird and wonderful tale. This all adds an extra piquancy to the feast of treats waiting for you in the East of England.

Find out more

web www.visiteastofengland.com

Southend Pier

www.openbritain.net

Hatfield House

Tourist Information Centres

Tourist Information Centres are a mine of information about local and regional accommodation, attractions and events. Visit them when you arrive at your destination or contact them before you go:

Aldeburgh	152 High Street	01728 453637	atic@suffolkcoastal.gov.uk
Aylsham	Bure Valley Railway	01263 733903	aylsham.tic@broadland.gov.uk
Beccles	The Quay	01502 713196	becclesinfo@broads-authority.gov.uk
Bedford	Old Town Hall	01234 221712	touristInfo@bedford.gov.uk
Bishop's Stortford	2 Market Square	01279 655831	tic@bishopsstortford.org
Braintree	Town Hall Centre	01376 550066	tic@braintree.gov.uk
Brentwood	Pepperell House	01277 200300	michelle.constable@brentwood.gov.uk
Burnham on Crouch	1 High Street	01621 784962	burnhamtic@one-place.org.uk
Bury St Edmunds	6 Angel Hill	01284 764667	tic@stedsbc.gov.uk
Cambridge	Peas Hill	01223 457577	info@visitcambridge.co.uk
Chelmsford	8 Dukes Walk	01245 283400	chelmsfordvisitor.information@firstgroup.com
Clacton	Town Hall	01255 686633	clactontic@tendring.gov.uk
Colchester	1 Queen Street	01206 282920	vic@colchester.gov.uk
Cromer	Louden Road	0871 200 3071	cromerinfo@north-norfolk.gov.uk
Deepdale Information	Deepdale Farm	01485 210256	info@deepdalefarm.co.uk
Diss	Meres Mouth	01379 650523	dtic@s-norfolk.gov.uk

Downham Market	The Priory Centre	01366 383287	downham-market.tic@west-norfolk.gov.uk
Dunstable	Priory House	01582 890270	tic@dunstable.gov.uk
Ely	Oliver Cromwell's House	01353 662062	tic@eastcambs.gov.uk
Felixstowe	91 Undercliff Road West	01394 276770	ftic@suffolkcoastal.gov.uk
Flatford	Flatford Lane	01206 299460	flatfordvic@babergh.gov.uk
Great Yarmouth	Maritime House	01493 846346	tourism@great-yarmouth.gov.uk
Harwich	Iconfield Park	01255 506139	harwichtic@btconnect.com
Hertford	10 Market Place	01992 584322	tic@hertford.gov.uk
Holt	3 Pound House	0871 200 3071	holtinfo@north-norfolk.gov.uk
Hoveton	Station Road	01603 782281	hoveton.info@broads-authority.gov.uk
Hunstanton	Town Hall	01485 532610	hunstanton.tic@west-norfolk.gov.uk
Ipswich	St Stephen's Church	01473 258070	tourist@ipswich.gov.uk
King's Lynn	The Custom House	01553 763044	kings-lynn.tic@west-norfolk.gov.uk
Lavenham	Lady Street	01787 248207	lavenhamtic@babergh.gov.uk
Letchworth Garden City	33-35 Station Road	01462 487868	tic@letchworth.com
Lowestoft	East Point Pavilion	01502 533600	touristinfo@waveney.gov.uk
Luton	Luton Central Library	01582 401579	touristinformation@luton.gov.uk
Maldon	Wenlock Way	01621 856503	tic@maldon.gov.uk
Newmarket	Palace House	01638 667200	tic.newmarket@forest-heath.gov.uk
Norwich	The Forum	01603 213999	tourism@norwich.gov.uk
Peterborough	3-5 Minster Precincts	01733 452336	tic@peterborough.gov.uk
Saffron Walden	1 Market Place	01799 524002	tourism@saffronwalden.gov.uk
Sandy	10 Cambridge Road	01767 682728	tourism@sandytowncouncil.gov.uk
Sheringham	Station Approach	0871 200 3071	sheringhaminfo@north-norfolk.gov.uk
Southend-On-Sea	Pier Entrance	01702 215620	vic@southend.gov.uk
Southwold	69 High Street	01502 724729	southwold.tic@waveney.gov.uk
St Albans	Town Hall	01727 864511	tic@stalbans.gov.uk
St Neots	The Old Court	01480 388788	stneots.tic@huntsdc.gov.uk
Mid Suffolk	Museum of East Anglian Life	01449 676800	tic@midsuffolk.gov.uk
Sudbury	Town Hall	01787 881320	sudburytic@babergh.gov.uk
Waltham Abbey	2-4 Highbridge Street	01992 652295	tic@walthamabbey-tc.gov.uk
Wells-next-the-Sea	Staithe Street	0871 200 3071	wellsinfo@north-norfolk.gov.uk
Wisbech	2-3 Bridge Street	01945 583263	tourism@fenland.gov.uk
Witham	Town Hall	01376 502674	ticwitham@braintree.gov.uk
Woodbridge	Station Buildings	01394 382240	wtic@suffolkcoastal.gov.uk
Wymondham	Market Cross	01953 604721	wymondhamtic@btconnect.com

East of England | Bedfordshire/Cambridgeshire

Sandy | Acorn Cottage

Enjoy England ★★★★
Units: 4   Sleeps: 2–8
Open: All year

Low season p/w:
£250.00
High season p/w:
£800.00

Mrs Margaret Codd, Highfield Farm, Tempsford Road, Sandy SG19 2AQ   t 01767 682332   e margaret@highfield-farm.co.uk

highfield-farm.co.uk   2D1

Converted barn in a courtyard on an arable farm. Wooden floors on one level throughout.

General: ... Unit: ...

Sandy | Holiday Inn Garden Court

AA   ★★★

Girtford Bridge, London Road, Sandy, Bedfordshire SG19 1NA
t 01767 692220   e sandysales@holidayinns.co.uk

holidayinn.co.uk

Access: ...   General: ...   Room: ...

Cambridge | Cherry Hinton Caravan Club Site

Enjoy England ★★★★★

(60)   £12.00–£17.75
(60)   £12.00–£17.75
(6)

60 touring pitches
Open: All year

Shop: 0.8 miles
Pub: <0.5 miles

Lime Kiln Road, Cherry Hinton, Cambridge CB1 8NQ
t 01223 244088

caravanclub.co.uk   2D1

Imaginatively landscaped site set in old quarry, bordered by nature trail and set within an area of SSI. It's a ten minute bus journey from site into the city centre. Take a guided walk or punt along the River Cam.

Location: Head to Fulbourn on A11. At roundabout in Fulbourn head to Cambridge. Left at trafficlights. Left into Lime Kiln Road.

Access: ...
General: ...
Pitch: ...

Cambridge | Crowne Plaza Cambridge

AA   ★★★★

Downing Street, Cambridge, Cambridgeshire CB2 3DT
t 0871 942 9180   e reservations-cpcambridge@ihg.com

crowneplaza.com/cambridgeuk

Access: ...   General: ...   Room: ...

East of England | **Cambridgeshire**

Huntingdon | **Houghton Mill Caravan Club Site** THE CARAVAN CLUB

Enjoy England ★★★★

Mill Street, Houghton, Huntingdon, Cambridgeshire PE28 2AZ
t 01480 466716

(65) £13.70–£19.55
(65) £13.70–£19.55
(8)

caravanclub.co.uk

3A2

65 touring pitches
Open: 3rd April - 9 November

Shop: 0.5 miles
Pub: 0.5 miles

Situated on the banks of the Great Ouse with spectacular views across to the National Trust's Houghton Mill with milling demonstrations every Sunday. There's an abundance of footpaths and bridleways for walkers, horse riders and cyclists.

Location: Continue through market square of Houghton Village into Mill Street, church on right. Site entrance on left before last house.

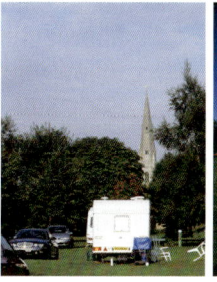

Access:
General:
Pitch:

Little Downham | **Wood Fen Lodge**

Enjoy England ★★★

6 Black Bank Road, Little Downham, Ely CB6 2UA
t 01353 862495 e info@woodfenlodge.co.uk

woodfenlodge.co.uk

©Britainonview – Britain on View

GETTING THERE IS NOT A PROBLEM!

OPEN BRITAIN

See Getting there….. and back section (p364)
Everything you need for a hassle-free journey

For symbols see pg 24

189

East of England | Cambridgeshire/Essex

Peterborough | Ferry Meadows Caravan Club Site

Enjoy England ★★★★★

🚐 (252) £13.70–£19.55
🚍 (252) £13.70–£19.55
⛺ (6)

252 touring pitches
Open: All year

Shop: 1 mile
Pub: <0.5 miles

Ham Lane, Peterborough, Cambridgeshire PE2 5UU
t 01733 233526

caravanclub.co.uk   3A1

The perfect family holiday site, ideally located in a country park with steam trains, lake, cycle and walking trails and many sporting facilities. Enjoy sailing, windsurfing and fishing or head to Peterborough for ice skating, bowling, shopping and theatre.

Location: From any direction, on approaching Peterborough, follow the brown signs to Nene Park and Ferry Meadows.

Access:
General:
Pitch:

St Ives | The Raptor Foundation

Mrs Elizabeth Blows, Chief Executive, The Heath, St Ives Road, Woodhurst, Cambridgeshire PE28 3BT   t 01487 741140   e heleowl@aol.com

raptorfoundation.org.uk

Access: abc   General: Unit:

Wisbech St. Mary | Common Right Barns

Enjoy England ★★★★

Mrs Teresa Fowler, Common Right Barns, Plash Drove, Tholomas Drove, Peterborough PE13 4SP   t 01945 410424   e teresa@commonrightbarns.co.uk

commonrightbarns.co.uk

Ashdon | Hill Farm Holiday Cottages

Enjoy England ★★★

Mrs Annette Bel, Hill Farm Holiday Cottages, Radwinter Road, Ashdon, Saffron Walden CB10 2ET   t 01799 584881
e hillfarm-holiday-cottages@hotmail.co.uk

hillfarm-holiday-cottages.co.uk

Basildon | Holiday Inn Basildon

AA ★★★

Waterfront Walk, Basildon, Essex SS14 3DG
t 0870 400 9003   e reservations.basildon@ihg.com

holiday-inn.co.uk

AS

Access: abc   General: Room:

East of England | **Essex**

Bradfield | **Curlews**

AS

Enjoy England ★★★★
Open: All year

Rooms per night:
s: £50.00–£60.00
d: £60.00–£75.00

Shop: 1 mile
Pub: <0.5 miles

Station Road, Bradfield, Manningtree CO11 2UP
t 01255 870890 e margherita@curlewsaccommodation.co.uk
curlewsaccommodation.co.uk

3C2

Experience accommodation at its best. Luxury single, double and twin B&B rooms plus in addition customised self-catering suite to NAS M2 standard. Most rooms with views over the Stour estuary and farmland.

Location: Take A120 towards Harwich turning left at Horsley Cross onto B1035. Turn right at TV mast 1½ miles to Curlews.

Access:
General:
Room:

Brentwood | **Holiday Inn Brentwood**

AA ★★★

Brook Street, Brentwood, Essex CM14 5NF
t 0870 400 9012 e brentwoodm25@ihg.com
holiday-inn.co.uk

Access: General: Room:

Chelmsford | **Boswell House Hotel**

Enjoy England ★★

118/120 Springfield Road, Chelmsford CM2 6LF
t 01245 287587 e boswell118@aol.com
boswellhousehotel.co.uk

Chigwell | **Vitalise Jubilee Lodge**

AS

Grange Farm, High Road, Chigwell, Essex IG7 6DP
t 020 8501 2331 e jubileelodge@vitalise.org.uk
vitalise.org.uk

Access: General: Room:

HUDSONs

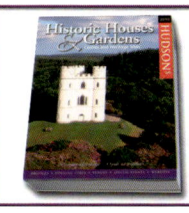

Hudson's is the definitive guide to historic houses & gardens.

Up to date information on over 2000 properties with clear information symbols for accessibility and facilities.

Historic Houses & Gardens
Castles and Heritage Sites

Order online at:
www.hhgroup.co.uk/hudsons

For symbols see pg 24

East of England | **Essex**

Clacton-On-Sea | Groomhill

Units: 1 Sleeps: 7
Open: All year

Low season p/w:
£240.00

High season p/w:
£540.00

Livability Self catering holidays, PO Box 36, Cowbridge, Vale of Glamorgan CF71 7TN
t 08456 584478   f 01446 775060   e selfcatering@livability.org.uk

livability.org.uk 3B3

Our adapted 3 bedroom bungalow is set in a quiet part of Clacton-on-Sea.

Access:
General: Unit:

Halstead | The White Hart

Enjoy England   ★★★

15 High Street, Halstead CO9 2AA
t 01787 475657

innpubs.co.uk

Mersea Island | Waldegraves, Holiday Park

AA   ★★★★
Enjoy England   ★★★★

Units: 16   Sleeps: 6
Open: March - November

Low season p/w:
£220.00

High season p/w:
£450.00

Shop: <0.5 miles
Pub: <0.5 miles

Mersea Island, Colchester, Essex CO5 8SE
t 01206 382898   e holidays@waldegraves.co.uk

waldegraves.co.uk 3B3

16 luxury holiday homes, wheelchair friendly, available to hire for week, midweek and weekend breaks. This is fully self catering consisting of 2 bedrooms, sleeps 5, lounge, dining area, wc & shower. Level grassed camping and caravan pitches available.

Location: B1025 to Mersea, take left towards East Mersea. Take second turning on right follow tourist board signs to Waldegraves.

Access:

General:

Unit:

Saffron Walden | Fishermans Lodge

Mrs Westerhuis, Rockells Farm, Duddenhoe End, nr. Saffron Walden, Essex CB11 4UY   t 01763 838053

General: Unit:

East of England | Essex/Hertfordshire/Norfolk

St. Osyth | The Cartlodge at Lee Wick Farm
Enjoy England ★★★★ Mr Robert Clarke, The Cartlodge, The Barn, Lee Wick Lane, St Osyth, Clacton-on-Sea CO16 8ES t 01255 823031 e info@leewickfarm.co.uk
leewickfarm.co.uk

Walton on the Naze | Bufo Villae Guest House
Enjoy England ★★★★ 31 Beatrice Road, Walton-on-the-Naze, Frinton-on-Sea CO14 8HJ
t 01255 672644 e bufovillae@btinternet.com
bufovillae.co.uk

Cheshunt | YHA Lee Valley Village
Enjoy England ★★★★ Windmill Lane, Cheshunt, Waltham Cross EN8 9AJ
t 01992 628392 e leevalley@yha.org.uk
yha.org.uk

Hemel Hempstead | Holiday Inn Hemel Hempstead
AA ★★★ Breakspear Way, Hemel Hempstead, Hertfordshire HP2 4UA
t 0870 400 9041 e hemelhempsteadm1@ihg.com
holiday-inn.co.uk

Access: abc **General:** **Room:**

Stevenage | Holiday Inn Stevenage
AA ★★★★ St George's Way, Stevenage SG1 1HS
t +44 01438 722727 e info@histevenage.com
holidayinn.co.uk

Access: abc **General:** **Room:**

Aylmerton | Roman Camp Inn
Enjoy England ★★★ Holt Road, Aylmerton, Sheringham NR11 8QD
t 01263 838291 e enquiries@romancampinn.co.uk
romancampinn.co.uk

Access: abc **General:** **Room:**

Bacton | Primrose Cottage
Enjoy England ★★★ Mr & Mrs Allen Epton, Primrose Cottage, Coast Road, Bacton, Norwich NR12 0EW t 01692 650667 e holiday@cablegap.co.uk
cablegap.co.uk

Beeston | Holmdene Farm
Enjoy England ★★★ Mrs Gaye Davidson, Holmdene Farm, Syers Lane, Beeston, King's Lynn PE32 2NJ t 01328 701284
holmdenefarm.co.uk

For symbols see pg 24

East of England | Norfolk

Cromer | Seacroft Caravan Club Site

Enjoy England ★★★★★

🚐 (130) £14.60–£23.20
🚓 (130) £14.60–£23.20
⛺ (30)

130 touring pitches
Open: 3 April – 4 January
Shop: 1 mile

Access:
General:
Pitch:

Runton Road, Cromer, Norfolk NR27 9NJ
t 01263 514938

caravanclub.co.uk   3C1

Ideal site for a family holiday with leisure complex including bar, restaurant, entertainment plus an outdoor heated swimming pool. The surrounding area offers plenty to attract all ages, including golf, sea and fresh water fishing and birdwatching.

Location: Turn left off A149 (Cromer-Sheringham). Site entrance on left in 1 mile.

Diss | Ivy House Farm Cottages (Owl Cottage)

Enjoy England ★★★★
Units: 1   Sleeps: 1–7
Open: All year
Low season p/w: £580.00
High season p/w: £1100.00

Paul Bradley, Owner, Wortham, Diss, Norfolk IP22 1RD
t 01379 898395   e prjsbrad@aol.com

ivyhousefarmcottages.co.uk

The lounge and bedroom open by french windows onto the garden that surrounds Owl Cottage.

Access: General: Unit:

East Harling | Berwick Cottage

Enjoy England ★★★★

Mrs Miriam Toosey, Berwick Cottage, The Lin Berwick Trust, Upper East Street, Sudbury CO10 1UB   t 01787 372343

thelinberwicktrust.org.uk

East Runton | Incleborough House

Enjoy England ★★★★★   AS

Lower Common, East Runton, Cromer NR27 9PG
t 01263 515939   e enquiries@incleboroughhouse.co.uk

incleboroughhouse.co.uk

Access: General: Room:

194   www.openbritain.net

East of England | Norfolk

Edgefield | Wood Farm Cottages

Enjoy England ★★★★ Mrs Diana Jacob, Wood Farm Cottages, Wood Farm, Plumstead Road, Edgefield, Melton Constable NR24 2AQ t 01263 587347
e info@wood-farm.com

wood-farm.com

Foxley | Moor Farm Stable Cottages

Enjoy England ★★★-★★★★★ Paul Davis, Moor Farm Stable Cottages, Moor Farm, Foxley, Fakenham NR20 4QP t 01362 688523 e mail@moorfarmstablecottages.co.uk

moorfarmstablecottages.co.uk

Fritton | Fritton Lake Country World

Enjoy England ★★★★ Mr Brian Humphrey, Fritton Lake Country World, Beccles Road, Fritton, Great Yarmouth NR31 9HA t 01493 488208

great-yarmouth.angle.uk.com/attractions/frittonlake.cgi

Gissing | Bluebell Cottage

Enjoy England ★★★★
Units: 4   Sleeps: 2-8
Open: All year

Low season p/w: £255.00
High season p/w: £767.00

Mrs Cathy Smith, Malthouse Farm, Malthouse Lane, Gissing, Norfolk IP22 5UT
t 01379 658021 e bookings@norfolkcottages.net

norfolkcottages.net   3B2

Restored single storey former dairy in courtyard complex with indoor swimming pool in rural Norfolk.

Access:
General: Unit:

Gissing | Honeysuckle Cottage

Enjoy England ★★★★
Units: 4   Sleeps: 2-8

Low season p/w: £453.00
High season p/w: £1346.00

Malthouse Farm, Malthouse Lane, Gissing, Norfolk IP22 5UT
t 01379 658021 e bookings@norfolkcottages.net

norfolkcottages.net   3B2

Converted two storey old granary in small courtyard complex with swimming pool in rural Norfolk.

Access: General: Unit:

Gissing | Malthouse Farm Cottages

Enjoy England ★★★★ Mrs Cathy Smith, Norfolk Cottages, 17 Owen Road, Diss IP22 4ER
t 01379 658021 e bookings@norfolkcottages.net

norfolkcottages.net

For symbols see pg 24   195

East of England | **Norfolk**

Gissing | **Primrose Cottage**

Enjoy England ★★★★
Units: 4   Sleeps: 2-8
Open: All year

Low season p/w:
£255.00
High season p/w:
£767.00

Malthouse Farm, Malthouse Lane, Gissing, Norfolk IP22 5UT
t 01379 658021   e bookings@norfolkcottages.net

norfolkcottages.net   3B2

Restored single storey former dairy in courtyard complex with indoor swimming pool in rural Norfolk.

Access:
General: Unit:

Gissing | **Rose Cottage**

Enjoy England ★★★★
Units: 4   Sleeps: 2-8
Open: All year

Low season p/w:
£453.00
High season p/w:
£1346.00

Malthouse Farm, Malthouse Lane, Gissing, Norfolk IP22 5UT
t 01379 658021   e bookings@norfolkcottages.net

norfolkcottages.net   3B2

Sensitively restored oak barn in small courtyard complex with indoor swimming pool. One of four.

Access: General: Unit:

Great Snoring | **Vine Park Cottage**

Enjoy England ★★★★

Thursford Road, Great Snoring, Fakenham NR21 0PF
t 01328 821016   e rita@vineparkcottagebandb.co.uk

vineparkcottagebandb.co.uk

Happisburgh | **Boundary Stables**

Enjoy England ★★★★
Units: 4   Sleeps: 1-6
Open: All year

Low season p/w:
£230.00
High season p/w:
£771.00

Mr & Mrs Julian & Elizabeth Burns, Boundary Stables, Grub Street, Happisburgh, Mundesley NR12 0RX
t 01692 650171   e bookings@boundarystables.co.uk

boundarystables.co.uk

Recently converted stables provide excellent accommodation in a rural setting. All are single storey.

General: Unit:

Happisburgh | **Nicholson Cottage**

Enjoy England ★★★★

Norfolk Country Cottages, Carlton House, Market Place, Reepham, Norwich NR10 4JJ   t 01603 871872   e info@norfolkcottages.co.uk

norfolkcottages.co.uk

East of England | Norfolk

Horning | King Line Cottages

Enjoy England ★★★–★★★★★
Units: 5   Sleeps: 9
Open: All year except Xmas and New Year
Low season p/w: £305.00
High season p/w: £1875.00
Shop: 0.5 miles

Access:
General:
Unit:

Mr Robert King, 4 Pinewood Drive, Horning NR12 8LZ
t 01692 630297   e info@norfolk-broads.co.uk

norfolk-broads.co.uk   3C1

King Line Cottages, English Tourist Board 4 star rated, consists of six holiday homes, overlooking one of the most picturesque parts of the River Bure at Horning Ferry. These cottages have been awarded an English Tourist Board accessibility rating 2.

Location: Norwich ringroad A1042, left A1151 through Wroxham, right turn onto A1062 to Horning. Right into Lower Street, right Ferry Road.

Hunstanton | Caley Hall Hotel   AS

AA   ★★★
Enjoy England   ★★★
Open: All year except Xmas and New Year
Rooms per night:
s: £50.00–£200.00
d: £80.00–£200.00
p/p half board:
d: £75.00–£125.00
Meals: £20.00–£30.00

Old Hunstanton Road, Old Hunstanton, Hunstanton PE36 6HH
t 01485 533486   e mail@caleyhallhotel.co.uk

caleyhallhotel.co.uk   3B1

The bar, restaurant and chalet style rooms have been converted from 17thC farm buildings.

Access:
General: Room:

Hunstanton | Foxgloves Cottage

Enjoy England   ★★★★

Terry & Lesley Heade, Foxgloves Cottage, 29 Avenue Road, Hunstanton PE36 5BW   t 01485 532460   e deepdenehouse@btopenworld.com

smoothhound.co.uk/hotels/deepdene.html

Kelling | The Pheasant Hotel

Enjoy England   ★★

Coast Road, Kelling, Blakeney NR25 7EG
t 01263 588382   e enquiries@pheasanthotelnorfolk.co.uk

pheasanthotelnorfolk.co.uk

For symbols see pg 24   197

East of England | **Norfolk**

Little Snoring | Jex's Farm Barn

Enjoy England ★★★★ Stephen & Lynn Harvey, Jex's Farm Barn, Jex Farm, Little Snoring, Fakenham NR21 0JJ t 01328 878257 e farmerstephen@jexfarm.wanadoo.co.uk
jexfarm.co.uk

Mundesley | Overcliff Lodge

Enjoy England ★★★★ 46 Cromer Road, Mundesley NR11 8DB
t 01263 720016 e enquiries@overclifflodge.co.uk
overclifflodge.co.uk

Norwich | Express by Holiday Inn - Norwich AS

Norwich Sports Village, Drayton High Road, Norwich NR6 5DU
t 01603 780 010
hiexpress.co.uk

Access: **General:** **Room:**

Norwich | Holiday Inn Norwich AS

AA ★★★ Ipswich Road, Norwich, Norfolk NR4 6EP
t 0870 400 9060 e reservations-norwich@ichotelsgroup.com
holiday-inn.co.uk

Access: **General:** **Room:**

Sandringham | Park House Hotel AS

Enjoy England ★★
Open: All year
Rooms per night:
s: £110.00-£158.00
d: £186.00-£288.00
p/p half board:
d: £108.00-£173.00
Meals: £15.00-£17.50

Shop: 1.5 miles
Pub: 1.5 miles

Sandringham PE35 6EH
t 01485 543000 e parkinfo@lcdisability.org
parkhousehotel.org.uk   3B1

Located on the Royal Sandringham Estate, the hotel has 8 single and 8 twin rooms and is adapted for people with mobility difficulties/disabilities with or without carers/companions. The hotel is fully accessible and care is available if required.

Location: From King's Lynn follow A149 towards Hunstanton, follow brown tourists signs. Park House is on right before Sandringham Visitor Centre.

Access:

General:

Room:

198   www.openbritain.net

East of England | **Norfolk**

Sandringham | **The Sandringham Estate Caravan Club Site**

Enjoy England ★★★★★
(136) £14.60–£21.45
(136) £14.60–£21.45
136 touring pitches
Open: All year
Shop: 1 mile
Pub: 1 mile

Glucksburg Woods, Sandringham, Norfolk PE35 6EZ
t 01553 631614

caravanclub.co.uk 3B1

Set in the heart of the Royal Estate. Take a walk to Sandringham House, the famous residence of the Royal Family and enjoy the Country Park - kids will love the nature trails, land train ride and adventure playground.

Location: A149 from King's Lynn (Hunstanton). Right onto B1439 (West Newton). Site on left after 0.5 miles.

Access:
General:
Pitch:

Sandringham (6 miles) | **Oyster House**   AS

Enjoy England ★★★★
Open: All year except Xmas and New Year
Rooms per night:
s: £45.00–£75.00
d: £68.00–£75.00

Lynn Road, West Rudham PE31 8RW
t 01485 528327   e oyster-house@tiscali.co.uk

oysterhouse.co.uk 3B1

17th-century farmhouse set in country gardens. Ideal base for North Norfolk Coast, Sandringham, Wells.

Access: General: Room:

Sheringham | **Sheringham YHA**

Enjoy England ★★

1 Cremers Drift, Sheringham NR26 8HX
t 0870 770 6024   e sheringham@yha.org.uk
yha.org.uk

OPENBRITAIN.NET
The one-stop-shop for all your travel needs. Go online and see how we can help you get in, out ...and about.

East of England | **Norfolk/Suffolk**

Thetford | 'Next Door' at Magdalen House

Enjoy England ★★★★
Units: 1 Sleeps: 1-2
Open: All year

Low season p/w: £300.00
High season p/w: £450.00

Keith & Lorna Cootes, Magdalen House, 18 Buntings Lane, Methwold, Thetford, Norfolk IP26 4PR
t 01366 727255   e bandb@magdalenhouse.co.uk

magdalenhouse.co.uk

3B2

Luxury apartment for two in peaceful surroundings. 4 star rated, access level 2, see website

Access:
General: Unit:

Titchwell | Titchwell Manor Hotel

Enjoy England ★★★
Near Brancaster, Titchwell, King's Lynn PE31 8BB
t 01485 210221   e margaret@titchwellmanor.com

titchwellmanor.com

Wells-Next-The-Sea | Wells-next-the-Sea YHA

Enjoy England ★★★★
Church Plain, Wells-next-the-Sea NR23 1EQ
t 01328 711748   e wellsnorfolk@yha.org.uk

yha.org.uk

Wendling | Greenbanks

Enjoy England ★★★★
Wendling, Dereham NR19 2AB
t 01362 687742   e jenny@greenbankshotel.co.uk

greenbankshotel.co.uk

Aldeburgh | Brudenell Hotel

Enjoy England ★★★
The Parade, Aldeburgh IP15 5BU
t 01728 452071   e info@brudenellhotel.co.uk

brudenellhotel.co.uk

Blaxhall | Blaxhall YHA

Enjoy England ★★★
Heath Walk, Blaxhall, Woodbridge IP12 2EA
t 0870 770 5702   e blaxhall@yha.org.uk

yha.org.uk

Combs | Jackbridge Cottage

Enjoy England ★★★★
Ian & Teresa Pemberton, Jackbridge Cottage, Jacks Lane, Great Finborough, Stowmarket IP14 2NQ
t 01449 672177   e pembertons@jackbridgefarm.plus.com

East of England | **Suffolk**

Cotton | **Coda Cottages**
Enjoy England ★★★★ Mrs Kate Sida-Nicholls, 2 Park Farm, Dandy Corner IP14 4QX
t 01449 780076 e codacottages@dandycorner.co.uk
codacottages.co.uk

Access: | General: | Unit:

Cratfield | **School Farm Cottages**
Enjoy England ★★★★ Mrs Claire Sillett, School Farm Cottages, Church Road, Cratfield, Halesworth IP19 0BU t 01986 798844 e schoolfarmcotts@aol.com
schoolfarmcottages.com

Edwardstone | **Sherbourne Farm Lodge Cottages**
Enjoy England ★★★★ Mrs Anne Suckling, Sherbourne Farm Lodge Cottages, Sherbourne House Farm, Edwardstone, Sudbury CO10 5PD
t 01787 210885 e enquiries@sherbournelodgecottages.co.uk
sherbournelodgecottages.co.uk

Haughley | **Red House Farm Cottages**
Enjoy England ★★★–★★★★ Mrs Mary Noy, Red House Farm, Station Road, Haughley, Stowmarket IP14 3QP t 01449 673323

General: | Unit:

Henley | **Damerons Farm Holidays**
Enjoy England ★★★★ Mr & Mrs Wayne & Sue Leggett, Damerons Farm Holidays, Main Road, Henley, Ipswich IP6 0RU t 01473 832454 e info@dameronsfarmholidays.co.uk
dameronsfarmholidays.co.uk

Ipswich | **Holiday Inn Ipswich**
London Road, Ipswich, Suffolk IP2 0UA
t 0871 942 9045 e reservations.ipswich@ihg.com
holidayinn.co.uk

Access: | General: | Room:

Lowestoft | **Hotel Victoria**
Enjoy England ★★★ Kirkley Cliff, Lowestoft NR33 0BZ
t 01502 574433 e info@thehotelvictoria.co.uk
thehotelvictoria.co.uk

OPEN BRITAIN — PLANNING A DAY OUT? WHY NOT MAKE IT A SHORT-BREAK? Fabulous 'Places to Stay' in every region

For symbols see pg 24

East of England | **Suffolk**

Lowestoft | **Pakefield Caravan Park**   AS

Enjoy England ★★★★
🚐 (361)
🚙 (12)   £17.00–£20.00
🏠 (12)   £125.00–£535.00
385 touring pitches
Open: 1st March – 30th November

Shop: <0.5 miles
Pub: 0.5 miles

Access:
General:
Pitch:

Arbor Lane, Pakefield, Lowestoft NR33 7BQ
t 01502 561136

pakefieldpark.co.uk   3C1

Pakefield Caravan Park is a level and accessible site situated within close proximity of the beach and the local shops. The park offers comfortable holiday accommodation with a layout suitable for some disabled customers. Further details available on request.

Location: 2 miles south of Lowestoft off main A12. Look out for main brown tourist signs

Mickfield | **Read Hall Cottage**

Enjoy England   ★★★★★

Mr & Mrs Andrew & Andrea Stewart, Read Hall Cottage, Read Hall, Mickfield, Stowmarket IP14 5LU   t 01449 711366   e info@readhall.co.uk

readhall.co.uk

Middlewood Green | **Leys Farmhouse Annexe**

Enjoy England   ★★★

Mrs Heather Trevorrow, Blacksmith's Lane, Middlewood Green, Earl Stonham, Stowmarket IP14 5EU   t 01449 711750   e leysfarmhouse@btinternet.com

leysfarmhouseannexe.co.uk

Nayland | **Gladwins Farm Self Catering Cottages**   AS

Enjoy England
★★★★–★★★★★

Units: 8   **Sleeps:** 2–8
Open: All year

Low season p/w:
£245.00
High season p/w:
£1955.00

Mrs Pauline Dossor, Partner, Harpers Hill, Nayland, Colchester CO6 4NU   t 01206 262261   e gladwinsfarm@aol.com

gladwinsfarm.co.uk   3B2

In Suffolk's Constable Country with marvellous views and fishing. Not far from the sea.

Access: **General:**   **Unit:**

202   www.openbritain.net

East of England | **Suffolk**

Oulton Broad | Ivy House Country Hotel

Ivy Lane, Oulton Broad, Suffolk NR33 8HY
t 01502 501353
ivyhousecountryhotel.co.uk

Saxmundham | Bluebell, Bonny, Buttercup & Bertie

AS

Enjoy England ★★★★
Units: 4   Sleeps: 2-4
Open: All year

Low season p/w:
£275.00
High season p/w:
£515.00

Mrs Margaret Gray, Park Farm, Sibton, Saxmundham IP17 2LZ
t 01728 668324   e mail@sibtonparkfarm.co.uk
sibtonparkfarm.co.uk   3D2

Four single storey cottages, each sleeping 2 - 4. Ideal centre for birdwatching, history, music.

Access: General: Unit:

Southwold | Newlands Country House

AS

Enjoy England ★★★★
Open: All year

Rooms per night:
s: £60.00-£95.00
d: £95.00-£110.00

72 Halesworth Road, Reydon, Southwold IP18 6NS
t 01502 722164   e info@newlandsofsouthwold.co.uk
newlandsofsouthwold.co.uk   3C2

Newlands Country House is only a mile from the town centre of Southwold.

Access:
General: Room:

Sudbury | Denis Duncan House

Scotland ★★★★

Mrs. Miriam Toosey, Eastgate House, Upper East Street, Sudbury, Suffolk CO10 1UB   t 01787 372343   e info@thelinberwicktrust.org.uk
thelinberwicktrust.org.uk

Wangford | The Plough Inn

Enjoy England ★★★★

London Road, Wangford, Southwold, Beccles NR34 8AZ
e enquiries@the-plough.biz
the-plough.biz

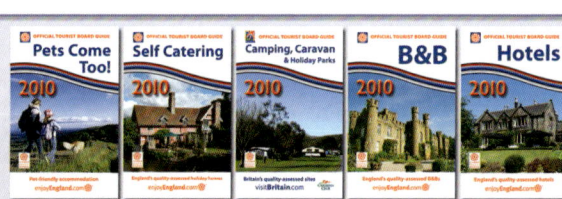

Looking for something else?

If you haven't found what you are looking for in OpenBritain, VisitBritain's Official Tourist Board Guides offer a wide choice of assessed accommodation which may meet your needs.

For symbols see pg 24   203

East of England | Suffolk/Attractions

Wattisfield | Jayes Holiday Cottages   AS

Enjoy England ★★★
Units: 2   Sleeps: 2-4
Low season p/w: £165.00
High season p/w: £400.00

Mrs Denise Williams, Walsham Road, Wattisfield, Diss IP22 1NZ
t 01359 251255   e info@jayesholidaycottages.co.uk
jayesholidaycottages.co.uk   3B2

Set in quiet countryside, our specially adapted cottages overlook a large pond with fishing facilities.

Access: General: P S   Unit:

Wattisham | Wattisham Hall Holiday Cottages

Enjoy England ★★★★
Mr & Mrs Jeremy & Jo Squirrell, Wattisham Hall Holiday Cottages, Wattisham Hall, Wattisham, Ipswich IP7 7JX
t 01449 740240   e enquiries@wattishamhall.co.uk
wattishamhall.co.uk

Wickham Skeith | Netus Barn

Enjoy England ★★★
Ms Joy Homan, Netus Barn, Street Farm, Wickham Skeith, Eye IP23 8LP
t 01449 766275   e joygeoff@homansf.freeserve.co.uk
netusbarn.co.uk

Harrold | Harrold Odell Country Park

Carlton Road, Harrold, Bedford MK43 7DS
t 01234 720016   e ed.burnett@bedscc.gov.uk
hocp.co.uk

Luton | Wrest Park

Open: For opening hours and prices, please call 0870 333 1181 or visit www.english-heritage.org.uk/properties

Silsoe, Luton, Bedfordshire MK45 4HS
t 0870 333 1181   e customers@english-heritage.org.uk
english-heritage.org.uk/wrestpark

With acres of breathtaking landscape, take a stroll, let the children play or simply relax.

Access: General: P

Chelmsford | RHS Garden Hyde Hall

Westerns Approach, Rettendon, Chelmsford, Essex CM3 8AT
t 01245 400256   e info@rhs.org.uk
rhs.org.uk

East of England | **Attractions**

Colchester | Colchester Museums

Colchester Museums, see website for details

colchestermuseums.org.uk

Saffron Walden | Audley End House & Gardens

Open: For opening hours and prices, please call 0870 333 1181 or visit www.english-heritage.org.uk/properties

Audley End, Saffron Walden, Essex CB11 4JF
t 0870 333 1181   e customers@english-heritage.org.uk

english-heritage.org.uk/audleyend

Experience working kitchens and a fantastic day out, in one of England's grandest country homes.

Access: **General:**

Norwich | Fairhaven Woodland and Water Gardens

School Road, South Walsham, Norwich, Norfolk NR13 6DZ
t 01603 270449   e fairhavengarden@btconnect.com

fairhavengarden.co.uk

Access: **General:**

Sandringham | Sandringham House

Estate Office, Sandringham, Norfolk PE35 6EN
t 01553 612908   e visits@sandringhamestate.co.uk

sandringhamestate.co.uk

Framlingham | Framlingham Castle

Open: For opening hours and prices, please call 0870 333 1181 or visit www.english-heritage.org.uk/properties

Framlingham, Suffolk IP13 9BP
t 0870 333 1181   e customers@english-heritage.org.uk

english-heritage.org.uk/framlinghamcastle

Get active, take the wall walk, see breathtaking views, relax and picnic in the grounds.

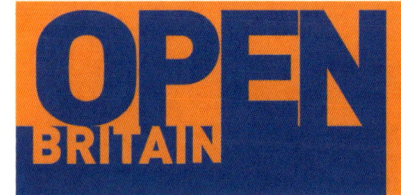

Access: **General:**

OPEN BRITAIN

DECIDED WHERE TO GO?
SEE ATTRACTIONS FOR WHAT TO DO
Ideas and information at the end of each regional section

©Britainonview / Martin Brent

For symbols see pg 24

Norwich Bus Station

your accessible gateway to Norfolk – Shopmobility available here

www.norfolk.gov.uk/passengertransport
or call 0344 800 8003.
For bus information call traveline
0871 200 22 33 (10p per minute from landlines).

Norfolk County Council
at your service

OpenBritain | East of England

Welcome to The Broads

Go to our website and look under the Visiting section for easy access information

Broads Authority
The Broads - a member of the National Park family

www.broads-authority.gov.uk

Colchester

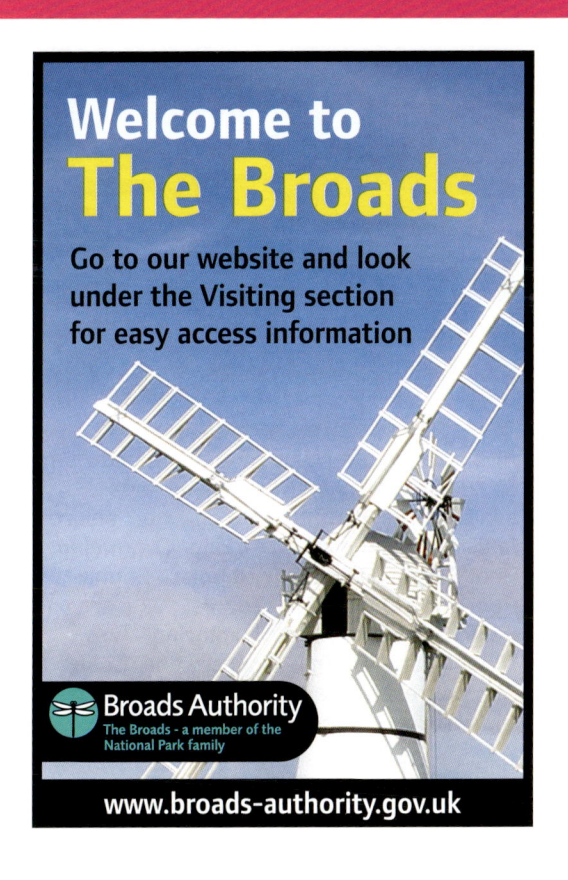

For more information about disabled facilities in the area please call

01206 282 700.

Colchester Borough Council
PO Box 884, Town Hall, Colchester
Essex CO1 1FR

www.colchester.gov.uk

---

up to 60% off high street prices

PROUD TO BE FULLY DDA COMPLIANT

OPENING TIMES
Monday to Saturday 10am - 6pm
Sunday 11am - 5pm
Bank Holidays 10am - 5pm

T: 01255 479595

- Free parking
- Regular events
- Adventure Play Area
- Fully pedestrianised shopping malls
- Premier Card scheme giving further discounts and offers

www.clactonfactoryoutlet.com

Access for All at Colchester and Ipswich Museum Service

Colchester and Ipswich Museum Service is committed to providing access to its museums, collections and services to as wide an audience as possible.

Inclusive thinking is always the way forward. **Colchester and Ipswich Museum Service** incorporates access into all new projects, large or small and it is central to the culture of the service and its staff.

Throughout the museums a range of facilities is available including British Sign Language interpreted events, Braille and tactile facilities, ramped and level access and much more.

Visit **www.colchestermuseums.org.uk** for more information and to download an access brochure.

Colchester and Ipswich Museum Service
01206 282931
Textphone users dial 18001 followed by the full number you wish to call

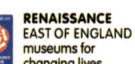

Colchester IPSWICH

RENAISSANCE EAST OF ENGLAND
museums for changing lives

207

OpenBritain | East of England

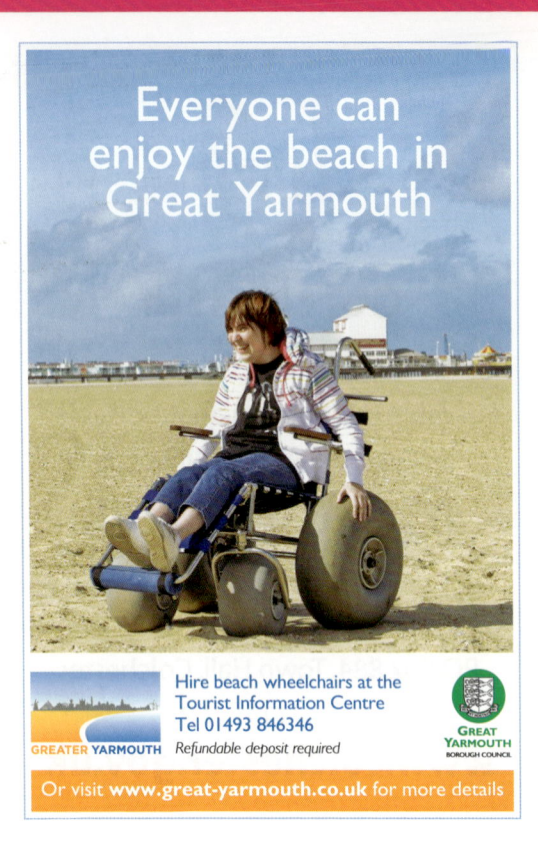

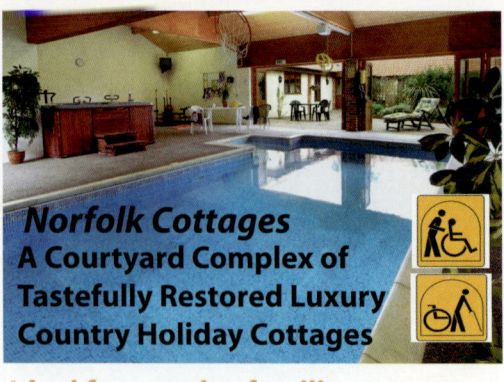

Everyone can enjoy the beach in Great Yarmouth

Hire beach wheelchairs at the Tourist Information Centre
Tel 01493 846346
Refundable deposit required

GREATER YARMOUTH
GREAT YARMOUTH BOROUGH COUNCIL

Or visit www.great-yarmouth.co.uk for more details

Norfolk Cottages
A Courtyard Complex of Tastefully Restored Luxury Country Holiday Cottages

Ideal for couples, families or groups

All Cottages offer wet rooms and bedrooms on the ground floor. Additional aids available many at no extra charge. Leisure facilities include Heater Indoor Swimming Pool & Spa with overhead hoist, Sauna, Pool and Table Tennis Tables. We are Perfectly situated for exploring the Norfolk and Suffolk Country and Coast. Short breaks available for that special Birthday or Anniversary.

Tel: 01379 658 021
www.norfolkcottages.net

enjoyEngland.com
SELF CATERING
EXCELLENCE IN ENGLAND
Tourism Awards 2004
Silver Winner

Huntingdonshire
DISTRICT COUNCIL

We are pleased to be associated with RADAR

Huntingdonshire District Council

Environmental Management Division

Pathfinder House, St Mary's Street,
Huntingdon PE29 3TN

Tel: 01480 388321

Visit rescued horses, ponies and donkeys FOR FREE! at Redwings Horse Sanctuary

Three visitor centres in Norfolk*, Essex and Warwickshire. Open daily from 10am seven days a week all year round
(except Christmas Eve, Christmas Day and New Years Day)

Enquiries for all centres including accessibility and special events

0870 040 0033
or www.redwings.co.uk

REDWINGS HORSE SANCTUARY
Registered Charity No. 1068911
Incorporating Ada Cole Memorial Stables

*Open 28 March to 1 November 2009

REDWINGS SILVER JUBILEE 1984-2009

OpenBritain | East of England

Tendring — The Essex Sunshine Coast

Clacton • Frinton • Walton • Brightlingsea • Manningtree
Harwich • Jaywick • St Osyth • Dovercourt • Mistley

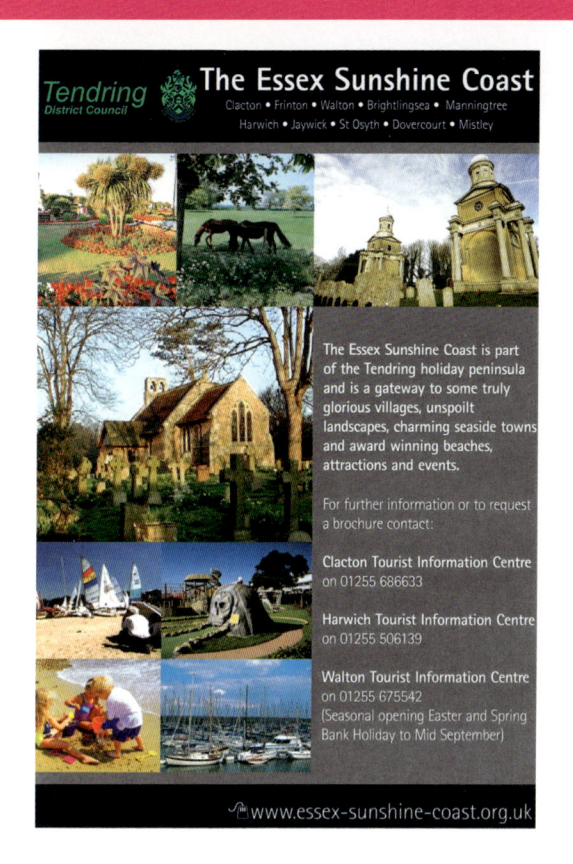

The Essex Sunshine Coast is part of the Tendring holiday peninsula and is a gateway to some truly glorious villages, unspoilt landscapes, charming seaside towns and award winning beaches, attractions and events.

For further information or to request a brochure contact:

Clacton Tourist Information Centre
on 01255 686633

Harwich Tourist Information Centre
on 01255 506139

Walton Tourist Information Centre
on 01255 675542
(Seasonal opening Easter and Spring Bank Holiday to Mid September)

www.essex-sunshine-coast.org.uk

Fenland — Cambridgeshire
Fenland District Council

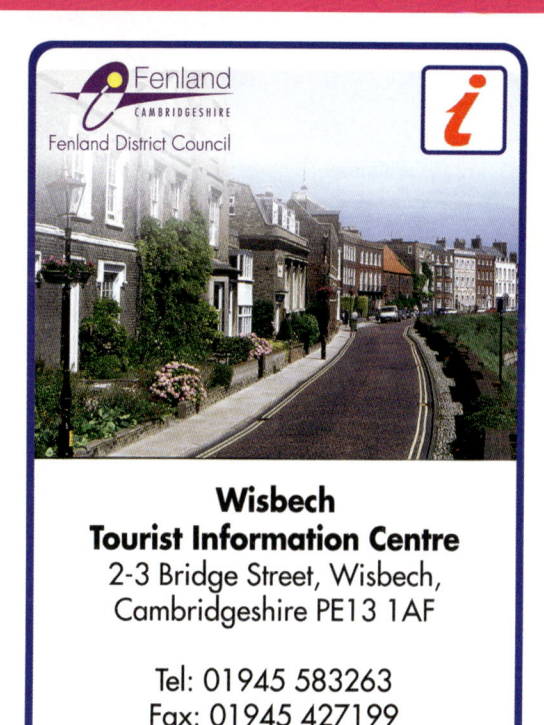

Wisbech Tourist Information Centre
2-3 Bridge Street, Wisbech,
Cambridgeshire PE13 1AF

Tel: 01945 583263
Fax: 01945 427199
email: tourism@fenland.gov.uk
website: www.fenland.gov.uk

GREAT VALUE, GREAT FUN, GREAT HOLIDAYS
GREAT YARMOUTH'S Vauxhall 5 STAR HOLIDAY PARK

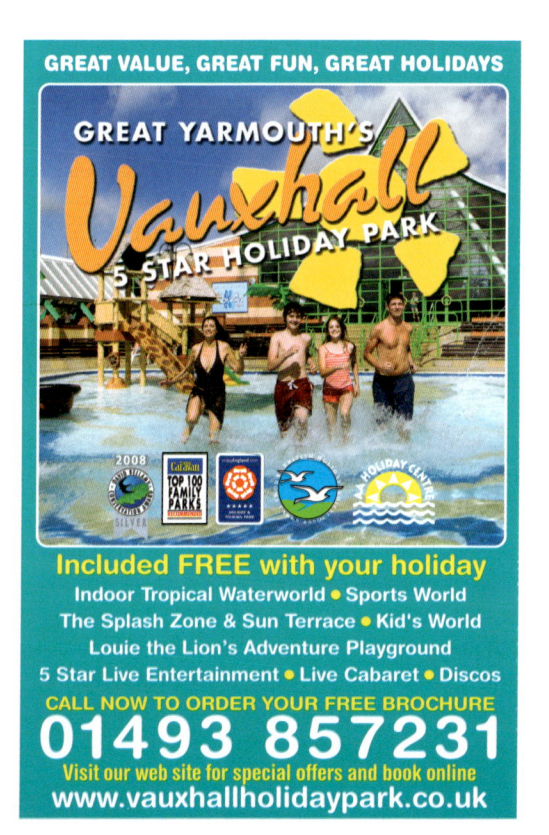

Included FREE with your holiday
Indoor Tropical Waterworld • Sports World
The Splash Zone • Sun Terrace • Kid's World
Louie the Lion's Adventure Playground
5 Star Live Entertainment • Live Cabaret • Discos

CALL NOW TO ORDER YOUR FREE BROCHURE
01493 857231

Visit our web site for special offers and book online
www.vauxhallholidaypark.co.uk

Year round access at Harrold Odell Country Park

Open every day of the year, the park is a haven for wildlife. There is a river, two lakes, meadow and woodland. The 2.5km surfaced route around the large lake is good for wheelchair users. The visitor centre and toilets are wheelchair accessible, the car park has designated spaces for elderly and disabled.

Harrold Odell Country Park is situated between Harrold and Odell villages to the north west of Bedford. Follow the signs from the A6 at Sharnbrook.

T: 01234 720016 W: www.hocp.co.uk

BEDFORD BOROUGH COUNCIL

Sandringham
House, Museum & Gardens
Her Majesty The Queen's country retreat in 60 acres of gardens is fully accessible throughout (land train available).

Open daily Easter Saturday to mid-July and early August to end October

Full details on www.sandringhamestate.co.uk
or telephone 01553 612908

209

The Duchess

Something for everyone!

The six counties of the East Midlands – Derbyshire, Leicestershire, Lincolnshire, Northamptonshire, Nottinghamshire and Rutland, are steeped in history and tradition. Magnificent ancient castles provide a unique glimpse into the region's royal connections. Grand stately homes sit amidst beautiful landscaped gardens and imposing Cathedrals hide interesting architectural secrets. Visitors to these inspiring buildings can step back in time to gain first hand experience of an 'England of old'.

This is a destination where the awe inspiring countryside, from the sweeping green hills of the **Peak District** to the picturesque Lincolnshire coast has captured the imagination of movie makers, providing the backdrops to numerous films.

Chatsworth, **Kedleston**, **Hardwick Hall**, **Burghley House** and **Lincoln Cathedral** have all played host to major Hollywood blockbusters including *Elizabeth*, *The Golden Age*, *Pride and Prejudice*, *The Duchess* and *The Da Vinci Code* to name a few.

Undoubtedly it is the rich heritage that attracts many visitors to the East Midlands, however the region also takes pride in futuristic attractions such as the **National Space Centre**. With good accessibility, the UK's largest attraction dedicated to space provides hours of breath taking discovery.

The region's cultural credentials have also been given a boost with the recent opening of a collection of contemporary new arts venues including; **Curve** in Leicester, **Quad** in Derby, the **New Art Exchange** and **Nottingham Contemporary** all of which offer easy access to wide variety of visual and performance arts.

Offering something for everyone, the East Midlands has wide appeal and welcomes visitors from all walks of life. For those who love to shop there is a choice of cosmopolitan cities such as **Nottingham**, **Derby**, **Leicester** and **Lincoln**, which offer designer boutiques alongside leading high street stores. Alternatively, for a shopping experience, visitors can choose from the region's abundant historic market towns such as **Ashbourne**, **Bakewell**, **Oundle**, **Stamford**, **Melton Mowbray** and **Oakham**.

For thrill seekers, world class motor sports venues including **Silverstone** and **Donington Park** provide spectacular entertainment. Motor sport has been at the heart of the East Midlands for decades, and the region hosts many exciting and prestigious events.

The East Midlands is also proving to be a magnet for business travellers boasting a wide range of conference facilities with excellent access policies. Venues such as **Imago** in Leicestershire and **East Lodge** in Derbyshire, have been awarded for having excellent accessibility credentials at the region's 2009 tourism awards.

OpenBritain | East Midlands

Derwent Valley

Motorsports

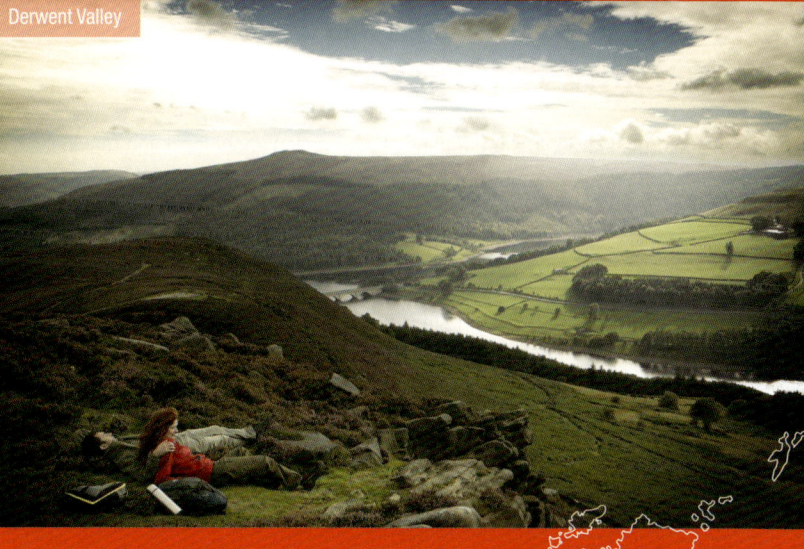

East Midlands

Derbyshire
Leicestershire
Lincolnshire
Northamptonshire
Nottinghamshire

▶ Families visiting the East Midlands need not struggle to find things to appeal, there is an array of venues that delight both children and parents. From historic attractions such as from **Calke Abbey**, one of the National Trust's most child friendly and fun properties located in South Derbyshire, **Rutland Water**, Europe's largest man made lake and a haven for wildlife, to the **Natureland Seal Sanctuary** in Skegness, which features a range of aquatic animals, has excellent accessibility and a strong focus on conservation, education and entertainment.

For gardening enthusiasts the East Midlands is a horticultural delight, some of the best gardens to visit include **Barnsdale Gardens** in Rutland, **Teversal Manor** in Nottingham and **Coton Manor** in Northamptonshire.

Whether visiting for a day or staying for a longer break, the East Midlands offers a wide range of accessible venues, whether as a cultural break, for outdoor pursuits or simply to relax and unwind.

Find out more

web www.discovereastmidlands.com

Barnsdale

Tourist Information Centres

Tourist Information Centres are a mine of information about local and regional accommodation, attractions and events. Visit them when you arrive at your destination or contact them before you go:

Ashbourne	13 Market Place	01335 343666	ashbourneinfo@derbyshiredales.gov.uk
Ashby-De-La-Zouch	North Street	01530 411767	ashby.tic@nwleicestershire.gov.uk
Bakewell	Old Market Hall	01629 813227	bakewell@peakdistrict-npa.gov.uk
Brackley	2 Bridge Street	01280 700111	tic@southnorthants.gov.uk
Brigg	The Buttercross	01652 657053	brigg.tic@northlincs.gov.uk
Buxton	The Crescent	01298 25106	tourism@highpeak.gov.uk
Castleton	Buxton Road	01433 620679	castleton@peakdistrict-npa.gov.uk
Chesterfield	Rykneld Square	01246 345777	tourism@chesterfield.gov.uk
Cleethorpes	42-43 Alexandra Road	01472 323111	cleetic@nelincs.gov.uk
Derby	Assembly Rooms	01332 255802	tourism@derby.gov.uk
Hornsea	120 Newbegin	01964 536404	hornsea.tic@eastriding.gov.uk
Leicester	7/9 Every Street	0906 294 1113	info@goleicestershire.com
Lincoln	9 Castle Hill	01522 873213	tourism@lincoln.gov.uk
Matlock	Crown Square	01629 583388	matlockinfo@derbyshiredales.gov.uk
Northampton	Guildhall Road	01604 838800	northampton.tic@northamptonshireenterprise.ltd.uk
Nottingham City	1-4 Smithy Row	08444 775 678	tourist.information@nottinghamcity.gov.uk
Ollerton	Sherwood Heath	01623 824545	sherwoodheath@nsdc.info
Oundle	14 West Street	01832 274333	oundletic@east-northamptonshire.gov.uk
Ripley	Town Hall	01773 841488	touristinformation@ambervalley.gov.uk
Sleaford	Advice Centre, Money's Yard	01529 414294	tic@n-kesteven.gov.uk
Swadlincote	Sharpe's Pottery Museum	01283 222848	Jo@sharpespotterymuseum.org.uk

East Midlands | **Derbyshire**

Ashbourne | **Ancestral Barn** — AS

Enjoy England ★★★★★ Mr & Mrs S Fowler, Church Farm, Stanshope, Ashbourne, Derbyshire DE6 2AD
t 01335 310243
dovedalecottages.co.uk

General: Unit:

Bakewell | **Chatsworth Park Caravan Club Site**

Enjoy England ★★★★★ Baslow, Bakewell, Derbyshire DE45 1PN
t 01246 582226

(120) £15.00–£22.50
(120) £15.00–£22.50
120 touring pitches
Open: All year
Shop: 1 mile
Pub: 1 mile

caravanclub.co.uk 4B2

Breathtaking setting in walled garden on the Estate, with views of the sheep-cropped rolling countryside to the west. Children will love the farmyard and adventure playground. Visit the house with its beautifully proportioned rooms, paintings and formal gardens.

Location: From Bakewell onto A619. In 3.75 miles turn right at roundabout (signposted Sheffield). Site entrance on right 150yds.

Access:
General:
Pitch:

OPEN BRITAIN

"The one-stop-shop for all your travel needs"

Become a member of OpenBritain today.

Share your own travel and accommodation experiences and help Britain become more open!

visit **www.openbritain.net**

OPENBRITAIN.NET

East Midlands | Derbyshire

Brassington | Hoe Grange Holidays

AS

Enjoy England ★★★★
Units: 2   Sleeps: 2-8
Open: All year

Low season p/w:
£375.00
High season p/w:
£800.00

Shop: 4 miles
Pub: 4 miles

Hoe Grange, Brassington DE4 4HP
t 01629 540262   e info@hoegrangeholidays.co.uk

hoegrangeholidays.co.uk　　　　4B2

Two award winning log cabins: a real 'home from home', fully equipped kitchen, open plan lounge, spacious bedrooms and luxurious whirlpool bath. Excellent disabled facilities including wet-room shower, mobile hoist and profile bed. Service dogs welcome. Short breaks available.

Location: Working farm, close to Carsington Water, Chatsworth, Dovedale, market towns of Ashbourne, Bakewell, and Matlock.

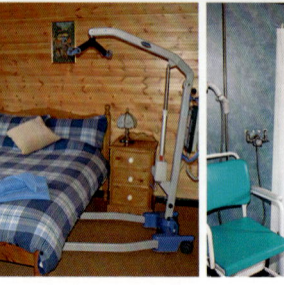

Access:
General:
Unit:

Buxton | Grin Low Caravan Club Site

THE CARAVAN CLUB

Enjoy England ★★★★★

(117)   £12.00–£17.75
(117)   £12.00–£17.75
(12)

117 touring pitches
Open: 27 March - 9 November

Shop: 1.8 miles
Pub: 0.5 miles

Grin Low Road, Ladmanlow, Buxton, Derbyshire SK17 6UJ
t 01298 77735

caravanclub.co.uk　　　　4B2

Conveniently placed for exploring the Peak District. Buxton, with its colourful Pavilion Gardens and Opera House offering a wide range of events, makes a great day or evening out. The Peak District National Park is ideal for walkers and cyclists.

Location: Turn left off A53 (Buxton to Leek) at Grin Low signpost, left in 300yds into site approach road.

Access:
General:
Pitch:

214　　　　www.openbritain.net

East Midlands | **Derbyshire**

Buxton | **Northfield Farm**
Enjoy England ★★★ Mrs Elizabeth Andrews, Flash, Nr Buxton, Derbyshire SK17 0SW
t 01298 22543   e info@northfieldfarm.co.uk
northfieldfarm.co.uk

Access: — General: — Unit: —

Chesterfield | **High Hazels**
National Trust, High Hazels, Hardwick Hall, Chesterfield, Derbyshire
t 0844 8002070
nationaltrustcottages.co.uk/north_of_england/

Derby | **Jurys Inn Derby**
AA ★★★ King Street, Derby DE1 3DB
t 01332 621000   e jurysinnderby@jurysinns.com
derbyhotels.jurysinns.com

Access: — General: — Room: —

Earl Sterndale | **Wheeldon Trees Farm**
Enjoy England ★★★★ Deborah & Martin Hofman, Wheeldon Trees Farm, Earl Sterndale, Buxton SK17 0AA   t 01298 83219   e stay@wheeldontreesfarm.co.uk
wheeldontreesfarm.co.uk

Hartington | **Ash Tree Cottage**
Enjoy England ★★★★ Mrs Clare Morson, Ash Tree Cottage, Nettletor Farm, Mill Lane, Buxton SK17 0AN   t 01298 84247   e nettletorfarm@btconnect.com

Milford | **The Ebenezer Chapel**
Enjoy England ★★★
Units: 1   Sleeps: 2-22
Open: All year
Low season p/w: £1000.00
High season p/w: £1795.00

Derbyshire Holidays, PO Box 7649, Belper, Derbyshire DE56 9DT
t 01332 840564   f 01773 825573
e ann.wayne@derbyshire-holidays.com
derbyshire-holidays.com   4B2

An 1846 riverside stone chapel, situated in the village of Milford in the Derwent Valley.

General: — Unit: —

Nr Hartington | **Old House Farm Cottages**
Enjoy England ★★★★ Mrs Sue Flower, Old House Farm Cottages, Old House Farm, Newhaven, Buxton SK17 0DY   t 01629 636268   e s.flower1@virgin.net
oldhousefarm.com

General: — Unit: —

For symbols see pg 24

East Midlands | Derbyshire/Leicestershire

Old Brampton | Chestnut and Willow Cottages

Enjoy England ★★★★ Mr & Mrs Jeffrey & Patricia Green, Chestnut and Willow Cottages, Priestfield Grange, Old Brampton S42 7JH
t 0800 141 2926 e patricia_green@btconnect.com

Leicester | Holiday Inn Leicester

129 St Nicholas Circle, Leicester, Leicestershire LE1 5LX
t 0870 400 9048 e leicestercity.reservations@ihg.com

holiday-inn.co.uk

Access: | **General:** | **Room:**

Leicester | Leicester Marriott

AS

Open: All year

Rooms per night:
s: £85.00-£159.00
d: £95.00-£169.00

p/p half board:
d: £106.45-£211.90
Meals: £21.45-£36.00

Shop: 0.5 miles
Pub: 0.5 miles

Smith Way, Grove Park, Enderby, Leicester LE19 1SW
t 01162 820100 e cork.regional.reservations@marriott.com

leicestermarriott.co.uk

4C3

The Leicester Marriott Hotel has 12 accessible king rooms, two of which have roll in showers. All areas in the hotel are accessible including Mixx Restaurant, Tanners Bar, Atrium, Leisure Club and bedrooms.

Location: Conveniently located minutes from M1 J21 with easy access to M6/M69/A14 and 4 miles from Leicester city centre.

Access:
General:
Room:

©Britainonview / - Britain on View

GETTING THERE IS NOT A PROBLEM!

OPEN BRITAIN See Getting there..... and back section (p364)
Everything you need for a hassle-free journey

216 www.openbritain.net

East Midlands | Leicestershire/Lincolnshire

Loughborough | imago at Burleigh Court   AS

Enjoy England ★★★★
Open: All year except Xmas and New Year

Rooms per night:
s: £79.00-£107.00
d: £99.00-£129.00
p/p half board:
d: £100.00-£128.00
Meals: £21.00-£26.00

Shop: 2 miles
Pub: 2 miles

Access:
General:
Room:

Loughborough University, Loughborough, Leicestershire LE11 3TD
t 08450 364624   e info@welcometoimago.com
welcometoimago.com   4C3

imago at Burleigh Court is one of the Midlands largest 4 star accredited residential conference centres and hotel offering accommodation ranging from the last word in luxury to unmatched quality and value.

Location: Leave junction 23 of the M1, taking the A512 Ashby Road to Loughborough. Turn right at first roundabout, into Holywell Way.

Market Harborough | Best Western Three Swans Hotel   AS

AA ★★★
Open: All year

Rooms per night:
s: £70.00-£98.50
d: £79.00-£113.00
p/p half board:
d: £65.00-£81.50
Meals: £9.00-£35.00

21 High Street, Market Harborough, Leicestershire LE16 7NJ
t 01858 466644   e sales@threeswans.co.uk
bw-threeswanshotel.co.uk   4C3

16thC coaching inn, 61 bedrooms, purpose built conference and event centre. Excellent food and service.

Access: General: Room:

Moira | YHA National Forest

Enjoy England ★★★★
48 Bath Lane, Moira, Ashby-de-la-Zouch DE12 6BD
t 0870 770 6141   e nationalforest@yha.org.uk
yha.org.uk

Alford | Half Moon Hotel

Enjoy England ★★★
25-28 West Street, Alford LN13 9DG
t 01507 463477   e halfmoonalford25@aol.com
halfmoonhotelalford.com

East Midlands | Lincolnshire

Belchford | Poachers Hideaway

Enjoy England
★★★★-★★★★★★

Jacki Harris, Flintwood Farm, Belchford LN9 5QN
t 01507 533555 e info@poachershideaway.com

poachershideaway.com

Access: General: Unit:

Blyton | Blyton (Sunnyside) Ponds

Enjoy England ★★★

Sunnyside Farm, Station Road, Blyton, Gainsborough DN21 3LE
t 01427 628240 e blytonponds@msn.com

blytonponds.co.uk

Boston | Crewyard Cottages

Enjoy England ★★★★

Colin Ash, Crewyard Cottages, Everards, Highgate, Leverton, Boston PE22 0AW
t 01205 871389 e gina@gina31.wanadoo.co.uk

crewyardholidaycottages-boston.co.uk

Burgh-On-Bain | Bainfield Lodge

Enjoy England ★★★★

Marian Walker, Bainfield Leisure, Bainfield House, Main Road, Market Rasen LN8 6JY   t 01507 313540 e dennis.walker1@btinternet.com

bainfieldholidaylodge.co.uk

Cleethorpes | Tudor Terrace Guest House

Enjoy England ★★★★

11 Bradford Avenue, Cleethorpes DN35 0BB
t 01472 600800 e tudor.terrace@ntlworld.com

tudorterrace.co.uk

Covenham St. Bartholomew | Westfield Mews & Lodges

Enjoy England
★★★★-★★★★★★

Mrs J Cream, Westfield Mews & Lodges, Westfield House, Covenham St Bartholomew, Louth LN11 0PB   t 01507 363217

Donington | Browntoft House

Enjoy England ★★★★

Browntoft Lane, Donington PE11 4TQ
t 01775 822091 e finchedward@hotmail.com

browntofthouse.co.uk

Goulceby | Bay Tree Cottage

Enjoy England ★★★★

Gordon Reid, Bay Tree Cottage, Goulceby Post, Ford Way, Goulceby, Louth LN11 9WD   t 01507 343230 e info@goulcebypost.co.uk

goulcebypost.co.uk

East Midlands | Lincolnshire

Hagworthingham | Kingfisher Lodge

Enjoy England ★★★★ Nick Bowser, E.W. Bowser & Son Ltd, The Estate Office, Leverton, Boston PE22 0AA t 01205 870210 e office@ewbowser.com

meridianretreats.co.uk

Hogsthorpe | Helsey House Cottages

AS

Enjoy England ★★★★
Units: 2 Sleeps: 4-5
Open: All year

Low season p/w: £310.00
High season p/w: £450.00

Mrs Elizabeth Elvidge, Joint Owner, Helsey, Hogsthorpe, nr. Skegness, Lincolnshire PE24 5PE
t 01754 872927 e eaepcs@yahoo.co.uk

helseycottages.co.uk 4D2

Rural location close to beaches. Special needs/autistic families welcome. Ring to discuss your needs.

Access:
General: Unit:

Horncastle | Best Western Admiral Rodney Hotel

Enjoy England ★★★ North Street, Horncastle LN9 5DX
t 01507 523131 e reception@admiralrodney.com

bestwestern.co.uk/admiralrodneyhotel

Hubberts Bridge | Elms Farm Cottages

AS

Enjoy England
★★★★-★★★★★
Units: 8 Sleeps: 2-5
Open: All year

Low season p/w: £340.00
High season p/w: £490.00

Carol Emerson, The Elms, Hubberts Bridge, Boston PE20 3QP
t 01205 290840 f 01205 290840 e carol@elmsfarmcottages.co.uk

elmsfarmcottages.co.uk 3A1

Relax and enjoy the Lincolnshire countryside from our 4 & 5 Star Award Winning Cottages. Elm Farm Cottages are all fully equipped and furnished to a high standard with level floor access. Five cottages with shower rooms suitable for wheelchairs.

Location: 2 miles from Historic Boston on the A1121 at Hubberts Bridge. Ideally situated for the Lincolnshire Fens, Wolds and Coast.

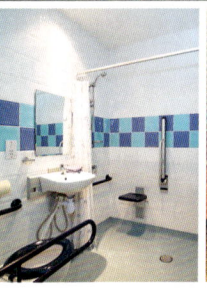

Access:
General:
Unit:

For symbols see pg 24

East Midlands | Lincolnshire

Ingoldmells | Ingoldale Park

Enjoy England ★★★★ Cathryn Whitehead, Ingoldale Park, Roman Bank, Ingoldmells PE25 1LL
t 01754 872335   e ingoldalepark@btopenworld.com
ingoldmells.net

Kirkstead | Kirkstead Old Mill Cottage

Enjoy England ★★★★ Tattershall Road, Woodhall Spa LN10 6UQ
t 01526 353637   e barbara@woodhallspa.com
woodhallspa.com

Lincoln | Cliff Farm Cottage

Enjoy England ★★★★
Units: 1   Sleeps: 4
Open: All year

Low season p/w: £350.00
High season p/w: £390.00

Rae Marris, Cliff Farm, North Carlton, Lincoln LN1 2RP
t 01522 730475   e info@cliff-farm-cottage.co.uk
cliff-farm-cottage.co.uk

4C2

Situated 3 miles north of historic Lincoln, charming cottage on working arable farm. Rural retreat.

Access: ☺   General: P   Unit:

Maltby Le Marsh | Ash & Chestnut Holiday Cottages

Enjoy England ★★★★ Ann Graves, Farmhouse B&B Cottages and Caravans, Grange Farm, Maltby le Marsh, Alford LN13 0JP   t 01507 450267   e anngraves@btinternet.com
grange-farmhouse.co.uk

Maltby Le Marsh | The Granary and Yew Tree Holiday Cottage

Enjoy England ★★★★ Ann Graves, Farmhouse B&B Cottages and Caravans, Grange Farm, Maltby le Marsh, Alford LN13 0JP   t 01507 450267   e anngraves@btinternet.com
grange-farmhouse.co.uk

Martin | The Manor House Stables

Enjoy England ★★★★ Sherry Forbes, The Manor House Stables, The Manor House, Timberland Road, Martin LN4 3QS   t 01526 378717   e sherryforbes@hotmail.com
manorhousestables.co.uk

HUDSONs

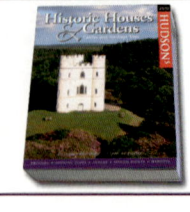

Hudson's is the definitive guide to historic houses & gardens.

Up to date information on over 2000 properties with clear information symbols for accessibility and facilities.

Historic Houses & Gardens
Castles and Heritage Sites

Order online at:
www.hhgroup.co.uk/hudsons

East Midlands | Lincolnshire/Northamptonshire

North Somercotes | Nursery Cottage   AS

Enjoy England ★★★★
Units: 3   Sleeps: 2-4
Open: All year
Low season p/w: £300.00
High season p/w: £450.00

Mrs Linda Libell, Meals Farm, Marsh Lane, North Somercotes LN11 7NT   t 01507 358256   e nurserycottage@hotmail.co.uk

mealsfarm.com   4D2

Modern, luxurious cottages in peaceful rural setting close to beach/nature reserve and market towns.

Access: abc   General: Unit:

Skegness | Chatsworth

Enjoy England ★★★
16 North Parade, Skegness PE25 2UB
t 01754 764177   e info@chatsworthskegness.co.uk
chatsworthskegness.co.uk

Woodhall Spa | Mill Lane Holiday Cottage

Enjoy England ★★
Ian Williamson, Mill Lane Holiday Cottages, 72 Mill Lane, Woodhall Spa LN10 6QZ   t 01526 353101   e janewill89@hotmail.com
skegness.net/woodhallspa.htm

Woodhall Spa | Petwood Hotel

Enjoy England ★★★
Open: All year
Rooms per night:
s: £95.00
d: £145.00
p/p half board:
d: £95.00
Meals: £23.95

Stixwould Road, Woodhall Spa LN10 6QG
t 01526 352411   e reception@petwood.co.uk

petwood.co.uk   4D2

The Petwood Hotel is an attractive building set in 30 acres of mature woodland.

Access:
General: Room:

Woodhall Spa | Wayside Cottage

Enjoy England ★★★
Ian Williamson, Mill Lane Holiday Cottages, 72 Mill Lane, Woodhall Spa LN10 6QZ   t 01526 353101   e janewill89@hotmail.com
skegness.net/woodhallspa.htm

Corby | Holiday Inn Corby-Kettering   AS

AA ★★★
Geddington Road, Corby, Northamptonshire NN18 8ET
t 01536 401020   e reservations@hicorby.com
www.holidayinn.co.uk

Access: abc   General: Room:

For symbols see pg 24   221

East Midlands | Northamptonshire/Nottinghamshire

Crick | Holiday Inn Rugby-Northampton

Junc 18 M1, Crick, Northamptonshire NN6 7XR
t 0871 9429059 e rugbyhi@ihg.com
ichotelsgroup.com

Access: General: Room:

Laxton | Spanhoe Lodge

AS

AA ★★★★★
Enjoy England ★★★★★
Open: All year

Rooms per night:
s: £85.00-£100.00
d: £90.00-£110.00
Meals: £10.00-£20.00
Shop: 4 miles
Pub: 1.5 miles

Laxton, nr. Corby, Northamptonshire NN17 3AT
t 01780 450328 e stay@spanhoelodge.co.uk
spanhoelodge.co.uk   4C3

Peace & tranquillity await you at this luxuriously appointed 5 Star GOLD accommodation. Our large, ground floor interconnecting rooms with fridges are adjacent to parking - one has a "wheel-in" wetroom. We serve gourmet breakfasts & cater for special diets.

Location: From A43 (Stamford - Corby) Take turning, sign posted Laxton. Go through village, after 0.5 mile Spanhoe Lodge on right.

Access:
General:
Room:

Wigsthorpe | Nene Valley Cottages

AS

Enjoy England ★★★★★
Units: 3   Sleeps: 2-4
Open: All year

Low season p/w:
£250.00
High season p/w:
£600.00

Heather Ball, The Cottage, Glapthorn PE8 5QB
t 01832 273601 e stay@nenevalleycottages.co.uk
nenevalleycottages.co.uk   4D3

Luxurious converted barns in secluded setting with Gold Award. One cottage is fully M3I compliant.

General: Unit:

Edwinstowe | Sherwood Forest Youth Hostel

Enjoy England ★★★★

Forest Corner, Edwinstowe, Mansfield NG21 9RN
t 0870 770 6026 e sherwood@yha.org.uk
yha.org.uk

222   www.openbritain.net

East Midlands | **Nottinghamshire**

Holbeck | **Browns**

Enjoy England ★★★★★ The Old Orchard Cottage, Holbeck, Worksop S80 3NF
t 01909 720659   e browns@holbeck.fsnet.co.uk
brownsholbeck.co.uk

Nottingham | **Harts Hotel**   AS

AA ★★★★   Park Row, Nottingham, Nottinghamshire NG1 6GN
Open: All year   t 0115 988 1900   e reception@hartshotel.co.uk
Rooms per night: **hartsnottingham.co.uk**   4C2
s: £121.50–£206.50
d: £135.00–£220.00   Hart's is Nottingham's highest rated Boutique hotel and award winning restaurant.
Meals: £25.00–£50.00

Access: General: Room:

Nottingham | **Holiday Inn Nottingham**

AA ★★★   Castle Bridge Road, Castle Marina Park, Nottingham NG7 1GX
t +44 0 115 9935000
holiday-inn.co.uk

Access: General: Room:

Nottingham | **Vitalise Skylarks**   AS

Adbolton Road, West Bridgford, Nottingham, Nottinghamshire NG2 5AS
t 0115 982 0962   e skylarks@vitalise.org.uk
vitalise.org.uk

Access: General: Room:

OPEN BRITAIN

Join today!

Become a member of OpenBritain today.

Share your own travel and accommodation experiences and help Britain become more open!

visit **www.openbritain.net**

For symbols see pg 24   223

East Midlands | **Nottinghamshire/Attractions**

Worksop | Clumber Park Caravan Club Site — THE CARAVAN CLUB

Enjoy England ★★★★★

🚐 (183) £14.60–£21.55
🚚 (183) £14.60–£21.55
183 touring pitches
Open: All year
Shop: 5 miles
Pub: 5 miles

Lime Tree Avenue, Clumber Park, Worksop, Nottinghamshire S80 3AE t 01909 484758

caravanclub.co.uk   4C2

There's a great feeling of spaciousness here, for the 20 acre site is set within 4,000 acres of parkland. Set in the heart of Sherwood Forest, also visit Nottingham Castle and the watersports centre at Holme Pierrepont.

Location: From junction of A1 and A57, take A614 signposted Nottingham for 0.5 miles. Turn right into Clumber Park site.

Access:
General:
Pitch:

Bolsover | Bolsover Castle

Open: For opening hours and prices, please call 0870 333 1181 or visit www.english-heritage.org.uk/properties

Castle Street, Bolsover, Derbyshire S44 6PR
t 0870 333 1181   e customers@english-heritage.org.uk
english-heritage.org.uk/bolsovercastle

Enjoy a family day out, there's lots to discover and places to rest and picnic.

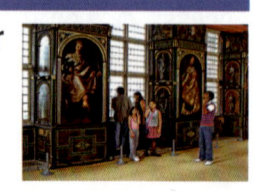

Access: **General:**

Sutton Cheney | Bosworth Battlefield Visitor Centre & Country Park

Sutton Cheney, Nuneaton, Leicestershire CV13 0AD
t 01455 290429   e bosworth@leics.gov.uk
bosworthbattlefield.com

Lincoln | Lincoln Cathedral

Minster Yard, Lincoln, Lincolnshire LN2 1PZ
t 01522 561600   e visitors@lincolncathedral.com
lincolncathedral.com

Access: **General:**

East Midlands | **Attractions**

Kenilworth | Kenilworth Castle & Elizabethan Garden

Open: For opening hours and prices, please call 0870 333 1181 or visit www.english-heritage.org.uk/properties

Kenilworth, Warwickshire CV8 1NE
t 0870 333 1181 e customers@english-heritage.org.uk
english-heritage.org.uk/kenilworth

With its new wheelchair accessible Elizabethan garden, restored gatehouse and exhibitions, there's lots to entertain.

Access: **General:**

Ollerton | Rufford Abbey Country Park

Ollerton, Nottinghamshire NG22 9DF
t 01623 822944 e info.rufford@nottscc.gov.uk
nottinghamshire.gov.uk

Great Witley | Witley Court

Open: For opening hours and prices, please call 0870 333 1181 or visit www.english-heritage.org.uk/properties

Great Witley, Worcestershire WR6 6JT
t 0870 333 1181 e customers@english-heritage.org.uk
english-heritage.org.uk/witleycourt

Explore a stunning romantic ruin, beautiful woodland walks and Parterre Gardens and the spectacular fountains.

Access: **General:**

OPEN BRITAIN DECIDED WHERE TO GO? SEE ATTRACTIONS FOR WHAT TO DO
Ideas and information at the end of each regional section

For symbols see pg 24

225

UpenBritain | East Midlands

The Thomas Centre

A *Unique* holiday park for everyone, designed for groups with communication impaired people.

Safe, Stunning and Just Perfect!

All year round short breaks and holidays, for families, young adults and residential groups!

The Thomas Centre is a contemporary barn development, which provides luxury self-catering holiday accommodation for families, or groups with communication impaired people.

Set in private grounds in Lincolnshire between the Wolds and the coast, the **4* and 5* plus**, stunning accommodation includes bungalows built to M2 disabled regulations.

Facilities on the 25 acre park include a private **indoor heated swimming pool, woodland, a community room, outdoor playing fields and indoor play barn with pool table, skittle alley** and more.

The Thomas Centre is also available for residential field trips and has conference facilities for group bookings.

www.thethomascentre.co.uk

"It's so lovely to come to relax in a place surrounded by fields and countryside. There was a lot to see and do. We shall definitely come here again!"
A happy guest.

For booking enquiries please contact Jan Crean on 01507 363463

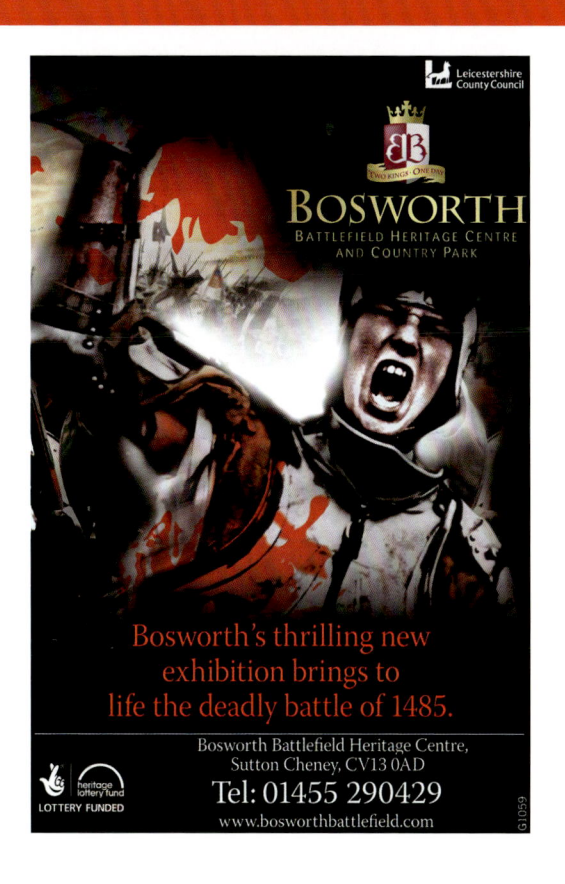

OpenBritain | East Midlands

BOSWORTH
BATTLEFIELD HERITAGE CENTRE AND COUNTRY PARK

Leicestershire County Council

Bosworth's thrilling new exhibition brings to life the deadly battle of 1485.

Bosworth Battlefield Heritage Centre,
Sutton Cheney, CV13 0AD
Tel: 01455 290429
www.bosworthbattlefield.com

LOTTERY FUNDED — heritage lottery fund

Grosvenor Centre Northampton
Where the shops are
all under one roof

GROSVENOR CENTRE

Tel: 01604 637268
www.grosvenorshoppingcentre.co.uk

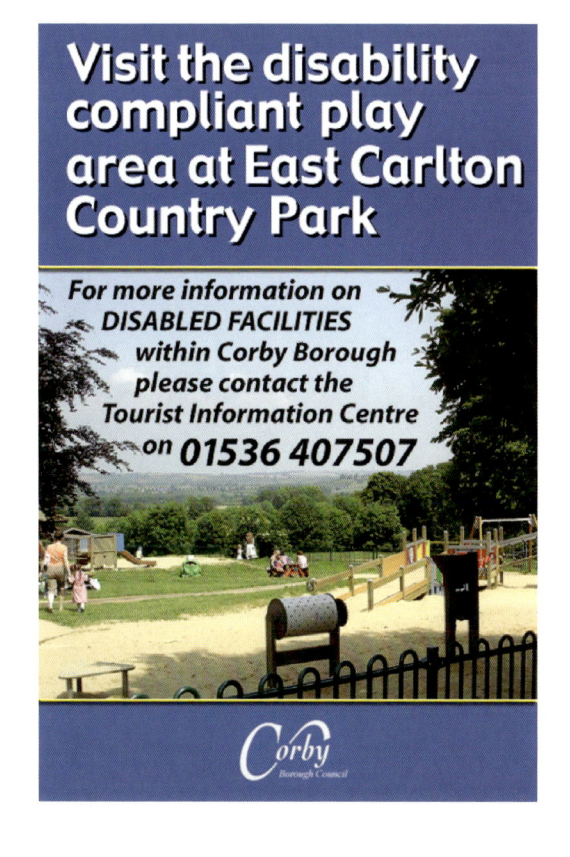

Visit the disability compliant play area at East Carlton Country Park

For more information on **DISABLED FACILITIES** within Corby Borough please contact the Tourist Information Centre on **01536 407507**

Corby Borough Council

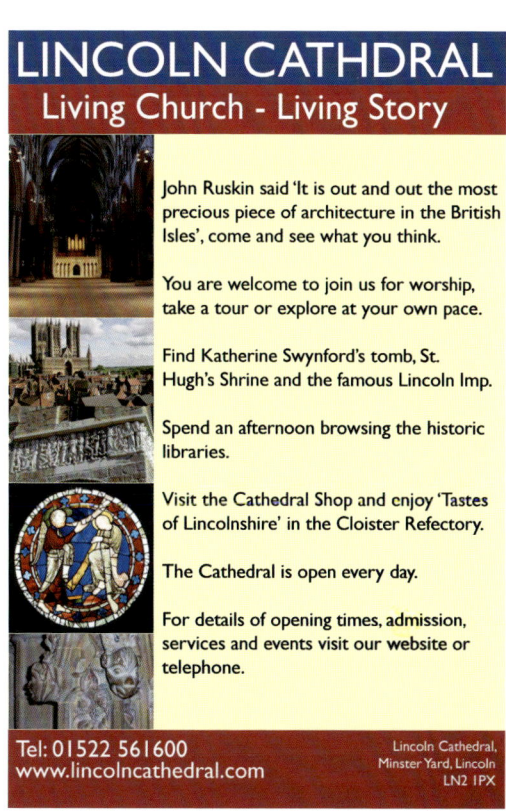

LINCOLN CATHDRAL
Living Church - Living Story

John Ruskin said 'It is out and out the most precious piece of architecture in the British Isles', come and see what you think.

You are welcome to join us for worship, take a tour or explore at your own pace.

Find Katherine Swynford's tomb, St. Hugh's Shrine and the famous Lincoln Imp.

Spend an afternoon browsing the historic libraries.

Visit the Cathedral Shop and enjoy 'Tastes of Lincolnshire' in the Cloister Refectory.

The Cathedral is open every day.

For details of opening times, admission, services and events visit our website or telephone.

Tel: 01522 561600
www.lincolncathedral.com

Lincoln Cathedral,
Minster Yard, Lincoln
LN2 1PX

Explore ...... Newark & Sherwood

Outdoor Activity Centres,
Country Parks,
Museums,
Historic Buildings,
Craft Centres,
Ancient Forests,
Cafes / Restaurants,
Cycle Hire,
Market Towns,
Garden Centres ...
And so much more ...

Email: tourism@nsdc.info
Website: www.visitnewarkandsherwood.co.uk

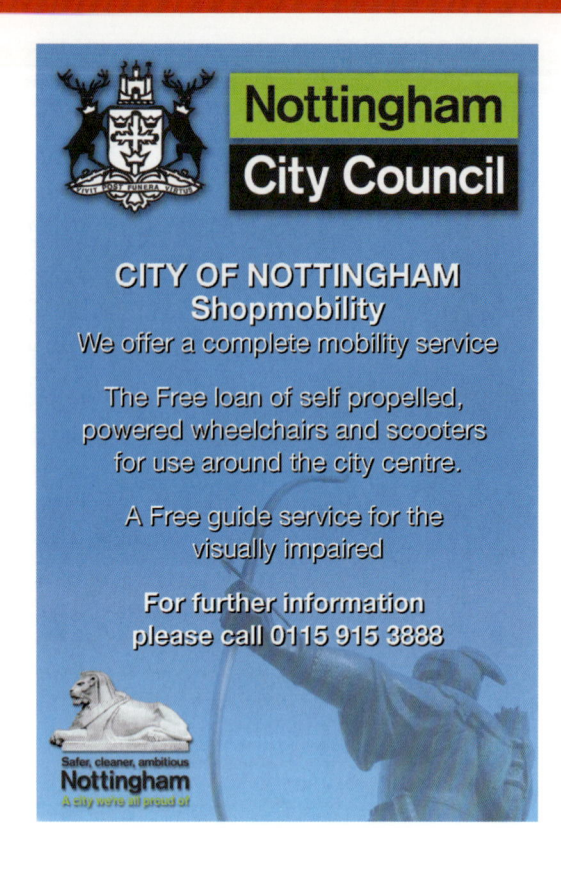

NEWARK & SHERWOOD DISTRICT COUNCIL

Nottingham City Council

CITY OF NOTTINGHAM
Shopmobility
We offer a complete mobility service

The Free loan of self propelled, powered wheelchairs and scooters for use around the city centre.

A Free guide service for the visually impaired

For further information please call 0115 915 3888

Safer, cleaner, ambitious
Nottingham
A city we're all proud of

NORTH SHORE

Ideal for family holidays by the sea!

Come and visit us on the East Coast

We have Pemberton Sovereign Caravan Holiday homes, specially designed for wheelchair users.

Pets are welcome too in selected units!

Shops and licensed club on site.

Public transport to and from site entrance.

NORTH SHORE
HOLIDAY CENTRE,
SKEGNESS, PE25 1SL

TEL. (01754) 763815
(01754) 762051

WWW.NORTHSHORE-SKEGNESS.CO.UK

Home of Robin Hood

Nottinghamshire

Explore the home of legends with easily accessible attractions and hotels.

To plan a trip best suited to you, call **08444 77 5678** and request a copy of the Nottinghamshire essential guide.

www.robinhoodbreaks.com

OpenBritain | East Midlands

RENISHAW HALL & GARDENS

A DAY OUT FOR ALL THE FAMILY

BEAUTIFUL CLASSICAL ITALIAN GARDENS
THE 400-YEAR-OLD HOME OF THE SITWELLS
CHILDREN'S FAIRYTALE GARDEN
PERFORMING ARTS GALLERY
SITWELL MUSEUM AND FILM
JOHN PIPER GALLERY
THE GALLERY CAFE
GIFT SHOP AND RESIDENT ARTIST
EXCELLENT DISABLED ACCESS

GROUP TOURS CAN BE BOOKED

RENISHAW, DERBYSHIRE - M1 JUNCTION 30
01246 432 310   WWW.RENISHAW-HALL.CO.UK

Bruce Wake Charitable Trust
ASSISTING THE PROVISION OF LEISURE FACILITIES FOR THE DISABLED

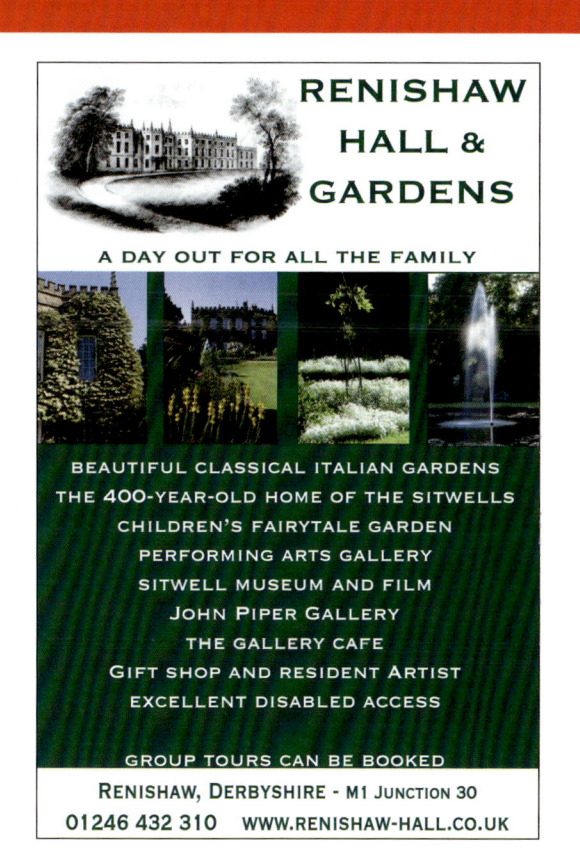

A Charitable Trust assisting the provision of leisure facilities for the disabled.
Ayston, Oakham, Rutland LE15 9AE
Tel & Fax: (01572) 822183
E-mail: wake@webleicester.co.uk
Website: www.brucewaketrust.co.uk

Operates three boats designed for use by disabled people, based at Upton-on-Severn between Tewkesbury and Worcester.

Two are narrowboats designed for a wheelchair user and family with berths for 6 - 7 people for holidays on the rivers and canals of the south west Midlands.

One is a wide-beamed boat for use on the rivers Severn and Avon and the Gloucester-Sharpness Canal.

All three boats have two hydraulic lifts, a hoist over a bed and a specially designed WC / shower.

Rates: from £550 - £700 (2009 / 2010)

Rufford Abbey Country Park

- Historic parkland & abbey ruins
- Restaurant & cafe
- Contemporary sculpture & craft exhibitions
  - Children's Garden

Open daily (except Xmas Day).
Free admission. Car parking £3.

Tel: 01623 821338
www.nottinghamshire.gov.uk/ruffordcp
Free loan of wheelchairs and mobility scooters.

Nottinghamshire County Council

©Britainonview / - Britain on View

GETTING THERE IS NOT A PROBLEM!

OPEN BRITAIN See Getting there….. and back section (p364)
Everything you need for a hassle-free journey

229

OpenBritain | Heart of England

Ironbridge with views of Telford town

The Heart of England – central, accessible, unmissable!

Welcome to The Heart of England – home to England's heritage and culture. From **Stratford-upon-Avon**, the birthplace of Shakespeare, to our world heritage site of **Ironbridge Gorge**, from the imposing **Warwick Castle** to '**The Potteries**' – home to the famous Wedgwood brand. From the iconic **Royal Shakespeare Company** to the **City of Birmingham Symphony Orchestra** and **Birmingham Royal Ballet**.

Welcome to The Heart of England – home to world-class festivals and events. From annual events that celebrate our heritage such as Darwin birthday celebrations in **Shrewsbury** to the Much Wenlock Olympian Games. From food and drink festivals such as **Ludlow**, real ale festivals, asparagus, plum and apple festivals to internationally acclaimed events such as the **V Festival**, **Three Choirs Festival** and **Artsfest**.

Welcome to The Heart of England – home to quintessential English countryside. From Worcestershire's market town of Broadway – gateway to **The Cotswolds**, to Shropshire and Herefordshire with their **Black and White Village Trails** to the imposing **Trentham Estate** – England's largest garden restoration project and the dozens of Capability Brown designed landscape gardens.

Welcome to The Heart of England – home to great English food and drink. Devour home made traditional food in country inns and pubs, experience Michelin ▶

230   www.openbritain.net

OpenBritain | Heart of England

Warwick Castle

Wedgwood

Heart of England

Herefordshire	Warwickshire
Shropshire	West Midlands
Staffordshire	

▶ starred restaurants in Ludlow and Birmingham, sample Black Country 'faggots' and Staffordshire oatcakes, the Birmingham 'Balti' and a myriad of local cheeses. Be quenched by Bass beer, Bulmers cider, wine, perry, and discover the micro-breweries of the countryside.

Welcome to The Heart of England – home to a great accessible welcome from our accommodation providers – hotels, caravanning sites such as Poston Mill, bed and breakfast establishments like Hidelow House. From our attractions such as **Cadbury World**, the **Heritage Motor Centre** at Gaydon, **RAF Cosford** and **Drayton Manor Theme Park** to the many National Trust properties such as **Attingham Park** near Shrewsbury with its accessible walks, and **Croombe Park** near Worcester with its mobility buggies.

Not only will you find this a region that's easy to get to – at the heart of the UK road, rail and canal network, it's a region that's easy to get around. Just go to www.visittheheart.co.uk for a full list of accessible –friendly attractions and accommodation that are sure to deliver exactly what you're looking for.

Find out more

web www.visittheheart.co.uk ■

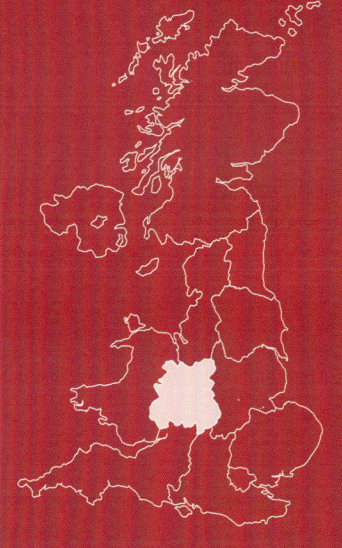

G Force at Drayton Manor

www.openbritain.net

OpenBritain | Heart of England

RAF Cosford

Heart of England countryside

Tourist Information Centres

Tourist Information Centres are a mine of information about local and regional accommodation, attractions and events. Visit them when you arrive at your destination or contact them before you go:

Bewdley	Load Street	01299 404740	bewdleytic@wyreforestdc.gov.uk
Birmingham	The Rotunda	0844 888 3883	callcentre@marketingbirmingham.com
Bridgnorth	The Library	01746 763257	bridgnorth.tourism@shropshire.gov.uk
Church Stretton	Church Street	01694 723133	churchstretton.scf@shropshire.gov.uk
Coventry Cathedral	Coventry Cathedral	024 7622 5616	tic@cvone.co.uk
Hereford	1 King Street	01432 268430	tic-hereford@herefordshire.gov.uk
Ironbridge	Ironbridge Gorge Museum Trust	01952 884391	tic@ironbridge.org.uk
Leamington Spa	The Royal Pump Rooms	01926 742762 I	eamington@shakespeare-country.co.uk
Leek	Stockwell Street	01538 483741	tourism.services@staffsmoorlands.gov.uk
Lichfield	Lichfield Garrick	01543 412112	info@visitlichfield.com
Ludlow	Castle Street	01584 875053	ludlow.tourism@shropshire.gov.uk
Malvern	21 Church Street	01684 892289	malvern.tic@malvernhills.gov.uk
Oswestry	Mile End	01691 662488	tic@oswestry-bc.gov.uk
Ross-On-Wye	Swan House	01989 562768	tic-ross@herefordshire.gov.uk
Rugby	Little Elborow Street	01788 533217	visitor.centre@rugby.gov.uk
Shrewsbury	The Music Hall	01743 281200	visitorinfo@shrewsbury.gov.uk
Solihull	Central Library	0121 704 6130	artscomplex@solihull.gov.uk
Stafford	Gatehouse Theatre	01785 619619	tic@staffordbc.gov.uk
Stoke-On-Trent	Victoria Hall, Bagnall Street	01782 236000	stoke.tic@stoke.gov.uk
Stratford-Upon-Avon	Bridgefoot	0870 160 7930	stratfordtic@shakespeare-country.co.uk
Tamworth	29 Market Street	01827 709581	tic@tamworth.gov.uk
Warwick	The Court House	01926 492212	touristinfo@warwick-uk.co.uk
Worcester	The Guildhall	01905 728787	touristinfo@cityofworcester.gov.uk

Heart of England | Herefordshire

Ewyas Harold | Old King Street Farm
Enjoy England ★★★★ Robert Dewar, Old King Street Farm, Ewyas Harold, Golden Valley HR2 0HB
t 01981 240208   e info@oldkingstreetfarm.co.uk
oldkingstreetfarm.co.uk

Hereford | Grafton Villa Farm Cottages
Enjoy England ★★★★
Units: 3   Sleeps: 2-6
Open: All year
Low season p/w: £250.00
High season p/w: £580.00

Mrs Jennie Layton, Owner, Grafton Villa, Grafton, Hereford HR2 8ED   t 01432 268689   e jennielayton@ereal.net
graftonvilla.co.uk

2A1

Gorgeous, award winning holiday cottages set within the farmhouse walled gardens overlooking farmland - perfect.

Access: abc   General: P S   Unit:

Ledbury | Old Kennels Farm
Enjoy England ★★★-★★★★★ Owner, Old Kennels Farm, Bromyard Road, Ledbury HR8 1LG

Leintwardine | Mocktree Barns Holiday Cottages
Enjoy England ★★★ Clive & Cynthia Prior, Mocktree Barns Holiday Cottages, Leintwardine, Ludlow SY7 0LY   t 01547 540441   e mocktreebarns@care4free.net
mocktreeholidays.co.uk

Leominster | YHA Leominster
Enjoy England ★★★★ The Priory, Leominster HR6 8EQ
t 01568 620517   e leominster@yha.org.uk
yha.org.uk

Little Tarrington | Hereford Camping and Caravanning Club Site
Enjoy England ★★★★★ Little Tarrington, Hereford HR1 4JA
t 01432 890243   e enquiries@millpond.co.uk
campingandcaravanningclub.co.uk/hereford

Looking for something else? If you haven't found what you are looking for in OpenBritain, VisitBritain's Official Tourist Board Guides offer a wide choice of assessed accommodation which may meet your needs.

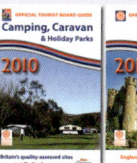

For symbols see pg 24

Heart of England | Herefordshire

Malvern | Hidelow House Cottages

Enjoy England
★★★★-★★★★★
Units: 3 Sleeps: 2-12
Open: All year
Low season p/w: £295.00
High season p/w: £2800.00
Pub: 2.5 miles

Access:
General:
Unit:

Mrs Pauline Diplock, Proprietor, Acton Green, Acton Beauchamp, Worcester WR6 5AH t 01886 884547 e openb@hidelow.co.uk

hidelow.co.uk

3 outstanding award-winning holiday cottages (sleeping 2, 5 and 12 people) in rural but accessible Elgar country. With a wide selection of assistance aids available and carers if required, we aim to provide worry-free holidays for disabled guests and their carers.

Location: From M5 J7, take A44, A4440, then A4103 at top of hill towards Bromyard. After 2mls turn left at signboard.

Michaelchurch Escley | Holt Farm

Enjoy England ★★★★

Nick Pash, Holt Farm, Michaelchurch Eskley, c/o Hideaways, Shaftesbury SP7 0HQ t 01747 828170 e enq@hideaways.co.uk

hideaways.co.uk/property.cfm/h189

Ross on Wye | Portland House

AA ★★★★

Whitchurch, Ross on Wye, Herefordshire HR9 6DB
t 01600 890757 e info@portlandguesthouse.co.uk

portlandguesthouse.co.uk

Access: General: Room:

Ross on Wye | Trevase Granary

Enjoy England ★★★★★

Mrs Liz Pursey, Trevase Granary, Trevase Farm, St Owens Cross HR2 8ND
t 01989 730210 e stay@trevasecottages.co.uk

trevasecottages.co.uk

Access: General: Unit:

Whitchurch | Tump Farm Holiday Cottage

Enjoy England ★★★

Mrs Debbie Williams, Tump Farm Holiday Cottage, Tump Farm, Whitchurch, Ross-on-Wye HR9 6DQ t 01600 891029 e clinwilcharmaine@hotmail.com

www.openbritain.net

Heart of England | Shropshire

Albrighton | Boningale Manor Barns
Enjoy England ★★★★ Owner, Boningale Manor Barns, Holyhead Road, Albrighton WV7 3AT

Broseley | Coalport YHA
Enjoy England ★★★ c/o John Rose Building, High Street, Telford TF8 7HT
t 0870 770 5882 e ironbridge@yha.org.uk
yha.org.uk

Corfton | Goosefoot Barn Cottages
Enjoy England ★★★★
Units: 4 Sleeps: 2-4
Open: All year
Low season p/w: £210.00
High season p/w: £485.00

Mrs Sally Loft, Goosefoot Barn Cottages, Pinstones, Diddlebury, Craven Arms SY7 9LB
t 01584 861326 e info@goosefootbarn.co.uk
goosefootbarn.co.uk   4A3

Fully-equipped cottages in Corvedale, near Ludlow. Twin and Double bedrooms all En Suite. Short breaks.
Access: abc
General: Unit:

Craven Arms | Tugford Farm Holiday Cottages
Enjoy England ★★★★ Tugford, Craven Arms, Shropshire SY7 9HS
t 01584 841259 e tugfordfarm@yahoo.co.uk
tugford.com

Access: General: Room:

Fishmore | Fishmore Hall
Enjoy England ★★★ Fishmore Road, Ludlow, Ludlow SY8 3DP

fishmorehall.co.uk

Lyth Bank | Lyth Hill House
Enjoy England ★★★★ 28 Old Coppice, Lyth Hill, Shrewsbury SY3 0BP
t 01743 874660 e bnb@lythhillhouse.com
lythhillhouse.com

Rowton | Church Farm Self Catering
Enjoy England ★★★ Mrs Virginia Evans, Church Farm, Rowton, Wellington, Telford TF6 6QY
t 01952 770381 e churchfarm49@beeb.net
churchfarmshropshire.co.uk

For symbols see pg 24

Heart of England | Shropshire/Staffordshire

Shrewsbury | Newton Meadows
Enjoy England ★★★★ Mr & Mrs Simcox, Wem Road, Harmer Hill, Shrewsbury, Shropshire SY4 3DZ
t 01939 290346 f 01939 290346 e e.simcox@btopenworld.com
newtonmeadows.co.uk

Access: General: Unit:

Stanton Lacy | Sutton Court Farm Cottages
Enjoy England ★★★-★★★★★ Mrs Jane Cronin, Sutton Court Farm, Little Sutton, Ludlow SY8 2AJ
t 01584 861305 e enquiries@suttoncourtfarm.co.uk
suttoncourtfarm.co.uk

Strefford | Strefford Hall Self Catering - Robins & Swallows Nest
Enjoy England ★★★★ Mrs Caroline Morgan, Strefford Hall, Strefford, Craven Arms SY7 8DE
t 01588 672383
streffordhall.co.uk

Telford | Holiday Inn Telford/Ironbridge
AA ★★★ St Quentin Gate, Telford, Shropshire TF3 4EH
t 01952 527000 e Hi.reception@southwatereventgroup.com
southwatereventgroup.com

Access: General: Room:

Tugford | Tugford Farm B&B
Enjoy England ★★★★ Tugford Farm, Craven Arms SY7 9HS
t 01584 841259 e tugfordfarm@yahoo.co.uk
tugford.com

Wheathill | The Malthouse
Mr & Mrs Brian & Janet Russell, The Malthouse, Bridgnorth WV16 6QT
t 01244 356666 e info@sykescottages.co.uk

Wroxeter | Wroxeter Hotel
Enjoy England ★★★ Wroxeter, Shrewsbury SY5 6PH
t 01743 761256 e info@thewroxeterhotel.co.uk
thewroxeterhotel.co.uk

Ilam | Beechenhill Farm Cottages
Enjoy England ★★★★ Alexandra Gray, Beechenhill Farm, Beechenhill Farm, Ilam, Ashbourne DE6 2BD t 01335 310274 e beechenhill@btinternet.com
beechenhill.co.uk

Heart of England | **Staffordshire**

Ilam | **The Cottage by the Pond**

Units: 1 Sleeps: 2-6
Open: All year

Low season p/w: £260.00
High season p/w: £720.00

Sue Prince, Beechenhill Farm, Ilam, Ashbourne, Derbyshire DE6 2BD t 01335 310274 e beechenhill@btinternet.com

beechenhill.co.uk 4B2

Specially converted barn for all on organic dairy farm in Peak District National Park.

Ilam | **YHA Ilam Hall**

Enjoy England ★★★

Ilam, Ashbourne DE6 2AZ
t 0870 770 5876 e ilam@yha.org.uk
yha.org.uk

Stanshope | **Dale Bottom Cottage**

Enjoy England
★★★★-★★★★★★

Mrs Sue Fowler, Church Farm, Milldale, Nr Alstonefield, Ashbourne DE6 2GD
t 01335 310243 e sue@fowler89.fsnet.co.uk
dovedalecottages.co.uk

Stoke-On-Trent | **Holiday Inn Stoke-on-Trent**

AA ★★★

Clayton Road, Newcastle-under-Lyme, Staffordshire ST5 4DL
t 0870 400 9077 e wendy.wortley@ihg.com
holidayinn.co.uk

Stoke-on-Trent | **Quarry Walk Park** AS

AA ★★★★
Enjoy England ★★★★
Units: 14 Sleeps: 2-6
Open: All year

Park Managers, Quarry Walk, Coppice Lane, Freehay, Alton, Staffordshire ST10 1RQ
t 01538 723412 e Quarry@quarrywalkpark.co.uk
quarrywalkpark.co.uk 4B2

14 luxurious log cabins with private hot tubs, 46 acres of woodland, quiet and relaxing.

OPEN BRITAIN

DECIDED WHERE TO GO?
SEE ATTRACTIONS FOR WHAT TO DO
Ideas and information at the end of each regional section

©Britainonview / Martin Brent

For symbols see pg 24 237

Heart of England | Warwickshire/West Midlands

Knightcote | Arbor Holiday & Knightcote Farm Cottages

Enjoy England ★★★★★
Units: 5   Sleeps: 4-10
Open: All year
Low season p/w: £453.00
High season p/w: £1708.00

Mr & Mrs Craig Walker, The Bake House, Knightcote, Southam CV47 2EF   t 01295 770637   e fionawalker@farmcottages.com

farmcottages.com   2C1

Award winning self-catering farm cottages in a quiet location - near to Stratford and Warwick.

Access: General: Unit:

Lighthorne | Church Hill Farm B & B

Enjoy England ★★★★
Lighthorne, Warwick CV35 0AR
t 01926 651251   e sue@churchillfarm.co.uk

churchhillfarm.co.uk

Stratford-Upon-Avon | The Stratford

Enjoy England ★★★★
Arden Street, Stratford-upon-Avon CV37 6QQ
t 01789 271000   e thestratford@qhotels.co.uk

qhotels.co.uk/hotels

Birmingham | Chapel Lane Caravan Club Site   THE CARAVAN CLUB

Enjoy England ★★★★★
(99)   £13.70–£19.55
(99)   £13.70–£19.55
99 touring pitches
Open: All year
Shop: 0.5 miles
Pub: 1 mile

Chapel Lane, Wythall, Birmingham, West Midlands B47 6JX
t 01564 826483

caravanclub.co.uk   4B3

A quiet, rural area yet convenient for Birmingham (9 miles) and the NEC (13 miles). Visit Cadbury's World, explore the surrounding countryside and local canals, or visit fascinating museums about our industrial heritage.

Location: M42 j3 onto A435 to Birmingham. At roundabout take 1st exit, Middle Lane. Turn right at church; site on right.

Access:
General:
Pitch:

238   www.openbritain.net

Heart of England | West Midlands/Worcestershire

Birmingham | Holiday Inn Birmingham City Centre
AA ★★★
Smallbrook Queensway, Birmingham, West Midlands B5 4EW
t 0870 400 9008　e reservations-birminghamcity@ihg.com
holidayinn.co.uk

Birmingham | Holiday Inn Birmingham M6 Junction 7
Chapel Lane, Great Barr, Birmingham, West Midlands B43 7BG
t 0871 9429009　e reservations-birminghamgreatbarr@ichhotelsgroup.com
holiday-inn.co.uk

Coventry | Holiday Inn Coventry M6 J2
AA ★★★
Hinckley Road, Walsgrave, Coventry, West Midlands CV2 2HP
t 0870 400 9021　e reservations-coventrym6@ihg.com
holiday-inn.co.uk

Chaddesley Corbett | Brockencote Hall
Enjoy England ★★★
Chaddesley Corbett, Nr Kidderminster DY10 4PY
t 01562 777876　e info@brockencotehall.com
brockencotehall.com

Redditch | White Hart Inn
Enjoy England ★★★
157 Evesham Road, Headless Cross, Redditch B97 5EJ
t 01527 545442　e enquiries@whitehartredditch.co.uk
whitehartredditch.co.uk

Worcester | The Manor Coach House
AS
Enjoy England ★★★★
Open: All year except Xmas and New Year

Rooms per night:
s: £45.00
d: £70.00

Hindlip Lane, Hindlip, Worcester WR3 8SJ
t 01905 456457　e info@manorcoachhouse.co.uk
manorcoachhouse.co.uk

Beautiful B&B, semi-rural location close to Worcester/M5. Five rooms, one with disabled access, full wetroom.

OPENBRITAIN.NET
The one-stop-shop for all your travel needs. Go online and see how we can help you get in, out ...and about.

For symbols see pg 24

Heart of England | Worcestershire/Attractions

Worcester | Roseland Bungalow Annexe
Enjoy England ★★★★
Mr & Mrs Guy & Mary Laurent, Clifton, Severn Stoke, Worcester WR8 9JF
t 01905 371463　e guy@roselandworcs.demon.co.uk
roselandworcs.demon.co.uk

Access: 　General: P　Unit:

Goodrich | Goodrich Castle
Open: For opening hours and prices, please call 0870 333 1181 or visit www.english-heritage.org.uk/properties

Goodrich, Ross-on-Wye, Herefordshire HR9 6HY
t 0870 333 1181　e customers@english-heritage.org.uk
english-heritage.org.uk/goodrich

Relive the history with our free audio tour. Explore the keep and maze of rooms.

Access: 　General: P

Tamworth | Drayton Manor
near Tamworth, Staffordshire B78 3TW
t 0844 472 1950　e info@draytonmanor.co.uk
draytonmanor.co.uk

Stratford-Upon-Avon | Royal Shakespeare Company RSC
The Courtyard Theatre, Southern Lane, Stratford-Upon-Avon, Warwickshire CV37 6BB　t 01789 296655　e ticketqueries@rsc.org.uk
rsc.org.uk

Birmingham | Cadbury World
Linden Road, Bournville, Birmingham, West Midlands B30 2LU
t 0845 450 3599
cadburyworld.co.uk

Edgbaston | Birmingham Botanical Gardens & Glasshouses
Westbourne Road, Edgbaston, Birmingham B15 3TR
t 01214 541860　e admin@birminghambotanicalgardens.org.uk
birminghambotanicalgardens.org.uk

Access: 　General: P

Walsall | New Art Gallery
Gallery Square, Walsall WS2 8LG
t 01922 654400　e WilkinsonC@walsall.gov.uk

www.openbritain.net

OpenBritain | Heart of England

Discover Trentham

- Stunning gardens with Lake, Adventure Play and Maze
- Monkey Forest with 140 Barbary Macaques
- Shopping Village and Garden Centre
- Choice of coffee shops & restaurants
- Ample free parking

The Trentham Estate

The Trentham Estate, Trentham, Stoke-on-Trent, Staffs ST4 8AX.
Tel: (01782) 646 646
www.trentham.co.uk   5 minutes from J15, M6

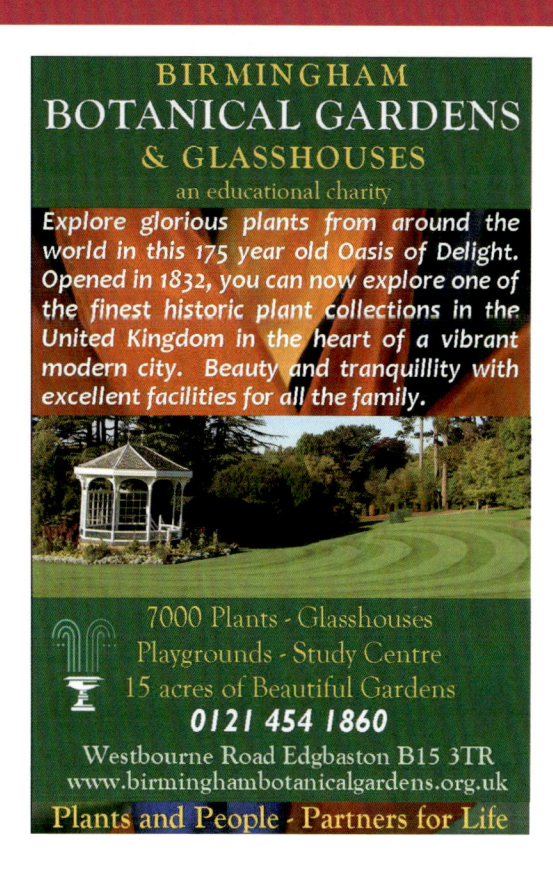

BIRMINGHAM BOTANICAL GARDENS & GLASSHOUSES
an educational charity

Explore glorious plants from around the world in this 175 year old Oasis of Delight. Opened in 1832, you can now explore one of the finest historic plant collections in the United Kingdom in the heart of a vibrant modern city. Beauty and tranquillity with excellent facilities for all the family.

7000 Plants - Glasshouses
Playgrounds - Study Centre
15 acres of Beautiful Gardens
0121 454 1860
Westbourne Road Edgbaston B15 3TR
www.birminghambotanicalgardens.org.uk
Plants and People - Partners for Life

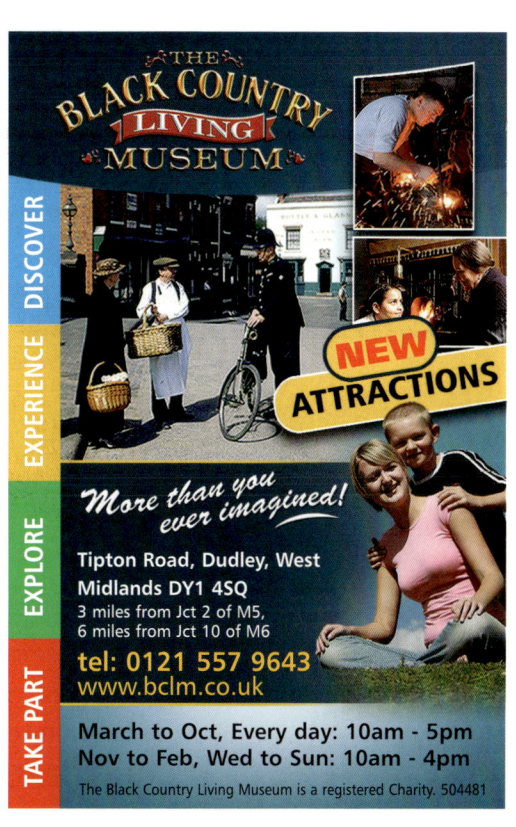

THE BLACK COUNTRY LIVING MUSEUM

DISCOVER • EXPERIENCE • EXPLORE • TAKE PART

NEW ATTRACTIONS

More than you ever imagined!

Tipton Road, Dudley, West Midlands DY1 4SQ
3 miles from Jct 2 of M5,
6 miles from Jct 10 of M6
tel: 0121 557 9643
www.bclm.co.uk

March to Oct, Every day: 10am - 5pm
Nov to Feb, Wed to Sun: 10am - 4pm
The Black Country Living Museum is a registered Charity. 504481

Cadbury WORLD

Where Chocolate comes to Life!

Visit the amazing new Advertising Avenue zone at Cadbury World. Stroll down our chocolate street and take a peek through the windows to bring sweet memories flooding back. Enjoy everything from unforgettable Cadbury commercials and jingles to great TV advertising moments that had the whole nation talking – including an unmissable live performance by a certain ape. With a whole day's worth of multi-sensory chocolatey fun to be had, Cadbury World is a fantastic day out!

FOURTEEN AMAZING ZONES. ONE FANTASTIC DAY OUT.
BOOK NOW ON 0845 450 3599 OR VISIT CADBURYWORLD.CO.UK

---

enjoy Rugby

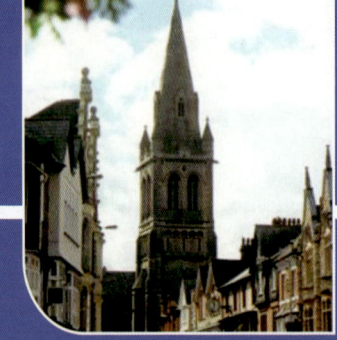

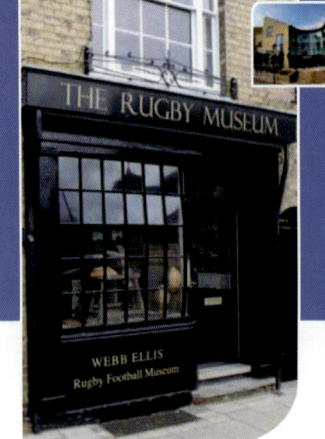

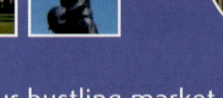

Discover how our bustling market town influenced the world with its Sporting History, Literary Heritage and Scientific Legacy.
Enjoy Rugby - more than just a game.

For an information pack contact Rugby Visitor Centre on
Tel: **01788 533217**
Email: visitor.centre@rugby.gov.uk
www.enjoyrugby.info

RUGBY - THE BIRTHPLACE OF THE GAME
RUGBY COUNCIL

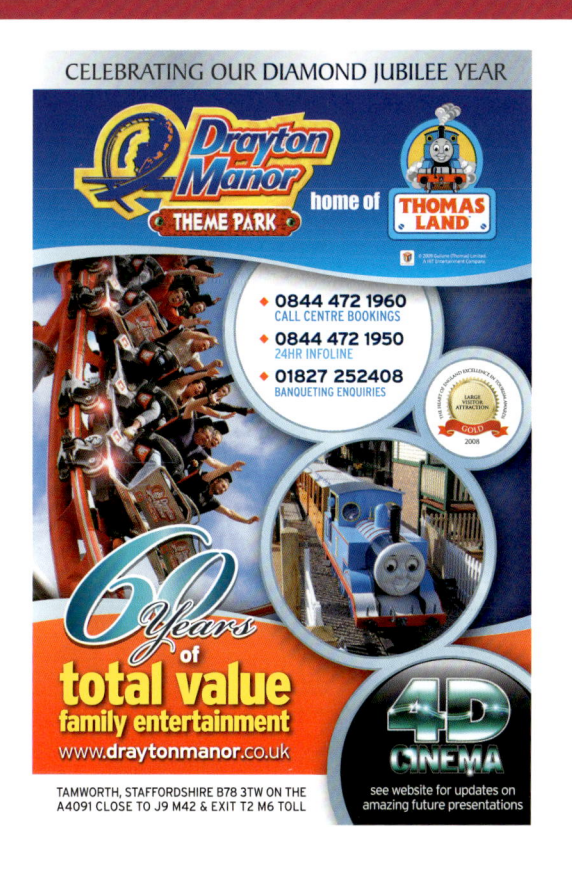

OpenBritain | Heart of England

Drayton Manor Theme Park

CELEBRATING OUR DIAMOND JUBILEE YEAR

home of THOMAS LAND

- 0844 472 1960 CALL CENTRE BOOKINGS
- 0844 472 1950 24HR INFOLINE
- 01827 252408 BANQUETING ENQUIRIES

60 Years of total value family entertainment

www.draytonmanor.co.uk

4D CINEMA — see website for updates on amazing future presentations

TAMWORTH, STAFFORDSHIRE B78 3TW ON THE A4091 CLOSE TO J9 M42 & EXIT T2 M6 TOLL

The New Art Gallery Walsall

■ Relax ■ Imagine ■ Explore ■ Discover
Free admission
Open 7 days

The New Art Gallery Gallery Square
Walsall WS2 8LG

Tel: 01922 654400
www.artatwalsall.org.uk

Walsall Council

ARTS COUNCIL ENGLAND

HERITAGE MOTOR CENTRE
THE ROAD TO A GREAT DAY OUT

MUSEUM | SHOP | CAFÉ | ACTIVITIES AND MUCH MORE

Home to the world's largest collection of historic British cars

An award winning attraction with excellent facilities for the less able visitor

T: 01926 641188
E: enquiries@heritage-motor-centre.co.uk
www.heritage-motor-centre.co.uk

Interactive zones
Disabled parking
Wide gangways

QUALITY ASSURED VISITOR ATTRACTION

HERITAGE MOTOR CENTRE

JUNCTION 12 M40 WARWICKSHIRE

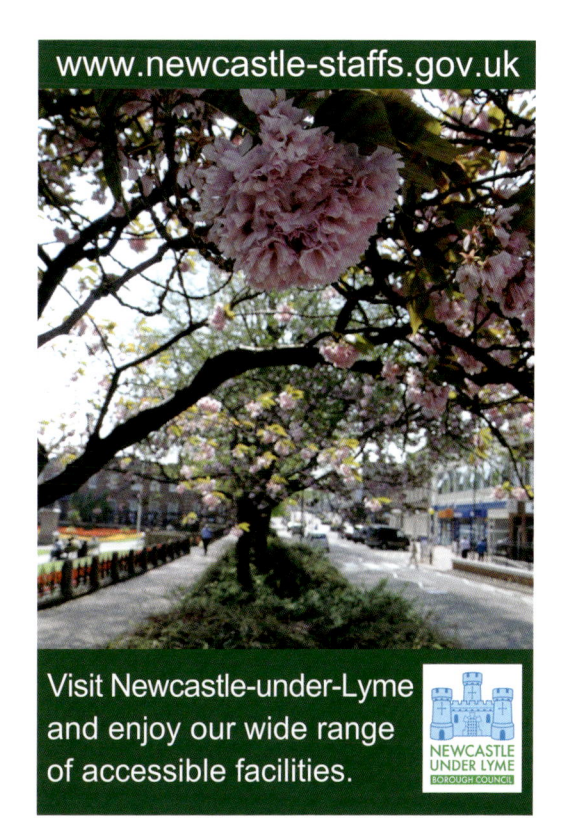

www.newcastle-staffs.gov.uk

Visit Newcastle-under-Lyme and enjoy our wide range of accessible facilities.

NEWCASTLE UNDER LYME BOROUGH COUNCIL

OpenBritain | Heart of England

SHREWSBURY

Goodness Gracious Great Days Out!

For information on visiting historic Shrewsbury, events, accessible accommodation, Shopmobility, and audio version of our brochure...

...call Shrewsbury Visitor Information on **01743 281200**
Email: visitorinfo@shropshire.gov.uk
Visit www.visitshrewsbury.com

Tamworth Castle offers guided and specialist tours to suit you!
Call **01827 709632**
or email: heritage@tamworth.gov.uk

Take a tour through Tamworth's History with a Heritage Guided Tour
Call **01827 709581**
or email: tic@tamworth.gov.uk

Tamworth Borough Council

Staffordshire County Council

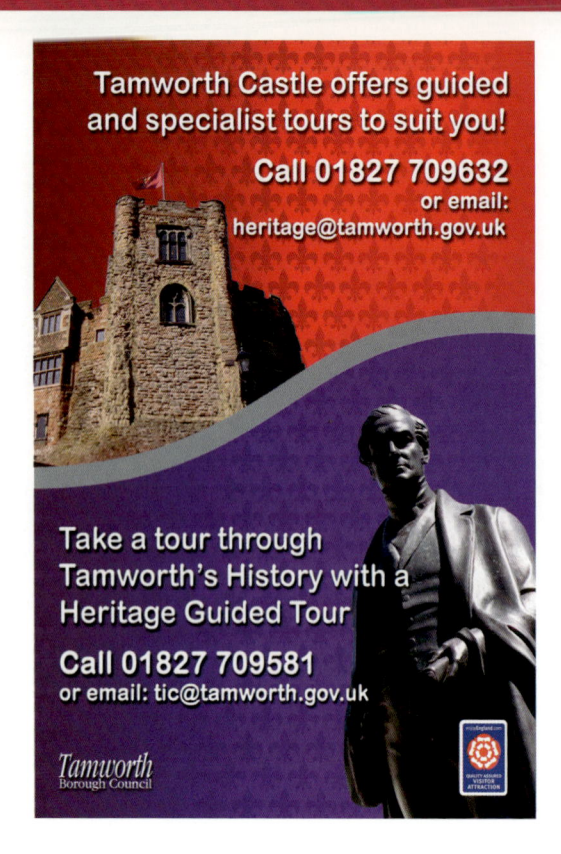

Country Parks with Facilities for Disabled People

Cannock Chase Country Park
Visitor Centre with RADAR keyed toilets and accessible café. Self-guided trail for the visually impaired and is wheelchair friendly (taped commentary available), 3 electric scooters for use on marked routes free of charge.

Apedale Country Park, Chesterton
Wheelchair route to viewpoint.

RADAR keyed toilets and wheelchair accessible visitor centre at:
Consall Nature Park, Wetley Rocks.
Deep Hayes Country Park, Cheddleton.
Greenway Bank Country Park, Knypersley.
Oakamoor Picnic area, Cheadle.

Contact 01785 277264

Come to **Twycross Zoo**
and bring out the animal in you.

Burton Road, Atherstone, Warwickshire, CV9 3PX
Tel: 01827 880250
www.twycrosszoo.org

The definitive guide to Britain's finest

Historic Houses & Gardens
Castles and Heritage Sites

Open to visitors

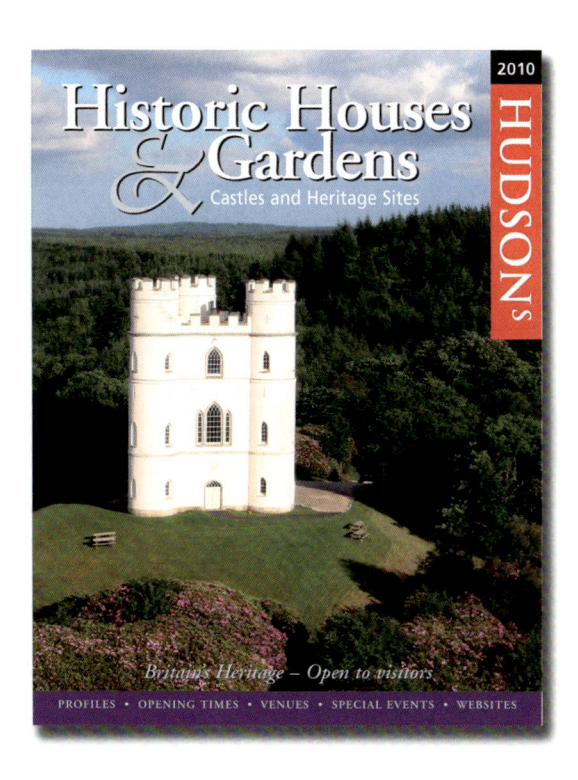

HUDSONs 2010

THE MUST HAVE GUIDE FOR GREAT DAYS OUT
SPECIAL OFFER ONLY £11.00 (normally £14.95) free p&p
Order online at: www.hhgroup.co.uk/hudsons or T: 01603 813319

OpenBritain | Yorkshire & Humber

Welcome to Yorkshire

Yorkshire and Humber is a region full of variety and you will be spoiled for choice by the many things to see and do and the places to go. Explore the great outdoors and get a feel for culture with the numerous galleries and museums, or discover which cities are the key to a night of lively entertainment.

As England's largest county Yorkshire and Humber is an exciting and diverse destination for all budgets. It's also one of the most accessible regions within the UK. High speed trains from London to the cities of York, Leeds, Sheffield, Doncaster and Hull can take as little as 90 minutes, and with three major airports, the region is a popular destination with visitors from across the globe.

A region full of inspiration, Yorkshire and Humber offers a variety of cultural sights to satisfy all tastes. From galleries and exhibitions to interactive museums and bold stately homes, these wonderful attractions are scattered across the region, enabling you to have the chance to explore more fully what Yorkshire has to offer. Take a trip to the coast and enjoy miles of clean golden beaches, take a tour around locations featured in internationally renowned literature and movies, immerse yourself in history within the region's historic houses and gardens, enjoy a designer shopping experience and take a piece of Yorkshire home.

The following is a small sample of what's on offer, with full accessible information on
www.yorkshire.com/disabled-go

Explore Yorkshire's industrial past at the **Magna Science Centre** in Rotherham or visit the **1853 Gallery at Salts Mill** in Bradford to wonder at over 400 works by Yorkshire artist David Hockney. The mill also houses a diner providing food and drinks in fine surroundings. Discover **the Parsonage in Haworth**, the former home of the Brontë sisters. Be transported back in time in **Hull's Museum Quarter**, visit the **Streetlife Transport Museum** or have a fun filled day out at **the world's only submarium, The Deep**, and experience the dramatic story of the world's oceans, from the dawn of time and into the future.

Gunnerside, Yorkshire Dales

Famous for miles of heritage coastline, castles, stately homes and churches, as well as being home to around 2663 ancient monuments, Yorkshire has a colourful sense of heritage and evidence of past lives are around every corner. Visit **Wakefield Cathedral** or **Cusworth Hall** in Doncaster. Take a tour of the stunning **Castle Howard** near York, **Harewood House** in Leeds and **Barley Hall** in York, all will amaze you with their magical settings and sense of grandeur.

What's so special about the Yorkshire countryside is that the best views are there for everyone to see; you don't have to climb a mountain or trek for miles. Many roads cross the moorland plateau and there are plenty of viewpoints where you can really take in the unique atmosphere of such a special place. And don't forget there are outdoor activities which can be suitable for a much wider range of people than you think and many venues have specialist instructors who are there to help. ▶

Haworth

OpenBritain | Yorkshire & Humber

Roche Abbey

Victoria Quarter, Leeds

Yorkshire & Humber

North Yorkshire
West Yorkshire
Hull & East Yorkshire
South Yorkshire

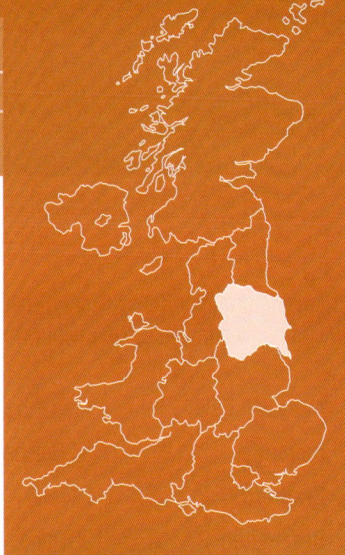

▶ Few places can be better than the **North York Moors** for people who really want to enjoy spectacular countryside but are not very mobile. The North York Moors National Park Authority has developed eight fully accessible routes for heavy duty wheelchairs and pushchairs through woodland, along riversides, by lakes, overlooking the Heritage Coast, through the heart of the moorland and around the fortifications at Cawthorn Roman Camp.

In the **Yorkshire Dales** there are many great places to visit however mobile you are. A number of accessible trails have been developed, some suitable for wheelchairs, accessible fishing platforms, as well as farms and waterfalls that can be visited.

Yorkshire and Humber has spectacular scenery, world class attractions, a year round calendar of festivals and events, vibrant cities alive with culture, and locally produced food and drink served in welcoming country inns and award winning restaurants. Find out more on **www.yorkshire.com** which lists a whole range of information on getting out and about and enjoying Yorkshire to the full, whatever your needs may be.

Find out more

web www.yorkshire.com/disabled-go

The Deep

OpenBritain | Yorkshire & Humber

Castle Howard

Tourist Information Centres

Tourist Information Centres are a mine of information about local and regional accommodation, attractions and events. Visit them when you arrive at your destination or contact them before you go:

Aysgarth Falls	Aysgarth Falls NP Centre	01969 662910	aysgarth@yorkshiredales.org.uk
Beverley	34 Butcher Row	01482 391672	beverley.tic@eastriding .gov.uk
Bradford	City Hall	01274 433678	tourist.information@bradford.gov.uk
Bridlington	25 Prince Street	01262 673474	bridlington.tic@eastriding.gov.uk
Danby	The Moors Centre, Lodge Lane	01439 772737	moorscentre@northyorkmoors-npa.gov.uk
Doncaster	The Blue Building	01302 734309	tourist.information@doncaster.gov.uk
Filey	John Street	01723 383637	tourismbureau@scarborough.gov.uk
Grassington	National Park Centre	01756 751690	grassington@yorkshiredales.org.uk
Guisborough	Priory Grounds	01287 633801	guisborough_tic@redcar-cleveland.gov.uk
Halifax	Piece Hall	01422 368725	halifax@ytbtic.co.uk
Harrogate	Royal Baths	01423 537300	tic@harrogate.gov.uk

OpenBritain | Yorkshire & Humber

Hawes	Dales Countryside Museum	01969 666210	hawes@yorkshiredales.org.uk
Haworth	2/4 West Lane	01535 642329	haworth@ytbtic.co.uk
Hebden Bridge	Visitor and Canal Centre	01422 843831	hebdenbridge@ytbtic.co.uk
Helmsley	Helmsley Castle	01439 770173	helmsley.tic@englishheritage.org.uk
Holmfirth	49-51 Huddersfield Road	01484 222444	holmfirth.tic@kirklees.gov.uk
Huddersfield	3-5 Albion Street	01484 223200	huddersfield.tic@kirklees.gov.uk
Hull	1 Paragon Street	01482 223559	tourist.information@hullcc.gov.uk
Humber Bridge	North Bank Viewing Area	01482 640852	humberbridge.tic@eastriding.gov.uk
Ilkley	Station Road	01943 602319	ilkleytic@bradford.gov.uk
Knaresborough	9 Castle Courtyard	0845 389 0177	kntic@harrogate.gov.uk
Leeds	Gateway Yorkshire	0113 242 5242	tourinfo@leeds.gov.uk
Leeming Bar	The Yorkshire Maid	01677 424262	leeming@ytbtic.co.uk
Leyburn	4 Central Chambers	01748 828747	tic.leyburn@richmondshire.gov.uk
Malham	National Park Centre	01969 652380	malham@yorkshiredales.org.uk
Malton	Market Place	01653 600048	maltontic@btconnect.com
Otley	Otley Library	01943 462485	otleytic@leedslearning.net
Pateley Bridge	8 High Street	0845 389 0177	pbtic@harrogate.gov.uk
Pickering	Ropery House	01751 473791	pickeringtic@btconnect.com
Reeth	National Park Centre	01748 884059	reeth@yorkshiredales.org.uk
Richmond	Friary Gardens	01748 828742	tic.richmond@richmondshire.gov.uk
Ripon	Minster Road	01765 604625	ripontic@harrogate.gov.uk
Rotherham	40 Bridgegate	01709 835904	tic@rotherham.gov.uk
Scarborough	Brunswick Shopping Centre	01723 383636	tourismbureau@scarborough.gov.uk
Scarborough	Harbourside TIC	01723 383636	tourismbureau@scarborough.gov.uk
Settle	Town Hall	01729 825192	settle@ytbtic.co.uk
Sheffield	14 Norfolk Road	0114 2211900	visitor@yorkshiresouth.com
Skipton	35 Coach Street	01756 792809	skipton@ytbtic.co.uk
Sutton Bank	National Park Centre	01845 597426	suttonbank@northyorkmoors-npa.gov.uk
Thirsk	49 Market Place	01845 522755	thirsktic@hambleton.gov.uk
Todmorden	15 Burnley Road	01706 818181	todmorden@ytbtic.co.uk
Wakefield	9 The Bull Ring	0845 601 8353	tic@wakefield.gov.uk
Wetherby	Library & Tourist Info. Centre	01937 582151	wetherbytic@leedslearning.net
Whitby	Langborne Road	01723 383637	whitbytic@scarborough.gov.uk
Withernsea	131 Queen Street	01964 615683	withernsea.tic@eastriding.gov.uk
York	The De Grey Rooms	01904 550099	info@visityork.org
York Railway Station	Outer Concourse	01904 550099	info@visityork.org

www.openbritain.net

Yorkshire & Humber

Bailiff Bridge | The Lodge @ Dirkby Hall

Enjoy England ★★★★ Birkby Hall, Birkby Lane, Brighouse HD6 4JJ
t 01484 400321 e thelodge@birkbyhall.co.uk
birkbyhall.co.uk

Bolton Abbey | Strid Wood Caravan Club Site — THE CARAVAN CLUB

Enjoy England ★★★★★ Bolton Abbey, Skipton, North Yorkshire BD23 6AN
t 01756 710433

(57) £13.70–£19.55
(57) £13.70–£19.55

caravanclub.co.uk   4B1

57 touring pitches
Open: 27 March - 4 January
Shop: 4 miles
Pub: 3 miles

One of the prettiest Club sites and part of the Bolton Abbey Estate in open glades surrounded by woodland and the glorious Yorkshire Dales. Within the boundaries of the estate are miles of footpaths through moors, woods and farmland.

Location: B6160 from A59 Bolton Bridge roundabout; after 3m turn right into car park. Do not approach on B6160 from north.

Access:
General:
Pitch:

Bridlington | The Bay View Hotel

Enjoy England ★★ 52 South Marine Drive, Bridlington YO15 3JJ
t 01262 674225 e info@bay-view-hotel.com
bay-view-hotel.com

Bridlington | Providence Place   AS

Enjoy England ★★★★ 11 North View Terrace, Bridlington YO15 2QP
t 01262 603840 e enquiries@providenceplace.info
providenceplace.info

Access: **General:**   **Room:**

Brighouse | Holiday Inn Leeds/Brighouse

AA ★★★ Clifton Village, Brighouse, West Yorkshire HD6 4HW
t 0870 400 9013 e reservations-brighouse@ihg.com
holiday-inn.co.uk

Access: **General:**   **Room:**

www.openbritain.net

Yorkshire & Humber

Buckden | **Dalegarth and The Ghyll Cottages**

Enjoy England ★★★★
Units: 3 Sleeps: 2-6
Open: All year

Low season p/w: £387.00
High season p/w: £722.00

Shop: <0.5 miles
Pub: <0.5 miles

Access:
General:
Unit:

Mr & Mrs David Lusted, Proprietors, 11 Dalegarth, Buckden BD23 5JU t 01756 760877 e info@dalegarth.co.uk

dalegarth.co.uk

5B3

Level access; downstairs En Suite double or twin bedroom with spa bath & level deck shower. Additional bedroom(s)/bathroom upstairs. Ground floor wheelchair friendly. Secluded sunny garden; stunning views yet close to village centre. Use of nearby indoor heated pool.

Location: Buckden, Upper Wharfedale, between Skipton (30 min) and Aysgarth (20 min) on B6160. Convenient for visiting Wensleydale, Nidderdale, Swaledale, Malhamdale.

Clapham | **New Inn Hotel**

Enjoy England ★★★

New Inn Hotel, Clapham LA2 8HH
t 01524 251203 e info@newinn-clapham.co.uk
newinn-clapham.co.uk

Crow Edge | **Lazy Daisy's**

Enjoy England ★★★-★★★★★

Sally Howe, Lazy Daisy's, Daisy Hill Farm, Flouch S36 4HH
t 01226 763001 e daisyhillfarm@tiscali.co.uk
lazydaisys.co.uk

Drewton | **Rudstone Walk Country Accommodation**

Enjoy England ★★-★★★★★

Laura Greenwood, Rudstone Walk Country Accommodation, South Cave HU15 2AH t 01430 422230 e office@rudstone-walk.co.uk
rudstone-walk.co.uk

Drewton | **Rudstone Walk Country B&B**

Enjoy England ★★★★

South Cave, Beverley HU15 2AH
t 01430 422230 e office@rudstone-walk.co.uk
rudstone-walk.co.uk

For symbols see pg 24

Yorkshire & Humber

Ebberston | Cow Pasture & Swallow-Tail Cottages

Enjoy England ★★★-★★★★

David & Brenda Green, Studley House Farm, 67 Main Street, Ebberston YO13 9NR t 01723 859285 e brenda@yorkshireancestors.com

studleyhousefarm.co.uk

Ellerby | Ellerby

Enjoy England ★★★★

Rooms per night:
s: £55.00-£75.00
d: £85.00-£110.00
Meals: £9.00-£25.00

Ryeland Lane, Ellerby, Saltburn-by-the-Sea TS13 5LP
t 01947 840342 e relax@ellerbyhotel.co.uk

ellerbyhotel.co.uk   5D2

Run by the Alderson family since 1985 and located in a beautiful country, coastal setting.

Access: abc
General: Room:

Fellbeck | Brimham Rocks Cottages

Enjoy England ★★★★

Deborah Gray, Brimham Rocks Cottages, High North Farm, Fellbeck HG3 5EY
t 01765 620284 e brimhamrockscottages@yahoo.com

brimham.co.uk

Filey | 5 Leys Holiday Accommodation

Enjoy England ★★★★★

Mrs Kerry Welsby, 5 Leys Bar, Restaurant & Holiday Accommodation, 7-10 The Beach, Filey YO14 9LA t 0845 094 5051 e kerry@icflimited.co.uk

5leys.co.uk

Filey | Muston Grange Farm

Enjoy England ★★★

Units: 5   Sleeps: 5
Open: All year

Low season p/w:
£295.00
High season p/w:
£590.00

David & Gillian Teet, Muston Road, Filey, North Yorkshire YO14 0HU t 01723 516620 e info@thecottagesfiley.co.uk

thecottagesfiley.co.uk   5D3

Group of five cottages, one being wheelchair friendly. Close to Filey on Yorkshire Coast.

Access: abc   General: Unit:

Become a member of OpenBritain today.
Share your own travel and accommodation experiences and help Britain become more open!

OPEN BRITAIN

visit www.openbritain.net

252   www.openbritain.net

Yorkshire & Humber

Flamborough | Flamborough Rock Cottages

Enjoy England ★★★
Units: 1   Sleeps: 2-8
Low season p/w: £390.00
High season p/w: £675.00

Mrs J Geraghty, 13 Dog & Duck Square, Bridlington YO15 1NB
t 01262 850996   e jannicegeraghty@hotmail.com

flamboroughrockcottages.co.uk

5D3

Well equipped cottage in pretty fishing village on Yorkshire's Heritage Coast. Enclosed courtyard at rear.

Gateforth | Lund Farm Cottages

Enjoy England ★★★★

Mr Chris Middleton, Lund Farm Cottages, Lund Farm, Gateforth YO8 9LE
t 01757 228775   e lundfarm@talktalk.net

lundfarm.co.uk

Harwood Dale | The Grainary

Enjoy England ★★★★

Harwood Dale, Scarborough YO13 0DT
t 01723 870026   e grainary@btopenworld.com

grainary.co.uk

Helmsley | Helmsley YHA

Enjoy England ★★★★

Carlton Lane, Helmsley YO62 5HB
t 01439 770433   e helmsley@yha.org.uk

yha.org.uk

High Catton | The Courtyard at High Catton Grange

Enjoy England ★★★★-★★★★★

Sheila Foster, High Catton Grange, High Catton, York YO41 1EP
t 01759 371374   e foster-s@sky.com

highcattongrange.co.uk

Ilkley | Westwood Lodge, Ilkley Moor

Enjoy England ★★★★-★★★★★

Tim Edwards, Westwood Lodge Ilkley Moor, Westwood Drive, Ilkley LS29 9JF
t 01943 433430   e welcome@westwoodlodge.co.uk

westwoodlodge.co.uk

Ingleton | Riverside Lodge

Enjoy England ★★★★

24 Main Street, Ingleton LA6 3HJ
t 01524 241359   e info@riversideingleton.co.uk

riversideingleton.co.uk

For symbols see pg 24

Yorkshire & Humber

Kelfield | The Dovecote Barns York

Enjoy England ★★★★★ Mrs Brigita Bramley, The Dovecote Barns York, Manor Farm, Kelfield YO19 6RG   t 01757 249332   e enquiries@dovecotebarnsyork.co.uk
dovecotebarnsyork.co.uk

Kirkbymoorside | The Cornmill

Enjoy England ★★★★ Kirby Mills, Kirkbymoorside YO62 6NP
t 01751 432000   e cornmill@kirbymills.co.uk
kirbymills.co.uk

Access: abc   **General:**   **Room:**

Kirkbymoorside | Low Hagg Holidays

Enjoy England ★★★★ Mr J Lee, Low Hagg Holidays, Low Hagg, Starfitts Lane, York YO62 7JF
t 01751 430500
lowhaggfarm.com

Leeds | Crowne Plaza Leeds

AA ★★★★ Wellington Street, Leeds, West Yorkshire LS1 4DL
t 0871 942 9170   e sales.cpleeds@ihg.com
leeds.crowneplaza.com

Access: **General:**   **Room:**

Leeds | Weetwood Hall Conference Centre & Hotel

Enjoy England ★★★★ Otley Road, Leeds, West Yorkshire LS16 5PS
t 0113 230 6000   e reservations@weetwood.co.uk
weetwood.co.uk   4B1

Open: All year

Rooms per night:
s: £69.00-£155.00
d: £69.00-£155.00
p/p half board:
d: £54.50-£97.50
Meals: £22.00

Built around a 17th century Manor House, Weetwood Hall offers extensive hotel services and facilities.

Access: **General:**   **Room:**

Leven | Agape

Enjoy England ★★★★ Heron House, Beverley Road, Beverley HU17 5PA
t 01964 541316   e enquiries@stayatagape.co.uk
stayatagape.co.uk

OPEN BRITAIN

GETTING THERE IS NOT A PROBLEM!
See Getting there.....
and back section (p364)
Everything you need for a hassle-free journey

©BritainonView - Britain on View

254   www.openbritain.net

Yorkshire & Humber

Levisham, nr Pickering | Lowstead Farm Cottage AS

Units: 1   Sleeps: 1-4
Low season p/w:
£270.00
High season p/w:
£420.00

Mrs Susan Pearson, Lowstead Farm, Levisham, Pickering, North Yorkshire YO18 7NL   t 01751 460043   e lowsteadfarm@gmail.com

lowsteadfarm.co.uk   5D3

A two-bedroomed cottage with beautiful views.

Access: General: Unit:

Lockton | YHA Lockton

Enjoy England   ★★★★   The Old School, Lockton, Nr. Pickering YO18 7PY
t 01751 460376   e lockton@yha.org.uk
yha.org.uk

Newton-On-Rawcliffe | Mel House Cottages

Enjoy England   ★★★★   John Wicks, Let's Holiday, Mel House, Newton-on-Rawcliffe YO18 8QA
t 01751 475396   e holiday@letsholiday.com
letsholiday.com

Newton-On-Rawcliffe | Sunset Cottage

Enjoy England   ★★★★   Pat Anderson, Mrs Anderson's Country Cottages, Boonhill Cottage, Newton-on-Rawcliffe YO18 8QF   t 01751 472172   e bookings@boonhill.co.uk
boonhill.co.uk/sunset.htm

Northallerton | Lovesome Hill Farm

Enjoy England   ★★★★   Northallerton DL6 2PB
t 01609 772311   e lovesomehillfarm@btinternet.com
lovesomehillfarm.co.uk

Pickering | Eastgate Cottages

Enjoy England
★★★★-★★★★★★   Kevin & Elaine Bedford, Eastgate Cottages Ltd, 117 Eastgate, Pickering YO18 7DW   t 01751 476653   e info@eastgatecottages.co.uk
eastgatecottages.co.uk

HUDSONs

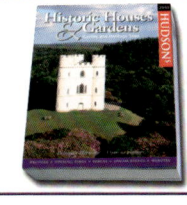

Hudson's is the definitive guide to historic houses & gardens.

Up to date information on over 2000 properties with clear information symbols for accessibility and facilities.

Historic Houses & Gardens
Castles and Heritage Sites

Order online at:
www.hhgroup.co.uk/hudsons

For symbols see pg 24   255

Yorkshire & Humber

Pickering | Keld Head Farm Cottages

Enjoy England ★★★★
Units: 9 Sleeps: 2-8
Open: All year
Low season p/w: £210.00
High season p/w: £1090.00
Shop: <0.5 miles
Pub: 0.5 miles

Penny & Julian Fearn, Keld Head, Pickering YO18 8LL
t 01751 473974 e julian@keldheadcottages.com
keldheadcottages.com

5D3

At the gateway to the North York Moors, a picturesque group of stone cottages with beamed ceilings, stone fireplaces. Furnished with emphasis on comfort and relaxation. Six cottages are easy access single storey. Large accessible gardens with garden house.

Location: In open countryside, off A170, yet an easy paved walk to Pickering centre. Scarborough, Whitby, York are a short drive.

General:
Unit:

Preston | Little Weghill Farm

Enjoy England ★★★★
Weghill Road, Preston, Hull HU12 8SX
t 01482 897650 e info@littleweghillfarm.co.uk
littleweghillfarm.co.uk

OPEN BRITAIN

Join today!

Become a member of OpenBritain today.

Share your own travel and accommodation experiences and help Britain become more open!

visit **www.openbritain.net**

Yorkshire & Humber

Richmond | Hargill House Caravan Club Site

Enjoy England ★★★★

🚐 (86) £10.45–£15.90
🚙 (86) £10.45–£15.90

86 touring pitches
Open: 27 March – 9 November

Shop: 1 mile
Pub: 1 mile

Access:
General:
Pitch:

Gilling West, Richmond, North Yorkshire DL10 5LJ
t 01748 822734

caravanclub.co.uk

5C3

A tranquil site in the old town of Richmond with breathtaking views over the Yorkshire Dales. It's Herriot country, and you'll find many of the locations used in the famous series. It's also where the artist Turner travelled and painted.

Location: Leave A1 at Scotch Corner onto A66. After 1.5m turn left at crossroads. Site entrance is 100yds on left.

Saltwick Bay | Whitby Holiday Park - Holiday Homes

Enjoy England ★★★★ Whitby Holiday Park, Saltwick Bay, Whitby YO22 4JX

Scarborough | The Scarborough Travel and Holiday Lodge

Enjoy England ★★★ 33 Valley Road, Scarborough YO11 2LX
t 01723 363537 e enquiries@scarborough-lodge.co.uk
scarborough-lodge.co.uk

Sewerby | Field House Farm Cottages

Enjoy England ★★★★–★★★★★ Mr & Mrs Foster, Field House Farm Cottages, Jewison Lane, Sewerby YO16 6YG t 01262 674932 e john.foster@farmline.com
fieldhousefarmcottages.co.uk

Slaithwaite | The Mistal Bed and Breakfast

Enjoy England ★★★★★ The Mistal, Cop Hill Side, Huddersfield HD7 5XA
t 01484 845404 e carolineandphil1@tiscali.co.uk
themistal.co.uk

Yorkshire & Humber

Sleights | Groves Dyke Holiday Cottage
Enjoy England ★★★ Niall Carson, Groves Dyke, Woodlands Drive, Sleights YO21 1RY
t 01947 810220 e relax@grovesdyke.co.uk
grovesdyke.co.uk

Stape | Rawcliffe House Farm
Enjoy England ★★★★ Duncan & Jan Allsopp, Rawcliffe House Farm, Stape YO18 8JA
t 01751 473292 e stay@rawcliffehousefarm.co.uk
rawcliffehousefarm.co.uk

Summerbridge | Helme Pasture Lodges & Cottages
Enjoy England ★★★★ Mrs Rosemary Helme, Helme Pasture Lodges & Cottages, Hartwith Bank, Summerbridge, Harrogate HG3 4DR
t 01423 780279 e info@helmepasture.co.uk
helmepasture.co.uk

Thornton Dale | Easthill Farm House and Gardens
Enjoy England ★★★★ Mrs Diane Stenton, Easthill Farm House and Gardens, Wilton Road, Thornton Dale, Pickering YO18 7QP t 01751 474561
e info@easthill-farm-holidays.co.uk
easthill-farm-holidays.co.uk

Thorpe Bassett | The Old Post Office
Enjoy England ★★★★ Sandra Simpson, S Simpson Cottages, The Old Post Office, Thorpe Bassett YO17 8LU t 01944 758047 e ssimpsoncottages@aol.com
ssimpsoncottages.co.uk

Wakefield | Holiday Inn Leeds-Wakefield M1 J40
AS
Queens Drive, Ossett, Wakefield, West Yorkshire WF5 9BE
t 0870 400 9082 e reservations-wakefield@ihg.com
holiday-inn.co.uk

Access: .: abc 🐕 🏨 😊 ♿ ♿ ♿ **General:** 🛏 🍴 ✕ 🍽 P ❄ 🔥 ♿ **Room:** 🛏 📺 🔐 📻 S ☕

Whitby | Captain Cook's Haven
Enjoy England ★★★★ Anne Barrowman, Captain Cook's Haven, Larpool Lane, Whitby YO22 4NE
t 01947 893573 e mail@hoseasons.co.uk
whitbyholidayhomes.co.uk

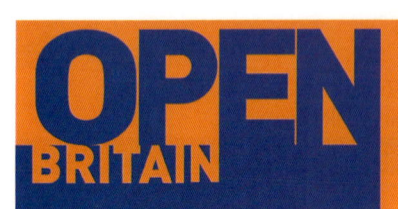

OPEN BRITAIN
PLANNING A DAY OUT? WHY NOT MAKE IT A SHORT-BREAK?
Fabulous 'Places to Stay' in every region

Yorkshire & Humber

Whitby | Carlton House Holiday Accommodation

Enjoy England ★★★★
Units: 1   Sleeps: 2-4
Open: All year

Low season p/w:
£440.00
High season p/w:
£610.00

Ms Vicki Clayton, Manager, Carlton House Apartments, 5 Royal Crescent, Whitby, North Yorkshire YO21 3EJ
t 01947 602868   e phillip.moore1@btconnect.com

carltonhouseapartments.co.uk   5D3

4* apartment with high quality facilities close to the heart of Whitby town.

General: [symbols]   Unit: [symbols]

Whitby | Whitby YHA

Enjoy England ★★★★
East Cliff, Whitby YO22 4JT
t 01947 602878
yha.org.uk

Wrelton | Beech Farm Cottages

Enjoy England ★★★★-★★★★★★
Rooney Massara, Beech Farm Cottages, Wrelton YO18 8PG
t 01751 476612   e holiday@beechfarm.com
beechfarm.com

Yapham | Wolds View Holiday Cottages

Enjoy England ★★★★-★★★★★
Margaret Woodliffe, Wolds View Holiday Cottages, Mill Farm, Yapham YO42 1PH   t 01759 302172   e info@woldsview.co.uk

York | Best Western Monkbar Hotel

Enjoy England ★★★
St. Maurice's Road, York YO31 7JA
t 01904 638086   e sales@monkbarhotel.co.uk
bestwestern.co.uk/monkbarhotel

York | Express by Holiday Inn York - East

AS

Malton Rd, York YO32 9TE
t 01904 438 660
hiexpress.co.uk

Access: [symbols]   General: [symbols]   Room: [symbols]

York | The Groves

Enjoy England ★★★
St. Peters Grove, York YO30 6AQ
t 01904 559777   e info@thegroveshotelyork.co.uk
thegroveshotelyork.co.uk

For symbols see pg 24

Yorkshire & Humber

York | Holiday Inn York

Tadcaster Road, York, North Yorkshire YO24 1QF
t 0870 400 9085   e reservations-york@ihg.com

holidayinn.co.uk

Access: abc   General: Room:

York | Rowntree Park Caravan Club Site

THE CARAVAN CLUB

Terry Avenue, York, North Yorkshire YO23 1JQ
t 01904 658997

caravanclub.co.uk   4C1

Enjoy England ★★★★★

(102) £14.60–£21.45
(102) £14.60–£21.45
(6)

102 touring pitches
Open: All year

Shop: <0.5 miles
Pub: <0.5 miles

On the banks of the river Ouse in the heart of York, this popular site is just a few minutes' walk from the city centre. York is a feast, there's so much to see and do.

Location: A64 onto A19 (York). After 2 miles join one-way system. Keep left. Left at caravan sign. Right onto Terry Avenue.

Access:

General:

Pitch:

Looking for something else?

OFFICIAL TOURIST BOARD GUIDE
Pets Come Too! 2010
Pet-friendly accommodation
enjoyEngland.com

OFFICIAL TOURIST BOARD GUIDE
Self Catering 2010
England's quality-assessed holiday homes
enjoyEngland.com

OFFICIAL TOURIST BOARD GUIDE
Camping, Caravan & Holiday Parks 2010
Britain's quality-assessed sites
visitBritain.com

OFFICIAL TOURIST BOARD GUIDE
B&B 2010
England's quality-assessed B&Bs
enjoyEngland.com

OFFICIAL TOURIST BOARD GUIDE
Hotels 2010
England's quality-assessed hotels
enjoyEngland.com

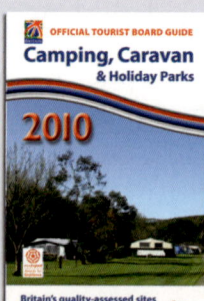

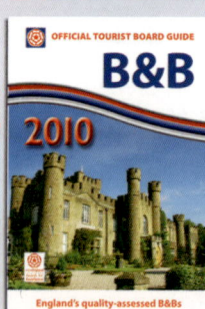

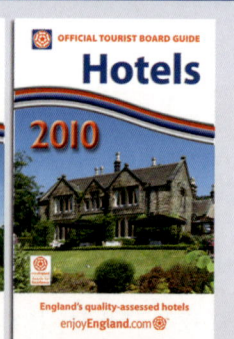

If you haven't found what you are looking for in OpenBritain, VisitBritain's Official Tourist Board Guides offer a wide choice of assessed accommodation which may meet your needs.

Yorkshire & Humber | **Attractions**

York | South Newlands Farm Self Catering

AS

Enjoy England ★★★★
Units: 3   Sleeps: 6
Open: All year

Low season p/w:
£295.00
High season p/w:
£550.00

Shop: 1 mile
Pub: 1 mile

Mrs Peggy Swann, South Newlands Farm, Selby Road, Riccall, York YO19 6QR
t 01757 248203   e info@southnewlandsfarm.co.uk

southnewlandsfarm.co.uk   4C1

Our aim is to provide excellent accommodation for people of all ages and abilities, generously proportioned rooms, ample wheelchair access, flat entry showers, double and twin bedrooms, lawn and paved patio all make for a comfortable and enjoyable stay.

Location: A19 York-Selby. From York pass 2 signs for Riccall take next left. From Selby pass turnoff A163 take next right.

Access:
General:
Unit:

York | Stakesby Holiday Flats

Enjoy England ★★★-★★★★★

Mr Anthony Bryce, Stakesby Holiday Flats, 4 St George's Place, York YO24 1DR   t 01904 611634   e ant@stakesby.co.uk

stakesby.co.uk

Brodsworth | Brodsworth Hall & Gardens

Open: For opening hours and prices, please call 0870 333 1181 or visit www.english-heritage.org.uk/properties

Brodsworth, Near Doncaster, South Yorkshire DN5 7XJ
t 0870 333 1181   e customers@english-heritage.org.uk

english-heritage.org.uk/brodsworth

Brodsworth Hall is a unique family day out. Explore the country house and beautiful gardens.

Access: General:

Harrogate | RHS Garden Harlow Carr

Crag Lane, Harrogate, North Yorkshire HG3 1QB
t 01423 565418   e harlowcarr@rhs.org.uk

rhs.org.uk

For symbols see pg 24   261

Yorkshire & Humber | **Attractions**

Helmsley | North York Moors National Park

The Old Vicarage, Bondgate, Helmsley, York YO62 5BP
t 01439 770657   e c.jagger@northyorkmoors-npa.gov.uk

Leeds | Henry Moore Institute

74 The Headrow, Leeds, Yorkshire LS1 3AH
t 0113 246 7467

henry-moore-fdn.co.uk

Access:

Leyburn | Yorkshire Dales National Park Authority

Yoredale, Bainbridge, Leyburn, North Yorkshire DL8 3EL
t 0870 1666333   e rachel.briggs@yorkshiredales.org.uk

Rievaulx | Rievaulx Abbey

Open: For opening hours and prices, please call 0870 333 1181 or visit www.english-heritage.org.uk/properties

Rievaulx, Nr Helmsley, North Yorkshire YO62 5LB
t 0870 333 1181   e customers@english-heritage.org.uk

english-heritage.org.uk/rievaulx

Take a day out to find peace amongst the atmospheric ruins of Rievaulx Abbey.

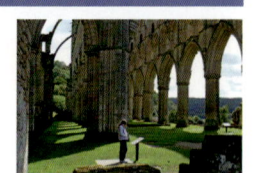

Access: **General:**

Scarborough | Scarborough Castle

Open: For opening hours and prices, please call 0870 333 1181 or visit www.english-heritage.org.uk/properties

Castle Road, Scarborough, North Yorkshire YO11 1HY
t 0870 333 1181   e customers@english-heritage.org.uk

english-heritage.org.uk/scarboroughcastle

Enjoy a fun family day out visiting Scarborough Castle! Explore over 2,500 years of history!

Access: **General:**

OPEN BRITAIN

DECIDED WHERE TO GO?
SEE ATTRACTIONS FOR WHAT TO DO
Ideas and information at the end of each regional section

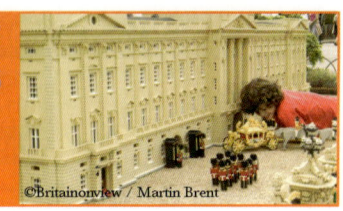

©Britainonview / Martin Brent

www.openbritain.net

Yorkshire & Humber | **Attractions**

Whitby | **Whitby Abbey**

Open: For opening hours and prices, please call 0870 333 1181 or visit www.english-heritage.org.uk/properties

Whitby, North Yorkshire YO22 4JT
t 0870 333 1181   e customers@english-heritage.org.uk
english-heritage.org.uk/whitby

The iconic ruins of Whitby Abbey offer a great family day out with great views.

Access: General:

York | **Jorvik Viking Centre**

Coppergate, York, North Yorkshire YO1 9WT
t 01904 543400   e jorvik@yorkat.co.uk
jorvik-viking-centre.co.uk

York | **York Minster**

Church House, Ongleforth, York YO1 7JN
t 0844 939 0011   e info@yorkminster.org
yorkminster.org

Jorvik Viking Centre

For symbols see pg 24

OpenBritain | Yorkshire & Humber

WHY PAY MORE

Total care, total freedom

Brook Miller Mobility offer a complete service to give you total care, total freedom and total satisfaction. We are a dedicated company with a reputation that means everything to us and a great deal more to you.

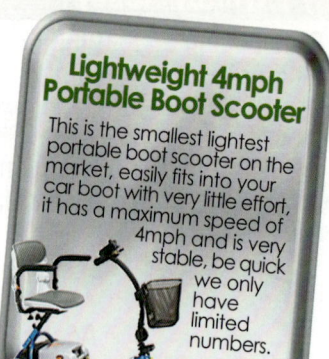

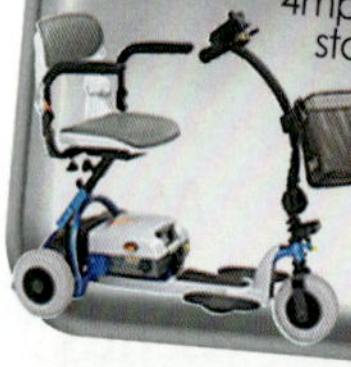

Lightweight 4mph Portable Boot Scooter
This is the smallest lightest portable boot scooter on the market, easily fits into your car boot with very little effort, it has a maximum speed of 4mph and is very stable, be quick we only have limited numbers.

Three Wheeled Walker
Available in Red, Blue or chrome finish, this three wheel walker is a very manoeuvrable walking aid for indoors or outdoors. It also benefits from loop brakes, carry ban and basket. Folds neatly for easy storage and car transportation.

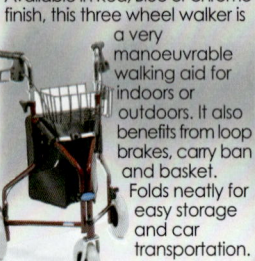

Lightweight Aluminium Wheelchair
Our best seller this high quality lightweight aluminium wheelchair is available in both transit and self propel versions. It has a folding back and detachable footrests and folds neatly into the back of a vehicle for transportation, also ideal for holiday use.

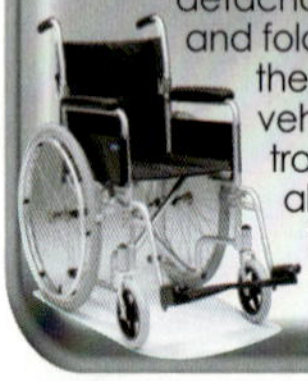

4mph Motability Scooter
A full size Motability scooter which will take up to 21 stone in weight, with a range of 20 miles on a full charge it's ideal for going to the shops, park or even the pub, features include swivel and slide seat with adjustable armrests, adjustable folding tiller, battery charger included available in Blue, Red and Champagne.

FREE DELIVERY TO YOUR DOOR

Electric Adjustable Bed
This bed makes relaxation and a good nights sleep an affordable and very comfortable reality. It has a five fold adjustable base and adjusts to support the five key areas; knees, hips, neck, back and head. Choice of mattress including memory foam.

Riser Recliner Arm Chair
This is the best value Electric Recliner Chair on the market. It represents quality at an excellent price. It features a distinct lift, rest and recline motion including a full excellent full snooze position.

Bath Lift Battery Powered Lift Risers and Recliners
For many people in life, bathing becomes difficult. This bath lift provides a fresh approach to this problem. It lifts, lowers and reclines easily and quietly and is designed to fit most baths. Simple to operate with excellent comfort, safety and reliability.

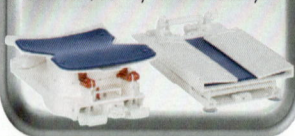

Many more products in store. See our online catalogue at: **www.brookmiller.com**

Unit 1A,
Elland Lane,
Elland, Halifax,
West Yorkshire,
HX5 9DZ

Motability

BROOK MILLER
MOBILITY LIMITED

FREEPHONE
0800 0644454
E-MAIL office@brookmiller.com

Opening Times:
Mon - Fri 9:00am - 5:30pm
Sat 9:00am - 12:30pm

HOME DEMONSTRATION SERVICE AVAILABLE, FULL WORKSHOP AND SERVICE FACILITIES.

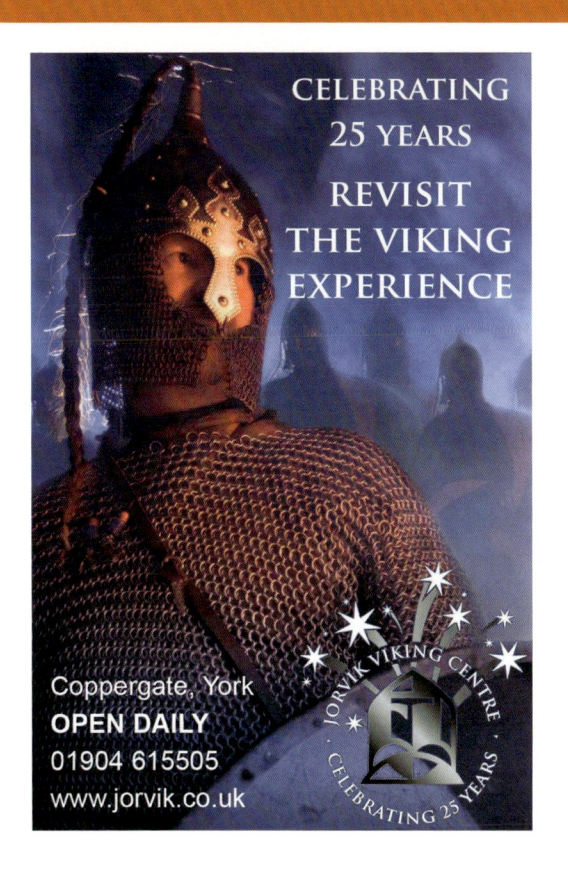

OpenBritain | Yorkshire & Humber

CELEBRATING 25 YEARS
REVISIT THE VIKING EXPERIENCE

Coppergate, York
OPEN DAILY
01904 615505
www.jorvik.co.uk

JORVIK VIKING CENTRE — CELEBRATING 25 YEARS

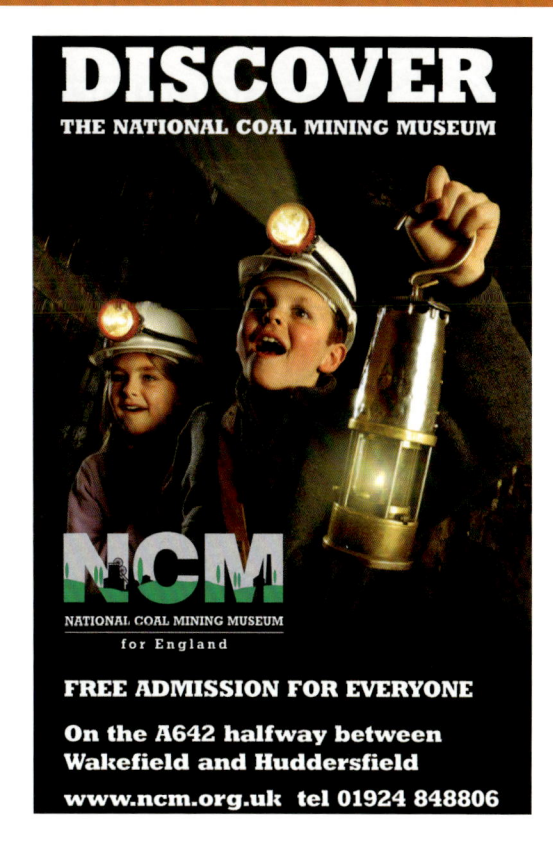

DISCOVER
THE NATIONAL COAL MINING MUSEUM

NCM
NATIONAL COAL MINING MUSEUM for England

FREE ADMISSION FOR EVERYONE

On the A642 halfway between Wakefield and Huddersfield

www.ncm.org.uk   tel 01924 848806

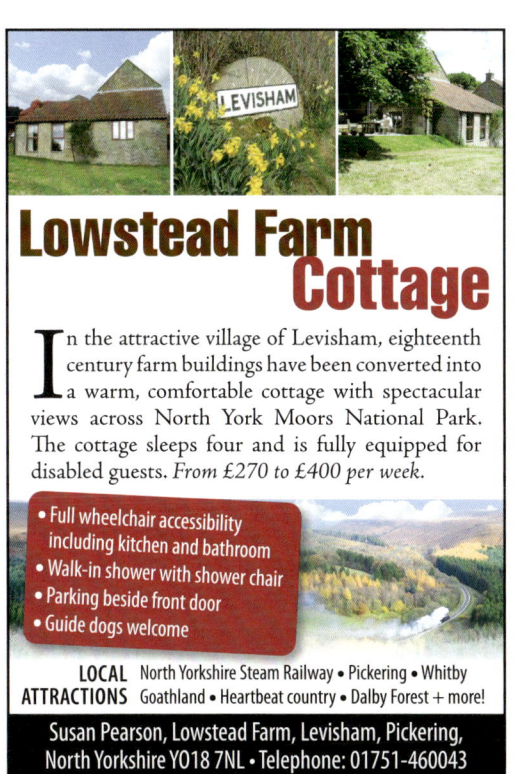

Lowstead Farm Cottage

In the attractive village of Levisham, eighteenth century farm buildings have been converted into a warm, comfortable cottage with spectacular views across North York Moors National Park. The cottage sleeps four and is fully equipped for disabled guests. *From £270 to £400 per week.*

- Full wheelchair accessibility including kitchen and bathroom
- Walk-in shower with shower chair
- Parking beside front door
- Guide dogs welcome

LOCAL ATTRACTIONS North Yorkshire Steam Railway • Pickering • Whitby
Goathland • Heartbeat country • Dalby Forest + more!

Susan Pearson, Lowstead Farm, Levisham, Pickering, North Yorkshire YO18 7NL • Telephone: 01751-460043
email: lowsteadfarm@gmail.com • www.lowsteadfarm.co.uk

NORTH BAY RAILWAY SCARBOROUGH

NORTH BAY RAILWAY, SCARBOROUGH

A THIRD FULL SIZE RAILWAY TRAVELLING BETWEEN PEASHOLM PARK AND SCALBY MILLS STATIONS, THROUGH BEAUTIFUL PARKLAND OUT TO THE NORTH BAY AND THE SEA LIFE CENTRE

OPEN WEEKENDS FEBRUARY TO EASTER THEN DAILY UNTIL NOVEMBER PLUS SANTA SPECIALS AND BETWEEN CHRISTMAS AND NEW YEAR

£3.00 ADULT RETURN / £2.50 CHILD RETURN

£2.50 ADULT SINGLE / £2.00 CHILD SINGLE

DOGS WELCOME

ALL OUR FACILITIES ARE 100% DISABLED FRIENDLY ON TRAINS FOR SEATED WHEELCHAIR PASSENGERS AND IN OUR CAFÉ BISTRO WHICH IS OPEN DAILY 10.00 A.M. TO 5.30 P.M. EVENING MEALS THURSDAY TO SATURDAY FROM 6.30 P.M.

SEE OUR WEBSITES: WWW.NBR.ORG.UK
AND WWW.GLASSHOUSEBISTRO.CO.UK
FOR FURTHER INFORMATION AND A PDF OF OUR CURRENT LEAFLET

OpenBritain | Yorkshire & Humber

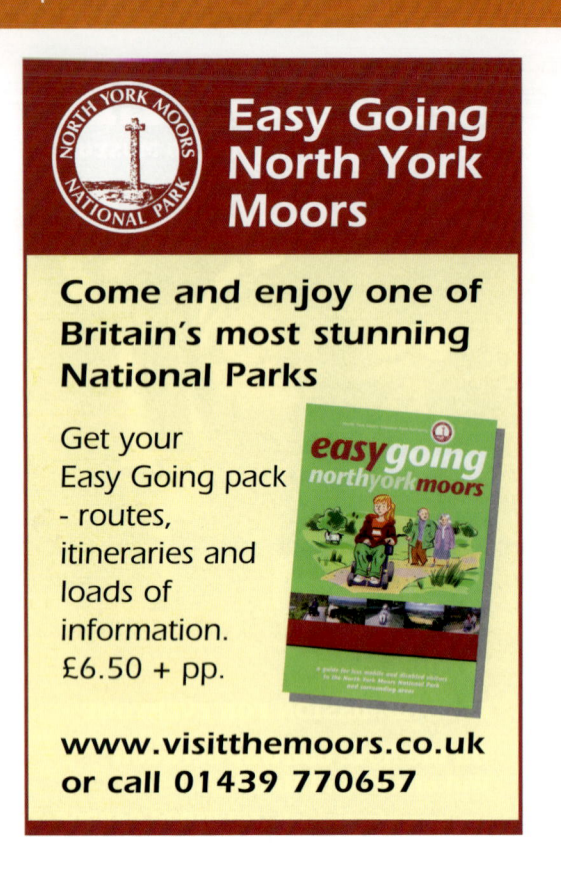

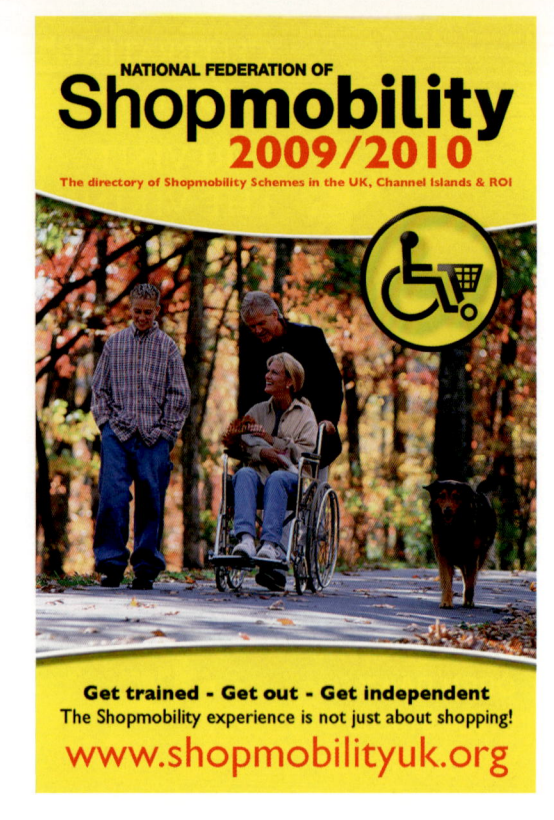

Easy Going North York Moors

Come and enjoy one of Britain's most stunning National Parks

Get your Easy Going pack - routes, itineraries and loads of information. £6.50 + pp.

www.visitthemoors.co.uk
or call 01439 770657

NATIONAL FEDERATION OF Shopmobility 2009/2010

The directory of Shopmobility Schemes in the UK, Channel Islands & ROI

Get trained - Get out - Get independent
The Shopmobility experience is not just about shopping!

www.shopmobilityuk.org

Explore, enjoy, discover
Dalby the Great Yorkshire Forest

- Visitor Centre & Shop
- Environment exhibition
- Restaurant
- Courtyard café
- Courtyard craft area
- Mountain bike hire
- Walks & trails for all
- World Class cycle trails
- Picnic areas
- Barbecues
- Orienteering
- Go Ape

Admission charges apply. Annual Membership ticket available
Further information 01751 460295
www.forestry.gov.uk

visit YORK MINSTER
it's simply The Heart of Yorkshire

Open daily: admission charges apply
0844 939 0016   www.yorkminster.org

Henry Moore Institute

- Discover sculpture from ancient to modern
- Changing exhibitions programme
- Sculpture reference library
- Talks, tours and events
- Wheelchair access from Cookridge St
- Lift to all floors
- Induction loops
- Braille and large print information
- Free admission

The Headrow, Leeds, LS1 3AH Open Daily (Closed Bank Holidays)
Recorded Information Line: 0113 234 3158 www.henry-moore.ac.uk

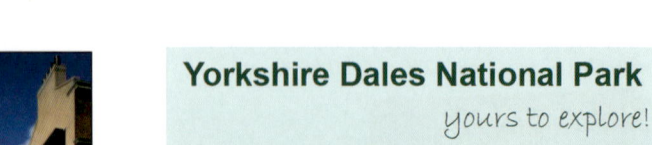

Yorkshire Dales National Park
yours to explore!

For FREE copies of our publications 'The Visitor 2010' and 'Access for All' call 0300 456 0030 or visit
www.yorkshiredales.org.uk

YORKSHIRE DALES National Park

one of Britain's breathing spaces

OPENBRITAIN.NET

The one-stop-shop for all your travel needs.

Go online and see how we can help you get in, out ...and about.

- Fully searchable database of accommodation, days out and where to eat and drink
- MyOpenBritain trip planner
- User reviews, blogs and forums

Join today!

OpenBritain | Northwest

Liverpool

Striking landscapes and vibrant cityscapes

An exciting and dynamic region, England's Northwest is full of striking landscapes and vibrant cityscapes. From the elegant and ancient city of Chester to the inspirational vistas of the Lake District, and from the award winning industrial heritage of Manchester to the outstanding cultural attractions of Liverpool, there is so much to see and do in England's Northwest. Add to these a spectacular coastline with Britain's favourite seaside resorts, and the delightfully undiscovered countryside of Lancashire, and you won't know where to start.

Individual and edgy, **Manchester** is a place like no other. From **Manchester Art Gallery's** Pre-Raphaelites to the cool and contemporary **Urbis**, it's a dramatic mix of old and new. The city's industrial legacy lives on in its trail-blazing spirit, with cutting edge festivals and events all year round. Manchester is synonymous with sport, but equally famed for its vibrant cultural scene and fantastic nightlife; this is the original 24-hour city.

Elegant and ancient, the city of **Chester** is full of 21st century delights. This walled Roman city is the perfect place to treat yourself; indulge in some seriously sophisticated retail therapy or pamper yourself in luxurious spa hotels. **Chester's Rows** are unique to the city and these two-tiered shopping galleries are accessible to all. And when it comes to spectacular gardens, Cheshire can boast some of the finest examples in the world, including the glorious **Ness Botanic Gardens**.

Liverpool is truly awe-inspiring; with more museums and galleries than anywhere else outside London and the iconic architecture of its World Heritage Site, this really is a world-class city. With eight venues in the **National Museums Liverpool family**, not to mention the **Beatles story** and **Tate Liverpool**, it's easy to see why Liverpool remains a Capital of Culture.

Head North from Liverpool and discover a spectacular coastline sprinkled with Britain's favourite seaside resorts, including bold and bright **Blackpool** with its famous illuminations and white-knuckle rides; **Sandcastle Waterpark** is always a favourite. Lancashire is also home to the **Forest of Bowland**, **Ribble Valley** and **Pendle Hill**, all areas of renowned natural beauty where it's easy to get out and about, as well as top notch cuisine and plenty of farm fresh produce. ▶

Northwest

Chester and Cheshire
Cumbria - The Lake District
Blackpool and Lancashire
Manchester
Liverpool and Merseyside

▶ The spectacular vistas of the **Lake District**, the country's best outdoor playground, are inspirational at any time of year. Home to England's highest mountain and deepest lake, here you can follow the footsteps of the Romantic poets at **Dove Cottage** and the **Wordsworth Museum** or try your hand at something a little more vigorous with countless outdoor activity providers eager to show you the ropes whatever your ability.

England's Northwest is also home to England's **Golf Coast**, the highest concentration of championship links courses in the world. Add to this a sporting heritage that is second to none – the professional football game was born here and **Aintree Racecourse** is home to the most famous steeplechase on earth, the renowned John Smiths Grand National – and you're spoilt for choice.

With the myriad events, performances, exhibitions and gigs that keep the region buzzing all year long, we guarantee you'll be hooked.

Find out more

web www.visitenglandsnorthwest.com

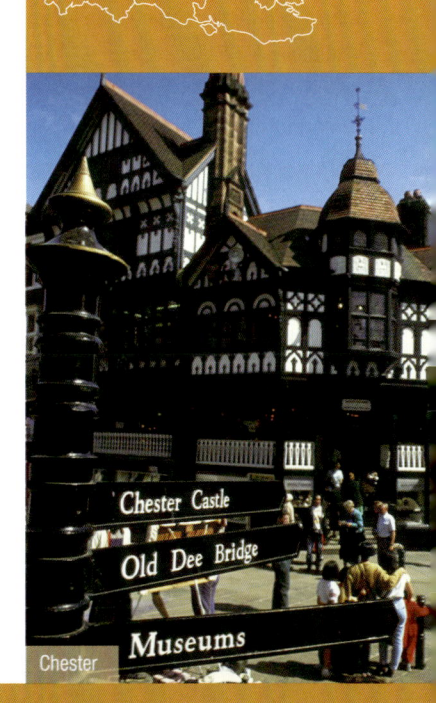

OpenBritain | Northwest

Wastwater

Royal Lytham and St Annes

Bowland Forest

Tourist Information Centres

Tourist Information Centres are a mine of information about local and regional accommodation, attractions and events. Visit them when you arrive at your destination or contact them before you go:

Accrington	Town Hall	01254 380293	tourism@hyndburnbc.gov.uk
Altrincham	20 Stamford New Road	0161 912 5931	tourist.information@trafford.gov.uk
Ashton-Under-Lyne	Council Offices	0161 343 4343	tourist.information@tameside.gov.uk
Barnoldswick	The Council Shop	01282 666704	tourist.info@pendle.gov.uk
Barrow-In-Furness	Forum 28	01229 876505	touristinfo@barrowbc.gov.uk
Blackburn	50-54 Church Street	01254 53277	visit@blackburn.gov.uk
Blackpool	1 Clifton Street	01253 478222	tic@blackpool.gov.uk
Bolton	Central Library Foyer	01204 334321	tourist.info@bolton.gov.uk
Bowness	Glebe Road	015394 42895	bownesstic@lake-district.gov.uk
Burnley	Burnley Bus Station	01282 664421	tic@burnley.gov.uk
Bury	The Met Arts Centre	0161 253 5111	touristinformation@bury.gov.uk
Carlisle	Old Town Hall	01228 625600	tourism@carlisle-city.gov.uk

Chester	Town Hall	01244 402111	tis@chester.gov.uk
Cleveleys	Victoria Square	01253 853378	cleveleystic@wyrebc.gov.uk
Clitheroe	12-14 Market Place	01200 425566	tourism@ribblevalley.gov.uk
Congleton	Town Hall	01260 271095	tourism@congleton.gov.uk
Coniston	Ruskin Avenue	015394 41533	mail@conistontic.org
Ellesmere Port	McArthur Glen Outlet Village	0151 356 7879	cheshireoaks.cc@visitor-centre.net
Fleetwood	Old Ferry Office	01253 773953	fleetwoodtic@wyrebc.gov.uk
Garstang	Council Offices	01995 602125	garstangtic@wyrebc.gov.uk
Kendal	Town Hall	01539 725758	kendaltic@southlakeland.gov.uk
Keswick	Moot Hall	017687 72645	keswicktic@lake-district.gov.uk
Knutsford	Council Offices	01565 632611	ktic@macclesfield.gov.uk
Lancaster	29 Castle Hill	01524 32878	lancastervic@lancaster.gov.uk
Liverpool City Centre	Whitechapel	0151 233 2459	contact@liverpool08.com
Liverpool Albert Dock	Anchor Courtyard	0151 233 2008	08place@liverpool.com
Liverpool John Lennon Airport	Arrivals Hall, South Terminal	0906 680 6886	info@visitliverpool.com
Lytham St Annes	Town Hall, St Annes Rd West	01253 725610	touristinformation@fylde.gov.uk
Macclesfield	Macclesfield	01625 504114	informationcentre@macclesfield.gov.uk
Manchester	Lloyd Street	0871 222 8223	touristinformation@marketingmanchester.co.uk
Morecambe	Old Station Buildings	01524 582808	morecambetic@lancaster.gov.uk
Nantwich	Civic Hall	01270 537359	touristi@crewe-nantwich.gov.uk
Northwich	The Arcade	01606 353534	tourism@valeroyal.gov.uk
Oldham	12 Albion Street	0161 627 1024	ecs.tourist@oldham.gov.uk
Pendle Heritage Centre	Park Hill	01282 661701	heritage.centre@pendle.gov.uk
Pendle, Discover	Boundary Mill Sores	01282 856186	discoverpendle@pendle.gov.uk
Penrith	Middlegate	01768 867466	pen.tic@eden.gov.uk
Preston	The Guildhall	01772 253731	tourism@preston.gov.uk
Rochdale	Touchstones	01706 924928	tic@link4life.org
Salford	The Lowry, Pier 8	0161 848 8601	tic@salford.gov.uk
Southport	112 Lord Street	01704 533333	info@visitsouthport.com
St Helens	The World of Glass	01744 755150	info@sthelenstic.com
Stockport	Staircase House	0161 474 4444	tourist.information@stockport.gov.uk
Warrington	The Market Hall	01925 428585	informationcentre@warrington.gov.uk
Whitehaven	Market Hall	01946 598914	tic@copelandbc.gov.uk
Wigan	62 Wallgate	01942 825677	tic@wlct.org
Wilmslow	Rectory Fields	01625 522275	i.hillaby@macclesfield.gov.uk
Windermere	Victoria Street	015394 46499	windermeretic@southlakeland.gov.uk

North West | Cheshire

Acton Bridge | Wall Hill Farm Guesthouse

Enjoy England ★★★★★
Open: All year

Rooms per night:
s: £45.00–£52.00
d: £68.00–£75.00

Acton Lane, Acton Bridge, Northwich CW8 3QE

wallhillfarmguesthouse.co.uk 4A2

Five star luxury guest house with 7 double/twin bedrooms with En Suite facilities.

Access: General: Room:

Bosley | Strawberry Duck Cottage

Enjoy England ★★★

Mr B Carter, Strawberry Duck Cottage, Bryer Cottage, Bullgate Lane, Bosley, Macclesfield SK11 0PP
t 01260 223591   e 2007@strawberryduckholidays.co.uk

strawberryduckholidays.co.uk/

Bosley | Woodcroft

Enjoy England ★★

Mrs Dorothy Gilman, Woodcroft, Tunstall Road, Bosley, Macclesfield SK11 0BB

farmstay.co.uk

Cheshire | Higher Farm Bed & Breakfast

AA ★★★★

Higher Farm, Barton, Malpas, Cheshire SY14 7HU
t 01829 782422   e info@higherfarm.co.uk

higherfarm.co.uk

Access: General: Room:

"The one-stop-shop for all your travel needs"

OPEN BRITAIN

Become a member of OpenBritain today.

Share your own travel and accommodation experiences and help Britain become more open!

visit www.openbritain.net

OPENBRITAIN.NET

North West | Cheshire

Chester | Chester Fairoaks Caravan Club Site

Enjoy England ★★★★★

🚐 (100) £14.60-£21.45
🚙 (100) £14.60-£21.45
⛺ (5)

100 touring pitches
Open: All year

Shop: 0.5 miles
Pub: <0.5 miles

Access:
General:
Pitch:

Rake Lane, Little Stanney, Chester, Cheshire CH2 4HS
t 0151 3551600

caravanclub.co.uk   4A2

A tranquil site edged with oak trees six miles from the walled city of Chester with its famous zoo, historic sites, and excellent entertainment and shopping. Take an open-top bus or walk around the walls to absorb the colourful atmosphere.

Location: Travel towards Queensferry on A5117 from M53. Turn left in Little Stanney at signpost Chorlton. Site 0.25 miles on left.

Chester | Crowne Plaza Chester   AS

AA ★★★★
Trinity Street, Chester, Cheshire CH1 2BD
t 0871 4234896 e cpchester@qmh-hotels.com
crowneplaza.com/chester

Access: General: Room:

Chester | Holiday Inn Chester South   AS

AA ★★★
Wrexham Road, Chester, Cheshire CH4 9DL
t 0870 400 9019 e reservations-chester@ihg.com
holidayinn.co.uk

Access: General: Room:

Ellesmere Port | Holiday Inn Ellesmere Port/Cheshire Oaks

Enjoy England ★★★
Centre Island, Waterways, Ellesmere Port CH65 2AL
t 0151 356 8111 e reception@hiellesmereport.com
hiellesmereport.com

Hulme Walfield | Sandhole Farm Bed & Breakfast

Enjoy England ★★★★
Manchester Road (A34), Hulme Walfield, Congleton CW12 2JH
t 01260 224419 e veronica@sandholefarm.co.uk
sandholefarm.co.uk

For symbols see pg 24

North West | Cheshire/Cumbria

Macclesfield | Kerridge End Holiday Cottages   AS

Enjoy England ★★★★★
Units: 3   Sleeps: 1-6
Open: All year

Low season p/w:
£300.00
High season p/w:
£800.00

Mr Ivor Williams, Owner, Kerridge End, Rainow, Macclesfield, Cheshire SK10 5TF
t 01625 424220   e info@kerridgeendholidaycottages.co.uk

kerridgeendholidaycottages.co.uk   4B2

Cheshire's 'Self Catering Holiday of the Year' and 'Access for All Tourism Award' winners 2009.

Access: abc
General: Unit:

Pulford | Grosvenor Pulford Hotel & Karma Spa

Enjoy England ★★★★

Wrexham Road, Pulford, Chester CH4 9DG
t 01244 570560   e reservations@grosvenorpulfordhotel.co.uk

grosvenorpulfordhotel.co.uk

Runcorn | Holiday Inn Runcorn

AA ★★★

Wood Lane, Beechwood, Runcorn, Cheshire WA7 3HA
t 0870 400 9070   e reservations-runcorn@ihg.com

holiday-inn.co.uk

Access: abc   General: Room:

Warrington | Holiday Inn Warrington

AA ★★★

Woolston Grange Avenue, Woolston, Warrington, Cheshire WA1 4PX
t 01925 838779

holidayinn.co.uk

Access: abc   General: Room:

Ambleside | Nationwide Bungalow

Units: 1   Sleeps: 7

Low season p/w:
£240.00
High season p/w:
£550.00

Livability Self catering holidays, PO Box 36, Cowbridge, Vale of Glamorgan CF71 7TN
t 08456 584478   f 01446 775060   e selfcatering@livability.org.uk

livability.org.uk   5A3

Fully accessible 4 bedroom bungalow set in the heart of Cumbria close to Lake Windermere.

Access:
General: Unit:

OPEN BRITAIN

GETTING THERE IS NOT A PROBLEM!
See Getting there..... and back section (p364) Everything you need for a hassle-free journey

274   www.openbritain.net

North West | Cumbria

Ambleside | Rothay Manor

AA ★★★
Enjoy England ★★★

Beds: 3 suites

Open: All year except 3rd to 28th January 2010.

Rooms per night:
s: £95.00-£150.00
d: £145.00-£225.00
p/p half board:
d: £105.00-£190.00
Meals: £32.00-£48.00

Shop: <0.5 miles
Pub: <0.5 miles

Access:
General:
Room:

Rothay Bridge, Ambleside LA22 0EH
t 01539 433605 e hotel@rothaymanor.co.uk

rothaymanor.co.uk   5A3

Country House hotel in the heart of the Lake District, close to Ambleside and the head of Windermere lake. Family owned and run for over 40 years, it is renowned for the warm, comfortable, friendly atmosphere, excellent food and wine.

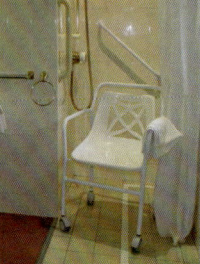

Arnside | YHA Arnside

Enjoy England ★★★

Oakfield Lodge, Redhills Road, Arnside LA5 0AT
t 01524 761781 e arnside@yha.org.uk
yha.org.uk

Bailey | Bailey Mill

Mrs Pamela Copeland, Bailey, Newcastleton, Roxburghshire TD9 0TR
t 01697 748617
baileycottages-riding-racing.com

Access: **General:** **Unit:**

Bassenthwaite | Parkergate

Enjoy England ★★★★

Ian & Jane Phillips, Parkergate, Bassenthwaite, Keswick CA12 4QG
t 01768 776376 e info@parkergate.co.uk
parkergate.co.uk

Bowness-On-Solway | The Old Chapel

Enjoy England ★★★

Bowness-on-Solway, Wigton, Bowness-on-Solway CA7 5BL
t 01697 351126 e oldchapelbowness@hotmail.com
oldchapelbownessonsolway.com

For symbols see pg 24

North West | Cumbria

Carlisle | Old Brewery Residences

Enjoy England ★★★

Dee Carruthers, Impact Housing Association, Old Brewery Residences, Bridge Lane, Carlisle CA2 5SR   t 01228 597352   e deec@impacthousing.org.uk

impacthousing.org.uk

Cockermouth | Irton House Farm

Enjoy England ★★★★
Units: 6   Sleeps: 2–6
Open: All year

Low season p/w: £365.00
High season p/w: £825.00

Isel, Cockermouth, Cumbria CA13 9ST
t 017687 76380   e joan@irtonhousefarm.co.uk

disabled-holiday.net

5A3

Self-catering cottages for up to 6 people, specially designed for wheelchair accessibility. Quiet, rural location.

General: Unit:

Gatebeck | Barkinbeck Cottage

Enjoy England ★★★

Mrs Ann Hamilton, Barkin House Barn, Gatebeck, Kendal LA8 0HX
t 01539 567122   e barkinhouse@yahoo.co.uk

barkinbeck.co.uk

Access: General: P   Unit:

Grange-over-Sands | Meathop Fell Caravan Club Site

Enjoy England ★★★★★

(131) £13.70–£19.55
(131) £13.70–£19.55
131 touring pitches
Open: All year

Shop: 3 miles
Pub: 2 miles

Grange-over-Sands, Cumbria LA11 6RB
t 01539 532912

caravanclub.co.uk

5A3

This gentle, peaceful site is an ideal base to explore the Lake District. You'll find literary associations everywhere, from Wordsworth to Beatrix Potter. Windermere and Coniston are great for water-based activities.

Location: M6 jct 36, A590 (Barrow). After 3 miles take slip road A590 (Barrow). At 1st roundabout follow International Camping signs.

Access:
General:
Pitch:

276

www.openbritain.net

North West | **Cumbria**

Grange-Over-Sands | Netherwood Hotel

Enjoy England ★★★ Lindale Road, Grange-over-Sands LA11 6ET
t 01539 532552 e enquiries@netherwood-hotel.co.uk
netherwood-hotel.co.uk

Grasmere | Rothay Lodge & Apartment

Enjoy England ★★★★ Lindsay Rogers, Rothay Lodge & Apartment, c/o 54A Trevor Road, West Bridgford NG2 6FT t 0115 923 2618 e enquiries@rothay-lodge.co.uk
rothay-lodge.co.uk

Hawkshead | Restharrow

National Trust, Restharrow, nr Hawkshead, Cumbria
t 0844 8002070
nationaltrustcottages.co.uk/north_of_england/lake_district/

Ings | Meadowcroft Country Guest House

Enjoy England ★★★★
Open: All year except Xmas

Rooms per night:
s: £50.00-£60.00
d: £70.00-£90.00

Ings, Windermere, Cumbria LA8 9PY
t 01539 821171 e info@meadowcroft-guesthouse.com
meadowcroft-guesthouse.com   5A3

Your comfort at Meadowcroft will be our priority.

Access: General: Room:

Historic Houses & Gardens
Castles and Heritage Sites
2010

Hudson's is the definitive guide to historic houses & gardens - open to visitors.

Up to date information on over 2000 properties with clear information symbols for accessibility and facilities.

HUDSONs

All you need for fabulous days out

For symbols see pg 24   277

North West | Cumbria

Kendal | Low Park Wood Caravan Club Site

Enjoy England ★★★★

🚐 (141) £13.70–£19.55
🚛 (141) £13.70–£19.55
141 touring pitches
Open: 27 March – 9 November
Shop: 3 miles
Pub: 1 mile

Sedgwick, Kendal, Cumbria LA8 0JZ
t 01539 560186

caravanclub.co.uk   5B3

Set in extensive National Trust woodland, on the site of a 19thC gunpowder mill this peaceful country site is a haven for birdwatchers, fishermen and wild-flower enthusiasts. Kendal, a small market town famous for its mint cake, isn't far.

Location: M6 jct 36 onto A590 (South Lakes). After 3 miles take slip road (Milnthorpe, Barrow) at roundabout; follow caravan signs.

Access:
General:
Pitch:

Longthwaite | Borrowdale YHA

Enjoy England ★★★★

Longthwaite, Borrowdale, Keswick CA12 5XE
t 0870 770 5706   e borrowdale@yha.org.uk
yha.org.uk

Longtown | Bessiestown Farm Country Guesthouse

Enjoy England ★★★★★

Catlowdy, Longtown, Carlisle CA6 5QP
t 01228 577219   e info@bessiestown.co.uk
bessiestown.co.uk

Penrith | Howscales

Enjoy England ★★★★

Liz Webster, Kirkoswald, Penrith CA10 1JG
t 01768 898666   e liz@howscales.co.uk
howscales.co.uk

Access: General: Unit:

OPENBRITAIN.NET

The one-stop-shop for all your travel needs. Go online and see how we can help you get in, out ...and about.

North West | Cumbria

Southwaite | Southwaite Green
AS

Enjoy England ★★★★★
Units: 4   Sleeps: 1-6
Open: All year

Low season p/w:
£410.00
High season p/w:
£880.00

Mrs Marna McMillin, Southwaite Green, Lorton, Cockermouth CA13 0RF   t 01900 821055   e info@southwaitegreen.co.uk

southwaitegreen.co.uk   5B2

Specially designed cottage on award winning eco holiday site in spectacular Western Lakes setting.

Access: abc   General: Unit:

Staveley | Avondale

Enjoy England ★★★

Helen Hughes, Avondale, 2 Lynstead, Thornbarrow Road, Windermere LA23 2DG   t 07811 670260   e enquiries@avondale.uk.net

avondale.uk.net

St Bees | Springbank Farm Lodges
AS

Enjoy England ★★★★

Mrs Carole Woodman, Springbank Farm, High Walton, St Bees, Cumbria CA22 2TY   t 01946 822375   e stevewoodman@talk21.com

springbanklodges.co.uk

Access: abc   General: Unit:

Tebay | Primrose Court
AS

Enjoy England ★★★★
Units: 3   Sleeps: 6
Open: All year

Low season p/w:
£270.00
High season p/w:
£620.00

Primrose Cottage, Orton Road, Tebay, Cumbria CA10 3TL
t 015396 24791

primrosecottagecumbria.co.uk   5B3

Superb village location close M6. Quiet, spacious, level accommodation. Suitable wheelchairs, 2 bedrooms, 2 bathrooms.

Access: General: Unit:

Threlkeld | Scales Farm Country Guest House

Enjoy England ★★★★

Scales, Threlkeld, Penrith CA12 4SY
t 01768 779660   e scales@scalesfarm.com

scalesfarm.com

Thurstonfield | The Tranquil Otter

The Lough, Thurstonfield, Carlisle, Cumbria CA5 6HB
t 01228 576661

thetranquilotter.co.uk

For symbols see pg 24

North West | Cumbria

Whinfell | Cobblestone Cottage & Wallers Barn

Enjoy England ★★★ Diane Barnes, Topthorn Holiday Cottages, Topthorn Farm, Whinfell, Kendal LA8 9EG   t 01539 824252   e info.barnes@btconnect.com

topthorn.com

Windermere | Birch Cottage

Enjoy England ★★★★
Units: 5   Sleeps: 2-6
Open: All year

Low season p/w: £280.00
High season p/w: £650.00

Mrs PM Fanstone, Deloraine Holiday Homes, Helm Road, Bowness-on-Windermere, Cumbria LA23 2HS
t 015394 45557   e info@deloraine.demon.co.uk

deloraine.co.uk   5A3

Luxury fully wheelchair accessible cottage. Well equipped with private gardens. Located in central Lakes.

Access:
General: Unit:

Windermere | Braithwaite Fold Caravan Club Site

Enjoy England ★★★★

(66) £13.70–£19.55
(66) £13.70–£19.55

66 touring pitches
Open: 27 March - 9 November

Shop: 1 mile
Pub: <0.5 miles

Glebe Road, Bowness-on-Windermere, Windermere, Cumbria LA23 3HB   t 01539 442177

caravanclub.co.uk   5A3

An attractively laid out site, close to the shores of Windermere and within easy walking distance of the town. Windermere has an excellent sailing centre from which you can enjoy sailing, windsurfing and canoeing.

Location: From A592 follow signs for Bowness Bay, in 300yds turn right into Glebe Road. Site on right.

Access:
General:
Pitch:

Windermere | Lake District Disabled Holidays

Enjoy England ★★★★ Stuart & Jane Higham, Mitchelland Farm, off Crook Road, Nr Bowness-on-Windermere, Kendal, Cumbria. LA8 8LL   t 01539 447421

lakedistrictdisabledholidays.co.uk

Access: General: Unit:

North West | Cumbria/Lancashire

Windermere | Linthwaite House Hotel

AA ★★★
Enjoy England ★★★
Open: All year

Rooms per night:
s: £150.00–£508.00
d: £162.00–£520.00
p/p half board:
d: £89.00–£299.00
Meals: £25.00–£50.00

Crook Road, Windermere, Cumbria LA23 3JA
t 01539 488600   e stay@linthwaite.com
linthwaite.com

Luxurious country house hotel set in 14 acres beautiful grounds with a sublime hilltop location.

Access: | General: | Room:

Alston | Proven House

Enjoy England ★★★★

Mrs Kathleen English, Laneside Farm, Alston Lane, Alston PR3 3BN
t 01772 782653   e kenglish56@hotmail.co.uk
theprovenhouse.co.uk/

Access: | General: | Unit:

Barnacre | Barnacre Cottages

Enjoy England ★★★★★

Mr Terence Sharples, Barnacre Cottages, The Old Shippon, Arkwright Farm, Eidsforth Lane, Preston PR3 1GN   t 01995 600918
e sue@barnacre-cottages.co.uk
barnacre-cottages.co.uk

Blackpool | The Beach House

Enjoy England ★★★★★

Mrs Estelle Livesey, The Beach House, 204 Queens Promenade, Blackpool FY2 9JS   t 01253 826555   e info@thebeachhouseblackpool.co.uk
thebeachhouseblackpool.co.uk

Blackpool | Big Blue Hotel

Enjoy England ★★★★

Pleasure Beach Blackpool, Ocean Boulevard, Blackpool FY4 1ND
t 0845 367 3333   e reservations@bigbluehotel.com
bigbluehotel.com

Blackpool | Holmsdale

Enjoy England ★★★

6-8 Pleasant Street, Blackpool FY1 2JA
t 01253 621008   e stay@holmsdalehotel-blackpool.com
holmsdalehotel-blackpool.com

Blackpool | Langtrys

Enjoy England ★★★

36 King Edward Avenue, Blackpool FY2 9TA
t 01253 352031   e david.webb7@virgin.net
langtrysblackpool.co.uk

North West | Lancashire

Blackpool | The Lawton
Enjoy England ★★★ 58-66 Charnley Road, Blackpool FY1 4PF
t 01253 753471   e thelawtonhotel@gmail.com
thelawtonhotel.co.uk

Access: | General: | Room:

Blackpool | Norbreck Castle Hotel
Enjoy England ★★ Queens Promenade, Blackpool FY2 9AA
t 0871 222 0031   e res722@britanniahotels.com
britanniahotels.com

Blackpool | Promenade Apartments
Enjoy England ★★-★★★ Mrs Christine Phillips, Promenade Apartments, 361 South Promenade, Blackpool FY1 6BJ   t 01253 346061
selfcateringflatinblackpool.com

Blackpool | St Elmo
Enjoy England ★★★ 20-22 Station Road, Blackpool FY4 1BE
t 01253 341820   e hotelstelmo@hotmail.co.uk
hotelstelmo.co.uk

Bleasdale | Bleasdale Cottages
Enjoy England ★★★★ Mr Gardner, Bleasdale Cottages, Lower Fairsnape Farm, Bleasdale, Nr Preston PR3 1UY   t 01995 61343   e robert_gardner1@tiscali.co.uk
bleasdalecottages.co.uk

Bolton | Holiday Inn Bolton Centre
AA ★★★★ 1 Higher Bridge Street, Bolton, Lancashire BL1 2EW
t 01204 879988   e gmsbol@moathousehotels.com
holiday-inn.co.uk

Access: | General: | Room:

Caton | The Croft - Ground Floor Apartment
Enjoy England ★★★★ Mrs Sue Brierly-Hampton, The Croft - Ground Floor Apartment, 4 The Croft, Caton, Lancaster LA2 9QG   t 01524 770725   e suebrierly@hotmail.com

Chipping | The Gibbon Bridge Hotel
Enjoy England ★★★★ Chipping, Forest of Bowland, Preston PR3 2TQ
t 01995 61456   e reception@gibbon-bridge.co.uk
gibbon-bridge.co.uk

North West | Lancashire

Forton | Cleveley Mere Boutique Lodges

Enjoy England ★★★★ Owner, Cleveley Mere Boutique Lodges, Cleveley Lodge, Cleveley Bank Lane, Forton PR3 1BY

Lancaster | Holiday Inn Lancaster

AA ★★★ Waterside Park, Caton Road, Lancaster, Lancashire LA1 3PA
t 0870 400 9047   e lancaster@ihg.com
holidayinn.co.uk

Access: / General: / Room:

Langho | Mytton Fold Hotel and Golf Complex   AS

Enjoy England ★★★ Hotel & Golf Complex, Langho, Nr Blackburn BB6 8AB
Open: All year except Xmas
t 01254 240662   e reception@myttonfold.co.uk
myttonfold.co.uk

Rooms per night:
s: £57.00-£59.50
d: £92.00-£95.00
p/p half board:
d: £65.00
Meals: £20.00-£25.45

Award winning (2009) family owned and run. Set in the picturesque Ribble Valley, Lancashire.

Access: / General: / Room:

Lytham St. Annes | The Chadwick Hotel

Enjoy England ★★★ South Promenade, Lytham St Annes FY8 1NP
t 01253 720061   e info@thechadwickhotel.com
thechadwickhotel.com

Morecambe | Eden Vale Luxury Holiday Flats

Enjoy England ★★★ Mr Jason Coombs, 338 Marine Road, Morecambe LA4 5AB
t 07739 008301   e jicoombs@talktalk.net
edenvalemorecambe.co.uk

Newton in Bowland | Stonefold Holiday Cottage

Enjoy England ★★★★ Ms Helen Blanc, Stonefold Holiday Cottage, Slaidburn Road, Newton-in-Bowland, Citheroe BB7 3DL   t 07966 582834
stonefoldholidaycottage.co.uk

Poulton-Le-Fylde | Hardhorn Breaks

Enjoy England ★★★★ Mr Pawson, Hardhorn Breaks, High Bank Farm, Fairfield Rd, Poulton Le Fylde FY6 8DN   t 01253 890422   e blackpoolnick@btinternet.com
highbank-farm.com

For symbols see pg 24

283

North West | Lancashire/Greater Manchester

Quernmore | Knotts Farm Holiday Cottages

Enjoy England ★★★★ Knotts Farm Holiday Cottages, Quernmore, Lancaster LA2 9LU
e stay@knottsfarm.co.uk

knottsfarm.co.uk

Ribble Valley | Pinfold Farm

Enjoy England ★★★★
Units: 1   Sleeps: 6
Open: All year

Low season p/w: £420.00
High season p/w: £520.00

Mr Alan Davies, Preston Road, Ribchester PR3 3YD
t 01254 820740   e davies-pinfold@yahoo.co.uk

pinfoldfarm.co.uk   4A1

Bungalow close to the historic village of Ribchester with its Roman Museum and great pubs.

Access: General: P S   Unit:

Ribchester | Riverside Barn

Enjoy England ★★★★★ Riverside, Ribchester, Nr Preston PR3 3XS
t 01254 878095   e relax@riversidebarn.co.uk

riversidebarn.co.uk

Southport | Sandy Brook Farm

Enjoy England ★★★ Mrs Wendy Core, Sandy Brook Farm, Wyke Cop Road, Southport PR8 5LR
t 01704 880337   e sandybrookfarm@gmail.co.uk

sandybrookfarm.co.uk

Southport | Sandy Brook Farm B&B

Enjoy England ★★★ Wyke Cop Road, Scarisbrick, Southport PR8 5LR
t 01704 880337   e sandybrookfarm@gmail.com

sandybrookfarm.co.uk

Turton | Clough Head Farm

Enjoy England ★★★★ Mrs Ethel Houghton, Clough Head Farm - Self Catering, Broadhead Road, Turton BL7 0JN   t 01254 704758   e ethelhoughton@hotmail.co.uk

cloughheadfarm.co.uk

Ardwick | Macdonald Manchester Hotel

London Road, Manchester M1 7JG
t 0844 8799000   e enquiries@macdonald-hotels.co.uk

macdonald-hotels.co.uk

North West | Greater Manchester

Bury | Burrs Country Park Caravan Club Site

Enjoy England ★★★★★

(85) £13.70–£19.55
(85) £13.70–£19.55
85 touring pitches
Open: All year
Shop: 1.5 miles
Pub: <0.5 miles

Woodhill Road, Bury, Lancashire BL8 8BN
t 0161 761 0489

caravanclub.co.uk

4B1

On a historic mill site, Burrs offers easy access to relaxing river and countryside walks, the adjacent East Lancashire Steam Railway and Manchester. There are many opportunities for outdoor pursuits in the country park, such as climbing, abseiling and canoeing.

Location: From A676 (signposted Ramsbottom), follow signs for Burrs Country Park.

Access:
General:
Pitch:

Denshaw | Cherry Clough Farm House Accommodation

Enjoy England ★★★★★

Cherry Clough Farm, Denshaw, Oldham OL3 5UE
t 01457 874369   e info@cherryclough.co.uk

cherryclough.co.uk

Manchester | Hilton Manchester Deansgate

303 Deansgate, Manchester M3 4LQ
t 0161 870 1600   e sales.manchesterdeansgate@hilton.com

hilton.co.uk/manchesterdeansgate

Manchester | Ibis Hotel Manchester

96 Portland Street, Manchester M1 4GX
t 0161 2340600

ibishotel.com

Manchester | Luther King House

Enjoy England ★★★

Brighton Grove, Wilmslow Road, Manchester M14 5JP
t 0161 224 6404   e reception@lkh.co.uk

lkh.co.uk

For symbols see pg 24

285

North West | Greater Manchester/Merseyside

Manchester | Manchester YHA

Enjoy England ★★★★ Potato Wharf, Castlefield, Manchester M3 4NB
t 0870 770 5950 e manchester@yha.org.uk
yha.org.uk

Manchester | Midland Hotel

Enjoy England ★★★★ Peter Street, Manchester M60 2DS
t 0161 236 3333 e midlandreservations@qhotels.co.uk
themidland.co.uk

Manchester Airport | Bewleys Hotel Manchester Airport

AA ★★★
Rooms per night:
s: £65.00–£155.00
d: £73.95–£163.95
p/p half board:
d: £99.00
Meals: £21.95

Outwood Lane, Manchester Airport, Manchester M90 4HL
t 0044 161 498 1390 e manchester@bewleyshotels.com
bewleyshotels.com   4B2

Contemporary, relaxed and informal, ideal for leisure and business travellers for terminals 1 and 3

Access: **General:** **Room:**

Manchester Airport | Crowne Plaza Manchester Airport

Terminal 3, Ringway Road, Manchester Airport M90 3NS
t 0870 400 9055 e reservations-manchesterairport@ihg.com
www.crowneplaza.co.uk

Access: **General:** **Room:**

Salford | Lowry Hotel

50 Dearmans Place, Chapel Wharf, Salford M3 5LH
t 0161 827 4000
thelowryhotel.com

Ainsdale | Willowbank Holiday Home and Touring Park

AA ★★★
Enjoy England ★★★★★

(87) £12.35–£16.90
(87) £12.35–£16.90
(228)

Open: 1st March to 10th January

Coastal Road, Ainsdale, Southport PR8 3ST
t 01704 571566 e info@willowbankcp.co.uk
willowbankcp.co.uk

Within walking distance of the National Trust nature reserve and Sefton Coastline.

Access: **General:** **Pitch:**

286   www.openbritain.net

North West | **Merseyside**

Birkenhead | Mersey View - East Float Dock 2

Enjoy England ★★★★-★★★★★★ Owner, Mersey View - East Float Dock 2, Mill 1, Dock Road, Birkenhead CH41 1DN

Haydock | Holiday Inn Haydock

Lodge Lane, Newton-le-Willows, Merseyside WA12 0JG
t 0870 400 9039 e reservations-haydock@ihg.com
holiday-inn.co.uk

Access: **General:** **Room:**

Liverpool | Holiday Inn Liverpool City Centre

Enjoy England ★★★ Lime Street, Liverpool L1 1NQ
t 0151 709 7090 e reservations@hiliverpool.com
hiliverpool.com

Liverpool | Hotel Ibis

27 Wapping, Liverpool, Merseyside L1 8LY
t 0151 706 9800
ibishotel.com

Liverpool | Staybridge Suites Liverpool   AS

Enjoy England ★★★★ 21 Keel Wharf, Liverpool L3 4FN
t 0151 703 9700
staybridge.co.uk

Access: **General:** **Room:**

Liverpool | YHA Liverpool International

Enjoy England ★★★★ 25 Tabley Street, off Wapping, Liverpool L1 8EE
t 0870 770 5924 e liverpool@yha.org.uk
yha.org.uk

Southport | Vitalise Sandpipers   AS

Fairway, Southport, Merseyside PR9 0AL
t 01704 538388 e sandpipers@vitalise.org.uk
vitalise.org.uk

Access: **General:** **Room:**

West Kirby | Herons Well Cottage

Enjoy England ★★★★★ Mrs Glynis Lavelle, Owner, Three Lanes End Farm, West Kirby, Wirral CH48 1PT t 0151 625 1401 e HeronsWell@btinternet.com
HeronsWell.co.uk

Access: **General:** **Unit:**

For symbols see pg 24

287

North West | Attractions

Necton | Ness Botanic Gardens
Ness, Necton, Cheshire CH64 4AY
t 0151 353 0123 e nessgdns@liverpool.ac.uk
nessgardens.co.uk

Blackpool | Sandcastle Waterpark
South Beach, Blackpool FY4 1BB
t 01253 343602 e info@sandcastle-waterpark.co.uk
sandcastle-waterpark.co.uk

Manchester | Manchester Art Gallery
Mosley Street, Manchester M2 3JL
t Booking: 020 7452 3000 / Information: 020 7452 3400
manchestergalleries.org

Manchester | Royal Exchange Theatre Company
St Annes Square, Manchester M2 7DH
t 0161 833 9833 e box.office@royalexchange.co.uk
royalexchangetheatre.org.uk

Salford | Salford Museum & Art Gallery
Peel Park, The Crescent, Salford, Lancashire M5 4WU
t 0161 778 0800 e salford.museum@salford.gov.uk
salford.gov.uk/salfordmuseum

Liverpool | The Conference Centre at Lace
Tuneside Ltd, Croxteth Drive, Sefton Park, Liverpool L17 1AA
t 0151 5221092 e n.hitchen@rcaol.co.uk
conferenceatlace.co.uk

Access: .: abc ✈ ☺ ♿ ♨ 🅿 ⚿ᴳ General: 🅿 ⚿ ♿

OPEN BRITAIN — PLANNING A DAY OUT? WHY NOT MAKE IT A SHORT-BREAK?
Fabulous 'Places to Stay' in every region

OpenBritain | Northwest

TRAMPER
All terrain electric buggies

Available **Free** at Beacon Fell and Wycoller Country Parks in Lancashire. They can also be used on many of our guided walks and events.

BOOKING ESSENTIAL
Call 01772 534709

Lancashire County Council

Lancashire's Country Parks are beautiful but sometimes challenging places. Access can be difficult due to the gradients and the rough nature of the terrain. To make sites more accessible Lancashire County Council provide Tramper all terrain electric vehicles to borrow **free** of charge. Beacon Fell is the best introduction to using these vehicles. A first time user will be given a one to one induction by one of our Rangers. Once the user and the Ranger are happy that the control of the tramper has been mastered the user is free to explore at their leisure.

The result is a true countryside experience including rough paths and steep gradients. Users often come back tired and sometimes muddy, but they come back happy!!

User Comment
"for someone who was a keen walker prior to my disability this has been a great experience, thank you."

www.lancashire.gov.uk/environment/countryside

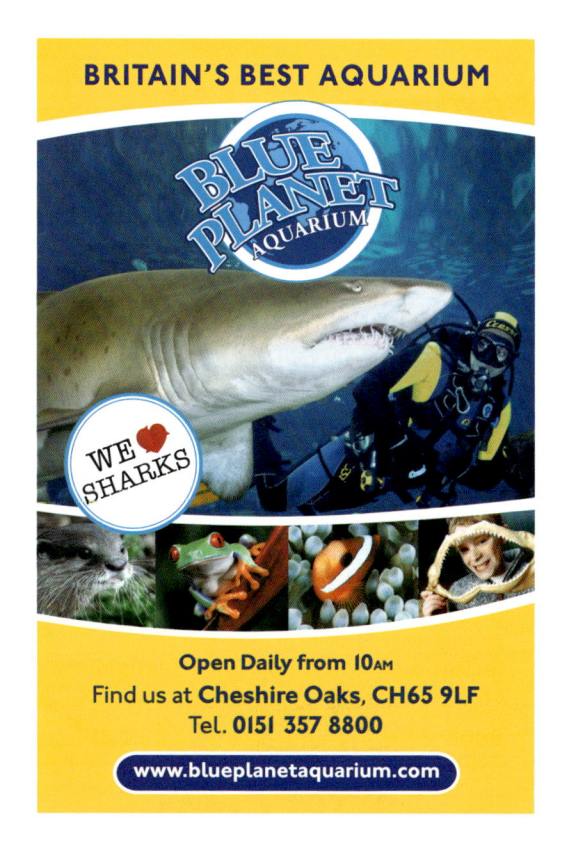

BRITAIN'S BEST AQUARIUM

BLUE PLANET AQUARIUM

WE ♥ SHARKS

Open Daily from 10AM
Find us at **Cheshire Oaks, CH65 9LF**
Tel. **0151 357 8800**

www.blueplanetaquarium.com

---

the **Quay** to a great **day out!**

lowryoutletmall.com

LOWRY OUTLET MALL
FAMOUS BRANDS DISCOUNT SHOPPING
SALFORD QUAYS

Upto **50% discount** off high street prices

Great group discounts and incentives available

Easy disabled access

For more information, contact
Terry Douglas
tel: 0161 848 1850
email: terry.douglas@emerson.co.uk

OpenBritain | Northwest

Welcome Explore Discover Relax
Manchester Art Gallery

Manchester Art Gallery,
Mosley Street,
Manchester M2 3JL
Tel: 0161 235 8888
Textphone: 0161 235 8893
www.manchestergalleries.org

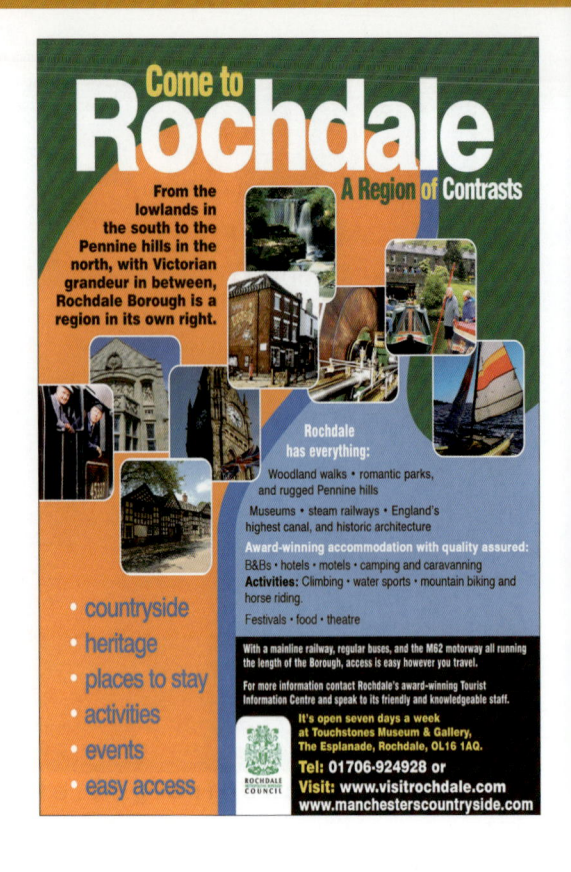

MANCHESTER CITY COUNCIL

Come to Rochdale
A Region of Contrasts

From the lowlands in the south to the Pennine hills in the north, with Victorian grandeur in between, Rochdale Borough is a region in its own right.

Rochdale has everything:
Woodland walks • romantic parks, and rugged Pennine hills
Museums • steam railways • England's highest canal, and historic architecture
Award-winning accommodation with quality assured: B&Bs • hotels • motels • camping and caravanning
Activities: Climbing • water sports • mountain biking and horse riding.
Festivals • food • theatre

With a mainline railway, regular buses, and the M62 motorway all running the length of the Borough, access is easy however you travel.

For more information contact Rochdale's award-winning Tourist Information Centre and speak to its friendly and knowledgeable staff.

It's open seven days a week at Touchstones Museum & Gallery, The Esplanade, Rochdale, OL16 1AQ.
Tel: 01706-924928 or
Visit: www.visitrochdale.com
www.manchesterscountryside.com

- countryside
- heritage
- places to stay
- activities
- events
- easy access

MANCHESTER CITY COUNCIL

For more information on Public Facilities and Access at many attractions, why not telephone for more details before you travel?

Please telephone for all enquiries
0161 957 8315

Autumn/Winter
Royal Exchange Theatre

4 November – 5 December
The Entertainer
Audio Described: 28 Nov 2.30pm
BSL: 1 Dec 7.30pm

9 December – 23 January 10
Blithe Spirit
Audio Described 16 Jan 4pm
BSL 19 Jan at 7.30pm

27 January – 20 February
A Raisin In The Sun
Audio Described 13 Feb 2.30pm
BSL 19 Feb 7.30pm

The Royal Exchange Theatre is comitted to improving access for all theatre-goers. We have wheelchair spaces, infra red assisted hearing facilities and our brochure is available on CD and in large print and in Braille.

Book now on **0161 833 9833**
royalexchange.co.uk

290

OpenBritain | Northwest

Sandcastle Waterpark

The UK's Largest Indoor Waterpark

- 18 Slides & attractions
- Accessible friendly
- Dedicated Safety Hotline 01253 340721
- Open all year round

Sandcastle Waterpark
South Beach, Blackpool, FY4 1BB
T. 01253 340700/343602
www.sandcastle-waterpark.co.uk

The Sandcastle Waterpark Team is committed to Guest Service Excellence

---

Silver Award – Large Visitor Attraction of the Year 2008

Tullie House Museum & Art Gallery

FREE ADMISSION to ages 18 and under

Enjoy a fun-filled day out for all the family!

Something for everyone, from fine art to interactive fun. We have a variety of exhibitions and events throughout the year.

Tel **01228 618718** or visit **www.tulliehouse.co.uk**

Open daily, all year except: 25th/26th December & 1st January.

Tullie House, Castle Street, Carlisle CA3 8TP
Email: enquiries@tulliehouse.co.uk

Bendrigg Trust
Activity Courses for All

- All abilities/disabilities catered for
- Qualified and experienced staff
- Centre situated in beautiful countryside
- Wide variety of activities
- All courses 'tailor-made'
- Open throughout the year

For a free brochure and further information contact:

Trevor Clarke, Bendrigg Lodge, Old Hutton, Kendal, Cumbria LA8 0NR
Tel: 01539 723766   Fax: 01539 722446   email: office@bendrigg.org.uk
www.bendrigg.org.uk   registered charity no. 508450

ROTHAY MANOR
HOTEL & RESTAURANT

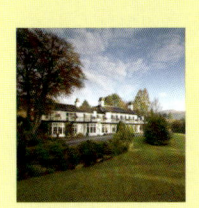

Award-winning, family owned
Lake District hotel

Comfortable, relaxed & friendly
Good Food Guide for 41 years

Wheelchair accessible rooms
Designated parking area
National Accessible Scheme
Level 2 mobility

Rothay Bridge, Ambleside, Cumbria
LA22 0EH   Tel: 015394 33605
e-mail: hotel@rothaymanor.co.uk
www.rothaymanor.co.uk

For information about mobility and accessibility in Preston

www.visitpreston.com

Preston City Council

Or contact the TIC on 01772 253731

Salford Heritage Service is your ticket to the past ...

Stroll down the Lark Hill Place, our authentic Victorian Street at Salford Museum and Art Gallery.

Trace your family tree at Salford Local History Library.

Exhibitions • Activities • Workshops • Events

Salford Museum and Art Gallery / Local History
Peel Park, Crescent, Salford M5 4WU

0161 778 0800

Mon - Fri 10am - 4.45pm. Sat / Sun 1pm - 5pm

www.salford.gov.uk/museums

291

OpenBritain | **Northwest**

A tranquil setting...
in stunning Cumbrian countryside

Southwaite Green offers a unique experience – 5 star luxury with deep green principles. Eco-holiday accommodation, fully adapted for disabled use and access.

southwaite green
eco-holidays - naturally good

visit **www.southwaitegreen.co.uk**,
or call **01900 821055** for details & brochure

OFFICIAL TOURIST BOARD GUIDE

Enjoy Every Minute
Enjoy England
Enjoy The Books

Now available in good bookshops and online at...

enjoyEngland.com

Pets Come Too! 2010 — Pet-friendly accommodation — enjoyEngland.com

---

OPEN LONDON
Coming soon.... early 2010

The new **OpenLondon** guide is the definitive guide for visitors to London with access needs. The guide contains everything required to enjoy London to the full.

OPEN LONDON 2010 — The definitive guide to accessible London — **NEW**

LONDON DEVELOPMENT AGENCY | VISIT LONDON visitlondon.com | MAYOR OF LONDON

www.openbritain.net | openlondon@hhgroup.co.uk | 01603 813740

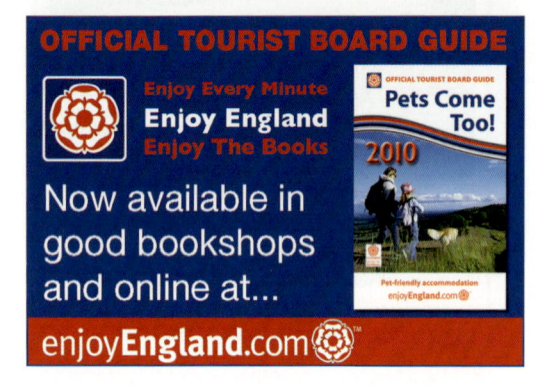

OPEN BRITAIN

PLANNING A DAY OUT? WHY NOT MAKE IT A SHORT- BREAK?
Fabulous 'Places to Stay' in every region

OPEN BRITAIN

2010 – Dates for your diary

2010

New Year's Day	1st Jan
Moving & Handling People	28th – 29th Jan
Kidz in the Middle	11th Mar
The Care Show	30th – 31st Mar
Good Friday	2nd Apr
Easter Monday	5th Apr
Naidex Roadshow	20th -22nd Apr
Early May Bank Holiday	3rd May
Liberation Day (Channel Islands)	9th May
Spring Bank Holiday	31st May
Kidz South	24th June
The Mobility Roadshow	1st – 3rd July
Summer Bank Holiday	30th Aug
Beyond Boundries Live!	11th – 12th Sept
enABLE 2010	TBC
Kidz up North	TBC
Christmas Bank Holiday	27th Dec
Boxing Day Holiday	28th Dec

If there is an event going on in your area that you think we should know about, let us know!

info@openbritain.net

OpenBritain | **North East**

Bamburgh Castle

Coastline, castles, countryside and culture

Hartlepool's Maritime Experience

World-famous for our friendliness and hospitality, come and share our passion for this wonderful region of coastline and castles, countryside and culture!

Want to experience our tranquil countryside and undiscovered coastline? Head for **Kielder**, where you can take a cruise on Europe's largest man-made lake, wander miles of forest paths and stay in a wheelchair-accessible forest village. Or take a boat trip from **Seahouses**, on the **Northumberland Coast Area of Outstanding Natural Beauty**, to see breeding puffins and grey seals on the **Farne Islands**.

NewcastleGateshead Quayside

OpenBritain | North East

North East

Co. Durham

Northumberland

Tyne and Wear

Tees Valley

Love your history? Come and marvel at **Hadrian's Wall**, still marking the northernmost limit of the Roman Empire after almost 2,000 years. You'll find amazing interactive exhibits and events at several of its forts, including **Segedunum** and **Arbeia** in North and South Tyneside respectively. You can board **HMS Trincomalee**, the oldest warship still afloat, at **Hartlepool's Maritime Experience** in Tees Valley. And at **Beamish**, an open air museum in Durham, you can travel back in time to 1825 and 1913 via an easy-access bus, to visit the town, farm, manor house and colliery village.

Our cities are alive with world-class culture and fantastic shopping. Visit **mima**, **Middlesbrough's Institute of Modern Art**, or **BALTIC, Centre for Contemporary Art**, on NewcastleGateshead's Quayside, for vibrant and often highly provocative exhibitions. Nearby, **The Sage Gateshead**, an award-winning centre for music, offers breathtaking waterfront views and access to its café, restaurant and library whether you're attending a concert or not. Or why not treat yourself to some retail therapy at **MetroCentre**, Europe's largest shopping and leisure complex, or see beautiful glass being hand-made at the **National Glass Centre**, Sunderland?

Find out more

web visitnortheastengland.com/access

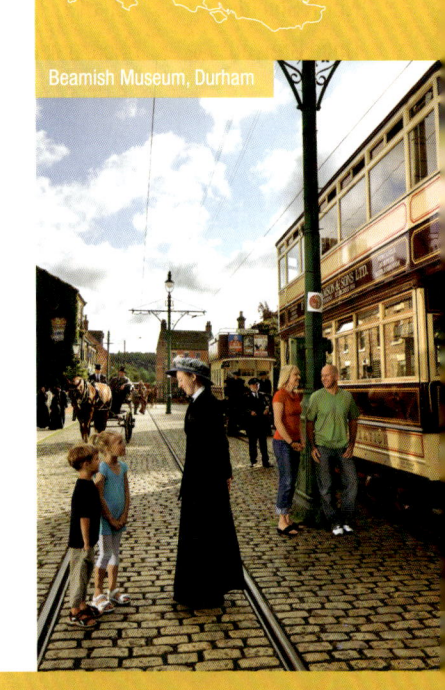

Beamish Museum, Durham

www.openbritain.net

Tourist Information Centres

Tourist Information Centres are a mine of information about local and regional accommodation, attractions and events. Visit them when you arrive at your destination or contact them before you go:

Alnwick	2 The Shambles	01665 511333	alnwicktic@alnwick.gov.uk
Amble	Queen Street Car Park	01665 712313	ambletic@alnwick.gov.uk
Barnard Castle	Woodleigh, Flatts Road	01833 690909	tourism@teesdale.gov.uk
Bellingham	The Heritage Centre, Hillside	01434 220616	bellinghamtic@btconnect.com
Berwick-Upon-Tweed	106 Marygate	01289 330733 t	ourism@berwick-upon-tweed.gov.uk
Bishop Auckland	Town Hall Ground Floor	01388 604922	bishopauckland.touristinfo@durham.gov.uk
Corbridge	Hill Street	01434 632815	corbridgetic@btconnect.com
Craster	Craster Car Park	01665 576007	crastertic@alnwick.gov.uk
Darlington	13 Horsemarket	01325 388666	tic@darlington.gov.uk
Durham	2 Millennium Place	0191 384 3720	touristinfo@durhamcity.gov.uk
Gateshead	Central Library	0191 433 8420	tic@gateshead.gov.uk
Gateshead	The Sage Gateshead	0191 478 4222	tourism@gateshead.gov.uk
Haltwhistle	Railway Station	01434 322002	haltwhistletic@btconnect.com
Hartlepool	Hartlepool Art Gallery	01429 869706	hpooltic@hartlepool.gov.uk
Hexham	Wentworth Car Park	01434 652220	hexham.tic@tynedale.gov.uk
Middlesbrough	99-101 Albert Road	01642 729700	middlesbrough_tic@middlesbrough.gov.uk
Morpeth	The Chantry	01670 500700	morpeth.tic@northumberland.gov.uk
Newcastle-Upon-Tyne	8-9 Central Arcade	0191 277 8000	tourist.info@newcastle.gov.uk
North Shields	Unit 18, Royal Quays	0191 2005895	ticns@northtyneside.gov.uk
Once Brewed	Northumberland NP Centre	01434 344396	tic.oncebrewed@nnpa.org.uk
Peterlee	4 Upper Yoden Way	0191 586 4450	touristinfo@peterlee.gov.uk
Redcar	West Terrace	01642 471921	redcar_tic@redcar-cleveland.gov.uk
Rothbury	Northumberland NP Centre	01669 620887	tic.rothbury@nnpa.org.uk
Saltburn By Sea	3 Station Buildings	01287 622422	saltburn_tic@redcar-cleveland.gov.uk
Seahouses	Seafield Car Park	01665 720884	seahousesTIC@berwick-upon-tweed.gov.uk
South Shields	South Shields Museum & Gallery	0191 454 6612	museum.tic@s-tyneside-mbc.gov.uk
South Shields	Sea Road	0191 455 7411	foreshore.tic@s-tyneside-mbc.gov.uk
Stanhope	Durham Dales Centre	01388 527650	durham.dales.centre@durham.gov.uk
Stockton-On-Tees	Stockton Central Library	01642 528130	touristinformation@stockton.gov.uk
Sunderland	50 Fawcett Street	0191 553 2000	tourist.info@sunderland.gov.uk
Whitley Bay	Park Road	0191 2008535	ticwb@northtyneside.gov.uk
Wooler	The Cheviot Centre	01668 282123	woolerTIC@berwick-upon-tweed.gov.uk

North East | Co. Durham

Barnard Castle | East Briscoe Farm Cottages

Enjoy England ★★★★
Units: 5　Sleeps: 1-5
Open: All year

Low season p/w:
£195.00
High season p/w:
£525.00

Baldersdale, Barnard Castle, Co. Durham DL12 9UL
t 01833 650087

eastbriscoe.co.uk

Five award winning cottages set in beautiful countryside. One wheelchair accessible, one limited mobility accessible.

Access:　General:　Unit:

Bowes | Mellwaters Barn

Enjoy England ★★★★　East Mellwaters Farm, Stainmore Road, Barnard Castle DL12 9RH

mellwatersbarn.co.uk

Cockfield | Stonecroft and Swallows Nest

AS

Enjoy England ★★★★
Units: 2　Sleeps: 4
Open: All year

Low season p/w:
£160.00
High season p/w:
£340.00

Mrs Alison Tallentire, Stonecroft and Swallows Nest, Lowlands Farm, Cockfield, Bishop Auckland DL13 5AW
t 01388 718251　e info@farmholidaysuk.com

farmholidaysuk.com

5C2

Beautifully renovated cottages, comfortable, cosy, own gardens/parking, friendly working farm, fantastic countryside, everyone welcome

Access:　General:　
Unit:

Looking for something else?

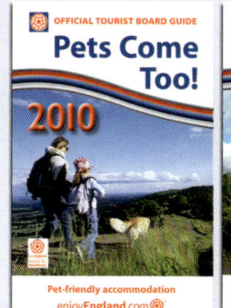

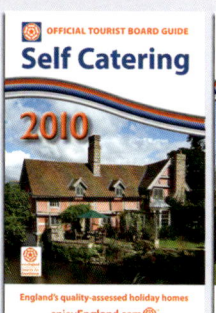

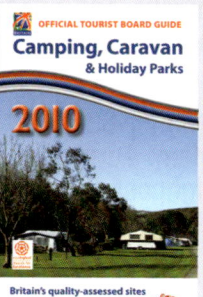

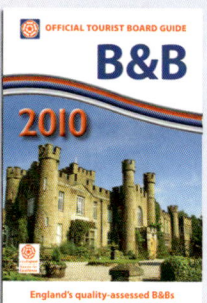

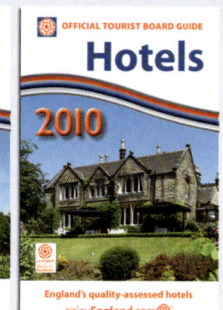

- Pets Come Too! 2010 — Pet-friendly accommodation — enjoyEngland.com
- Self Catering 2010 — England's quality-assessed holiday homes — enjoyEngland.com
- Camping, Caravan & Holiday Parks 2010 — Britain's quality-assessed sites — visitBritain.com
- B&B 2010 — England's quality-assessed B&Bs — enjoyEngland.com
- Hotels 2010 — England's quality-assessed hotels — enjoyEngland.com

OFFICIAL TOURIST BOARD GUIDE

If you haven't found what you are looking for in OpenBritain, VisitBritain's Official Tourist Board Guides offer a wide choice of assessed accommodation which may meet your needs.

For symbols see pg 24

North East | Co. Durham

Cornriggs | Alice & Nelly's Cottages

Enjoy England ★★★★★
Units: 2 Sleeps: 5-6
Open: All year

Low season p/w: £320.00
High season p/w: £510.00

Shop: 1.5 miles
Pub: 1 mile

Mrs Janet Elliot, Cornriggs Cottages, Low Cornriggs Farm, Cornriggs, Bishop Auckland DL13 1AQ
t 01388 537600 e cornriggsfarm@btconnect.com

britnett.net/lowcornriggsfarm 5B2

Both cottages are a very high standard with accommodation on one level. Level entrances, wide doors, large rooms and corridors. Roll in accessible showers, handrails and space by WC. Patio area, flat parking area. Home baking, meals.

Access:
General:
Unit:

Durham | The Grange Caravan Club Site

Enjoy England ★★★★★
(76) £13.70–£19.55
(76) £13.70–£19.55
(12)

76 touring pitches
Open: All year

Shop: 1 mile
Pub: 1.5 miles

Meadow Lane, Durham DH1 1TL
t 0191 384 4778

caravanclub.co.uk 5C2

An open, level site within easy reach of the picturesque city of Durham with walks from the site into the city. Durham is steeped in history, and a visit to Durham Cathedral and Castle is a must.

Location: A1(M) jct 62, A690 towards Durham. Turn right after 50m. Signposted Maureen Terrace and brown caravan sign.

Access:
General:
Pitch:

298 www.openbritain.net

North East | Co. Durham

Eggleston | Stable Court

Enjoy England ★★★★ Owner, Stable Court, High Shipley, Eggleston, Barnard Castle DL12 0DP

stablecourt.co.uk

Frosterley | Cromer House Camping Barn

48 Front Street, Frosterley, Bishop Auckland DL13 2QS
t 01388 526632 e inquiries@cromerhousecampingbarn.co.uk

cromerhousecampingbarn.co.uk

Access: abc **General:**   **Room:**

Gainford | East Greystone Farm Cottages

Enjoy England ★★★★
Units: 2 Sleeps: 1-4
Open: All year

Low season p/w: £275.00
High season p/w: £460.00

Mrs Sue Hodgson, Main Road, Gainford DL2 3BL
t 01325 730236 e sue@holidayfarmcottages.co.uk

holidayfarmcottages.co.uk   5C3

Situated in glorious rolling Teesdale countryside. Peaceful retreat. Ideal base to relax or explore.

Access: **General:**   **Unit:**

High Hesleden | The Ship Inn

Enjoy England ★★★★ Main Street, High Hesleden TS27 4QD
t 01429 836453 e sheila@theshipinn.net

theshipinn.net

Ingleton | Mill Granary Cottages

Enjoy England ★★★★★ Mr & Mrs Richard & Kate Hodgson, Mill Granary Cottages, Middleton House, Ingleton, Darlington DL2 3HG t 01325 730339 e info@millgranary.co.uk

millgranary.co.uk

Quebec | Hamsteels Cottages

Enjoy England ★★★★
Units: 3 Sleeps: 2-8
Open: All year

Low season p/w: £250.00
High season p/w: £560.00

Mrs June Whitfield, Hamsteels Cottages, Hamsteels Hall, Hamsteels Lane, Quebec DH7 9RS
t 01207 520388 e june@hamsteelshall.co.uk

hamsteelshall.co.uk

Attractive stone bungalows in open countryside very spacious with all facilities. Close to Durham/Beamish.

Access:
General: **Unit:**

For symbols see pg 24   299

North East | Co. Durham/Northumberland

Stockton on Tees | White Water Park Caravan Club Site

Enjoy England ★★★★★

(115) £10.45–£15.90
(115) £10.45–£15.90
(5)

115 touring pitches
Open: All year
Shop: 1 mile
Pub: 0.5 miles

Access:
General:
Pitch:

Tees Barrage, Stockton-on-Tees, Co Durham TS18 2QW
t 01642 634880

caravanclub.co.uk　　　　　　　　　　　　　　5C3

Pleasantly landscaped site, close to the largest white-water canoeing and rafting course in Britain. Nearby Teesside Park is great for shopping, restaurants, cinema and bowling. Birdwatchers, wildlife enthusiasts and walkers will enjoy 30 miles of coastline close by.

Location: Come off the A66 Teesside Park. Follow Teesdale sign, go over Tees Barrage Bridge, turn right. Site 200yds on left.

Winston | Alwent Mill Cottage

Enjoy England ★★★★　　Mrs Libby Hampson, Alwent Mill Cottage, Alwent Mill, Alwent Mill Lane, Darlington DL2 3QH　　t 01325 730479　　e libby@alwentmill.co.uk

Alnwick | Bog Mill Farm Holiday Cottages

Enjoy England ★★★★-★★★★★　　Mrs Ann Mason, Bog Mill Farm Holiday Cottages, Bog Mill Farm, Alnwick NE66 3PA　　t 01665 604529　　e stay@bogmill.co.uk

bogmill.co.uk

Alnwick | Doxford Cottages

Enjoy England ★★★★★　　Ms Sue Pringle, Manager, Doxford Cottages, Doxford Estate, Chathill NE67 5DW　　t 01665 589393　　e stay@doxfordcottages.co.uk

doxfordcottages.co.uk

Access:　**General:**　**Unit:**

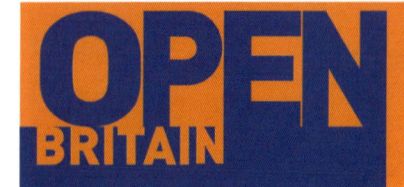

OPEN BRITAIN

DECIDED WHERE TO GO?
SEE ATTRACTIONS FOR WHAT TO DO
Ideas and information at the end of each regional section

©Britainonview / Martin Brent

North East | **Northumberland**

Bardon Mill | **High Shield**

Enjoy England ★★★★
Units: 1   Sleeps: 1-2
Low season p/w: £350.00
High season p/w: £495.00

Michael, High Shield, Bardon Mill, Hexham, Northumberland NE47 7AJ
t 01434 340188   f 01434 344791   e highshield@btinternet.com

highshield.co.uk

Spacious accommodation with stunning views from cottage and garden terrace. Situated half-way along Hadrian's Wall.

Access: General: P   Unit:

Belford | **Elwick Farm Cottages**

Enjoy England ★★★★
Mrs Roslyn Reay, Elwick Farm Cottages, Elwick, Belford NE70 7EL
t 01668 213242   e w.r.reay@talk21.com

elwickcottages.co.uk

Belford | **Outchester & Ross Farm Cottages**

Enjoy England ★★★★-★★★★★
Mrs Shirley McKie, Outchester & Ross Farm Cottages, 1 Cragview Road, Belford NE70 7NT   t 01668 213336   e stay@rosscottages.co.uk

rosscottages.co.uk

Bellingham | **Brownrigg Lodges**

AS

Enjoy England ★★★
Mrs Morag MacLeod, Brownrigg, Bellingham NE48 2HR
t 01434 220272   e mac.kent@virgin.net

brownrigglodges.com

Access: General: P   Unit:

Berwick-Upon-Tweed | **Bowsden bed and breakfast**

Enjoy England ★★★★
Open: Closed February open otherwise
Rooms per night:
s: £35.00-£45.00
d: £60.00-£80.00

West View, Bowsden, Berwick Upon Tweed TD15 2TW
t 01289 388731   e bfieldsend@btconnect.com

bowsdenbedandbreakfast.co.uk   5B1

Homely accommodation in sleepy village between Wooler, Berwick and 6 miles off Holy Island.

Access: General: Room:

Berwick-Upon-Tweed | **Meadow Hill Guest House**

Enjoy England ★★★★
Duns Road, Berwick-upon-Tweed TD15 1UB
t 01289 306325   e christineabart@aol.com

meadow-hill.co.uk

For symbols see pg 24

North East | **Northumberland**

Berwick-Upon-Tweed | West Ord Holiday Cottages

Enjoy England ★★★-★★★★★ Mrs Carol Lang, West Ord Holiday Cottages, West Ord Farm, Berwick-upon-Tweed TD15 2XQ t 01289 386631 e stay@westord.co.uk
westord.co.uk

Cornhill-On-Tweed | Collingwood Arms Hotel

Enjoy England Main Street, Cornhill on Tweed TD12 4UH
t 01890 882424 e enquiries@collingwoodarms.com
collingwoodarms.com

Craster | Craster Pine Lodges

Enjoy England ★★★★ Mr & Mrs Michael & Fyona Robson, Craster Pine Lodges, 19 Heugh Road, Alnwick NE66 3TJ t 01665 576286 e pinelodges@barkpots.co.uk
crasterpinelodges.co.uk

Crookham | The Coach House

Enjoy England ★★★★

Open: All year except Xmas

Rooms per night:
s: £45.00-£85.00
d: £90.00-£104.00
Meals: £22.95

Access:
General:
Room:

Crookham, Cornhill-on-Tweed, Northumberland TD12 4TD
t 01890 820293 e stay@coachhousecrookham.com
coachhousecrookham.com

5B1

Seventeenth Century Dower house with spacious En Suite bedrooms in a rustic courtyard. Perfect to explore Scottish Borders, Northumberland coast and Alnwick. Unsurpassed hospitality in extremely comfortable surroundings. Fine fresh home cooked food. Fully licensed. Your home in the country.

Location: Located outside the village of Crookham. Ten miles north of Wooler, Four miles south of Coldstream, on the A697.

Doxford | Doxford Hall Hotel & Spa

Enjoy England ★★★★ Doxford Hall, Chathill NE67 5DN
doxfordhall.com

302 www.openbritain.net

North East | **Northumberland**

Falstone | Falstone Barns

Enjoy England ★★★★★ Mrs Nicolette Forster, Falstone Barns, Falstone Farm, Hexham NE48 1AA
t 01434 240251 e redstone@btinternet.com
falstonebarns.com

Haydon Bridge | Grindon Cartshed

Enjoy England ★★★★
Open: All year
Rooms per night:
s: £49.00
d: £70.00
Meals: £19.00

Haydon Bridge, Hexham, Northumberland NE47 6NQ
t 01434 684273 e cartshed@grindon.force9.co.uk
grindon-cartshed.co.uk   5B2

Cosy barn conversion nestled in Hadrian's Wall country. Spectacular rural views. An ideal relaxing base.

Access: abc
General: **Room:**

Haydon Bridge | Shaftoe's

Enjoy England ★★★★ 4 Shaftoe Street, Haydon Bridge NE47 6BJ
t 01434 684664 e bookings@shaftoes.co.uk
shaftoes.co.uk

Hexham | The Hytte

Enjoy England ★★★★★
Units: 1 **Sleeps:** 8
Open: All year
Low season p/w: £550.00
High season p/w: £960.00

Mr & Mrs S R Gregory, The Hytte, Bingfield, Hexham NE46 4HR
t 01434 672321 e sgregory001@tiscali.co.uk
thehytte.com   5B2

Norwegian style mountain lodge with grass roof, sleeps eight, four accessible bedrooms. Sauna and hot-tub.

Access: abc
General: **Unit:**

Hexham | The Old Farmhouse

Units: 1 **Sleeps:** 1-5
Open: All year
Low season p/w: £265.00
High season p/w: £505.00

Mrs J A Armstrong, Grindon Farm, Haydon Bridge, Hexham, Northumberland NE47 6NQ e chris@grindonfarm.co.uk
grindonfarm.co.uk   5B2

Cosy barn conversion nestled in Hadrian's Wall country. Spectacular rural views. An ideal relaxing base.

Access: abc **General:**   **Unit:**

For symbols see pg 24

North East | **Northumberland**

Hexham | Peel Bothy

National Trust, Peel Bothy, nr Hexham, Northumberland
t 0844 8002070
nationaltrustcottages.co.uk/north_of_england/

Kielder | Calvert Trust Kielder

Enjoy England ★★★★
Units: 10   Sleeps: 6-7
Open: All year

Low season p/w: £265.00
High season p/w: £779.00

Calvert Trust Kielder Water & Forest Park, Kielder Water, Kielder NE48 1BS   t 01434 250232   e enquiries@calvert-kielder.com
calvert-trust.org.uk/kielder   5B1

4-star Scandinavian style lodges, located in the beautiful Kielder Water & Forest Park.

Longhirst | Longhirst Hall

Enjoy England ★★★

Longhirst NE61 3LL
t 01670 791348   e enquiries@longhirst.co.uk
longhirst.co.uk

Longhorsley | Beacon Hill

Enjoy England ★★★★★
Units: 15   Sleeps: 2-6
Open: All year

Low season p/w: £240.00
High season p/w: £1635.00

Mr Alun Moore, Doxford Estate, Chathill NE67 5DW
t 01670 780900   e alun@doxfordcottages.co.uk
beaconhill.co.uk   5C1

3 mobility M2 cottages. 5 star. Ramped access, level entry showers. All rooms accessible.

Longhorsley | Macdonald Linden Hall Hotel

Enjoy England ★★★★

Longhorsley NE65 8XF
t 0870 194 2123   e lindenhall@macdonald-hotels.co.uk
lindenhall-hotel.co.uk

Become a member of OpenBritain today.
Share your own travel and accommodation experiences and help Britain become more open!

visit www.openbritain.net

OPEN BRITAIN

304   www.openbritain.net

North East | **Northumberland**

Lucker | **Lucker Hall Steading**

AS

Owner, Lucker Hall Steading, Lucker, Belford NE70 7JQ

Enjoy England
★★★★-★★★★★

Units: 19 **Sleeps:** 2-18
Open: All year

Low season p/w:
£369.00
High season p/w:
£497.00

Shop: 2 miles
Pub: <0.5 miles

alnwickcastlecottages.co.uk 5C1

Superbly spacious cottages for 2 designed with level entry and walk-in shower in a tiny village close to Bamburgh. Alnwick Castle and grounds are just a 15 minute drive away. There are other delightful groundfloor cottages accommodating upto 6.

Location: In the centre of a tiny village, 5 mins from A1 and the beach at Bamburgh.

Access:
General:
Unit:

Morpeth | **Beacon Hill Farm**

Enjoy England
★★★★-★★★★★

Units: 15 **Sleeps:** 2-7
Open: All year

Low season p/w:
£290.00
High season p/w:
£1800.00

Alun Moore, Beacon Hill Farm, Longhorsley, Morpeth, Northumberland NE65 8QW
t 01670 780900 e alun@beaconhill.co.uk

beaconhill.co.uk 6D3

3 mobility M2 cottages. 5 star, ramped access, level entry showers. All rooms accessible.

Access: abc
General: **Unit:**

Newbrough | **Carr Edge Farm**

Enjoy England ★★★★

Newbrough NE47 5EA
t 01434 674788 e stay@carredge.co.uk

carredge.co.uk

OPEN BRITAIN

GETTING THERE IS NOT A PROBLEM!
See Getting there.....
and back section (p364)
Everything you need for a hassle-free journey

For symbols see pg 24

305

North East | **Northumberland**

Newcastle upon Tyne | **Burradon Farm Houses and Cottages** AS

Units: 2   Sleeps: 3-4
Open: All year

Low season p/w:
£375.00

High season p/w:
£650.00

Mrs Judith Younger, Owner, Burradon Farm, Cramlington, Northumberland NE23 7ND
t 0191 2683203   e judy@burradonfarm.co.uk

burradonfarm.co.uk   5C2

15 Luxury self catering units near town and country ideally suited for holidays and business.

Access:
General: Unit:

North Charlton | **The Reading Rooms**

Enjoy England   ★★★★

Mrs Jane Robson, The Reading Rooms, Northumberland Cottages, The Old Stable Yard, Chathill NE67 5DE
t 01665 589434   e enquiries@northumberlandcottages.com

Powburn | **River Breamish Caravan Club Site** THE CARAVAN CLUB

Enjoy England   ★★★★★

(79) £12.00–£17.95
(79) £12.00–£17.95
(7)

79 touring pitches
Open: 27 March - 2 November

Shop: 0.8 miles
Pub: 0.8 miles

Access:
General:
Pitch:

Powburn, Alnwick, Northumberland NE66 4HY
t 01665 578320

caravanclub.co.uk   5B1

This site is set amid the Cheviot Hills, with excellent walking and cycling in the immediate area. A footbridge in Branton takes you over the river to the delightful Breamish Valley. There is a National Park Centre at Ingram.

Location: Take A697 from A1. In 20 miles (just past Powburn) turn left at service station on right. Site on right.

Shilbottle | **Village Farm**

Enjoy England   ★★★-★★★★★

Mrs Crissy Stoker, Village Farm, Town Foot Farm, Alnwick NE66 2HG
t 01665 575591   e crissy@villagefarmcottages.co.uk

villagefarmcottages.co.uk

North East | **Northumberland**

Slaley | Rye Hill Farm (Old Byre)

Enjoy England ★★★★
Units: 1   Sleeps: 2
Open: All year

Low season p/w: £350.00
High season p/w: £700.00

Mrs Elizabeth Courage, Rye Hill Farm (Old Byre), The Old Byre, Slaley NE47 0AH   t 01434 673259   e info@ryehillfarm.co.uk

ryehillfarm.co.uk   5B2

Wonderful rural views. Modern barn conversion on working farm. 3 En Suite bedrooms. Underfloor heating.

Access: General: Unit:

Wark | Battlesteads Hotel

Enjoy England ★★★★

Wark, Hexham, Northumberland NE48 3LS
t 01434 230209   e info@battlesteads.com

battlesteads.com

Access: General: Room:

Wooler | Crookhouse Cottages

Enjoy England ★★★★
Units: 2   Sleeps: 2-12
Open: All year

Low season p/w: £470.00
High season p/w: £950.00
Shop: 4 miles
Pub: 4 miles

Lynney Holden, Crookhouse Cottages, Crookhouse, Kirknewton, Wooler, Northumberland NE71 6TN
t 01668 216113   e stay@crookhousecottages.co.uk

crookhousecottages.co.uk

A small traditional Northumbrian Steading, superior accommodation in a secluded, tranquil location with outstanding views of the College Valley and Cheviots. Two 4 star luxury cottages, each sleeping 4-6, can easily transform into one to sleep 12+. Dogs welcome.

Location: A697, 3 miles north of Wooler, turn left to Lanton, single track for 3 miles over cattle grids & uphill.

Access:
General:
Unit:

Wooler | Fenton Hill Farm Cottages

Enjoy England ★★★★

Mrs Margaret Logan, Fenton Hill Farm Cottages, Fenton Hill Farm, Wooler NE71 6JJ   t 01668 216228   e stay@fentonhillfarm.co.uk

fentonhillfarm.co.uk

North East | Tyne and Wear/Attractions

Gateshead | Hilton Newcastle Gateshead

Bottle Bank, Gateshead NE8 2AR
t 01914 909700 e reservations.newcastle@hilton.com
hilton.co.uk/newcastlegateshead

Marley Hill | Hedley Hall Country Cottages

Enjoy England ★★★★

Mrs Brenda Fraser, Hedley Hall Country Cottages, Hedley Hall, Hedley Lane, Nr Sunniside, Newcastle-upon-Tyne NE16 5EH
t 01207 231835 e hedleyhall@aol.com
hedleyhallcountrycottages.com/

Durham | Barnard Castle

Open: For opening hours and prices, please call 0870 333 1181 or visit www.english-heritage.org.uk/properties

Barnard Castle, Durham DL12 8PR
t 0870 333 1181 e customers@english-heritage.org.uk
english-heritage.org.uk/barnardcastle

Above the banks of the River Tees is one of northern England's largest medieval castles.

Access: **General:**

Alnwick | The Alnwick Garden

Denwick Lane, Alnwick, Northumberland NE66 1YU
t 01665 511350 e info@thealnwickgarden.com
alnwickgarden.com

Belsay | Belsay Hall, Castle & Gardens

Open: For opening hours and prices, please call 0870 333 1181 or visit www.english-heritage.org.uk/properties

Belsay, Northumberland NE20 0DX
t 0870 333 1181 e customers@english-heritage.org.uk
english-heritage.org.uk/belsayhallcastleandgardens

With something to delight and inspire everyone, Belsay Hall is a wonderful family day out.

Access: **General:**

OPENBRITAIN.NET
The one-stop-shop for all your travel needs. Go online and see how we can help you get in, out ...and about.

North East | **Attractions**

Hexham | Northumberland Park Authority

Eastburn, South Park, Hexham, Northumberland NE46 1BS
t 01434 605555

northumberland-national-park.org.uk

Prudhoe | Prudhoe Castle

Open: For opening hours and prices, please call 0870 333 1181 or visit www.english-heritage.org.uk/properties

Prudhoe, Northumberland NE42 6NA
t 0870 333 1181   e customers@english-heritage.org.uk

english-heritage.org.uk/prudhoecastle

Explore the fortress remains, visit the exhibition and enjoy play and picnics in the grounds.

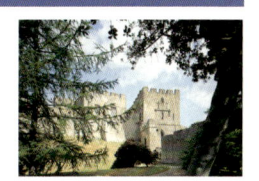

Access: .: ✈ ♿ ♿   **General:** 🔲 ♿

Warkworth | Warkworth Castle & Hermitage

Open: For opening hours and prices, please call 0870 333 1181 or visit www.english-heritage.org.uk/properties

Warkworth, Northumberland NE65 0UJ
t 0870 333 1181   e customers@english-heritage.org.uk

english-heritage.org.uk/warkworthcastleandhermitage

One of the most impressive fortresses in northern England offers a fun family day out.

Access: ♿ ♿ ✕ ♿ ♿   **General:** P 🔲 ❋ ♿

Historic Houses & Gardens
Castles and Heritage Sites
2010

Hudson's is the definitive guide to historic houses & gardens - open to visitors.

Up to date information on over 2000 properties with clear information symbols for accessibility and facilities.

All you need for fabulous days out

HUDSON's

For symbols see pg 24   309

OpenBritain | North East

adapt-ABILITY

Freephone 0800 0 92 5092
www.adapt-ability.co.uk

- Buy or Hire
- FREE Home Demonstration
- Sales, Service & Repair
- New & Pre-owned
- Home Delivery Services
- Wheelchair & Scooter Service

WHEELCHAIRS, SCOOTERS, BATHLIFTS, WALKING FRAMES, TOILET & BATHROOM AIDS, DINING AIDS, COMMODES, HIGH SEAT & RISER CHAIRS, KITCHEN AIDS, WIDE FITTING SHOES & SLIPPERS, BEDS STAIRLIFTS and lots more!

Finance Available (Written details on request)

Showroom:
M. Whitfield Ltd.,
Sanderson Street,
Coxhoe, City of Durham,
DH6 4DF
Tel: 0191 377 3705

NEBULISERS
Supplied, serviced or repaired. Coutesy Nebuliser while we service yours

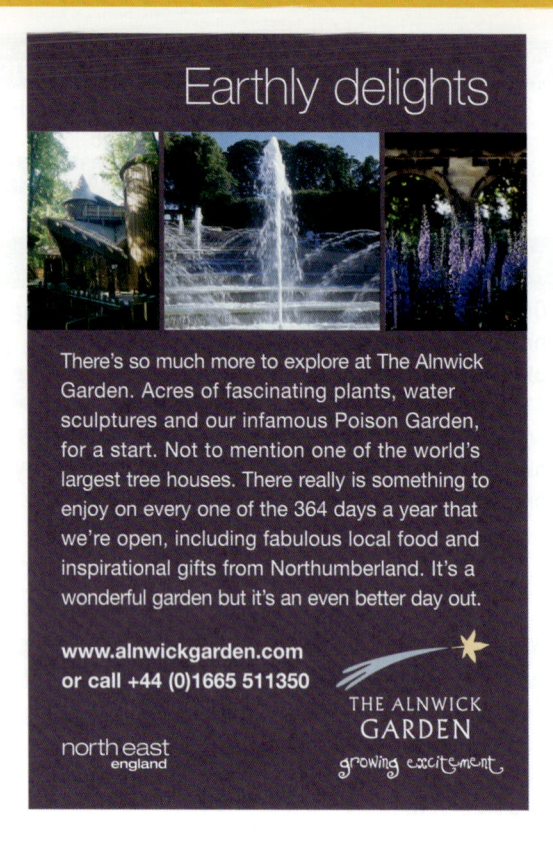

Earthly delights

There's so much more to explore at The Alnwick Garden. Acres of fascinating plants, water sculptures and our infamous Poison Garden, for a start. Not to mention one of the world's largest tree houses. There really is something to enjoy on every one of the 364 days a year that we're open, including fabulous local food and inspirational gifts from Northumberland. It's a wonderful garden but it's an even better day out.

www.alnwickgarden.com
or call +44 (0)1665 511350

north east england

THE ALNWICK GARDEN
growing excitement

Bow Well House

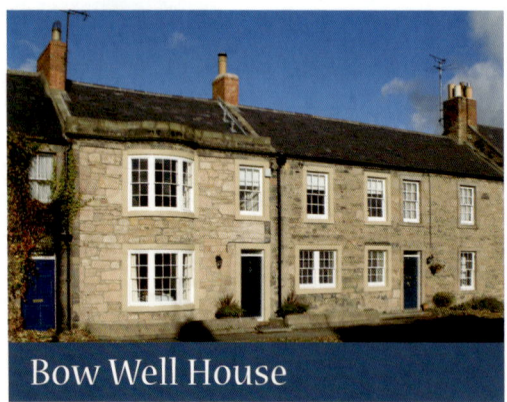

Beautifully refurbished listed building located in the heart of the delightful conservation village of Norham.

Bow Well House****
23 Castle Street
Norham
Nr Berwick Upon Tweed
Northumberland
TD15 2LQ

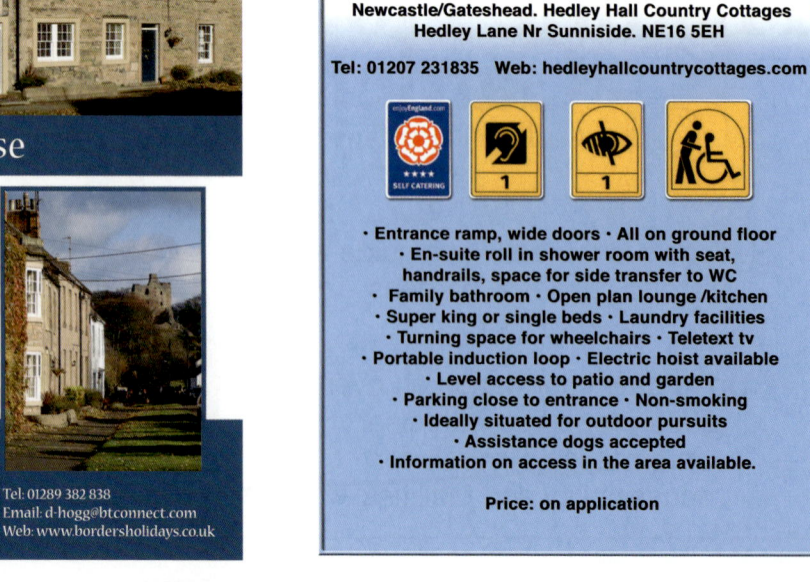

Tel: 01289 382 838
Email: d-hogg@btconnect.com
Web: www.bordersholidays.co.uk

Hedley Hall
country cottages

Newcastle/Gateshead. Hedley Hall Country Cottages
Hedley Lane Nr Sunniside. NE16 5EH

Tel: 01207 231835   Web: hedleyhallcountrycottages.com

- Entrance ramp, wide doors • All on ground floor
- En-suite roll in shower room with seat, handrails, space for side transfer to WC
- Family bathroom • Open plan lounge /kitchen
- Super king or single beds • Laundry facilities
- Turning space for wheelchairs • Teletext tv
- Portable induction loop • Electric hoist available
- Level access to patio and garden
- Parking close to entrance • Non-smoking
- Ideally situated for outdoor pursuits
- Assistance dogs accepted
- Information on access in the area available.

Price: on application

OpenBritain | North East

Northumberland National Park
Space to explore...

Milecastle 39, Hadrian's Wall

Walltown, Hadrian's Wall | Scottish Blackface Tup | River North Tyne, Falstone

Pick up our 2009 Visitor Guide or log onto our website - your essential guide for a memorable visit Or contact the National Park Centre at Once Brewed
T: +44 (0) 1434 344296   E: tic.oncebrewed@nnpa.org.uk

NATIONAL PARKS
Britain's breathing spaces
www.northumberlandnationalpark.org.uk

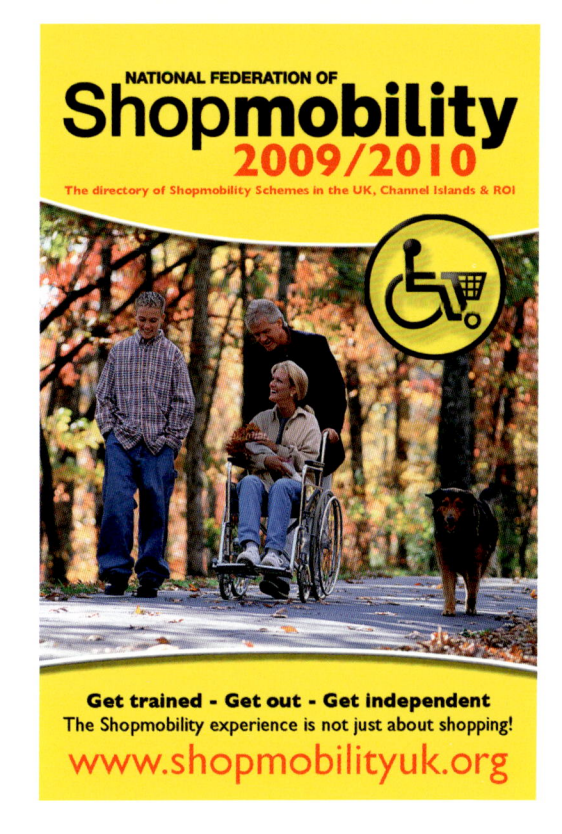

NATIONAL FEDERATION OF Shopmobility 2009/2010
The directory of Shopmobility Schemes in the UK, Channel Islands & ROI

Get trained - Get out - Get independent
The Shopmobility experience is not just about shopping!
www.shopmobilityuk.org

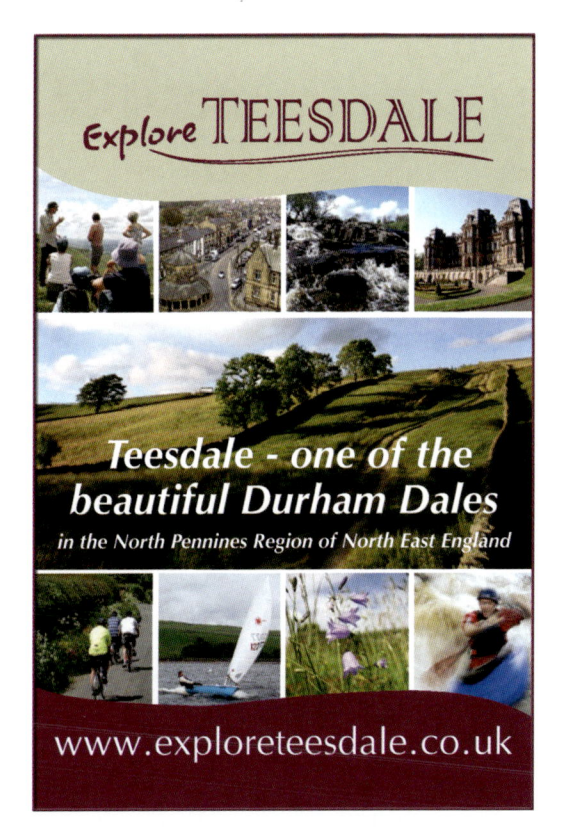

explore TEESDALE

Teesdale - one of the beautiful Durham Dales
in the North Pennines Region of North East England

www.exploreteesdale.co.uk

OPENBRITAIN.NET

The one-stop-shop for all your travel needs.

Go online and see how we can help you get in, out ...and about.

- Fully searchable database of accommodation, days out and where to eat and drink
- MyOpenBritain trip planner
- User reviews, blogs and forums

Join today!

311

Scott's View looking west over the River Tweed and the Eildon Hills

Scotland. For the holiday of a lifetime.

Scotland's stunning scenery and fascinating heritage make for memorable holidays. For such a small country, there is a lot to see and do and you don't have to travel far to enjoy the variety of breath-taking landscapes from the **Border hills** to the **forests of Perthshire**, from the **fertile farmlands of the North East** to the **Highland mountains and glens**.

The castles, gardens, historic houses and the wildlife are the main reasons for people to visit Scotland, but just as important are the people and the traditional culture. In the summer there are **Highland games** where pipe bands play, Highland dancers in their colourful kilts come under the stern eye of the judges, and strong men toss the caber! Scotland also has a **busy festival scene** throughout the year – folk, rock and Celtic music, theatre and film, jazz and poetry; just take your pick!

The main cities of **Edinburgh** and **Glasgow** are cosmopolitan, with a rich mix of cultures, which means that the shops, the pubs, the restaurants and the clubs provide a range of places to go, once you have visited the most popular of visitor attractions – **Edinburgh Castle** and Glasgow's **Kelvingrove Museum**, as well as the myriad of other attractions, such as the **National Museum of Scotland** and the **Royal Botanic Garden** in Edinburgh, and the medieval **Cathedral** and the **Burrell Collection** in Glasgow. But to get to know Scotland well and to understand her heritage, you should explore the countryside and visit some of the historic castles such as **Floors Castle, Lennoxlove House, Hopetoun House** and **Balmoral Castle**, all family homes with connections reaching back through the centuries.

Two organisations are responsible for much of Scotland's built heritage and both ensure that they do all they can to make access possible for visitors who may find it difficult to get around, despite the fact that their properties were built centuries ago! ▶

OpenBritain | Scotland

Highland Games

Edinburgh Castle

Scotland

315	Visitor Information Centres
318	**Accommodation**

▶ **Historic Scotland** has over seventy castles, abbeys and monuments in its care, from **Skara Brae** in Orkney to **Sweetheart Abbey** in the South West. **Stirling Castle**, for centuries the home of Scotland's monarchs, is one of the most splendid, but **Urquhart Castle** on the banks of **Loch Ness** is on everyone's list of places to visit. **The National Trust for Scotland** looks after historic houses and gardens; among their most visited are **Culzean Castle** in Ayrshire and **Crathes Castle and Gardens** on Royal Deeside. A new attraction for 2010 is the **Robert Burns' Birthplace Museum** near Ayr, where the life of Scotland's national poet is celebrated.

Also on everyone's list to visit are **whisky distilleries**, where visitors are given a guided tour – finishing off with a dram of malt whisky, the "water of life". By their nature, distilleries are not easy places to get around, but **Auchentoshan** on the outskirts of Glasgow, **Dewar's World of Whisky** at Aberfeldy and **Dallas Dhu** in Moray are all accessible.

An important feature of Scotland as a destination is the sense of homecoming for many thousands of visitors whose ancestors emigrated to North America or Australia and New Zealand or to South America or moved south of the border to seek their fortune in England. No matter how long ago their ancestors left Scotland, the diaspora Scots are welcomed home! Many want to find out where their family came from and this is made easy by the **Scotlandspeople Centre** in Edinburgh, where records are held and staff are on hand to help. ▶

Live it. Visit *Scotland*.
visitscotland.com

Culzean Castle

www.openbritain.net   313

OpenBritain | Scotland

Kelvingrove Museum
A Whisky Distillery
Glasgow Cathedral
Royal Botanic Gardens

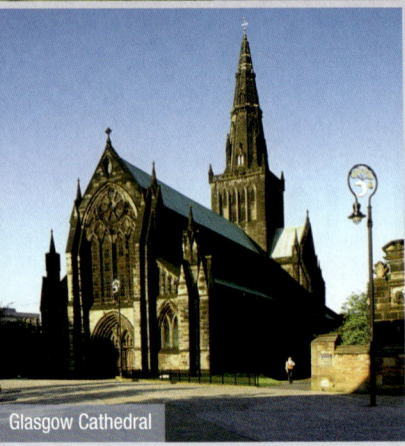

Live it. Visit Scotland.
visitscotland.com

Get in touch

For general information and advice on accommodation:

VisitScotland

t +44 (0) 131 625 8635
e info@visitscotland.com
web www.visitscotland.com

Accessible accommodation:
www.visitscotland.com/
accommodation/
accessiblescotland

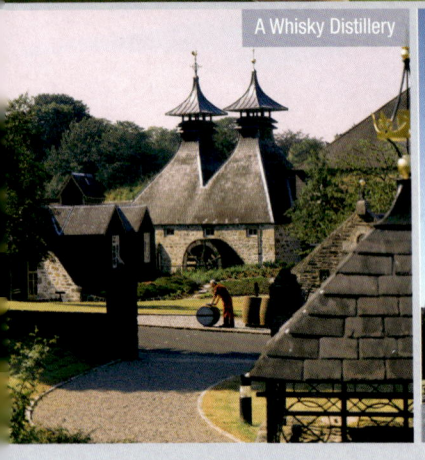

▶ Scotland prides itself on its food, with an emphasis on **fresh produce locally sourced**. The grass-fed beef, the spring lamb and the seafood are among the best in the world and restaurants often concentrate on these, so you can enjoy the best of Scotland's food. But the ethinic diversity of the Scots means that there is a range of ethnic restaurants – you can dine out in a different country every night.

There are **a hundred visitor information centres** where you can find out what's on where; the staff are a mine of information on their area – and much further afield.

Where to stay

Finding the right place to stay is important; there is a wide choice of bed and breakfasts, guest houses, hotels, self-catering of all kinds, and hostels, all inspected by VisitScotland. If you prefer somewhere where easier access is certain, then **VisitScotland** can help you find it.

Accessibility

VisitScotland, the national tourist board, operates a scheme whereby accommodation and visitor attractions are checked for their accessibility for visitors with a mobility impairment. In serviced accommodation the assessment covers bedrooms, bathrooms and all public areas; in self-catering everything is checked. Attractions are assessed for the attraction itself e.g. castle, museum, plus the catering outlet, the shop and the toilets. There are three categories of awards, see page 21 for details.

The check is carried out every three years by one of VisitScotland's trained Quality Advisors, who use criteria drawn up in discussion with relevant organisations. Details of the accommodation (and the criteria) appear on the **VisitScotland.com** website where you can search by category and by town or village. Or you can contact VisitScotland who will do all they can to help you find the right accommodation. ■

Visitor Information Centres

Visitor Information Centres are a mine of information about local and regional accommodation, attractions and events. Visit them when you arrive at your destination or contact them before you go.

All the Visitor Information Centres listed below can give you detailed information on all of Scotland *and* book your accommodation wherever you want to go. You can email **info@visitscotland.com** for information and to book your holiday.

Aberdeen	23 Union St, Aberdeen AB11 5BP	+44 (0) 1224 252212
Aberfeldy	The Square, Aberfeldy PH15 2DD	+44 (0) 1887 820276
Aberfoyle	Trossachs Discovery Centre, Main St, Aberfoyle FK8 3UQ	+44 (0) 1877 382352
Abington	Welcome Break Services, Junction 13, off M74, Biggar ML12 6RG	+44 (0) 1864 502571
Alford*	Old Station Yard, Main St, Alford AB33 8FD	+44 (0) 1975 562052
Anstruther*	Scottish Fisheries Museum, Harbourhead, Anstruther KY10 3AB	+44 (0) 1333 311073
Arbroath	Harbour Visitor Centre, Fishmarket Quay, Arbroath DD11 1PS	+44 (0) 1241 872609
Ardgarten*	Glen Croe, By Arrochar G83 7AR	+44 (0) 1301 702432
Aviemore	7 The Parade, Grampian Rd, Aviemore PH22 1PP	+44 (0) 1479 810930
Ayr	22 Sandgate, Ayr KA7 1BW	+44 (0) 1292 290300
Ballater	Old Royal Station, Station Square, Ballater AB35 5RB	+44 (0) 13397 55306
Balloch	Old Station Building, Balloch Rd, Balloch G83 8LQ	+44 (0) 1389 753533
Banchory*	Bridge St, Banchory AB31 5SX	+44 (0) 1330 822000
Banff*	Collie Lodge, St Mary's Car Park, Low St, Banff AB45 1AU	+44 (0) 1261 812419
Biggar*	155 High St, Biggar ML12 6SD	+44 (0) 1899 221066
Blairgowrie	26 Wellmeadow, Blairgowrie PH10 6AS	+44 (0) 1250 872960
Bo'ness	Bo'ness Station, Union St, Bo'ness EH15 9AQ	+44 (0) 1506 826626
Bowmore	The Square, Main St, Bowmore, Islay PA43 7JP	+44 (0) 1496 810254
Braemar	The Mews, Mar Rd, Braemar AB35 5YP	+44 (0) 1339 741600
Brechin	Pictavia Centre, Brechin Castle Centre, Haighmuir, Brechin DD9 6RL	+44 (0) 1356 623050
Brodick	The Pier, Brodick, Arran KA27 8AU	+44 (0) 1770 303774 +44 (0) 1770 303776
Callander	Ancaster Sq, Callander FK17 8ED	+44 (0) 1877 330342
Campbeltown	MacKinnon House, The Pier, Campbeltown PA28 6EF	+44 (0) 1586 552056
Castle Douglas*	Market Hill Car Park, Castle Douglas DG7 1AE	+44 (0) 1556 502611
Castlebay*	Main St, Castlebay, Barra HS9 5XD	+44 (0) 1871 810336
Craignure	The Pierhead, Craignure, Mull PA65 6AY	+44 (0) 1680 812377
Crail*	Museum & Heritage Centre, 62-64 Marketgate, Crail KY10 3TL	+44 (0) 1333 450869
Crathie	The Car Park, Crathie, By Ballater AB35 5UL	+44 (0) 13397 42414
Crieff	High St, Crieff PH7 3HU	+44 (0) 1764 652578
Daviot Wood*	The Picnic Area, Daviot Wood (A9), By Inverness IV2 5ER	+44 (0) 1463 772971
Drumnadrochit	The Car Park. Drumnadrochit IV63 6TX	+44 (0) 1456 459086

OpenBritain | Scotland

Dufftown*	The Clock Tower, Dufftown AB55 4AD	+44 (0) 1340 820501
Dumbarton (Milton)*	A82 Northbound, Milton, Dumbarton G82 2TZ	+44 (0) 1389 742306
Dumfries	64 Whitesands, Dumfries DG1 2RS	+44 (0) 1387 253862
Dunbar*	143A High St, Dunbar EH42 1ES	+44 (0) 1368 863353
Dundee	Discovery Point, Discovery Quay, Dundee DD1 4XA	+44 (0) 1382 527527
Dunfermline	1 High St, Dumfermline KY12 7DL	+44 (0) 1383 720999
Dunkeld	The Cross, Dunkeld PH8 0AN	+44 (0) 1350 727688
Dunoon	7 Alexandra Parade, Dunoon PA23 8AB	+44 (0) 1369 703785
Dunvegan	2 Lochside, Dunvegan, Skye IV55 8WB	+44 (0) 1470 521878
Durness	Sango, Durness IV27 4PZ	+44 (0) 1971 511368
Edinburgh	3 Princes St, Edinburgh EH2 2QP	+44 (0) 131 473 3844
Edinburgh Airport	Edinburgh International Airport, Edinburgh EH12 9DN	+44 (0) 131 473 3120 +44 (0) 131 473 3213
Elgin	Elgin Library, Cooper Park, Elgin, Moray IV30 1HS	+44 (0) 1343 562608 +44 (0) 1343 562614
Eyemouth*	Auld Kirk, Manse Rd, Eyemouth TD14 5JE	+44 (0) 1890 750678
Falkirk	Falkirk Wheel, Lime Road, Tamfourhill, Falkirk FK1 4RS	+44 (0) 1324 620244
Fort William	15 High Street, Fort William PH33 6DH	+44 (0) 1397 701801
Fraserburgh*	3 Saltoun Square, Fraserburgh AB43 9DA	+44 (0) 1346 518315
Glasgow	11 George Square, Glasgow G2 1DY	+44 (0) 141 204 4400
Glasgow Airport	International Arrivals Hall, Glasgow Airport, Paisley PA3 2ST	+44 (0) 141 848 4440
Grantown-on-Spey*	54 High St, Grantown-on-Spey PH26 3EH	+44 (0) 1479 872242
Gretna	Unit 10 Gateway Outlet Village, Glasgow Rd, Gretna DG16 5GG	+44 (0) 1461 337834
Hawick	Heart of Hawick Tower Mill, Kirkstile, Hawick TD9 0AE	+44 (0) 1450 373993
Helensburgh*	Clock Tower, East Clyde St, Helensburgh G84 7PA	+44 (0) 1436 672642
Huntly*	9A The Square, Huntly AB54 8BR	+44 (0) 1466 792255
Inveraray	Front St, Inveraray PA32 8UY	+44 (0) 1499 302063
Inverness	Castle Wynd, Inverness IV2 3BJ	+44 (0) 1463 252401
Inverurie*	18 High St, Inverurie AB51 3XQ	+44 (0) 1467 625800
Jedburgh	Murray's Green, Jedburgh TD8 6BE	+44 (0) 1835 863170
Kelso	Town House, The Square, Kelso TD5 7HF	+44 (0) 1573 228055
Kirkcaldy	The Merchant's House, 339 High St, Kirkcaldy KY1 1JL	+44 (0) 1592 267775
Kirkcudbright*	Harbour Square, Kirkcudbright DG6 4HY	+44 (0) 1557 330494
Kirkwall	The Travel Centre, West Castle Street, Kirkwall, Orkney KW15 1GU	+44 (0) 1856 872856
Lanark	Horsemarket, Ladyacre Rd, Lanark ML11 7LQ	+44 (0) 1555 661661
Largs*	Booking Office, Railway Station, Largs KA30 8AN	+44 (0) 1475 689962
Lerwick	Market Cross, Lerwick, Shetland ZE1 0LU	+44 (0) 1595 693434

Lochboisdale*	The Pier Rd, Lochboisdale, South Uist HS8 5TH	+44 (0) 1878 700286
Lochgilphead*	29 Lochnell St, Lochgilphead PA31 8JL	+44 (0) 1546 602344
Lochinver*	Assynt Visitor Centre, Lochinver IV27 4LX	+44 (0) 1571 844373
Lochmaddy*	Pier Rd, Lochmaddy, North Uist HS6 5AA	+44 (0) 1876 500321
Melrose	Abbey House, Abbey St, Melrose TD6 9LG	+44 (0) 1896 822283
Moffat*	Churchgate, Moffat DG16 9EG	+44 (0) 1683 220620
Newton Stewart*	Dashwood Square, Newton Stewart DG8 6EQ	+44 (0) 1671 402431
Newtongrange*	Scottish Mining Museum, Newtongrange EH22 4QN	+44 (0) 131 663 4262
North Berwick	1 Quality St, North Berwick EH39 4HJ	+44 (0) 1620 892197
North Kessock*	Picnic Site, North Kessock IV1 1XB	+44 (0) 1463 731836
Oban	Albany St, Oban PA34 4AN	+44 (0) 1631 563122
Paisley	9A Gilmour St, Paisley PA1 1DD	+44 (0) 141 889 0711
Peebles	23 High St, Peebles EH45 8AG	+44 (0) 1721 723159
Perth	Lower City Mills, West Mill St, Perth PH1 5QP	+44 (0) 1738 450600 +44 (0) 1738 636103
Pirnhall	M9/M80 Junction 9 Service Area, Pirnhall FK7 8EU	+44 (0) 1786 814111
Pitlochry	22 Atholl Rd, Pitlochry PH16 5BX	+44 (0) 1796 472215
Portree	Bayfield House, Bayfield Rd, Portree, Skye IV51 9EL	+44 (0) 1478 614906
Rothesay	Isle of Bute Discovery Centre, Victoria St, Rothesay PA20 0AH	+44 (0) 1700 502151
Selkirk*	Halliwell's House, Selkirk TD7 4BL	+44 (0) 1750 20054
Southwaite	M6 Service Area, Southwaite, Carlisle CA4 0NS	+44 (0) 1697 473445
St Andrews	70 Market St, St Andrews KY16 9NU	+44 (0) 1334 472021
Stirling	41 Dumbarton Rd, Stirling FK8 2QQ	+44 (0) 1786 475019
Stonehaven*	66 Allardice St, Stonehaven AB39 2AA	+44 (0) 1569 762806
Stornoway	26 Cromwell St, Stornoway, Lewis HS1 2DD	+44 (0) 1851 703088
Stranraer	28 Harbour St, Stranraer DG9 7RA	+44 (0) 1776 702595
Stromness*	Ferry Terminal Building, Pier Head, Stromness KW16 1BH	+44 (0) 1856 850716
Strontian*	Strontian, Ardnamurchan PH36 4HZ	+44 (0) 1967 402382
Sumburgh	Sumburgh Airport, Wilsness Terminal, Sumburgh ZE3 9JP	+44 (0) 1595 460905
Tarbert	The Pier, Tarbert, Harris HS3 3DG	+44 (0) 1859 502001
Tarbert Loch Fyne*	Harbour St, Tarbert Loch Fyne PA29 6UD	+44 (0) 1880 820429
Tarbet*	Tarbet Loch Lomond, By Arrochar G83 7DE	+44 (0) 1301 702260
Thurso*	Riverside Rd, Thurso KW14 8BU	+44 (0) 1847 893155
Tobermory*	The Pier, Main St, Tobermory, Mull PA75 6NU	+44 (0) 1688 30218
Tyndrum	6 Main Street, Tyndrum FK20 8RY	+44 (0) 1838 400324
Ullapool*	Argyle St, Ullapool IV26 2UB	+44 (0) 1854 612486

*seasonal opening

Scotland | **Aberdeenshire**

Aberdeen | **Copthorne Hotel**
Scotland ★★★★ 122 Huntly Street, Aberdeen AB10 1SU
e reservations.aberdeenemill-cop.com
milleniumhotels.com

Aberdeen | **Express by Holiday Inn**
Scotland ★★★ Chapel Street, Aberdeen AB10 1SQ
e reservations@hieaberdeen.co.uk
hieaberdeen.co.uk

Aberdeen | **Express By Holiday Inn Aberdeen City Centre**
Chapel Street, Aberdeen AB10 1SQ
t 01224 623500
hieaberdeen.co.uk

Access: General: Room:

Aberdeen | **Hilton Double Tree Hotel**
Scotland ★★★★ Beach Boulevard, Aberdeen AB24 5EF
e sales.doubletreeaberdeen@hilton.com
patiohotels.com

Aberdeen | **King's Hall**
Scotland ★★ University of Aberdeen, Aberdeen AB24 3FX
t 01224 273444 e conf.events@abdn.ac.uk
abdn.ac.uk/confevents

Aberdeen | **The Marcliffe Hotel and Spa**
Scotland ★★★★★ North Deeside Road, Cults, Aberdeen AB15 9YA
e enquiries@marcliffe.com
marcliffe.com

Aberdeen | **Thistle Aberdeen Airport Hotel**
Scotland ★★★★ Aberdeen Airport, Argyll Road, Dyce, Aberdeen AB21 0AF
e aberdeenairport@thistle.co.uk
thistlehotels.com

Aberdeen | **Thistle Aberdeen Altens**
Scotland ★★★ Souterhead Road, Altens, Aberdeen AB12 3LF
e stephen.gow@thistle.co.uk
thistlehotels.com

www.openbritain.net

Scotland | Aberdeenshire/Angus

Aberdeen | University of Aberdeen, King's Hall
Scotland ★★ Kings College, Regent Walk, Aberdeen AB24 3FX
e conf.events@abdn.ac.uk
abdn.ac.uk/confevents

Access: General: Room:

Ballater | Crathie Opportunity Holidays   AS
Scotland ★★★★ Ms Maggie MacAlpine, The Manse Courtyard, Crathie, Ballater,
Units: 4   Sleeps: 4-6 Aberdeenshire AB35 5UL
Low season p/w: t 01339 742 100   f 01339 742 002   e info@crathieholidays.org.uk
£295.00
High season p/w: crathieholidays.org.uk   7D3
£650.00
Four beautifully restored cottages, designed and equipped to the highest standard for disabled people.

Access: General: Unit:

Ballater | Glenernan Guest House
Scotland ★★★ 37 Braemar Road, Ballater, Aberdeenshire AB35 5RQ
t 01339 753111   e enquiries@glenernanguesthouse.com
glenernanguesthouse.com

Access: General: Room:

Turriff | Ashwood
Scotland ★★★ Mrs. Joan Johnson, Delgatie Castle Trust Self Catering, Delgatie Castle, Turriff, Aberdeenshire AB53 5TD   t 01888 563479   e joan@delgatiecastle.com
delgatiecastle.com

Turriff | Deveron Lodge B&B Guesthouse
Scotland ★★★★ Bridgend Terrace, Turriff, Aberdeenshire AB53 4ES
t 01888 563613   e deveron.lodge@gmx.com
deveronlodge.com

Access: General: Room:

Westhill | Holiday Inn Aberdeen West
Scotland ★★★★ Westhill Drive, Westhill, Aberdeenshire AB32 6TT
e reservations@hiaberdeenwest.co.uk
holiday-inn.com/aberdeenwest

Brechin | Northern Hotel
Scotland ★★★ 2 Clerk Street, Brechin, Angus DD9 6AE
e info@northern-hotel.co.uk
northern-hotel.co.uk

For symbols see pg 24   319

Scotland | Angus/Argyll & Bute

By Dundee | Forbes of Kingennie - Glen Esk
Scotland ★★★★ Ms. Gail Forbes, Forbes of Kingennie (SC), Omachie Farm, Kingennie, By Dundee, Angus DD5 3RE t 01382 350777 e info@forbesofkingennie.com
forbesofkingennie.com

Dundee | West Park Centre
Scotland ★★★ 319 Perth Road, Dundee, Angus DD2 1NN
t 01382 647171 e natalia.murray@westpark.co.uk
westparkcentre.com

Ardmaddy | Ardmaddy Castle Holiday Cottages - The Lodge
Scotland ★★★★ Ardmaddy Castle, Oban, Argyll PA34 4QY

Ardmaddy | Caddleton Farmhouse AS
Scotland ★★★★
Units: 5 Sleeps: 4-12
Open: All year
Low season p/w: £351.00
High season p/w: £2112.00

Mrs Minette Struthers, Owner, Ardmaddy Castle Holiday Cottages, Ardmaddy Castle, By Oban, Argyll PA34 4QY
t 01852 300353 e ardmaddycastle@btopenworld.com

Five 4* cottages-stunning rural location nr Oban overlooking the sea. Hillwalking, wildlife, fishing, boats.

Access:
General: Unit:

Benderloch | Port Selma Lodges AS
Mr & Mrs Jan & Willie Orr, Port Selma Lodges, Tigh-an-Tuim, Benderloch, Oban, Argyll PA37 1QP t 01631 720224 e willieorr@btinternet.com
portselma.co.uk

General: P Unit:

By Helensburgh | Rosslea Hall Hotel
Scotland ★★★ Ferry Road, Rhu, By Helensburgh, Argyll & Bute G84 8NF
e rossleahall@mckeverhotels.co.uk
mckeverhotels.co.uk

Campbeltown | Dalnaspidal Guest House
Scotland ★★★★★ Dalnaspidal, Tangy, Kilkenzie, Campbeltown PA28 6QD
e relax@dalnaspidal-guesthouse.com
dalnaspidal-guesthouse.com

Scotland | Argyll & Bute

Campbeltown | Dunvalanree
Scotland ★★★★ Port Righ, Carradale, Campbeltown, Argyll PA28 6SE
e bookin@dunvalanree.com
dunvalanree.co.uk

Access: General: Room:

Isle of Mull | Ard Mhor House
Scotland ★★★ Pier Road, Salen, Isle of Mull, Argyll PA72 6JL
e davidclowes@ardmhorguesthouse.fsnet.co.uk
ardmhor-guesthouse.co.uk

Kinlochleven | Tigh-Na-Cheo
Scotland ★★★★ Garbhein Road, Kinlochleven, Argyll PH50 4SE
e reception@tigh-na-cheo.co.uk
tigh-na-cheo.co.uk

Oban | North Ledaig Caravan Club Site
Scotland ★★★★★
(230) £14.50–£22.50
(50) £14.50–£22.50
280 touring pitches
Open: 26/03/2010 to 01/11/2010
Pub: 2 miles

Connel, Oban PA37 1RU
t 01631 710291
caravanclub.co.uk

6B1

We are situated right on shore with fabulous views over the sea to the Isle of Mull. Enjoy a peaceful escape or an activity holiday touring the local area, visiting gardens or cruising to the off-shore islands.

Location: From south, turn at Connel onto A828 (sign posted Fort William), site is on left about 1 mile.

Access:
General:
Pitch:

Oban | Wide Mouthed Frog
Scotland ★★★ Dunbeg, Oban, Argyll PA37 1PX
e enquiries@widemouthedfrog.co.uk
widemouthedfrog.com

For symbols see pg 24

Scotland | Argyll & Bute/Dumfries & Galloway

Strontian | Ariundle Bunkhouse
Scotland ★★★★ Ariundle, Strontian PH36 4JA
t 01967 402279 e info@Ariundle.co.uk
ariundle.co.uk

Strontian | Honeysuckle
Scotland ★★★★★ Susanna Barber, Acharacle, Argyll PH36 4JA
t 01967 402226
bluebellcroft.co.uk

Auldgirth | The Byre
Scotland ★★★★ Ms Zan Kirk & Mr J Kirk, Low Kirkbride, Auldgirth DG2 0SP
t 01387 820258 e lowkirkbride@btinternet.com
lowkirkbridebyre.com

General: Unit:

Castle Douglas | Balcary Bay Hotel
Scotland ★★★ Shore Road, Auchencairn, Castle Douglas DG7 1QZ
e reservations@balcary-bay-hotel.co.uk
balcary-bay-hotel.co.uk

Dalbeattie | Kerr Cottage
Scotland ★★★★ Port Road, Dalbeattie, Dumfries & Galloway DG5 4AZ
e l.wilbur@site-electrical.co.uk
kerrcottage.co.uk

Dumfries | Ae Farm Cottages
Scotland ★★-★★★★ Mr. David Stewart, Gubhill Farm, Ae Forest, Dumfries DG1 1RL
t 01387 860 648 e david@creaturefeature.co.uk
aefarmcottages.co.uk

General: Unit:

Dumfries | Gubhill Farm - Shepherd's Flat
Scotland ★★-★★★★ Mr D Stewart, Ae Forest Cottages, Dumfries DG1 1RL
e david@creaturefeature.co.uk
aefarmcottages.co.uk

Dumfries | Smiths @ Gretna Green
Scotland ★★★★ Gretna Green, Dumfries, Dumfries & Galloway DG16 5EA
e info@smithsgretnagreen.com
smithsgretnagreen.com

Scotland | Dumfries & Galloway/Dundee

Gretna | The Garden House Hotel
Scotland — ★★★ — Sarkfoot Road, Gretna, Dumfriesshire DG16 5EP
e june@gardenhouse.co.uk
gardenhouse.co.uk

Gretna | Hunters Lodge Hotel
Scotland — ★★★ — Annan Road, Gretna, Dumfriesshire DG16 5DL
t 01461 338214 e reception@hunterslodgehotel.co.uk
hunterslodgehotel.co.uk

Kirkcudbright | Fludha Guest House
Scotland — ★★★★★ — Fludha, Tongland Road, Kirkcudbright, Dumfries & Galloway DG6 4UU
e stay@fludha.com
fludha.com

Lochmaben | The Crown Hotel
Scotland — ★★ — Bruce Street, Lochmaben, Dumfriesshire DG11 1PD
e lorraine@crownlochmaben.freeserve.co.uk
crownlochmaben.co.uk

Moffat | Lochhouse Farm Retreat Centre
Scotland — ★★★ — Lochhouse Farm Retreat Centre, Beattock, Moffat, Dumfriesshire DG10 9SG
e accommodation@lochhousefarm.com
lochhousefarm.com

Stranraer | Culmore Bridge Cottages
Scotland — ★★★★ — Mr. J.W. Sime, Oak Cottage, Sandhead, Stranraer DG9 9DX
t 01776 830539 e jandmsime@aol.com
culmorebridge.co.uk

Broughty Ferry | The Fisherman's Tavern Hotel
Scotland — ★★ — 10-16 Fort Street, Broughty Ferry, Dundee DD5 2AD
e bookings@fishermans-tavern-hotel.co.uk
fishermanstavern.co.uk

Dundee | The Landmark Hotel
Scotland — ★★★★ — Kingsway West, Invergowrie, Dundee DD2 5JT
t 01382 641122
thelandmarkdundee.co.uk

For symbols see pg 24

Scotland | East Ayrshire/East Lothian/Edinburgh

Kilmarnock | Park Hotel

Scotland ★★★★ Rugby Road, Kilmarnock, Ayrshire KA1 2DP
t 01563 545999 e nh@theparkhotelayrshire.co.uk
theparkhotelayrshire.co.uk

Haddington | Maitlandfield House Hotel

Scotland ★★★★ 24 Sidegate, Haddington, East Lothian EH41 4BZ
e info@maitlandfieldhouse.co.uk
maitlandfieldhouse.co.uk

Edinburgh | Ardgarth Guest House

Scotland ★★★ 1 St. Mary's Place, Portobello, Edinburgh EH15 2QF
t 0131 669 3021 e stay@ardgarth.com
ardgarth.com

Access: **General:** **Room:**

Edinburgh | Atholl Brae - The Harland

Scotland ★★★★
Units: 1   Sleeps: 1-6
Open: All year

Low season p/w: £398.00
High season p/w: £948.00

Shop: <0.5 miles
Pub: <0.5 miles

Flat 10, 6 Pilrig Heights, Edinburgh EH6 5BF
t 01721 730679 home and fax mobile - 07732 730177 e stay@athollbrae.co.uk
athollbrae.co.uk

4 Stars, Assisted Wheelchair Access (Visit Scotland). Friendly, personal service. Lift. Bedroom 1 - king-sized bed, En Suite, balcony. Bedroom 2 - 2 singles. Further bathroom. Cots, highchairs, folding beds. Car park off-street or multi-storey. Gym, internet.

Location: The apartment address is - Flat 10, 6 Pilrig Heights, Edinburgh, EH6 5BF. - Google map on our web-site www.athollbrae.co.uk

General:
Unit:

Edinburgh | Edinburgh City Centre (Morrison St) Premier Inn

Scotland 1 Morrison Street Link, Edinburgh EH3 8DN
e edinburghccmorrisonst.pti@whitbread.com
premiertravelinn.com

Scotland | Edinburgh

Edinburgh | Express By Holiday Inn
Scotland — ★★★ — Picardy Place, Edinburgh EH1 3JT
e sales@hieedinburgh.co.uk
hiexpress.com/edinburghetyet

Edinburgh | Fraser Suites Edinburgh
Ms. Laura Carrick, 12-26 St Giles Street, Edinburgh EH1 1PT
t +44 0 131 221 7200   e sales.edinburgh@frasershospitality.com
edinburgh.frasershospitality.com/

Access: [symbols]   General: [symbols]   Unit: [symbols]

Edinburgh | Gillis Centre
Scotland — ★★★ — 100 Strathearn Road, Edinburgh EH9 1BB
t 0131 6238933   e gilliscentre@staned.org.uk
gilliscentre.org.uk

Access: [symbols]   General: [symbols]   Room: [symbols]

Edinburgh | Holiday Inn Edinburgh
AA — ★★★★ — 132 Corstophine Road, Edinburgh EH12 6UA
t 0871 9429026   e edinburghhi@ihg.com
holiday-inn.co.uk

Access: [symbols]   General: [symbols]   Room: [symbols]

Edinburgh | Holiday Inn Express - Edinburgh, Royal Mile
AS
300 Cowgate, Edinburgh EH1 1NA
t 0871 423 4876
hiexpress.co.uk

Access: [symbols]   General: [symbols]   Room: [symbols]

Edinburgh | Jurys Inn Edinburgh
Scotland — ★★★ — 43 Jeffrey Street, Edinburgh EH1 1DH
e ann-marie_verdon@jurysdoyle.com
jurysinn.com

Edinburgh | Marriott Dalmahoy Hotel & Country Club
AS
AA — ★★★★ — Kirknewton, Nr. Edinburgh EH27 8EB
Scotland — ★★★★ — t 0131 333 1845   e uk.north.sales.office@marriotthotels.com
marriottdalmahoy.co.uk

Access: [symbols]   General: [symbols]   Room: [symbols]

Edinburgh | Novotel Edinburgh Centre
Scotland — ★★★★ — 80 Lauriston Place, Edinburgh EH3 9DE
e iuge.vanooteghem@accor.com
novotel.com

For symbols see pg 24

Scotland | Edinburgh/Fife

Edinburgh | Ramada Mount Royal Hotel
Scotland ★★★ 53 Princes Street, Edinburgh EH2 2DG
e linda.watson@ramadajarvis.co.uk
ramadajarvis.co.uk

Edinburgh | Thistle Edinburgh
Scotland ★★★★ 107 Leith Street, Edinburgh EH1 3SW
e helen.parker@thistle.co.uk
thistlehotels.com/edinburgh

Leith | Express By Holiday Inn
Scotland ★★★ Saltire Leisure, Britannia Way, Ocean Drive, Leith, Edinburgh, Lothian EH6 6LA
hiex-edinburgh.com

Burntisland | Kingswood Hotel
Scotland ★★★ Kinghorn Road, Burntisland, Fife KY3 9LL
e rankin@kingswoodhotel.co.uk
kingswoodhotel.co.uk

Dunfermline | Express by Holiday Inn - Fife
AA ★★★ Leslie Roundabout, Leslie Road, Glenrothes, Fife KY6 3EP
t 01592 745509   e ebhi-glenrothes@btconnect.com
hiexpress.co.uk

Access: General: Room:

Dunfermline | Express By Holiday Inn Dunfermline
Scotland ★★★ Halbeath, Dunfermline, Fife KY11 8DY
e info@hiexpressdunfermline.co.uk
hiexpress.com/dunfermline

Elie | Lobster Pot Cottage
Scotland ★★★★ Mrs Kim Kirkaldy, Incharvie Farmhouse, Kilconquhar, Elie, Fife KY9 1JU
t 01333 340 640   e kirkaldy2004@hotmail.com
lobster-pot.co.uk

General: Unit:

Kinghorn | Bay Hotel
Scotland ★★★ Burntisland Road, Kinghorn, Fife KY3 9YE
e thebayhotel@pettycur.co.uk
thebayhotel.net

Scotland | **Fife/Glasgow**

St. Andrews | **The Old Station Country Guest House**
Scotland ★★★★ Stravithie Bridge, St Andrews, Fife KY16 8LR
e info@theoldstation.co.uk
theoldstation.co.uk

Glasgow | **Carlton George Hotel**
Scotland ★★★★ 44 West George Street, Glasgow G2 1DH
e resgeorge@carltonhotels.co.uk
carltonhotels.co.uk

Glasgow | **Fraser Suites Glasgow**
Scotland ★★★★ Ms. Susan Anderson, 1-19 Albion Street, Glasgow G1 1LH
t 0141 5534288 e sales.glasgow@frasershospitality.com
frasershospitality.com

Access: General: Unit:

Glasgow | **Glasgow Hilton**
Scotland ★★★★★ 1 William Street, Glasgow G3 8HT
e sales.glasgow@hilton.com
hilton.co.uk/glasgow

Glasgow | **Glasgow Marriott**
Scotland ★★★★ 500 Argyle Street, Anderston, Glasgow G3 8RR
t 0141 226 5577 e mhrs.gladt.frontdesk@marriotthotels.com
marriott.co.uk/gladt

Access: General: Room:

Glasgow | **Holiday Inn**
Scotland ★★★★ 161 West Nile Street, Glasgow G1 2RL
e carolynn.morrison@higlasgow.com
higlasgow.com

Glasgow | **Jurys Inn Glasgow**
Scotland ★★★ 80 Jamaica Street, Glasgow G1 4QG
e jurysinnglasgow@jurysdoyle.com
jurysdoyle.com

Glasgow | **Premier Inn Glasgow City Centre South**
Scotland ★★★ 80 Ballater Street, Glasgow G5 0TW
e sales@tulipinnglasgow.co.uk
tulipinnglasgow.co.uk

For symbols see pg 24

Scotland | Highland

Achnasheen | The Torridon
Scotland ★★★★ Torridon, Achnasheen, Ross-Shire IV22 2EY
e dan@thetorridon.com
lochtorridonhotel.com

Aviemore | Braeriach High Range Holiday Lodges
Scotland ★★★-★★★★★ Mr. F Vastano, High Range Holiday Lodges, Grampian Road, Aviemore, Inverness-Shire PH22 1PT t 01479 810636 e info@highrange.co.uk
highrange.co.uk

Farr | Rowan, Woodpecker, Mountain View
Scotland ★★★★ Inverarnie House, Inverness IV2 6XA
t 01808 521467/521747 e farquharforbes@onetel.com

Fort William | Bluebell Croft, Honeysuckle House and Rose Cottage   AS
Scotland ★★★★★ Mrs Sukie Barber, Strontian, Ardnamurchan, Highlands PH36 4JA
t 01967 402226 e billandsukie@bluebellcroft.co.uk
bluebellcroft.co.uk

Access: General: Unit:

Gairloch | Willow Croft
Scotland ★★★ Mrs Beryl Leslie, 40 Big Sand, Gairloch, Ross-Shire IV21 2DD
t 01445 712448 e bigsand@waitrose.com
sites.ecosse.net/iml

Access: General: P Unit:

Inverness | Dalvourn Holidays
Scotland ★★★★ Mr F Forbes, Inverarnie House, Inverarnie, Inverness IV2 6XA
t 01808 521467

Inverness | Kingsmills Hotel Inverness Ltd
Scotland ★★★★ Culcabock Road, Inverness IV2 3LP
e craig.ewan@kingsmillshotel.com
kingsmills.com

Inverness | Lochletter Lodges
Scotland ★★★ Miss Mary Brook, Lochletter Lodges, Balnain, Drumnadrochit, Inverness IV63 6TJ t 01456 476 313 e info@lochletter.com
lochletter.com

Scotland | Highland

Inverness | The Lodge at Daviot Mains
Scotland ★★★★★ Daviot, Inverness IV2 5ER
e info@daviotlodge.co.uk
daviotlodge.co.uk

Isle of Skye | Cuillin Hills Hotel
Scotland ★★★★ Portree, Isle of Skye IV51 9QU
e info@cuillinhills-hotel-skye.co.uk
cuillinhills-hotel-skye.co.uk

Isle of Skye | La Bergerie
Scotland ★★★★ Mrs Chantal MacLeod, 33 Lochbay, Waternish, Isle Of Skye IV55 8GD
t 01470 592282   f 01470 592 282   e enquiries@la-bergerie-skye.co.uk
la-bergerie-skye.co.uk

General: [symbols]   Unit: [symbols]

Kincraig | Loch Insh Chalets - Drumguish
Scotland ★★-★★★★ Mr. Andrew Freshwater, Loch Insh Log Chalets, Loch Insh Chalets Ltd, Insh Hall, Kincraig, Inverness-shire PH21 1NU
t 01540 651 272   e office@lochinsh.com
lochinsh.com

Nairn | Covenanters' Inn
Scotland ★★★ Auldearn, Nairn IV12 5TG
e covenanters@aol.com
covenanters-inn.co.uk

OPEN BRITAIN

Join today!

Become a member of OpenBritain today.

Share your own travel and accommodation experiences and help Britain become more open!

visit **www.openbritain.net**

For symbols see pg 24

329

Scotland | **Highland**

Nairn | **Lovat Lodge**

Beds: 15 single, 5 double, 6 twin

Open: All year

p/p half board:
d: £30.00-£60.00

Shop: 0.5 miles
Pub: 1 mile

Thurlow Road, Nairn IV12 4EZ
t 01667 453298   e info@lovatlodgehotel.co.uk

lovatlodgehotel.co.uk   7C3

A hotel with a difference, Lovat Lodge is specifically designed to meet the needs of the mature and disabled guest. All rooms have ensuite showers and there are no single room supplements. Special weekly half-board rates available.

Location: Nairn is located 15 miles east of Inverness and is easily accessible by road, rail and air.

Access:
General:
Room:

Nairn | **Windsor Hotel**

Scotland   ★★★   16 Albert Street, Nairn, Inverness-shire IV12 4HP

Newtonmore | **Crubenbeg House**

Scotland   ★★★★   Falls of Truim, Newtonmore PH20 1BE
                     t 01540 673300   e enquiries@crubenbeghouse.com
                     crubenbeghouse.com

Access: **General:**   **Room:**

Nr Fort William | **Isles of Glencoe Hotel & Leisure Centre**

Scotland   ★★★   Ballachulish, Nr Fort William PH49 4HL
                     e gm.glencoe@foliohotels.com
                     foliohotels.com

Portree | **Number 6**

Scotland   ★★★   Mrs. Margaret MacDonald, Maligan, Achachork, Portree, Isle Of Skye IV51 9HT
                     t 01478 613 167   e No6chalet@aol.com

330   www.openbritain.net

Scotland | Highland/Inverclyde/Moray/North Ayrshire

Spean Bridge | Old Pines Hotel and Restaurant
Scotland ★★★ Gairlochy Road, Spean Bridge, Inverness-Shire PH3 4EG
e enquiries@oldpines.co.uk
oldpines.co.uk

Thurso | Park Hotel
Scotland ★★★ Oldfield, Thurso, Caithness KW14 8RE
e reception@parkhotelthurso.co.uk
parkhotelthurso.co.uk

Thurso | Pentland Lodge House
Scotland ★★★★ Pentland Lodge House, Granville Street, Thurso, Caithness KW14 7JN
t 01847 895103 e info@pentlandlodgehouse.co.uk
pentlandlodgehouse.co.uk

Access: General: Room:

Greenock | Express by Holiday Inn
Scotland ★★★ Cartsburn, Greenock PA15 4RT
e greenock@expressbyholidayinn.net
hiexpressgreenock.co.uk

Greenock | James Watt College
Scotland ★★ Halls of Residence, Waterfront Campus, Custom House Way, Greenock, Renfrewshire PA15 1EN   e kfullerton@jameswatt.ac.uk

Lossiemouth | Ceilidh B&B
Scotland ★★★ 34 Clifton Road, Lossiemouth, Moray IV31 6DJ
t 01343815848 e ceilidhbandb@btconnect.com
ceilidhbandb.co.uk

Access: abc   General: Room:

Brodick | Auchrannie Spa Resort
Scotland ★★★★ Auchrannie Spa Resort, Brodick, Isle of Arran KA27 8BZ
e resort@auchrannie.co.uk
auchrannie.co.uk

Irvine | Gailes Hotel and Restaurant
Scotland ★★★ Marine Drive, Gailes, Irvine, Ayrshire KA11 5AE
e janette.mitchell@gaileshotel.com

Scotland | **North Ayrshire/North Lanarkshire/Orkney/Perth and Kinross**

Irvine | Menzies Irvine
Scotland ★★★ 46 Annick Road, Irvine KA11 4LD
e irvine.hotel@menzieshotels.co.uk
menzieshotels.co.uk

Isle of Arran | Kildonan Hotel
Scotland ★★★ Kildonan, Isle of Arran KA27 8SE
e info@kildonanhotel.com
kildonanhotel.com

Motherwell | Express By Holiday Inn
Scotland ★★★ Strathclyde Country Park, 1 Hamilton Road, Motherwell, Lanarkshire ML1 3RB
e james.rush@ichotelgroup.com
hiexpress.com

Motherwell | Motherwell College
Scotland Dalzeil Drive, Motherwell ML1 2DD
e Information@motherwell.co.uk
motherwell.ac.uk

Kirkwall | Auldkirk Apartments
Scotland ★★★★ Mr. Robert Clouston, Clouston Properties, 5 Clumly Avenue, Kirkwall, Orkney KW15 1YU t 01856 875488 e enquiries@r-clouston.co.uk

Kirkwall | Lav'rockha Guest House
Scotland ★★★★ Inganess Road, St. Ola, Kirkwall, Orkney KW15 1SP
e lavrockha@orkney.com
lavrockha.co.uk

Blairgowrie | Glenbeag Mountain Lodges - Clashmore
Scotland ★★★-★★★★ Mr. David Stewart, Glenbeag Mountain Lodges, Spittal of Glenshee, Perthshire PH10 7QE t 01250 885204 e logcabins@glenbeag.co.uk
glenbeag.co.uk

General: Unit:

Crieff | Phase 1 & Phase 2 Lodges
Scotland ★★★-★★★★★★ Ms. Lynne Anderson, Crieff Hydro Hotel (Self Catering), Crieff Hydro Hotel, Crieff, Perthshire PH7 3LQ t 01764 655555 e enquiries@crieffhydro.com
crieffhydro.com

Scotland | **Perth and Kinross/Renfrewshire/Scottish Borders**

Forgandenny | Battledown Bed & Breakfast
Scotland ★★★★ Battledown, Forgandenny, Perthshire PH2 9EL
e dunsire9@aol.com
battledown.net

Glenshee | New Steading Cottage/Old Steading Cottage
Scotland ★★★★
Units: 2   Sleeps: 2-4
Open: All year

Low season p/w:
£315.00
High season p/w:
£550.00

Sue Smith, Dalnoid Holiday Cottages, Dalnoid Farmhouse, Glenshee, Blairgowrie, Perthshire PH10 7LR
t 01250 882200   e info@dalnoid.co.uk
dalnoid.co.uk   6C1

Single-storey cottages both sleep 4. King-size with En Suite and twin. Large open-plan kitchen/lounge/dining area.

Access: General: Unit:

Perthshire | The Gleneagles Hotel
Scotland ★★★★★ Auchterarder, Perthshire PH3 1NF
e anness.black@gleneagles.com
gleneagles.com

Glasgow Airport | Holiday Inn Glasgow Airport
AA ★★★ Abbotsinch, Paisley, Renfrewshire PA3 2TR
t 0870 400 9031   e reservations-glasgow@ihg.com
holidayinn.co.uk

Access: General: Room:

Paisley | Express by Holiday Inn Glasgow Airport
Scotland ★★★ St Andrew's Drive, Glasgow Airport, Paisley PA3 2TJ
e gm.glasgowairport@expressbyholidayinn.co.uk
hiex-glasgow.com

Berwickshire | The Wheatsheaf at Swinton
Scotland ★★★★ Main Street, Berwickshire TD11 3JJ
e chris@wheatsheaf-swinton.co.uk
wheatsheaf-swinton.co.uk

Coldstream | Cotoneaster
Scotland ★★★ Mrs S Brewis, Leet Villa, Leet St, Coldstream, Berwickshire TD12 4BJ
t 01890 882173   e suebrewis@tiscali.co.uk
littleswinton.co.uk

Access: General: Unit:

Scotland | **Scottish Borders**

Coldstream | Little Swinton Cottages
Scotland ★★★ Mrs Sue Brewis, Leet Villa, Leet Street, Coldstream, Berwickshire TD12 4BJ
t 01890 882173 e suebrewis@tiscali.co.uk
littleswinton.co.uk

Access: **General:** **Unit:**

Hawick | Whitchester Christian Guest House
Scotland ★★★ Borthaugh, Hawick, Roxburghshire TD9 7LN
e enquiries@whitchester.org.uk
whitchester.org.uk

Access: **General:** **Room:**

Melrose | Eildon Holiday Cottages   AS
Scotland ★★★-★★★★★ Mrs Jill Hart, Dingleton Mains, Melrose, Scottish Borders TD6 9HS
t 01896 823 258 e info@eildon.co.uk
eildon.co.uk   6C2

Units: 6   Sleeps: 2-6
Open: All year
Low season p/w: £294.00
High season p/w: £777.00
Shop: 0.5 miles
Pub: 0.5 miles

Winner of Holiday Care Service award for the best self-catering accommodation for disabled people in Britain. On slopes of Eildon Hills in the beautiful Scottish Borders. 40 mins. from Edinburgh. Category 1 accessibility. Two cottages with overhead ceiling hoists.

Location: From Melrose centre, take Dingleton Road for ½ mile. Turn left into Melrose Golf Club and past the clubhouse.

Access:
General:
Unit:

Nr Hawick | Mosspaul
Scotland ★★★ Teviothead, Nr Hawick, Scottish Borders TD9 0LP
e mosspaulinn@aol.com
mosspaulinn.com

Peebles | Cringletie House Hotel
AA ★★★★ Edinburgh Road, Peebles EH45 8PL
Scotland ★★★★ t 01721 725750 e enquiries@cringletie.com
cringletie.com

Access: **General:** **Room:**

334   www.openbritain.net

Scotland | Shetland/South Ayrshire/South Lanarkshire

Bressay | Northern Lights Holistic Spa
Scotland ★★★★ Sound View Uphouse, Bressay, Shetland ZE2 9ES
e northernlightsholisticspa@fsmail.net

Shetland | Burrastow House
Scotland ★★★★ Walls, Shetland ZE2 9PD
e burr.hs@zetnet.co.uk
users.zetnet.co.uk/burrastow-house

Ayr | Daviot House
AA ★★★★ 12 Queens Terrace, Ayr, Ayrshire, KA7 1DU KA7 1DU
Scotland ★★★★ t 01292 269678 e daviothouse@hotmail.com
daviothouse.co.uk

General: Room:

Ayr | Ramada Jarvis
Scotland ★★★ Dalblair Road, Ayr KA7 1UG
e gm.ayr@ramadajarvis.co.uk
ramadajarvis.co.uk

Turnberry | The Westin Turnberry Resort
Scotland ★★★★★ Turnberry, Ayrshire KA26 9LT
e turnberry@westin.com
westin.com/turnberry

Biggar | The Glenholm Centre
Scotland ★★★ Broughton, Biggar, Lanarkshire ML12 6JF
t 01899 830 408 e info@glenholm.co.uk
glenholm.co.uk

New Lanark | New Lanark Mill Hotel
Scotland ★★★ Mill Number One, New Lanark Mills, Lanark, South Lanarkshire ML11 9DB
t 01555 667200 e hotel@newlanark.org
newlanark.org

Access: General: Room:

OPEN BRITAIN
PLANNING A DAY OUT? WHY NOT MAKE IT A SHORT-BREAK?
Fabulous 'Places to Stay' in every region

For symbols see pg 24

Scotland | Stirling/West Dunbartonshire/Western Isles

Dunblane | Cambushinnie Croft

Scotland ★★★★
Units: 1 Sleeps: 1-6
Open: All year

Low season p/w:
£510.00
High season p/w:
£950.00

Mrs Fiona Lyle, Mid Cambushinnie Farm, Cromlix, Dunblane, Perthshire FK15 9JU   t 01786 880631/ 07977135071   f 01786 880631   e info@cambushinniecroft.co.uk

cambushinniecroft.co.uk

6C1

Modern, comfortable house in stunning countryside on family farm yet centrally located to explore Scotland.

Access:
General: Unit:

Stirling | Express by Holiday Inn - Stirling

Scotland ★★★
Springkerse Business Park, Stirling FK7 7XH
e gm.stirling@expressholidayinn.co.uk
expressstirling.co.uk

Stirling | Stirling Management Centre

Scotland ★★★
University of Stirling Campus, Stirlang FK9 4LA
e smc.sales@stir.ac.uk
smc.stir.ac.uk

Clydebank | The Beardmore Hotel & Conference Centre

Scotland ★★★★
Beardmore Street, Clydebank G81 4SA
e info@beardmore.scot.nhs.uk
the beardmore.com

Loch Lomond | De Vere Cameron House

Scotland ★★★★★
Cameron House, Loch Lomond, Dunbartonshire G83 8QZ
e shona.brierton@cameronhouse.co.uk
devere.co.uk

Isle of Lewis | The Cross Inn

Scotland ★★★
Cross, Ness, Isle Of Lewis HS2 0SN
e info@crossinn.com
crossinn.com

South Uist | Crossroads

Scotland ★★★
Crossroads, Stoneybridge, South Uist HS8 5SD
e macrury.321@tiscali.co.uk

336

www.openbritain.net

Scotland | Western Isles/Attractions

Stornoway | Broad Bay House
Scotland ★★★★★ Back, Nr Stornoway, Isle of Lewis HS2 0LQ
t 01851 820990 e stay@broadbayhouse.co.uk
broadbayhouse.co.uk

Access: General: Room:

Stornoway | Tigh-nan-Eilean
Scotland ★★★-★★★★★ Mr. Murdo MacLeod, 17 Uigen, Uig, Stornoway, Isle of Lewis HS2 9H5
t 01851 672377 e murdomac@btinternet.com
mountainviewholidays.co.uk

Aberdeen | David Welch Winter Gardens
Duthie Park, Polmuir Road, Aberdeen, Aberdeenshire AB11 7TH
t 01224 583310 e wintergardens@aberdeencity.gov.uk
aberdeencity.co.uk

Edinburgh | Scottish Parliament
Edinburgh EH99 1SP
t 0131 348 5000 e gordon.stewart@scottish.parliament.uk
scottish.parliament.uk

North Queensferry | Deep Sea World
Battery Quarry, North Queensferry, Fife, Scotland KY11 1JR
t 01383 411880
deepseaworld.com

Orkney | Corrigall Farm Museum
Harray, Orkney KW17 2JR
t 01856 771411 e museum@orkney.gov.uk
orkney.gov.uk

Orkney | Kirbuster Museum
Birsay, Orkney KW17 2LR
t 01856 771 268
orkney.gov.uk

Orkney | The Orkney Museum
Tankerness House, Broad Street, Kirkwall, Orkney KW15 1DH
t 01856 873535
orkney.gov.uk

For symbols see pg 24

Scotland | **Attractions**

Orkney | **Scapa Flow Visitor Centre & Museum**

Lyness, Hoy, Orkney KW16 3NU
t 01856 791300
orkney.gov.uk

Orkney | **St. Magnus Cathedral**

Broad Street, Kirkwall, Orkney KW15 1NX
t 01856 874894
orkney.gov.uk

St Magnus Cathedral

LOOK FORWARD TO IMPROVED ACCESS

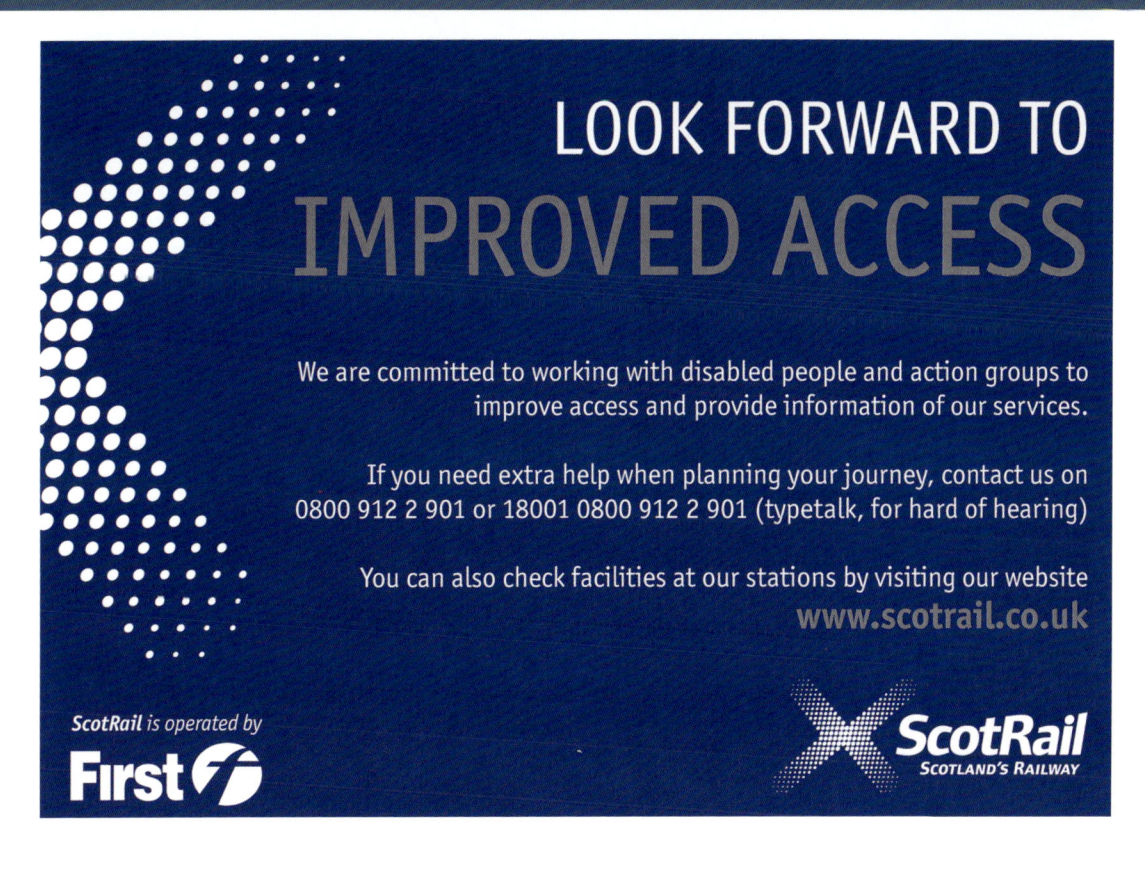

We are committed to working with disabled people and action groups to improve access and provide information of our services.

If you need extra help when planning your journey, contact us on 0800 912 2 901 or 18001 0800 912 2 901 (typetalk, for hard of hearing)

You can also check facilities at our stations by visiting our website www.scotrail.co.uk

ScotRail is operated by **First**

ScotRail SCOTLAND'S RAILWAY

Shetland Island Council - Ferry Services
Meet the Local Wildlife And See the Sights

With Shetland's Inter-Island Ferries, 95 Sailings Daily to 8 Islands

www.shetland.gov.uk/ferries

OpenBritain | Scotland

EVERYONE IS WELCOME UNDER THE SEA

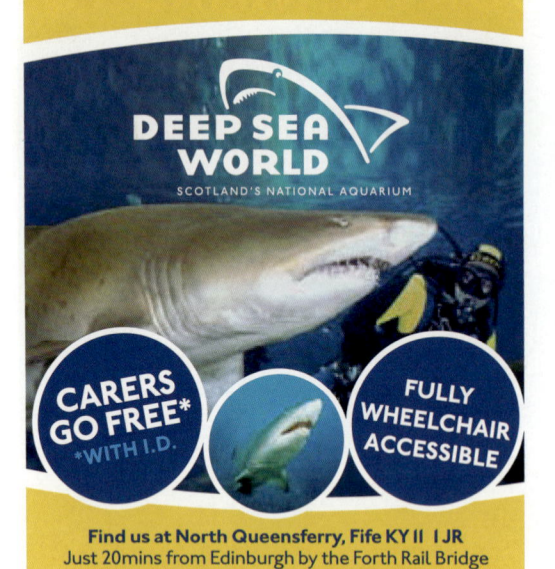

DEEP SEA WORLD
SCOTLAND'S NATIONAL AQUARIUM

CARERS GO FREE* *WITH I.D.

FULLY WHEELCHAIR ACCESSIBLE

Find us at North Queensferry, Fife KY11 1JR
Just 20mins from Edinburgh by the Forth Rail Bridge
Open Daily from 10am t: 01383 411880

www.deepseaworld.com

Enabled shopping

With easy access to a huge range of shops and restaurants all under one roof, we'll make sure your trip to The Centre is a great day out.

- Relaxed atmosphere with over 155 shops & restaurants.
- Disabled parking right by the entrances.
- Dedicated disabled washrooms.
- Friendly customer service team always on hand.
- Easy access & navigation with lifts to the Wintergarden.
- Induction loops & Deaf Alerter Systems.
- Registered Assistance dogs welcome.
- Lothian Shop Mobility Scheme Tues - Sat: 01506 442744.

For more info or assistance call
01506 432 961

www.shopthecentre.co.uk

the centre

East Ayrshire COUNCIL

Our public toilet facilities are at Burns Mall Kilmarnock and Tanyard Cumnock also Mauchline APC at Loudoun Street

All facilities are at ground level with no steps

FAIRPRICE MOBILITY (Scotland)

Suppliers of Mobility Equipment at Discounted Prices

Discounted Scooters, Wheelchairs & Stairlifts

Scotland's Favourite Family Run Mobility Supplier

Because we care

- Scooters • Electric & Manual Wheelchairs
- Riser / Recliner chairs • Stairlifts • Walking Aids
- Adjustable Beds • Bathrooms
- Batteries & Much More!

Open 8am till late

Need a price, just call:
0800 389 7603

Carberry Place, Kirkcaldy, KY1 3NQ
(Behind Asda)

OpenBritain | Scotland

Forestry Commission Scotland

Great Access

Explore your forests!

Come in and enjoy!

Many of our forests, woodlands and visitor centres offer great access opportunities if you have a disability

On wheels All-ability trails suitable for wheelchairs

With a 4-legged friend Dogs are welcome everywhere

With your senses Experience the natural environment all around you

For more information about access to your forests, call us on 0845 367 3787 or visit www.forestry.gov.uk/scotland

---

THE ROMAN CAMP COUNTRY HOUSE HOTEL

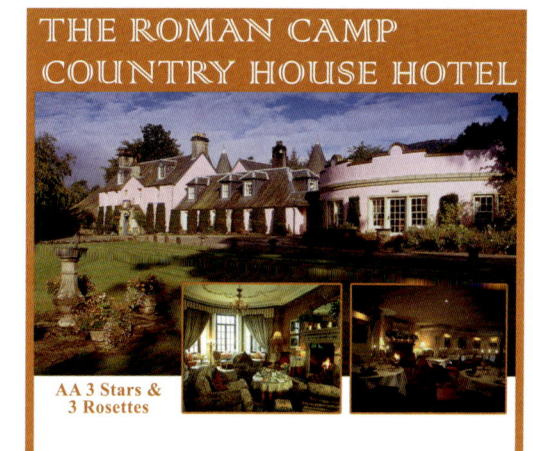

AA 3 Stars & 3 Rosettes

Nestling in 20 acres of secluded gardens on the banks of the River Tieth, in the Trossachs National Park, you'll find our country retreat. Built as a hunting lodge in 1625, all the public rooms and seven of our bedrooms are on the ground floor giving good accessibility. The hotel has wonderful period lounges including silk lined drawing room and oak panelled library. Our restaurant with 3 AA rosettes is ranked as one of the top 10% of UK establishments.

www.romancamphotel.co.uk
Tel: 01877 330003
Fax: 01877 331533
The Roman Camp Hotel, Callander, Perthshire FK17 8BG

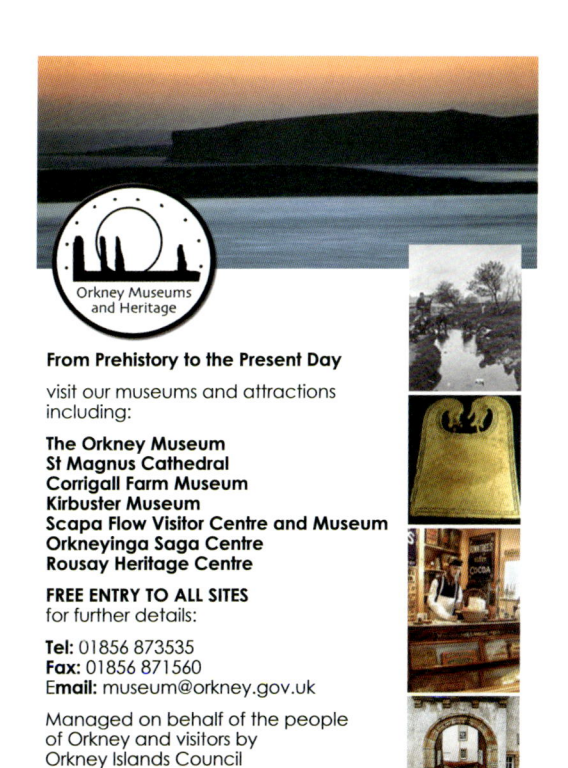

Orkney Museums and Heritage

From Prehistory to the Present Day

visit our museums and attractions including:

**The Orkney Museum
St Magnus Cathedral
Corrigall Farm Museum
Kirbuster Museum
Scapa Flow Visitor Centre and Museum
Orkneyinga Saga Centre
Rousay Heritage Centre**

FREE ENTRY TO ALL SITES
for further details:

Tel: 01856 873535
Fax: 01856 871560
Email: museum@orkney.gov.uk

Managed on behalf of the people of Orkney and visitors by Orkney Islands Council

---

RUSKO HOLIDAYS

Luxurious 4 star "haven in the hills" with Grade 1 Wheelchair accessibility award. sleeps 4 - 6 people and charming Victorian cottage with Grade 3 Accessibility (sleeps 4), set amid stunning Scottish Scenery in beautiful South West Scotland.

Rusko Holidays, Gatehouse of Fleet, Castle Douglas, DG7 2BS   Tel: **01557814215**
Email: **info@ruskoholidays.co.uk**
Website: **www.ruskoholidays.co.uk**

OpenBritain | Scotland

the Scottish Parliament
Discover it for yourself

- Guided tours
- Exhibition
- Café
- Shop

Visit Scotland's 'Landmark for 21st century democracy'

Find out about the Scottish Parliament, its Members and what we do. See Parliament in action and, depending on when you visit, take a guided tour of this iconic landmark.

To book a visit:
0131 348 5200 / 0800 092 7600
sp.bookings@scottish.parliament.uk
www.scottish.parliament.uk

OPEN MONDAY – SATURDAY, ADMISSION FREE
Next to Holyrood Park, Our Dynamic Earth, the Palace of Holyroodhouse and the Queen's Gallery

The Scottish Parliament
Pàrlamaid na h-Alba

Duthie Park
The David Welch Winter Gardens

The Gardens have been open since 1899. Many of the original features are still intact which complement the wide range of plant collections at the Gardens. The park is a unique facility in Northern Scotland which you are welcome to tour from 9.30am daily

Admission is free - though donations are always welcome. Staff are on hand to answer questions.

The David Welch Winter Gardens, Duthie Park
Polmuir Road, Aberdeen AB11 7TH
T: 01224 585310 F: 01224 210532 E: wintergardens@aberdeencity.gov.uk

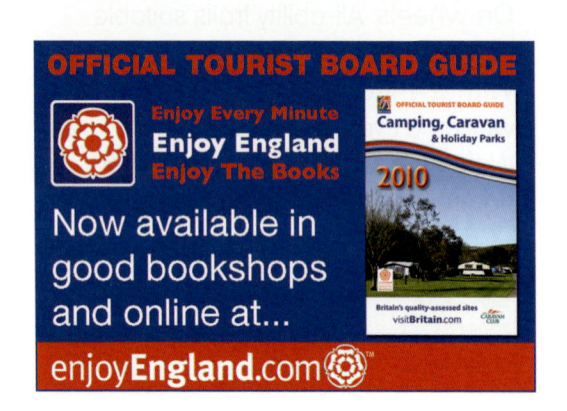

OFFICIAL TOURIST BOARD GUIDE

Enjoy Every Minute
Enjoy England
Enjoy The Books

Now available in good bookshops and online at...

enjoyEngland.com

Camping, Caravan & Holiday Parks 2010
Britain's quality-assessed sites
visitBritain

NATIONAL FEDERATION OF
Shopmobility
2009/2010

The directory of Shopmobility Schemes in the UK, Channel Islands & ROI

Get trained - Get out - Get independent
The Shopmobility experience is not just about shopping!

www.shopmobilityuk.org

Historic Houses & Gardens
Castles and Heritage Sites
2010

HUDSONs — 2010

All you need for fabulous days out

2010 EDITION AVAILABLE NOW
SPECIAL OFFER ONLY £11.00 (normally £14.95) free p&p
Order online at: www.hhgroup.co.uk/hudsons

OpenBritain | Wales

National Botanic Garden of Wales

Accessibility reaches new heights in Wales

The tourism industry in Wales provides opportunities for staying in traditional resorts, large cities, country towns or more rural locations. Well established resorts for families that are set within mostly level terrain, are to be found around most of the coast. In the North these include Rhyl, Colwyn Bay and Llandudno. Aberdovey, Barmouth and Towyn are on the West coast and Tenby and Porthcawl in the south. Hillier sections of the coast have many historic towns, some with castles such as Harlech, Caernarfon and Conwy or with attractive harbours like New Quay.

But the landscape in Wales is changing through a greater awareness, bringing with it a variety of accessible solutions to satisfy our individual lifestyles. A common factor linking attractions; restaurants; museums and accommodation is the provision of an Access Statement that, in giving accurate and up-to-date information, allows you, the visitor, the choice of where to visit.

There is a saying here in Wales that "you don't have to flatten Snowdon for us all to walk over", illustrating the fact that access is not just about physical features. Take for instance, cordless kettles; personal loop systems; suction support rails; large print menus; easy grip cutlery; bath seats. These little things make a BIG difference to many and the tourism industry is alive to this, and have them to hand.

Let's take a brief tour across this accessible tapestry, starting with yes, that Mountain, the roof of Wales - **Snowdon**. Several heritage railways horizontally criss-cross the face of Wales — Vale of Rheidol, Bala, Ffestiniog, Talyllyn, Llanberis, Welshpool, Fairbourne, Welsh Highland (Portmadog) but the **Snowdon Mountain Railway** climbs vertically from Llanberis to the summit at 3650 ft.

And at the summit, **Hafod Eryri**, has a welcome for all. A lift complements steps from the station platform to the level floor of the new Visitor Centre. Views are audio described from window vantage points. Baby change and toilet facilities are designed inclusively. ▶

OpenBritain | Wales

Cardiff Food Festival

Tl-y-Llyn, Snowdonia

Wales

347	Tourist Information Centres
349	**Accommodation**

▶ Perhaps mountains are not for you, rather the coast, visible from the summit of **Yr Wyddfa**. There are several award winning beaches; bays, headlands and harbours are dotted along the 750 miles of coastline, which is the subject of more access initiatives to create **The All Wales Coastal Path**. If you are lucky you could spot dolphins along the coast of **Cardigan Bay**. A Pembrokeshire initiative using a wheelchair attachment allows you to dip your toes in the sea without getting beached!

Of National Parks, there are three, **Brecon Beacons**, **Snowdonia** and a coastal one in **Pembrokeshire**, all of which have easy access routes for families with pushchairs and wheelchair users.

Gardens large and small will delight the senses at all seasons, with perhaps the most fascinating ones being the **National Botanic Garden of Wales** in Carmarthenshire, and also the walled gardens at **Aberglasney** that may evoke poetry from your inner self…as it has in poets since 1477.

The past is always around you wherever you travel, with Roman legends fact and fiction at for instance **Llangollen** and **Caernarfon**. Castles are our forte – hanging over a cliff face at **Harlech**; on a hilltop at **Llandielo**, and on river estuaries at **Conwy** and **Caernarfon**. Once built to keep the enemy at bay, new initiatives such as those at Caernarfon and Cardiff allow more and more people through their fortified ramparts. ▶

Visit Wales
Croeso Cymru

Harlech Castle

www.openbritain.net

345

OpenBritain | Wales

Caernarfon

Llanerchaeron

Hafod Eryri Visitors Centre - Summit of Snowdon (Yr Wyddfa)

Visit Wales
Croeso Cymru

Get in touch

For general information and advice on accommodation:

Visit Wales

t 08708 300 306
e info@visitwales.co.uk
web www.visitwales.co.uk

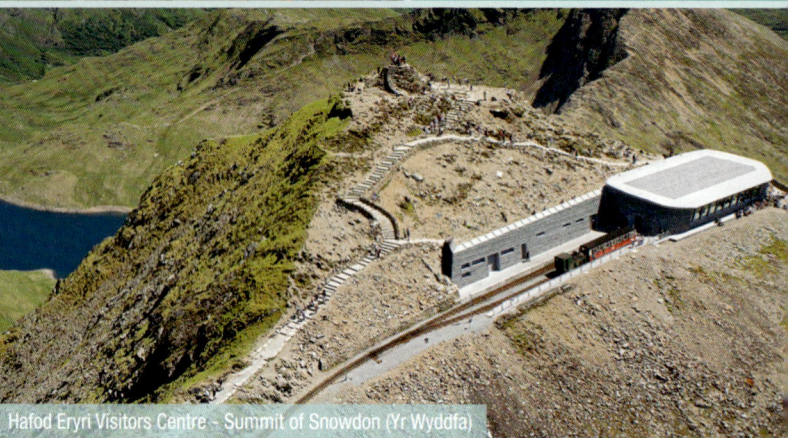

▶ As opposed to Castles, motorways are a rarity in Wales, being confined mostly to the South. This creates more opportunities to drink in the countryside along quieter roads, passing cottages, hostels, caravan parks, farms and Country Houses in idyllic settings just waiting to greet you.

At some of these you can fish a lake for your dinner from a safe platform or an adapted wheely boat, as on **Tal-y-Llyn**, under the shadow of the **Cader Idris** mountain ridge.

You could have a film show after dinner, in a purpose built cinema in the once cellar of one country house near **Aberaeron**, without hardly leaving your seat. On clear nights, starry skies put on another show in the unspoilt darkness and complete quietness of the countryside.

Witness the agricultural activity at many of the **Farm Stay** Cottage properties with, if you time if right, the smell of shoeing the family pony as the horn receives the hot shoe, or the bleating of new born spring lambs.

Or just sink into the luxurious splendour of days gone by, amidst the smell of beeswax on the antique furniture, as the chiming of the grandfather clock announces dinner.

And food is high on the menu, not only on the dinner plate, but at the many local farmers markets and Food Festivals held throughout the year.

Accessibility is not an extra on your bill, but a natural consequence of accommodating you, the visitor and ensuring a quality holiday experience.

Let Wales touch all your senses and speak to you through its sights, sounds, smells and tastes...giving a real Sense of Place...and that Place is Wales. ■

Tourist Information Centres

Tourist Information Centres are a mine of information about local and regional accommodation, attractions and events. Visit them when you arrive at your destination or contact them before you go:

Aberaeron	The Quay	01545 570602	aberaerontic@ceredigion.gov.uk
Aberdulais Falls	The National Trust	01639 636674	aberdulaistic@nationaltrust.org.uk
Aberdyfi*	The Wharf Gardens	01654 767321	tic.aberdyfi@eryri-npa.gov.uk
Abergavenny	Swan Meadow	01873 853254	abergavenny.ic@breconbeacons.org
Aberystwyth	Terrace Road	01970 612125	aberystwythtic@ceredigion.gov.uk
Bala *	Pensarn Road	01678 521021	bala.tic@gwynedd.gov.uk
Bangor *	Town Hall	01248 352786	bangor.tic@gwynedd.gov.uk
Barmouth	The Station	01341 280787	barmouth.tic@gwynedd.gov.uk
Barry Island *	The Promenade	01446 747171	barrytic@valeofglamorgan.gov.uk
Beddgelert *	Canolfan Hebog	01766 890615	tic.beddgelert@eryri-npa.gov.uk
Betws y Coed	Royal Oak Stables	01690 710426	tic.byc@eryri-npa.gov.uk
Blaenau Ffestiniog *	High Street	01766 830360	tic.blaenau@eryri-npa.gov.uk
Blaenavon *	World Heritage Centre	01495 742333	Blaenavon.tic@torfaen.gov.uk
Borth *	Cambrian Terrace	01970 871174	borthtic@ceredigion.gov.uk
Brecon	Cattle Market Car park	01874 622485	brectic@powys.gov.uk
Bridgend	Bridgend Designer Outlet	01656 654906	bridgendtic@bridgend.gov.uk
Caerleon	5 High Street	01633 422656	caerleon.tic@newport.gov.uk
Caernarfon	Oriel Pendeitsh	01286 672232	caernarfon.tic@gwynedd.gov.uk
Caerphilly	The Twyn	029 2088 0011	tourism@caerphilly.gov.uk
Cardiff	The Old Library	08701 211 258	visitor@cardiff.gov.uk
Cardigan	Theatr Mwldan	01239 613230	cardigantic@ceredigion.gov.uk
Carmarthen	113 Lammas Street	01267 231557	carmarthentic@carmarthenshire.gov.uk
Chepstow	Castle Car Park	01291 623772	chepstow.tic@monmouthshire.gov.uk
Conwy	Castle Buildings	01492 592248	conwytic@conwy.gov.uk
Dolgellau	Ty Meirion	01341 422888	tic.dolgellau@eryri-npa.gov.uk
Fishguard Harbour	Ocean Lab	01348 872037	fishguardharbour.tic@pembrokeshire.gov.uk
Fishguard Town	Town Hall	01437 776636	fishguard.tic@pembrokeshire.gov.uk
Harlech *	Llys y Graig	01766 780658	tic.harlech@eryri-npa.gov.uk
Haverfordwest	Old Bridge	01437 763110	haverfordwest.tic@pembrokeshire.gov.uk

OpenBritain | Wales

Holyhead	Stena Line	01407 762622	holyhead@nwtic.com
Knighton	Offa's Dyke Centre	01547 528753	oda@offasdyke.demon.co.uk
Llanberis *	41b High Street	01286 870765	llanberis.tic@gwynedd.gov.uk
Llandovery	Heritage Centre	01550 720693	llandovery.tic@breconbeacons.org
Llandudno	Library Building	01492 577577	llandudnotic@conwy.gov.uk
Llanelli	Millennium Coastal Park Visitor Centre	01554 777744	DiscoveryCentre@carmarthenshire.gov.uk
Llanfairpwllgwyngyll	Station Site	01248 713177	llanfairpwll@nwtic.com
Llangollen	Y Chapel	01978 860828	llangollen@nwtic.com
Merthyr Tydfil	14a Glebeland Street	01685 727474	tic@merthyr.gov.uk
Milford Haven *	94 Charles Street	01646 690866	milford.tic@pembrokeshire.gov.uk
Mold	Library Museum & Art Gallery	01352 759331	mold@nwtic.com
Monmouth	Market Hall	01600 713899	monmouth.tic@monmouthshire.gov.uk
Mumbles	The Methodist Church	01792 361302	info@mumblestic.co.uk
New Quay *	Church Street	01545 560865	newquaytic@ceredigion.gov.uk
Newport	Museum & Art Gallery	01633 842962	newport.tic@newport.gov.uk
Newport (Pembs) *	2 Bank Cottages	01239 820912	NewportTIC@Pembrokeshirecoast.org.uk
Oswestry Mile End	Mile End Services	01691 662488	oswestrytourism@shropshire.gov.uk
Oswestry Town	The Heritage Centre	01691 662753	ot@oswestry-welshborders.org.uk
Pembroke	Visitor Centre	01437 776499	pembroke.tic@pembrokeshire.gov.uk
Penarth *	Penarth Pier	029 2070 8849	penarthtic@valeofglamorgan.gov.uk
Porthcawl *	Old Police Station	01656 786639	porthcawltic@bridgend.gov.uk
Porthmadog	High Street	01766 512981	porthmadog.tic@gwynedd.gov.uk
Presteigne *	The Judge's Lodging	01544 260650	presteignetic@powys.gov.uk
Pwllheli	Min y Don	01758 613000	pwllheli.tic@gwynedd.gov.uk
Rhyl	Rhyl Childrens Village	01745 355068	rhyl.tic@denbighshire.gov.uk
Saundersfoot *	The Barbecue	01834 813672	saundersfoot.tic@pembrokeshire.gov.uk
St Davids	The Grove	01437 720392	enquiries@stdavids.pembrokeshirecoast.org.uk
Swansea	Plymouth Street	01792 468321	tourism@swansea.gov.uk
Tenby	Upper Park Road	01834 842402	tenby.tic@pembrokeshire.gov.uk
Welshpool	The Vicarage Gardens Car Park	01938 552043	ticwelshpool@btconnect.com
Wrexham	Lambpit Street	01978 292015	tic@wrexham.gov.uk

*seasonal opening

Wales | Carmarthenshire

Carmarthen | Coedllys Country House   AS

AA ★★★★★ Coedllys Uchaf, Llangynin, Carmarthen, Carmarthenshire SA33 4JY
t 01994 231455   e vah53@btinternet.com

Access: 🐾🏛☺ General: ✕P♿✿ Room: 📺☕

Felingwm Uchaf | Allt-y-Golau Farmhouse   AS

AA ★★★★
Enjoy England ★★★★
Allt-y-Golau Uchaf, Felingwm Uchaf, Carmarthenshire SA32 7BB
t 01267 290455   e alltygolau@btinternet.com
alltygolau.com

Access: abc 🐾🏛 General: 🐴🍴✿ Room: 🛁🚾📺☕

Pendine | Clyngwyn Farm Self Catering Cottages

Visit Wales ★★★ Mrs Jean Stuckey, Clyngwyn Farm, Marros, Pendine, Carmarthenshire SA33 4PW   t 01994453214   e clyngwyn@tiscali.co.uk

Access: 🅷🐾🏛 General: 🐴📺P🆂 Unit: 🛁♨♿♿📝✿

Whitland | Homeleigh Country Cottages

Visit Wales ★★★★
Mrs Morfydd Turner, Red Roses, Whitland, Carmarthenshire SA34 0PN   t 01834 831765   e enquiries@homeleigh.org
homeleigh.org

Units: 6   **Sleeps:** 2-7
Open: All year except Xmas and New Year
Low season p/w: £320.00
High season p/w: £1030.00
Shop: 5 miles
Pub: <0.5 miles

6 spacious cottages to offer a warm welcome to guests who need a little extra help to make their holiday perfect. Disabled aids included in price, eg. electric bed, wheel in shower chair, commode, walking frame. Hoist available to hire.

Location: M4 to Wales. A40 Carmarthen, A477 St. Clears/Tenby, Red Roses B4314 Pendine. Homeleigh Country Cottages 300m on left.

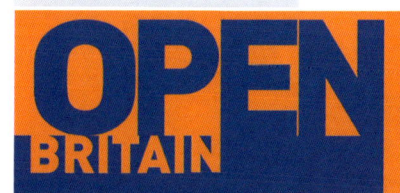

Access:
🅷🐾🏛☺🚾
General:
🐴📺P🆂
Unit:
🛁♿♨♿📝📺🆂♿
♿✿

OPEN BRITAIN

DECIDED WHERE TO GO?
SEE ATTRACTIONS FOR WHAT TO DO
Ideas and information at the end of each regional section

©Britainonview / Martin Brent

For symbols see pg 24   349

Wales | Ceredigion/Conwy

Aberaeron | Ty Mawr Mansion Country House — AS

Open: All year except Xmas and New Year

Rooms per night:
s: £110.00-£180.00
d: £120.00-£280.00

p/p half board:
d: £85.00-£200.00
Meals: £24.95-£45.95

Cilcennin, Ceredigion SA48 8DB
t 01570 470033   e info@tymawrmansion.co.uk

tymawrmansion.co.uk   8A2

Beautiful family run 5 star restaurant with rooms including our 2 AA Rosette restaurant.

Access: abc 🐕 ♿
General: 🍴 🍷 P ❀ ♿   **Room:** 🛏 S

Lampeter | Falcondale Mansion Hotel — AS

Falcondale Drive, Lampeter, Ceredigion SA48 7RX
t 01570 422910   e info@falcondalehotel.com

Access: abc 🐕 ♿ WC   **General:** 🍴 🍷 P ❀ ♿   **Room:** ☕

Abergele | Plas Farm Caravan Park — AS

AA ★★★
Visit Wales ★★★

Plas Yn Betws, Abergele, Conwy LL22 8AU
t 01492 680250   e sianplas@live.co.uk

Access: 🐕 ☺ WC ♿   **General:** 🚿 🚗 🏕 WP   **Pitch:** 🚐 🚙 🎒

Llandudno | Esplanade Hotel

AA ★★

Promenade, Llandudno, Gwynedd LL30 2LL
t 01492 860300   e info@esplanadehotel.co.uk

esplanadehotel.co.uk

Access: .: abc WC ♿   **General:** 🍴 🍷 ♿   **Room:** 🛏 ☕

Llandudno | The Queens Hotel — AS

Clonmel Street, The Promenade, Llandudno, Conwy LL30 2LE
t 01492 877218   e info@queenshotel.wanadoo.co.uk

Access: 🐕   **General:** 🍴 🍷 ❀ ♿   **Room:** ☕

OPENBRITAIN.NET

The one-stop-shop for all your travel needs.

Go online and see how we can help you get in, out...and about.

350   www.openbritain.net

Wales | Conwy/Denbighshire/Gwynedd

Llandudno | The West Shore

Visit Wales ★★★
Open: All year

Rooms per night:
s: £25.00-£50.00
d: £50.00-£100.00
p/p half board:
d: £40.00-£70.00
Meals: £14.95
Shop: <0.5 miles
Pub: <0.5 miles

Access:
General:
Room:

West Parade, Llandudno, Conwy LL30 2BB
t 01492 876833   e westshore@livability.org.uk

livability.org.uk   8B1

The West Shore is a fully adapted wheelchair accessible hotel with 18 en suite bedrooms all with level access shower. Located on the west shore of Llandudno with stunning views across the Conwy Estuary towards the Snowdonia National Park.

Location: Conveniently located just off the A55 North Wales coast road, close to the historic castle town of Conwy.

Ruthin | Number 5   AS

Visit Wales ★★★★
Units: 1   **Sleeps:** 5
Open: All year

Low season p/w:
£300.00
High season p/w:
£450.00

Mrs K Benton, Rhos Isa, Gellifor, Ruthin, Denbighshire LL15 1RY
t 01824707691   e kellybenton@btinternet.com

number5wales.co.uk   8B1

Beautiful, centrally heated disabled-friendly bungalow set in a tranquil part of North Wales.

Access: **General:**   **Unit:**

Aberdaron | Manaros   AS

Visit Wales ★★★★

1 Dolfor, Aberdaron, Gwynedd LL53 8BP
t 01758 760652   e enquiries@aberdaronbandb.co.uk

aberdaronbandb.co.uk

Access: **General:**   **Room:**

Bethesda | Bryn Llys (Care of Joys of Life)   AS

Visit Wales ★★★★

Dr Wendy Jones, Coed Y Parc, Bethesda, Gwynedd LL57 4YW
t 01248602122   e joysoflife@tiscali.co.uk

thejoysoflife.co.uk

Access: **General:**   **Unit:**

For symbols see pg 24

Wales | Gwynedd

Bethesda | Hafan (Care of Joys of Life) — AS

Visit Wales ★★★★★
Units: 1 Sleeps: 2-4
Open: All year

Low season p/w: £695.00
High season p/w: £850.00

Dr Wendy Jones, The Joys of Life Country Park, Coed Y Parc, Bethesda, Gwynedd LL57 4YW
t 01248602122 e joysoflife@tiscali.co.uk

thejoysoflife.co.uk 8A1

Well equipped stone cottage in country park, with Snowdonia Mountain views. Close to coastal castles.

Access:
General: Unit:

Bethesda | Joys Of Life Country Park B&B — AS

Visit Wales ★★★★

Coed Y Parc, Bethesda, Gwynedd LL57 4YW
t 01248 602122 e joysoflife@tiscali.co.uk

thejoysoflife.co.uk

Access: General: Room:

Blaenau Ffestiniog | Bryn Elltyd — AS

Visit Wales ★★★
Open: All year

Rooms per night:
s: £30.00-£45.00
d: £60.00-£80.00
p/p half board:
d: £44.00-£59.00
Meals: £14.00

Bryn Elltyd ECO Guest House, Tanygrisiau, Blaenau Ffestiniog, Gwynedd LL41 3TW t 01766 831356 mob 07905 568127
e info@brynelltyd.com

brynelltyd.com

Heart of Snowdonia, stunning rural location Guardian recommended. Mainline station 3k; Drive on beach 28k

Access:
General: Room:

Caernarfon | Cae'r Dderwen

Mrs E Jones, Cae'r Dderwen, Ffordd Pant, Caernarfon, Gwynedd LL54 5RL
t 01286677870 e hendy@hendycaernarfon.co.uk

General: Unit:

Caernarfon | Old School Guest House — AS

Visit Wales ★★★
Open: All year

Rooms per night:
s: £35.00-£48.00
d: £31.00-£38.00
p/p half board:
d: £48.00-£58.00
Meals: £17.00-£20.00

Bwlch Derwen, Pant Glas, North West Snowdonia, Gwynedd LL51 9EQ t 01286 660701 e oldschoolpantglas@talk21.com

oldschool-henysgol.co.uk 8A1

Wales Tourist Board 3-star. Peaceful location, perfect for the attractions of Snowdonia & Llyn Peninsula.

Access:
General: Room:

352 www.openbritain.net

Wales | Gwynedd/Monmouthshire/Pembrokeshire

Dolgellau | Pen-y-Lon   AS
Visit Wales ★★★★ Mr & Mrs Michael Senior, Pentre Bach, Llwyngwril, Nr. Dolgellau, Gwynedd LL37 2JU t 01341 250294 e cottages@pentrebach.com
pentrebach.com

Access: | General: | Unit:

Abergavenny | Garden Flat
Visit Wales ★★★★ Mrs A Kellett, 11 Lansdown Road, Abergavenny, Monmouthshire NP7 6AN
t 01873 857903 e dr.kellett@btinternet.com

General: | Unit:

Chepstow | Cwrt-Y-Gaer (Self-catering)   AS
Visit Wales ★★★ Mr John Llewellyn, Cwrt-Y-Gaer, Wolvesnewton, Chepstow, Monmouthshire NP16 6PR t 01291 650700 e john.llewellyn11@btinternet.com

Access: | General: | Unit:

Amroth | Amroth Bay Holidays   AS
Visit Wales ★★★★ Mr & Mrs Clark, Pendeilo Leisure, Amroth, Norberth, Pembrokeshire SA67 8PR
Units: 2   Sleeps: 1-2
Open: March to October
t 01834 831 259 e pendeiloholidays@aol.com
pendeilo.co.uk   8A3

Low season p/w: £195.00
High season p/w: £425.00

Superb, coastal location, gently sloping. Comfortable, cosy farm conversion; peaceful secluded setting. Beach 1.25m. Sat/TV.

Access: | General: | Unit:

GETTING THERE IS NOT A PROBLEM!
OPEN BRITAIN See Getting there..... and back section (p364)
Everything you need for a hassle-free journey

For symbols see pg 24

Wales | Pembrokeshire

Boncath | Clynfyw Countryside Centre AS

Visit Wales ★★★★
Units: 4   Sleeps: 4-6
Open: All year

Low season p/w: £220.00
High season p/w: £600.00

Jim Bowen, Abercych, Boncath, Pembrokeshire SA37 0HF
t 01239 841236   e jim.clynfyw@virgin.net

clynfyw.co.uk   8A2

Twin and single rooms with En Suite wetrooms. Four independent cottages with private decking/garden. Close proximity so can easily be run together for larger groups. Close to coastal path, mountains and Teifi Valley - Lovely!

Location: B4332 between Cenarth and Boncath North Pembrokshire. Buses to Cenarthy. Train to Carmarthen. One hour north-west of Swansea.

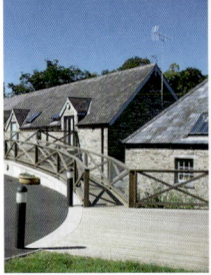

Access:
General:
Unit:

Boncath | Eden House Country Guest Accommodation AS

Visit Wales ★★★★

Penlanfeigan, Boncath, Pembrokeshire SA37 0JE
t 01239 841499   e light.warriors@talk21.com

eden-housebb.co.uk

Access: **General:**   **Room:**

Castlemartin | Cornerstone Cottage

Mrs Christine Neve, 2 Pound Cottages, Castlemartin, Pembroke, Pembrokeshire SA71 5HN   t 01646 661369

Self-catering, two bedroom, detached cottage; stone walls and floors. Two miles from Freshwater West.

General: **Unit:**

HUDSONs

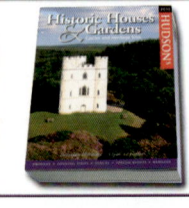

Hudson's is the definitive guide to historic houses & gardens.

Up to date information on over 2000 properties with clear information symbols for accessibility and facilities.

Historic Houses & Gardens
Castles and Heritage Sites

Order online at:
www.hhgroup.co.uk/hudsons

Wales | Pembrokeshire/Powys

Maenclochog | Twmpath Guest House
AS

Open: All year

Rooms per night:
s: £35.00
d: £70.00

p/p half board:
d: £30.00
Meals: £15.00

Maenclochog, Pembrokeshire SA66 7RL
t 01437 532990 e enquire@twmpath.co.uk

twmpathguesthouse.co.uk 8A3

Family run. Heart of Pembrokeshire. Quality homemade food. Wonderful views. Ideal for all activities.

Access: **General:** **Room:**

Brecon | Old Radnor Barn Bed & Breakfast
AS

Visit Wales ★★★★

Open: All year except Xmas

Rooms per night:
s: £45.00-£60.00
d: £65.00-£80.00

p/p half board:
d: £90.00-£120.00
Meals: £15.00-£20.00

Shop: <0.5 miles
Pub: <0.5 miles

Station Yard, Talgarth, Brecon, Powys LD3 0PE
t 01874 712102 e groves@oldradnorbarn.com

oldradnorbarn.com 8B3

Croeso! Welcome to the Old Radnor Barn. We are pleased to offer two ground floor bedrooms, one double, one K/size/twin both benefit from level approach and wide access doors, bathrooms are wheelchair accessible with grab rails and shower seating.

Location: Follow A479 signs Talgarth. Follow signs for Car Park, we are just off the western end of High street.

Access:

General:

Room:

Brecon | Wye Knot Stop

Visit Wales ★★★★

Open: All year except Xmas

Rooms per night:
s: £35.00
d: £60.00

Llyswen, Brecon, Powys LD3 0UR
t 01874 754247 e info@wyeknotstop.co.uk

wyeknotstop.co.uk

4 star B&B in the Wye Valley, views of the Black mountains, nr. Hay-on-Wye.

Access: **General:** **Room:**

Wales | Powys

Builth Wells | Penrheol Farm   AS

Visit Wales ★★★★ Mrs Anne Brooks, Llanynis, Builth Wells, Powys LD2 3HH
t 01982 553853 e penrheol@btinternet.com
penrheol.co.uk

General: ... Unit: ...

Llandrindod Wells | The Metropole   AS

AA ★★★ Temple Street, Llandrindod Wells, Powys LD1 5DY
Visit Wales ★★★ t 01597 823700
metropole.co.uk

Access: ... General: ... Room: ...

Llanfair Caereinion | Madog's Wells   AS

Visit Wales ★★★★★ Mrs Ann & Michael Reed, Madog, Llanfair Caereinion, Welshpool, Powys SY21 0DE t 01938 810446 e info@madogswells.co.uk
Units: 3 **Sleeps:** 1–6
Open: All year
Low season p/w: £100.00
High season p/w: £530.00

madogswells.co.uk   8B2

3 cottages, 2 spacious and 1 cosy, sleep 6, 6 and 3 in quiet countryside.

Access: ... General: ... Unit: ...

Welshpool | Lake Vyrnwy Hotel & Spa   AS

AA ★★★★ Lake Vyrnwy, LLanwddyn, Powys, Mid Wales SY10 0LY
Visit Wales ★★★★ t 01691 870692 e info@lakevyrnwyhotel.co.uk
Open: All year
Rooms per night:
s: £95.00–£190.00
d: £120.00–£215.00
p/p half board:
d: £87.50–£126.50
Meals: £39.95

lakevrynwyhotel.co.uk   8B2

Lake Vyrnwy Hotel & Spa enjoys one of the finest locations in Wales.

Access: ... General: ... Room: ...

OPENBRITAIN.NET

The one-stop-shop for all your travel needs.
Go online and see how we can help you get in, out ...and about.

- Fully searchable database of accommodation, days out and where to eat and drink
- MyOpenBritain trip planner
- User reviews, blogs and forums

Wales | Rhondda, Cynon, Taff/Flintshire/Attractions

Pontyclun | The Vale Resort AS

AA	★★★★

Open: All year

Rooms per night:
s: £70.00-£282.00
d: £70.00-£292.00
p/p half board:
d: £22.00-£35.00
Meals: £22.00-£35.00

Shop: 4 miles
Pub: 2 miles

Access:
General:
Room:

Hensol, Pontyclun, Mid Glamorgan CF72 8JY
t 01443 667 800   e b.danielsen@vale-hotel.com

vale-hotel.com   8B3

The Vale Resort is one of the UK's leading destinations for golf, spa and family breaks offering spacious accommodation in its luxuriously appointed four star hotel. The Vale boasts two championship golf courses, Wales' largest spa and superb conference facilities.

Location: Ideally located just 3 minutes from junction 34 of the M4. 15 minutes from Cardiff city centre and international airport.

Axton | Meadowcroft Guest House AS

Visit Wales   ★★★★★

Llanasa Road, Axton, Holywell, Flintshire CH8 9DH
t 01745 570785   e helen@meadowcroftguesthouse.net

meadowcroftguesthouse.net

Access: General: Room:

Cardiff | New Theatre Cardiff

Park Place, Cardiff CR10 3LN
t 0292 087 8889   e MSmith@cardiff.gov.uk

Brynslencyn | Anglesey Sea Zoo and Farm

Brynsiencyn, Anglesey, Wales LL61 6TQ
t 01248 430411   e info@angleseyseazoo.co.uk

angleseyseazoo.co.uk

Machynlleth | Centre For Alternative Technology

Machynlleth, Powys SY20 9AZ
t 01654 705952

cat.org.uk

For symbols see pg 24

Harriet Davis Seaside Holiday Trust for Disabled Children
(Registered Charity No. 1015096)

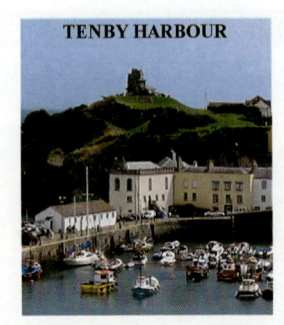

TENBY HARBOUR

The Trust provides self-catering holiday houses in Pembrokeshire for families with disabled children. Harriet's House, Giltar View and The Wheelabout are in the Tenby area and have been adapted and equipped to provide for children who are wheel-chair dependant. All have profiling beds, hydraulic baths, hoists, showering aids and special seating. The Wheelabout, has an indoor heated swimming pool and a large garden. Harriet's House is on Tenby Harbour and Giltar View overlooks the South Beach. All have convenient parking. Caerwen, in Narberth, has been adapted for use by families with children with autism and other learning disabilities. The house and garden have been made secure and there is a large soft playroom.

For more details see the Trust's website: www.harriet-davis-trust.org.uk
Contact the Trust at: Harriet Davis Trust, Tindle House, Warren Street, Tenby. SA70 7JY
Telephone: 01834 845197   Email: helen@harriet-davis-trust.freeserve.co.uk

Bodelwyddan Castle Hotel, North Wales   Telephone number 01745 585088

Warner Leisure Hotels

Exclusively for adults.

Fantastic evening entertainment and stylish en suite accommodation.

Home of the National Portrait Gallery's Victorian Collection - free admission for hotel guests

Bodelwyddan is just under an hour from Snowdonia and Chester, 10 minutes from the seaside town of Rhyl, and half an hour away from the Victorian pier at Llandudno

Breakfast and three course evening meals in St Davids Restaurant

- Heated indoor swimming pool • Spa pool • Sauna
- Steam room • Tropicarium • Fitness studio
- Four rink indoor bowls complex • All weather Crown Green bowling arena • Late lounge for optional evening entertainment and shows • Hair and beauty salon featuring Decleor health and beauty therapies

Wheelchair accessible rooms : 9 these have a lower bathside rails by the toilet and on the side of the bath

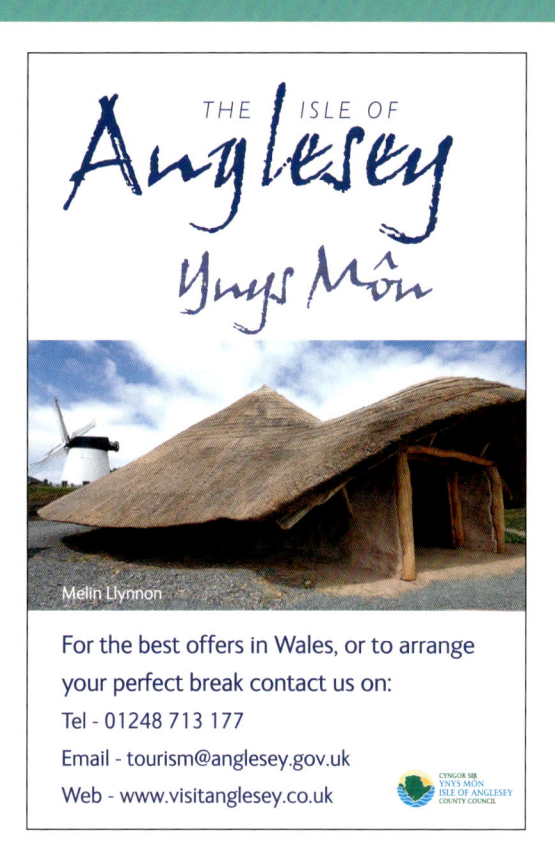

OpenBritain | Wales

THE ISLE OF Anglesey / Ynys Môn

Melin Llynnon

For the best offers in Wales, or to arrange your perfect break contact us on:
Tel - 01248 713 177
Email - tourism@anglesey.gov.uk
Web - www.visitanglesey.co.uk

CYNGOR SIR YNYS MÔN ISLE OF ANGLESEY COUNTY COUNCIL

BANK FARM

Bank Farm Leisure Park is situated on the beautiful Gower Peninsula in the village of Horton. We have facilities for camping, touring and motor caravans and self catering accommodation. There is a licensed bar and restaurant on site and a shop, swimming pool and childrens play area.

Our bungalows are situated at the Bank Farm holiday complex about five minutes walk from the main facilities. They are double glazed and are of sound brick-built construction with a tiled pitched roof. They have two bedrooms, a lounge/dining area, kitchen and bathroom and are fully equipped with a colour television, fridge, cooker, microwave, cutlery and crockery. Bedding is available on request. All heating and electricity is included in the price. There is a dedicated parking space for each bungalow.

Telephone: 01792 390228 / 01792 390452 Fax: 01792 391282
Email: bankfarmleisure@aol.com Website: www.bankfarmleisure.co.uk

Anglesey Sea Zoo — for a splashing day out!

Anglesey Sea Zoo the largest aquarium in Wales

over 150 british species from octopusses and seahorses to sharks and sunstars for you to get up-close and personal with!

open all year round!

includes the Lobster hatchery of Wales, an eerie shipwreck brimming with conger eels and a big-fish forest full of huge sea bass and sharks

daily fish feeding at 2.30pm and presentation at 12.00 noon. some days you can see a diver underwater! flexible education packages available

from kids to grown-ups, a great day out guaranteed! fully licensed bistro, gift shop, adventure play area, giant octojump bouncy castle and crazy golf

full wheelchair access throughout the site and disabled toilet. group discounts available. free coach parking

www.angleseyseazoo.co.uk
t. 01248 430411

Centre for Alternative Technology / Canolfan y Dechnoleg Amgen

- 7 acres of interactive displays on eco living
- On-site info service, shop and café
- Accessible water powered cliff railway
- Organic garden displays
- To discuss your requirements please call 01654 705950

Assisted wheelchair access. Some woodland paths

Guide dogs welcome

www.cat.org.uk

Machynlleth, Powys, Mid Wales, SY20 9AZ
01654 705950 • info@cat.org.uk

359

OpenBritain | Wales

Cyngor Sir Ceredigion - yn ymrwymedig i wella eich teithiau ar fws.

Mae pob llwybr craidd y bysiau sy'n teithio trwy Geredigion nawr yn cael eu gwasanaethu gan fysiau modern a chyfforddus sy'n cydymffurfio â DDA, sy'n cynnwys:

- Mynediad lefel isel
- Mynediad hygyrch i rai sy'n defnyddio cadair olwyn
- Cyhoeddiadau gweledol a chlywedol am arosfannau bws

Dewch i deithio'n gyfforddus ac mewn steil trwy sir hyfryd Ceredigion yng ngorllewin Cymru - i gael gwybodaeth am amserlenni a siwrneiau, cysylltwch â Traveline ar 0871 200 22 23

Ceredigion County Council - committed to improving your travel by bus.

All core bus routes travelling through Ceredigion are now serviced by modern and comfortable DDA compatible buses which include:

- Low level access
- Easily accessible for wheelchair users
- Visual and audio announcement of bus stops

Come and travel in style and comfort through the beautiful west Wales county of Ceredigion - for timetable and journey information contact Traveline on 0871 200 22 23

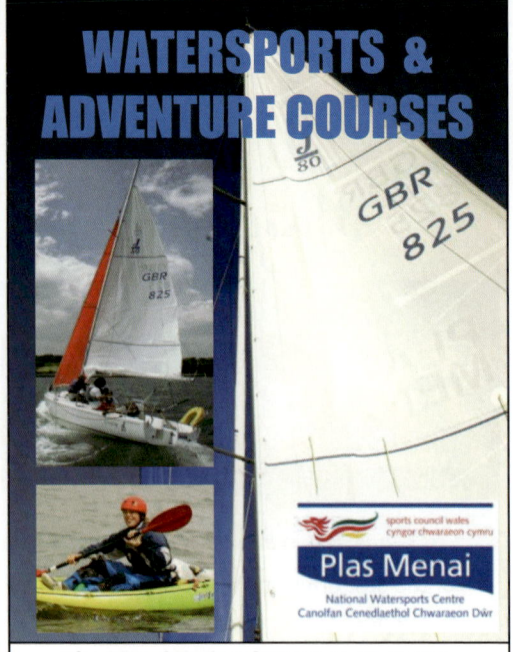

WATERSPORTS & ADVENTURE COURSES

Plas Menai

sports council wales
cyngor chwaraeon cymru

National Watersports Centre
Canolfan Cenedlaethol Chwaraeon Dŵr

Plas Menai National Watersports Centre
Caernarfon, Gwynedd, LL55 1UE
01248 670 964   info@plasmenai.co.uk
www.plasmenai.co.uk

Our commitment to you...

St David's Hall and the **New Theatre**, Cardiff have a range of services to assist disabled customers. Contact us for a copy of our Access Guide.

NEW THEATRE 029 2087 8889
ST DAVID'S HALL 029 2087 8444
www.newtheatrecardiff.co.uk/access
www.stdavidshallcardiff.co.uk/access

NEW THEATRE

St David's Hall
Neuadd Dewi Sant

Enjoy Snowdonia
feel good in pure air

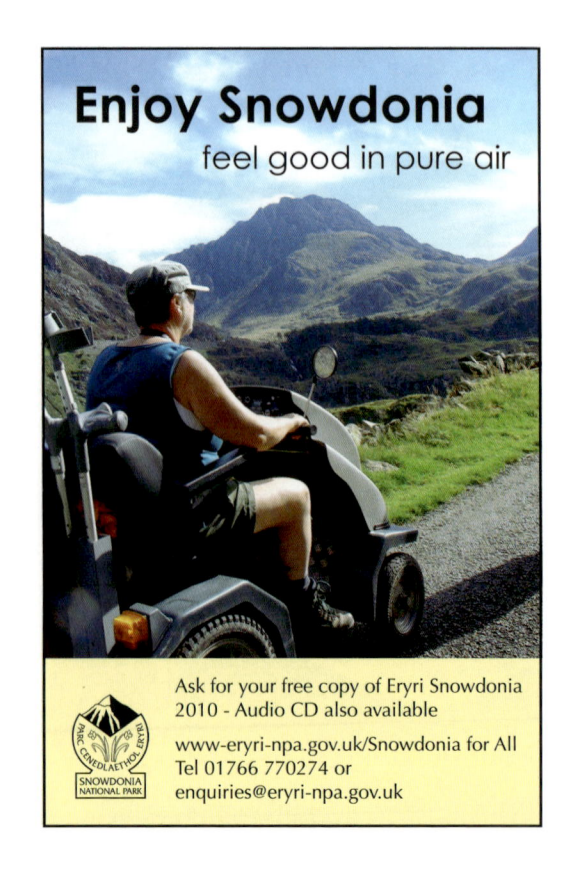

Ask for your free copy of Eryri Snowdonia 2010 - Audio CD also available
www-eryri-npa.gov.uk/Snowdonia for All
Tel 01766 770274 or
enquiries@eryri-npa.gov.uk

SNOWDONIA NATIONAL PARK
PARC CENEDLAETHOL ERYRI

360

OpenBritain | Wales

Wheelchair Hire Scheme

P.I.P.P.A.
Physically Impaired People of Pembrokeshire Association

The Basement
Haverfordwest Registry Office
Tower Hill
Haverfordwest
Pembrokeshire
SA65 9LX
01437 760999

Ynysymaengwyn Caravan & Camping Park

This is a Local Authority owned site, situated in the grounds of an old Manor House and woodlands, offers good facilities and is an ideal base for hikers, Climber, fishing, cycling and walking. Approximately one mile from the local town And safe sandy beach ideal for all watersports.

- Daffodil Award   • Walking & Cycling Award

To make a booking please write, phone or email the Site Managers Mr. & Mrs. Blunden
www.ynysy.co.uk   Email: Rita@ynysy.co.uk

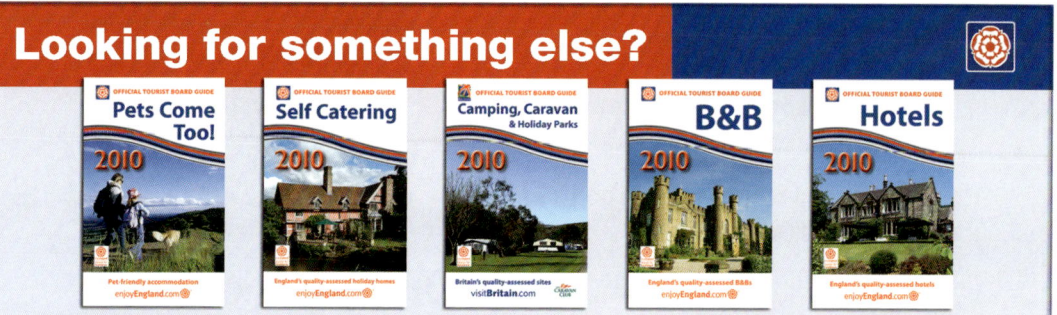

Looking for something else?

- Pets Come Too! 2010 — Pet-friendly accommodation — enjoyEngland.com
- Self Catering 2010 — England's quality-assessed holiday homes — enjoyEngland.com
- Camping, Caravan & Holiday Parks 2010 — Britain's quality-assessed sites — visitBritain.com
- B&B 2010 — England's quality-assessed B&Bs — enjoyEngland.com
- Hotels 2010 — England's quality-assessed hotels — enjoyEngland.com

If you haven't found what you are looking for in OpenBritain, VisitBritain's Official Tourist Board Guides offer a wide choice of assessed accommodation which may meet your needs.

©Britainonview / Rod Edwards

OPEN BRITAIN — DECIDED WHERE TO GO? SEE ATTRACTIONS FOR WHAT TO DO
Ideas and information at the end of each regional section

361

BRIG-AYD CONTROLS Ltd

Driving and lifting aids for disabled drivers and passengers

Hoists

Wheelchair Hoists to suit saloons, hatchbacks, estates, people carriers and 4x4`s

Five models 30kg, 75kg, 100kg, 150kg and patented 120kg fully automatic telescopic hoist

The Basil person hoist with a safe working load of 120kg

Remote radio control available on 100kg, 150kg and telescopic hoists

Driving Aids

Single lever hand controls for light and easy operation of throttle and brake.

Cruise Control and Electric Clutch systems fitted.

New Electric Throttle and Brake Hand control.

Twin flip throttle pedal transfers for left or right foot operation.

Steering knobs with quick release and a choice of grips.

Parking brake easy release mechanisms.

Infra Red hand controls.

Seat adaptations (eg swivel seats).

Contact us for a quote or to find your nearest fitter of these quality products

Telephone: 01707 322322   Fax: 01707 394149

sales@brig-aydcontrols.co.uk

www.brig-aydcontrols.co.uk

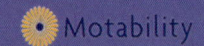

Motability

OPENBRITAIN.NET

The one-stop-shop for all your travel needs.

Go online and see how we can help you get in, out ...and about.

- Fully searchable database of accommodation, days out and where to eat and drink
- MyOpenBritain trip planner
- User reviews, blogs and forums

Join today!

OpenBritain | Getting there... and back

Getting there...

Kindly supported by: **HIGHWAYS AGENCY**

www.highways.gov.uk

OpenBritain | Getting there... and back

366	Travel planning
370	Air travel
390	Road travel
404	Rail travel
412	Sea travel

"Twenty years from now you will be more disappointed by the things you didn't do than by the ones you did do. So throw off the bowlines, sail away from the safe harbor. Catch the trade winds in your sails. Explore. Dream. Discover." – Mark Twain

and back

As a wheelchair user for over 50 years, I am at last slowly beginning to find that necessary changes are being taken seriously and about time too! I always say things start to happen when people see £ signs in their eyes and, with the vast numbers of disabled people, the potential market is immense and do you blame them?

There are plenty of opportunities that disabled people can avail themselves of like the Disabled Persons Railcard, discounts on ferry operators and Eurotunnel, favourable rates at large hotel chains, car leasing through Motability and so on. Many of these opportunities are run through charities like Tourism for All and Mobilise and require an annual membership fee but they are small in comparison with the benefits on offer.

Although after taking a holiday, it is always nice to say 'there's no place like home' but wouldn't it be nice to say 'home and away' for the same experience?

Sir William Lawrence Bt OBE
Chairman, Tourism for All UK

www.openbritain.net/openbritain/travel

HIGHWAYS AGENCY

OpenBritain | Getting there... and back | **Travel planning**

Travel planning

Deciding between different means of transport for any particular journey depends on a range of individual factors and practical considerations that can include price, time, convenience and personal requirements and preferences. Security concerns require longer check-in times, which may make the overall time spent on flying between some cities longer than on a rail journey.

The journey may be anticipated as an enjoyable or relaxing experience: an overnight ferry crossing or railway journey may be used as such before or after a visit to a major city. If a person's regular means of transport is a private car, the convenience or lack or lack of alternative transport will be a major consideration. If a car has been substantially altered to meet the disabled owner's needs, then the difficulty/impossibility of hiring an alternative mode of transport away from home may require enduring long ferry routes and/or long driving times.

To make choices effectively one needs to know the available options — and these are always changing. Eurostar's links to St Pancras and King's Cross stations have increased these options for many people. Buses that can carry passengers in wheelchairs and wheelchair-accessible taxis have been of great benefit — although many local railway stations require the use of steps, as do the majority of long-distance coaches.

367	Information sources
367	The internet
367	National key scheme for toilets
367	Concessionary fares
368	Information sources (listing)

Top tip

- In general, if assistance may be required at any point in the journey advance notification will usually be required.

Information sources

County and unitary councils have some responsibilities for public transport for most of England and Wales, through a public transport information officer. Most publish specific information for disabled passengers. In major conurbations passenger transport executives oversee this facility. In Greater London, public transport planning and regulation of all forms of public transport and other functions are carried out by Transport for London. In Scotland, Regional Transport Partnerships deal with transport planning and some have more direct functions. The main public transport operations in Northern Ireland include Ulster Bus, Metro bus services in Belfast, NI Rail and Goldline coach services.

Detailed listings for these organisations are on page 368

The internet

Some sources of information are only available through the web. Information can be updated than in print and from the point of view of the transport companies or other providers, it costs less to provide and update information through the internet than in print.

Using the internet to make bookings is widespread and recommended. If assistance is required a telephone call is also advisable. People who do not have the use of a computer may, understandably, be irritated by an assumption that the internet is not only the major way of obtaining information but also that other methods are inferior. This is not helped when web addresses are publicised without other contact information being given. In general, assistance is available for people who want to start using the internet – a good starting point would be a local library/Ideas store.

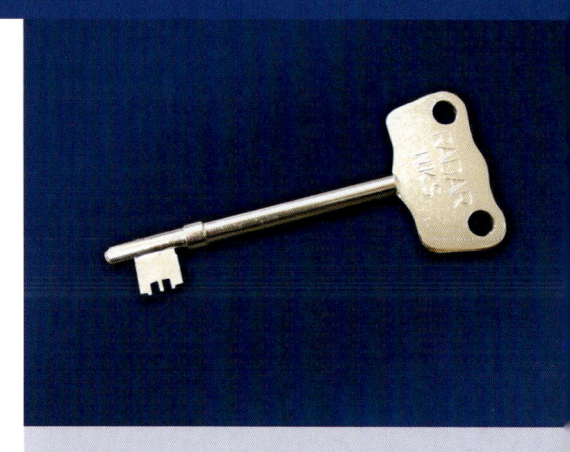

National key scheme for toilets

The NKS is used widely throughout the UK. The principle of the NKS is that if local authorities and other organisations decide to lock toilets for disabled people to prevent misuse they should use a standard lock. Local authorities taking part should have arrangements for disabled people in their area to obtain a NKS key that can be used throughout the country. If you have difficulty obtaining a key (price £3.50) contact RADAR on **020 7250 3222** or through **www.radar.org.uk.** RADAR also maintains a list of the toilets fitted with the NKS list, which is published annually in the National Key Scheme Guide and is updated on **www.directenquiries.co.uk; t 01344 360101**, **e customerservices@directenquiries.com.**

Concessionary fares

Separate national concessionary fares schemes exist in England, Northern Ireland, Scotland and Wales. In England and Wales, free travel is available for people aged 60+ and qualifying disabled people. Individual local bodies may offer more extensive concessions – such as extending the concession to all buses or other forms of public transport, or widening the range of disabled people covered. Applications should be made to local authorities, PTEs or their agents.

OpenBritain | Getting there... and back | **Travel planning**

Information sources

Door-to-door

e dptac@dft.gsi.gov.uk
web www.dptac.gov.uk/door-to-door

This is an internet source of regularly updated information for disabled people on all forms of transport.

GMPTE

9 Portland Street, Piccadilly Gardens,
Manchester M60 1HX
t 0871 200 2233 textphone 0871 200 2233
web www.gmpte.com

Highlands & Islands RTP

Building 25, Inverness Airport, Inverness IV2 7JB
t 01667 460464 web www.hitrans.org.uk

MerseyTravel

24 Hatton Garden, Liverpool L3 2AN
t/textphone 0151 227 5181
web www.merseytravel.gov.uk

Metro

Wellington House, 40-50 Wellington Street
Leeds LS1 2DE
t 0113 251 7272 web www.wymetro.com

Network West Midlands

Centro House, 16 Summer Lane,
Birmingham B19 3SD
t 0121 200 2700 textphone 0871 200 2233
web www.centro.org.uk

Nexus

Nexus House, St James Boulevard
Newcastle upon Tyne NE1 4AX
t 0191 203 3333 e contactus@nexus.org.uk
web www.nexus.org.uk

North East RTP

27-29 King Street, Aberdeen AB24 5AN
t 01224 625524 web www.nestrans.org.uk

Shetland TP

11 Hill Lane, Lerwick ZE1 0HA
t 01595 744868 e info@shetland.gov uk
web www.shetland.gov.uk/transport
Also see Shetland Islands Council t 01595 693535

South East RTP

1st Floor, Hoptoun Gate, 8B MacDonald Road
Edinburgh EH7 4LZ
t 0131 524 5150 web www.sestran.gov.uk

South West PT

c/o Dumfries & Galloway Council, Kirkbank House
English Street, Dumfries, DG1 2HS
t 01387 260102 web www.dumgal.gov.uk

South Yorkshire PT

11 Broad Street West, Sheffield S1 2BQ
t 0114 276 7575 web www.travelsouthyorkshire.com

Strathclyde PT

Consort House, 12 West George Street,
Glasgow G2 1HA
t 0141 3326811 e enquiry@spt.co.uk
web www.spt.co.uk

Tayside & Central RTP

Bordeaux House, 31 Kinnoull Street, Perth PH1 5EN
t 01738 475775   web www.tactran.gov.uk

Translink

Central Station, Belfast BT1 3PB
t 028 9066 6630   textphone 028 9035 4007
web www.translink.co.uk

Timetables and a guide are available in alternative formats. Website can be used with Browsealoud.

Transport for London

Travel Information, 55 Broadway, London SW1H 0BD
t 020 7222 1234   textphone 020 7222 1234
e travinfo@tfl.gov.uk   web www.tfl.gov.uk

Traveline

t 0871 200 2233   web www.traveline.org.uk

Traveline is a partnership of transport operators and local authorities formed to provide impartial advice and comprehensive information about public transport within England, Scotland and Wales.

Useful websites

Mobilise

web www.mobilise.info/

Mobilise was formed in 2005 from a merger of two charities, the Disabled Drivers' Association and the Disabled Drivers' Motor Club. Mobilise is not just an organisation for drivers, they also campaign for and support passengers, scooter and wheelchair users, families and carers. The organisation is run by and for disabled people and their core belief is that personal mobility impacts on every aspect of disabled people's lives.

By leading in the fight to improve mobility and access Mobilise seek to promote a better way of life for all disabled people irrespective of age, gender or race; and to end discrimination and segregation.

When it comes to finding solutions to the mobility problems that their members face, they believe that choice and affordability are paramount. They work closely with Motability in a role that ensures the benefits of co-operation and the ability to be constructively critical when necessary. They also participate in mobility events at dealerships throughout country as a way of engaging with the public and publicising the services we provide.

Transport for All

web www.transportforall.org.uk/

Transport for All provides specialised advice, information, advocacy and training to both service users and providers of accessible transport in London. The organisation can help with all your general enquiries regarding accessible transport in the capital and are contacted every day about service information, complaints, appeals and application assistance.

They have also published a comprehensive 48 page booklet containing information, contact numbers and helpful tips about all of London's Transport services and travel schemes.

OpenBritain | Getting there... and back | Air travel

Air travel

Since July 2007 it is illegal for an airline, travel agent or tour operator in Europe to refuse a booking on the grounds of disability or to refuse to embark a disabled person who has a valid ticket and reservation under EC Regulation 1107/206. In Britain, the rules mean that anyone who has been refused boarding on the grounds of disability or reduced mobility may complain to the Commission on Equalities and Human Rights (CEHR). The Commission will advise them and could refer the matter to the Civil Aviation Authority (CAA), which has the power to prosecute. An airline could face an unlimited fine if found guilty.

371	Safety and security
371	Minimum requirements
372	General air enquiries
373	Airports
388	Fear of flying

Airports are required to organise the provision of services required by disabled passengers to board, disembark and transit between flights, with the airlines providing those services on board the aircraft. Airports may provide the services or contract them out. Passengers should not be charged for such services. Procedures must be in place to ensure information is gathered and exchanged so that the smooth operation of the service to passengers and all staff dealing directly with travellers should receive disability awareness and equality training.

Top tip

- Book assistance in advance: With air travel, more organisations may be involved than with other forms of transport, particularly if the flight is by charter aircraft as part of a holiday package. There can be failures in the communication chain; it is advisable to check that appropriate messages have been passed on and to emphasise the importance of the requests.

Safety and security

Airlines have to ensure that passengers understand the emergency instructions given at take-off. Accompanied passengers with sensory impairments or learning disabilities are asked to make themselves known, although they may consider that they do not need any particular assistance. Airlines may choose not to provide any particular safety instruction services, such as large print information or sub-titled videos.

Security enhancements - Anyone leaving a vehicle unattended outside a terminal should expect it to be removed. At some airports disabled people are helped into the building by a short free-parking period at the nearest car park. Wheelchair users/other disabled people obviously can not go through the regular metal detectors and can ask to be searched in private. Security staff are instructed to take particular care in re-packaging any luggage belonging to visually impaired people whom they search. A form of certification, such as a passport or driving licence is required for domestic flights.

Medicine and injections - Any medicines should be carried in hand luggage and contained in their original packaging. It is advisable to have a note saying what these medicines are, both to satisfy security personnel and to obtain further supplies if anything goes wrong. Despite the general ban on sharp objects, people who require injections must have a letter explaining the medical need for it, usually from their doctor.

Heightened security - At times of heightened security, additional restrictions may be imposed, relating to the use of private cars and even taxis in the area around airport terminals and on what may be taken onto aircraft.

Minimum requirements

The minimum requirements for assistance are laid down in the EC regulation; see Access to Air Travel for Disabled Persons and Persons with Reduced Mobility – Code of Practice 2008. This takes account of matters such as the wider definition of disability in the Disability Discrimination Act than in the regulation, although the regulation does include people with a temporary impairment.

Depending on the airline and the size of the aircraft, there may be an on-board wheelchair for transport to the seat, and it may be possible to request a seat in a particular area. The seats behind emergency exits, which have more space, will be allocated to people who are perceived as having the dexterity and strength to open the doors if necessary.

Most pieces of equipment are carried free of charge. Larger items, including wheelchairs, are carried in the hold. Smaller items, such as sticks and crutches, can be taken into the cabin, although will have to be stowed away. Check with the airline on any equipment, particularly if it may be required during the flight. Some airlines impose a weight limit on equipment that can be loaded into their hold.

DPTAC

The Disabled Persons Transport Advisory Committee (DPTAC) is an independent organisation; meetings are usually held in London. www.dptac.gov.uk explains the activities of its working groups, and focuses on air travel, buses, ferries, motoring, rail, taxis and walking. DPTAC has a travel guide for disabled people – 'Door to Door'.

Contact DPTAC, Great Minster House, 76 Marsham Street, London SW1P 4DR
t 020 7944 8011   e dptac@dft.gsi.co.uk

General air enquiries

Holiday Taxis

1st Floor Martlet Heights' 49 The Martlets,
Burgess Hill, West Sussex RH15 9NN
t 0870 444 1880   textphone info@holidaytaxis.com
web www.holidaytaxis.com

Holiday Taxis arrange for its clients to be transferred between the airport and their hotel. This avoids the need to use transfer buses, find car hire offices, etc while also dealing with luggage. The service is available at airports serving a large number of cities and resorts in Europe, USA, the Caribbean, North Africa and the Middle East.

A wide range of vehicles are offered, from a standard saloon car taxi for up to 4 passengers, to people-carriers and minibuses and coaches for larger groups. At about 25 destinations, mainly in Europe, there are vehicles that have been adapted for wheelchair users. Individuals or travel agents and tour operators can make bookings.

Aetas Services

141 boulevard MacDonald 75019 Paris
t +33 (0)1 30 53 69 97
web www.aetas.fr

Aetas have vehicles that can carry wheelchair users and other disabled people on transfers to and from Paris airports and rail stations within the Paris region and the rest of France.

Air Transport Users Council

CAA House, 45-59 Kingsway, London WC2B 6TE
t 020 7240 6061
web www.caa.co.uk/auc

The AUC is the consumer council for passengers of the British aviation industry. It is funded through the Civil Aviation Authority with an independent council and secretariat. It can take up complaints against airlines and airports when customers' previous written complaints have not been satisfactorily dealt with and offer advice in other cases. There is advice on many matters relating to air travel on the website.

Aviatours Ltd

Eglinton Road, Rushmoor, Farnham GU10 2DH
t 01252 793250   e fearofflying@aviatours.co.u
web www.aviatours.co.uk

ResortHoppa.com

Oakfield House, Small Heath Business Park,
Talbot Way, Birmingham B10 0HJ
t 0871 855 0350   web www.resorthoppa.com

ResortHoppa provides pre-booked transfers between airports and popular holiday destinations in Europe and beyond. These may be through shuttle services, often using coaches and minibuses, or private transfers by car or larger vehicles depending on the size of the booking. Folded, manual wheelchairs are carried without extra charge for passengers who transfer to a standard seat.

OPENBRITAIN.NET

The one-stop-shop for all your travel needs.
Go online and see how we can help you get in, out ...and about.

- Fully searchable database of accommodation, days out and where to eat and drink
- MyOpenBritain trip planner   • User reviews, blogs and forums

Airports

In the past at most British airports, airlines have been responsible for any assistance required by disabled passengers from the check-in desk on departure and to baggage reclaim on arrival. This has now changed as a result of European Union regulation (EC) 1107/2006 so that the airline is only responsible for services on the aircraft with the airport being required to ensure that assistance as far as boarding and from disembarkation. Airports can contract out the provision of assistance, perhaps to airlines, and should establish procedures to ensure that advance requests and information are passed on smoothly to those involved. At the time of writing few Airports have published their revised arrangements.

Aberdeen Airport

Dyce, Aberdeen AB1 7DU
t **0844 481 6666**   textphone **0141 585 6161**
web **www.aberdeenairport.com**

By Road - Aberdeen Airport is 7 miles north of the city centre off the A96. It has scheduled services to around 35 domestic and European destinations.

Parking - There are parking spaces for Blue Badge holders in the short-stay car park close to a telephone help point for people who need assistance in getting to the terminal. There are also bays for disabled motorists in the long-stay park close to the Customer Service office. The buses between there and the terminal are accessible to wheelchair users. For assistance, information or if you need to take your Blue Badge with you for use elsewhere call **0844 335 1000**.

By Public Transport - The nearest rail station to the airport is Dyce, a short taxi ride away, which is used by trains between Aberdeen and Inverness. There are regular bus services into central Aberdeen, some using low-floor vehicles. Information can be obtained from Stagecoach Bluebird on **01224 212266** or First Bus on **01224 650565**. Wheelchair accessible cars can be ordered from Comcab by calling **01224 725728**, booking office **01224 775555**.

Accessiblity - The terminal is accessible with toilets for disabled people in both landside and airside areas. There are help points for requesting assistance on the terminal forecourt, in baggage reclaim and at a number of places ▶ around the terminal. There are reserved seating areas for passengers with special needs and induction loops have been installed and are signposted.

Assistance for disabled passengers through the airport and on and off the aircraft is provided by G4S. It is requested that any assistance is requested at least 48 hours before flying, and preferably as far in advance as possible. Therefore in addition to contacting the airline of your requirements, it is suggested that you separately contact G4S on **01224 725767**.

Belfast City George Best Airport

Airport Road, Belfast BT3 9JH
t **028 9093 9093**
web **www.belfastcityairport.com**

By Road - Belfast City Airport has scheduled services mainly to other airports in Britain and Ireland.

Parking - There are spaces designated for disabled motorists in the short-stay car park near the Terminal entrance. These are available at the long-term rate by paying at the Information Desk. A telephone for requesting assistance is located in the car park.

By Public Transport - It is about 5km east of Belfast city centre off the A2. A shuttle bus service runs between the Airport Terminal and Sydenham Rail Halt for rail services to destinations elsewhere in Ireland. There is an express Airlink bus service between the airport and the Belfast Europa Bus Station at 20 minute intervals during the day and also regular services between Sydenham and the city centre. There are also regular Airporter coach services between the airport and Londonderry. Wheelchair accessible taxis are available on the rank.

Accessiblity - All areas of the Terminal are accessible with a lift between the floors, toilets for disabled people at each level and lowered counters at the Information Desk and other public enquiry points. Induction loops are installed at check-in areas and the Information Desk, where there is also a textphone. A public BT Textphone that can send emails is also available. An alerter linked to the fire alarm can be obtained from the Information Desk by deaf and hard-of-hearing travellers. A number of staff members are trained to basic sign language level. An excrcise area for assistance dogs is available outside the terminal.
An Ambulift is available for boarding the aircraft.

Belfast International Airport

Belfast, BT29 4AB
t 028 9448 4848
e infodesk@bfs.aero
web www.belfastairport.com

By Road - Belfast International Airport is near Antrim 18 miles north-west of Belfast city centre. It has scheduled flights to destinations in Britain, Europe and North America and also a number of chartered services.

Parking - There is an area for passengers to be set down outside the terminal. When picking up people drivers should use the 10-minute free period in the short-stay car park and collect passengers from the Meeting Point. There are also medium and long-term car parks on site with an accessible bus between the long-stay car park and the terminal entrance.

To pre-book or get information in long-stay parking call Q-park 0870 195 9689 or see www.qparkni.com.

By Public Transport - The frequent Airport Express coach service, using a low floor vehicle, between the airport and central Belfast is operated by Ulsterbus. For information on onward connections by bus or rail and also local bus services contact **Translink** 028 9066 6630 or www.translink.co.uk. Coach services from the Airport to Derry, whether direct, through Omagh or via Coleraine are operated by **AirPorter 028 7126 9996**. For information in taxis contact **Belfast International Airport Taxi Company** on 028 9448 4353.

Accessiblity - The Terminal is on 2 floors with lifts between and with toilets in all areas. Assistance, including a porter service, can be requested from helpline telephones at the entrance and elsewhere in the building. The Information Desk has a low counter and low level; text telephones are available.

An Ambilift is available to airlines boarding or disembarking passengers with impaired mobility, which needs to be pre-booked.

Birmingham International Airport

Birmingham B26 3QJ
t 0844 576 6000
textphone 0121 767 8084
web www.bhx.co.uk

By Road - Birmingham International Airport has scheduled and chartered services to around 100 destinations in Europe, North America and the Middle East. It is located 8 miles east of central Birmingham and near M42 J6.

Parking - The Rapid Drop-Off parking area near the terminal can be used by Blue Badge holders for up to 30 minutes without charge, by taking their badge to the NCP Desk in Terminal One. There are spaces for disabled motorists in both long and short-stay car parks, which have call-for-assistance buttons at their entrances

By Public Transport - The airport is next to Birmingham International Station, from where there are direct services to many destinations around the country as well as frequent services to Birmingham New Street from where other connections can be made. The Air-Rail link between the airport and the station is accessible to disabled people and makes the transfer every 2 minutes. The airport has its own bus/coach station serving both long-distance National Express coaches and local bus services. Information on which of the latter use accessible buses can be obtained from **Network West Midlands 0121 200 2700**. Metered taxis that can carry a passenger in a wheelchair are available on the taxi rank. Information on these can be obtained on **0121 782 3744**.

Accessiblity - The terminal building is accessible with lifts between floors and toilets for disabled people in all areas. There is a Textphone at the Terminal 1 Information Desk and staff who can use sign language both there and at the Special Assistance Reception Desk on the ground floor of Terminal 1. Deaf Alerters, linked to the fire alarm, are also available. Wheelchairs are available and anyone needing assistance to get to check-in should call **0121 767 7878** or Textphone **0121 767 8084**.

Wheelchairs and a special lift to help with boarding are available.

Blackpool International Airport

Squires Gate Lane, Blackpool FY4 2QY
t 0871 855 6868
e info@blackpoolairport.com
web www.blackpoolinternational.com.

By Road - The airport is close to the end of the M55 north of Blackpool town centre. It has flights to over 25 destinations in Britain, Ireland and Southern Europe.

Parking - There is a set-down and pick-up point in front of the terminal and both short and long- stay car parks are nearby.

By Public Transport - Taxis and nearby local buses provide a service into town and the nearby Squires Gate Station has an hourly rail service to Preston.

Accessiblity - The terminal building, which was extended and modernised in 2006, is accessible and has lowered check-in desks and pay phones and toilets for disabled people in all areas. A mobile lift is available for boarding.

Bournemouth International Airport

Christchurch BH23 6SE
t 01202 364000
web www.bournemouthairport.com

By Road - Bournemouth Airport is 6 miles north east of Bournemouth and signposted from the A338 and the A31. It handles both scheduled and holiday flights to an increasing number of destinations.

Parking - There are parking spaces for disabled motorists in Car Park 1 opposite the terminal and also a set-down/pick-up area. Assistance can be provided to and from the long-stay car park.

By Public Transport - The Bournemouth Airport Shuttle operates at hourly intervals using buses with a space for a passenger in a wheelchair and a low-level floor. Contact **Discover Dorset 01202 557007**. www.bournemouth-airport-shuttle.co.uk. Buses stop at Bournemouth Travel Interchange for passengers using South West Trains, Southern and CrossCountry rail services. Taxis to and from the airport can be booked from **United Taxis 01202 556677**. ▶

▶ **Accessiblity** - The terminal is single storey with automatic doors. The Information Desk is just inside the entrance and from there staff can provide assistance or a wheelchair if required. Toilets for disabled people are located in the main terminal and the Arrivals Hall; there are wide aisles in shops and restaurants.

A lift and ambulance chairs are available for boarding and exiting. In bad weather wheelchair capes are available for crossing to the aircraft.

Bristol International Airport

Bristol BS48 3DY
t 0870 121 2747
textphone 01275 473670
e specialassistance@bristolairport.co.uk
web www.bristolairport.co.uk

By Road - The airport is 8 miles south of central Bristol off the A38 and is among the most rapidly growing in the country.

Parking - Although cars cannot be left unattended beside the terminal, there is a pick-up area 100m from the Terminal. There are help buttons at car park barriers, which have designated bays for blue badge holders. Buses equipped with ramps are available for transfers from the long-stay car park.

By Public Transport - There is an express coach service between the Airport and Central Bristol including the bus station and Bristol Temple Meads railway station. Through tickets are available. This runs at 20-minute intervals but cannot carry passengers in wheelchairs. The taxi company serving the airport has minibuses adapted for disabled passengers. Contact **Checker Cars 01275 475000** or **bristol@checkercars.com**.

Accessiblity - The terminal has lifts between floors, Braille signs, special assistance points and toilets for disabled people. There is an induction loop and wheelchairs are available without charge.
To arrange assistance call the **OCS** Special Assistance Desk **0871 334 4444**.

Cardiff International Airport

Vale of Glamorgan CF62 3BD
t **01446 711111**
web **www.cwlfly.com**

By Road - The airport is on the outskirts of Rhoose, 12 miles west of Cardiff and 10 miles from M4 junction 33. It has scheduled flights to over 40 domestic and international destinations.

Parking - There are designated parking bays for disabled motorists in both the short and long-stay car parks close to call-for assistance points. There is a ramp from the short-stay/business car park to the terminal. For long-stay parking enquiries contact **NCP 01446 710 313**.

Places can be booked at discounted rates by pre-booking online. Passengers can be dropped off near the Terminal entrance and picked-up from the short-stay car park.

By Public Transport - Rhoose Cardiff International rail station has regular services to Cardiff Central and Bridgend. There is an accessible shuttle bus between the station and the airport that is free to people with a rail ticket. Express bus services that can carry passengers in wheelchairs run between the airport and central Cardiff, both non-stop and via Barry. Taxis are available and can be booked by calling **Checker Cars** on **01446 711474** or **cardiff@checkercars.com**.

Accessiblity - There are dropped kerbs at the entrances to the terminal, which has lifts to all floors. There are toilets for disabled people in all areas. The Information Desk has a Minicom and is equipped with an induction loop, which are also fitted at most check-in desks and other areas. Information is given visually on monitor screens and also by public address announcements. Wheelchairs are available and passengers can stay in their own wheelchairs up to boarding.

There is an assistance service to board aircraft and an Ambulift for those who cannot manage aircraft steps.

City of Derry Airport

Airport Road, Eglinton,
Co. Londonderry BT47 3GY
t **028 7181 0784**
web **www.cityofderryairport.com**

By Road - The airport is 7 miles north east of the city, off the A2 Londonderry-Coleraine main road. It has scheduled domestic services and also a number of chartered flights.

Parking - There are spaces for Blue Badge Holders in the car parks adjacent to the terminal and concessionary rates are available.

By Public Transport - Ulsterbus operates various services between the airport and the main Foyle Street Bus Station in the city centre for onward services by bus and rail. For information contact **Translink 028 9066 6630** or **www.translink.co.uk**. There is a taxi rank outside the temminal.

Accessiblity - There is a ramp into the terminal and all the passenger facilities are on the ground floor with toilets for disabled people off the main concourse and the departure lounge. An induction loop is installed.

Wheelchairs are available, and the airport has stairclimbers for use both by airlines to assist in loading and disembarking passengers and also for wheelchair users who may need to go to the first floor conference room or administrative offices. Advance booking for these is requested.

Coventry Airport

Siskin Parkway West, Coventry CV3 4PB
t **024 7630 8600** e **info@coventryairport.co.uk**
web **www.coventryairport.co.uk**

By Road - Coventry Airport is to the south-east of Coventry. In addition to holiday flights it has scheduled budget services to 14 overseas destinations.

Parking - Parking spaces for Blue Badge holders are available. These cannot be booked in advance. ▶

▶ **By Public Transport -** There is an hourly bus service between the airport and the city centre and Coventry railway station. This uses vehicles that can carry wheelchair users. For information see www.traveldecourcey.com. To book a taxi contact **Central Taxis 024 7633 3333.**

Accessiblity - The present small terminal has all public areas on the ground floor with an accessible entrance. An induction loop is available. For assistance or wheelchair loan book in advance or contact **Thompsonfly** Customer Services **024 7633 3333.**

Durham Tees Valley Airport

Darlington DL2 1LU
t **01325 332811** e **information@dtva.co.uk**
web **www.durhamteesvalleyairport.com**

By Road - Durham Tees Valley Airport is 10 miles east of Darlington on the A26.

Parking - There is a set down/pick-up area at the side of the terminal. Designated spaces for disabled motorists are located at the front of the main car park.

By Public Transport - There is a regular Sky Express bus link to Darlington Town Centre and Darlington Station, from where there are frequent rail services to Newcastle, York and elsewhere around the country. The Sky Express service is free to people flying from or to the airport; see **www.skyexpress.co.uk**. There are also local bus services. There is a taxi rank at the airport, for information call **07855 642947.**

Accessiblity - The terminal building was designed to be accessible to disabled passengers. There is an induction loop at the Information Desk.

Wheelchairs and an Ambulift are available and should be booked in advance.

East Midlands Airport

Castle Donington, Derby DE74 2SA
t **0871 919 9000** textphone **0845 108 8545**
web **www.eastmidlandsairport.com**

By Road - East Midlands Airport is between Derby, Leicester and Nottingham and close to the M1 Junctions 23a and 24. It has scheduled flights to many domestic, European and Mediterranean destinations and also handles chartered flights.

Parking - There are designated spaces for blue badge holders in the Short Stay Car Park where there are also help points connected to customer services staff. The long and medium stay car parks have accessible shuttle buses to the terminal. The Pick-up zone is situated at the terminal side of the short stay car park.

By Public Transport - At present the nearest rail stations are Loughborough (8 miles) and Long Eaton (5 miles), both served by East Midlands Trains. The new East Midlands Parkway Station is open a couple of miles away with regular shuttle buses to the airport. A regular express Skylink service, using wheelchair accessible buses runs between the airport and central Nottingham with connections with Nottingham Station and the NET tram system. There is also a half-hourly accessible Skylink service to Leicester. Local buses serve Derby, Long Eaton and Loughborough Stations and National Express coaches to towns in the Midlands and Yorkshire.

Accessiblity - The Terminal building is accessible, being mainly on the ground floor with a lift the 1st floor part of the Departure Lounge. First aid rooms can be used for medication if required. There are two lounges equipped for passengers needing assistance in the Departure area. Wheelchairs are available free of charge. A booklet 'Access: a guide for passengers with a disability' is available or can be downloaded from the website.

Become a member of OpenBritain today.
Share your own travel and accommodation experiences and help Britain become more open!

visit www.openbritain.net or call 01603 813740

OpenBritain | Getting there... and back | **Air travel**

Edinburgh Airport

Edinburgh, EH12 9DN
t **0844 481 8989**   textphone **0141 585 6161**
e **baascotlandmediacentre@baa.com**
web **www.edinburghairport.com**

By Road - Edinburgh Airport is west of the city, off the A8. It is used by over 40 airlines flying to around 90 destinations. The airport has direct flights to 25 different foreign countries. The first phase of a new £40m departure lounge is planned to open in November 2009; £240m is being invested in developing the airport over the next 10 years.

Parking - Blue Badge holders can use the designated bays in the multi-storey short-stay car park free for 15 minutes for set-down/pick-up purposes. This is linked to the terminal by a covered walkway. Both short and long-stay car parks have designated spaces and help buttons. People wishing to take their Blue Badge for use elsewhere should contact the car park operator via the help button or by visiting the customer services points. For further information on parking t **0844 335 1000**.

By Public Transport - The 100 express Airlink bus service, which uses wheelchair accessible buses, connects the airport with central Edinburgh including Edinburgh Waverley Station for onward journeys by First Scotrail and National Express East Coast. There are plans for both direct rail and tram links to the airport. Airlink also stops at Haymarket Station for some local services. For further information contact Lothian Buses t **0131 555 6363**,
e **mail@lothianbuses.com** or got to **www.flybybus.com**. There is also an Airdirect service, again using easy access buses, between the airport and Inverkeithing Station in Fife providing a more direct transport link to the East of Scotland. Accessible taxis are usually available on the airport taxi rank. Information on taxis can be obtained from Executive Onward Travel t **0131 333 2255**.

Accessiblity - The terminal building is accessible with reserved seating areas for disabled passengers and others with special requirements and toilets for disabled people in all areas. All payphones can be used by hearing aid users and there is a Textphone in the international arrivals area. In addition to the car parks there are help points in the coach station taxi ranks and several places within the Terminal. ▶

▶ Assistance for disabled passengers through the airport and on and off the aircraft is provided by THS. It is requested that any assistance is requested at least 48 hours before flying, and preferably as far in advance as possible. In addition to contacting the airline concerning your requirements, it is suggested that you separately contact THS on t **0131 344 3449**.

Exeter International Airport

Exeter EX5 2BD
t **01392 367433**
web **www.exeter-airport.co.uk**

By Road - The airport is east of Exeter off the A30 near M5 junction 29. Vehicles using the drop-off area must be attended at all times.

Parking - Designated bays for Blue Badge holders are located near the pay station in the short-stay car park 1, from where assistance can be called for transfer into the terminal. Car park 2 is for car rental/return, disability and Blue Badge spaces, charged at standard rate.
There are also designated spaces by the Shuttle Bus Shelter in car parks 3 and 4. Pre-booking discount of 30% if booking online.

By Public Transport - There are bus services that normally use low-floor buses, during the day between the airport and Exeter St Davids Station for First Great Western and South West Trains services. Call the taxi operator at the airport, Corporate Cars **01392 362000** for information or booking.

Accessiblity - The entrances to the terminal buildings are ramped and have automatic doors. The information desks are equipped with induction loops and information sheets in Braille are available at check-in and security areas. Deaf or hard of hearing passengers should make themselves known so that they can be alerted to announcements. Assistance, including wheelchair loan if required, can be provided to the boarding gate and between the aircraft and final point of departure from the airport.

Low-floor coaches with ramps are used between the terminal and the aircraft and an Ambulift, which must be booked in advance through the airline, is available for people who would have difficulty with the aircraft steps.

Glasgow Airport

Paisley, PA3 2ST
t 0844 481 5555   textphone 01224 725082
web www.glasgowairport.com

By Road - Glasgow Airport is to the west of Glasgow, near Paisley, off the M8, junction 28. It is the busiest airport in Scotland, handling services to 80 destinations by 40 airlines.

Parking - There is a drop-off/pick-up zone for Blue Badge holders on the ground floor of short-stay car park 2 giving 30 minutes free parking. Users should take their ticket and Blue Badge to the customer service desk in the car park for validation. There are spaces for Blue Badge holders in car parks 1, 2 and 3 close to the terminal. The multi-storey car park 2 has a height limit of 2 metres. People who wish to take their Blue Badge with them should contact the customer services office in car park 2. There are also reserved spaces for disabled motorists in the long-stay car parks and to ensure accessible transport to the terminal disabled people are advised to contact BAA information line on **0870 850 2825.**

By Public Transport - Paisley Gilmour Street railway station is 2 miles from the airport and has regular services to Glasgow Central. The bus service to the station is accessible. Arriva operate a regular Glasgow Flyer bus service into central Glasgow, including both main railway stations and Buchanan Street bus station. The Airport Link service serves other points in the city including Charing Cross bus station. These, and a number of other local bus services, use vehicles that can carry a passenger in a wheelchair. A direct rail link between the Airport and Glasgow Central Station is planned for completion by the end of 2010. Wheelchair-accessible taxis are available at the airport. Contact the warden controlling the taxi rank at the arrivals end of the terminal.

Accessiblity - The terminal building has reserved seating areas for disabled passengers on the ground floor and the International Departure Lounge, unisex toilets in most toilet areas and induction loops in marked areas. Help points are located in car parks, outside the terminal, in the T2 check-in area and the baggage reclaim hall. A public text phone is located in the 1st floor shopping area. ▶

▶ Assistance for disabled passengers through the airport, including to and from car parks, and on and off the aircraft is provided by THS (Scotland). It is requested that any assistance is requested at least 48 hours before flying, and preferably as far in advance as possible. Therefore, in addition to contacting the airline of your requirements, it is suggested that you separately contact THS on **0141 842 7700** or **info@thsscotland.co.uk**.

Glasgow Prestwick Airport

Aviation House, Prestwick KA9 2PL
t 0871 223 0700
web www.gpia.co.uk

By Road - Prestwick Airport, north of Ayr, is just over 30 miles south west of Glasgow. It handles scheduled services to 25 domestic and European destinations and chartered flights to 11 holiday destinations.

Parking - It can be reached from the A77. Two short-term car parks are close to the Terminal entrance, both with designated bays for Blue Badge holders. Car park 1 is free of charge for the first 30 minutes on producing a valid Blue Badge at the car park information desk and should be used to set down and pick up passengers. Spaces in the medium and long-stay car parks can be booked 24 hours in advance (**0871 2222 883**) and are linked to the terminal by accessible shuttle bus.

By Public Transport - Prestwick Airport Station has regular half-hourly train services (hourly on Sundays) from Glasgow Central Station. The station has a lift to each platform, a unisex toilet and is linked to the Terminal by a covered walkway. Discounted fares are available from any First ScotRail Station. There are also express bus services to Glasgow Buchanan Street Bus Station. Taxis, of various sizes, serving the airport can carry wheelchair users. Contact **Ayr Black Cabs 01292 284545/471600** or **ayrblackcabs@aol.com**.

Accessiblity - The Terminal is accessible with a lift between the ground and upper floors and toilets for disabled people on the ground floor and in departure lounges. A stairlift provides access to the Aviator Suite.

Wheelchairs are available. Staff assist disabled passengers who are pre-boarded, without charge.

Guernsey Airport

La Falaize, Forest, Guernsey GY8 0DS
t 01481 237766   e airport@gov.gg
web www.guernsey-airport.gov.gg

By Road - Guernsey Airport is in the south of the island, 4 miles from St Peter Port. There are scheduled inter-island flights and also services to destinations in England, France, Germany and the Netherlands.

Parking - There are designated spaces for disabled motorists in the car park and a set down/pick up point for blue badge holders by the Terminal entrance.

By Public Transport - The regular Island Coastway bus service between the Airport and St Peter Port can carry passengers in wheelchairs and accessible vehicles are used on some other services around Guernsey.
Taxis that can carry folded wheelchairs can be pre-booked, **01481 244444**.

Accessiblity - All areas of the Terminal, which opened in 2004, are accessible to wheelchair users. There are toilets for disabled people in both the main concourse and the arrivals hall.

A hoist for boarding is provided by Flybe. Other passengers unable to manage aircraft steps may have to be carried.

Highlands & Islands Airports Ltd

Inverness Airport, Inverness IV2 7JB
t 01667 462455   web www.hial.co.uk

By Road - HIAL, owned by Ministers in the Scottish Government, operates 11 airports providing commercial, tourist and emergency air services in northern Scotland. HIAL Airports are Inverness (see below), Sumburgh in Shetland, Kirkwall, Wick, Stornoway, Benbecula, Barra (the world's only beach airport with scheduled services), Tiree, Islay, Campbelltown and Dundee.

Accessiblity - Facilities at the smaller airports are not extensive but all have basically accessible terminals and most have Ambulifts for passengers who cannot use the steps to the aircraft. Information on each of these is available on the above website.

Humberside International Airport

Kirmington, North Lincolnshire DN39 6YH
t 01652 688456   web www.humbersideairport.com

By Road - Humberside Airport is between Scunthorpe and Grimsby off the A18, near the end of M180. It has scheduled flights to Amsterdam, for connections to many other destinations, and Aberdeen. There are also many charter flights to holiday destinations.

Parking - There are spaces designated for Blue Badge holders in the nearby short-stay car park with charges at standard rather than short- stay rates. There is a help point to call for assistance into the terminal. It is possible to book spaces in the long-stay car parks by calling **0871 360 2946**.

By Public Transport - An express coach service between Hull and Grimsby calls at the Airport from Monday to Saturday. The nearest rail station is Barnetby, 3 miles away, which has regular services to Doncaster for connections to other destinations. Taxis can be booked **01652 688132**.

Accessiblity - The public parts of the Terminal are on the ground floor and incorporate unisex toilets for disabled passengers in all area. A First Aid room is available.
An Ambulift is available for boarding and disembarking.

Inverness Airport

t 01667 464000   f 01667 462041
web www.hial.co.uk/inverness-airport

By Road - Inverness Airport has over 300 scheduled flights a week to airports throughout Britain. There are also a number of holiday charter flights.

Parking - The airport is 9 miles east of the city, situated just off the A96. The car park has designated parking bays for disabled motorists and there is also a designated set down/pick up point for disabled passengers at the entrance to the Terminal.

By Public Transport - There are regular bus services to the railway and bus stations in central Inverness using a low floor bus. The taxi company serving the airport (**Central Highland Taxis 01463 222222**) has vehicles that can carry passengers in wheelchairs. ▶

▶ **Accessiblity** - The terminal is single storey and smoke free. There are unisex toilets for disabled people. Assistance dogs can be exercised in the dog walk area. Anyone who may need assistance should contact the Airport Information Desk on **01667 464000**. An Ambulift and stairclimbers are available for the boarding and disembarkation of disabled passengers.

Isle of Man Airport

Ballasalla, Isle of Man IM9 2AS
t **01624 821600**   web **www.iom-airport.com**

By Road - Isle of Man (Ronaldsway) Airport is at the south of the Island near Castletown but less than an hour's drive from all points on the Island. There are currently 5 airlines flying between the Isle of Man and airports in Britain and Ireland.

Parking - There are designated spaces for Blue Badge holders in both the main and the long-stay car parks. There are also reserved spaces outside the terminal to set down or pick up disabled passengers.

By Public Transport - Bus services run between the airport and Douglas and other major towns. For information on low floor buses and on arrangements for disabled passengers on their railways, contact **Isle of Man Transport**, Banks Circus, Douglas IM1 5PT. **01624 662525**. **info@busandrail.dtl.gov.im** **www.iombusandrail.info**

Accessiblity - Within the terminal there is a lift to the first floor, toilets for disabled people, lowered pay phones and an induction loop for announcements. Vehicles to lift wheelchair users to the aircraft are available, the use of which is arranged through the airline.

Jersey Airport

St Peter, Jersey JE1 1BY
t **01534 446000**   e **information@jerseyairport.com**
web **www. jerseyairport.com**

By Road - The airport is located near the coast, west of St Helier and has flights to and from over 30 airports in Britain and Ireland.

Parking - There is a taxi rank and set down/pick up point outside the terminal. ▶

▶ **By Public Transport** - There is a regular bus service between the Airport and St Helier. Most of the public bus services on Jersey use vehicles that can carry a passenger in a wheelchair. Contact **Connex Transport Jersey 01534 877772**. **www.mybus.je**

Accessiblity - The terminal building is largely on the ground floor with a lift to the viewing gallery and restaurant. There are toilets for disabled people in the departure lounge and the arrivals area. Wheelchairs are available free of charge. Boarding and disembarking assistance can be provided with advanced notice through the airline.

Leeds Bradford International Airport

Leeds LS19 7TU
t **0871 288 2288**
web **www.lbia.co.uk**

By Road - The airport is 11 miles from central Leeds and 7 miles from Bradford, signposted from the M1, M62 and A1. It is the largest airport in the region with flights to 74 domestic and international destinations.

Parking - There are reserved spaces for Blue Badge holders in the short stay car park. Stays of over 24 hours in these can be charged at the pre-booked long stay rate to people who call **0113 391 3295** or contact the Information Desk as soon as possible. There is also an intercom to call for assistance if required.

By Public Transport - There are regular bus services, usually using low floor buses that can carry a passenger in a wheelchair, between the airport and mainline rail stations in Leeds and Bradford. For further information call **0113 245 7676** or see **www.wymetro.com**.

Leeds Airport Service provides a service between the airport terminal building and the long-stay car park.

The **Yorkair Coach** operates between the airport and York station, **01904 883000** or **www.yorkaircoach.com**. Joint rail/bus ticketing is available on these services.

Accessiblity - For wheelchairs and assistance contact Interserve **0113 391 1607**. An Ambulift is available for boarding and getting off the plane.

OpenBritain | Getting there... and back | Air travel

Liverpool John Lennon Airport

South Terminal, Liverpool L24 1YD
t **0870 129 8484**
web www.liverpoolairport.com

By Road - The airport is 7 miles south of central Liverpool at Speke and signposted from the M56, M57 and M62. It has scheduled services to over 50 destinations in Britain and Europe and also chartered holiday flights.

Parking - There is a set down/pick up area opposite the terminal and designated parking spaces for disabled motorists at the front of the short-stay and long-stay 1 car parks. Pre-book for discounts. There are no disabled parking bays within long-stay car park 2.

By Public Transport - There are regular bus services, using vehicles that can carry wheelchair users between the Airport and Liverpool South Parkway from where there are Merseyrail and Northern Rail services to central Liverpool and other destinations in the North West and the Midlands. From Lime Street Station there are main line connections. There are also other local bus services from the airport, including a night bus service into the City Centre. Mersey Travel has an information point for information about public transport in the area located in the Airport Tourist Information Centre. A taxi rank is located in front of the terminal by the arrivals area. For information about taxis at the airport contact **Mersey Cabs** on **0151 733 3393**.

Accessiblity - The terminal building is accessible and has toilets for disabled people and low level payphones.

Wheelchairs are available and there is an Ambulift for passengers unable to use the aircraft steps. These services should be requested when booking a flight.

London City Airport

Royal Docks, London E16 2PX
t **020 7646 0088** e **CSC1@londoncityairport.com**
web www.londoncityairport.com

By Road - London City Airport is 5 miles east of the City of London and 10 miles from the West End. It handles flights in comparatively small aircraft to 30 domestic and European destinations for predominately for business travellers.

Parking - There are designated spaces for disabled motorists in the car park close to the terminal. However, the long-term car park is not far away. A valet parking service is available which could be useful to some disabled people. There is no additional charge for this beyond the parking fee.

By Public Transport - A station on the accessible Docklands Light Railway is integrated into the terminal. This is served by trains from Bank and Canning Town where it connects with the Jubilee Line for accessible transfers to London Bridge, Waterloo and Stratford rail stations. The DLR line continues south of the Thames to Woolwich. Local buses that can carry wheelchair users stop near the airport and there is a taxi rank where accessible cabs can be obtained.

Accessiblity - The terminal has toilets for disabled people, a first-aid room and a lift from the concourse to the departure lounge and to the apron for boarding.

For assistance when passing through the airport or boarding and disembarking, contact Customer Services **020 7646 0000** or **cssupervisor@londoncityairport.com**.

OPENBRITAIN.NET

The one-stop-shop for all your travel needs.
Go online and see how we can help you get in, out ...and about.
Fully searchable database of accommodation, days out and where to eat and drink

London Gatwick Airport

Gatwick, West Sussex RH6 0NP
t **0844 335 1802**
textphone **01293 513179**
web **www.gatwickairport.com**

By Road - Gatwick, the second busiest airport in UK, is 28 miles south of London off the M23 junction 9.

Parking - For the South Terminal there is a set down area on the Lower Forecourt including an area specifically for disabled people. The Orange Short-stay car park 3 is now the dedicated area for passengers being picked up. There are spaces for Blue Badge holders in the short-stay multi-storey car parks beside each of the terminals. These are near help points and signposted accessible routes into the terminal. They are subject to a height limit of 2 metres but there is a parking area for higher vehicles nearby. For information on both short and long-term parking call **0844 335 1000**.

Travel-Care Gatwick is an independent agency, with charitable status, offering assistance to anyone at the airport who has a problem. It is located in The Village, South Terminal and is open during office hours 7 days a week. **01293 504283**.

Help-me-Park offers a meet and greet parking service at both Gatwick Terminals avoiding the need for disabled members of a family to be dropped off or having to hang around while another member of the party parks the car or the use of transfer coaches. They can be contacted via **0870 300 6009** or **www.help-me-park.com**.

By Public Transport - Gatwick Station is immediately beside the South Terminal. In addition to the frequent non-stop services to London Victoria by Gatwick Express, there are also direct rail services to other London terminals and elsewhere in southern England. There are also CrossCountry services on a number of longer routes. The airport is well served by long-distance coach services although these cannot carry passengers in wheelchairs. Local bus services into Crawley do use accessible vehicles. **Checker Cars** operate taxis from Gatwick and can supply cars with swivel seats, contact **0800 747737**. **bookings@checkercars.com**. ▶

▶ **Accessiblity** - As with all multi terminal airports, it is important to make sure that you know which you will be using before setting out or making arrangements to be met. The South and North Terminals are linked by a frequent transit system that has level entrances and space for wheelchair users. The terminals have lifts or ramps for changes in level, toilets for disabled people near or in toilets blocks, reserved seating areas and induction loops. In addition to the short stay car parks and the railway and coach stations, help points are located on terminal forecourts, baggage reclaim halls and on some of the long pedestrian routes around the buildings.

Assistance for disabled passengers through the airport, including to and from car parks, and on and off the aircraft is provided by G4S. It is requested that any assistance is requested at least 48 hours before flying, and preferably as far in advance as possible. Therefore in addition to contacting the airline of your requirements, it is suggested that you separately contact **G4S** on **01293 505599**.

London Heathrow Airport

234 Bath Road, Hayes, UB3 5AP
t **0844 335 1801** textphone **020 8745 7950**
web **www.heathrowairport.com**

By Road - Heathrow, situated on the western edge of Greater London near the M4 and M25, has more international flights than any other airport in the world with 90 airlines serving 180 destinations in over 90 countries. It has 5 terminals with Terminals 1, 2 and 3 being grouped together in the centre of the airport, Terminal 4 on the southern edge and Terminal 5 at the west.

Parking - Short-stay car parks by each terminal have spaces for blue badge holders near routes into the terminal and help points where assistance can be called. People who wish to take their blue badge with them to notify the car park operator can also use the help points. The general height limit in multi-storey car parks is 2 meters. Higher cars than this can park on the ground floor of car park 3 for terminals 1, 2 & 3 or the roof of car park 4. There are also designated spaces in the business and long stay car parks for which the operators can provide information on the accessibility of their transfer arrangements. For other information on parking at Heathrow or for pre-booking call **0844 335 1000**. ▶

▶ **By Public Transport** - Heathrow is linked by train to Paddington in central London using the accessible, nonstop Heathrow Express service and also the Heathrow Connect service that also serves some stations in west London. Both go to Terminals 1, 2 and 3 with Heathrow Connect continuing to Terminal 4 while Heathrow Express goes to Terminal 5. There are also London Underground (Piccadilly Line) services to and from all terminals at the airport. Although the underground stations at Heathrow can be reached without using stairs or escalators the same is true of few other underground stations particularly in central London. For information call **020 7222 1234** or see **www.tfl.gov.uk**.

The central bus station at the airport is close to Terminals 1, 2 & 3 and is equipped with a help point for people needing assistance to get into the Terminal. Local bus services, long distance coach services and also the coaches linking with the rail network at Reading, Woking, Feltham and elsewhere use this. Many coach services also serve Terminals 4 and 5. Although most of the local bus services can carry passengers in wheelchairs, this is not yet a regular feature of coach services. Accessible taxis are available on taxi ranks.

The rail services can be used without charge to get between Terminal 4, Terminal 5 and Terminals 1, 2 & 3. An alternative is the Heathrow Help Bus, a free, accessible service for disabled passengers and those with heavy luggage. The bus serves all terminals and the central bus station and can be called from help points, the information desk or by phoning **020 8745 6261**.

Accessiblity - There are help points at the entrances to the terminals, in the baggage reclaim halls and along routes with long walking distances as well as in car parks and stations. Lifts and ramps are provided for changes of level. Most toilets blocks contain a unisex WC for disabled passengers. Induction loops have been installed at various points in the terminals and their locations are indicated. Text pay phones are sited in the arrivals area of each terminal. Airbridges between the terminal and the aircraft are used for most flights at Heathrow.

Assistance is provided for disabled passengers through the airport, including to and from car parks, and on and off the aircraft is provided. It is requested that any assistance is requested at least 48 hours before flying, and preferably as far in advance as possible. ▶

▶ Therefore in addition to contacting the airline of your requirements, it is suggested that you separately contact:

- Terminal 1 – Mitie on **020 8745 2165**
- Terminal 2 – Mitie on **020 8745 2195**
- Terminal 3 – OCS on **020 8745 2227**
- Terminal 4 – Mitie on **020 8745 2357**
- Terminal 5 – OCS on **020 3165 0285**

Terminal 5 opened in March 2008 and will handle British Airways flights. As this changeover is completed there will be changes to the Terminals used by other airlines and major developments in the existing area over forthcoming years.

Travel-Care Heathrow is an independent social work agency offering assistance to anyone at the airport who has a problem. It can be contacted on weekday office hours through help points or on **020 8745 7495**

London Luton Airport

Navigation House, Airport Way, Luton LU2 9LY
t **01582 405100** e **disabledfacilities@ltn.aero**
web **www.london-luton.com**

By Road - The airport is to the south of Luton town centre, two miles from M1 junction 10. It has scheduled flights to a large number of domestic, European and Mediterranean airports and also chartered flights to holiday destinations.

Parking - A set down and pick-up area is located near the terminal with a strictly enforced 10 minute time limit during which vehicles must be attended at all times. Cars with a Blue Badge can use spaces in the nearby short-term car park without charge for the first hour. There are designated parking bays for disabled people in all car parks with Special Assistance points in those for mid- and long-stay car parks, which also have accessible transfer buses to the terminal.

Parking places can be booked online in advance at a discounted rate. Users of powered wheelchairs should contact APCOA parking, which manages a variety of airport car parks, on **0845 303 7387** **www.apcoa.co.uk** ▶

▶ **By Public Transport** - The Hire Car Centre is accessible, has a Special Assistance Help Point and is served by an accessible shuttle bus from the terminal.

There is also a shuttle bus between the airport and Luton Parkway Station, which is served by Capital Connect and East Midlands trains to London and parts of South East England and the Midlands. Local buses and a range of longer distance coach services also serve the airport. Among these, the Green Line 757 Express route to and from Central London has some coaches that are equipped with lifts. At present passengers wishing to use this service are asked to give a day's notice so that the correct vehicles can be put into the schedule – www.greenline.co.uk.

Luton Taxis with a fleet of wheelchair accessible vehicles operates from the airport **01582 735555**.

Accessiblity - The Terminal has been rebuilt over recent years during which accessible features were incorporated. The large automatic revolving entrance doors can be slowed and two can be set open.

A Special Assistance Waiting Area is available for disabled people while cars are being parked or collected. Assistance telephones are located around the terminal and porters can give help or act as escorts to the check-in desks. Wheelchairs can be borrowed without charge from beside the entrance and near the checkout desks. Information points have lowered desks for wheelchair users and check-in desks and airport service counters are fitted with induction loops. There are toilets for disabled people in all main areas. There are covered walkways to the aircraft.

Boarding and disembarking are normally via steps to the aircraft. Aviance Care Assistants will pre-board disabled passengers using an Ambulift if appropriate. On return Aviance staff will escort disabled passengers as far as the baggage reclaim hall, after which free assistance, if required will be available from porters. A booklet, "Access and Facilities Guide for Customers with Disabilities", is available in normal or large print, on the website or on a CD – contact **01582 405100** or **disabledfacilities@ltn.aero** All general information leaflets can be obtained in large print.

London Stansted Airport

Enterprise House, Bassingbourne Road, Stansted, Essex CM24 1QW
t **0844 335 1803** textphone **01279 663725**
web **www.stanstedairport.com**

By Road - Stansted is Britain's 3rd busiest airport with flights to 160 destinations in 36 countries. It is located north of London and south of Cambridge off the M11, junctions 8 and 8A.

Parking - There are designated spaces for Blue Badge holders in all car parks, including the short-stay car parks close to the terminal. There are help buttons in the short-stay areas and at the bus shelters in the mid and long-stay car parks. Transfer buses can carry passengers in wheelchairs. Blue Badge holders wanting to take their badge with them should contact the car park operator on arrival. For further information or pre-booking **0844 355 1000**.

By Public Transport - Stansted Airport Station is directly under the terminal with lifts and escalators to the platforms. There are frequent Stansted Express train to London Liverpool Street and also stopping trains to London. There is also a regular service between Stansted and Birmingham with connections to other parts of the rail network at Cambridge, Peterborough and Leicester. At the time of writing few of the long-distance coach services to and from the airport can carry passengers in wheelchairs. Wheelchair accessible taxis can be booked from **Checker Cars 0800 747 737**.

Accessiblity - There are help points outside the terminal entrance doors for people needing assistance to check-in. The main areas of the terminal are on one level with lifts to the upper level catering outlets. There are toilets, some fitted with the National Key Scheme Lock, for disabled people in the main concourse and the departure lounge. Reserved seating areas have induction loops and low level flight information screens. Induction loops are also fitted in other areas and there are public text phones in the satellite two departure lounge and the international arrivals area. Most boarding gates are off satellites, which are reached by an accessible rail transit system. However, even using this the distances to travel can be quite long for many disabled people who do not usually use a wheelchair. ▶

▶ Assistance for disabled passengers through the airport, including to and from car parks, and on and off the aircraft is provided by Mitie. It is requested that any assistance is requested at least 48 hours before flying, and preferably as far in advance as possible. In addition individuals and groups who are unfamiliar with airport procedures can request an escort service either through security and the departure lounge to the aircraft or from the aircraft to the Arrivals area in the main terminal. This should be booked in advance by calling **Aviation Location Services** on **07715 171316**.

Manchester Airport

Manchester, M90 1QX
t **0871 271 0711** (general enquiries)
t **090 10 10 1000** (flight information)
t **0871 310 2200** (car park bookings)
web **www.manchesterairport.co.uk**

By Road - Manchester Airport is the UK's third largest airport and the busiest outside the London area with flights to over 200 destinations worldwide. It is located 10 miles south of central Manchester off the M56.

Parking - Cars cannot wait or be left unattended outside the Terminals although there are areas where passengers can be set down and picked up. The short-stay car parks near each terminal have bays reserved for blue badge holders near the lifts. There are also reserved spaces near the entrance or reception office of each of the long-stay car parks. However, disabled people can also make arrangements to keep their car in the short-stay parks at long-term rates by calling **0871 310 2200**. The same number should be used by people wishing to take their Blue Badge for use elsewhere.

By Public Transport - There is a transport interchange with lifts or ramps between levels for Manchester Airport's rail, bus and coach stations and covered walkways to each of the terminals. There are frequent rail services to Manchester Piccadilly Station and also direct services to destinations in northern and central England. Many Transpennine Express train routes terminate at Manchester Airport. Future plans include extending the Metronet tram service to the airport. National Express has wheelchair accessible coaches on the 538 route serving Manchester Airport from Scotland and the Midlands. ▶

▶ Information on local bus services, including those using accessible vehicles, can be obtained from GMPTE **0161 228 7811**. There are taxi ranks outside each Terminal and some of the taxis serving the airport can carry passengers in wheelchairs. For information call **0161 489 2313**.

Accessiblity - The Terminals are accessible with ramps or lifts for changes of level and toilets for disabled people in all areas. Assistance can be obtained by using the courtesy telephones by entrances and elsewhere. Customer Service Agents are available to assist passengers with hearing difficulties and additional voice announcements are made in areas where there are induction loops. However, this is a large and quite complex airport. All 3 Terminals have their own car parks. It is not necessary to pre-book parking.

Special vehicles are available to transfer passengers who are unable to walk between the terminal and the aircraft; contact the terminal manager.

Newcastle International Airport

Woolsington, Newcastle upon Tyne, NE13 8BZ
t **0871 882 1121**
textphone **0191 214 3333**
e **enquiries@newcastleinternational.co.uk**
web **www.newcastleinternational.co.uk**

By Road - Newcastle International is off the A1 north of Newcastle city centre. It acts as a regional airport with flights to almost 100 destinations by scheduled and chartered operators. An area to set down and pick up passengers is located at the front of the short-stay car park. There are designated parking bays for disabled people in both short and long-stay car parks with assistance points nearby. The shuttle bus to and from the long-stay car park can carry passengers in wheelchairs.

By Public Transport - The Tyne & Wear Metro system, which provides accessible connections to rail services at Newcastle Central Station, has a station at the airport terminal. There are also a number of local bus services. Airport Taxis are the only company that can use the taxi rank at the airport entrance. They have wheelchair accessible vehicles and operate both locally and for longer distances. Contact Airport Taxis **0191 214 6969** or see **www.airport-taxis.co.uk** ▶

▶ **Accessiblity** - The entrance to the terminals has large revolving doors that can be slowed down for disabled people. The Information Desk has a lowered counter. There are lifts between the ground floor to the 1st floor departure lounge, security area and departure gates. Toilets for disabled people are on both levels.

For passengers who use or require a wheelchair, assistance will be provided by the airport's airside operations or community service teams and will be taken through security and on to the aircraft and on their return to Newcastle. There is no charge for use of wheelchairs or cabin lifts for boarding, but it should be noted that the latter have no space for more than one person accompanying a disabled person. For information about services for disabled passengers at the airport call **0871 882 1121.**

Norwich International Airport

Amsterdam Way, Norwich NR6 6JA
t **01603 420653** web **www.norwichairport.co.uk**

By Road - The airport is to the north of Norwich off the A140 and handles domestic and international flights, both schedules and chartered.

Parking - Both long and short-stay car parks are close to the terminal and there are designated bays for disabled people opposite the entrance. For information contact **NCP** on **0845 050 7080**.

By Public Transport - Rail passengers should use local buses or taxis from Norwich Station. There is a taxi rank at the airport and information can be obtained from **Norwich Airport Taxis** on **01603 424 044**.

Accessiblity - The terminal building is single storey and has toilets for disabled people in the main concourse and the departure lounge. Assistance can be provided and advance notice is requested.

Robin Hood Airport Doncaster Sheffield

Heyford House, First Avenue, Doncaster DN9 3RH
t **0844 481 7777** web **www.robinhoodairport.com**

By Road - Robin Hood Airport Doncaster Sheffield is the UK's newest airport having opened in 2005. The airport currently offers both scheduled and holiday flights to over 35 worldwide destinations. ▶

▶ **Parking** - Robin Hood Airport is located just 7 miles from Doncaster and 25 miles from Sheffield and offers excellent access by road, rail and bus. The airport is located within 20 minutes of 5 major motorway networks including the A1(M), M1, M18, M62 and M180. Disabled passengers can park just yards from the terminal building in designated spaces for Blue Badge holders at the front of the main passenger car park.

By Public Transport - There is an hourly, dedicated bus service, the 707 Airport Arrow, between the Doncaster Transport Interchange and the airport that uses accessible buses; for further information call **01302 330330**. Through ticketing is available from any National Express East Coast rail station. For information and booking taxis call **01302 625555**.

Accessiblity - The terminal is mainly on the ground floor with a lift to the 1st floor catering and retail areas. The reception desk has an induction loop and there are toilets for disabled people in all areas. Wheelchairs are available. For assistance call **01302 625099**.

Southampton Airport

Southampton, SO18 2NL
t **0844 481 7777** textphone **023 8062 7032**
web **www.southamptonairport.com**

By Road - Southampton Airport offers flights by 14 airlines to 40 destinations. The Airport is north of Southampton near Eastleigh and the M3/M27 interchange.

Parking - There are designated spaces for Blue Badge holders in the main short-stay car park and disabled people wishing to take their badge with then should notify the car parks customer services office on the ground floor. Help Points are available for assistance with transferring luggage to the terminal or if the ticket payment slot is out of reach in the short-stay car park and also by the bus stop in the long-stay car park.

By Public Transport - Southampton Airport Parkway Station is immediately outside the airport and is also equipped with a Help Point for passengers needing assistance. There are frequent services to Southampton Central and London Waterloo stations and others on services operated by South West Trains. However, there is a footbridge to the northbound platform, for services towards London. Assistance with an alternative route may be provided. ▶

OpenBritain | Getting there... and back | Air travel

▶ The U1 bus service, which can carry passengers in wheelchairs, runs 4 times an hour from the airport via the University to central Southampton, including the main railway station and the Red Funnel ferry terminals for the Isle of Wight. This service is operated by UniLink **023 8059 5974**. Other bus services at the airport are by First Southampton **023 8022 4854**.

Accessiblity - The terminal is mainly single storey, with a lift to the upper floor departure lounge. Assistance can be requested at the information desk.

There are toilets for disabled people in the main concourse and the departure lounge. Reserved seating areas for disabled passengers have been provided. Induction loops are fitted in these areas and elsewhere in the terminal. Text payphones are available in the main concourse and the departure lounge.

Assistance for disabled passengers through the airport, including to and from car parks, and on and off the aircraft is provided by Aviance. It is requested that any assistance is requested at least 48 hours before flying, and preferably as far in advance as possible. Therefore in addition to contacting the airline of your requirements, it is suggested that you separately contact Aviance on **023 8062 7391**.

Southend Airport

Southend-on-Sea SS2 6YF
t 01702 608100
e enquiries@southendairport.net
web www.southendairport.net

By Road - London Southend Airport is located just north of Southend. At present it is used for scheduled services to Jersey and also some chartered flights.

Accessiblity - It has a single-storey terminal and assistance is provided for disabled passengers by Southend Handling 01702 608 150.

A major development for a new terminal and more extensive services is planned. There are plans for a new railway station on the line between Southend and London Liverpool Street to be completed by 2010. At present the nearest rail station is Rochford, a short taxi ride away. Flybe runs a weekly service to Jersey.

Fear of flying

A number of organisations run courses for people who are scared of flying. These include:

Aviatours Ltd

Eglinton Road, Rushmoor, Farnham GU10 2DH
t **01252 793250**   e **fearofflying@aviatours.co.uk**
web **www.aviatours.co.uk**

Virgin Atlantic Flying without Fear

PO Box 289, Betchworth RH3 7WX
t **01423 714900**   e **info@flyingwithoutfear.info**
web **www.flyingwithoutfear.info**

Virtual Aviation

Sheraton House, Castle Park, Cambridge CB3 0AX
t **01799 530105**   e **info@virtualaviation.co.uk**
web **www.virtualaviation.co.uk**

BROOK MILLER
MOBILITY LIMITED

KIA MOTORS
The Power to Surprise™

Brook Miller Mobility are more than just 'Motability Specialists', we are a company dedicated to providing solutions to a multitude of mobility problems. The company was built on foundations of customer care and professionalism.
We believe the service and products we offer are without equal, our customers seem to think so too as they come back time after time.

Talk to Brook Miller Mobility, you'll discover people that listen and a depth of understanding that can only be achieved through years of dedication.

Brook Miller Motability, our reputation means everything to us and a great deal more to you.

Kia Sedona Centro.
Long Floor Rear Access Wheelchair Vehicle

Kia Sedona Access.
Rear Access Wheelchair Vehicle

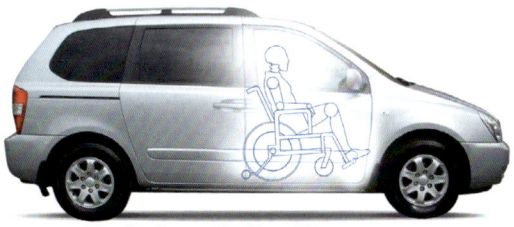

Kia Sedona Up Front Passenger:
Side Access

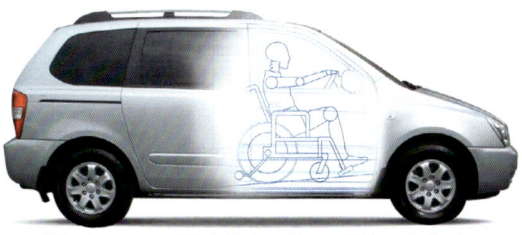

Kia Sedona Pilot: Drive From Wheelchair

FREE HOME DEMONSTRATION ON VEHICLES ANYWHERE IN THE UK MAINLAND

Unit 1A,
Elland Lane,
Elland, Halifax,
West Yorkshire,
HX5 9DZ

Motability

BROOK MILLER
MOBILITY LIMITED

FREEPHONE
0800 0644454
E-MAIL office@brookmiller.com

Opening Times:
Mon - Fri 9:00am - 5.30pm,
Sat 10:00am - 1:30pm

www.brookmiller.com

OpenBritain | Getting there... and back | Road travel

Road travel

Motoring

For many disabled people, motoring is the major means of independent mobility. General motoring organisations provide particular services for their disabled members and provide advice/assistance with route planning and insurance.

The Highways Agency is responsible for the motorways and major trunk roads in England and has duties in relation to construction and maintenance as well as safety and traffic management. Regional leaflets outlining planned road works, regional events likely to cause congestion and other news/advice are published quarterly.
Contact the Information Line t 0845 750 4030 or t 0102 335 8300
web www.highways.gov.uk

Information on main roads elsewhere in the UK is available from:
TrafficWatch N. Ireland t 0845 712 3321 web www.trafficwatchni.com
Traffic Scotland t 0800 028 1414 web www.trafficscotland.org
Traffic Wales t 0845 602 6020 web www.traffic-wales.com

Taxis

Information on companies and independent drivers with accessible vehicles should be available from local authorities. Two national websites with information on taxi companies with accessible vehicles are web www.transportdirect.info and web www.traintaxi.co.uk

391	Road travel in London
391	London taxis
391	Driving abroad
392	Door-to-door & community transport
392	Park and ride
392	Coaches
392	Bus services
394	Motoring organisations
394	Car hire (listings)
399	Coach travel (listings)
400	Coach hire (listings)

top tip

- The 100% London Congestion Charge discount applies to the person who is the Blue badge holder and not the vehicle that is being used.

390   HIGHWAYS AGENCY   www.highways.gov.uk

Road travel in London

Two particular factors affect disabled people using cars in central London:

On street parking - the Blue Badge Scheme does not apply in the City of London, Kensington & Chelsea, Westminster and the southern part of Camden. There are a limited number of marked parking spaces for Blue Badge holders and the badge may also be recognised for reserved bays in car parks. The location of Blue Badge spaces, car parks other useful information is shown in "Blue Badge Parking Guide" price £4.99 from bookshops or the publishers.
t 020 7952 0456 web www.thepieguide.com

An interactive map showing parking bays for Blue Badge holders in over 100 towns and cities and spaces on Red Routes in London as well as parking rules for all councils in the UK is at www.direct.gov.uk/bluebadgemap

Congestion Charge – disabled people's cars that are exempt from Vehicle Excise Duty are also exempt from the Central London Congestion Charge. Blue Badge holders can register for 100% discount from the charge. Registration takes 10 days to be administered and costs £10. The initial registration lasts for a year but can be renewed for free. It is possible to register both for long-term vehicles or those used on a short-term basis such as hire cars. t 0845 900 1234 web www.cclondon.com

London taxis

In London, which has a different system to the rest of the country, all licensed taxis must be able to carry a passenger in a standard wheelchair. All of the 'London black cabs' manufactured since 1989 must have space to carry a passenger in a manual wheelchair and carry or be equipped with a ramp. Computer Cab plc operates a booking service for taxis in the London area using wheelchair accessible black cabs. Their drivers have the necessary licence and experience with disabled people through their provision of services to disabled London Taxicard Users. Contact Computer Cab t **020 7908 0207** (cash bookings – there is a £2 booking fee); customer services t **020 7286 2728**
e **customerservices@comcab.co.uk;**
web **www.comcab.co.uk**; for information about international airport transport services go to www.cabchargeinternational.com

Car hire

For some journeys it may be appropriate to hire a car or other vehicle that has been adapted for a disable driver or that can carry a passenger in a wheelchair. There are organisations that include both major car hire companies with outlets throughout the country and elsewhere including ports, airports, major railway stations and also more specialist organisations.

See page 394 for listings.

Driving abroad

Advice is available from motoring organisations and at **www.fco.gov.uk**

The Blue Badge is recognised throughout most of Europe, giving British Blue Badge holders the same parking arrangements as local disabled people. However, the concessions vary from country to country. For more information contact the **Institute of Advanced Motorists, IAM House, 510 Chiswick High Road, London W4 5RG, www.iam.org.uk 020 8996 9600.**

OpenBritain | Getting there... and back | Road travel

Door-to-door and community transport

Special transport schemes exist in some localities for disabled people who are not able to use public transport. The principle is that a disabled person can phone to book an adapted vehicle to carry them on a specific door-to-door journey. More general Community Transport schemes exist where no other public transport is available, often but not exclusively in rural areas. Generally, community transport schemes use vehicles adapted to carry disabled people. The demand for such a service is always likely to exceed the resources available, so a variety of restrictions are likely to be in place – people may be limited to a number of journeys in any given period of time, journeys may be limited to a particular administrative area, for example. Essentially, all special transport schemes are locally run with their own priorities

Park and ride

These schemes usually provide secure parking areas on the approaches to towns with transport into the town centres, thereby avoiding some parking problems and reducing congestion. In many instances the transport provided is by accessible buses or other vehicles, for example trams. Information on Park and Ride schemes can be obtained from the appropriate local authorities;
web www.parkandride.net and www.transportdirect.info.

Coaches

Costs are generally lower than alternative means of transport. Coach stops in towns are often close to local transport services and are usually adjacent to passenger terminals at ports and airports. Drivers can provide some assistance and information when getting on and off, however finding information can be difficult.

Coaches are in general inaccessible for disabled people, particularly for wheelchair users and others with impaired mobility, due to the shallow steps and steep narrow entrances. A few operators have pioneered more accessible services, and from 2006 all new vehicles used for scheduled services have to capable of carrying disabled passengers.

The situation will improve, but it will be some time before all the existing vehicles have been replaced and staff trained. Coaches available for private hire or used on holidays are not covered even by the accessibility regulations for those on scheduled services. However, some coach companies do have adapted vehicles.
See page 399 for listings.

Bus services

Regulations have come into effect ensuring that all new buses are equipped with lifts or ramps with a level floor space to carry a passenger in a wheelchair, and incorporate features such as colour contrasted handrails, easy to operate bell-pushes etc. In London all general bus routes have been served with accessible buses since 2006, but elsewhere older vehicles may continue to be in use for years.

In some areas travel training is available to disabled people who may need assistance and encouragement to use accessible buses and other forms of public transport, for example the GMPTE in Greater Manchester
web www.gmpte.com has a travel Training Guide that can be downloaded. 'Coolmove' is a network of people involved with independent travel training
e info@coolmove.org.uk   web www.coolmove.org.uk

Freedom to explore....

bbnav
blue badge enhanced GPS navigation

BBNav is not only a great SatNav for all the family but is the first designed specifically to support the needs of disabled drivers and those caring for the disabled.

BBNav offers drivers detailed information about on-street disabled parking, including Blue Badge and red route parking bays, as well as colour coded mapping for local council rules for parking on yellow lines. Covers 150 major cities and towns across the UK including all of the London boroughs.

BBNav also includes over 20,000 Points of Interest to support people with disabilities including hotels with disabled facilities and Radar toilet locations.

Key features include:-

- Navigate directly to over 10,000 Blue Badge and Red Route parking bays
- Over 3,500 disabled accessible car parks
- On-map local council parking concessions
- Six months free safety camera alerts
- 4.3" wide touch screen
- Bluetooth hands free connectivity

**Available from Halfords and other selected high street stores
For more information please visit www.bbnav.co.uk**

Motoring organisations

AA

Norfolk House, Priestly Road, Basingstoke RG24 9NY
t 0870 5500 600   textphone 0870 243 2456
web www.theaa.com

Disabled Motorists' Federation

c/o 145 Knoulberry Road, Blackfell,
Washington NE37 1JN
t 0191 416 3172   e jkillick2214@yahoo.co.uk
web www.freewebs.com/dmfed

A grouping of local organisations of disabled motorists.

Green Flag Assistance

Cote Lane, Leeds LS28 5GF
t 0113 390 4000   web www.greenflag.com

Motability

Goodman House, Station Approach, Harlow CM20 2ET
t 0845 456 4566   textphone 01279 632213
web www.motability.co.uk

RAC Motoring Services

Great Park Road, Bradley Stoke, Bristol BS32 4QN
t 0870 572 2722   e info@citylink.co.uk
web www.rac.co.uk

The Mobilise Organisation

Ashwellthorpe, Norfolk NR16 1EX
t 01508 489449   e enquiries@mobilise.info
web www.mobilise.info

Mobilise, formed from a merger of the Disabled Drivers' Association and the Disabled Drivers Motor Club, can advise their members on a wide range of matters including concessions on ferries and tolls.

Car hire

Adapted Vehicle Hire Ltd

43-49 Gunnersbury Lane, Acton, London W3 8ED
t 0845 257 1670   e admin@avhldt.com
web www.avhltd.com

This company has a variety of vehicles for hire including those with adaptations and fittings for disabled drivers and that are accessible to wheelchair users.

Atlas Vehicle Conversions Ltd

3 Aysgarth Road, Waterlooville, Hampshire PO7 7UG
t 023 9226 5600   web www.avcltd.co.uk

In addition to selling adapted cars, Atlas has a number of accessible vehicles for hire including the Renault Kangoo, which can carry one passenger in a wheelchair and a minibus with removable seats that can carry up to two wheelchair users. Daily, weekly and monthly terms are available with special rates for weekends. Drivers must be over 25.

Autobility

Tower Garage, Main Road, Abernethy, Perth PH2 9JN
t 0800 298 9290   web www.autobility.co.uk

Autobility has cars and vans that can carry people in wheelchairs for hire on weekend, weekly and monthly rates. From it's base in Scotland this family-run company can arrange delivery throughout Britain and deliver vehicles to airports and rail stations. Used wheelchair accessible vehicles are available for sale.

Avis

Trident House, Station Road, Hayes UB3 4DJ
t 0844 581 0147   web www.avis.co.uk

Avis can fit Lynx hand controls to any automatic cars in its fleet. These controls are designed for people with good upper body function and hand dexterity. This service is available at all its UK rental locations with 48 hours notice.

Brotherwood Automobility

Lambert House, Pillar Box Lane, Beer Hackett, Sherborne, Dorset DT9 6QP
t 01935 872605   e sales@brotherwood.com
web www.brotherwood.com

Brotherwood has long experience of converting cars for wheelchair users and have a range of cars available for long or short term hire from it's premises in North Dorset.

Budget Rent-a-Car

Park Road, Bracknell RG12 2BW
t 0800 072 0644   e info@quotezone.co.uk
web www.budget.co.uk

Budget has Lynx hand controls that can be fitted to most automatic cars in its hire fleet. These are available with 48 hours notice from all their rental locations with advice and test drives available if required.

Hertz Rent-a-Car

700 Bath Rd, Cranford, Middlesex TW5 9SW
t 0870 844 8844 (Reservations)
web www.hertz.co.uk

Hertz can fit hand controls to cars from all its locations in the UK, most of those in North America and the main entry points in Western Europe for any length of hire and also for periods of 5 days or more in a number of other European countries. Advanced reservation of 48 hours for this service is required in Britain and 72 hours elsewhere.

Olympic (South) Ltd

153-157 Kingston Road, Wimbledon,
London SW19 1LJ
t 020 8543 9737   e admin@olympic-cars.co.uk
web www.olympic-cars.co.uk

OSL has a variety of vehicles for hire including wheelchair accessible vans and minibuses and drivers with wide experience of disability. These are available for outings and transfers to and from stations and airports in the London area.

Pyehire

Ovangle Road, Morcambe LA3 3PF
t 01524 598598   web www.pyemotors.co.uk

Pyehire has a range of self-drive accessible vehicles that can carry between 1 and 4 passengers in wheelchairs and 2-8 other people. These are available on daily or weekly hire.

Thorntrees Garage

Wigan Road, Leyland, Lancashire PR25 5SB
t 01772 622688   e vicki@thorntreesgarage.co.uk
web www.thorntreesgarage.co.uk

Cars and vans that can carry passengers in wheelchairs are available for hire for between 1 day and 6 months. Thorntrees Garage is near M6 J28 and the M61 and M65 or customers can be picked up from Preston mainline rail station from where there are direct services from many parts of the country including Manchester Airport.

Wheelchair Accessible Vehicles

Unit H4, Morton Park, Darlington DL1 4PH
t 01325 389900.
e hire@wheelchairaccessiblevehicles.co.uk
web www.wheelchairaccessiblevehicles.co.uk

This company has for hire a range of self-drive adapted vans that can carry wheelchair users. Delivery or collection from Darlington Station can be arranged at additional cost.

Wheelchair Travel

1 Johnston Green, Guildford GU2 9XS
t 01483 233640   e info@wheelchair-travel.co.uk
web www.wheelchairtravel.co.uk

Wheelchair Travel is a well-established self-drive rental company with wheelchair accessible cars and minibuses available for any period of domestic and continental use by both UK and non-UK licence holders. Minibuses have lifts, wheelchair securing points and seatbelts. Fiat Doblo cars can carry a wheelchair user, driver and 2 passengers. Cars with fixed hand controls are also available. Vehicles can be delivered to home, hotel or airport. A wheelchair taxi service using luxury adapted minibuses is also offered.

At Perrys we believe our Motability commitment and track record are second to none. And to give you even greater confidence to choose us to meet your needs we introduce...

PERRYS Motability
the one stop shop

Do you receive higher rate mobility allowance? If so you could exchange it for a new car right here

SOME MODELS AVAILABLE WITH NO ADVANCE PAYMENT

Taxed, insured, serviced and ready to drive away' it's all included

Trouble free motoring for everyone in receipt of the Mobility allowance, if you don't drive, you can nominate another driver.

Sound good? Then all you need to do is contact us and discover how Motability seamless motoring can benefit you.

WORRY-FREE MOTORING ASSURED

- Friendly and experienced Motability trained Specialists!
- Perrys proven track record with motability customers
- Automatic demonstrators available for test drives
- Trouble free, no stress Complete Aftersales Service at no extra cost!
- Disabled access to all our showrooms
- Excellent disabled parking facilities on site
- If you are a new to scheme customer we will also take your old car as Part Exchange!

Vauxhall Corsa & Astra from NIL ADVANCE

Citroën C1, C2 & C3 from NIL ADVANCE

Kia Picanto & Rio from NIL ADVANCE
KIA MOTORS — The Power to Surprise

Mazda 2 from NIL ADVANCE

Renault Clio & Twingo from NIL ADVANCE

Ford Fiesta, Fusion & Focus from NIL ADVANCE

Peugeot 107, 207 & 308 from NIL ADVANCE

Also covering the following other manufacturers:

SEAT auto emoción · FIAT · CHEVROLET · LAND ROVER · JAGUAR

Ask for our Motability specialist at any of our sites listed below

Perrys Rotherham Chevrolet 0845 293 9543	Perrys Rotherham Kia 0845 293 9577	Perrys Aylesbury Peugeot 0845 293 9561	Perrys Aylesbury Vauxhall 0845 293 9547
Perrys Huddersfield Citroen 0845 293 9544	Perrys Burnley Kia 0845 293 9579	Perrys Portsmouth Peugeot 0845 293 9562	Perrys Preston Vauxhall 0845 293 9572
Perrys Barnsley Citroen 0845 293 9545	Copley Land Rover 0845 293 9553	Perrys Bolton Peugeot 0845 293 9563	Perrys Leyland Vauxhall 0845 293 9573
Perrys Milton Keynes Citroen 0845 293 9560	Rocar Moores Land Rover 0845 293 9554	Perrys Blackburn Peugeot 0845 293 9564	Perrys Swinton Vauxhall 0845 293 9574
Perrys Aylesbury Commercial Centre 0845 293 9546	Luton Land Rover 0845 293 9555	Perrys Nelson Peugeot 0845 293 9565	Perrys Doncaster Vauxhall 0845 293 9575
Perrys Aylesbury Fiat 0845 293 9547	Perrys Preston Mazda 0845 293 9556	Perrys Clitheroe Peugeot 0845 293 9566	Perrys Barnsley Vauxhall 0845 293 9576
Perrys Portsmouth Fiat 0845 293 9548	Perrys Huddersfield Mazda 0845 293 9557	Perrys Aylesbury Renault 0845 293 9567	Perrys Rotherham Vauxhall 0845 293 9577
Perrys High Wycombe Ford 0845 293 9549	Perrys Blackburn Mazda 0845 293 9558	Perrys Aylesbury SEAT 0845 293 9568	Perrys Huddersfield Vauxhall 0845 293 9578
Perrys Aylesbury Ford 0845 293 9550	Perrys Barnsley Mazda 0845 293 9559	Perrys Broadstairs Vauxhall 0845 293 9569	Perrys Burnley Vauxhall 0845 293 9579
Perrys Huddersfield Jaguar 0845 293 9551	Perrys Portsmouth Mazda 0845 293 9562	Perrys Dover Vauxhall 0845 293 9570	Perrys Clitheroe Vauxhall 0845 293 9580
Perrys Preston Kia 0845 293 9552	Perrys Milton Keynes Peugeot 0845 293 9560	Perrys Canterbury Vauxhall 0845 293 9571	Perrys Colne Vauxhall 0845 293 9581
			Perrys Bury Vauxhall 0845 293 9582

www.PERRYS.co.uk/motability

Worry-free means everything is included

- Use your Mobility allowance
- Breakdown cover
- Road tax
- Insurance
- Servicing and maintenance
- Replacement tyres and windscreen
- 100,000 mileage allowance
- Specialist advice

WORRY-FREE MOTORING ASSURED

Motability
The leading car scheme for disabled people

www.motability.co.uk

Not sure if you qualify for a Motability car? Call 0800 953 4002

Expect more...

| RENAULT KANGOO | FIAT DOBLO | FIAT QUBO AUTOMATIC | RENAULT ESPACE |

Advanced payments from just £50

• New vehicles • Used vehicles • Car adaptations • Home demonstrations

Holden Mobility
Heigham Street, Norwich NR2 4TF

0845 612 6665
www.holdenmobility.co.uk

Coach travel

National Express

Ensign Court, 4 Vicarage Road, Birmingham B15 3ES
t 0871 781 8181 (bookings) or t 0121 423 8479 (disabled persons travel helpline)
textphone 0121 455 0086
web www.nationalexpress.com

National Express operates Britain's largest network of long distance coach services serving around 1000 destinations including city centres, small towns, airports and major ferry terminals. Folding wheelchairs can be carried and drivers can give some assistance on all services. Information on facilities for disabled people at National Express Coach Stations is available from the Helpline, on the website and in a booklet, "Serving our disabled customers". They are also the UK partner of Eurolines with services through Ireland and Continental Europe. National Express is introducing coaches equipped with a lift at the main entrance door and space for a passenger in a wheelchair. These also have less steep steps than previous models, no internal steps and a larger, though not wheelchair accessible toilet. These new vehicles are being rolled out across their network with the intention that they will become the norm by 2012.

At present accessible coaches are used for all or most services on the following routes:

240	Leeds-Sheffield-Coventry-Heathrow-Gatwick
314	Liverpool-Stoke-Birmingham-Coventry-Northampton-Bedford-Cambridge
333	Blackpool-Bolton-Manchester-Stoke-Bristol-Yeovil-Weymouth-Poole-Bournemouth
337	Coventry-Leamington-Stratford-Cheltenham-Bristol-Exeter-Torbay
341	Burnley-Blackburn-Bolton-Manchester-Birmingham-Weston-Exeter-Torquay
390	Hull Docks-Leeds-Manchester
403	Bath-Swindon-Chippenham-Heathrow-London
538	The Midlands-Manchester Airport-Manchester-Preston-Carlisle-Scotland
560	Barnsley-Sheffield-London
562	Hull-Doncaster-London
591	Edinburgh-Newcastle-London
737	Oxford-High Wycombe-Luton Airport-Stansted
767	Nottingham-Leicester-Luton Airport-Stansted

Goldline Translink

t 028 9066 6630   e marketing@translink.co.uk
textphone 028 9038 7505   web www.translink.co.uk

Megabus

Customer Services, Stagecoach in Perth, Inveralmond Industrial Estate, Perth PH1 3EE
t 0900 160 0900
web www.megabus.com

Megabus has a growing network of inter-city services using double deck buses, most of which radiate from London to around 40 cities. Wheelchairs cannot be carried.

Oxford Tube

Customer Services, Freepost SCE 15567, Oxford OX4 2RY
t 01865 772250
web www.oxfordtube.com

Oxford Tube has services at frequent intervals through the day, and at least hourly overnight, between Victoria in London and Gloucester Green in Oxford with additional stops in each city, one of which is at Thornhill Park & Ride on the outskirts of Oxford. All of their 25 vehicles can carry one passenger in a wheelchair and have easy access to the lower deck. Guide dogs are carried free of charge. Drivers can usually assist with luggage.

Scottish Citylink Coaches Ltd

Buchanan Bus Station, Killermont Street, Glasgow G2 3NP
t 0870 550 5050   e info@citylink.co.uk
web www.citylink.co.uk

Citylink is the largest network of inter-city coaches in Scotland serving some 200 destinations. Wheelchair accessible vehicles are in use on its regular service between Edinburgh and Glasgow. Scottish holders of the Entitlement Card for disabled and elderly people can travel free on Citylink services within Scotland.

Victoria Coach Station

164 Buckingham Palace Road, London SW1W 9TP
web www.victoriacoachstation.com or www.tfl.gov.uk

Passengers with impaired mobility can pre-book mobility assistance from the Mobility Lounge, t 020 7027 2520 for assistance on and off the coaches. This service is free, although if you require a porter for luggage, a payment may be expected. Customers can arrange to be set down or picked up by taxi, minicab or private car at the Mobility Lounge. There are toilets for disabled people in the Mobility Lounge and in Arrivals and Departures.

Coach hire

Belle Vue (Mancheser) Ltd

The Travel Centre, Discovery Park, Crossley Road Stockport SK4 5DZ
t 0161 947 9477 t 07790 270036 (emergency)
web www.bellevue-mcr.com

Britannia Coaches

Britannia House, Hollow Wood Road, Dover CT17 0UB
t 01304 228111 t 07968 570727 (emergency)
web www.britannia-coaches.co.uk

Bugler Coaches

29 Victoria Buildings, Lower Bristol Road, Bath BA2 3EH
t 01225 444 422 e info@buglercoaches.co.uk
web www.buglercoaches.co.uk

Caldew Coaches

6 Caldew Drive, Dalston, Carlisle CA5 7NS
t 01228 711690/710963
e caldewcoachesltd@aol.com
web www.caldewcoaches.co.uk

Chalfont Line

Chalfont House, 4 Providence Road, West Drayton Middlesex UB7 8HJ
t 01895 459540 web www.chalfont-line.co.uk

Community Transport Association UK

Highbank, Halton Street, Hyde, Cheshire SK14 2NY
t 0870 774 3586
web www.communitytransport.com

CTA UK gives advice and support on establishing and improving community transport schemes and provides training. Transport schemes for elderly and disabled people, including escorting people on public transport and providing volunteer drivers, are provided by a number of community organisations including British Red Cross and WRVS.

Coopers Tours

Aldred Close, Norwood Industrial Estate, Killamarsh, Sheffield S21 2JF
t 0114 248 2859 e specialtravel@cooperstours.co.uk
web www.cooperstours.co.uk

Copeland Tours

1005 Uttoxeter Road, Meir, Stoke on Trent ST3 6HE
t 01782 334466 e enquiry@copelandtours.co.uk
web www.copelandtours.co.uk

Cruisers Ltd

Unit M, Kingsfield Business Centre, Redhill, Surrey RH1 4DP
t 01737 770036 web www.cruisersltd.co.uk

Golden Stand Coaches (Southern)

13 Waxlow Road, London NW10 7NY
t 020 8961 9974 e info@goldenstand.co.uk
web www.goldenstand.co.uk

H C Chambers & Son

Chambers Bus Garage, High Street, Bures,
Suffolk CO8 5AB
t 01787 227233
web www.chamberscoaches.co.uk

Hatts Travel

Foxham, Chippenham, Wiltshire SN15 4NB
t 01249 740444   e info@hattstravel.co.uk
web www.hattstravel.co.uk

John Flanagan

2 Reddish Hall Cottages, Broad Lane, Grappenhall
Warrington WA4 3HA
t 01925 266115
web www.flanagancoaches.co.uk

London Hire

14 Dock Offices, Surrey Quays, Lower Road,
London SE16 2XU
t 0845 257 4257
e lauras@londonhireltd.com
web www.londonhireltd.com

MCT Group Travel

Nethan Street Depot, Nethan Street,
Motherwell ML1 3TF
t 01698 253091
e enquiries@mctgrouptravel.com
web www.mctgrouptravel.co.uk

Meridian Line Travel

Unit 2, Wireless Station Park, Chestnut Lane
Bassingbourne, Royston, Herts SG8 5JH
t 01763 241999
e meridianline@dial.pipex.com
web www.mltravel.co.uk

Reliance Travel

Unit 8, Norfolk Road, Gravesend, Kent DA12 2PS
t 01474 322002   e info@reliance-travel.co.uk
web www.reliance-travel.co.uk

Star Coaches of Batley

t 01924 477111   web www.star-coaches.com

Star Coaches of Batley private coach hire service in West Yorkshire covers a wide area through all the major towns and cities in Yorkshire and beyond.

Tellings Golden Miller

Building 16300 MTZ, Electra Avenue
London Heathrow Airport, Hounslow TW6 2DN
t 020 8757 4700   e info@tellings.co.uk
web www.tellingsgoldenmiller.co.uk

Translinc

Jarvis House, 157 Sadler Road, Lincoln LN6 3RS
t 01522 503400   e enquiries@translinc.co.uk
web www.translinc.co.uk

Travel De Courcey

Rowley Drive, Coventry CV3 4FG
t 024 7630 2656   web www.traveldecourcey.com

Making travel easier

HIGHWAYS AGENCY

The key to a safe and reliable car journey starts before you turn the ignition, explains Alison Beare from the Highways Agency.

A few minutes planning before you set off is time well spent. It can save you much more time and inconvenience in the long run.

As well as checking a map so you know where you're going, it's well worth checking the weather and traffic conditions – even if you're already familiar with the route.

Only ten percent of delays are caused by roadworks. The vast majority of frustrating hold-ups are caused by accidents or simply the sheer number of vehicles on the roads. That's why live traffic information has become so useful. With that knowledge you can allow the right amount of time for your journey – or change your plans if it's really bad.

Most of our network is free-flowing most of the time, but it never harms to check before you leave.

The Highways Agency website provides live updates from many thousands of traffic sensors and CCTV cameras. You can see how the traffic is flowing, what the signs are saying and even check the view from those cameras.

Our automatic phone system provides live updates or you can talk to a Highways Agency operator. Both these services can take calls from a textphone.

Travel information on the move

The traffic situation can change rapidly, especially at rush hour or during one of the holiday getaways, so keep listening to the car radio for bulletins. If you have a DAB digital radio you can check the Highways Agency's own station Traffic Radio too.

Warnings of delays and major incidents, plus travel time information and advice will be flashed up on the overhead message signs. And when you take a break, which you should do at least every two hours on a long journey, you can check our website from your mobile phone. (Remember it is illegal and dangerous to use a mobile while driving)

Highways Agency control centre

Useful information

Route planning: www.transportdirect.info

Live traffic information
for England: www.highways.gov.uk/traffic
London: www.tfl.gov.uk
Scotland: www.trafficscotland.org
Wales: www.traffic-wales.com
Northern Ireland: www.trafficwatchni.com

Phone lines:
Live traffic info: 08700 660 115*
All other calls: 08457 50 40 30*

My Way magazine

For more information for disabled road users call 08457 50 40 30 or visit www.highways.gov.uk/disability

* calls to 08457 and 08700 numbers can cost up to 8p/min from landlines, but are free from some providers. Mobiles usually cost more

Disabled Persons Railcard

£18 For a one-year Railcard

Get 1/3 off rail fares for you...

...and a companion...

Only £48 For a three-year Railcard

You qualify if you meet any one of the criteria below:

- ✓ You receive Attendance Allowance
- ✓ You receive Disability Living Allowance (at either the higher or lower rate for getting around or the higher or middle rate for personal care)
- ✓ You are registered as having a visual impairment
- ✓ You have epilepsy and have repeated attacks or are currently prohibited from driving because of epilepsy
- ✓ You are registered as deaf or use a hearing aid
- ✓ You receive severe disablement allowance
- ✓ You receive War Pensioner's Mobility Supplement for 80% or more disability
- ✓ You are buying or leasing a vehicle through the Motability scheme

To find out how to apply see the leaflet 'Rail Travel Made Easy' (available at stations) or contact us:

Web
www.disabledpersons-railcard.co.uk

Email
disability@atoc.org

Telephone
0845 605 0525

Textphone
0845 601 0132

Rail travel

The Trains

All newly-built trains that have come into service since 1998 must incorporate access features, including spaces for passengers travelling in manual wheelchairs, visible and audible information and appropriate toilet facilities. Many trains introduced before 1998 have some of these features, either inherently or following refurbishment. Some pre-1998 carriages will be used for the next 10 years or so.

The Stations

These often date from the Victorian era and represent the range of disability access levels. The process of adapting premises is lengthy and has concentrated on larger stations and those that were being modernised in any event. Many smaller stations rely on the approach to platforms by steps; however, an Access for All programme funded by the Department of Transport is underway and is due to provide step-free routes and other access improvements for more than 200 stations.

Mind the Gap!

A remaining potential problem is the gap or step that exists between the train and the platform. There are portable ramps at stations and on trains, although staff need to be available to place and remove the ramp as well as providing assistance when required. In spite of continuing improvements, the railway system still has problem areas and many disabled passengers will need help at some points of their journey.

405	Disabled person's railcard
405	Underground railways
405	Wheelchairs and powered scooters
406	General rail enquiries
406	Train operating companies
410	Light railways and trams

Top tips

- Book assistance: recommended 24 hours in advance. This allows the stations involved time to allocate appropriately trained staff and for them to check their equipment.

- Taxi assistance: TrainTaxi is a database providing information on the availability of taxis at rail, underground and tramsystems - **www.traintaxi.co.uk**

Disabled person's railcard

Some disabled people can get the Disabled Person's Railcard, which gives a third-off most rail fares for the cardholder and an adult companion. The qualifying criteria are:
- registered as visually impaired
- registered deaf
- have epilepsy, and are disabled by repeated attacks
- receipt of Attendance Allowance
- receipt of Disability Living Allowance (at either rate of the mobility component or the higher or middle level of the care component)
- receipt of Severe Disablement Allowance
- receipt of war or Service Disablement Pension for 80% or more disability
- buying or leasing a vehicle through Motability.

For further information on the railcard go to
web www.disabledpersons-railcard.co.uk or
t 0845 605 0525, textphone 0845 601 0132.

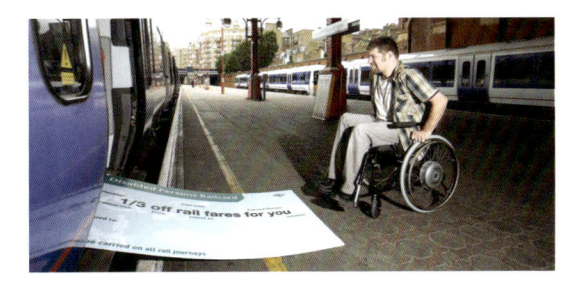

Underground railways

There are two long-established underground systems – London and Glasgow.

London – an increasing number of stations have a step-free access to platforms and there is a commitment that 25% of stations will have step-free access by 2010. Contact web www.tfl.gov.uk or for detailed information on each station go to web www.directenquiries.com

Glasgow – staff can assist disabled passengers who can manage the steps to the platforms. For information on each station for blind and partially sighted people go to web www.describe-online.com or t 0845 128 4025 or web www.spt.co.uk, t 0141 332 6811;
e enquiry@spt.co.uk

Wheelchairs and powered scooters

Most trains can accommodate wheelchairs that are up to 700mm wide and 1200mm long and that have a combined weight for the wheelchair and passenger of up to the safe working load of the portable ramp (between 230kg and 300kg).

However, scooters are of a far wider variety of sizes and weights. There can be problems caused by exceeding the safe load or tipping backwards on the ramp and being unable to manoeuvre safely inside the train. While many train companies accept scooters that are within the dimensions given above, there are some that only carry folded scooters or require the users to obtain a special pass. There have been some examples of rigidly restrictive rules being relaxed over the last year or so. However, at present anyone thinking of making a rail journey with a scooter should check on the policy of the train operator(s) involved.

Accessibility rail maps

National Rail has produced maps showing accessibility around Britain's rail network. For links and other information go to www.openbritain.net/openbritain/travel

OpenBritain | Getting there... and back | **Rail travel**

General rail enquiries

National Rail Enquiries

t 0845 748 49 50
textphone 0845 605 0600
web www.nationalrail.co.uk

National Rail Enquiries provides up-to-date information on train timetables, disruptions to services and also has information on the accessibility of individual stations.

Network Rail

40 Melton Street, London NW1 2EE
t 020 7557 8000
textphone 18001 0845 7114141
web www.networkrail.co.uk

Network Rail owns and operates the track, signals and other infrastructure of Britain's rail network. Although this includes the stations, most of these are managed by individual train operating companies. However, Network Rail does directly run 17 major stations including 10 London terminals, Birmingham New Street, Edinburgh Waverley, Gatwick, Glasgow Central, Leeds, Liverpool Lime Street and Manchester Piccadilly.

Passenger Focus

Freepost WA1521,
Warrington WA4 6GB
t 0845 302 2022
textphone 0845 850 1354
e advice@passengerfocus.org.uk
web www.passengerfocus.org.uk

Passenger Focus is the independent body established by Government to represent the interests of rail passengers. They can take up complaints when no satisfactory response has been obtained from the relevant train operating company or other service provider, perhaps if assistance that had been booked was not provided.

They can also advise on making complaints and welcome hearing of people's experiences even when they are not formally representing them.

Train operators

Arriva Trains Wales

St Mary's House, 47 Penarth Road,
Cardiff CF10 5DJ
t 0845 300 3005   textphone 0870 410 0355
web www.arrivatrainswales.co.uk

Arriva Trains Wales operates rail services in Wales and the border counties, including services to Cardiff Airport and ferry ports at Holyhead, Fishguard and Pembroke Dock. A regularly up-dated booklet, 'Guide for Customers with Disabilities', gives information on services and accessibility of the stations. It is available from staffed stations in Wales, the above address or can be downloaded from the website.

C2C

Freepost ADM3968, Southend SS1 1ZS
t 01702 357640   textphone 0845 712 5988
web www.c2c-online.co.uk

C2C operates services between London and Southend through East London and South Essex.

Chiltern Railways

Banbury IIC, Merton Street, Banbury, Oxon OX16 4RN
t 0845 6005 165 textphone 0845 7078 051
web www.chilternrailways.co.uk

Chiltern runs trains from London to Aylesbury and through Banbury to Birmingham, Kidderminster and Stratford-upon-Avon.

CrossCountry

t 0844 811 0125   textphone 0844 811 0126
web www.crosscountrytrains.co.uk

CrossCountry has a network of long distance routes, from Aberdeen to Penzance, all of which use Birmingham New Street Station as a terminus or for connections. Airports that are directly served by CrossCountry trains include Birmingham, Gatwick, Southampton and Stansted.

East Midland trains

t 0845 712 5678 textphone 0845 707 8051
e getintouch@eastmidlandtrains.co.uk
web www.eastmidlandstrains.co.uk

East Midlands has mainline services between St Pancras International in London and Sheffield, Nottingham, Derby and Leicester and also local services around the eastern Midlands with extensions into East Anglia and the North West. At St Pancras there are connections with Eurostar services. Luton and East Midlands Airports can be reached from East Midlands services, with transfers to the latter improved with the opening of East Midlands Parkway Station.

Eurostar

Eurostar House, Waterloo Station, London SE1 8SE
t 0870 518 6186 web www.eurostar.com

Eurostar train services currently run through the Channel Tunnel from London St Pancras International to Brussels and Paris. This provides straightforward connections for passengers from services to St Pancras and also into the adjacent King's Cross Station. It is also close to Euston Station for passengers from the North West and West Midlands.

Some services stop at Ebbsfleet International, off M25 J2, at Ashford International in Kent, where there are connections to many stations in southeast England, and Lille where connections can be made to high speed rail services for many cities across France. There are also simple connections at Brussels to destinations in the rest of Belgium, Germany and the Netherlands. The Paris terminal of Eurostar is quite close to Gare d'Est for accessible high-speed rail services to Eastern France and parts of Germany and Switzerland. Eurostar operates some direct services to Disneyland Paris all year, to ski resorts in the French Alps in the winter and to Avignon in the south of France in the summer.

There are spaces for passengers in a wheelchair on each Eurostar train. These are available at the lowest available standard class fare for the wheelchair user and a companion. These spaces should be booked in advance on 0870 518 6186.

All Eurostar stations are accessible. Assistance can be provided on request at check-in although anyone who may need help is asked to arrive as early as possible. Assistance dogs covered by the "Passports for Pets" scheme can be carried.

First Capital Connect

Customer Relations, Freepost ADM 3973,
London SW1Y 1YP
t 0800 058 2844 textphone 0800 975 1052
web www.firstcapitalconnect.co.uk

Operates rail services through central London from Brighton and south-west London to Bedford, serving both Gatwick and Luton Airports and the Eurostar Terminal at St Pancras International and also from London King's Cross and Moorgate to Cambridge through Hertfordshire.

First Great Western

Customer Services, Freepost SWB 40576
Plymouth PL4 6ZZ
t 0800 197 1329 e fgw@custhelp.com
textphone 0800 294 9209
web www.firstgreatwestern.com

Operates InterCity services between London Paddington and the West of England and South Wales and also regional and local services through the west country, the Thames Valley and the Cotswolds. It also has a service to Gatwick Airport from Reading. Heathrow airport can be reached on the Heathrow Connect service from stations in west London and by a coach link service from Reading. The Night Riviera service operates overnight between Paddington and Penzance. Significant improvements to the disabled facilities are in progress for First Great Western high speed trains.

First Scotrail

PO Box 7030, Fort William PH33 6WX
t 0800 912 2901 textphone 0800 912 2899
web www.firstscotrail.com

Operates both long distance and local rail services in Scotland. Tickets to include bus transfers are available for Aberdeen, Edinburgh and Glasgow Airports, while Prestwick International Airport has its own rail station. Inclusive rail and ferry fares are available to and from Scottish stations for Stena services between Stranraer and Belfast and for many of the Caledonian MacBrayne services to the islands off the west coast. First Scotrail also operates the Caledonian Sleepers between London Euston and Aberdeen, Edinburgh, Fort William, Glasgow and Inverness and a number of intermediate stations. These incorporate a berth that can be used by a wheelchair user.

OpenBritain | Getting there... and back | Rail travel

First Transpennine Express

Customer Relations, Admail 3876, Freepost Manchester M1 9YB
t 0800 107 2149 (Assisted Travel)
textphone 0800 107 2061   web www.tpexpress.co.uk

Transpennine Express has regional services from Manchester and Liverpool to Yorkshire, Humberside, the North East and southern Cumbria. Many of their routes are direct to and from Manchester Airport. Through tickets are also available to a number of other airports on their network including Leeds/Bradford from Leeds, Liverpool John Lennon from Liverpool Lime Street, Robin Hood from Doncaster and Durham Tees Valley from Darlington. Barnetby, on the hourly service to Cleethorpes is the nearest station to Humberside.

Gatwick Express

52 Grosvenor Gardens, London SW1W 0AV
t 0845 850 1530   web www.gatwickexpress.co.uk

Services run non-stop between Gatwick Airport and London Victoria Station every 15 minutes during the day. As there are staff on both the trains and the platforms, assistance can usually be provided even without advanced notice. All trains have spaces for passengers in wheelchairs.

Grand Central Railway

River House, 17 Museum Street, York YO1 7DJ
t 0845 603 4852 (Customer Services)
e info@grandcentralrail.com
web www.grandcentralrail.com

Grand Central operates direct services between London King's Cross and Sunderland, Hartlepool and North Yorkshire. Plans are in place for a service between London and West Yorkshire.

Heathrow Express

Customer Services, Freepost RLXYETJG-XKZS, London W2 6LG
t 0845 600 1515   web www.heathrowexpress.com

The Heathrow Express runs non-stop at frequent intervals between London Paddington and Heathrow. Each of their trains has two spaces for wheelchair users in Express (or standard) Class, by an accessible toilet, and one on First Class. Railcard holders can obtain discounted fares at Heathrow Express ticket offices, or for holders of the Disabled Persons Railcard on the train. The trolley barriers at the Heathrow platforms can be raised by Customer Service Assistants to give access to wheelchair users. A free service for disabled people needing assistance or help with luggage between the Heathrow platforms and airport check-in is available and can be pre-booked by calling Skycaps 020 8745 6011/5727.

Hull Trains

Premier House, Ferensway, Hull HU1 3UF
t 0845 071 0222   textphone 0845 678 6967
e customer.services@hulltrains.co.uk
web www.hulltrains.co.uk

Hull Trains operates inter-city services between Hull and London King's Cross. There is a bus link between Hull Station and Ferry Terminal. The company won the Enhanced Accessibility Rail Award at RADAR's 2006 People of the Year Awards following a poll among disabled railcard holders.

Island Line

Ryde St Johns Road Station, Ryde, Isle of Wight PO33 2BA
t 0800 528 2100   textphone 0800 692 0792
web www.island-line.com

Island Line operates rail services between Ryde and Shanklin on the Isle of Wight. Passengers from Wightlink Catamaran services can connect with services at Ryde Pier Head and those from Hovertravel at Ryde Esplanade where there is a new transport interchange. Disabled people needing assistance for journeys entirely on Island Rail call 01983 562492; for those on journeys from the mainland call 0845 605 0440. Textphone: 0845 605 0441.

London Midland

t 0870 010 1296   textphone 0845 707 8051
web www.londonmidland.com

London Midlands operates services between London Euston and Birmingham, via Northampton and also local services around the western Midlands and to the North West. Among the airports served are Birmingham and Liverpool.

London Overground

t 0870 601 4867   textphone 0845 721 5988
web www.tfl.gov.uk

London Overground, part of Transport for London, runs train services between London Euston and Watford Junction, Richmond and Stratford, Gospel Oak and Barking and Willesden Junction and Clapham Junction. Although primarily used for local journeys, it can be a useful means of avoiding changing stations in Central London. The East London Line extension, currently under construction, will provide additional links with eastern and southern parts of Greater London.

Merseyrail

Rail House, Lord Nelson Street Liverpool L1 1JF
t 0151 702 2071 (Mobility Helpline)
textphone 0151 702 2071   web www.merseyrail.org

Merseyrail provides local rail services over most of Merseyside and the Wirral. The primary connection with is at Liverpool Lime Street. There is an ongoing programme to improve interchange links to accessible bus services with MerseyTravel (see www.merseytravel.gov.uk).

National Express East Anglia

Customer Relations, Grosvenor House,
112-114 Prince of Wales Road, Norwich NR1 1NS
t 0800 028 2878   textphone 0845 606 7245
web www.nationalexpress.com

National Express East Anglia operates Intercity and local services from London Liverpool Street and local services throughout East Anglia. These include Stansted Express trains between London and Stansted Airport and also services to Harwich International for ferry services to Denmark, Germany and Holland.

National Express East Coast

t 0845 722 5444
textphone 0856 720 2067
web www.youreastcoast.co.uk

National Express East Coast runs long-distance services between London and Scotland through Yorkshire and North East England. The London terminal is King's Cross which is next to the Eurostar Terminal at St Pancras International. Established connections for other means of transport can be made at Newcastle for both the airport and ferries to Darlington for Humberside Airport, Leeds for Leeds/Bradford Airport and Doncaster for Robin Hood Airport.

Northern Rail

Customer Relations, PO Box 208, Leeds LS1 2BU
t 0845 600 8008
textphone 0845 604 5608
e assistance@northernrail.org
web www.northernrail.org

Northern Rail operates local and regional rail services across northern England. A booklet, "A Guide for Customers with Disabilities" is available from their staffed stations and can be downloaded from the website. There are connections to Inter-City services at many locations and services to Manchester Airport and Liverpool South Parkway for Liverpool John Lennon Airport.

South West Trains

Customer Service Centre, Overline House,
Blechynden Terrace, Southampton SO15 1GW
t 0800 528 2100   textphone 0800 692 0792.
web www.southwesttrains.co.uk

South West Trains run from London Waterloo through south-west London, Surrey, Berkshire, Hampshire, Dorset and parts of Wiltshire and Devon. There are also services to Bristol, Brighton and Reading allowing connections to many other parts of the national rail network. Interchanges include Southampton Airport Parkway that adjoins Southampton Airport, Feltham, Woking and Reading that all have coach links to Heathrow, Portsmouth Harbour and Lymington Pier for Wightlink services to the Isle of Wight and Weymouth for services to the Channel Islands.

OpenBritain | Getting there... and back | Rail travel

Southeastern Trains

PO Box 63428, London SE1P 5FD
t 0800 783 4524 (assisted travel)
textphone 0800 783 4548
web www.southeasternrailway.co.uk

South Eastern operates services in southeast London, Kent and parts of East Sussex. Stations served include Ashford International for connections to Eurostar and Dover Priory for transfer to Dover Ferry Port. It also has services from Kent to Gatwick. A booklet 'Helping you access our railway network' and a station map guide 'Planning an accessible journey with southeastern' are available.

Southern

PO Box 277, Tonbridge TN9 2ZP
t 0800 138 1016
textphone 0800 138 1018
e comments@southernrailway.com
web www.southernrailway.com

Southern trains serve much of south London, Surrey and Sussex and parts of Kent and Hampshire. Among the stations served regularly is Gatwick Airport and there are also direct services between Brighton to Ashford International, for Eurostar, and from East Croydon to Watford Junction, which can avoid the need to change stations in London for people travelling between the south coast and the Midlands and north west of England. From June 2008 the Gatwick Express and Southern franchise merged.

Virgin Trains

Meridian, 85 Smallbrook Queensway,
Birmingham B5 4HA
t 0845 744 3366 (JourneyCare)
textphone 0845 744 3367
web www.virgintrains.co.uk

Virgin Trains operates InterCity services between London Euston, the west Midlands, north west England and Scotland. Many Virgin services stop at Birmingham International for Birmingham International Airport. Other destinations include Holyhead Ferry Terminal, Gatwick Airport and Reading for transfers to Heathrow Airport.

Wrexham & Shropshire

The Pump House, Coton Hill,
Shrewsbury SY1 2DP
textphone 0845 260 5200 (Customer Services)
e info@wrexhamandshropshire.co.uk
web www.wrexhamandshropshire.co.uk

Operates direct services between London Marylebone and Wrexham, Shrewsbury and Telford, with connections for other rail services at Wolverhampton, Tame Bridge Parkway and Banbury. Trains are being renovated to include spaces for wheelchair users and adapted toilets.

Light Railways and Trams

Blackpool Transport Services

Rigby Road, Blackpool FY1 5DD
t 01253 473001
e jean.cox@blackpooltransport.com
web www.blackpooltransport.com

Blackpool's old tram system survived the tram services closures of the 1960s. It was not designed for use by disabled people but upgrades are planned for 2011.

Croydon Tramlink

5 Suffolk House, George Street, Croydon CR0 1PE
t 020 8681 8300   web www.tfl.gov.uk/trams

Croydon Tramlink crosses southern greater London between Wimbledon and Beckenham through central Croydon with lines to New Addington and Elmers End. It has accessible connections with the national rail network at Wimbledon, East Croydon, (where there are trains to Gatwick Airport) and Beckenham Junction. At Wimbledon there are passenger lifts providing connections to other rail services as well as from street level. There are tactile strips along the length of each stop to assist blind and partially sighted people. Wheelchair users can easily board and alight; next to the wheelchair space is an intercom to speak to the driver in an emergency and a stop request button, both at low level.

Greater Manchester

Metrolink House, Queens Road, Manchester M8 0RY
t 0161 205 2000   e customerservices@metrolink.co.uk
web www.metrolink.co.uk

Metrolink has services to Manchester Piccadilly Station from Altrincham, Bury and Eccles, via Salford Quays and also through services between Altrincham and Bury. Where required – mainly sections that had been railway lines – lifts have been provided to the platforms. Most platforms have tactile edges for visually impaired passengers and all platforms have designated wheelchair/pushchair access points for step-free access. Each tram has designated disabled/pushchair areas with its own emergency and information call points. Bus interchanges and Park & Rides have been established at several points and the service provides an accessible link between Victoria and Piccadilly stations. A £1bn investment project is ongoing to replace all Metrolink tram track, with 4 new tram lines now under construction. There are lower fares and free travel for some disabled people.

London Docklands

t 020 7363 9700   textphone 020 7093 0999
e cservice@dlr.co.uk   web www.dlr.co.uk

The Docklands Light Railway operates an expanding network of routes from the City of London through east and south-east London. It was designed from the outset to be accessible by disabled people, with carriage entrances level with the platforms. There is an extension by covered walkway with London City Airport. The line extension to Woolwich Arsenal Station is completed. Other useful accessible interchanges with the national rail network are at Greenwich, Lewisham and Stratford. Until 2010 construction is taking place on DLR. Persons over 18 who live in Greater London should check the Travel Mentoring Scheme.

Nottingham

t 0115 950 6070   e travelcentre@nctx.co.uk
web www.thetram.net

NET (Nottingham Express Transit) runs from Hucknell, north of Nottingham, through the city centre to Nottingham railway station. It also has a branch to Phoenix Park Park & Ride near M1 Junction 26. NET incorporates 5 free Park & Ride sites. There are accessible buses to Nottingham East Midlands Airport.

Sheffield

t 0114 272 8282
e enquiries@supertram.com
web www.supertram.com

Stagecoach Supertram has 3 light rail routes, which go through the city centre, and 5 Park & Ride sites that give easy access to the rail station, shopping areas, the 2 universities, the cathedral, sports arenas and entertainment venues. All platforms are accessible and the trams accommodate wheelchair users, have priority seating and low-level driver alert buttons. The Supertram Link bus service extends the network. Staff are trained in disability awareness.

Tyne & Wear

Nexus House, St James Boulevard, Newcastle upon Tyne NE1 4AX
t 0191 203 3207   textphone 0191 303 3216
e contactus@nexus.org.uk
web www.nexus.org.uk

There are ramps or lifts to all platforms. There is a gap/step between platforms and train that may be difficult for some wheelchair users. Work on the second and final phase of a £7m modernisation project at Sunderland Station is now underway. Newcastle Central, Sunderland, Heworth and Metro Centre have level, ramped or lift access to all stations. You can book assistance when travelling on mainline services for your complete journey with the operator that you start your journey from. A Metro Access Guide is available on request from Nexus.

West Midlands

Travelcare, Travel West Midlands, PO Box 3565, Birmingham B1 3JR
t 0121 254 7272   web www.travelmetro.co.uk

The Metro Tram runs from Birmingham Snow Hill to Wolverhampton through West Bromwich. All stations have step-free access. There are Park & Ride sites along the route and bus interchanges. Concessionary travel passes are available for blind and disabled persons.

Sea travel

There are many journeys within the British Isles and beyond using sea and air travel, or for which a ferry is appropriate. Many people will make their choice based on personal taste, convenience and cost. A particular advantage of ferries for some disabled people, especially drivers, is that they can take their cars with them and so do not have to hire one, possibly with adaptations, at their destination. Also, motorists are not as restricted in the amount of luggage that they take with them, up to the capacity of the car. Equipment remains under the control of the ferry passenger whether directly of left in the car – unlike with air travel, where it may have to be carried in the hold.

When deciding between sea and air travel, factors that need to be taken into account include the ability to move around, availability of toilets designed for disabled people and the chance to relax during a long journey. This can be relevant to some channel crossings where there may be a choice between longer driving distances and length of crossing times.

Port assistance

Port accessibility will vary from location to location but the only real difficulty you should encounter is if the port is too small or too shallow for the ship to dock. In such cases you will have to transfer from the ship to the dockside by tender. Many of these smaller boats are now able to convey wheelchairs, but you are advised to confirm this beforehand. Try and get confirmation regarding the suitability for disabled travellers of the onshore tours.

412	Ferry services
412	Port assistance
413	Ferry/cruise operators
413	Boarding
413	Assistance dogs
414	Ferry companies

Top tip

- If a passenger needs assistance or information, get in touch with the ferry operator in advance, preferably at the time of booking, and get to the port in good time.

- Depending on the ferry operator, your pet may have to remain in the car for the duration of the crossing. Other than registered guide dogs accompanying a visually impaired passenger, your pet will not be allowed access to any area other than the designated pet areas on any ferry.

Ferry/cruise operators

Ferry companies and cruise operators will often insist that a disabled passenger be accompanied by an able-bodied companion for the journey, depending on the nature and extent of the disability. One reason for this is that in the event of rough seas, a disabled passenger may encounter difficulties. If you are planning to take the journey alone you should discuss this possibility with the company first.

Ferries can vary from large modern ships used on international journeys, which in most cases are accessible with lifts between decks, toilet facilities and adapted cabins, through to much simpler vessels on estuary crossings with open car decks that may be accessible by virtue of their lack of facilities, and the short space of time that they are used.

When travelling by sea, note that getting around the ship can be difficult in rough weather; in catering areas furniture will be more likely to be fixed or difficult to move. Doors, particularly to deck areas, will usually be heavy and many staircases will be steep.

Cabins for the disabled, especially on more modern ships, are usually placed with better access to all public areas and lifts. They are designed with wider doorways, hand bars, low level controls, low door peep holes and specially designed spacious bathrooms. It is worth checking that balcony suites have ramps onto the verandah, that outside decks can be reached without assistance and that lifts are wide enough for your wheelchair.

Some cruise companies may ask that you are medically fit to travel, and provide proof of this, before travelling. It is essential that you confirm any requirements that the ferry or cruise company may have before booking your trip.

Try and give the cruise company you are travelling with as much notice as possible of your disability. They may ask that you book through their reservation centre in order that any requirements you may have can be noted on your booking, which will avoid any confusion later on. For this reason it is important that you are frank about your disability and any special needs you may have. Also some of the company's fleet of ships may be more disabled friendly than others.

Boarding

Boarding procedures will vary depending on whether you travel with a vehicle or as a foot passenger. If any member of a party travelling by car has impaired mobility this must be brought to the attention of the boarding staff, so that the car may be parked near the lift. This will require early check-in but does not necessarily mean early boarding.

Boarding is usually via a ramped walkway (which may be long) for foot passengers, although there may be a step or a steep lip when entering or leaving the ship. In some instances foot passengers use the car deck and its associated lifts. Some people who do not usually use a wheelchair may be advised to use one for boarding and disembarking

Assistance dogs

If you are considering taking an assistance dog on a cruise you must inform the cruise company and ensure your dog complies with the Pet Travel Scheme. You will also be responsible for clearing up after your dog. However, you may not be allowed to take your dog ashore in many foreign countries, so you should check this before travelling, along with any vaccinations that may be required for your dog. On board cruise ships Braille facilities are fairly standard, with lift buttons, deck numbers and cabin numbers in Braille. You should also be able to request a menu in Braille.

For deaf and hearing-impaired passengers, many cruises have special equipment such as telephone amplifiers, and lights that indicate someone has knocked on the cabin door, or that the smoke alarm has been activated.

Ferry companies

Brittany Ferries

Millbay, Plymouth, PL1 3EW
t 0871 244 0744 **textphone** 0871 244 0425
web www.brittanyferries.co.uk

Plymouth	▶ Roscoff / Santander
Poole	▶ Cherbourg
Portsmouth	▶ Caen / Cherbourg / St Malo
Cork	▶ Roscoff

Brittany Ferries is the major operator on the Western Channel with the above routes from England and Ireland, Normandy, Brittany and Spain:

The ships include both fast and traditional ferries with lifts between decks and toilets for disabled people, details available from the above telephone number. Those used on overnight crossings have some cabins designed for wheelchair users, which should be booked by telephone. If assistance is likely to be required it should be requested as far in advance as possible and disabled passengers are asked to check in at least 1 hour before departure.

Caledonian MacBrayne Ltd

The Ferry Terminal, Gourock, PA19 1QP
t 0800 066 50000 (Enquiries)
e reservations@calmac.co.uk.
web www.calmac.co.uk

Sails to 24 destinations on the west coast of Scotland.

A variety of vessels are in use. The timetable indicates whether there are facilities for disabled passengers. Anyone who may need assistance should notify the company when booking and checking in. Fare concessions for disabled drivers are available on production of appropriate documents.

Celtic Link Ferries

t 0844 576 8834 (Reservations)
web www.celticlinkferries.com

Rosslare	▶ Cherbourg

Celtic Link operates an overnight service for vehicles and their passengers three times a week between Rosslare and Cherbourg. The crossing takes 18-20 hours. There is a lift between the car and passenger decks but no specific facilities for disabled passengers.

Condor Ferries

Ferry Terminal Building, Weymouth DT4 8DX
t 0845 609 1024
e reservations@condorferries.co.uk
web www.condorferries.com

Weymouth	▶ Guernsey / Jersey / St Malo
Poole	▶ Guernsey / Jersey / St Malo
Portsmouth	▶ Guernsey / Jersey / Cherbourg

Condor Ferries operates a fast ferry service from the south coast ports of Weymouth and Poole to the Channel Islands of Jersey and Guernsey, and the French port of St Malo. A conventional ferry service also operates daily all year round excluding Sundays from Portsmouth to the Channel Islands and a Sunday service operates from Portsmouth to Cherbourg from May until September, recommended for taking caravans and motor homes.

On the fast ferries there is a lift from the car deck to the main cabin level where most of the passenger facilities are located including access to the outside viewing decks and a toilet for disabled passengers. The conventional ferry has two cabins with toilet facilities adapted for disabled passengers. Passengers with a hearing impairment can obtain information and make bookings at sign-it5@hotmail.com. Any passengers who require assistance must do so at the time of booking.

OPENBRITAIN.NET
The one-stop-shop for all your travel needs. Go online and see how we can help you get in, out ...and about.

OpenBritain | Getting there... and back | Sea travel

DFDS Seaways

Scandinavia House, Parkeston, Harwich CO12 4QG

International Ferry Terminal, Royal Quays,
North Shields NE29 6EE

t 0871 522 9955 e travel.sales@dfds.co.uk
web www.dfds.co.uk

| Harwich | ▶ Esbjerg (west coast of Denmark) |
| Newcastle | ▶ Ijmuiden (near Amsterdam) |

DFDS operate the above services which carry both foot and vehicle passengers.

The ferry terminal at Harwich is next to Harwich International railway station, there are coaches that connect with sailings to and from the main stations at Newcastle and Amsterdam and regular bus services from the terminal at Esbjerg.

Eurotunnel

UK Terminal, Ashford Road, Folkestone CT18 8XX
t 0870 535 3535   web www.eurotunnel.com

Eurotunnel carries cars and other vehicles with their passengers on frequent shuttle trains through the Channel Tunnel between the outskirts of Folkestone and Calais. For disabled people an advantage of this service is that they can stay in their car throughout the 35-minute journey if they wish. Drivers of cars carrying disabled people should arrive at least 45 minutes ahead of their booked departure time make themselves known at check-in. Vehicles carrying anyone who may need assistance in the event of an emergency will be loaded at the front of the shuttle. The single-storey Terminal Buildings, with shops and catering outlets, have low level telephones and toilets for disabled people. Eurotunnel is approved under PETS and can therefore carry assistance dogs with appropriate documentation.

Hovertravel Ltd

Quay Road, Ryde,
Isle of Wight PO33 2HB
t 01983 811000
e info@hovertravel.co.uk
web www.hovertravel.co.uk

Southsea   ▶ Ryde (Isle of Wight)

Hovertravel operates a fast crossing for foot passengers between Southsea and Ryde by hovercraft – the only hovercraft service in British waters. There is a lift for boarding and spaces for two passengers in wheelchairs on each craft. Their most modern craft has an additional wheelchair space and an induction loop. The terminals have adjacent parking, toilets for disabled people and wheelchairs for transfer to and from the craft. There is a shuttle bus service between the Southsea Terminal
t 023 9281 1000 and rail stations in Portsmouth. There are easy connections to bus and rail at the Ryde Terminal.

Irish Ferries

Contact Centre, PO Box 19,
Alexandra Road Ferryport, Dublin 1
t + 35 31 0818 300 400
e info@irishferries.com
web www.irishferries.com

UK office: Corn Exchange,
Brunswick Street, Liverpool L2 7TP
t 08717 300 400 web www.irishferries.co.uk

| Holyhead | ▶ Dublin |
| Pembroke | ▶ Rosslare |

Irish Ferries is Ireland's leading ferry company carrying passengers and their cars between Ireland, Great Britain and France. All vessels have toilets and lifts for disabled passengers, designated seating areas and adapted cabins as well as port terminals which have been built to be accessible. Advance notification at the time of booking is requested if passengers feel they have more specific requirements. All information for disabled passengers can be found on their website under 'More Information' and anyone with more specific requests should contact the Disability Officers directly through the Contact Centre or e disabilityofficer@irishferries.com

www.openbritain.net/openbritain/travel   HIGHWAYS AGENCY   415

Isle of Man Steam Packet Co.

Imperial Buildings, Douglas, Isle of Man IM1 2BY
t 0871 222 1333   web www.steam-packet.com

Liverpool	▶ Douglas (Isle of Man)
Heysham	▶ Douglas (Isle of Man)
Belfast	▶ Douglas (Isle of Man)
Dublin	▶ Douglas (Isle of Man)

Operates services to Douglas from Heysham and Liverpool all year and from Belfast and Dublin from late March to September. The 'Ben-my-Chree' ferry on the Heysham route has a lift to all decks and two cabins adapted for disabled passengers. The Liverpool service uses Super SeaCats that have lifts for disabled people. However the SeaCats on the Belfast and Dublin services cannot be used by wheelchair users. A new large fast ferry came into service in 2009 and a new terminal in Liverpool is now in use. When making a reservation please notify the company of any assistance that may be required.

Isles of Scilly Steamship Co

Isles of Scilly Travel Centre, Quay Street, Penzance TR18 4BZ
t 0845 710 5555   e sales@islesofscilly-travel.co.uk
web www.islesofscilly-travel.co.uk

Penzance	▶ St Mary's

The 'Scillonian III' makes a return journey between Penzance and St Mary's 6 days a week from spring to autumn with additional Sunday services in August and a reduced service in winter. The Penzance terminal is a 15-minute walk or a short taxi journey from Penzance Station. Passengers can board and disembark using wheelchairs. Powered scooters have to be carried as cargo but a manual wheelchair is available for scooter users; this should be requested in advance.
There is a stair lift on the main staircase on board to which wheelchair users have to transfer independently. Information on services between St Mary's and the other islands can also be obtained from the Tourist Information Centre t 01720 424031. For information on Shop Mobility Scheme see web www.gopenzance.com or t 01736 351792.

John O'Groats Ferries

Ferry Office, John O'Groats, Caithness KW1 4YR
t 01955 611353   e info@jogferry.co.uk
web www.jogferry.co.uk

John O'Groats	▶ Burwick (South Ronaldsay)

A ferry service for foot passengers operates from May to September. The ferry can carry passengers in wheelchairs for the 40-minute crossing although there is no lift between decks and at tidal extremes it is necessary to use a different deck when getting off from that used on boarding. Staff can provide help but it is advisable to check in advance. The large car park at John O'Groats has a toilet fitted with the NKS lock for disabled people.

Coach transfers are available from Burwick to Kirkwall and between John O'Groats and Thurso and Wick rail stations. There is also an express coach service to and from Inverness. There are no specific facilities for disabled passengers on the coach connections although folded wheelchairs can be carried.

LD Lines

Continental Ferry Port, Wharf Road, Portsmouth PO2 8QW
t 0844 576 8836   e mailto:booking@ldlines.co.uk
special assistance t +33 2 35 19 78 78
web www.ldlines.com

Portsmouth	▶ Le Havre
Dover	▶ Boulogne
Newhaven	▶ Dieppe
Rosslare	▶ Cherbourg / Le Havre

LD Lines operates ferry services between Portsmouth and Le Havre with day and night sailings in each direction. Disabled passengers and those with animals are asked to check in 90 minutes before departure. The main vessel on the route, 'Norman Spirit', has lifts between decks and toilets for disabled passengers. However, there are no adapted cabins and the reclining seats have fixed armrests, although in rows of no more than two. LD Lines also operates services between Newhaven and Dieppe (in association with Transmanche Ferries), a new fast ferry service (since June 2009) between Dover and Boulogne and a new service (from September 2009) between Cherbourg and Rosslare.

North Link Ferries

Kiln Corner, Ayre Road, Kirkwall, Orkney KW15 1QX
t 0845 6000 449 (Reservations),
t 01856 885500 (Administration)
e info@northlinkferries.co.uk
e reservations@northlinkferries.co.uk
web www.northlinkferries.co.uk

Aberdeen	▶ Kirkwall / Lerwick
Scrabster	▶ Stromness
Kirkwall	▶ Lerwick

Operates ferry services to Orkney and Shetland from Aberdeen and between Scrabster in Caithness and Stromness on Orkney, using three modern vessels. Each has toilets for disabled passengers and lifts between decks. Those used for overnight sailings have 4 cabins designed for disabled people of which two have enhanced facilities including hoists.

Concessionary rates and special boarding arrangements are available for disabled people. There are toilets for disabled people at each of NorthLink's terminals, and people using powered wheelchairs can board at all ports except Scrabster. Advance notice of passengers requiring assistance is appreciated.

Norfolk Line

Norfolk House, Eastern Docks, Dover CT16 1JA
t 0870 870 1020   web www.norfolkline.com

12 Quays Terminal, Tower Road, Birkenhead CH41 1FE
t 0844 499 0007 (UK) or   t 01 819 2999 (Ireland)
web www.norfolkline.com

Dover	▶ Kirkwall / Lerwick
Dover	▶ Dunkirk
Liverpool	▶ Belfast / Dublin
Rosyth	▶ Zeebrugge

Norfolk Line operates a round-the-clock car ferry service using modern vessels. Ferries to France, Ireland, Scotland, Belgium and Dover. Foot passengers and coaches are not carried. Advance notice is requested for passengers who may need assistance.

Orkney Ferries

Shore Street, Kirkwall, Orkney KW15 1LG
t 01856 872044   e info@orkneyferries.co.uk
web www.orkneyferries.co.uk

Orkney Mainland to 13 of the smaller islands.

Facilities for disabled passengers vary according to the vessels used.

P&O Ferries

Channel House, Channel View Road, Dover CT17 9TJ
t 0871 664 5645   e help@poferries.com
web www.poferries.com

Dover	▶ Calais
Hull	▶ Rotterdam / Zebrugge
Portsmouth	▶ Bilbao

Advice on the facilities on the ship is available when booking and at least 48 hours notice is requested for any assistance that may be required.

P&O Irish Sea

Larne Harbour, Larne BT40 1AW
t 0871 664 4999   textphone 01304 223090
web www.poirishsea.com

Liverpool	▶ Dublin
Troon	▶ Larne
Cairnryan	▶ Larne

Operates both fast craft and conventional ferries between Larne and Cairnryan and fast craft on a summer seasonal service between Larne and Troon. On board there are lifts between car and passenger decks and toilets for disabled passengers. A minibus is available at both terminals for foot passengers. There is also a car ferry service between Dublin and Liverpool. However, the vessels used for this do not have lifts between the car deck and the main passenger areas. Advice on the suitability of vessels is available when booking and at least 48 hours notice is requested for any assistance that may be required.

Pentland Ferries

Pier Road, St Margaret's Hope, South Ronaldsay
Orkney KW17 2SW
t 01856 831226   t Gill's Bay 01955 611773
web www.pentlandferries.co.uk

Gill's Bay ▶ St Margaret's Hope (South Ronaldsay)

Operates car ferries on the 1-hour crossing between Gill's Bay in Caithness and St Margaret's Hope on the southern Orkney island of South Ronaldsay. No specific facilities are available for disabled passengers.

Red Funnel Ferries

12 Bugle Street, Southampton SO14 2JY
t 0845 155 2442   e post@redfunnel.co.uk
web www.redfunnel.co.uk

Southampton ▶ Cowes

Operates both car ferries and hi-speed passenger services between Southampton and Cowes on the Isle of Wight. Ferries have lifts and there are toilets for disabled passengers on board and at terminals. At Southampton a free bus service, which can carry wheelchair users, links the ferry terminals with the main railway station and the city centre.

SeaFrance

Whitfield Court, Honeywood Close,
Whitfield, Kent CT16 3PX
t 0871 423 7119   web www.seafrance.com

Dover ▶ Calais

SeaFrance operates vehicle and foot passenger ferries between Dover and Calais. The vessels used are modern with facilities for disabled passengers. Advance notice of any assistance that may be required is requested. Any car driver carrying a disabled passenger should advise the call centre or click the box on the website when booking and should also make themselves known at check-in.

Shetland Islands Council Ferry

Port Administration Building, Stella Ness,
Shetland ZE2 9QR
t 01806 244219   e ferries@sic.shetland.gov.uk
web www.shetland.gov.uk/ferries
t Shetlands Island Council 01595 693 535

Shetland Islands Council operates 13 ferries serving 9 islands from 16 terminals.

Facilities for disabled passengers at terminals, which are often unmanned and built around 30 years' ago, and on board, vary. Crew members can give assistance if required especially if passengers indicate their needs when booking or on arrival at the terminal.
To discuss requirements in advance call the above number. Information on facilities for disabled passengers at terminals and on board ferries is available on a website hosted by Disability Shetland.
www.shetlandcommunities.org/disabilityshetland/shetland-access-guide

SpeedFerries Ltd

Hoverport, Western Docks, Dover CT17 9TG
t 0871 222 7456
e customerservice@speedferries.com
web www.speedferries.co.uk

Dover ▶ Boulogne

SpeedFerries operate a fast, 55-minute crossing between their sole-use terminals at Dover and Boulogne for vehicles and their passengers. There is a ramped approach from the car deck to the main passenger lounge and cafeteria, where there are toilets for disabled people, although there are steps to an upper deck level. Early check-in may be required for appropriate loading. Disabled people who may need assistance can make bookings through the call centre, rather than the website, without the £10 charge that is otherwise incurred. Foot passengers cannot be carried.

OPENBRITAIN.NET — The one-stop-shop for all your travel needs.

Stena Line

Stena House, Station Approach,
Holyhead LL65 1DQ
t 08705 707070 (Reservations)
e info.uk@stenaline.com
web www.stenaline.co.uk

Harwich	▶ Hook of Holland
Fleetwood	▶ Larne
Stranraer	▶ Belfast
Holyhead	▶ Dublin / Dun Laoghaire
Fishguard	▶ Rosslare

Stena Line operates 18 ferry routes across Europe and offers a ferry travel service to Ireland, Britain and Holland. There is a range of hotel breaks, self-catering and landbreak holidays, with the option to travel by car, rail, coach or on foot.

Two new superferries will be introduced to the Harwich and the Hook route, which will offer 30% more capacity and improved onboard facilities.

At present there are 2 crossings daily – day and overnight sailing. Assistance can be provided at both ports and on board, although as much notice as possible is requested. Pets can travel free of charge to Ireland; dogs must stay in the vehicle.

Transeuropa Ferries

t 0184 359 5522
e info@transeuropaferries.com
web www.transeuropaferries.com

Ramsgate ▶ Ostend

TransEuropa Ferries runs ferries for vehicles and their passengers from Ramsgate to Ostend on a crossing time of approximately 4 hours; 8 sailings per day cater to passengers with cars. The crossings do not carry foot passengers.

Facilities for disables passengers on board the ships vary. Although some can carry passengers in wheelchairs, two have no lifts from the car deck and two others have small lifts with entrance steps. Therefore it is essential that anyone who cannot manage stairs notify the company at the time of booking. Guide and assistance dogs cannot be carried.

Transmanche Ferries

t 0870 420 1267 (Reservations)
web www.transmancheferries.com

Newhaven ▶ Dieppe

Transmanche has ferries for vehicles and foot passengers between Newhaven in Sussex and Dieppe in Normandy. Wheelchairs are available in both terminals to assist in transfer to the vessels and there are lifts between the car and passenger decks. One of the vessels has a 4-person cabin that has been adapted for disabled passengers. The terminal at Newhaven is within walking distance of Newhaven Town railway station and there is an adapted minibus between the ship and terminal at Dieppe.

Wightlink Isle of Wight Ferries

PO Box 59, Portsmouth PO1 2XB
t 0871 376 1000
e bookings@wightlink.co.uk
web www.wightlink.co.uk

Portsmouth	▶ Fishbourne / Ryde
Lymington	▶ Yarmouth

Wightlink operates car ferries on the Portsmouth-Fishbourne and Lymington-Yarmouth routes and FastCat catamaran services for foot passengers only between Portsmouth and Ryde. The vessels on the Portsmouth-Fishbourne service are equipped with lifts and toilets for disabled passengers and new vessels have been introduced onto the Lymington-Yarmouth route. Wheelchairs are available at all terminals and Wightlink can give contact details of companies with accessible taxicabs on the island. A Wightlink Disabled Persons Card is available giving discounted fares.
For assistance t 023 9281 2011.

Map 1

Location Maps

Every place name featured in the regional accommodation sections of this OpenBritain guide has a map reference to help you locate it on the maps which follow. For example, to find Colchester, Essex, which has 'Map ref 3B2', turn to Map 3 and refer to grid square B2.

All place names appearing in the regional sections are shown with orange circles on the maps. This enables you to find other places in your chosen area which may have suitable accommodation – the place index (at the back of this guide) gives page numbers.

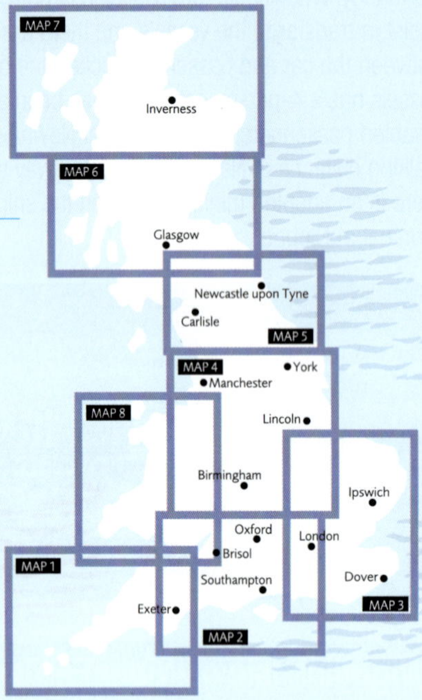

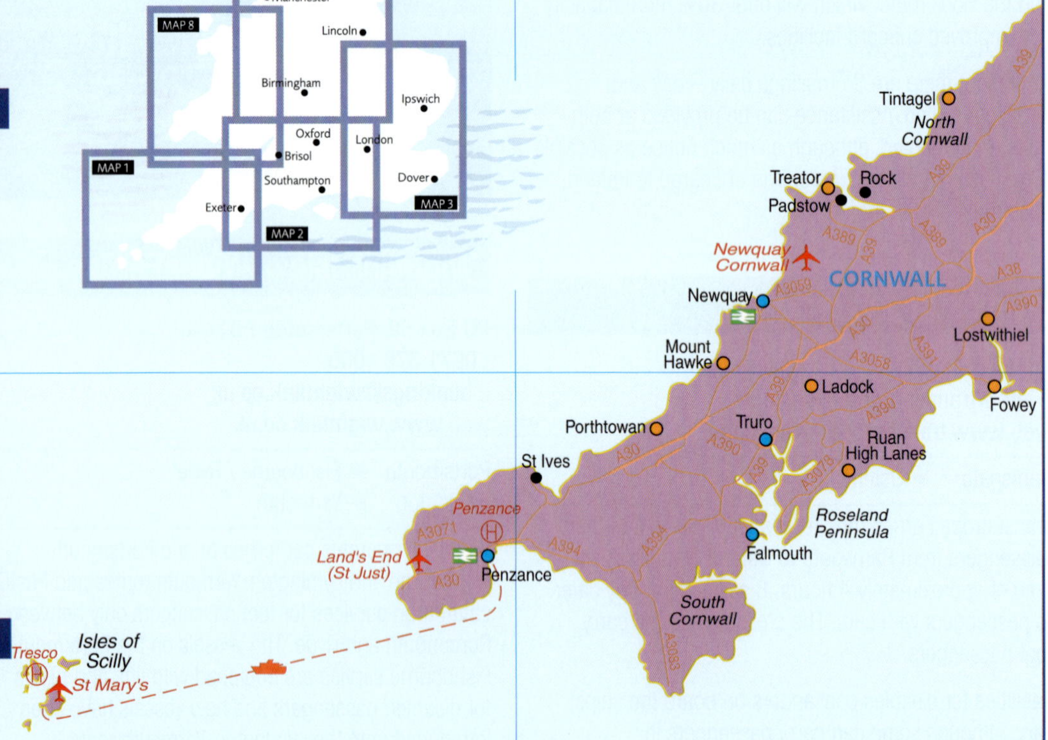

Key to regions: South West England | Wales

Map 1

Map 2

Key to regions: South West England | Wales | South East England | London | East of England | East Midlands | Heart of England

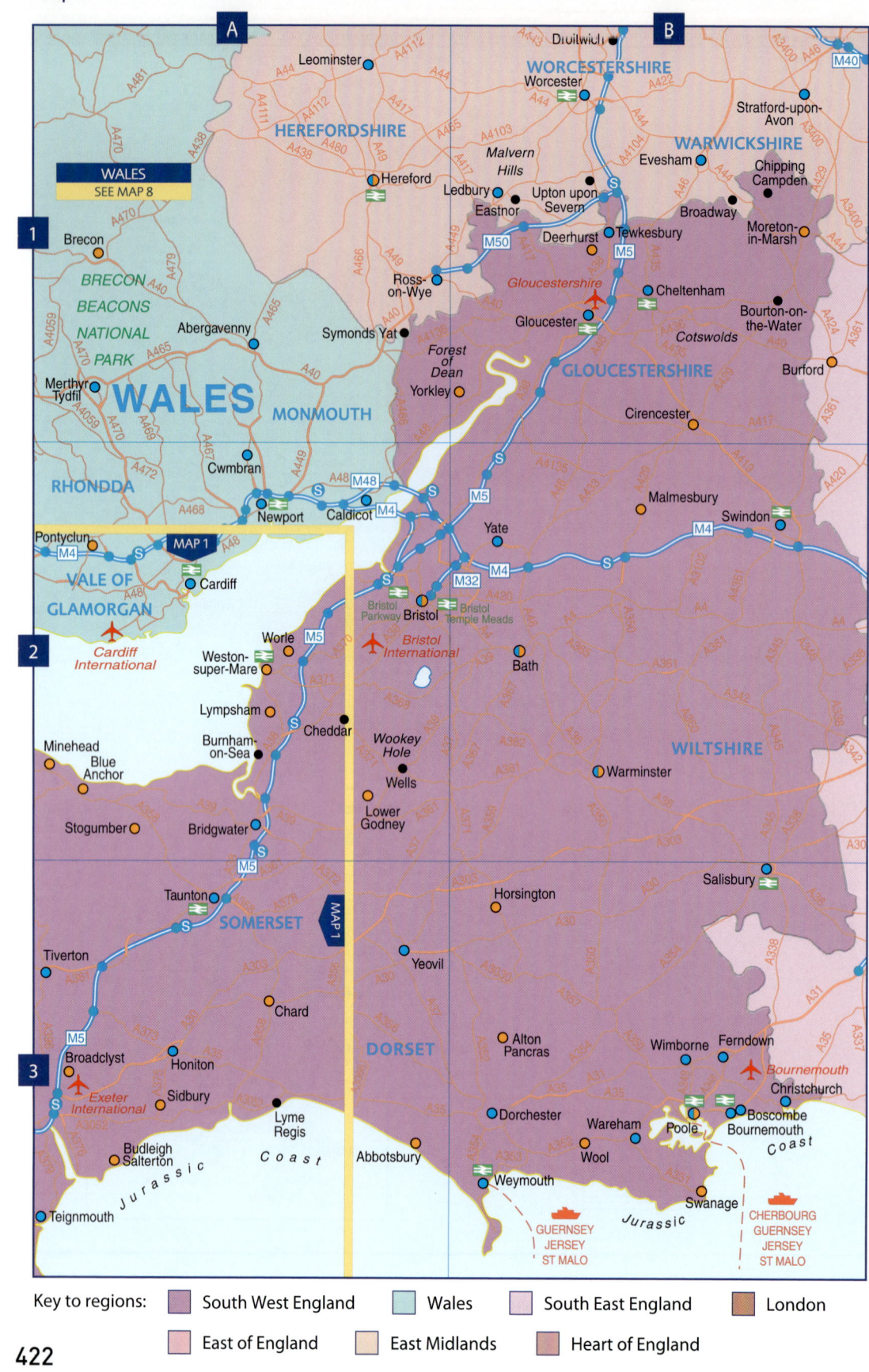

422

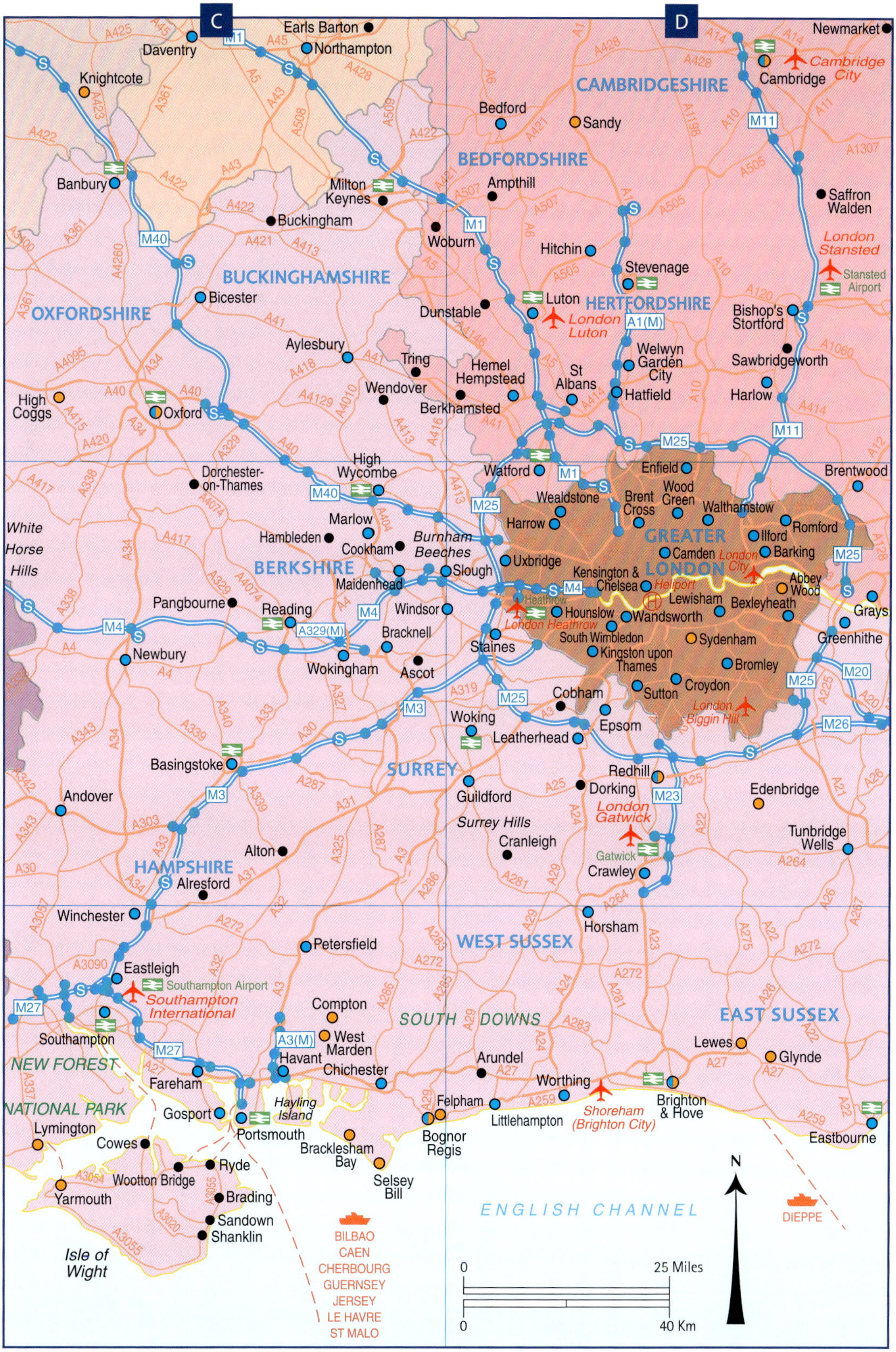

Accommodation   Shopmobility Centres   Accommodation/Shopmobility Centres

Map 3

Map 3

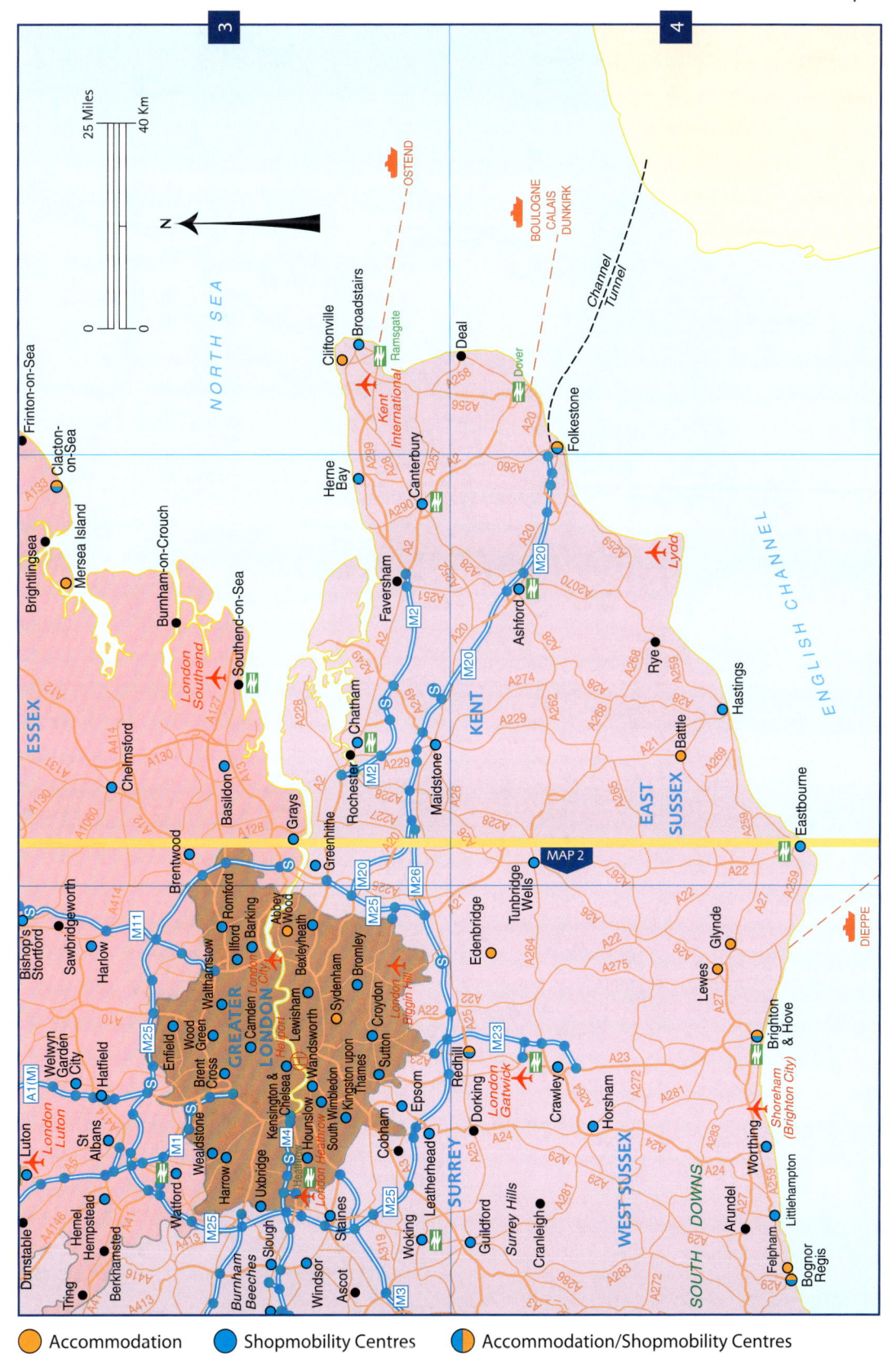

Key to regions: East of England, East Midlands, Heart of England, Yorkshire, North West England, Wales

Map 4

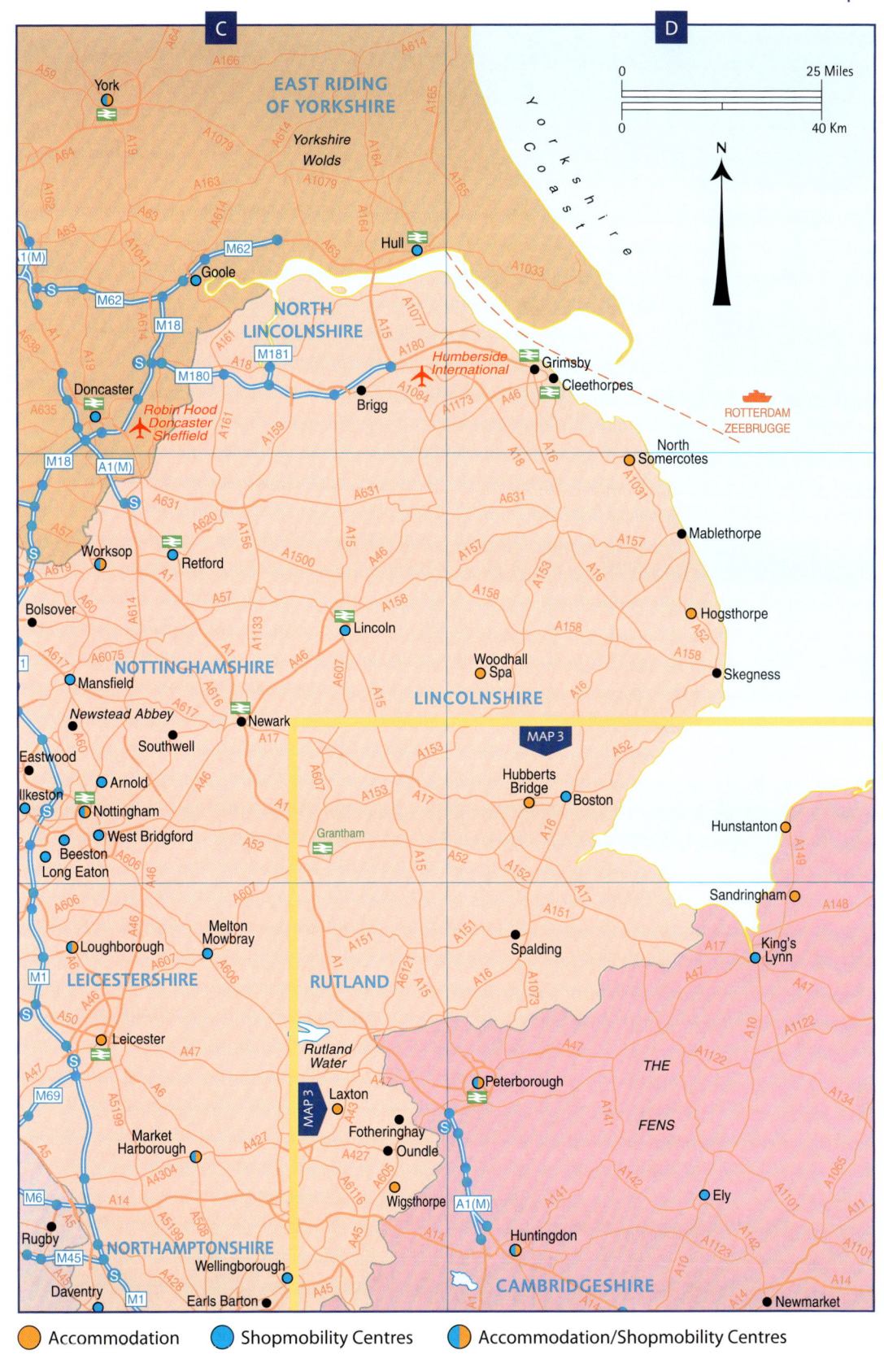

Map 5

Map 5

- Accommodation
- Shopmobility Centres
- Accommodation/Shopmobility Centres

Map 6

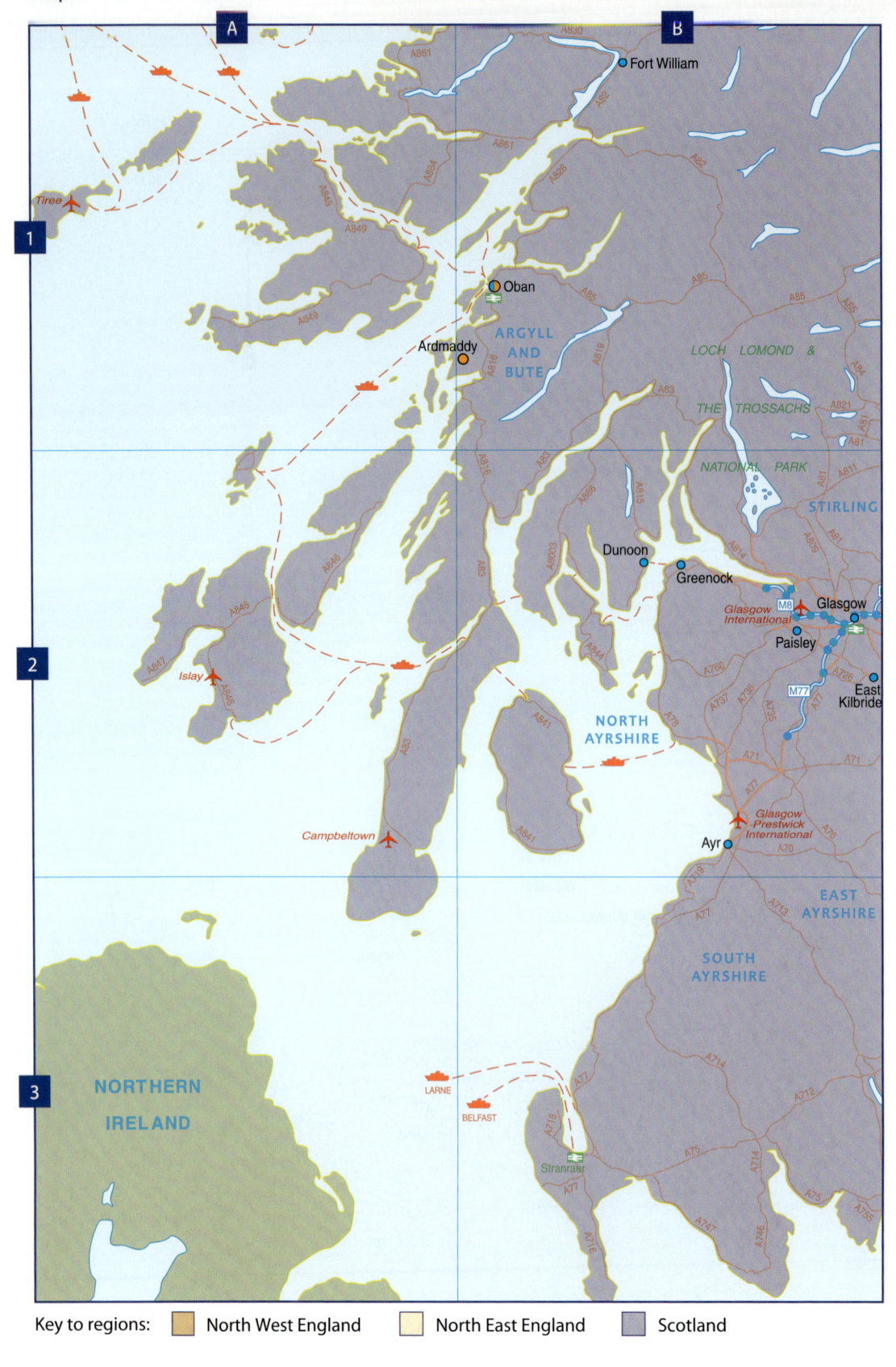

Map 6

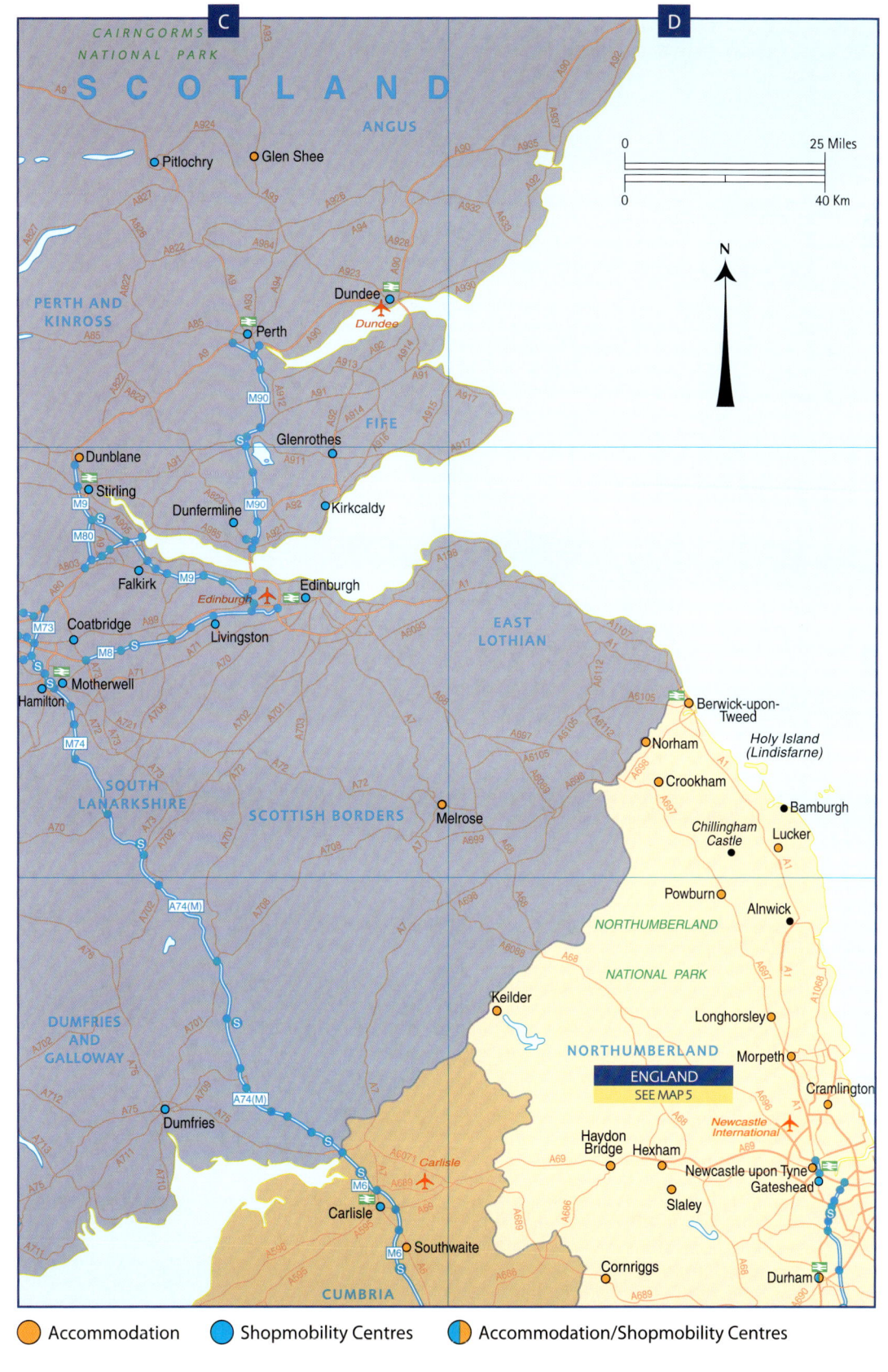

Accommodation • Shopmobility Centres • Accommodation/Shopmobility Centres

Map 7

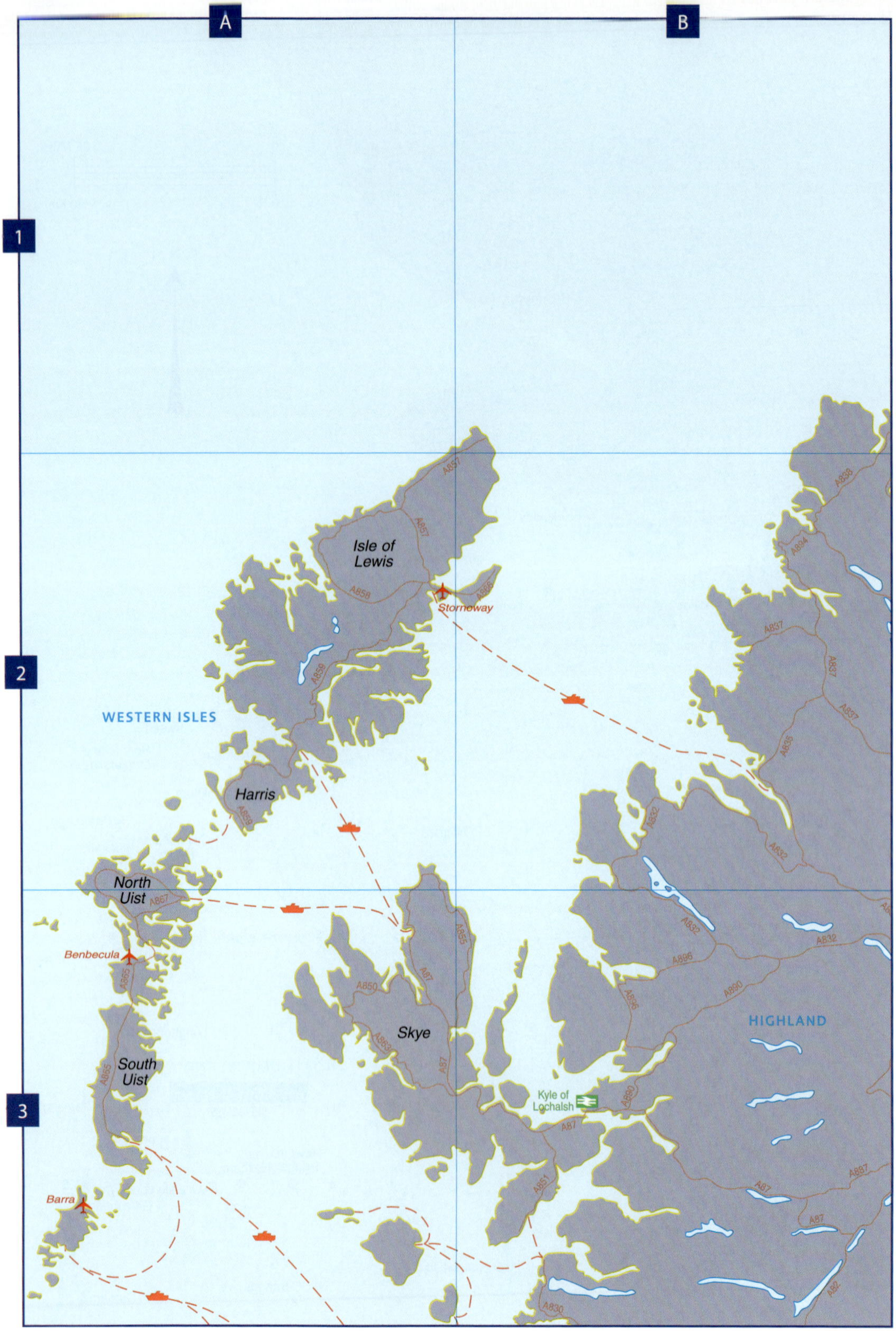

Key to regions: Scotland

Map 7

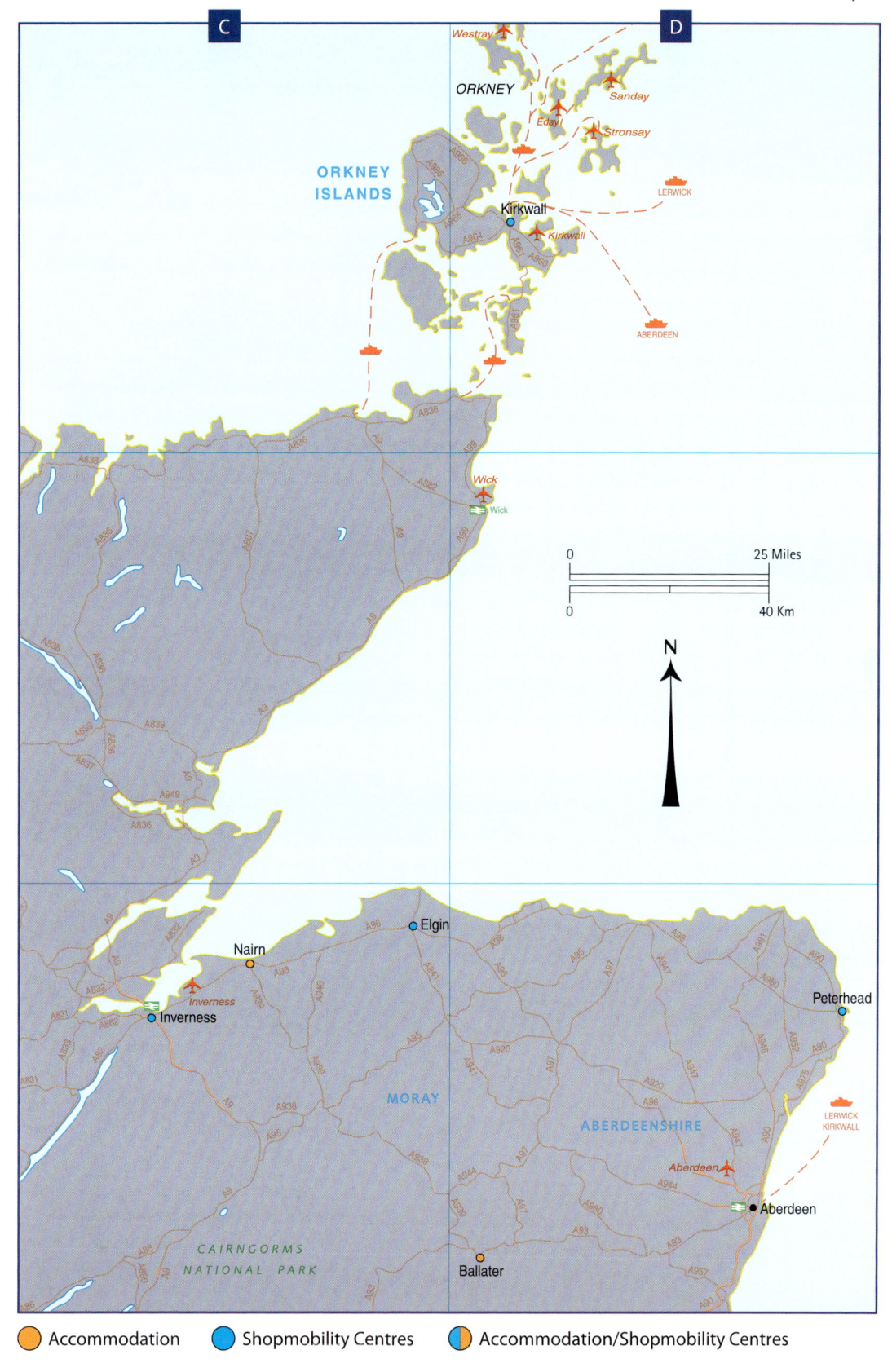

Map 8

National Accessible Scheme index

🚶 Mobility level 1

Abbotsbury South West
  Character Farm Cottages ★★★★ 109
Alston North West
  Proven House ★★★★ 281
Alton Pancras South West
  Bookham Court ★★★★★ 109
Aylmerton East of England
  Roman Camp Inn ★★★ 193
Bardon Mill North East
  High Shield ★★★★ 301
Bath South West
  Carfax Hotel ★★★ 116
Belchford East Midlands
  Poachers Hideaway ★★★★ - ★★★★★ 218
Blackpool North West
  The Lawton ★★★ 282
Boscastle South West
  The Old Coach House ★★★★ 92
Brassington East Midlands
  Hoe Grange Holidays ★★★★ 214
Bridlington Yorkshire & Humber
  Providence Place ★★★★ 250
Bridport South West
  Tamarisk Farm Holiday Cottages
  ★★★★ 110
Buckland Brewer South West
  West Hele ★★★★ 104
Budleigh Salterton South West
  Badgers Den ★★★★ 104
Burnham on Sea South West
  Wall Eden Farm ★★★ 117
Buxton East Midlands
  Northfield Farm ★★★ 215
Chewton Mendip South West
  The Garden House ★★★★★ 118
Compton South East
  The Barn ★★★★ 153

Compton South East
  The Bull Pen ★★★★ 153
Cotton East of England
  Coda Cottages ★★★★ 201
Davidstow South West
  Pendragon Country House ★★★★★ 92
East Dean South East
  Beachy Head Holiday Cottages ★★★★ .. 150
East Runton East of England
  Incleborough House ★★★★★ 194
Edenbridge South East
  Hay Barn & Straw Barn ★★★★ 144
Ellerby Yorkshire & Humber
  Ellerby ★★★★ 252
Farnham South East
  High Wray ★★★ 147
Gainford North East
  East Greystone Farm Cottages ★★★★ ... 299
Godney South West
  Swallow Barn ★★★★ 119
Happisburgh East of England
  Boundary Stables ★★★★ 196
Haydon Bridge North East
  Grindon Cartshed ★★★★ 303
Hereford Heart of England
  Grafton Villa Farm Cottages ★★★★ 233
Hexham North East
  The Hytte ★★★★★ 303
High Littleton South West
  Greyfield Farm Cottages
  ★★★★ - ★★★★★ 119
Horning East of England
  King Line Cottages ★★★ - ★★★★ 197
Hubberts Bridge East Midlands
  Elms Farm Cottages ★★★★ - ★★★★★ ... 219
Hunstanton East of England
  Caley Hall Hotel ★★★ 197

Establishments listed here have a detailed entry in this guide **435**

OpenBritain | National Accessible Scheme index

🦽 Mobility level 1 cont.

Ings North West
 Meadowcroft Country Guest House ★★★★ 277

Kirkbymoorside Yorkshire & Humber
 The Cornmill ★★★★ 254

Langho North West
 Mytton Fold Hotel and Golf Complex ★★★ 283

Lanreath South West
 Bocaddon Holiday Cottages ★★★★ 94

Looe South West
 Tudor Lodges ★★★★ 94

Lostwithiel Fowey South West
 Hartswheal Stables ★★★★ 95

Lower Godney South West
 Double-Gate Farm ★★★★ 119

Lowestoft East of England
 Pakefield Caravan Park ★★★★ 202

Macclesfield North West
 Kerridge End Holiday Cottages ★★★★★ 274

Maidenhead South East
 Holiday Inn Maidenhead 140

Marazion South West
 Ocean Studios ★★★★ 96

Middlewood Green East of England
 Leys Farmhouse Annexe ★★★ 202

Minehead South West
 The Promenade ★★★ 120

Minehead South West
 Woodcombe Lodges ★★★★ 120

Morecambe North West
 Eden Vale Luxury Holiday Flats ★★★ 283

Mount Hawke South West
 Ropers Walk Barns ★★★★ 96

North Somercotes East Midlands
 Nursery Cottage ★★★★ 221

Northleigh South West
 Smallicombe Farm ★★★★ 105

Oxford South East
 Abbey Guest House ★★★★ 147

Penrith North West
 Howscales ★★★★ 278

Pickering Yorkshire & Humber
 Keld Head Farm Cottages ★★★★ 256

Plymouth South West
 Haddington House Apartments ★★★ 106

Porthtowan South West
 Rosehill Lodges ★★★★★ 97

Quebec North East
 Hamsteels Cottages ★★★★ 299

Ross on Wye Heart of England
 Portland House 234

Sandringham (6 miles) East of England
 Oyster House ★★★★ 199

Sandy East of England
 Acorn Cottage ★★★★ 188

Saxmundham East of England
 Bluebell, Bonny, Buttercup & Bertie ★★★★ 203

Southwaite North West
 Southwaite Green ★★★★★ 279

Torquay South West
 Atlantis Holiday Apartments ★★★ - ★★★★ 107

Torquay South West
 Crown Lodge ★★★★ 108

Treator South West
 Woodlands Country House ★★★★★ 100

Wattisfield East of England
 Jayes Holiday Cottages ★★★ 204

Weston-Super-Mare South West
 The Royal Hotel ★★★ 122

Windermere North West
 Linthwaite House Hotel ★★★ 281

Woodhall Spa East Midlands
 Petwood Hotel ★★★ 221

Wooler North East
 Crookhouse Cottages ★★★★ 307

Yealmpton South West
 Kitley House Hotel and Restaurant ★★★ 108

Yelverton South West
 Overcombe House ★★★★ 109

🦽 Mobility level 2

Abbotsbury South West
 Character Farm Cottages ★★★★ 109

Acton Bridge North West
 Wall Hill Farm Guesthouse ★★★★★ 272

Mobility level 2 cont.

Ainsdale North West
Willowbank Holiday Home and Touring Park ★★★★★ 286

Albaston South West
Todsworthy Farm Holidays ★★★★ 92

Alnwick North East
Doxford Cottages ★★★★★ 300

Alston North West
Proven House ★★★★ 281

Alton Pancras South West
Bookham Court ★★★★★ 109

Ambleside North West
Rothay Manor ★★★ 275

Aylmerton East of England
Roman Camp Inn ★★★ 193

Bath South West
Carfax Hotel ★★★ 116

Beaminster South West
Stable Cottage ★★★★ 109

Beesands South West
Beeson Farm Holiday Cottages ★★★★ .. 102

Bellingham North East
Brownrigg Lodges ★★★ 301

Bradfield East of England
Curlews ★★★★ 191

Brassington East Midlands
Hoe Grange Holidays ★★★★ 214

Bridlington Yorkshire & Humber
Providence Place ★★★★ 250

Buckden Yorkshire & Humber
Dalegarth and The Ghyll Cottages ★★★★ 251

Buckland Brewer South West
West Hele ★★★★ 104

Budleigh Salterton South West
Badgers Den ★★★★ 104

Chewton Mendip South West
The Garden House ★★★★★ 118

Compton South East
The Barn ★★★★ 153

Compton South East
The Bull Pen ★★★★ 153

Corfton Heart of England
Goosefoot Barn Cottages ★★★★ 235

Diss East of England
Ivy House Farm Cottages (Owl Cottage) ★★★★ 194

Earl Sternedale East Midlands
Wheeldon Trees Farm ★★★★ 215

East Runton East of England
Incleborough House ★★★★★ 194

Ellerby Yorkshire & Humber
Ellerby ★★★★ 252

Farnham South East
High Wray ★★★ 147

Flamborough Yorkshire & Humber
Flamborough Rock Cottages ★★★ 253

Fowey South West
South Torfrey Farm ★★★★★ 92

Frosterley North East
Cromer House Camping Barn 299

Gainford North East
East Greystone Farm Cottages ★★★★ ... 299

Gatebeck North West
Barkinbeck Cottage ★★★ 276

Gissing East of England
Honeysuckle Cottage ★★★★ 195

Gissing East of England
Rose Cottage ★★★★ 196

Godney South West
Swallow Barn ★★★★ 119

Happisburgh East of England
Boundary Stables ★★★★ 196

Haughley East of England
Red House Farm Cottages
★★★ - ★★★★ 201

Haydon Bridge North East
Grindon Cartshed ★★★★ 303

Hereford Heart of England
Grafton Villa Farm Cottages ★★★★ 233

Hexham North East
The Hytte ★★★★★ 303

High Cogges South East
Swallows Nest ★★★★ 146

Horning East of England
King Line Cottages ★★★ - ★★★★ 197

Hubberts Bridge East Midlands
Elms Farm Cottages ★★★★ - ★★★★★ ... 219

Hunstanton East of England
Caley Hall Hotel ★★★ 197

OpenBritain | National Accessible Scheme index

Mobility level 2 cont.

Ings North West
Meadowcroft Country Guest House ★★★★ 277

Knightcote Heart of England
Arbor Holiday & Knightcote Farm Cottages ★★★★★ 238

Langho North West
Mytton Fold Hotel and Golf Complex ★★★ 283

Lewes South East
Heath Farm ★★★★ 151

Llanfair Caereinion Wales
Madog's Wells 356

Longhorsley North East
Beacon Hill ★★★★★ 304

Looe South West
Tudor Lodges ★★★★ 94

Lostwithiel Fowey South West
Hartswheal Stables ★★★★ 95

Lower Godney South West
Double-Gate Farm ★★★★ 119

Lucker North East
Lucker Hall Steading ★★★★ - ★★★★★ .. 305

Malvern Heart of England
Hidelow House Cottages ★★★★ - ★★★★★ 234

Manchester Airport North West
Bewleys Hotel Manchester Airport 286

Minehead South West
The Promenade ★★★ 120

Minehead South West
Woodcombe Lodges ★★★★ 120

Mount Hawke South West
Ropers Walk Barns ★★★★ 96

Nayland East of England
Gladwins Farm Self Catering Cottages ★★★★ - ★★★★★ 202

Northleigh South West
Smallicombe Farm ★★★★ 105

Northleigh South West
Smallicombe Farm Self Catering ★★★★ .. 106

Nr Hartington East Midlands
Old House Farm Cottages ★★★★ 215

Oxford South East
Abbey Guest House ★★★★ 147

Penrith North West
Howscales ★★★★ 278

Polzeath South West
Manna Place ★★★★ 97

Ribble Valley North West
Pinfold Farm ★★★★ 284

Ross on Wye Heart of England
Portland House 234

Ross on Wye Heart of England
Trevase Granary ★★★★★ 234

Ruan High Lanes South West
Trenona Farm Holidays ★★★★ 98

Sandy East of England
Acorn Cottage ★★★★ 188

Shrewsbury Heart of England
Newton Meadows ★★★★ 236

Slaley North East
Rye Hill Farm (Old Byre) ★★★★ 307

Southwaite North West
Southwaite Green ★★★★★ 279

St Bees North West
Springbank Farm Lodges ★★★★ 279

Stathe South West
Walkers Farm Cottages ★★★★ 121

Torquay South West
Atlantis Holiday Apartments ★★★ - ★★★★ 107

Torquay South West
Crown Lodge ★★★★ 108

Treator South West
Woodlands Country House ★★★★★ .. 100

Wark North East
Battlesteads Hotel ★★★★ 307

Wattisfield East of England
Jayes Holiday Cottages ★★★ 204

West Kirby North West
Herons Well Cottage ★★★★★ 287

Weston-Super-Mare South West
The Royal Hotel ★★★ 122

Worcester Heart of England
The Manor Coach House ★★★★ 239

Yealmpton South West
Kitley House Hotel and Restaurant ★★★ 108

Yelverton South West
Overcombe House ★★★★ 109

National Accessible Scheme index | OpenBritain

Mobility level 2 cont.

Yorkley South West
2 Danby Cottages ★★★ 116

Mobility level 3 Independent

Albaston South West
Todsworthy Farm Holidays ★★★★ 92

Bridport South West
Tamarisk Farm Holiday Cottages
★★★★ 110

Bristol South West
Winford Manor ★★★ 113

Broadclyst South West
Hue's Piece ★★★★ 103

Buckland Brewer South West
West Hele ★★★★ 104

Corfe Castle South West
Mortons House Hotel ★★★ 110

Gissing East of England
Bluebell Cottage ★★★★ 195

Gissing East of England
Primrose Cottage ★★★★ 196

Godney South West
Swallow Barn ★★★★ 119

Kilkhampton South West
Forda Lodges & Cottages
★★★★ - ★★★★★ 94

Knightcote Heart of England
Arbor Holiday & Knightcote Farm Cottages ★★★★★ 238

Lincoln East Midlands
Cliff Farm Cottage ★★★★ 220

Looe South West
Tudor Lodges ★★★★ 94

Lostwithiel Fowey South West
Hartswheal Stables ★★★★ 95

Loughborough East Midlands
imago at Burleigh Court ★★★★ 217

Lower Godney South West
Double-Gate Farm ★★★★ 119

Malvern Heart of England
Hidelow House Cottages
★★★★ - ★★★★★ 234

Mount Hawke South West
Ropers Walk Barns ★★★★ 96

Sandringham East of England
Park House Hotel ★★ 198

Southwold East of England
Newlands Country House ★★★★ 203

Torquay South West
Crown Lodge ★★★★ 108

Weston-Super-Mare South West
The Royal Hotel ★★★ 122

Wigsthorpe East Midlands
Nene Valley Cottages ★★★★★ 222

Windermere North West
Lake District Disabled Holidays ★★★★ .. 280

Mobility level 3 Assisted

Albaston South West
Todsworthy Farm Holidays ★★★★ 92

Buckland Brewer South West
West Hele ★★★★ 104

Cockfield North East
Stonecroft and Swallows Nest ★★★★ 297

Compton South East
The Barn ★★★★ 153

Compton South East
The Bull Pen ★★★★ 153

Cornriggs North East
Alice & Nelly's Cottages ★★★★★ 298

Godney South West
Swallow Barn ★★★★ 119

Hexham North East
The Hytte ★★★★★ 303

Kielder North East
Calvert Trust Kielder ★★★★ 304

Kilkhampton South West
Forda Lodges & Cottages
★★★★ - ★★★★★ 94

Lanreath South West
Bocaddon Holiday Cottages ★★★★ 94

Looe South West
Tudor Lodges ★★★★ 94

Lostwithiel Fowey South West
Hartswheal Stables ★★★★ 95

Lostwithiel South West
Brean Park ★★★★★ 95

Lower Godney South West
Double-Gate Farm ★★★★ 119

Minehead South West
The Promenade ★★★ 120

Establishments listed here have a detailed entry in this guide

OpenBritain | National Accessible Scheme index

Mobility level 3 Assisted cont.

Mount Hawke South West
  Ropers Walk Barns ★★★★ 96
Pillaton South West
  Kernock Cottages ★★★★ - ★★★★★ 96
South Molton South West
  Stable Cottage ★★★★★ 107
Wattisfield East of England
  Jayes Holiday Cottages ★★★ 204
Yarmouth South East
  West Bay Club ★★★★ 143
York Yorkshire & Humber
  South Newlands Farm Self Catering
  ★★★★ 261

Hearing impairment level 1

Alston North West
  Proven House ★★★★ 281
Brassington East Midlands
  Hoe Grange Holidays ★★★★ 214
Corfe Castle South West
  Mortons House Hotel ★★★ 110
Hexham North East
  The Hytte ★★★★★ 303
Hubberts Bridge East Midlands
  Elms Farm Cottages ★★★★ - ★★★★★ ... 219
Kielder North East
  Calvert Trust Kielder ★★★★ 304
Loughborough East Midlands
  imago at Burleigh Court ★★★★ 217

Lowestoft East of England
  Pakefield Caravan Park ★★★★ 202
Maidenhead South East
  Holiday Inn Maidenhead 140
Oxford South East
  Abbey Guest House ★★★★ 147
St Bees North West
  Springbank Farm Lodges ★★★★ 279
Weston-Super-Mare South West
  The Royal Hotel ★★★ 122

Visual impairment level 1

Ainsdale North West
  Willowbank Holiday Home and
  Touring Park ★★★★★ 286
Alston North West
  Proven House ★★★★ 281
Brassington East Midlands
  Hoe Grange Holidays ★★★★ 214
Hexham North East
  The Hytte ★★★★★ 303
Hubberts Bridge East Midlands
  Elms Farm Cottages ★★★★ - ★★★★★ ... 219
Loughborough East Midlands
  imago at Burleigh Court ★★★★ 217
Lowestoft East of England
  Pakefield Caravan Park ★★★★ 202
Oxford South East
  Abbey Guest House ★★★★ 147
St Bees North West
  Springbank Farm Lodges ★★★★ 279

Index of Display Advertisers

Accor Hotels	28
Action for Blind People	46
Adapt-Ability	310
Adapted Car Hire	70
Age Concern	70
Allied Mobility	38
The Alnwick Garden	310
Amvale	74
Anglesey Sea Zoo	359
Arsenal Stadium Tours	182
Arundel Castle	161
ATOC	4 & 403
Bank Farm Leisure Park	359
Bath City Sightseeing	133
Bath Park & Ride	129
Bath-Knight	68
Beaulieu	161
Bendrigg Trust	291
Birmingham Botanical Gardens	241
The Black Country Living Museum	241
Blue Planet Aquarium	289
Bodelwyddan Castle Hotel	358
Bond Hotels	32
Bosworth Battlefield Heritage Centre	227
Bow Well House	310
Break	74
Breeze Buses	162
Bridgestone	74
Brig-Ayd Controls Ltd	362
The Bristol Hippodrome	129
British Airways	8
Broads Authority	207
Broadwindsor Craft and Design Centre	130
Brook Miller Mobility Limited	167, 264 & 389
Brotherwood Auto	48
Bruce Wake Charitable Trust	229
Bunn Leisure	162
Cadbury World	242
The Camping & Caravanning Club	44
Can be Done	74
Canterbury	161
Centre for Alternative Technology	359
The Centre	340
Ceredigion County Council	360
Christchurch	134
Clacton Factory Outlet	207
Colchester and Ipswich Museum Service	207
Colchester Borough Council	207
Collins Care	58
Come to Rochdale	290
Constables Mobility	58
Copthorne Tara Hotel	179
Cotswold Charm	130
Cotswold Wildlife Park and Gardens	162
DairyLand Farm World	133
Dalby Forest	266
Deep Sea World	340
Delichon	12
Devon County Council	131
Direct Mobility Hire	82
DirectGov	14 & 15
Disability Support Group (NE)	82
Discover Falmouth	131
Discover Royal Windsor	164
Donmar Warehouse	182
Drayton Manor Theme Park	243
Duthie Park	342
East Ayrshire Council	340
East Carlton Country Park	227
Easy Link UK	82
Enjoy Rugby	242
Enjoy Snowdonia	360

For symbols see pg 24

441

OpenBritain | Index of Display Advertisers

Etac	135
Explore Teesdale	311
Fairhaven Garden	84
Fairhaven Woodland	84
Fairprice Mobility (Scotland)	340
Fenland District Council	209
Fleet Air Arm Museum	134
Focke & Co (UK)	84
Forest Laboratories (UK) Ltd	84
Forestry Commission Scotland	341
Geffrye Museum	181
The General Estates Co Ltd	163
Gerald Simonds	60
Gloucester Cathedral	134
GM Coachwork	62
Great Yarmouth	208
Greenwich	181
Grosvenor Centre Northampton	227
Guildford Cathedral	166
Guildhall Art Gallery	179
Hall for Cornwall	131
Harpers Health & Fitness	160
Harriet Davis Seaside Holiday Trust for Disabled Children	358
Harrold Odell Country Park	209
Hastings & 1066 Country	163
Havant & Hayling Island	163
The Hawk Conservancy Trust	163
Hedley Hall	310
Henry Moore Institute	266
Heritage Motor Centre	243
Holden Mobility	398
Holiday Inn	56
Horniman Museum	181
Houses of Parliament	182
Huntingdonshire District Council	208
Hurley Riverside Park	166
Intercontinental Hotels	6
The Isle of Anglesey	359
Jane Austen's House Museum	166
John Greenan	52
Jorvik Viking Centre	265
Jubilee Sailing Trust	82
Lancashire County Council	289
Lee Valley Regional Park	177
Les Rocquettes Hotel	134
Lincoln Cathedral	227
London Borough of Barking & Dagenham	181
London Borough of Redbridge	183
London Canal Museum	182
The Look Out Discovery Centre	164
Lowry Outlet Mall	289
Lowstead Farm Cottage	265
Manchester Art Gallery	290
Manchester City Council	290
McArthur Glen	18
Mobilise	72
The Mobility Roadshow	62
Mobility Smart	42
Molten Rock	64
Monkey World	128
Motability	16
Motion Technology	54
MS Society	30
The National Coal Mining Museum	265
National Theatre	180
National Trust	78
The New Art Gallery Walsall	243
Newark & Sherwood District Council	228
Newquay Zoo	134
Nexus	66
Norfolk Cottages	208
North Bay Railway	265
North Shore	228
North York Moors National Park	266
Northumberland National Park	311
Norwich Bus Station	206
Nottingham City Council	228
The Nuffield Theatre	164
Orkney Museums and Heritage	341
P.I.P.P.A. Wheelchair Hire Scheme	361
Parkdean	78
PB Conversions	78
Plas Menai National Watersports Centre	360
Plymouth Gin Distillery	131
Quay Holidays	129

Index of Display Advertisers | OpenBritain

Redwings Horse Sanctuary	208
Rehab Prosthetics	78
Renaissance London Heathrow Hotel	180
Renishaw Hall & Gardens	229
RHS Garden Rosemoor	132
The Roald Dahl Museum and Story Centre	166
Robin Hood Breaks	228
The Roman Camp Country House Hotel	341
Rothay Manor	291
Royal Exchange Theatre	290
Royal Horticultural Society	26 & 27
Royal Military Police Museum	166
The Royal Parks	178
RSC	84
Rufford Abbey Country Park	229
Rusko Holidays	341
RYA Sailability	80
Salford Heritage Service	291
Sandcastle Waterpark	291
Sandringham House, Museum & Gardens	209
Scope Inclusion Team	80
Scotrail	339
The Scottish Parliament	342
Scout Holiday Homes Trust	80
Sharp and Nickless	84
Shetland Island Council Ferry Services	339
Shrewsbury	244
Sirus Automotive	64
Sissinghurst	165
South Devon Railway	132
South Somerset	132
Southwaite Green	292
Spinal Home Care	36
St David's Hall and New Theatre	360
St Michael's Without	134
Staffordshire County Council	244
Stairlifts from Help The Aged	70
STEAM	132
Sudeley Castle	134
Swallow Evacuation & Mobility Products	60
Tamworth Castle	244
Taunton's Shopmobility Centre	133
Tendring District Council	209
The Thomas Centre	226
Tower Park	133
Transpennine Express	68
Transportforall	182
The Trentham Estate	241
Tullie House Museum & Art Gallery	291
Twycross Zoo	244
Unwin Safety Systems	80
Vauxhall Holiday Park	209
Visit Cornwall	130
Visit Newcastle-under-Lyme	243
Visit Preston	291
Watercress Line	164
Westminster Cathedral	183
The Wheelyboat Trust	84
Winchester City Council	165
Wood Farm	133
Woodlands Family Theme Park	134
YHA	66
Ynysymaengwyn Caravan & Camping Park	361
York Minster	266
Yorkshire Dales National Park	266

For symbols see pg 24

Index by place name

A

Abbotsbury, *Dorset* 109
Aberaeron, *Ceredigion* 350
Aberdaron, *Gwynedd* 351
Aberdeen, *Aberdeenshire* .... 318, 319 & 337
Abergavenny, *Monmouthshire* 353
Abergele, *Conwy* 350
Acton Bridge, *Cheshire* 272
Ainsdale, *Merseyside* 286
Albaston, *Cornwall* 92
Alnwick, *Northumberland* .... 300 & 308
Alston, *Lancashire* 281
Alton, *Hampshire* 156
Alton Pancras, *Dorset* 109
Ambleside, *Cumbria* .... 274 & 275
Amroth, *Pembrokeshire* 353
Ardmaddy, *Argyll & Bute* 320
Ashbourne, *Derbyshire* 213
Ashford, *Kent* 143
Auldgirth, *Dumfries & Galloway* 322
Axton, *Flintshire* 357
Aylesbury, *Buckinghamshire* 140
Aylmerton, *Norfolk* 193
Ayr, *South Ayrshire* 335

B

Bailey, *Cumbria* 275
Bakewell, *Derbyshire* 213
Ballater, *Aberdeenshire* 319
Bardon Mill, *Northumberland* 301
Barnard Castle, *Co. Durham* 297
Basildon, *Essex* 190
Bath, *Somerset* .... 116 & 126
Battle, *East Sussex* .... 149 & 159
Beaminster, *Dorset* 109
Beaulieu, *Hampshire* 156
Beesands, *Devon* 102
Belchford, *Lincolnshire* 218
Bellingham, *Northumberland* 301
Belsay, *Northumberland* 308
Benderloch, *Argyll & Bute* 320
Berwick-Upon-Tweed, *Northumberland* ... 301

Bethesda, *Gwynedd* .... 351 & 352
Biggar, *South Lanarkshire* 335
Birmingham, *West Midlands* ... 238, 239 & 240
Blackpool, *Lancashire* .... 282 & 288
Blaenau Ffestiniog, *Gwynedd* 352
Blairgowrie, *Perth and Kinross* 332
Blandford Forum, *Dorset* 125
Blue Anchor, *Somerset* 117
Bodmin, *Cornwall* 92
Bognor Regis, *West Sussex* .... 151 & 152
Bolsover, *Derbyshire* 224
Bolton Abbey, *Yorkshire & Humber* 250
Bolton, *Lancashire* 282
Boncath, *Pembrokeshire* 354
Boscastle, *Cornwall* 92
Bracklesham Bay, *West Sussex* 152
Bracknell, *Berkshire* 155
Bradfield, *Essex* 191
Brassington, *Derbyshire* 214
Brecon, *Powys* 355
Brentwood, *Essex* 191
Bridgewater, *Somerset* 117
Bridlington, *Yorkshire & Humber* 250
Bridport, *Dorset* 110
Brighouse, *Yorkshire & Humber* 250
Brighton & Hove, *East Sussex* 149
Bristol, *Gloucestershire* .... 113 & 126
Brixham, *Devon* 103
Broadclyst, *Devon* 103
Brodsworth, *Yorkshire & Humber* 261
Brynslencyn, *Isle of Anglesey* 357
Buckden, *Yorkshire & Humber* 251
Buckland Brewer, *Devon* 104
Budleigh Salterton, *Devon* 104
Builth Wells, *Powys* 356
Burford, *Oxfordshire* .... 146 & 158
Burnham on Sea, *Somerset* 117
Bury, *Greater Manchester* 285
Buxton, *Derbyshire* .... 214 & 215

C

Caernarfon, *Gwynedd* 352
Cambridge, *Cambridgeshire* 188

Index by place name | OpenBritain

C continued

Campbeltown, *Argyll & Bute*	321
Cardiff, *Cardiff*	357
Carmarthen, *Carmarthenshire*	349
Castlemartin, *Pembrokeshire*	354
Chard, *Somerset*	118
Chelmsford, *Essex*	204
Chepstow, *Monmouthshire*	353
Cheshire, *Cheshire*	272
Chester, *Cheshire*	273
Chesterfield, *Derbyshire*	215
Chewton Mendip, *Somerset*	118
Chichester, *Hampshire*	156
Chigwell, *Essex*	191
Cirencester, *Gloucestershire*	114
Clacton-On-Sea, *Essex*	192
Cliftonville, *Kent*	144
Cockermouth, *Cumbria*	276
Cockfield, *Co. Durham*	297
Colchester, *Essex*	205
Coldstream, *Scottish Borders*	333 & 334
Compton, *West Sussex*	153
Corby, *Northamptonshire*	221
Corfe Castle, *Dorset*	110
Corfton, *Shropshire*	235
Cornriggs, *Co. Durham*	298
Cotton, *Suffolk*	201
Coventry, *West Midlands*	239
Cowes, *Isle of Wight*	157
Cranbrook, *Kent*	157
Craven Arms, *Shropshire*	235
Crick, *Northamptonshire*	222
Cromer, *Norfolk*	194
Crookham, *Northumberland*	302
Croydon, *Surrey*	147

D

Davidstow, *Cornwall*	92
Deal, *Kent*	157
Derby, *Derbyshire*	215
Diss, *Norfolk*	194
Dolgellau, *Gwynedd*	353
Dover, *Kent*	158
Downe, *Kent*	158
Dumfries, *Dumfries & Galloway*	322
Dunblane, *Stirling*	336
Dunfermline, *Fife*	326
Durham, *Co. Durham*	298 & 308

E

Earl Sterndale, *Derbyshire*	215
East Dean, *East Sussex*	150
East Grinstead, *West Sussex*	154
East Runton, *Norfolk*	194
Edenbridge, *Kent*	144
Edgbaston, *West Midlands*	240
Edinburgh, *Edinburgh*	324, 325 & 337
Elie, *Fife*	326
Ellerby, *Yorkshire & Humber*	252
Eynsford, *Kent*	158

F

Falmouth, *Cornwall*	124
Fareham, *Hampshire*	141
Farnham, *Surrey*	147
Felingwm Uchaf, *Carmarthenshire*	349
Felpham, *West Sussex*	154
Filey, *Yorkshire & Humber*	252
Flamborough, *Yorkshire & Humber*	253
Folkestone, *Kent*	145
Forest of Dean, *Gloucestershire*	114
Fort William, *Highland*	328
Fowey, *Cornwall*	92
Framlingham, *Suffolk*	205
Frosterley, *Co. Durham*	299

G

Gainford, *Co. Durham*	299
Gairloch, *Highland*	328
Gatebeck, *Cumbria*	276
Gissing, *Norfolk*	195 & 196
Glasgow Airport, *Renfrewshire*	333
Glasgow, *Glasgow*	327
Glenshee, *Perth and Kinross*	333
Gloucester, *Gloucestershire*	114 & 126
Glynde, *East Sussex*	150
Godney, *Somerset*	119
Goodrich, *Herefordshire*	240
Grange-over-Sands, *Cumbria*	276
Great Missenden, *Buckinghamshire*	155
Great Torrington, *Devon*	124
Great Witley, *Worcestershire*	225
Gretna, *Dumfries & Galloway*	323
Guildford, *Surrey*	147 & 158

H

Happisburgh, *Norfolk*	196
Harrogate, *Yorkshire & Humber*	261
Harrold, *Bedfordshire*	204

For symbols see pg 24

445

OpenBritain | Index by place name

H continued

Hastings, *East Sussex*	150
Haughley, *Suffolk*	201
Hawick, *Scottish Borders*	334
Hawkshead, *Cumbria*	277
Haydock, *Merseyside*	287
Haydon Bridge, *Northumberland*	303
Haywards Heath, *West Sussex*	154
Helmsley, *Yorkshire & Humber*	262
Helston, *Cornwall*	93
Hemel Hempstead, *Hertfordshire*	193
Hereford, *Herefordshire*	233
Hexham, *Northumberland*	303, 304 & 309
High Cogges, *Oxfordshire*	146
High Littleton, *Somerset*	119
High Wycombe, *Buckinghamshire*	140
Hogsthorpe, *Lincolnshire*	219
Honiton, *Devon*	105
Horley, *Surrey*	148
Horning, *Norfolk*	197
Hounslow, *Outer London*	172
Hubberts Bridge, *Lincolnshire*	219
Hunstanton, *Norfolk*	197
Huntingdon, *Cambridgeshire*	189

I

Ilam, *Staffordshire*	237
Ings, *Cumbria*	277
Ipswich, *Suffolk*	201
Isle of Purbeck, *Dorset*	110
Isle of Skye, *Highland*	329
Isle of Wight, *Isle of Wight*	157

J

Jersey, *Jersey*	101 & 102

K

Kendal, *Cumbria*	278
Kenilworth, *Warwickshire*	225
Kielder, *Northumberland*	304
Kilkhampton, *Cornwall*	94
Kirkbymoorside, *Yorkshire & Humber*	254
Knightcote, *Warwickshire*	238

L

Lampeter, *Ceredigion*	350
Lancaster, *Lancashire*	283
Langho, *Lancashire*	283
Lanreath, *Cornwall*	94
Laxton, *Northamptonshire*	222
Leeds, *Yorkshire & Humber*	254 & 262
Leicester, *Leicestershire*	216
Levisham, nr Pickering, *Yorkshire & Humber*	255
Lewes, *East Sussex*	151
Leyburn, *Yorkshire & Humber*	262
Lincoln, *Lincolnshire*	220 & 224
Liverpool, *Merseyside*	287 & 288
Llandrindod Wells, *Powys*	356
Llandudno, *Conwy*	350 & 351
Llanfair Caereinion, *Powys*	356
London - Kingston South, *Outer London*	173
London E16, *Inner London*	171
London E2, *Inner London*	174
London N1, *Inner London*	174
London N5, *Inner London*	174
London, Newbury Park, *Outer London*	173
London NW2, *Outer London*	173
London NW3, *Inner London*	174
London, *Outer London*	173 & 176
London SE19, *Outer London*	173
London SE2, *Inner London*	171
London SE9, *Inner London*	175
London SW1, *Inner London*	175
London SW6, *Inner London*	171
London SW7, *Inner London*	172
London W1, *Inner London*	172
London W2, *Inner London*	175
London W3, *Inner London*	172
London W4, *Inner London*	175
London WC1, *Inner London*	172
London WC2, *Inner London*	175
Longhorsley, *Northumberland*	304
Looe, *Cornwall*	94
Lossiemouth, *Moray*	331
Lostwithiel, *Cornwall*	95
Lostwithiel Fowey, *Cornwall*	95
Loughborough, *Leicestershire*	217
Lower Godney, *Somerset*	119
Lowestoft, *Suffolk*	202
Lucker, *Northumberland*	305
Luton, *Bedfordshire*	204
Lymington, *Hampshire*	141
Lympsham, Weston-Super-Mare, *Somerset*	120

M

Macclesfield, *Cheshire*	274
Machynlleth, *Powys*	357

446   www.openbritain.net

Index by place name | OpenBritain

M continued

Maenclochog, *Pembrokeshire* 355
Maidenhead, *Berkshire* 140
Malmesbury, *Wiltshire* 123
Malvern, *Herefordshire* 234
Manchester Airport, *Greater Manchester* 286
Manchester, *Greater Manchester* 288
Marazion, *Cornwall* 96
Market Harborough, *Leicestershire* 217
Melrose, *Scottish Borders* 334
Mersea Island, *Essex* 192
Middlewood Green, *Suffolk* 202
Milford, *Derbyshire* 215
Milton Keynes, *Buckinghamshire* 140
Minehead, *Somerset* 120
Modbury, *Devon* 105
Morecambe, *Lancashire* 283
Moreton-in-Marsh, *Gloucestershire* 115
Morpeth, *Northumberland* 305
Mount Hawke, *Cornwall* 96

N

Nairn, *Highland* 330
Nayland, *Suffolk* 202
Necton, *Cheshire* 288
New Alresford, *Hampshire* 156
New Lanark, *South Lanarkshire* 335
Newcastle upon Tyne, *Northumberland* ... 306
Newquay, *Cornwall* 124
Newtonmore, *Highland* 330
North Queensferry, *Fife* 337
North Somercotes, *Lincolnshire* 221
Northleigh, *Devon* .... 105 & 106
Norwich, *Norfolk* .... 198 & 205
Nottingham, *Nottinghamshire* 223
nr Amesbury, *Wiltshire* 126
Nr Andover, *Hampshire* 156
Nr Hartington, *Derbyshire* 215

O

Oban, *Argyll & Bute* 321
Okehampton, *Devon* 125
Ollerton, *Nottinghamshire* 225
Orkney, *Orkney Islands* .... 337 & 338
Oxford, *Oxfordshire* 147

P

Peebles, *Scottish Borders* 334
Pendine, *Carmarthenshire* 349

Penrith, *Cumbria* 278
Peterborough, *Cambridgeshire* 190
Pevensey, *East Sussex* 159
Pickering, *Yorkshire & Humber* 256
Pillaton, *Cornwall* 96
Plymouth, *Devon* .... 106 & 125
Polzeath, *Cornwall* 97
Pontyclun, *Rhondda, Cynon, Taff* 357
Poole, *Dorset* .... 111 & 125
Porthtowan, *Cornwall* 97
Portland, *Dorset* 125
Powburn, *Northumberland* 306
Prudhoe, *Northumberland* 309

Q

Quebec, *Co. Durham* 299

R

Redhill, *Surrey* 148
Ribble Valley, *Lancashire* 284
Richmond, *Yorkshire & Humber* 257
Rievaulx, *Yorkshire & Humber* 262
Rochester-Chatham, *Kent* 145
Ross on Wye, *Herefordshire* 234
Ruan High Lanes, *Cornwall* 98
Runcorn, *Cheshire* 274
Ruthin, *Denbighshire* 351

S

Saffron Walden, *Essex* .... 192 & 205
Salford, *Greater Manchester* 288
Salisbury, *Wiltshire* 127
Sandringham (6 miles), *Norfolk* 199
Sandringham, *Norfolk* .... 198, 199 & 205
Sandy, *Bedfordshire* 188
Saxmundham, *Suffolk* 203
Scarborough, *Yorkshire & Humber* 262
Selsey Bill, *West Sussex* 155
Shepperton, *Outer London* 174
Shrewsbury, *Shropshire* 236
Sidbury, *Devon* 107
Slaley, *Northumberland* 307
Slough, *Berkshire* 140
South Molton, *Devon* 107
Southampton, Eastleigh, *Hampshire* 141
Southampton, *Hampshire* .... 141 & 156
Southport, *Merseyside* 287
Southwaite, *Cumbria* 279
Southwold, *Suffolk* 203
St Agnes, *Cornwall* 99

For symbols see pg 24

447

S continued

St Bees, *Cumbria* 279
St Helen's, *Isle of Wight* 142
St Ives, *Cambridgeshire* 190
St Mawes, *Cornwall* 124
Stathe, *Somerset* 121
Stevenage, *Hertfordshire* 193
Stockton on Tees, *Co. Durham* 300
Stogumber, *Somerset* 121
Stoke-on-Trent, *Staffordshire* 237
Stornoway, *Western Isles* 337
Stratford-Upon-Avon, *Warwickshire* 240
Summercourt, *Cornwall* 124
Sutton Cheney, *Leicestershire* 224
Sutton, *Surrey* 148
Swanage, *Dorset* 112
Swindon, *Wiltshire* .... 123 & 127

T

Tamworth, *Staffordshire* 240
Taunton, *Somerset* 121
Tebay, *Cumbria* 279
Telford, *Shropshire* 236
Thetford, *Norfolk* 200
Thurso, *Highland* 331
Tilbury, *Essex* 156
Tintagel, *Cornwall* 99
Torquay, *Devon* .... 107 & 108
Totnes, *Devon* 125
Treator, *Cornwall* 100
Truro (7 miles), *Cornwall* 101
Truro, *Cornwall* 100
Turriff, *Aberdeenshire* 319

W

Wakefield, *Yorkshire & Humber* 258
Walsall, *West Midlands* 240
Wark, *Northumberland* 307
Warkworth, *Northumberland* 309
Warminster, *Wiltshire* .... 123 & 127
Warrington, *Cheshire* 274
Wattisfield, *Suffolk* 204
Wells, *Somerset* 121
Welshpool, *Powys* 356
West Drayton, *Outer London* 174
West Kirby, *Merseyside* 287
West Marden, *West Sussex* 155
Weston-Super-Mare, *Somerset* 122
Weymouth, *Dorset* 112
Whitby, *Yorkshire & Humber* .... 259 & 263
Whitland, *Carmarthenshire* 349
Wigsthorpe, *Northamptonshire* 222
Winchcombe, *Gloucestershire* 126
Windermere, *Cumbria* .... 280 & 281
Wisley, *Surrey* 159
Woking, *Surrey* 148
Wokingham, *Berkshire* 140
Woodchester, *Gloucestershire* 115
Woodhall Spa, *Lincolnshire* 221
Wooler, *Northumberland* 307
Worcester, *Worcestershire* .... 239 & 240
Worksop, *Nottinghamshire* 224
Worle, *Somerset* 122

Y

Yarmouth, *Isle of Wight* 143
Yealmpton, *Devon* 108
Yelverton, *Devon* 109
York, *Yorkshire & Humber* .... 259, 260, 261 & 263
Yorkley, *Gloucestershire* 116

Index by property name

0-9

1 Woodchester Lodge *Woodchester* 115
2 Danby Cottages *Yorkley* 116
5 Dolphin Quays *Poole* 111
1066 Battle of Hastings, Abbey & Battlefield *Battle* 159

A

Abbey Guest House *Oxford* 147
Abbey Wood Caravan Club Site *London SE2* 171
Acorn Cottage *Sandy* 188
Ae Farm Cottages *Dumfries* 322
Alderstead Heath Caravan Club Site *Redhill* 148
Alice & Nelly's Cottages *Cornriggs* 298
Allt-y-Golau Farmhouse *Felingwm Uchaf* .. 349
The Alnwick Garden *Alnwick* 308
Amroth Bay Holidays *Amroth* 353
Ancestral Barn *Ashbourne* 213
Anglesey Sea Zoo and Farm *Brynslencyn* 357
Arbor Holiday & Knightcote Farm Cottages *Knightcote* 238
Ardgarth Guest House *Edinburgh* 324
Arsenal Football Club *London N5* 174
Atholl Brae - The Harland *Edinburgh* 324
Atlantis Holiday Apartments *Torquay* 107
Audley End House & Gardens *Saffron Walden* 205

B

Badgers Den *Budleigh Salterton* 104
Bailey Mill *Bailey* 275
Barkinbeck Cottage *Gatebeck* 276
The Barn *Compton* 153
Barnard Castle *Durham* 308
Battlesteads Hotel *Wark* 307
Beach Lodge *Felpham* 154
Beachy Head Holiday Cottages *East Dean* 150
Beacon Hill Farm *Morpeth* 305
Beacon Hill *Longhorsley* 304

Beaulieu *Beaulieu* 156
Beeson Farm Holiday Cottages *Beesands* 102
Belsay Hall, Castle & Gardens *Belsay* 308
Bench Cottage and Little Bench *Lymington* 141
Best Western Premier Blunsdon House Hotel *Swindon* 123
Best Western The Mayfield House Hotel *Malmesbury* 123
Best Western Three Swans Hotel *Market Harborough* 217
Bewleys Hotel Manchester Airport *Manchester Airport* 286
Bibury Court Hotel *Cirencester* 114
Birch Cottage *Windermere* 280
Birch Hotel *Haywards Heath* 154
Birmingham Botanical Gardens & Glasshouses *Edgbaston* 240
Black Horse Farm Caravan Club Site *Folkestone* 145
Bluebell, Bonny, Buttercup & Bertie *Saxmundham* 203
Bluebell Cottage *Gissing* 195
Bluebell Croft, Honeysuckle House and Rose Cottage *Fort William* 328
Bocaddon Holiday Cottages *Lanreath* 94
Bolsover Castle *Bolsover* 224
Bookham Court *Alton Pancras* 109
Bosworth Battlefield Visitor Centre & Country Park *Sutton Cheney* 224
Boundary Stables *Happisburgh* 196
Bowsden bed and breakfast *Berwick-Upon-Tweed* 301
Braithwaite Fold Caravan Club Site *Windermere* 280
Brean Park *Lostwithiel* 95
Bristol Hippodrome *Bristol* 126
Broad Bay House *Stornoway* 337
Broad Park Caravan Club Site *Modbury* 105
Brodsworth Hall & Gardens *Brodsworth* ... 261
Brownrigg Lodges *Bellingham* 301
Bryn Elltyd *Blaenau Ffestiniog* 352

For symbols see pg 24

449

OpenBritain | Index by property name

B continued

Bryn Llys (Care of Joys of Life) *Bethesda* .. 351
The Bull Pen *Compton* 153
Burford Caravan Club Site *Burford* 146
Burradon Farm Houses and Cottages
    Newcastle upon Tyne 306
Burrs Country Park Caravan Club Site
    Bury 285
Buzzard Heights *Bridgewater* 117
The Byre *Auldgirth* 322

C

Caburn Cottages *Glynde* 150
Cadbury World *Birmingham* 240
Caddleton Farmhouse *Ardmaddy* 320
Cae'r Dderwen *Caernarfon* 352
Caley Hall Hotel *Hunstanton* 197
Calvert Trust Kielder *Kielder* 304
Cambushinnie Croft *Dunblane* 336
Cantley House Hotel *Wokingham* 140
The Captain's Quarter *Truro* 100
Carfax Hotel *Bath* 116
Carisbrooke Castle *Isle of Wight* 157
Carlton House Holiday Accommodation
    Whitby 259
Ceilidh B&B *Lossiemouth* 331
Centre For Alternative Technology
    Machynlleth 357
Chapel Lane Caravan Club Site
    Birmingham 238
Character Farm Cottages *Abbotsbury* 109
Chatsworth Park Caravan Club Site
    Bakewell 213
Cherry Hinton Caravan Club Site
    Cambridge 188
Chester Fairoaks Caravan Club Site
    Chester 273
Chiswick House & Gardens *London W4* 175
Churchtown Lodges *Bodmin* 92
Cliff Farm Cottage *Lincoln* 220
Clumber Park Caravan Club Site
    Worksop 224
Clynfyw Countryside Centre *Boncath* 354
Clyngwyn Farm Self Catering Cottages
    Pendine 349
The Coach House *Crookham* 302
Coda Cottages *Cotton* 201
Coedllys Country House *Carmarthen* 349
Colchester Museums *Colchester* 205

Combe House *Honiton* 105
The Conference Centre at Lace *Liverpool* 288
Cornerstone Cottage *Castlemartin* 354
The Cornmill *Kirkbymoorside* 254
Corrigall Farm Museum *Orkney* 337
Cotoneaster *Coldstream* 333
Cotswold Wild Life Park *Burford* 158
The Cottage by the Pond *Ilam* 237
Crathie Opportunity Holidays *Ballater* 319
Cringletie House Hotel *Peebles* 334
Cromer House Camping Barn *Frosterley* .. 299
Crookhouse Cottages *Wooler* 307
Crown Lodge *Torquay* 108
Crowne Plaza Cambridge *Cambridge* 188
Crowne Plaza Chester *Chester* 273
Crowne Plaza Heathrow *West Drayton* 174
Crowne Plaza Leeds *Leeds* 254
Crowne Plaza London - Docklands
    London E16 171
Crowne Plaza Manchester Airport
    Manchester Airport 286
Crubenbeg House *Newtonmore* 330
Crystal Palace Caravan Club Site
    London SE19 173
Curlews *Bradfield* 191
Cwrt-Y-Gaer (Self-catering) *Chepstow* 353

D

Dairyland Farm World *Summercourt* 124
Dalegarth and The Ghyll Cottages
    Buckden 251
David Welch Winter Gardens *Aberdeen* 337
Daviot House *Ayr* 335
Deep Sea World *North Queensferry* 337
Deveron Lodge B&B Guesthouse *Turriff* ... 319
Donmar Warehouse Theatre *London
    WC2* 175
Double-Gate Farm *Lower Godney* 119
Dover Castle *Dover* 158
Doxford Cottages *Alnwick* 300
Drayton Manor *Tamworth* 240
Dryslade Farm *Forest of Dean* 114
Dunvalanree *Campbeltown* 321

E

East Briscoe Farm Cottages *Barnard
    Castle* 297
East Greystone Farm Cottages *Gainford* .. 299
The Ebenezer Chapel *Milford* 215

450 www.openbritain.net

Index by property name | OpenBritain

E continued

Eden House Country Guest
  Accommodation *Boncath* 354
Eden Vale Luxury Holiday Flats
  Morecambe.. 283
Eildon Holiday Cottages *Melrose* 334
Ellerby *Ellerby* 252
Elms Farm Cottages *Hubberts Bridge*....... 219
Eltham Palace *London SE9*...................... 175
Engine House *Truro*................................. 100
Esplanade Hotel *Llandudno*..................... 350
Express by Holiday Inn - Fife *Dunfermline* 326
Express by Holiday Inn - Norwich *Norwich* 198
Express By Holiday Inn Aberdeen City
  Centre *Aberdeen*..................................... 318
Express by Holiday Inn Gloucester South
  Gloucester 114
Express by Holiday Inn London -
  Park Royal *London W3* 172
Express by Holiday Inn York - East *York*... 259

F

Fairhaven Woodland and Water Gardens
  Norwich 205
Falcondale Mansion Hotel *Lampeter* 350
The Farmhouse *Isle of Purbeck* 110
Farrell House *Bognor Regis*...................... 151
Felbridge Hotel and Spa *East Grinstead* ... 154
Ferry Meadows Caravan Club Site
  Peterborough 190
Fishermans Lodge *Saffron Walden* 192
Flamborough Rock Cottages
  Flamborough... 253
Forda Lodges & Cottages *Kilkhampton*..... 94
Framlingham Castle *Framlingham*............ 205
Fraser Suites Edinburgh *Edinburgh*.......... 325
Fraser Suites Glasgow *Glasgow* 327

G

Garden Flat *Abergavenny* 353
The Garden House *Chewton Mendip*........ 118
Geffrye Museum *London E2*..................... 174
Gillis Centre *Edinburgh* 325
Gladwins Farm Self Catering Cottages
  Nayland... 202
Glasgow Marriott *Glasgow*........................ 327
Glenbeag Mountain Lodges - Clashmore
  Blairgowrie.. 332
Glenernan Guest House *Ballater*.............. 319

The Glenholm Centre *Biggar* 335
Gloucester Cathedral *Gloucester*............. 126
Goodrich Castle *Goodrich* 240
Goosefoot Barn Cottages *Corfton* 235
Grafton Villa Farm Cottages *Hereford*....... 233
Grand Hotel *Hastings*............................... 150
Grandwood House *West Marden* 155
The Grange Caravan Club Site *Durham*.... 298
Greyfield Farm Cottages *High Littleton* 119
Grin Low Caravan Club Site *Buxton* 214
Grindon Cartshed *Haydon Bridge*............. 303
Groomhill *Clacton-On-Sea* 192
Guildford Cathedral *Guildford* 158

H

Haddington House Apartments *Plymouth*.. 106
Hafan (Care of Joys of Life) *Bethesda* 352
Hailes Abbey *Winchcombe*....................... 126
Hamsteels Cottages *Quebec*.................... 299
Hargill House Caravan Club Site
  Richmond 257
Harrold Odell Country Park *Harrold* 204
Harts Hotel *Nottingham*............................ 223
Hartswheal Stables *Lostwithiel Fowey* 95
Hawk Conservancy Trust *Nr Andover*....... 156
Hay Barn & Straw Barn *Edenbridge*.......... 144
Haycraft Caravan Club Site *Swanage*....... 112
Heath Farm *Lewes* 151
Helsey House Cottages *Hogsthorpe*......... 219
Henry Moore Institute *Leeds*.................... 262
Herons Well Cottage *West Kirby* 287
Hidelow House Cottages *Malvern* 234
High Hazels *Chesterfield*.......................... 215
High Shield *Bardon Mill* 301
High Wray *Farnham*................................. 147
Higher Farm Bed & Breakfast *Cheshire* 272
Hillhead Caravan Club Site *Brixham*......... 103
Hoe Grange Holidays *Brassington* 214
Holiday Inn - High Wycombe *High
  Wycombe* 140
Holiday Inn Ashford Central *Ashford*......... 143
Holiday Inn Aylesbury *Aylesbury* 140
Holiday Inn Basildon *Basildon*.................. 190
Holiday Inn Birmingham City Centre
  Birmingham 239
Holiday Inn Birmingham M6 Junction 7
  Birmingham 239
Holiday Inn Bolton Centre *Bolton*.............. 282
Holiday Inn Brent Cross *London NW2* 173
Holiday Inn Brentwood *Brentwood* 191

For symbols see pg 24   **451**

OpenBritain | Index by property name

H continued

Holiday Inn Bristol Filton *Bristol* 113
Holiday Inn Chester South *Chester* 273
Holiday Inn Corby-Kettering *Corby* 221
Holiday Inn Coventry M6 J2 *Coventry* 239
Holiday Inn Edinburgh *Edinburgh* 325
Holiday Inn Express - Edinburgh,
  Royal Mile *Edinburgh* 325
Holiday Inn Express - Newbury Park,
  London *London, Newbury Park* 173
Holiday Inn Fareham *Fareham* 141
Holiday Inn Garden Court *Sandy* 188
Holiday Inn Gatwick Airport *Horley* 148
Holiday Inn Glasgow Airport *Glasgow
  Airport* 333
Holiday Inn Gloucester-Cheltenham
  Gloucester 114
Holiday Inn Guildford *Guildford* 147
Holiday Inn Haydock *Haydock* 287
Holiday Inn Hemel Hempstead *Hemel
  Hempstead* 193
Holiday Inn Ipswich *Ipswich* 201
Holiday Inn Lancaster *Lancaster* 283
Holiday Inn Leeds-Wakefield M1 J40
  Wakefield 258
Holiday Inn Leeds/Brighouse *Brighouse* ... 250
Holiday Inn Leicester *Leicester* 216
Holiday Inn London - Bexley *London* 173
Holiday Inn London - Bloomsbury
  London WC1 172
Holiday Inn London - Kingston South
  London - Kingston South 173
Holiday Inn London - Regents Park
  London W1 172
Holiday Inn London Heathrow *West
  Drayton* 174
Holiday Inn London Kensington
  London SW7 172
Holiday Inn London Mayfair *London W1* 172
Holiday Inn London Shepperton
  Shepperton 174
Holiday Inn Maidenhead *Maidenhead* 140
Holiday Inn Milton Keynes *Milton Keynes* .. 140
Holiday Inn Norwich *Norwich* 198
Holiday Inn Nottingham *Nottingham* 223
Holiday Inn Oxford *Oxford* 147
Holiday Inn Plymouth *Plymouth* 106
Holiday Inn Rochester Chatham
  Rochester-Chatham 145

Holiday Inn Rugby-Northampton *Crick* 222
Holiday Inn Runcorn *Runcorn* 274
Holiday Inn Slough Windsor *Slough* 140
Holiday Inn Southampton - Eastleigh
  Southampton, Eastleigh 141
Holiday Inn Southampton *Southampton* ... 141
Holiday Inn Stevenage *Stevenage* 193
Holiday Inn Stoke-on-Trent *Stoke-On-
  Trent* 237
Holiday Inn Sutton *Sutton* 148
Holiday Inn Taunton M5 J25 *Taunton* 121
Holiday Inn Telford/Ironbridge *Telford* 236
Holiday Inn Warrington *Warrington* 274
Holiday Inn Woking *Woking* 148
Holiday Inn York *York* 260
Holton Lee - Gateway & Woodland
  Cottages *Poole* 111
Holton Lee - The Barn *Poole* 111
The Home of Charles Darwin,
  Down House *Downe* 158
Homeleigh Country Cottages *Whitland* 349
Honeysuckle Cottage *Gissing* 195
Hope Farm Cottages
  Lympsham, Weston-Super-Mare 120
Hotel L'Horizon *Jersey* 101
Houghton Mill Caravan Club Site
  Huntingdon 189
Houses Of Parliament *London SW1* 175
Howscales *Penrith* 278
Hue's Piece *Broadclyst* 103
Hunters Lodge Hotel *Gretna* 323
The Hytte *Hexham* 303

I

imago at Burleigh Court *Loughborough* 217
Incleborough House *East Runton* 194
Irton House Farm *Cockermouth* 276
Isolation Hospital 2 *Corfe Castle* 110
Ivy House Farm Cottages (Owl Cottage)
  Diss 194

J

Jane Austen's House and Museum *Alton* .. 156
Jayes Holiday Cottages *Wattisfield* 204
Jorvik Viking Centre *York* 263
Joys Of Life Country Park B&B *Bethesda* .. 352
Jurys Inn Chelsea *London SW6* 171
Jurys Inn Croydon *Croydon* 147
Jurys Inn Derby *Derby* 215

K

Keld Head Farm Cottages *Pickering*......... 256
Kenilworth Castle & Elizabethan Garden
  Kenilworth.. 225
Kenwood House *London NW3*................. 174
Kernock Cottages *Pillaton* 96
Kerridge End Holiday Cottages
  Macclesfield.. 274
King Line Cottages *Horning*..................... 197
Kirbuster Museum *Orkney*....................... 337
Kitley House Hotel and Restaurant
  Yealmpton 108

L

La Bergerie *Isle of Skye* 329
La Rocco Self-catering Apartments
  Jersey 101
Lake District Disabled Holidays
  Windermere... 280
Lake Vyrnwy Hotel & Spa *Welshpool*........ 356
The Lawton *Blackpool*.............................. 282
Leicester Marriott *Leicester* 216
Leys Farmhouse Annexe *Middlewood
  Green*... 202
Lincoln Cathedral *Lincoln* 224
Linthwaite House Hotel *Windermere*......... 281
Little Swinton Cottages *Coldstream*.......... 334
Lobster Pot Cottage *Elie*........................... 326
London Canal Museum *London N1* 174
Longleat Caravan Club Site *Warminster* ... 123
Longleat *Warminster*................................ 127
Look Out Discovery Centre *Bracknell* 155
Lovat Lodge *Nairn* 330
Low Park Wood Caravan Club Site
  Kendal... 278
Lowstead Farm Cottage *Levisham, nr
  Pickering* 255
Lucker Hall Steading *Lucker*..................... 305
Lullingstone Roman Villa *Eynsford*........... 158

M

Madog's Wells *Llanfair Caereinion* 356
Maison Des Landes Hotel *Jersey*............. 102
The Major's Quarter *Truro* 100
Manaros *Aberdaron*................................. 351
Manchester Art Gallery *Manchester* 288
Manna Place *Polzeath* 97
The Manor Coach House *Worcester*......... 239
Manor Farm *Wells* 121
Marble Hill House *London* 176

Marriott Dalmahoy Hotel & Country Club
  Edinburgh.. 325
Meadowcroft Country Guest House *Ings*... 277
Meadowcroft Guest House *Axton*............. 357
Meathop Fell Caravan Club Site
  Grange-over-Sands................................. 276
The Metropole *Llandrindod Wells*............. 356
Mid Hants Railway Plc *New Alresford* 156
Moreton-in-Marsh Caravan Club Site
  Moreton-in-Marsh................................... 115
Mortons House Hotel *Corfe Castle* 110
Muston Grange Farm *Filey* 252
Mytton Fold Hotel and Golf Complex
  Langho.. 283

N

Nationwide Bungalow *Ambleside* 274
Nene Valley Cottages *Wigsthorpe*............ 222
Ness Botanic Gardens *Necton*................. 288
New Art Gallery *Walsall*............................ 240
New Lanark Mill Hotel *New Lanark*........... 335
New Steading Cottage/Old Steading
  Cottage *Glenshee* 333
New Theatre Cardiff *Cardiff* 357
Newlands Country House *Southwold*........ 203
Newquay Zoo *Newquay* 124
Newton Meadows *Shrewsbury*................. 236
'Next Door' at Magdalen House *Thetford* .. 200
Normanhurst Court Caravan Club Site
  Battle... 149
North Ledaig Caravan Club Site *Oban*...... 321
North York Moors National Park *Helmsley* 262
Northfield Farm *Buxton* 215
Northumberland Park Authority *Hexham*... 309
Nuffield Theatre *Southampton* 156
Number 5 *Ruthin* 351
Nursery Cottage *North Somercotes*.......... 221

O

Ocean Studios *Marazion* 96
Okehampton Castle *Okehampton* 125
The Old Club House *St Helen's*................ 142
The Old Coach House *Boscastle* 92
The Old Farmhouse *Hexham*.................... 303
Old House Farm Cottages *Nr Hartington*... 215
Old Radnor Barn Bed & Breakfast *Brecon* 355
Old Sarum *Salisbury*................................ 127
Old School Guest House *Caernarfon*........ 352
The Orkney Museum *Orkney*.................... 337
Osborne House *Cowes* 157

For symbols see pg 24   **453**

OpenBritain | Index by property name

O continued

Overcombe House *Yelverton* 109
Oyster House *Sandringham (6 miles)* 199

P

Pakefield Caravan Park *Lowestoft* 202
Park House Hotel *Sandringham* 198
Peel Bothy *Hexham* 304
Pen-y-Lon *Dolgellau* 353
Pendennis Castle *Falmouth* 124
Pendragon Country House *Davidstow* 92
Penrheol Farm *Builth Wells* 356
Pentland Lodge House *Thurso* 331
Petwood Hotel *Woodhall Spa* 221
Pevensey Castle *Pevensey* 159
Pinfold Farm *Ribble Valley* 284
Plas Farm Caravan Park *Abergele* 350
Plymouth Gin *Plymouth* 125
Poachers Hideaway *Belchford* 218
Port Selma Lodges *Benderloch* 320
Portland Castle *Portland* 125
Portland House *Ross on Wye* 234
Primrose Cottage *Gissing* 196
Primrose Court *Tebay* 279
Primrose Hill Holidays *Blue Anchor* 117
The Promenade *Minehead* 120
Proven House *Alston* 281
Providence Place *Bridlington* 250
Prudhoe Castle *Prudhoe* 309
Putts Corner Caravan Club Site *Sidbury* ... 107

Q

Quarry Walk Park *Stoke-on-Trent* 237
The Queens Hotel *Llandudno* 350

R

The Raptor Foundation *St Ives* 190
Red House Farm Cottages *Haughley* 201
Renaissance London Heathrow Hotel
   Hounslow 172
Restharrow *Hawkshead* 277
RHS Garden Harlow Carr *Harrogate* 261
RHS Garden Hyde Hall *Chelmsford* 204
RHS Garden Rosemoor *Great Torrington* 124
RHS Garden Wisley *Wisley* 159
Rievaulx Abbey *Rievaulx* 262
River Breamish Caravan Club Site
   Powburn 306
Roald Dahl Museum and Story Centre
   Great Missenden 155
Roman Camp Inn *Aylmerton* 193
Ropers Walk Barns *Mount Hawke* 96
Rose Cottage *Gissing* 196
Rosehill Lodges *Porthtowan* 97
Roseland Bungalow Annexe *Worcester* 240
Rothay Manor *Ambleside* 275
Rowan Park Caravan Club Site *Bognor
   Regis* 152
Rowntree Park Caravan Club Site *York* 260
Royal Exchange Theatre Company
   Manchester 288
The Royal Hotel *Weston-Super-Mare* 122
Royal Military Police Museum *Chichester* 156
Royal Parks *London W2* 175
Royal Shakespeare Company RSC
   Stratford-Upon-Avon 240
Royal Signals Museum *Blandford Forum* .. 125
Rufford Abbey Country Park *Ollerton* 225
Rye Hill Farm (Old Byre) *Slaley* 307

S

Salford Museum & Art Gallery *Salford* 288
Sandcastle Waterpark *Blackpool* 288
The Sandringham Estate Caravan Club
   Site *Sandringham* 199
Sandringham House *Sandringham* 205
Scapa Flow Visitor Centre & Museum
   Orkney 338
Scarborough Castle *Scarborough* 262
Scottish Parliament *Edinburgh* 337
Seacroft Caravan Club Site *Cromer* 194
Seagulls *Selsey Bill* 155
Sheepcote Valley Caravan Club Site
   Brighton & Hove 149
Sissinghurst Castle Garden *Cranbrook* 157
Smallicombe Farm *Northleigh* 105
Smallicombe Farm Self Catering
   Northleigh 106
Smiths Court Hotel *Cliftonville* 144
South Newlands Farm Self Catering *York* 261
South Torfrey Farm *Fowey* 92
Southwaite Green *Southwaite* 279
Spanhoe Lodge *Laxton* 222
Springbank Farm Lodges *St Bees* 279
St. Magnus Cathedral *Orkney* 338
St Mawes Castle *St Mawes* 124
St Michaels Without *Bath* 126
Stable Cottage *Beaminster* 109

S continued

Stable Cottage *South Molton* 107
The Stables *Helston* 93
Staybridge Suites Liverpool *Liverpool* 287
STEAM - Museum of the Great Western Railway *Swindon* 127
Stonecroft and Swallows Nest *Cockfield* ... 297
Stonehenge *nr Amesbury* 126
Strid Wood Caravan Club Site *Bolton Abbey* 250
Sudeley Castle *Winchcombe* 126
Swallow Barn *Godney* 119
Swallows Nest *High Cogges* 146

T

Tamarack Lodge *Chard* 118
Tamarisk *Bracklesham Bay* 152
Tamarisk Farm Holiday Cottages *Bridport* 110
Tilbury Fort *Tilbury* 156
Todsworthy Farm Holidays *Albaston* 92
Tower Park *Poole* 125
Trenerry Farm *St Agnes* 99
Trenona Farm Holidays *Ruan High Lanes* 98
Trevase Granary *Ross on Wye* 234
Trewethett Farm Caravan Club Site *Tintagel* 99
Treworgans Farm Holidays *Truro (7 miles)* 101
Tudor Lodges *Looe* 94
Tugford Farm Holiday Cottages *Craven Arms* 235
Twmpath Guest House *Maenclochog* 355
Ty Mawr Mansion Country House *Aberaeron* 350

U

University of Aberdeen, King's Hall *Aberdeen* 319

V

The Vale Resort *Pontyclun* 357
Villa Ryall *Worle* 122
Vitalise Churchtown *Bodmin* 92
Vitalise Jubilee Lodge *Chigwell* 191
Vitalise Netley Waterside House *Southampton* 141
Vitalise Sandpipers *Southport* 287
Vitalise Skylarks *Nottingham* 223

W

Waldegraves, Holiday Park *Mersea Island* 192
Walkers Farm Cottages *Stathe* 121
Wall Eden Farm *Burnham on Sea* 117
Wall Hill Farm Guesthouse *Acton Bridge* .. 272
Walmer Castle & Gardens *Deal* 157
Warkworth Castle & Hermitage *Warkworth* 309
Weetwood Hall Conference Centre & Hotel *Leeds* 254
West Bay Club *Yarmouth* 143
West Hele *Buckland Brewer* 104
The West Shore *Llandudno* 351
Westminster Cathedral *London SW1* 175
Wheeldon Trees Farm *Earl Sterndale* 215
Whitby Abbey *Whitby* 263
Whitchester Christian Guest House *Hawick* 334
White Water Park Caravan Club Site *Stockton on Tees* 300
Wick House *Stogumber* 121
Willow Croft *Gairloch* 328
Willowbank Holiday Home and Touring Park *Ainsdale* 286
Wimborne & Ferndown Lions Club Caravans *Weymouth* 112
Winford Manor *Bristol* 113
Witley Court *Great Witley* 225
Woodcombe Lodges *Minehead* 120
Woodlands Country House *Treator* 100
Woodlands Leisure Park *Totnes* 125
Wrest Park *Luton* 204
Wye Knot Stop *Brecon* 355

Y

York Minster *York* 263
Yorkshire Dales National Park Authority *Leyburn* 262

OpenBritain

Published by: Tourism for All UK, c/o Vitalise, Shap Road Industrial Estate, Kendal LA9 6NT in partnership with RADAR and Shopmobility UK.

Chief Executive: Jennifer Littman

Chairman: Sir William Lawrence

Compilation, design, editorial, production and advertisement sales: Heritage House Group, Ketteringham Hall, Wymondham, Norfolk NR18 9RS
t 01603 813319

Publisher: Kate Kaegler

Production Manager: Sarah Phillips

Group Director: Kelvin Ladbrook

Cover design/photography:
Peter Moore Fuller/Nick McCann

Typesetting: PDQ Digital Media Solutions Ltd, Bungay, Suffolk

Maps: Based on digital map data © ESR Cartography, 2009-10-19

Printing and binding:
Burlington Press, Cambridge.

Photography credits: © Crown copyright 2009 Visit Wales; ATOC (Andrew Molyneux / Giles Park); Barrie Beattie; britainonview (Daniel Bosworth / Martin Brent / Rod Edwards / Pawel Libera / Ian Shaw / Jon Spaull / Tourism South East); Roz Gordon; Sharon Lucey; Nick McCann; Norman McNab; Diane Naylor; Mark Owen; photolibrary.com (Jim Craigmyle / Brian Mitchell / Huntstock / Imagesource / Creatas / John Short / David Ellis / Ls Pictures / Maisant Ludovic / Martin Ruegner / Medicimage / Chad Ehlers / Laurence Mouton / Lars Langemeier); Duncan Phillips; Phil Pinfield / Midhire; Alan Richardson; Simon Shepheard; Transport for London; Visit Scotland / Scottish Viewpoint. Special thanks to John Horncastle / ATOC, Carla Rinaldi / First Scotrail and Deborah Evans / London Development Agency for their kind assistance in image sourcing.

Important note: The information contained in this Guide has been published in good faith on the basis of information supplied to OpenBritain by the proprietors of the premises listed together with data supplied by Visit England, Visit Scotland and Visit Wales. Whilst all reasonable steps are taken, Tourism for All cannot guarantee the accuracy of the information contained within this Guide and accepts no responsibility for any error or misrepresentation. All liability for loss, disappointment, negligence or other damage caused by reliance on the information contained in this guide, or in the event of bankruptcy, or liquidation, or cessation of trade of any company, individual or firm mentioned, is hereby excluded to the fullest extent permitted by law. Please check carefully all prices, ratings and other details before confirming a reservation.

© Tourism for All 2010

ISBN 97880-85101-442-5

An OpenBritain guide.

OPENBRITAIN.NET